JAPAN IN THE 21ST CENTURY

二十一世紀の日本

JAPAN
IN THE 21ST CENTURY

ENVIRONMENT, ECONOMY, AND SOCIETY

PRADYUMNA P. KARAN

CARTOGRAPHY BY DICK GILBREATH

THE UNIVERSITY PRESS OF KENTUCKY

Note: This book includes a folded oversize map of Japan.

Publication of this volume was made possible in part by a grant
from the National Endowment for the Humanities.

Editorial and Sales Offices: The University Press of Kentucky
663 South Limestone Street, Lexington, Kentucky 40508-4008
www.kentuckypress.com

13 12 11 10 09   7 6 5 4 3

Library of Congress Cataloging-in-Publication Data

Karan, Pradyumna P. (Pradyumna Prasad)
  Japan in the twenty-first century : environment, economy, and society / Pradyumna P. Karan.
    p. cm.
  Includes bibliographical references and index.
  ISBN-10: 0-8131-2342-9 (alk. paper) — ISBN-10: 0-8131-9118-1 (pbk. : alk. paper)
  1. Japan. 2. Twenty-first century—Forecasts. I. Title: Japan in the 21st century. II. Title.
  DS806.K385 2004
  952.05—dc22   2004020797
  ISBN-13: 978-0-8131-9118-8 (pbk. : alk. paper)

 Member of the Association of
American University Presses

CONTENTS

Maps and Figures

Preface and Acknowledgments

Japan stands as one of the more intriguing nations in Asia. Despite Japan's important role as the second-largest economy in the world and a major trading and strategic partner of the United States, geographic studies of Japan in the United States have been relatively scarce. The standard English-language geography, *Japan: A Geography,* by Glenn Trewartha, was published in 1965. Momentous changes have taken place in every facet of the nation during the last four decades. In the early 1980s Japan's growing economic strength was a source of concern in the United States and Europe. Now there is worry about an economy that is slow to reform and grow. Fundamental problems such as banks overburdened by bad loans, a dangerous ratio of national debt to gross domestic product, a rigid labor market, a highly regulated economy, and an aging population and shrinking labor force have eroded Japan's ability to play a larger world role. Today Japan is a far different nation than it was in the 1980s.

This book discusses the land, people, and economy of Japan from a geographic perspective and identifies the demographic, economic, and environmental challenges facing the country in the twenty-first century. The text integrates important new research published in Japan and elsewhere during the last two decades. Maps, graphs, and photographs provide a gripping portrait of the new Japan.

I first became interested in the geography of Japan in the 1960s while spending several weeks each year in the country—on my way to field research in the Himalayas—to visit with Japanese Himalayanists. A visiting research professorship in 1985–86 at the Institute for the Study of Languages and Cultures of Asia and Africa, Tokyo, provided my first prolonged opportunity to travel throughout the Japanese islands.

In 1992–93, another visiting research professorship at the Tokyo University of Foreign Studies provided the opportunity for geographic field reconnaissance from Hokkaido to Kyushu. Professor Cotton Mather of the University of Minnesota, who had done extensive geographic research on Japan at the Office of Strategic Services in Washington, D.C., during World War II, accompanied me on these field trips. The idea for writing this book on challenges facing Japan in the twenty-first century from a geographic perspective originated in 1998 while I was doing field research in Atsumi Peninsula with Cotton Mather. I began work on the book in 2000 during my stay at Nagoya University on a research fellowship from the Japan Society for the Promotion of Science. The fellowship enabled me to travel again to all the Japanese prefectures and visit with people in various walks of life in both rural and urban areas: factory workers, farmers, grassroots activists, government officials, and academics. To those individuals whom I interviewed in Japan, I owe a debt of gratitude for revealing many rich details of their country's social and cultural geography. The book in many ways represents my personal observations and interactions with the Japanese people and their country.

My experiences were greatly enlarged and my observations confirmed through discussions with other professional geographers and scholars. Several individuals deserve specific mention. Professor Toshi Ikegawa (University of Hawaii—Windward Community College) helped prepare an earlier version of the section on physical geography that appears in chapter 2. Professor Jonathan Taylor (California State University at Fullerton) wrote the section on entertainment districts in Japanese cities that is included in chapter 8.

The generous help and hospitality of many friends and colleagues ensured the success of my field visits in Japan. In particular, I want to thank Shigeru Iijima, professor emeritus at the Tokyo Institute of Technology, who first introduced me to Japan in the early 1960s. I also thank Professor Hiroshi Ishii and other colleagues at the Institute for the Study of Languages and Cultures of Asia and Africa and the Tokyo University of Foreign Studies, who provided great fellowship in the field and helped me establish contacts with Japanese officials and scholars in various parts of the country. Field observations in Japan in the 1990s were greatly facilitated by President Kazuaki Imoto of IEC Kyushu International College, Yatsushiro, Kyushu, and former Prime Minister Morihiro Hosokawa. The University of Kentucky Field Research Station at Yatsushiro also helped with my research trips around the archipelago.

At Nagoya University I benefited immensely from discussions on various aspects of Japanese geography with Professors Kohei Okamoto, Tsunetoshi Mizoguchi, and Masatomo Umitsu. Graduate students at Nagoya—Toshibumi Takai, Yumiko Yonemoto, Yuichiro Nishimura, Daisuke Hirouchi, and Jun Tsuchiya—helped me contact other scholars and locate archival research materials. Kenji Ito of Meijo University; Kenkichi Nagao of the Institute for Economic Research, Osaka City University; Shii Okuno of the University of Marketing and Distribution Sciences, Kobe; Kazusei Kato of the Kansai University of Foreign Studies; Kenichi Nonaka of the Institute for the Study of Nature and Humanity, Kyoto; Koji Ohnishi of Toyama University; Shin'ichiro Sugiura of Kanazawa University; Shigeru Kobayashi of Osaka University; Noritaka Yagasaki of Tokyo Gakugei University; Toshio Mizuuchi of Osaka City University; Yuji Yamamoto of Osaka International University; Biren K. Jha, Barrister-at-Law in Tokyo; and Asabe Shin-ichi, independent journalist and television producer, provided many insightful comments on the geography of Japan and the challenges facing the country.

Professor Okamoto and his students at Nagoya University played a key role in the evolution of this book. They read the manuscript and made many constructive suggestions. Their meticulous comments were invaluable, and I am deeply indebted to them for the time they spent to read the text and brainstorm over parts of it, and for their unflagging interest. Professor Miranda Schreurs of the University of Maryland, Professor Todd Stradford of the University of Wisconsin–Platteville, and Professor Unryu Suganuma of Hokuriku University also read earlier drafts of the manuscript and offered encouraging, stimulating, and helpful comments. My students at the University of Kentucky in the Department of Geography and the Japan Studies Program provided many constructive comments. The book has benefited from the comments of all these individuals, but I alone am responsible for any errors.

Richard Gilbreath, Director of the University of Kentucky Cartographic Laboratory, edited the maps prepared by Donna Gilbreath, cartographer, and student cartographers Jeff Casperson, Jacqueline Goins, Dave McLaughlin, Tony Morris, Gina Poore, John Poskin, Whitney Walker, and Tony Zerhusen. I am grateful to all of them for their splendid work.

Note on Numerical Conversions

Most of the physical measures in this book are given in English units, with metric equivalents added for the convenience of readers who are more familiar with metric units. All references to tons, however, designate metric tons unless indicated otherwise.

For yen-to-dollar conversions, the rate of exchange at the time of writing, 109 yen to a dollar in June 2004, has been used throughout for the sake of simplicity.

Chapter 1   第 一 章

JAPAN AT THE CROSSROADS

Grappling with Changes

Japan. The name evokes thoughts of electronics, dials, lights, and numbers. This ancient civilization, with its Shinto shrines and Buddhist temples, is closely associated with all that is new and modern in our times. Looking outward, Japan sees what it has become since Hiroshima: a source of fury and wonder, the world's second-largest economy, a power without arms. Looking inward, Japan sees old ways shaken and new ones moving forward at a hectic pace.

What is Japan like? Who are the Japanese people?

What are the challenges that they face in the twenty-first century? Their characteristics collide: democracy and hierarchy; formality and chaos; the overfed wrestler and the shrunken tree; daring modernity and traditional skills; permissiveness and restrictiveness. In form, Japan is a parliamentary democracy. Yet a single party, the Liberal Democrats, was in power for almost all the years since World War II. In form, Japan is a capitalist, free enterprise society. Yet bureaucrats, businessmen, and politicians seem to collude for the greater glory of Japan. Is this real democracy? A real free enterprise society?

Some say Japan is continuous. It interweaves the

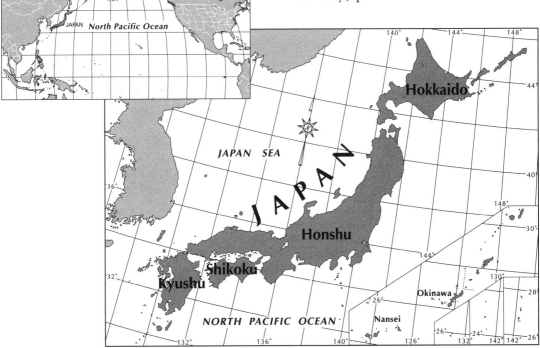

Fig. 1.1. Japan and the United States. Japan is America's neighbor across the Pacific. Tokyo is located about 3,000 miles (4,828 km) from the west coast of Alaska and a little over 6,000 miles (9,656 km) from Chicago. The four largest islands of Japan cover an area a bit smaller than California. Japan lies in the same latitude as the United States. The residents of the islands call their homeland Dai Nippon or Great Land of the Rising Sun.

1

tradition of temples with the discovery of cameras. It heeds parental voices even while recording them. It tells yesterday's time promptly, digitally. Japan is viewed as seamless: A garden. A blossom. A stone. A brook. The haiku that fuses them together. The wizened figure in a kimono who recites the haiku.

How do we assess such a culture? Where did the Japanese come from? Where are they going in the twenty-first century? And why are they as they are? Even more than most peoples, the Japanese have been shaped by their environment. From the dawn of their history, close communication and often precarious coexistence with nature have dominated almost all aspects of the national character and culture. In chapter 2, we will examine a few of the natural features of this island nation, which have played such an important role in the making of the Japanese. In the other chapters we will explore Japan's social, economic, and political structure as it affects Japan's twenty-first-century role in the world. We will try to understand its environment, culture, and economy within the context of geography, and you will find explanations that clarify much of what seems so contradictory about Japan and the Japanese.

All nations seek greatness, but few achieve it. During the past half century, Japan has attained this rare status. This claim will stand despite all of Japan's obvious flaws. The past fifty years constitute the greatest epoch of all Japanese history, outweighing the Heian age with its splendid writers, the Kamakura era with its great religious thinkers, the epoch of the warring states with its military heroes, and the Edo period with its unprecedented flowering of political reflection.

Between 1945 and 2000, more Japanese have lived more decently, enjoyed better health and more prosperity, while benefiting from greater freedom and peace, than at any other time in recorded history. This is a singular triumph. Even more astonishing, the postwar labors of the Japanese people have all but ensured that Japan's name will be added to that very select list of nations that have successively stood at the spear point of economic progress during those years.

Against enormous odds and the weight of history, Japan has transcended its obvious weaknesses (its physical constraints and its dependence on imported raw materials and export markets, for example) to play the predominant role in a historic transformation: the shift of the center of economic activity and initiative from the Atlantic to the Pacific. More than the decolonization of Asia and Africa, this marked the end of the long era of Western domination of world history. Japan's economic surge has helped to spark the revival of East Asian energies after two centuries of decline and turmoil. More importantly, the Japanese model has demonstrated that a people can successfully pursue their own destiny in defiance of economic laws and the iron cage of rationalization.

Unique among the advanced industrial nations, Japan developed a benevolent society in which many employees are valued throughout the whole of their working lives. The postwar Japanese family blunted

The high-speed, superexpress bullet train (*shinkansen*) symbolizes Japan's natural beauty and impressive technology. These high-speed trains travel almost silently and without vibration at more than 100 miles (161 km) per hour, and they run nearly the entire length of the country. Wind and earthquake detectors and rain gauges are installed along the entire line to warn of impending natural disasters. In case of an earthquake, the current is automatically shut down, and the train in the danger area stops; if there is high wind or heavy rain, the train's running speed is automatically reduced, or the train is stopped. Photo by P.P. Karan.

Despite modernization and urbanization, Japanese people have made major efforts to preserve their culture and tradition through a variety of festivals celebrated at various times during the year. A dance performance in Tokyo's Asakusa district at the Tanabata Matsuri is celebrated on the seventh day of the seventh month (July 7). Many festivals in Japan have their origins in tradition and are related to the annual cycle of planting, growing, and harvesting, which followed the four seasons. Festivals were observed when a major task in rice cultivation was completed. They gave rhythm to life in a village community. During the festivals many urban Japanese return to their former village homes. A large proportion of the population of metropolitan areas have rural roots, their families having lived in the cities only for two or three generations. Photo by P.P. Karan.

the pain of modernity. A delicate Japanese balance permitted the maximum division of labor (the father's total commitment to the workplace, matched by the full educational mobilization of the children, with the mother playing the role of indispensable family anchor). At the same time a higher standard of civilized life is reflected in the freedom of a woman to walk alone in the city, day or night, unafraid. That such freedom has been secure in this huge society almost without interruption through all the stresses and strains of the postwar era is astonishing.

Two decades ago Japan was praised as a nation with small government, balanced budget, and economic vitality. Japanologists such as Chalmers Johnson and Ezra Vogel described the Japanese state as a growth-oriented "developmental state" (Johnson 1982; Vogel 1979, 2000) in which the state bureaucracy, the Ministry of Finance and the Ministry of International Trade and Industry in particular,[1] collaborating with business associations and the Liberal Democratic Party, coordinated market activities and allocated resources efficiently to promote economic growth. One of the major institutional instruments of the developmental state system was the linkage of public and private finances, in which leading ministries controlled the Bank of Japan's finan-

Traditional Japanese clothing, such as the kimono worn by this woman, is no longer part of everyday life and is reserved for special ceremonial occasions. Japanese adopted Western-style clothing in the mid-nineteenth century. Until the recession of the 1990s the Japanese topped the list of big fashion spenders on clothing. Now, it's good-bye to designer suits as Japanese taste is drifting down-market. Photo by P.P. Karan.

---

[1] The central government underwent a major reorganization in January 2001, and the names of the ministries have changed.

cial policy as a means of growth-oriented economic policy. However, in the 1990s Japan's fiscal condition worsened, and its economic growth rate became one of the lowest in Asia (Yoichi 2000). The "Developmental Public Work State" failed.

As the twenty-first century began, a sense of greatness did not define Japan's mood. Fears of national stasis, even retreat, persisted despite evidence that the recent recession was at last easing. The 1980s taught the Japanese to celebrate their success; then the 1990s provoked the most severe crisis of national confidence since 1945. For the first time since the brutal ending of the Pacific War, the Japanese have been forced to brood on why countries decline and fall. Just a few years ago, Japan was a country so dedicated to extravagance that some restaurants even offered meals topped with gold dust, a tribute to corporate expense accounts, and executives were picking up Armani suits and patches of American real estate as if they were stuffing a gift bag with baubles. National spending soared. But now after several years of near-zero growth, many Japanese are anxious about their future.

The collapse of Japan's "bubble" economy is having a dramatic impact on consumer behavior. Traditionally, Japanese consumers placed overwhelming priority on a product's quality and on luxury brand names: Hermes scarves, Prada handbags, Rolex watches, fashion and leather goods from Louis Vuitton, Tiffany, Giorgio Armani, and Bvlgari. Since 1996 sales of luxury goods have declined by more than one-third, to 1.2 trillion yen ($10.8 billion), according to Yano Research Institute. That is a big change from the heady 1980s, when the average Japanese was flush with cash. But consumer behavior changed when the economy slipped into reverse more than a decade ago. The lifetime employment system began to crumble, disposable incomes declined, and consumers started to look harder at what they were buying. Young Japanese working women living with their parents have room in their budgets to shop for luxuries. The number of young working women is dwindling, however. Japan's population is aging rapidly, and the sluggish economy, rising unemployment, and higher taxes mean that the smaller new generation of young adults tends to have less to spend. Now economic uncertainty and political inertia have altered the tendency to shop for mainstream brands like Gap and its Japanese equivalent,

The idea of dressing down arrived in Japan in the 1990s with the recession. Uniqlo, a Japanese retailer, often called the clone of the Gap, is growing rapidly. Young women in Japan now tend to wear simple casual clothing sold at stores similar to Kmart and Target. Gone are the heady 1980s, when Japanese were dressed in the likes of Gucci and Hanae Mori; when Japanese companies seemed unstoppable; when some Japanese and Western commentators opined that Japan had developed a form of capitalism newer and better than that practiced elsewhere. All this now smacks of hubris. Photo by P.P. Karan.

Uniqlo. Japanese are becoming much more bargain-conscious and are willing to buy at Wal-Mart, which opened its first store in Yokohama in partnership with Seiyu, Japan's fourth-largest retailer. This price sensitivity is causing a revolution in the distribution of goods. Japanese consumers have stopped making weekend shopping forays to expensive department stores, opting instead for suburban discount centers. In the Tokyo and Osaka areas alone, there are at least eight major megamalls under construction hoping to take advantage of the changes. Most of these malls are American-inspired projects and feature America's best specialty retailers and American-style entertainment venues.

Large department stores such as Sogo collapsed in 2000 because they had borrowed heavily and over-expanded; they paid the price when real estate values fell in the 1990s. The squeeze on Sogo came about when banks faced new competition from overseas and a deregulated financial system, which could no longer keep shaky companies on life support forever. Japanese banks are cleaning up their balance sheets; in the

Despite the collapse of the asset-inflated economic bubble in 1990 and the general business slowdown, new shopping malls such as this one, called Apita, in suburban Nagoya, are being constructed all across the country in response to strong consumer demand by the young Japanese. The stores that fill the mall include outlets for Lands End, Gap, Starbucks Coffee, McDonald's, and Eddie Bauer. Each day cars jam the parking structures adjoining the shopping complex. Consumers are willing to spend on luxury items that are discounted and quality items that are inexpensive in shopping malls. Thanks to cheaper land in the 1990s and looser regulations, the shopping mall concept is taking root in suburban Japan. Photo by P.P. Karan.

short term this may result in job losses that will delay economic recovery. Most scholars say that Japan must swallow strong medicine in order to rise again.

Japanese banks are now shifting themselves from government control, while companies are casting off the control of banks. Strings of interdependence, which crisscross among Japanese companies two or three times, are being snipped one by one. For example, Nissan Motor Company, supported previously by the Industrial Bank of Japan, Japan's main bank, chose to survive as a member of France's Renault group, which introduced Western-style pricing and smashed entrenched and often costly corporate relationships.

Japan's elderly citizens have enough money (54 percent of the nation's personal assets), and they could revive the economy if they spent a little more. But fear of the future deters seniors from opening their wallets. Without strong evidence that a well-constructed social security system—one that could ease the anxiety senior citizens feel as their declining

years approach—is on the horizon, efforts to get older citizens to spend their life savings are unlikely to succeed.

Frugality is sweeping Japanese society as it enters the new millennium. Magazines offer suggestions for saving, telling readers that microwave cooking is half as expensive as gas-burner cooking and recommending baths rather than showers or small instead of large televisions. A long recession notwithstanding, shops dealing in used goods are going strong. The trend is endorsed by cheap prices and a changing awareness of consumers, who now value quality more than newness and who are also interested in environmental issues. A case in point is the recent rise in the number of secondhand golf-club shops, which were hard to come across a few years ago, and 100-yen stores (similar to the Dollar General stores in the United States). More than two hundred used-golf-club outlets opened in 2000, and about the same number have contracted to become part of Golf Partner, a franchise chain that opened in 1999. The rapid growth of shops selling used goods contrasts sharply with the slow growth in consumption. The Ministry of Economy, Trade, and Industry's Commercial Census shows that there were 10,568 used-goods retailers in Japan in 1999, an increase of 24.9 percent from 1997. That growth is astonishing considering that the overall number of retailers decreased 7.5 percent in the same period.

Until recently, many Japanese were unwilling to buy secondhand goods. But the negative feeling has been dying down, particularly among young people. In an Economic Planning Agency survey in August 2000, 47.9 percent of the respondents reported buying books and CDs at secondhand shops. About 31 percent had purchased used clothes, and about 24 percent had bought used children's wear. Consumers are more aware now than in the 1980s of the balance between price and quality, as evidenced by the extraordinary success of clothes retailer Uniqlo, which made its name with its own brand of clothing at reasonable prices. Japan's society may be moving from one filled with disposable goods to one that emphasizes recycled products.

Cost cutting has increased household savings in Japan, which have climbed to 21 percent of disposable income, from about 18.5 percent in 1991. Household savings were less than 5 percent in the United States. Savings cut domestic consumption and thus

Success turns sour. Sogo Department Store chain in Toyota City was closed in 2000. The financial collapse of Sogo, one of the largest chain stores in Japan, was a shocking reminder of Japan's economic problems. Sogo borrowed huge amounts of money from banks, overexpanded during the 1980s real estate boom, and paid the price when values fell in the 1990s. Sogo started in 1830 as a secondhand kimono shop, and it was a struggling 3-store department chain until 1962, when it became transformed into a retailing colossus with 41 outlets in Japan and overseas. Sogo opened stores near busy railway stations and bought nearby land. As business took off at the department store, surrounding land rose in value, providing collateral for further expansion. Trouble began as land prices fell after the burst of the bubble economy. By 1994 Sogo was in default, but it was still opening stores in 1998. When the end finally came in 2000, Sogo had racked up more than $17 billion in debt, making the corporate collapse one of the biggest in postwar Japanese history. Photo by P.P. Karan.

increase the trade surplus. In Japan, women often control the household purse strings, and one sign of the times is the dwindling allowances that wives give their husbands. It is the habit of parsimony that will help fortify the Japanese economy and society in the long run, because those billions are recycled into moneymaking investment projects throughout the international economy.

What a difference a dozen years can make! When the Japanese stock market was at its peak in 1989, many experts around the world foresaw Japan capturing global economic and industrial leadership. Japanese companies bought up chunks of Hollywood and New York real estate; they talked about their nation's gross national product surpassing America's in the twenty-first century. Many Japanese thought the twenty-first century would be the Japanese century. But after years of unremitting economic struggles since the 1990 burst of the "bubble economy," that seems unlikely. Japanese books, business magazines, and dailies are now arguing that—like Britain a century ago—Japan may be in an inexorable decline in international prestige and economic might.

Many business leaders and ordinary citizens say that unless the economy is freed of regulatory barriers, the bureaucracy is reorganized, and the approach to policymaking is changed, Japan's aging society and the flight of manufacturing industries to lower-wage countries will bring about even greater economic problems. About four-fifths of the Japanese economy, including the financial industry, lumbers through commerce under heavy regulation. Japan has outgrown the postwar set of restrictions and must replace them with more market-oriented capitalism. For the regulated swath of the economy, the transition toward market mechanisms is fraught with growing pains. The Japanese government has talked about transforming Japan's economy and the financial system but has not been able to accomplish much. The bureaucrats who sit at the apex of the current system don't share the conviction that change is needed—in their view the old machinery needs only a bit of tweaking. Meanwhile, the nation's political leaders have demonstrated neither the ability nor the inclination to push for real reforms.

The public wants politicians to reform Japan's economic structure and to exercise leadership in making a breakthrough in the current sluggish economic environment. This sentiment is a reflection of the political confusion and economic stagnation of the 1990s, which has been dubbed "the lost decade." In any country, although politics leads the economy, the economy can also move politics. Therefore, if an economic malaise caused by a crisis of politics persists for a long time, the power of the economic sector eventually will change the political structures. In Japan such a move has already begun at the local government level, as evidenced by the 2000 gubernatorial elections in Tochigi and Nagano, and it might not be long before the political scene at the national level is also transformed.

When is Japan going to recover, restructure, and take off again? The question is simple, the answer very complicated. There are daunting obstacles in the way of dynamic change, including a mountain of bad bank loans, excessive regulation, and informal as well as formal barriers to open markets. There is a real-time urgency. Not only does the world need Japan as an ongoing engine for growth, but growth is by far the best answer to Japan's government debt burden and the fiscal consequences of the nation's rapidly approaching demographic problems. Most Japanese accept that change is needed, but there is a lack of determination to implement any reforms that would cause real pain. Although deregulation and liberalization are recognized as important policy issues, several issues combine to keep the pace of change disappointingly slow. The rapid aging of the population has implications for the structure of the future labor force, the savings rate, and the government's budget. The banking system is heavily burdened by bad debt. The government's fiscal position has also deteriorated rapidly, largely owing to the implementation during the 1990s of successive fiscal stimulus packages (about $826 billion) and to the sluggish tax revenue growth.

Deflation. Recession. Huge public debts. Insolvent banks. Even amid this economic gloom, some Japanese are less worried than optimistic. Japan may not rival America in innovation, but it has repeatedly shown prowess in catching up with the West. It is a kind of social phenomenon that Japan as a country starts to move when it is triggered by pessimism. Japan maintains a hope for success and a sense of crisis as it faces the challenges of the twenty-first century. Given the resourcefulness that produced its postwar economic miracle, Japan is likely to emerge from a decade of stagnation and reestablish sustained economic growth.

This book discusses the challenges facing Japan in the twenty-first century in the context of the country's geography. Chapter 2 deals with environmental challenges and constraints. The historical and cultural roots of Japan, which provide the background for understanding the contemporary challenges, are the topic of chapter 3. A comprehensive account of the landscape and regions of the country, which provide the stage for the nation's development, is found in chapters 4 and 5.

Ancient Chinese culture and politics have influenced Japan. Religion in Japan, during much of its history, has centered on Shintoism and Buddhism. The philosophy of Confucianism, which respects humility and requires strict hierarchical relationships, deeply penetrated Japanese society. As a result Japanese culture differs from that of the West in many respects. The Tokugawa (Edo) era, which began in the early seventeenth century, established a closed-country policy that built a unique culture and societal system. In the latter half of the nineteenth century, Japan opened itself to external influence with the arrival of Commodore Perry's black ships. The Meiji Restoration, which more definitively opened Japan's door to the West, introduced European science, technology, and political systems and resulted in earnest efforts to build a modern state. Initially, Japan modeled itself after the German brand of constitutional monarchy and established an imperial parliament.

Because of its declining birthrate, Japan is facing an aging society. The average life expectancy in Japan is the highest in the world for both men and women. The challenges of demography, particularly those related to the aging society, are discussed in chapter 6. The problems of the rural and urban areas are described in chapters 7 and 8. The postwar political culture, attempts to reform the political system, and Japan's relations with its neighbors are analyzed in chapter 9. The end of World War II saw the Japanese economy developing swiftly, becoming the second-largest in the world, behind only the United States in terms of gross domestic product. However, the economic bubble burst in the 1990s owing to unchecked speculation, the appreciation of the yen, and the progression of information technology that propelled the globalization of Japanese companies. Economic challenges, including the shift in management methods from the one that had been established in Japanese culture and institutions, marked by the seniority system, lifetime employment, and group decision making, to a method that recognizes openness, fairness, and speed; industrial restructuring; and the problems of the postindustrial sector of the economy, are discussed in chapters 10, 11, and 12. Chapter 13 treats the impact of rapid development on environment and the citizens' movement to protect the local environment. Chapter 14 pulls together major ideas that bear on the challenges confronting Japan in the twenty-first century.

REFERENCES

Johnson, Chalmers. 1982. *MITI and the Japanese Miracle, 1925–75*. Stanford, CA: Stanford Univ. Press.

Vogel, Ezra. 1979. *Japan as Number One: Lessons for America*. London: Harper.

———. 2000. *Is Japan Still Number One?* Selangor Darul Ehsan, Malaysia: Pelanduk.

Yoichi, Masuzoe. 2000. *Years of Trial: Japan in the 1990s*. Tokyo: Japan Echo.

Chapter 2

第二章

Environmental Challenges and Constraints

What challenges and constraints does the natural environment offer to Japan? What is the influence of nature on the country's society and culture? What impact will the environmental challenges have on Japan's role in the twenty-first century? The Japanese dwell in a dynamic and ever-shifting, even though restricted, natural setting, from cold northern seas to tepid southern waters. There is striking diversity in geography and environment from region to region. These differences have been a major factor in creating the unique blend that is Japanese culture. A slender mountain range stretching down the middle forms the backbone of the island nation. There are basin lands between the mountains and small plains along the coast.

The Physical Setting of Japan

Physically, Japan is made up of a ragged chain of islands scattered as a crescent off the east coast of Asia. In terms of size, these islands are but a footnote to the great landmass of Asia. But that footnote is where the Japanese have carved out their life and developed their culture. The total area, about 146,000 square miles (378,000 sq km) is one-twenty-fifth the size of the United States, about the same size as Italy, and less than the area of California. Only three West European countries (France, Spain, and Sweden) are larger than Japan.

The elongated shape of the Japanese archipelago in the north-south direction has played an important role in shaping the country's natural and cultural landscapes. The entire archipelago covers 25 degrees of latitude, from 45° N to 20° N, about 1,740 miles (2,800 km) along the meridian. The four major islands cover a total north-south distance of nearly 1,150 miles (1,850 km), which is about the same as the distance between St. Paul and New Orleans or

between Seattle and Los Angeles. The northernmost part of Japan lies in the latitude of Maine, and the southern areas lie in the latitudes of southern Alabama. The southern chain of the small Nansei (Ryukyu) Islands extends more than 700 miles (1,100 km). The Nansei Islands, between Kyushu and Taiwan, lie in the latitude of the Florida Keys and central Mexico. The Izu and Ogasawara Islands extend more than 1,000 miles (1,600 km) between the capital city of Tokyo and the tropical Mariana Islands. This geographic reach of the Japanese islands is unusually long.

The Sea of Okhotsk, the Sea of Japan, the East China Sea, and the Pacific Ocean surround Japan. The three seas, which cover part of the Asian continental shelf, are shallower than the Pacific Ocean to the east. The Korea Strait between the Island of Tsushima and Korea is only 31 miles (50 km) wide and 500 feet (150 m) deep. In contrast, on the east side of Japan, the floor of the Pacific Ocean drops away quickly into the zones of tectonic subduction forming the Chishima-Kamchatka, Japan (Tuscarora), and Izu-Ogasawara trenches. One of the greatest ocean depths in the world is found in the Japan trench at 35,040 feet (10,680 m).

Another oceanic feature is that a cold surface ocean current, the Oyashio, from northern polar waters, meets with a strong warm surface current, the Kuroshio, from southern equatorial waters, off the east coast of Japan. The Oyashio, also known as the Chishima (Kuri) Current, literally means "parent" current because it has provided good fishing. The Kuroshio, also known as the Japan or Black Current, literally means "black" current and is named for its dark color. The Kuroshio is one of the strongest ocean currents in the world—as strong as the Gulf Stream. A tributary of the Kuroshio, the warm

Wakkanai, an ice-free port on Soya Strait between the Sea of Okhotsk and the Sea of Japan, is a major fishing center in northern Hokkaido. Wakkanai forms the northernmost tip of Japan at latitude 45° 31′ north, and Japan extends southwest from Hokkaido to the Ryukyu Islands, north of Taiwan. Photo by P.P. Karan.

Tsushima Current, enters the Sea of Japan through the Korea Strait and plays an important role in the climate of Japan.

GEOLOGIC STRUCTURE

The Japanese islands are located at the junction of major ever-shifting tectonic plates (see fig. 2.1). Some of these plates are enormous—the rocks underlying much of the Pacific Ocean, for example, rest on a single Pacific plate 6,210 miles (10,000 km) wide—whereas others span only a couple hundred miles. What distinguishes a plate, however, is that it moves as a cohesive body across the surface of the earth. The motion is slow, usually on the order of two inches or less per year. As a plate moves, it grinds or knocks against its neighbors; this plate-to-plate interaction produces the majority of the earthquakes in Japan.

The Japanese archipelago was created by crustal movements involving four major tectonic plates: the Pacific plate underlying the western Pacific, the Eurasian plate beneath the Asian landmass and the Sea of Japan, the North American plate in the north, and the Philippine plate to the south. Ocean deeps mark the lines of collision between the plates. The intermittent sliding of the ocean bed along the deeps results in earthquakes and tidal waves called tsunamis. The friction of movement deep beneath the western plates melts the surrounding crust, which spews forth as volcanoes that run along the entire island chain. The volcanic zones, many of which contain hot springs, have considerable value as tourist attractions.

The largest earthquakes have originated in the subducted Philippine and Pacific plates, although the havoc wrecked on Kobe by the 1995 Hanshin earthquake reveals the hazard posed by shallow crustal quakes to densely populated cities.

The complex geologic structure of the islands offers an explanatory framework for its complicated geomorphology (Yamazaki 1996), which in turn often provides meaningful explanations for the diverse physical and cultural landscapes of Japan. Two major geologic features of the Japanese islands are the Fossa Magna and the Median Tectonic Line.

The Fossa Magna is a great structural depression or rift valley in central Honshu created by block faulting. The western edge of the Fossa Magna is known as the Itoigawa-Shizuoka Line. The eastern edge is not clear because of volcanic activity in the Quaternary period, but it most likely runs through Naoetsu in Niigata Prefecture and Choshi in Chiba Prefecture.

The Fossa Magna divides northeastern from southwestern Japan. Northeast of the Fossa Magna, Honshu runs in a north-south direction, and to the southwest it runs east and west. In general, in the northeastern part of Japan, the Pacific Ocean side is geologically older than the Sea of Japan side. In contrast, in the southwestern part, the Pacific Ocean side is geologically younger than the Sea of Japan side.

The Median Tectonic Line is one of the major fault lines longitudinally dissecting the Japanese islands. The origin of the line is traced back to the

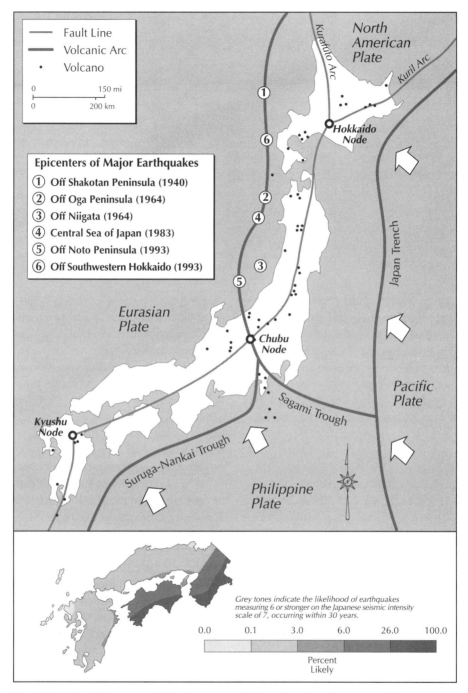

Fault Line
Volcanic Arc
Volcano

0 ———— 150 mi
0 ———— 200 km

Epicenters of Major Earthquakes

① Off Shakotan Peninsula (1940)
② Off Oga Peninsula (1964)
③ Off Niigata (1964)
④ Central Sea of Japan (1983)
⑤ Off Noto Peninsula (1993)
⑥ Off Southwestern Hokkaido (1993)

North American Plate

Kurafuto Arc

Kuril Arc

Hokkaido Node

Japan Trench

Eurasian Plate

Chubu Node

Pacific Plate

Kyushu Node

Sagami Trough

Suruga-Nankai Trough

Philippine Plate

Grey tones indicate the likelihood of earthquakes measuring 6 or stronger on the Japanese seismic intensity scale of 7, occurring within 30 years.

0.0   0.1   3.0   6.0   26.0   100.0

Percent Likely

Fig. 2.1. Continental plates around the Japanese archipelago. Based on Geographical Survey Institute, *National Atlas of Japan* (Tokyo: Japan Map Center, 1977).

A mountain village, north of Shizuoka, in the Fossa Magna belt of Japan. Fossa Magna is a large depressed land zone extending north–south (from Itoigawa in Niigata Prefecture on the Sea of Japan to the city of Shizuoka on the Pacific coast, via Lake Suwa) across the center of Honshu, the main island of Japan. This area consists of sedimentary, volcanic, and pyroclastic rocks. The Fossa Magna (Great Fissure Zone) was identified by Edmund Naumann, a German geologist, who taught at Tokyo University from 1875 to 1885 and helped establish a geology department in the Ministry of Agriculture and Commerce in 1878. The department later became the Geological Survey of Japan. Photo by P.P. Karan.

Cretaceous period when dinosaurs walked over the islands. It runs from the south of Lake Suwa, across the Kii Peninsula and Shikoku, to the center of Kyushu. The line divides southwestern Japan into the outer (*gaitai*) and inner (*naitai*) zones. A similar dislocation line (fault line) may exist in northeastern Japan; however, it is less obvious. The alignment of these fault lines demonstrates the basic arc-linear structure of the Japanese islands.

LANDFORMS

Mountain and hilly country makes up nearly 80 percent of the land area (see fig. 2.2). The major mountain ranges, following the arc-linear structure of the Japanese islands, run throughout the entire length of the four major islands. The mountain ranges form parallel chains separated by numerous basins. They have functioned as an effective barrier for human movements within the country. Most of the prefecture boundaries today, like the ancient ones, follow the ridges of these mountain ranges. Consequently, tunnels through the mountains are conspicuous features of the landscape of Japan today.

The mountains in Japan are rugged and steep-sided but not very high, usually less than 6,560 feet (2,000 m). Most of the higher mountains (higher than 9,840 ft or 3,000 m) are located in central Honshu, and this lofty mountain area is often called the Roof of Japan. It includes the precipitous Hida, Kiso, and Akaishi ranges, which run in a north-south direction and together are called the Japan Alps (see fig. 2.3). West of the Japan Alps and the Fossa Ma-

gna, the parallel (east–west) lines of mountains continue. They are broken by faults and subsidences in which the Setonaikai (Seto Inland Sea) and Lake Biwa have formed.

To the southeast of the Japan Alps, Japan's highest mountain, Mount Fuji (12,388 ft or 3,776 m), stands in isolation from other high mountains. This handsome composite volcano is located within the partly filled depression of the Fossa Magna. The eruption of Mount Fuji began about 700,000 years ago, and most recently it erupted in AD 1707.

Each summer Mount Fuji is visited and climbed by more than five thousand tourists and pilgrims. Trash left by the visitors has despoiled the environment, damaging the reputation of the Japanese for tidiness. In recent years volunteers have responded to the challenge of cleaning up the slopes of the dormant volcano to give Mount Fuji a makeover. In addition to the visitors, there are two thousand religious organizations registered around Mount Fuji, and the peak's base offers 117 golf courses. A thirty-four-square-mile area (88 sq km) on the mountain's eastern flank is used by the Japanese and American militaries for live-fire exercises. In many ways, Mount Fuji captures the jarring amalgam of spirituality and commercialization that is central to Japan's modern identity.

Within the complex mountain framework there are small areas of habitable land generally confined to the coastal margins. Most of these plains have been formed by either fluvial or marine deposition or erosion during the Quaternary period. Among these

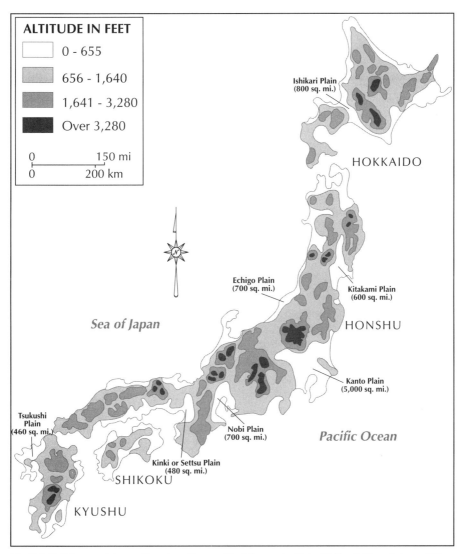

ALTITUDE IN FEET

0 - 655

656 - 1,640

1,641 - 3,280

Over 3,280

0   150 mi
0   200 km

Ishikari Plain
(800 sq. mi.)

HOKKAIDO

Echigo Plain
(700 sq. mi.)

Kitakami Plain
(600 sq. mi.)

Sea of Japan

HONSHU

Kanto Plain
(5,000 sq. mi.)

Tsukushi
Plain
(460 sq. mi.)

Nobi Plain
(700 sq. mi.)

Pacific Ocean

Kinki or Settsu Plain
(480 sq. mi.)

SHIKOKU

KYUSHU

Fig. 2.2. Relief map of Japan. Based on Geographical Survey Institute, *National Atlas of Japan* (Tokyo: Japan Map Center, 1977).

areas of relatively level land are the Kanto Plain around Tokyo, Ishikari in southeast Hokkaido, Echigo on the west coast of Honshu, Nobi around Nagoya, Kitakami north of Sendai on the Pacific coast of Honshu, Kinki or Settsu around Osaka at the eastern end of the Inland Sea, and Tsukushi, surrounding Kurume in western Kyushu. The distribution of alluvial plains, diluvial terraces, and a mountain zone in Saitama Prefecture of the Kanto region illustrates the pattern of terrain in Japan (see fig. 2.4). The plains consist of separate sections of alluvial lowland with finer earth materials, which blanket the downstream part of the plains, followed by degraded alluvium or diluvial upland, which flanks the mountains (Saito 1999; Ouchi 1996).

The alluvial lowland portion of the plain is most valuable for paddy cultivation and as the site for urban-industrial development. Intensive agriculture, with rice as the major crop, occupies about half of the lowlands (see fig. 2.5). The diluvial upland portion of the plain consists of relatively coarse materials forming a porous dry area with a deep water table. With water shortage and porous soil, the upland is used for orchards and nonirrigated crops such as wheat, barley, and vegetables. The margins of the uplands are used for tea growing. The higher areas

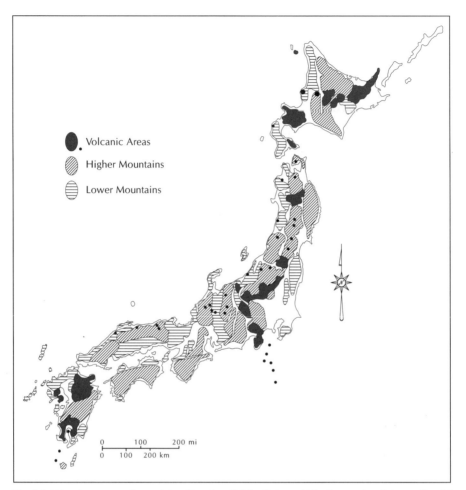

Fig. 2.3. Volcanic areas and mountains. Based on Yutaka Sakaguchi in *Geography of Japan,* Special Publication no. 4 (Tokyo: Association of Japanese Geographers, 1980).

flanking the mountains are covered with dense forest, varying from a broad-leaved type in the south to pines in the north; lumbering is a major activity.

The Nobi Plain, in which the city of Nagoya is located, is a fluvial lowland comprising an alluvial fan area adjacent to the mountains forming the piedmont plain, a natural levee area, and a deltaic region in the lower reaches. The natural levees, about 200–600 feet (61–183 m) wide, are densely developed. Large parts of the deltaic plain have been reclaimed. The Niigata Plain, an area of more than 77 square miles (200 sq km) on the west coast of Honshu, is alluvial lowland. The area experienced unusually high subsidence during geologic time, resulting in the absence of terraces.

In the interiors of the islands, there are many small, steep-sided basins, which are often surrounded by alluvial fans at the base of slopes. The major basins are Kofu, Nagano, and Yamagata. In Japanese history, a basin has been a particularly preferred place for an urban settlement. For example, the early capitals of Japan were placed in basins: Heijo-kyo was built in AD 710 in Nara Basin, and Heiankyo was built in AD 794 in Kyoto Basin. This tendency, which is discussed further below, is a key to understanding the Japanese people's perceptions and preferences with regard to landscapes, in relation to Confucianism, Taoism, and traditional geomancy (*husui* in Japanese or *feng shui* in Chinese).

The scarcity of level land is one of the salient features of the geography of Japan. Thus, the small areas of lowland, which contain not only most of the cultivated land but also all the major concentrations of population and industry, are of vital importance.

Mountains of the Chubu region. Part of the Japan Alps, these ranges extend through four prefectures and include five peaks over 10,000 feet (3,048 m). The Japanese archipelago is made up almost entirely of steep mountain areas with very few plains. High, precipitous mountains form the spine of Japan. Multipurpose dams have been constructed on many rivers to control flooding and provide irrigation, water, and power. Photo by P.P. Karan.

Mount Iwake (Iwakesan in Japanese) has an elegant conical peak 5,331 feet (1,625 m) high and is located in western Aomori prefecture in northern Honshu. It is also called Tsugaru Fuji. The summit abounds in alpine flora. Photo by Cotton Mather.

Field Report

Climbing Mount Fuji

Japan's highest peak, with its perfectly symmetrical cone, is undeniably spellbinding from afar. Up close, this dormant volcano is basically a collection of lava rocks and cinder-covered slopes. During the peak summer season, climbers must contend with the garbage on the slopes and such tourist kitsch as cone-shaped Fuji palm cakes with white frosting on top.

Yet what the Japanese affectionately call Fuji-san continues to draw 150,000 to 200,000 climbers annually from all walks of life. True, this is not Mount Everest. There are no death-defying thrills or sprawling base camps. Still, muscling and grunting one's way up to the summit is something of a personal challenge for amateur climbers. The views at the summit, whether of the nearby rugged mountain ranges of central Japan or of the Pacific coastline, can be immensely beautiful even when clouds at lower altitudes obscure the mountaintop from below.

Mount Fuji has always held a strong, sometimes bizarre, influence over the Japanese psyche (Abe 1992). Climbing of Fuji began as a religious ritual. Followers of Fujiko, a syncretic sect with both Buddhist and Shinto elements, consider Fuji sacred. Prior to the Meiji era (1868–1912), most believed that the volcano was the dwelling of Japan's Shinto gods. Even in a more secular Japan, numerous Buddhist sects, including the powerful Soka Gakkai (Value Creation Society), have set headquarters nearby. The notorious Aum Shinriko (Supreme Truth) cult prepared nerve gas at its Fuji-area base to launch a deadly attack on a subway station in Tokyo.

The climbing season runs from mid-June to mid-September, ending before bad weather and snow keep people away. To avoid the usual throng, many people decide to make a night climb, with the hope of catching the mountain's best sunrise view at about 5 a.m. A two-and-a-half-hour journey by bus from central Tokyo takes the climbers halfway up the volcano's north slope to Gogome, or Station Five. Although diehard enthusiasts start at the bottom of Mount Fuji, most begin the five-to-six-hour climb to the top from Gogome or a similar spot on the south side. Rest stations along the way and at the summit sell snacks and drinks. Climbers from the Fujiko sect originally divided the route to the summit into ten stations or stages (*gome*).

Most climbers breeze up gentle dirt slopes to the seven-thousand-foot-high Station Seven, a mile and a half up from Station Five. Then the heavy trudging begins in earnest as the terrain turns steep and rocky. The temperature plummets and high winds kick in. One hears a lot of encouraging sounds of "*gambatte*," or "hang in there." The pastel-colored outlines of a sunrise begin to appear on the horizon as climbers pass the historic lion-dog stone sculptures that guard the sacred grounds of the summit. When the sun finally shows itself, the Japanese national anthem is piped over a loudspeaker.

Walking around the summit's crater takes about an hour. On a clear day, one can enjoy a panoramic view of Honshu, Japan's primary island. But don't expect to see lava or smoke. Fuji last blew its top back in the early 1700s and has been inactive ever since.

Of course, the trip back is less tiring, but it is hardly a joyride. The main route down is a steep, zigzagging journey over loose gravel and rocks big enough to trip up the most nimble-footed. Climbers usually make it back to Gogome about 10 a.m. and sleep in the bus for most of the return trip to Tokyo.

These regions, however, represent a mere 16 percent of Japan's total land area. The foundation of the daily lives of the Japanese people is anchored in these small flatland areas. The industrialization of the post–Meiji Restoration era from about 1868 has increased the importance of these plains. The great majority of the population has moved steadily to the large cities located in these flatlands, and the natural beauty near the areas continues to be eroded. The mountain areas, which make up most of Japan's land area, are

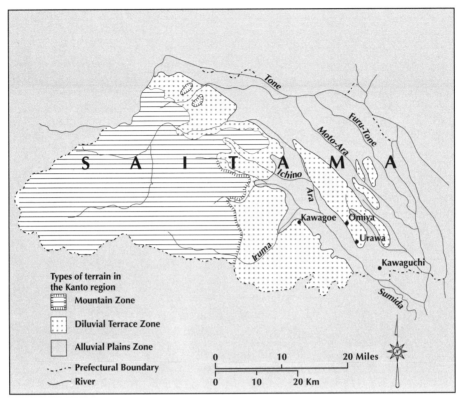

Fig. 2.4. Alluvial plains, diluvial terraces, and mountains, Saitama Prefecture. Based on Ron L. Andrews, *Japan: A Social and Economic Geography* (Melbourne: George Philip and O'Neil, 1971).

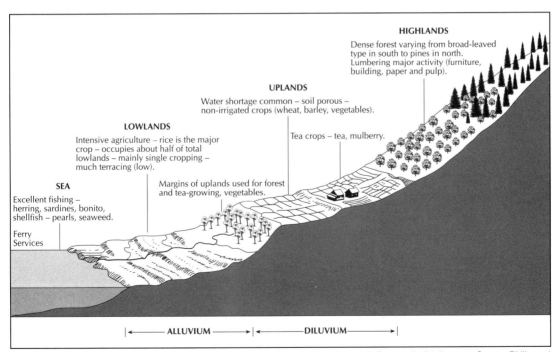

Fig. 2.5. Land use by terrain. Based on Ron L. Andrews, *Japan: A Social and Economic Geography* (Melbourne: George Philip and O'Neil, 1971).

progressively becoming depopulated. The flatlands are interrupted by mountain ranges. Along the coast one finds a variety of natural landscapes: quiet, sandy beaches, rough and rugged cliffs, gentle inland seas, and turbulent open ocean. Mountains and sea are the two primary elements of Japan. The evolution of the coastal plains of Japan has been investigated in detail by Masatomo Umitsu (1991, 1996).

RIVERS AND LAKES: DRAINAGE PATTERNS

"A series of rapids and falls" may be an appropriate description of the rivers of Japan. Because of heavy rainfall, the rivers have dissected mountains by rapid erosion, forming steep-sided valleys; the rivers often cause serious floods as they emerge from the mountains onto the lowland plains. Notable rivers in Japan include the Tone, Kiso, and Shinano Rivers. Comparing these "long" rivers of Japan with other famous rivers of the world, clearly the rivers in Japan are shorter in length, and their angles of base flow are steeper (see fig. 2.6).

Japan has numerous lakes, the largest of which is Lake Biwa, a freshwater lake with an area of 259 square miles (670 sq km). Most of the inland lakes were formed by volcanic activity. On the one hand, these lakes and mountains make splendid scenery, which attracts many tourists. On the other, most lagoons and seaside lakes are polluted with waste from urban and industrial areas and are inaccessible because artificial banks have been built along the shores of lagoons.

In contrast to the mountain ranges, which acted as barriers for people's movement, these water bodies, combined with the surrounding oceans and the Seto Inland Sea, have provided useful means of transportation since the early days of Japanese history. Like the tunnels through mountains, the numerous bridges are also conspicuous features of the landscape of Japan.

CLIMATES AND SEASONS

Japan lies in the temperate zone and at the northeastern fringe of monsoon Asia, which extends from Japan through the Korean Peninsula, China, and Southeast Asia to India. The climate of Japan varies considerably from place to place, largely due to the continental air currents from the northwest that dominate the winter weather and the oceanic air currents from the southeast that prevail in the summer months. The large latitudinal extent of Japan, the sheltering effect of the mountains, and the monsoonal airstream produce considerable climatic differences between north and south and between the western Sea of Japan side and the eastern Pacific side of the islands. Hiroshi Shitara (1978) and Takeshi Kawamura (1980) have summarized recent studies on the climate of Japan.

The elongated north-south direction of the Japanese islands produces a great variety of climates. The southern island chains, such as the Nansei and Ogasawara Islands, have a warm subtropical climate, whereas the northern island of Hokkaido has a cold subpolar climate. The rest of Japan has a warm-temperate to cool-temperate climate. Thus, there are four primary climatic zones in Japan: from north to south, these are the subpolar, cool-temperate, warm-temperate, and subtropical zones.

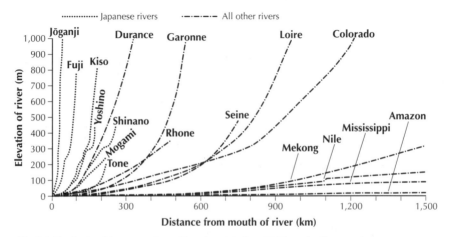

Fig. 2.6. Gradients of Japanese rivers. Based on data from K. Okamoto, Nagoya, Japan.

The temperature in the summer is more or less homogeneous over the archipelago; during the winter the temperature difference between the southern and northern parts becomes greater (that is, warmer in the south and much colder in the north). See figure 2.7. This difference between summer and winter results from the seasonal shift of the polar front, where a cold polar air mass meets a warm subtropical air mass over Japan. The position of the polar front shifts north during the summer; thus, most of the Japanese archipelago is covered by the subtropical air mass in summer. In contrast, the position of the polar front moves toward the south during the winter, and the archipelago comes under the influence of the polar air mass.

Another important factor is the central mountains. Because of the mountain ranges, the climate of Japan is further divided into two general types, the sun belt on the southeastern Pacific side and the snow belt on the northwestern Sea of Japan side. As with the primary climatic zones, the climatic difference between these two types is greater in winter than in summer. Both sides have a hot summer, although the Pacific side is more humid than the Sea of Japan side. In winter, prevailing northwesterly winds bring some of the heaviest snows in the world to the Sea of Japan side. The northwesterly winds, which blow out from the cold Siberian high pressure zone, cross over the Sea of Japan. The winds pick up heat and moisture from the warm Tsushima Current and form convectional cumulus and cumulonimbus clouds. This results in heavy snow on the Sea of Japan side, from 40 to 120 inches (1–3 m) annually. The recorded maximum is an unbelievable 470 inches (12 m). Then, as the winds move over the mountains, they have less moisture and are warmed up by adiabatic processes. As a result they bring clear, dry weather over the Pacific side.

There are two additional climate types, the inland type and the Inland Sea type. The inland type is characterized by a large seasonal temperature fluctuation, because the moderating maritime effect is less apparent in inland areas. This climate type occurs in central Hokkaido and the central highland areas of Honshu.

The Inland Sea type occurs around the Seto Inland Sea, which extends 280 miles (450 km) in the east-west direction and 9–34 miles (15–55 km) north-south. This area is surrounded by the Chugoku and Shikoku Mountains and thus receives a relatively small amount of precipitation: the annual precipitation at Okayama, a city on the Seto Inland Sea, is 48.2 inches (1,223 mm).

Most of Japan is under the influence of the Asian monsoon. The general direction of these seasonal winds is from the Pacific Ocean in the summer and from the Asian continent in the winter. As a consequence, Japan has four clearly distinguishable seasons. Hokkaido, which is located between 41 and 45 N latitude, normally does not experience a summer monsoon.

A marked rainy season about a month long, called *baiu* or plum rain (also called *tsuyu*), is a conspicuous feature of the summer monsoon in Japan and southern China, occurring between May and July (Murata 1987). During this period, a distinct stationary (stagnant) frontal zone, called the baiu front, develops over the Japanese archipelago and southern China. The frontal zone forms where the warm, moist subtropical air mass from the Pacific meets the cold, dry polar air mass from higher latitudes (Yamakawa 1984). Along this frontal zone, many

The Hokuriku region along the Sea of Japan receives heavy snowfall, which measures up to 10 feet (3 m) each winter. Cold Siberian air masses pick up moisture as they move over the Sea of Japan, and they bring heavy precipitation in the form of snow in coastal Hokuriku. Photo by Unryu Suganuma.

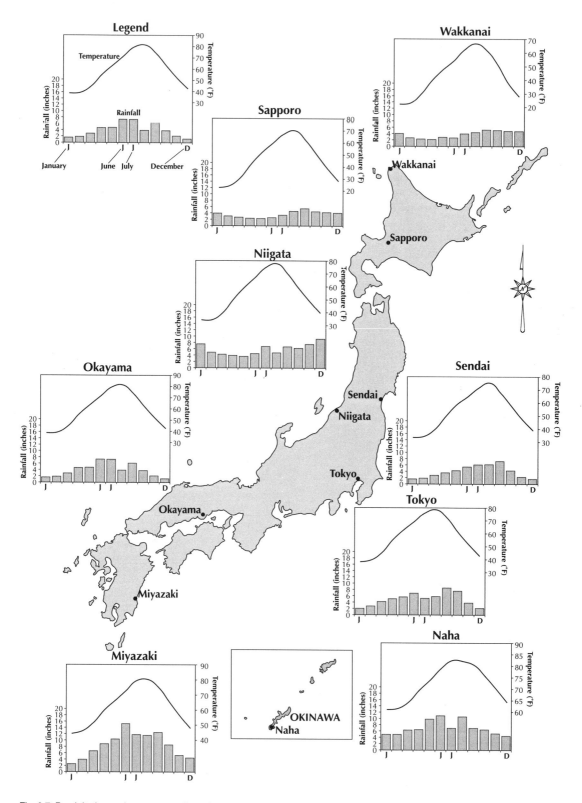

Fig. 2.7. Precipitation and temperature. Based on data from the Japan Meteorological Agency, Tokyo.

midlatitude cyclones (low pressure systems) develop rain and bring it to Japan. Toward the end of the baiu season, heavy rain often falls over Kyushu and the southern part of Chugoku. After the rainy season, the Japanese islands experience a bright, hot summer.

In autumn, from September to early October, a less marked (because of a smaller temperature contrast between the two air masses) but similar rainy season occurs. When a typhoon approaches this autumnal frontal zone, heavy rain may occur.

In most places in Japan, the annual precipitation exceeds 39 inches (1,000 mm) per year. Most of the precipitation comes from weather fronts, midlatitude cyclones, storms such as typhoons, summer and winter monsoons, and thunderstorms. The precipitation ranges between 30 and 160 inches (800–4,000 mm) per year. The annual precipitation of Tokyo, Nagoya, and Kyoto is 57.5, 62.0, and 65.7 inches, respectively (1,460, 1,575, and 1,669 mm). In comparison, that of Seattle, Los Angeles, St. Paul, and New Orleans is 28.8, 23.5, 32.2, and 52.7 inches, respectively (731, 597, 818, and 1,339 mm). This abundant precipitation is an important factor for the country's vegetation. In general, there is little north-south variation in annual precipitation in Japan. Hokkaido receives less precipitation than the rest of the country because the summer monsoon does not reach Hokkaido's high latitude. Topographical effects create special local climates in specific areas (Toritani and Hayashi 1996), and thermal environments of urban areas produce special features (Nakagawa 1996).

There are four distinct seasons in most parts of Japan. Summer, which is warm and humid, begins around the middle of July. It is preceded by a rainy season that usually lasts for about a month, except in Hokkaido, the northernmost major island, where there is no rainy season at all. Summer along the Pacific coast is hot and humid, whereas winter is generally dry and mild. Along the coast of the Sea of Japan, the summer is relatively dry, and there is heavy snowfall in the winter. The cities of Niigata and Kanazawa receive their peak precipitation in December in the form of snow, often as much as 25 inches (63.5 cm). The mountainous interior area is one of the snowiest regions in the world. Hokkaido is also characterized by fairly severe winters. Both of these regions (the mountainous interior and Hokkaido) are superb sites for winter sports.

Spring and autumn are the best seasons of the year, with balmy days and sunshine across the country. The northward passage of the *sakura zensen*—the cherry blossom front—in late March or early April, marking the onset of spring, is widely publicized in the media and in weather forecasts in Japan. It is the time when millions of people flock to public parks, ostensibly to view the blossoms, but in fact to enjoy the many hours of song and drink. From spring through summer a long wet season drags on, and when the summer heat at last withdraws its muggy clutches, the typhoon season arrives. Tropical depressions known as typhoons, generated to the southwest, travel a northern route, bending off to the northeast upon reaching Japan. About four major storms of this type assault Japan annually, bringing strong rains and winds and often leaving behind great damage and destruction.

The clearly defined change of seasons in Japan has added complexity and subtlety to the country's natural environment. For centuries the Japanese people have closely observed the cycle of the seasons, gradually developing the wisdom necessary to cope with seasonal changes. One concrete example of such wisdom is the Japanese roof. The traditional Japanese house has always been outfitted with openings in the outside walls, which were then overhung with long, low-slung eaves. These eaves block out the hot sunshine in the summer but allow the winter sun, which shines at a much lower angle, to slip in under them. During rains, these long eaves allow dwellers to leave the doors open, thereby cooling and brightening the interior. Another Japanese practice is to build a low wooden veranda under the eaves, making a place to sit down and actually be outside in the midst of nature while one is connected to the house itself. In short, the area beneath the roof is a unique space hard to define as either inside or outside, designed to allow the Japanese to become part of the natural world. At the opposite pole is the roof of a modern four-cornered building. Towering high-rises continue to multiply within Japan's cities, but the Japanese people have difficulty identifying with the roofs (or lack of them) of these structures.

Seasonal change, a factor so deeply tied to the Japanese consciousness, varies widely in essence and time according to geography. The diversity of the country's weather is most graphically demonstrated by measuring the pattern of the coming of spring.

The southernmost island, Okinawa, is alive with cherry blossoms in February, whereas Tokyo, located in approximately the latitudinal center of the nation, has its flower-viewing season in late March. The bloom line continues north through April, with the northernmost island, Hokkaido, heralding the coming of spring with the trees' pale pink blossoms in May. This extended celebration of spring takes more than 120 days from the southern end to the northern tip of the archipelago.

The cherry blossom is only a single example of the great concern of the Japanese for the tones of the different seasons. Northerners are delighted by the initial tidings of spring from the "deep south," and southerners feel an instinctive need to begin winter preparations when news roundups report the first frost in the north and the onset of autumn color (fig. 2.8). There are subtle weather variations even within the same district, and simply traveling from one area to another can bring a change in the weather and land variations. It is within this pattern that the people of the nation forge their daily modes of existence.

Vegetation Cover

An area's vegetation type is an indicator of its comprehensive ecological (biological) value and potential, because it reflects the combined effects of many environmental factors, such as climate, soils, geologic history, and geomorphology. It demonstrates the quality of the environment not only for plants, but also for animals, including humans. Thus, the vegetation type portrays the overall environmental characteristics of an area.

The forest type of vegetation dominates throughout the Japanese islands, obviously reflecting the climate pattern. Because of the abundant precipitation, forest-type vegetation can be found almost throughout the entire country. Also, the young volcanic materials that cover many areas of Japan provide a good substrate for the forest, though such soil may not be adequate for agriculture. As a result, the distribution pattern of different forest types over the Japanese islands is primarily determined by temperature, specifically the warmth of the summer and the coldness of the winter.

Today about 67 percent of Japan's land area is covered by forest (see fig. 2.9). However, almost no original (primeval) forests, or even a written record of them, remain because of the long history of human exploitation and occupation. Thus, the vegetation types shown on the map in figure 2.10 are potential climax vegetation (natural forest), the vegetation that would appear if the ecological plant succession of the area were allowed to proceed to a natural end. This is not the actual vegetation cover we see in today's Japan. Most of the standing forests are secondary forests, still in the regeneration process after being harvested. The best way to observe a replica of the original lowland forests of Japan is to visit a sacred forest (*chinju no mori*) enclosing a Shinto shrine. These are still well preserved in many places.

There are four primary forest types in Japan, named after the climatic zones. From north to south they are the subpolar, cool-temperate, warm-temperate, and subtropical forests. A transitional, or midtemperate forest appears in some areas between the cool- and warm-temperate forests.

Subpolar Zone Forest

The subpolar forest is an evergreen needle-leaf forest or taiga occurring in the eastern half of Hokkaido. This type of forest also appears in the high mountainous areas (subhighland areas) of Honshu, because the summer temperatures are not warm enough to support the cool-temperate forest at these high elevations. The subpolar forest is usually dominated by few tree species and has a simple species composition. In Japan, the dominant trees are maries fir (*oshirabiso*) and veiteles silver fir (*shirabiso*) on

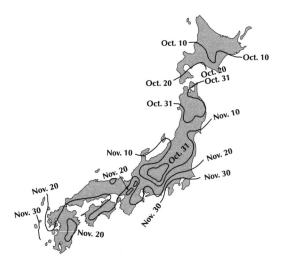

Fig. 2.8. Dates of autumn color. Based on data from the Japan Meteorological Agency, Tokyo.

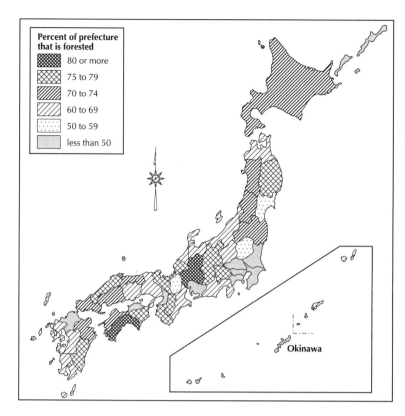

Fig. 2.9. Forest cover in prefectures, 2000. Japan Forestry Agency, Tokyo.

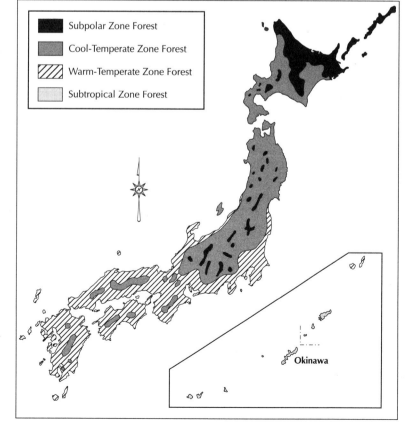

Fig. 2.10. Forest types. Based on Geographical Survey Institute, *National Atlas of Japan* (Tokyo: Japan Map Center, 1977).

Field Report

Hanami: *Cherry Blossoms, the Messengers of Spring*

In Japan, the harbinger of spring is the blooming of the *sakura* (cherry tree). As the days grow longer and the sun begins to warm the land, the tight flower buds of the cherry trees begin to open. The buds are quite unnoticeable until the pink petals begin to show here and there. Perhaps three or four days pass without much happening. But then one day, all the cherry trees suddenly bloom. In fact, they blossom so abruptly that you wake up one morning, surprised to find that your neighborhood is filled with the pink, hazy clouds of cherry blossoms.

The Japanese eagerly anticipate the sensational moment when the cherry blossoms open completely. People watch weather forecasts far in advance (often one or two weeks ahead) to try to gauge exactly when the sakura will start blooming. Indeed, information on the sakura zensen, or the cherry blossom front, is crucial for planning the exact timing for a hanami flower-viewing party. Why? Because the flowers begin to shed their petals just a few hours after they reach full bloom. If you do not plan properly, you will be too early. Worse still, the flowers could all be gone by the time you begin your party.

In addition to all the planning and preparation, it is important to consider finding space: someone must set out early in the morning to find the best cherry tree under which the *goza*, or straw mat, should be spread. Here again, skill is required to find the best location, since these goza will become the temporary living-room rugs that will hold all the food, drink, people, and perhaps karaoke sets.

Hanami parties sometimes start early in the morning and last until evening. Or they may begin in the evening, when lanterns are lit among the cherry trees, and continue late into the night. Many stalls selling yakitori (barbecued chicken), *yakisoba* (fried noodles), and drinks augment the crowd. This added activity intensifies the already high excitement and fervor of the people.

Hanami flower-viewing parties cannot be held without food and drink. Drink, in this case, often means sake, and it is purchased in full-sized *isshobin* glass bottles (containing about 1.9 qt or 1.8 liters). Although sake at Japanese pubs is usually served warm, ideally around body temperature, at hanami parties it is consumed cold—perhaps because there aren't any stoves to heat the sake, but also perhaps because it seems more romantic, or just because of the long tradition of Japanese people enjoying cold sake at hanami parties.

During the Heian era, hanami was a special, leisurely occasion enjoyed only by members of the imperial family. Over the centuries, hanami gradually became an event also for the common people. Although sometimes now it is taken over by fast food, people still gather under the cherry trees to enjoy these mystically beautiful flowers and toast the special occasion of hanami with sake. You can make the event all the more elegant by waiting for a cherry petal to drift into your sake glass from the tree above.

The seriousness of the Japanese people about cherry blossoms may seem almost humorous. However, cherry blossoms often arouse very typical Japanese sentiments among the people. Sometimes recalling scenes from Buddhist teachings, the fragile beauty of the cherry blossom is said to represent the brevity of life. This idea leads to the conclusion that "life is too short for worries, so you might as well enjoy it now," a sentiment that aptly fits many people at hanami parties.

The cherry blossom is also used to represent something that is short-lived. This is why couples in Japanese soap operas often pose under cherry trees—it is an indication that their love is almost over. Hara-kiri scenes in Japanese dramas are also frequently performed under cherry trees. Here again, these delicate flowers are used as a subtle reminder that life is often short and empty.

Cherry blossom time coincides with the beginning of the Japanese school year, and the sight of cherry trees in bloom often brings back memories of the first day of school. Over the centuries the Japanese have expressed their af-

(continued on the following page)

Honshu, and red and blue fir (*todomatsu*) and Japanese spruce (*ezomatsu*) on Hokkaido. Similar evergreen forests occur in Canada and northern Europe.

Cool-Temperate Forest

The cool-temperate forest is a deciduous broad-leaved (summer-green) forest. It occurs in the western half of Hokkaido, in the northeastern half of Honshu, and in the mountainous areas of southwestern Honshu. The distribution of this forest coincides with the cool-temperate climate zone. Cool-temperate forests usually have a simple composition dominated by few tree species. In Japan's case the dominant tree is beech (*buna*), with undergrowth of small bamboos (*sasa*). Similar deciduous forests occur widely in the cool-temperate climate zones of Europe, North America, and South America, though the bamboo understory occurs only in tropical Asia. In relatively warm, humid areas like western Europe and Japan, beech trees are dominant; but in the drier or cooler areas, oak trees become dominant.

Warm-Temperate Forest

The warm-temperate forest is an evergreen broad-leaved forest, which occurs in the warm-temperate climate of the southwestern part of Japan. Because of the abundant precipitation, especially during the summer, the evergreen broad-leaved forest of Japan is the laurel forest (*shoyojurin*), in contrast to the sclerophyllous forest, which occurs in the drier areas of other parts of the world. The laurel forest is a relatively mixed forest (not as complex as a tropical rain forest) composed of such trees as evergreen oaks, chinquapins, camphor trees, and camellias, with many undergrowth shrubs and vines. Compared to the subpolar and cool-temperate forests, the laurel forest has a more diverse composition.

Since the beginning of rice cultivation in Japan, in the third century BC or so, most of the Japanese people have lived in the laurel forest (lowland) areas of southwestern Japan. They cleared the forest for settlement and agriculture. As a result, almost no natural laurel forest remains today. The laurel forest is (or *was*, in most cases) a rather conspicuous feature of Japan and areas south extending to southeastern Asia. Some intriguing evidence suggests that the former existence of a conspicuous cultural region is associated with the peculiar environmental conditions of the laurel forest area.

In the southern part of the East Coast of North America, the climate type is fairly similar to the laurel forest areas of Japan. However, the laurel forest per se does not occur in the United States, except in Florida where the climate is warmer than in the similar areas of Japan. This is probably because the area receives less precipitation than Japan. Instead, deciduous broad-leaved forests are prominent all along the East Coast of the United States.

Some inland mountainous areas of Honshu, Shikoku, and Kyushu, which belong to the warm-temperate climate zone, experience relatively cold winter temperatures. In such areas, neither laurel forest nor deciduous broad-leaved forest occurs because the winter is too cold for the former and the summer is too warm for the latter. Instead, a transitional-type forest, the midtemperate forest, is present. This forest is dominated by firs, Japanese hemlocks, chestnuts, and *shide* (a type of magnolia). Other transitional-type forests may exist between the deciduous broad-leaved type and the evergreen needle-leaf type on Hokkaido.

Subtropical Forest

Subtropical rain forests occur in the Nansei and Ogasawara Islands. Diverse subtropical and tropical plants, such as banyan (*akou*), loquat (*inubiwa*), date palms, mangroves, screw pine (*adan*), hunek, beach heliotrope, monpa (*monpanoki*), and pongam (*kuroyona*), grow in these rain forests. Importantly, however, on the Nansei Islands, the trees belonging to the laurel forest also occur. Thus, the forest type of these islands is sometimes described as the warm-temperate/subtropical forest type. In contrast, the Ogasawara Islands are well known for their endemic flora (plants not found anywhere else), which is very different from that of the rest of Japan. This peculiarity is the result of the geologic history and geographic isolation of the Ogasawara Islands.

Natural Resources

Japan's natural resources are meager, and important materials such as oil and metals are scarce. Areas of good arable land are also severely limited. The main renewable resources are plants, forests, and fish. These are declining, however, primarily because of human activities such as overexploitation, shrinking acreage due to rapid urbanization, often-shortsighted land development policies, and a largely unconcerned public.

Forests

The forest resources of Japan *appear* substantial, based on the statistic (of 1995) that about 67 percent of the land area of Japan is still covered by forest, compared to figures of approximately 30, 36, 10, and 30 percent for the United States, Canada, the United Kingdom, and Germany, respectively. Of course the actual area covered by forest in Japan is not large because the country's total land area is small, but it still looks notable since 67 percent of the total land is in forest. The reality is not as bright or as simple as this percentage implies, however. The original laurel forests were almost entirely eradicated from lowland areas as rice cultivation spread, starting around the third century BC. Other forests have been heavily exploited for construction materials, fuel, fodder, and fertilizer since the early days of Japanese history.

The Japanese culture is based on wood and paper, in contrast to the mostly stone- and metal-based culture of the West. When large capital cities such as Nara (Heijokyo) and Kyoto (Heiankyo) were constructed, enormous numbers of trees (mainly cypress, which is one of the favored woods for building materials) were cut from nearby mountains. The scars of this heavy exploitation are still visible, even a thousand years later, on the mountains surrounding these cities. Also, some lowland plains are a consequence of the deforestation of these mountains and the resulting massive erosion, which filled the mouths of rivers with soil.

Kumazawa Banzan, a seventeenth-century Japanese scholar (of the Tokugawa shogunate period), noted that about 80 percent of the forests of Japan were gone. This alarming degradation of forest resources led many feudal lords and clans to undertake protective measures for the forests within their territories. They labored at reforestation, using valuable trees such as cedar and cypress. Japan's remaining beautiful forests owe much to those forward-thinking people.

After the Meiji Restoration in 1868, the new government attempted rapid westernization of the country, accompanied by development of a strong military. Exploitation of forests increased exponentially as the Japanese government tried to attain status as a major military power.

During World War II and the following hasty reconstruction periods, inevitable, drastic deforestation took place. It is important to remember that the climate of Japan is suitable for the growth of forests (see "Climates and Seasons," above). Also, the young volcanic soils have not lost their productivity after repeated deforestation by humans. Fortunately, as a result, it has been possible to recover forests over denuded mountains.

However, the recent rapid economic growth of Japan into a global economic power again brought heavy stress on the forests, including exploitation of even older, more pristine forests in the more remote areas of the Japanese islands. The Forestry Agency of Japan has promoted monotypic reforestation, using fast-growing, economically valuable tree species such as cedar, cypress, and especially larch. Much controversy surrounds the activities of the agency. Beginning in 2001, the forest-management policy in Japan has focused on environmental and ecological functions of the forest rather than lumber production. There is apprehension over the practice of monotypic reforestation using species that are not typical climax species of the areas involved and over an anachronistic self-generating budgetary system, which has resulted in the cutting of old, pristine forests merely for immediate income. Kazuhiro Ajiki (1988) has analyzed recent changes in forestry and its regional pattern in the Tohoku region of Japan. Government subsidies target the logging of forests and their replacement by serried ranks of industrial cedar. In this gloomy picture, nature serves commerce in Japan.

The small island of Yakushima, south of Kagoshima Prefecture, gives a glimpse of how Japan used to be. It is possible here to walk from semitropical forests fringing coral-reef beaches up into cool temperate forests and subalpine grassland, all within a single trek. Here, one can step into broad-leaved forests of the kind that used to cover much of southern Japan. Stump regeneration in the moist, moss-carpeted forests of the island has provided the perfect environment for the extraordinary *yakusugi*, the Yakushima cedars, some of which are more than two thousand years old.

As the price of wood in Japan rose, it became more economical to import cheaper wood from abroad. The forestry industry of Japan has declined because it cannot compete with the flood of cheaper imports. This brings up an important ecological point: forestry based on artificial reforestation is an attempt to shortcut natural ecological succession by planting trees (climax vegetation type) immediately on open land and skipping all the steps between the pioneer and climax stages. Apparently, continuous human intervention is required to maintain such a shortcut process. When the forestry industry declined, and along with it human effort, these artificial forests became overcrowded with seedlings and began losing their potential as resources. Obviously, a high percentage of remaining forest cover does not necessarily indicate effective long-term resource management.

Paradoxically, Japan's violation of old primeval forests does not preclude a love of wood and a familiar use of wooden objects. Temples, shrines, and houses are built of cedar and cypress, high quality timber redolent with cultural meaning and imagery. Bamboo is the principal wood for household objects and for arts and crafts. The numerous strains of bamboo grow well in humus-rich soil that has good drainage, a condition that prevails in much of Japan. Used for a host of objects ranging from arrows, walking sticks, paper, and *kadomatsu* (a traditional New Year's decoration) to basketry and furniture, it is also made into musical instruments like the *shakuhachi*, a Japanese bamboo flute, and powder whisks for the tea ceremony. Bamboo adds an aesthetic touch to gardens when it is used in the making of fences, which can be seen in both private gardens and the formal ones seen in Kyoto. This versatile wood, and others like it, is clearly here to stay. Ecophilosophy, though much dismissed in recent times, is embedded in the culture. The "roots" of Japan's wood culture are not dead. They just need to be gently rewatered.

Fisheries

Fisheries represent another major resource. The mixing of the two ocean currents, Kuroshio and Oyashio, off the coast of Japan provides a major fishing ground. As a consequence, Japanese people have developed a taste for seafood such as raw fish and seaweed. In the Japanese diet, fish and fish products are more prominent than meat. However, because of the

The fishing port of Nagahama, Ehime Prefecture, western Shikoku. In coastal fishing villages, people combine fishing with farming for a living. When large fishing vessels were introduced, deep-sea fishing emerged. Although modern commercial fishing is responsible for the bulk of Japan's fish production, traditional fishing techniques are still in use. The increasing demand for fish, combined with shrinking catches, has boosted Japan's imports of marine products. At present Japan is the leading importer of fish and marine products. Photo by Cotton Mather.

depletion of ocean stocks, accompanied by adverse environmental changes and stricter international fishing regulations in recent years, Japan's total annual fish catch has been diminishing rapidly. Now Japanese imports of fish are by far the largest in the world.

Traditional fishing in Japan was a coastal practice. Since early days, Japanese people have gathered fish and other marine foods on and near beaches. This coast-oriented behavior marks an important cultural trait of the Japanese people. Although the country is surrounded by open water, Japanese people rarely left the coasts for the open ocean during the period of isolation. Before the isolation policy in the Edo period (1603–1868), Japanese actively sailed out into the ocean. According to the noted Japanese historian Yoshihiko Amino, there were several Japanese communities (*nihonmachi*) in Southeast Asia in the sixteenth century.

Whaling in Japan was also traditionally a coastal practice. During the nineteenth century, however, American whalers frequented the oceans near Japan and significantly reduced the Japanese coastal whale catch. The decrease in the coastal whale catch encouraged Japanese fishers to go out into the open oceans.

The background of the whaling connection between the United States and Japan is as follows. American whaling flourished from the end of the eighteenth century to the early twentieth century, somewhat as portrayed in Herman Melville's *Moby-Dick* (1851). The primary purpose was to obtain oil for lamps, spermaceti for candles, and baleen (whalebone) for corsets, which were fashionable at the time (but not flesh for food). After 1812, for nearly one hundred years, whaling in the Pacific was a virtual American monopoly, and the practice drastically depleted whales in the area. By the first decade of the twentieth century, American whaling ground to a halt because of the scarcity of whales accompanied by the increasing use of petroleum and electricity.

Taiji in Wakayama Prefecture, Wada in Chiba Prefecture, Abashiri in Hokkaido, and Ayukawa, near the port of Oshika, in Miyagi Prefecture, are among the whaling stations still in existence that trace the tradition of their once-dominant livelihood back to the Meiji era. In Taiji, whalers in the seventeenth century developed the technique of driving the whales into nets before harpooning them. The town is considered a symbol of Japan's whaling culture, which

evolved from primitive whaling in the Jomon period (10,000 BC to 300 BC). Now whalers go hunting aboard 15–20-ton whaling boats equipped with harpoon guns. More than half of the people in Oshika were connected to whaling, either on the high seas or along the coast, before the international moratorium on commercial whaling took effect in 1988. Now the town's population has dwindled noticeably. Nihon Kinkai Ltd., based in Ayukawa, owns one of only five boats that continue to pursue whales off the Japanese coast. Minke whales used to be the coastal whalers' principal prey. The whalers target smaller creatures today, such as pilot whales and tsuchi whales, both of which are exempt from international treaty restrictions. Nihon Kinkai's president feels that rapidly aging staff, coupled with the absence of young people interested in learning hunting and cleaning techniques, will mean that the tradition will not survive the twenty-first century.

Most of the smaller specimens are sold in towns not far from the seas in which they are caught, but minkes taken from the Antarctic Ocean as part of the scientific program to study whales end up in markets throughout Japan. The organization in charge of Japan's whaling program is the Institute of Cetacean Research. Most of the 4 to 4.5 billion yen ($37–42 million) needed each year to support the whaling comes from the sale of whale meat. A 500-million-yen subsidy (about $46 million) furnished by the Fisheries Agency accounts for the rest. The body that outfits the fleets and supplies crew members is Kyodo Sempaku Kaisha Ltd. Its predecessor, Nihon Kyodo Hogei, was formed in 1976 when Taiyo Gyogyo (now Maruha Corporation), Nippon Suisan Kaisha Ltd., and Kyokuyo Company agreed to pool their crews and fleets. Today, Kyodo Sempaku is the only Japanese enterprise that still implements deep-sea whaling techniques. In 1998 Maruha quietly sold off its stake in Kyodo Sempaku to other shareholders, after the international environmental group Greenpeace promoted a boycott of Maruha products in Britain. Maruha's decision to sell was reached despite repeated pleas from the Fisheries Agency that it continue its association with the whaling outfit. Maruha also plans to discontinue its involvement in the production of canned whale meat. In 1992 the name of its professional baseball team was changed from the Yokohama Taiyo Whales to the Yokohama BayStars, as part of a policy directive by the team's administrators to drop all links with whaling. Other leading makers of marine products have voiced similar sentiments. This is partially due to business associations that traders and processors of these products in Japan have with people in antiwhaling nations such as the United States and New Zealand.

Many Japanese support whaling (Shima 1999), but most younger Japanese have never tasted whale meat. Japanese feel that fish of all species are being devoured by the overpopulation of whales, so the latter must be contained. By reducing the number of whales, hunters will spare for the fishers many of the salmon and sardines upon which whales feed. In support of this theory, Japan added two larger species—Bryde's and sperm whales—to the official list of whales authorized for hunting, a list that already featured minke. The move has prompted the threat of U.S. trade sanctions, largely because sperm whales have been designated as an endangered species under U.S. law for the past thirty years.

Minerals

Among nonmetallic resources, limestone is abundant on the Japanese islands. This is an important raw material for cement and other chemical industries. Limestone in Japan is often found mixed with other rock of oceanic origin, such as pillow lava and basalt. This indicates that the limestone of the Japanese islands originated as coral reefs of tropical oceanic islands and was carried to the subduction zone by tectonic plate movement.

Coal

Coal was a significant resource in the past. Most of the coal of Japan was formed in the early Tertiary period, when the climate was much cooler and the vegetation type was monotypic coniferous forest. The coal mines, especially in the Chikuho region of northern Kyushu, provided enough energy for the industrialization of the country in the early twentieth century. However, as the preferred energy source has shifted from coal to fossil oil since the 1960s, the demand for coal has dramatically declined. Also, because the coal deposits of Japan are rather thin, the high-grade coal is mostly depleted. As a result, many coal mines closed, and subsequently serious social problems occurred, associated with the unemployment of coal miners. Although the demand for coal has risen again since the oil crisis of the 1970s, many closed mines cannot be reopened economically because they have become flooded. High labor costs and the difficulty of mining have made the price of Japanese coal extremely high compared with that of imported coal. Japan has given up mining coal; in 2000 there were only two active mines. In 1986 Takashima coal mine in Nagasaki Prefecture closed after 118 years of operation (Nishihara and Saito 2002). In 1997 the decision was made to close the 108-year-old Miike Coal Mine in Omuta, Kyushu (Gilman 1997). The focus of government policy has shifted to securing a stable supply of foreign coal. Coal provided 17.9 percent of Japan's energy in 2000 (see fig. 2.11).

Oil and Natural Gas

For petroleum Japan is almost entirely dependent on imports from the Middle East and other areas. Most of the natural gas consumed in Japan is im-

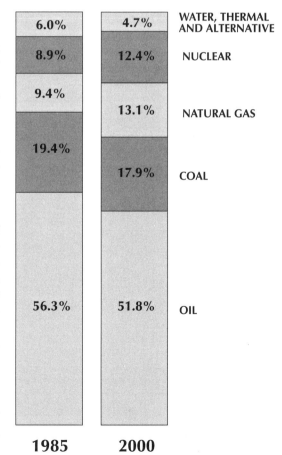

Fig. 2.11. Japan's energy sources. Based on *Japan Almanac, 2003* (Tokyo: Asahi Shimbun, 2003).

Field Report

Japan's Last Coal Mine

Hundreds of miners wearing helmets with headlamps emerged for the final time from Japan's last coal mine on January 31, 2002, marking the end of the industry that fueled the nation's miraculous post–World War II recovery. After eighty-two years of operation, the Taiheiyo Coal Mine Company closed its facility near Kushiro on the island of Hokkaido, because of high production costs and cheap imports. Each of the one thousand miners put out of work by the closure received a severance check of about $60,150. But because of Japan's lingering economic recession, many of them were going to be hard pressed to find new jobs. Many were second- or third-generation miners, but as a group the miners seemed resigned to the closure. A thirty-six-year old miner who had worked for Taiheiyo since he graduated from high school said: "I haven't really thought about what I'll do next. The coal mine has been my life. I have no training to do anything else."

Established in 1920, the Taiheiyo mine was a pillar of industry in Kushiro, an outpost of 190,000 people on Hokkaido's southeastern edge. Taiheiyo was one of hundreds of mining communities that took root in the late nineteenth and early twentieth centuries as the government turned to fossil fuels to power industrial expansion. With the coal came prosperity, helping Japan's sustained post-war growth. But by the late 1960s, Japan's mines began dying off. Falling global coal prices, competition from overseas, tougher environmental and safety regulations, and the switch to cheaper, cleaner fuels combined to reduce profits.

At their peak in 1940, Japanese mines produced 56 million tons of coal and employed more than 450,000 people. By 2000, the most recent year for which Trade Ministry figures are available, the last two domestic mines produced 3 million tons and employed 2,500. Taiheiyo's mine produced about 2.6 million tons of coal at its peak in 1977, but output dropped sharply within a few years. In 2001 it was just 1.23 million tons. By the end of 2001, Taiheiyo was Japan's only coal mine.

An important factor leading to the closing of the mine was the government's decision to end subsidies for domestically produced coal after March 31, 2002. Many blame globalization for the industry's demise. Global coal prices were about $30 per ton in 1999, compared with the $105 per ton Japanese producers charged, according to Trade Ministry figures.

Despite Taiheiyo's closure, coal consumption in Japan—the world's leading coal importer—is expected to remain steady. Domestic power plants and steelmakers use about 130 million tons of coal each year, most of it bought from Australia and China.

Taiheiyo mine's operator planned to reorganize as Kushiro Coal Mine Company, keeping five hundred workers and focusing on transferring technology to other mining countries in Asia over a five-year period. The company was also going to continue to collect coal that had already been mined from the coal beds more than 600 yards (550 m) beneath the ocean floor.

ported as liquid natural gas from Indonesia, Malaysia, Brunei, Australia, and other countries. Despite efforts to diversify energy sources, more than half of the country's energy (about 51.8%) comes from oil, and 13 percent from natural gas. Japan is more dependent on Middle East crude than it was in 1973, when the Organization of the Petroleum Exporting Countries organized its first worldwide embargo. As this oil shock rippled through Japan's economy, prices spiraled upward and panicked consumers. Memories of that event, considered ancient history to most Japanese, are returning to the forefront as turmoil in the Middle East grows. Japan's economy relies heavily on the export of autos and other goods for growth. A disruption of oil flows from the Middle East could idle Japanese factories and throw Japan back into deep recession. Japan remains confident that it can secure enough oil to offset any temporary loss of

Middle East crude. It also maintains a formidable stockpile of fuel, enough to last 171 days. Japanese also assume that some producers would increase output to make up for losses elsewhere, something the Saudis did during the Persian Gulf War.

Nevertheless, Japan remains dangerously tethered to developments in the Middle East. It imports more than 87 percent of its oil from the region, the highest percentage since 1969. Japanese refiners revamped their operations in the 1980s to accommodate Middle Eastern oil. Compounding matters, Japan's domestic oil market was deregulated in 1996, forcing refiners long cloistered from international competition to slash their capacity. Most are reluctant to invest in equipment needed to process other types of oil from Russia, Mexico, and beyond. The government's efforts to help companies find new oil have largely failed. Japan's Arabian Oil Company lost its concession to fields on the Saudi-Kuwait border (Karan and Abu Dawood 1990) in 2000. Losing the Arabian Oil concession has prompted Japan to try to win access to oil fields in Libya, Iran, and several Latin American countries. But here, Japanese companies must bid against global giants like Exxon Mobil and Royal Dutch/Shell, integrated refiners with deeper roots in the region and with the economies of scale to extract oil profitably. Japan still lacks oil companies with the capital and technology needed to explore large reserves of oil. For decades, the government-backed Japan National Oil Company provided low-cost financing to help the refiners. The public corporation has been criticized for racking up huge debts and encouraging companies to invest in projects that they may have otherwise avoided.

To keep factories humming and to maintain its living standards, Japan has focused on shaping domestic consumption habits. Japan has set a goal of increasing the natural gas share of its energy consumption to 20 percent in 2010 from 13 percent in 2002. Since Japan has little natural gas of its own, it must purchase it from Indonesia and elsewhere. And before shipping, the gas must be turned into liquid, driving up its cost. In 2001 Japan was unable to import natural gas from Aceh, Indonesia, because of separatist violence there. To diversify its energy sources away from the Middle East and Indonesia, Japan is hoping that Sakhalin in eastern Russia, about 25 miles (40 km) above Japan's northern tip, will become a major supplier of oil and gas. A consor-

tium of Japanese trading and oil companies plans to invest $13 billion in two gas and oil projects on Sakhalin and to build a pipeline from Sakhalin to Japan. Sakhalin's offshore oil and gas reserves compare favorably with those of Alaska's North Slope. In the production venture, Exxon Neftegas, Exxon Mobil's local unit, is the operating partner of a group that includes a Japanese company (the Sakhalin Oil and Gas Development Company), two Russian companies, and an Indian company. In the pipeline venture, Exxon Mobil's partner is the Japan Sakhalin Pipeline Company, whose shareholders include the Itochu Corporation, the Marubeni Corporation, and the Japan Petroleum Exploration Company. The Sakhalin group, anchored in Japan, includes Shell, Mitsui & Company, and the Mitsubishi Corporation.

In 2003 Sakhalin Energy Investment Company, a multinational oil and gas group based in Korsakov, started to work on a 500-mile (805-km) pipeline down the island to feed gas from an offshore operation to a large liquefied natural gas plant. From an ice-free terminal a few miles east of Korsakov, tankers will start supplying, in late 2006, a dozen gas terminals around Japan. Sakhalin Energy, the first energy producer on the island, has been pumping and exporting oil since 1999. A group led by Exxon Mobil is developing a Sakhalin offshore section, with the goal of producing oil in about three years. Sakhalin could supply 10 percent of Japan's oil and gas imports within a decade.

For half a century, Sakhalin was not accessible to Japanese investment. In the summer of 1945, Soviet troops expelled Japanese soldiers and settlers from the island's southern half, ending four decades of Japanese occupation. To this day, there is no World War II peace treaty between Russia and Japan. But now Japan is racing to engage its northern neighbor to take oil and gas from Sakhalin. Japan's newest consulate is in Yuzhno-Sakhalinsk. With about $2 billion scheduled to be spent on development on the island every year until the end of the decade, Sakhalin's 591,000 residents should be bracing for a major boom.

Nuclear Energy

In order to diversify its energy sources, Japan has promoted nuclear power, which over the past two decades has tripled to 12 percent of the country's

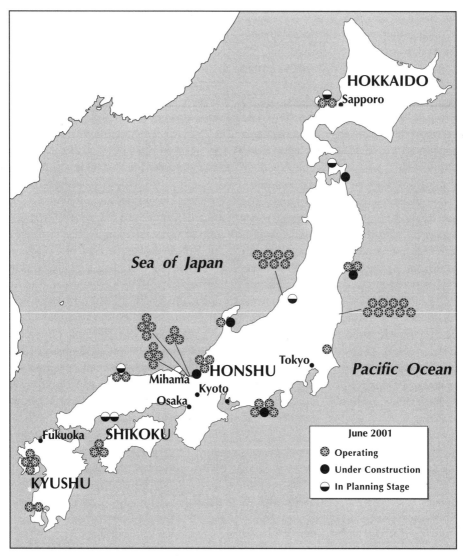

Fig. 2.12. Nuclear power in Japan, June 2001. Based on *Japan Almanac, 2003* (Tokyo: Asahi Shimbun, 2003).

energy mix. There were fifty-one nuclear power generation facilities in operation as of June 2001 (see fig. 2.12). Japan is banking heavily on conventional uranium-based nuclear power and an advanced system using plutonium to relieve its dependence on imported coal and oil. But the program has been hit by several accidents, including one in 1999 in Tokaimura, north of Tokyo, in which two workers died. More bad will was created in September 2002 when the country's largest utility, the Tokyo Electric Power Company, admitted to having falsified records at its nuclear plants for more than fifteen years. The revelation was particularly worrisome because gov-

ernment regulators knew about the problem two years earlier but did little to expose it.

Public anxiety over the nuclear industry's safety record will slow the growth of nuclear power. Antinuclear activists in Japan have seized upon accidents as evidence that many of Japan's nuclear reactors are aging and constitute a safety risk. The prototype reactor Monju is in mothballs because of an accident that occurred in the cooling system in 1995. There are also problems connected with the underground disposal of high-level radioactive waste. For one thing, it is difficult to find disposal sites in densely populated Japan. And it is enormously expensive to store such waste deep in the ground. With the economy projected to expand at 1.3 percent per year over the next decade, demand for electricity is likely to rise accordingly. The high cost of building and maintaining nuclear power plants is another reason Japan expects to add only a dozen new nuclear plants by 2010, down from as many as twenty that were planned (Yoshida 2000).

Other Energy Sources

Hot springs in Japan are sources of geothermal energy for power plants and greenhouse agriculture. But there has not been extensive development of this energy source. Hydroelectric, geothermal, and alternative sources accounted for 4.7 percent of Japan's energy consumption in 2000. In some parts of the country, wind power is being viewed as an important source. In 1998 Tomamae, Hokkaido, was among the six municipalities to receive central government subsidies to promote "green energy" projects. Tomamae has the most wind-power facilities in Japan. Fifty-two wind-power farms have been built since 1998, compared with twenty-one built in the decade before. Despite all the eagerness, Japan had an output capacity of only 83,000 kilowatts of electricity through wind power in 2000 (for comparison, the United States had a capacity of 2.14 million kilowatts, Germany 2.87 million kilowatts, and Denmark 1.42 million kilowatts).

NATURAL HAZARDS

Natural disasters are abundant on the Japanese archipelago, and their frequency and magnitude are important human concerns. If it were not for human concerns, these events would not be disasters at all, but merely natural phenomena, part of nature's cycle. With or without human presence, they occur repeatedly and beyond human control, as major catastrophes or minor disturbances. Often, however, inadequate preparation by the residents of an area increases the human impact of such occurrences. In addition, the significance of natural disasters to humans becomes greater with the expansion of human habitats into more risky areas. For example, even a moderate earthquake can cause serious damage if people live close to the epicenter, or if a building is not constructed well enough to withstand the tremors.

The natural environment of Japan accounts for numerous natural disasters. The Japanese archipelago is located over the highly active volcanic belt known as the Pacific Ring of Fire. Also, the archipelago is in the path of frequent typhoons (hurricanes) and midlatitude climatic disturbances. Furthermore, nearly 127 million people (about half the U.S. population) crowd the small flat areas scattered among the mostly mountainous islands, making the population very vulnerable to natural disasters.

Although the Japanese suffer from natural hazards, they still admire nature's graces. The Japanese attitude toward these hazards illuminates an interesting fact in the life of the country. In other industrial countries, nature seems to exist only as a half-forgotten backdrop to life. In Japan, a personal relationship is recognized between humans and nature. Nature is a reality, not an abstraction. It brings beauty and calamity to everyday life.

The particular beauties and tastes of Japan that appeal to the foreigner, and mean so much more to the Japanese, come for the most part from the loving attention given to things of nature. A rock garden, a single fish in a tiny pool, water coaxed to trickle through a hollow bamboo rod, a dwarf pine in a clay pot, the painstaking arrangement of fruit on a stand or flowers in a vase, the maple leaf on a woman's kimono to greet the coming of autumn—these are not matters simply of aesthetic or passive admiration of nature. The Japanese seem to be eager to cooperate with nature and help to nourish and embellish its various forms, because they respect them and consider them so important.

Nature is beloved, but it is also the enemy. Perhaps one reason its graces are so admired is that people are unable to escape its harshness. Earthquakes, fires, floods, and landslides remind Japan day after day of the importance of nature. The earth moves often in the great city of Tokyo. People make small jokes about the earthquakes—when they are over. But no matter how imposing with glass and chrome the buildings, and no matter how thick with automobiles the roads, the simple reality of nature can never be quite forgotten in a city that once was almost wiped out when the earth moved.

A renowned Japanese proverb lists the things people fear: "Earthquake, Thunder, Fire and Dad." For a country sitting on the active volcanic belt, earthquakes are inescapable natural events. About 500 to 1,000 noticeable earthquakes occur in Japan every year, and normally 3 or 4 of them cause notable damage to human life and property. About 35 devastating large quakes (of magnitude greater than 7.0) struck Japan between 1605 and 1995. In 2000 Mount Usu in southwestern Hokkaido erupted. Mount Oyama on Miyake Island, one of the Izu Islands, also began its volcanic activity in July 2000. According to statistics from the National Police Agency, in the year 2001 destruction caused by natural disasters resulted in 23 deaths, 344 injuries, total destruction of 62 homes, partial damage to 382 homes, flooding of 2,404 homes, and damage to 13,823 acres (5,594 ha) of farmland.

Major natural disasters in Japan, commonly short-term catastrophes, include earthquakes, tsunamis (tidal waves), volcanic eruptions, landslides, floods, typhoons, and midlatitude cyclones. Long-term disasters, the effects of which accumulate over years, include ground subsidence and the Yamase, a summer cold wind in Tohoku region.

Earthquakes and Tsunamis

Many earthquakes occur along the subduction zones where the Pacific and Philippine plates go under the Japanese archipelago. At a single location this type of earthquake would repeat every few hundred years, but of course the geology of Japan provides innumerable vulnerable locations. Other earthquakes, such as the devastating Hanshin-Awaji (Kobe) earthquake in 1995 (magnitude 7.2), occur along active fault lines in the inland areas (Earthquake Engineering Research Institute 1995). In Japan the active fault lines are concentrated in the Chubu and Kinki regions and imply the existence of a compressing force in the east-west direction in the middle part of Honshu. Often the secondary damages from an earthquake exceed the direct damage caused by the tremors and earth movements of the quake itself. Tsunamis (tidal waves) often cause serious secondary damage. Most are induced by the rapid movement of the ocean floor associated with an earthquake, but some come from volcanic eruptions and large landslides.

The Sanriku coast facing the Pacific Ocean in northeastern Honshu experiences one of the highest frequencies of tsunamis in the world. This coast parallels the Japan trench, along which frequent offshore earthquakes occur. Along this scenic coast, known as a *rias* (sawtooth) coast, mountain ridges descend into the ocean at nearly right angles to the coast. These indentations provide splendid protected harbors but also allow the buildup of high waves when a tsunami approaches. The term *tsu-nami*, which means literally "harbor wave," comes from this region.

Some of the most complex and menacing seismic faults are located off the coast of the Tokai region to the southwest of Tokyo. A powerful earthquake in this area could produce a tsunami 27 feet (8 m) high, which would reach the Tokyo waterfront within three to four minutes, before any safety precautions could be taken. Kumamoto (1999) has constructed seismic hazard maps for intraplate earthquakes based on historical records, paleoseismology data, and a time-dependent conditional earthquake recurrence model.

Earthquake Prediction   Japan has a multipronged government program to address its many seismic risks. Earthquake prediction is a primary focus of Japan's efforts to reduce losses from earthquakes. Six agencies participate in this program. The Japan Meteorological Agency (JMA) collects seismological data and oversees the prediction efforts (Disaster Prevention Bureau 1993). The Earthquake Assessment Committee, consisting of six eminent seismologists, is responsible for analyzing potentially anomalous data and reporting to the director of JMA a verdict of either imminent danger or no danger. The two options are designated black and white verdicts; a gray verdict, or a statement of intermediate probability, is not permitted. The Geodetic Council of Japan acts as an advisory body to the Ministry of Education, Culture, Sports, Science, and Technology with respect to earthquake prediction and oversees the development of five-year-program plans. Other agencies involved in the prediction effort include the Maritime Safety Agency, the Geological Survey of Japan, and the National Research Institute for the Earth Sciences and Disaster Prevention (part of the Ministry of Education, Culture, Sports, Science, and Technology). Now in its sixth five-year plan, the program has both harsh critics, which include an increasing number of Japanese scientists, and staunch defenders (Normile 1994). Limited access to data, opportunity costs for other areas of earthquake research, and the program's narrow focus on the Tokyo region are among the motivations for criticism.

With spending on the order of $100 million per year—a figure that does not include salaries—Japan's prediction program receives funding comparable to that of the entire U.S. National Earthquake Hazards Reduction Program (NEHRP). Initiated in 1963, the earthquake prediction program in Japan is one of the country's largest and oldest research projects. Pursuant to the 1978 Large-Scale Earthquake Countermeasures Act, ten regions have been designated for special monitoring. The Kanto-Tokai Observation Network, for example, continuously monitors crustal movements, using more than 250 seismometers, strain meters, and tilt meters. In addition, 167 Global Positioning System stations operate in this area.

The most recent plan for the prediction program, adopted in 1993, continues intensive observation of the Tokai region, which is expected to experience the effects of a great earthquake on the nearby Suruga trough. Scientists hope to detect the onset of the quake by monitoring seismicity, strain, and crustal deformation. Previous major quakes on the Suruga and Nankai troughs were preceded by rapid crustal uplift.

Earthquake Building Codes and Engineering

Earthquakes have caused massive death and destruction, and potentially damaging earthquakes are certain to occur in the future. Although earthquakes are uncontrollable, the losses they cause can be reduced by building structures that resist earthquake damage, matching land use to risk, developing emergency response plans, and other means. Early in the twentieth century, Japan established one of the first seismic design codes, based on the performance of certain buildings in Tokyo during the 1923 Great Kanto earthquake. The years since then have seen many advances in earthquake engineering research, seismic codes, and construction practices, because of investment on the part of both the government and the private sector.

The most recent code went into effect in 1981. The Japanese seismic design code differs from the current U.S. guidance document for building codes in that it calls for a two-stage design process. The first phase follows an analysis approach similar to that used in the NEHRP provisions; it is intended to avoid structural damage from frequent, moderate quakes. The second phase is an explicit assessment of the building's ability to withstand severe ground motions. In addition, Japanese buildings are typically designed to withstand more force than U.S.

buildings are. As a result, buildings in Japan tend to be stronger and stiffer than their U.S. counterparts and will likely suffer less damage during moderate or severe shaking.

Japanese construction companies annually spend a considerable amount on research and development, including testing of scaled building models in large in-house laboratories and research into passive and active control technologies. One result is that new technologies for seismic protection have been incorporated into new buildings at a faster rate than in the United States.

The government's engineering research facilities include a large-scale earthquake simulator that is operated by the National Research Institute for the Earth Sciences and Disaster Prevention but is also used by other agencies. Future evaluation of the seismic performance of the built environment will likely be aided by the large set of strong-motion data obtained from the Kobe earthquake in January 1995; the data set includes near-fault records that reflect rupture directivity and other effects encountered in the immediate vicinity of the fault.

Response and Recovery Within the National Land Agency, the Disaster Prevention Bureau was established in 1984 to develop disaster countermeasures through coordination with various ministries and agencies. The countermeasure framework has three primary parts: (1) making cities more disaster resistant, (2) strengthening disaster prevention systems (e.g., tsunami warning systems) and raising awareness, and (3) promoting earthquake prediction. One related effort has been to set up the Disaster Prevention Radio Communications Network to link agencies at the federal, prefectural, and municipal levels.

The primary responsibility for disaster response rests with local-level governments, which must ensure that adequate water, food, and medical supplies are available. As witnessed in the 1995 disaster, Kobe's capabilities were overstretched, and some argue that mechanisms for federal intervention were inadequate. Whether or to what degree Japan's earthquake research, mitigation, and response programs will change as a result of the Kobe disaster is not yet clear. It must be noted that the intensive monitoring programs intended to support Japan's prediction capability cover but a small portion of the nation.

Field Report

The Two Great Earthquakes of the Twentieth Century

According to traditional East Asian beliefs, the onset of new historical eras is marked by catastrophes. This was true for Commodore Matthew Perry's opening of Japan. Just months later, in December 1854, Japan was hit by three major earthquakes (including the Ansei) and tidal waves. The Ansei earthquake caused tsunamis that affected Shimoda, which had just become an open port by way of the Kanagawa Treaty between Japan and the United States. The two great earthquakes in 1944 (Tonankai earthquake) and 1945 (Mikawa earthquake) just before the end of World War II caused massive destruction and loss of life in the Tokai region. But the two major urban quakes of the twentieth century occurred on September 1, 1923, in Tokyo and on January 17, 1995, in Kobe.

The Great Kanto earthquake, the first of these two, was the deadliest quake in Japanese history, killing more than 100,000 in an urban population of 2.5 million and destroying or burning 64.5 percent of the houses in Tokyo. Following the earthquake the typhoid mortality rate jumped to 285 per 100,000 in 1924. The Great Kanto earthquake struck at 11:58 a.m., September 1, 1923, at a time when lunch was cooking in many homes. Fires started from these homes, and the tongues of small blazes soon merged into a massive firestorm, more than 547 yards (500 m) wide. Unstoppable, it steadily consumed everything in its path.

The earthquake and the fires reduced much of Tokyo-Yokohama into a wasteland in an instant. The disaster was the "death of old Tokyo and Yokohama." In the immediate aftermath, people wandered aimlessly through the rubble and the corpses, searching hopelessly for their separated relatives and friends. As the days progressed, many dramas of self-sacrifice and courage unfolded. People who were buried under heaps of bricks were rescued in the nick of time just before fires would have consumed them. Captains of ships, in a show of daring seamanship, maneuvered their vessels out of the blazing harbor set afire by spilled oil.

While such valiant relief and rescue operations were taking place at a frantic pace, corpses were being collected and cremated by the thousands under sheets of corrugated iron. Looters seized the opportunity to pocket the contents of many safes lying out unsecured in the midst of rubble. But such crimes paled in comparison to the atrocities committed against the Koreans. Police rounded up Koreans by the droves and tied them to telegraph poles; others were executed. Vigilante groups were formed in response to unfounded rumors that Koreans had lit the fires and that they were poisoning wells. As a result, as many as six thousand Koreans are thought to have died in the great quake's aftermath, after having escaped the maw of a natural cataclysm.

In Yokohama, the rubble lying in Yamashita-cho was dumped in the Bund area to form today's scenic Yamashita Park. To the southwest of Yokohama, below Suruga Bay, lies the epicenter of the overdue Tokai earthquake, which will badly jolt the Tokai region of central Japan. The epicentral area has been ominously quiet for too long—though the coastline has been sinking. Movement of the Pacific plate causes the quakes centered in the Kanto region. But the Philippine plate under the Tokai region is stronger and more active. The tension is expected to break with a quake measuring higher than 8 on the Richter scale, to be followed by a tsunami 10 to 13 feet (3 to 4 m) high. In 1979, 170 municipalities in the Tokai region, including 75 in Shizuoka prefecture, were designated areas for disaster relief measures. With scientific prediction Shizuoka plans to minimize the damage from the quakes. The earthquake-proof wharves at Shimizu will keep the port open to receive food and other aid sent by sea.

Few will ever forget what happened to Kobe and its surrounding areas at 5:46 a.m. on January 17, 1995. No other event in twentieth-century Japan, save for the Great Kanto earthquake and World War II, claimed so many lives and shattered so many hopes in a few seconds. Registering 7.2 on the Richter scale, the Hanshin

(continued on the following page)

Field Report: *The Two Great Earthquakes of the Twentieth Century* (continued)

earthquake was centered on a fault near Kobe. It began at a depth of 12.4 miles (20 km). The Philippine Sea plate moved in a northwest direction near Kobe, striking the Eurasian plate and causing that plate to buckle. The buckling resulted in a twisting motion and caused the destruction in Kobe. The earthquake killed more than 5,300, injured nearly 27,000, and left 300,000 homeless. It struck a crucial economic zone that encompasses Kobe, Japan's sixth-largest city and a major commercial hub, and Osaka, the nation's second-largest city and a financial center.

Many elevated expressways, bridges, and buildings collapsed because of flaws in engineering design (Esper and Tachibana 1998). The Japanese rely on brute strength in structural engineering. Support columns, especially those used to hold up roadways and train tracks, tend to be huge and brittle. When the ground shakes, the columns are meant to stand firm and resist collapse. In the United States support columns are made smaller and more flexible, or ductile, with the hope that although they may deform and sustain damage, they will not collapse. Newer Japanese buildings incorporate the American approach, but those built before 1983 and most elevated roadways followed the brute-strength approach. The Japanese approach works as long as ground motions occur in a range that has been anticipated, but the ground motions in Kobe were twice as large as expected (Whitaker et al. 1995).

The minorities and the poor suffered heavy losses in the Hanshin quake, as they had in the Great Kanto earthquake. Although nature was democratic in that the temblor rattled rich neighborhoods as well as poor ones, the consequences of the quake were not evenly spread. Frequently it was the poorer people's homes that collapsed and burned the occupants in rubble. Nagata Ward, a gritty industrial center just west of downtown Kobe, suffered some of the worst damage and worst fires. Here old traditional Japanese wooden houses with heavy tile roofs easily collapsed in the earthquake. Kobe's largest minority group, the Koreans living in this area, absorbed a disproportionate share of the disaster. There are about 700,000 ethnic Koreans in Japan, with many living in the region around Kobe and Osaka. About half of Kobe's 20,000 Korean residents lived in Nagata. The industry the Koreans dominated and which employed a majority of the people in Nagata—shoe production—was nearly destroyed. The shoe industry is not likely to be built to its prequake level and may wither to a fraction of its previous size, causing hardship to the Koreans. The scale of the disaster in Nagata Ward fell hard on another minority, a group known as the *burakumin*. The burakumin were Japan's official outcastes for more than a century; they were given jobs that were considered unclean, such as butchering and leather work. Many of Kobe's burakumin were clustered in Nagata Ward, and many relied on the small shoe workshops for jobs.

The earthquake zone in the Kobe region included some of the wealthiest parts of Japan, such as Ashiya, to the east of Kobe, where $5 million ranch-style homes peek out from behind stone walls. Ashiya was the setting for the novel *The Makioka Sisters*, Junichiro Tanizaki's portrayal of the life of a rich family in the 1930s. Here many of the homes came though unscathed; they were sturdy enough to withstand the shocks (Fukutome 1999). In the wealthy neighborhoods such as Ashiya, residents have built newer homes and have spent more money on better-quality construction. The affluent also tend to have larger rooms and often sleep on beds; poorer people sleep on futons on the floor of tiny rooms, so that a falling wardrobe is almost sure to hit them.

Volcanic Eruptions

Volcanic eruptions are another inescapable feature of Japan's geology. Based on the plate tectonics theory, there are two volcanic zones in Japan, the eastern and the western. The former is associated with the subduction of the Pacific plate, and the latter with that of the Philippine plate. In these zones, there are about fifty active and dormant volcanoes. Shikoku, Kinki, part of the Chugoku region, and the Kanto Plain are not included in the volcanic zones. Although no active vol-

Showa Shinzan, a volcanic hill 1,319 feet (402 m) high in the Usuzan volcano, south of Lake Toya in southwestern Hokkaido. Showa Shinzan's volcanic activity ended in 1945, but it still emits steam and sulfuric acid. Photo by P.P. Karan.

Fig. 2.13. Kikai Caldera and the area covered by volcanic ash from Kikai. Based on a map by K. Okamoto, Nagoya, Japan.

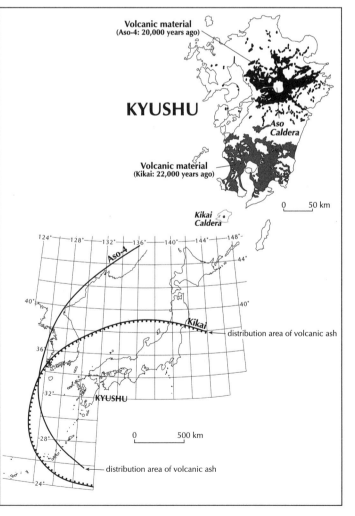

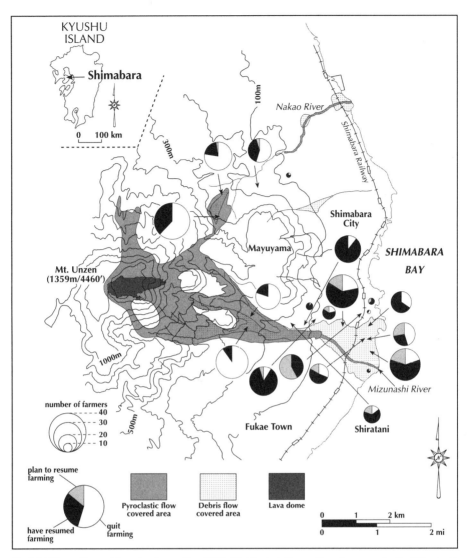

Fig. 2.14. Unzen-Fugendake volcanic eruption, 1990–95: Affected villages. Based on a map by Kenji Yamazaki, Tokyo.

canoes exist in these regions, blankets of volcanic ash give evidence of prehistoric volcanic activity.

The aftermath of an enormous prehistoric eruption of the Kikai Caldera off the south coast of Kyushu about seven thousand years ago is still visible today (see fig. 2.13). The eruption poured about 36 cubic miles (150 cu km) of volcanic material over the surrounding landscape. For comparison, the eruptions of Santorini (responsible for the devastation of the Minoan civilization in the Aegean Sea, which may have given rise to the legend of Atlantis), Krakatau, and Mount St. Helens produced about 10, 4, and 0.7 cubic miles (40, 17, and 3 cu km) of volcanic material,

respectively. The *nuée ardente,* or glowing cloud, from the Kikai eruption directly hit southern Kyushu and eradicated almost all the life forms it encountered. Meanwhile, the volcanic ash from the eruption blanketed wide areas of southwestern Japan. The ash probably did not kill humans, but it greatly affected the vegetation and altered human lives. Archaeological evidence shows that earthenware with indigenous Kyushu patterns disappeared after the eruption and that afterward pottery with the patterns of eastern Honshu and Korea spread into Kyushu. The volcanic debris from the Kikai Caldera and other prehistoric eruptions still provides an obstacle to agriculture, especially in southern Kyushu, because it forms a layer that is impermeable to the roots of crops.

The recent eruption of Mount Unzen (Fugendake) in 1990 (see fig. 2.14), after 190 years of dormancy, was not as large as the eruption of the Kikai Caldera. Indeed, next to the eruption of the Kikai Caldera, that of Unzen appears tiny. However, the effect this eruption had on the local population has been devastating, because the population density around the volcano is significantly higher today than in prehistoric days. Research by Kenji Yamazaki (2000), a geographer at Meiji University, revealed that 229 households from 12 communities at Fukae town and 438 households from 22 communities in Shimabara city were directly affected by the Unzen eruption. These families could not farm because of restrictions on living in and entering the area near the volcano where 1,574 acres (641 ha) of cultivated land are located.

Over the Japanese archipelago, many other enormous prehistoric volcanic eruptions took place, some exceeding the size of the eruption of the Kikai Caldera. Together, the eruptions of the Aira Caldera (Sakurajima) 22,000 years ago and that of Mount Aso 70,000 years ago released more than 48 cubic miles (200 cu km) of volcanic material. If such an enormous eruption occurred now in Japan, the damage to human life and property would be inconceivable.

The year 2000 was marked by unusually intense seismic and volcanic activity across Japan. Mount Usu, a volcano in southwest Hokkaido, erupted in March. Mount Oh on Miyake in Japan's Izu Islands erupted several times during the summer. The series of natural disasters has worn down islanders, and the economy is suffering. Around 2,200 residents—58 percent of the population—were evacuated in June after authorities warned that a major eruption was likely. Days later, when it seemed officials had overreacted and evacuees had returned home, there were more violent tremors, and on July 8 Mount Oh blew its top. The last full-scale eruption of Mount Oh had occurred in 1983, when lava poured down the slopes and engulfed four hundred buildings.

Normally as many as 30,000 Japanese tourists visit Miyake and the Izu chain each year, drawn by the sapphire Pacific waters, the coral reefs, the dolphins, and the hot springs. The spate of eruptions scared visitors away in 2000. Following the evacuation in September 2000, the residents of Miyake have been scattered across Japan. Many were still living in public housing in and around Tokyo in 2002, and others have chosen to move in with relatives. To provide the evacuees with opportunities to socialize with each other, voluntary organizations and local governments organized several events. Miyako no enmichi (the Festival of Miyake) was held at Akikawa Metropolitan High School in Akiruno, where 315 primary, middle, and high school students from Miyake continue their education and live together in a dormitory. About 1,000 evacuees enjoyed seeing familiar faces they had not seen since leaving the island. As of early 2002 it was not known when the evacuees would return to their homes in Miyake.

The forced evacuation order in the vicinity of Mount Usu was lifted in May 2000, but by December 2002 many residents had not returned home. It takes more than lifting an evacuation order to resettle a community. This is particularly true of those who lived and worked in the Toyako hot spring resort, located at the foot of Mount Usu and once one of Hokkaido's most popular tourist destinations. Most of the local residents were in service industries such as hotels and restaurants that relied on the resort. But the number of tourists dropped sharply in 2000 after the eruption.

Landslides

The young, mountainous Japanese archipelago experiences frequent landslides. Earthquakes, volcanic eruptions, and heavy rainfall, which are all common in Japan, can provoke them. Landslides favor areas with certain kinds of topography and certain geologic conditions. These are, in general, relatively steep slopes consisting of large amounts of unconsolidated materials in unstable conditions, such as the abrupt, steep slopes of volcanoes; hilly areas of soft tertiary sedimentation; and clay-rich slopes of heavily spa-weathered rocks. The shock from an earthquake or a volcanic eruption often triggers landslides on these slopes. A heavy rain also encourages landslides by expanding unstable materials, increasing the mass, and lubricating the sliding surface. The numerous active volcanoes in Japan, therefore, provide favorable conditions for large landslides. Many devastating landslides in Japan, including the enormous 1984 landslide on a sacred mountain, Ontake, in Nagano Prefecture, have happened on and around volcanoes.

Although this implies that the most of the land area of Japan is highly susceptible to disastrous landslides, in actuality the areas devastated by landslides are not yet widespread. Unless humans drastically alter it, the natural vegetation cover provides adequate protection against landslides. Deep forests with extra-heavy rainfall (nearly 400 inches or 10,000 mm per year) such as at Yakushima (Yaku Island) and the Kii Peninsula are examples of areas where the natural vegetation cover can protect from landslides. However, as soon as the balance is tipped by humans, the devastating effects of landslides and erosion proceed rather quickly.

Climatic Disasters

Climatic disasters in Japan are mostly associated with typhoons (hurricanes), midlatitude cyclones, and weather fronts. Every year, about thirty typhoons develop in the western Pacific. Usually two or three of them hit Japan and cause damage from wind and flooding.

Of the many midlatitude cyclones that annually cross the vicinity of the Japanese islands, three or four are seriously damaging. Because these midlatitude cyclones have much larger storm zones than typhoons do, the resulting damage is often nationwide. In contrast to typhoons, whose damage normally occurs in southwestern Japan, midlatitude cyclones are more likely to cause harm in the northern part of Japan.

Weather fronts that become stagnant around the Japanese archipelago often bring long rainy days in the baiu season, from May to July. Such rain often triggers landslides. Other climatic disasters of Japan include heavy snowfalls on the Sea of Japan coast in winter, frost damage, mountain fires caused by migratory anticyclones in spring, and abnormally high temperatures and dryness induced by foehn winds.

Solifluction by ground ice, or the slow downslope movement of materials caused by freezing and thawing of the ground, occurs in eastern Hokkaido, on the Pacific Ocean side of northeastern Honshu, and in mountain areas of the Chubu, Chugoku, and Shikoku regions, where the winter temperature is cold and no snow cover protects the ground from subfreezing temperatures. Solifluction damages roads, railroads, buildings, and underground utility lines.

A cold northeasterly wind called Yamase blows over the northeastern districts of Japan when anticyclones are located over or around the Sea of Okhotsk from the baiu season to summer. Since Yamase produces cold weather, the crops suffer damage in the Tohoku region.

Floods

Reflecting the midlatitude location of Japan off the east coast of the Asian continent, there are three general types of floods resulting from heavy rainfall in Japan. They are those associated with typhoons, the baiu season (plum rain), and the melting of snow (Nakano, Arai, and Mizutani 1980).

Typhoons often bring heavy localized rain, which may result in flooding. The area of typhoon rainfall is usually larger than that resulting from a heavy rain during the baiu season. Typhoon 17 in September 1976 ravaged the artificial levee of the Nagara River in Gifu Prefecture. More than four thousand houses were flooded. On September 11, 2000, over a twenty-four-hour period, Typhoon Saomai inundated the central Tokai area with more torrential rain than it had seen in a century. The Meteorological Agency reported as much as 32 inches (800 mm) of rain in some areas, the largest amount on record since 1891, when the agency began keeping records.

As many as nine people were killed and many injured as Typhoon Saomai's heavy rains began to wreak havoc in Nagoya, which was thoroughly unprepared for the deluge. Local authorities urged the residents of more than 200,000 households to evacuate and seek shelter at public facilities as the rains caused landslides and the Shonai and Shin Rivers burst their banks. Wading through water neck-deep in some areas, people fled their homes, many holding onto ropes to avoid being swept away. Nishibiwajima and Nishi Ward in Nagoya were the worst hit; Ground Self-Defense Force soldiers were called in to rescue about thirty people stranded on rooftops of flooded homes.

The weather also forced as many as fifty-two thousand people to spend the night sleeping on station platforms or on board stopped trains, as the heavy rains halted the shinkansen (bullet train), the entire Nagoya subway system, and local train lines.

Nagoya's industry was also affected: both Toyota and Mitsubishi Motor Corporations stopped production, being unable to reach their parts suppliers in Nagoya city. Some businesses remained closed for up to two days, because employees could not get to their workplaces.

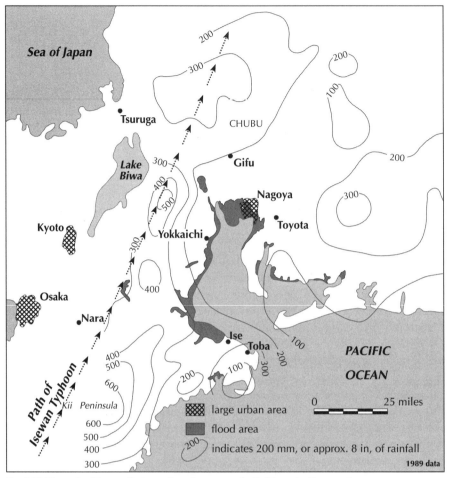

Fig. 2.15. The path of Isewan Typhoon. Based on a map by K. Okamoto, Nagoya, Japan.

Toward the end of each baiu season, the rain sometimes becomes a heavy downpour in the southwestern part of Japan, especially in western Kyushu. The rainfall is usually sharply localized and often reaches 10–15 inches (300–400 mm) per day. The local downpour that hit Nagasaki on July 23, 1982, brought severe flooding and landslides. The rain reached 7.4 inches (187 mm) per hour in some areas. Importantly, the damage in Nagasaki was augmented by human factors. Preparation for a disaster was poor in both private and public sectors. The public communication system did not function well during the emergency situation. Telephones and automobiles quickly became useless. These experiences revealed the weakness of a modern city overly dependent on high-tech equipment that may prove to be startlingly fragile in the face of natural disasters.

Flooding from the melting of snow occurs on the Sea of Japan coasts of Hokkaido and the northern part of Honshu (in the snow-belt areas; see "Climates and Seasons"). Compared with the floods caused by heavy rainfall associated with typhoons and the baiu season, those resulting from melting snow are generally smaller in size and longer (slower) in time scale.

An important type of flood results from the high tides associated with typhoons and other storms. This type of flood is becoming more frequent with the increase in land reclamation along the coast and the subsidence of coastal lands caused by the excessive use of groundwater. Isewan Typhoon, which hit the northern part of Ise Bay on September 26, 1959, inundated 50 percent of the city area of Nagoya for many days (see fig. 2.15). About 160,000 houses were damaged, and five thousand people died. The most

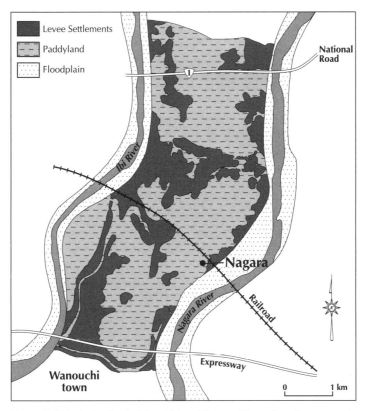

Fig. 2.16. Waju in the flood plain of Ibi and Nagara Rivers. Based on a map by K. Okamoto, Nagoya, Japan.

serious damage occurred in the reclaimed land areas surrounding the bay and in areas that had previously experienced subsidence from overuse of groundwater. The high tide—greater than 17 feet (5.3 m)—induced by the typhoon went over the artificial levee and submerged these mostly below-sea-level areas.

The large quantities of earth and sand washed down from the mountains by the Kiso, Ibi, and Nagara Rivers have led to the formation of natural dikes, which are slightly higher areas of land. Villages are located on these elevated portions of the land, and farmers grow rice within the confines of the natural dikes. In order to protect villages from flooding, key-shaped semicircular dikes were built upstream so as to fend off the direct onslaught of floodwaters. Because the downstream sides were left open, farmers were hard pressed to drain off the irrigated paddy water: the low ground would force the water from the downstream side into the paddies. Farmers also had to deal with seawater rushing in from Ise Bay. Embankments were built later on the

downstream side to protect the cultivated land; these embankments completed the full circle and are called *waju* or circular dikes (see fig. 2.16). Communities in the area surrounded by the circular dikes have raised the level of the ground to fend off floods.

Land Subsidence

Land subsidence is a significant long-term disaster in Japan today. Excessive pumping of groundwater for industrial and urban use causes ground subsidence. It results in compression of clay beds caused by depression of capillary pressure. As early as 1910–19 subsidence was observed in Tokyo's Koto Ward, and it was found in Osaka in the 1920s. Land subsidence leads to damage by floods and high tides and the destruction of buildings. The damage to industry during World War II reduced the industrial use of groundwater, thereby halting land subsidence temporarily. In the 1950s, when industry revived and groundwater demand increased rapidly, land subsidence began again, particularly in metropolitan areas. With the control of the rate of groundwater

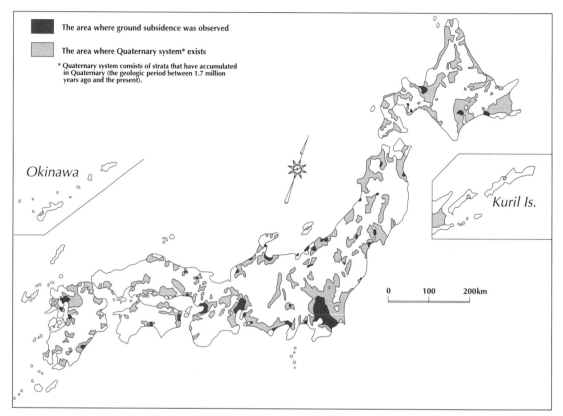

Fig. 2.17. Areas affected by ground subsidence. Based on data from the Japan Environmental Agency, Tokyo, 2000.

The lower courses of the rivers Kiso, Nagara, and Ibi contain *waju* (polder) settlements. Both the community and the fields in waju are surrounded by embankments for protection from flooding. The area extends from the city of Ogaki, Gifu Prefecture, in the north to the mouths of the three rivers in Aichi and Mie Prefectures in the south. The building of waju in this area dates back to 1319. Photo by P.P. Karan.

pumping in the 1960s, the rate of subsidence has slowed in metropolitan areas. However, in some regions large amounts of groundwater are pumped for tap water and agriculture as well as for industry. At present, marked ground subsidence is occurring in the suburbs of metropolitan Tokyo (the northern part of the Kanto Plain), rural regions such as Chikugo-Saga Plain, and Minami Uonuma in Niigata Prefecture, among other sites (see fig. 2.17).

In Niigata ground subsidence has intensified since the 1950s because of the pumping up of natural gas water. The lands below sea level, which extend along the coastal region, consist of 55 square miles (142 sq km) in the Niigata Plain, 48 square miles (124 sq km) in the Tokyo lowland, 143 square miles (370 sq km) in the Nobi Plain, 21 square miles (55 sq km) in the Osaka Plain, and 80 square miles (207 sq km) in the Saga Plain. The maximum subsidence is 15.03 feet (4.58 m) in Tokyo Koto Ward (1918–67), 4.95 feet (1.51 m) in Nobi Plain (1961–76), and 9.45 feet (2.88 m) in the Osaka Plain (1935–76).

Human-Caused Disasters

Many disasters are induced by human activities, and the threat of these long-term disasters to human well-being increases as human habitat spreads into more risky, marginal areas. Matsuda (1987) has noted the relationship between urban development and increasing flood hazard in the Kashio River basin in the western part of Yokohama city. Human response to typhoon disasters in Japan has been discussed by Osamu Nishikawa (1983).

The rate of soil erosion, or loss of fertile topsoil, has been significantly increased by human activities such as deforestation and agricultural practices throughout the already vulnerable rainy, mountainous country of Japan. Under agricultural land use, for example, the rate of soil erosion (about 0.5–100.0 t/ha/year) exceeds the rate of natural formation of topsoil (about 0.1–0.4 t/ha/year). As a result, the topsoil, which is often overlooked as an important natural resource, has been lost, resulting in serious long-term damage to agriculture. Also, carried by the short, rapid rivers of Japan, the eroded materials from upstream areas quickly reach the more level ground below and increase the threat of flooding by raising the river floor.

Human efforts to control the impact of soil erosion have resulted in another disaster of sorts, coastal erosion. To prevent flooding in downstream areas, many sand-control dams have been constructed upstream. Unfortunately, this artificial control measure, accompanied by the effects of many other dams constructed for power plants, has decreased the sand supply near the mouths of many rivers. The result is serious coastal erosion. In many areas, the coastline has retreated significantly and the encroaching sea threatens human settlements. The construction of breakwater levees, usually protected by tetrapods (four-legged concrete blocks that lessen the force of the waves) on the outer side, slows the process of coastal erosion. However, the aggressive waves that often occur in winter or during typhoons rapidly deteriorate these protective structures, forcing a continuous human struggle against coastal erosion.

Protection from Natural Hazards

To protect the population from natural hazards, Japan has developed a well-equipped system of seismic, meteorological, and volcanic monitoring mechanisms. Japan's monitoring technology has also progressed significantly as a result of improved information technology. September 1 is observed each year as Disaster Preparedness Day in Japan, and exercises are conducted on that day across the country to demonstrate preparations to cope with the hazards. Government policy on disaster protection is now placing more emphasis on stepping up cooperation among local residents in a disaster-stricken area.

Accurate prediction of volcanic eruptions can undoubtedly reduce damage. It is worth noting that no one was killed when Mount Usu in Hokkaido erupted in 2000, largely because there were accurate forecasts of how soon the volcano would erupt. These were complemented by local efforts to secure shelter for evacuees and preparation of a hazard map showing anticipated damage from pyroclastic flows from the mountain.

In 1979 the Central Disaster Prevention Council established crisis management procedures for the ministries and agencies of the central government and local governments. The procedures were amended in 1999 to reflect the social and economic changes that occurred during the twenty-year period since 1979 and to incorporate the lessons of the Great Hanshin earthquake of 1995. The updated plan pays more attention to assisting the elderly, children, the sick, and other segments of the population who would be most vulnerable to the threats posed by a catastrophic earthquake. New procedures for evacuating residents to indoor shelters in tsunami- and landslide-prone areas have been established. To minimize disruption of the lives of the people who live within the area stricken by disaster, the plan added measures to ensure that small-scale retail stores would remain open outside the evacuation zone. The plan adopted in 1999 represents a step forward because it adds more flexibility to the crisis management framework.

ALTERATION OF LANDFORMS BY HUMAN ACTIVITIES

The land of Japan has been modified considerably by human activities, such as artificial works to control rivers, reclamation of coastal areas and lakes, and excavation of mountain slopes. During the preindustrial period, land modification was on a small scale and was limited to draining marshes and reclaiming land for agriculture. Since the mid-nineteenth century, particularly during the twentieth century, the pace of change has been very rapid and on a large scale with the help of modern technology.

For more than four hundred years, Japanese have been attempting to change the courses of rivers to exploit the rice-growing potential of the lowlands, to protect the land from floods, and to use rivers as waterways to transport food from northern Japan. In most cases old river courses were used for channel alterations, but in some cases new channels were excavated to divert the flow. Today the major rivers of Japan are artificially controlled to prevent floods by construction of continuous dikes, shortcuts, and dams. Confined by continuous dikes, Japanese rivers have been prevented from developing their fluvial plains. The riverbeds have become higher than the surrounding plain as the debris is deposited between dikes. In general, rivers in Japan do not any longer have the natural levees and alluvial fans produced under physical geomorphic processes.

The Tone River basin offers a good example of human alteration of river channels. The Tone River flows across the Kanto Plain and presently drains into the Pacific Ocean at Choshi. It has a number of tributaries rising in the mountains surrounding the Kanto Plain. Originally the Tone flowed between the Omiya and Shimosa uplands toward Tokyo Bay. The Arakawa River joined the Tone to the east of the

Omiya upland, and the Irume River joined the Tone between the Omiya and Musashino uplands. The combined rivers drained into Tokyo Bay. The Watarase River, which now drains into the Tone, was an independent river flowing southward along the western margin of the Shimosa upland. The Kinu River, which also now drains into the Tone, flowed eastward into the Pacific Ocean. The lower reaches of the Tone were once the Kinu River. During the Tokugawa shogunate the Watarase River was connected to the Tone in 1621; the Arakawa River was diverted to flow into the Irume River in 1629. An artificial channel was dug to divert the Tone and the Watarase into the Kinu in 1632.

During the Edo period (1603–1868), rice and lumber from the Tohoku region and marine products from Ezo (now Hokkaido) were shipped to Edo via a circuitous route: they arrived in Choshi, Chiba Prefecture, were taken to Sekiyado, Ibaraki Prefecture, via the Tone River, and then down to their final destination via the Edogawa (*gawa* or "river" often appears as a suffix to Japanese river names). The route took about ten to fifteen days, depending on wind conditions. Goods that spoiled quickly were unloaded at various places, including Kioroshi, Chiba Prefecture, and carried overland to the Edogawa for transport into Edo.

After the Meiji Restoration, the amount of goods being transported increased, and a plan was begun in 1888 to build a canal that would reduce travel time. Dutch civil engineer Rouwenhorst Mulder (1848–1901) was engaged to design the canal and supervise its construction, and it was completed in 1890. About 2.2 million workers were involved in the building of the 5-mile (8-km) waterway from Funado, on the Tone, to Nishifukai, on the Edogawa. The canal served as a major transport route, and more than one hundred vessels passed through each day during peak seasons. However, as rail and road transport developed, canal traffic declined. In addition, bridges were destroyed one after another by floods, and the canal's life as a transportation route came to an end in 1941. The Tone Canal was then placed under the management of the central government.

At one point, the Tone Canal was intended to serve as a flood channel for the Tone. From 1975 on, it was temporarily renamed the Noda Waterway and was used to transfer water from the Tone River to the Edogawa to increase water supply in the metropolitan area. However, with the completion of the

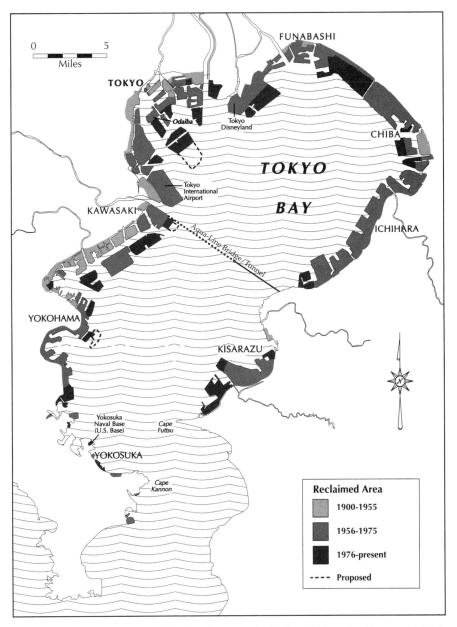

Fig. 2.18. Land reclamation in Tokyo Bay. Based on a map by the Tokyo Metropolitan Government, 2000.

North Chiba Water Conveyance Channel in 2000, the canal no longer serves this function. A wide variety of birds and insects now live in and along the canal, which is also home to dozens of flower and plant species. The canal is winding because it was built in harmony with the natural terrain. The aesthetics of the canal design have resulted in a beautiful sight.

The shoreline of Japan has been modified in many places by special works to control shoreline erosion, brought about by decreases in the sediment washed down by the rivers, by construction of dams, and by the building of ports and breakwaters on the coast. These changes are particularly striking on the coast of Niigata at the mouth of the Shinano River and along the coast of the Toyama Plain facing the Sea of Japan.

Perhaps the most outstanding example of man's role in changing the face of Japan can be observed in Tokyo Bay. Bit by bit, the bay has shrunk to feed Japan's hunger for its rare commodity: space. Recla-

on a large scale. Landforms in particular have been the target of efforts to maintain and control their stability. Civil engineering works to achieve stability have often generated other types of changes. Large-scale reclamation of swamps and other bodies of water for use as paddy fields, for example, has accelerated topographic change.

The conversion for farm use of a 1,095-acre (443-ha) area in Kisozaki, which straddles the border between Aichi and Mie Prefectures, is a good example of reclaiming land and thereby altering the land surface—in this case at a cost of 28.3 billion yen. But it is land that nobody wants now. It is located where the Kisogawa flows into Ise Bay, about 12 miles (20 km) southwest of central Nagoya. The central government spent 16 billion yen reclaiming the land and building embankments and waterways for irrigation. The Agriculture, Forestry, and Fisheries Ministry shouldered 11.2 billion yen of the cost. It also borrowed 4.8 billion yen from the state at 6.5 percent interest. By the end of fiscal 2000, the interest on the loan totaled 12.3 billion yen.

In 1966 the Mie prefectural government asked the ministry to undertake the reclamation project to increase available land for agricultural use. Neighboring Aichi Prefecture claimed a stake in the scheme after construction work started. To fend off the dispute over prefectural demarcation, the ministry's Tokai Agricultural Administration Office continued to oversee the project. The office had made the land fit for arable use by 1989, but by then there was no use for such a large tract of agricultural land because the number of farmers had declined.

The local business communities of the two prefectures pressed their cases to have warehouses built on the land so it could be used as a large distribution center or, alternatively, to have a theme park built there. To build a distribution center or a theme park would have required the investment of billions to raise the ground level, a project that the prefectural governments could not afford. The prefectural boundary dispute was finally settled in 1996. Mie Prefecture got 828 acres (335 ha) of the reclaimed land; the remaining 198 acres (80 ha), excluding a part to be used for an expressway, were allocated to Aichi Prefecture. Aichi and Mie Prefectures are now planning to build athletic grounds and camping areas on the land so that the land reclamation project will not have been a complete waste.

A bird's-eye view of reclaimed land in Kisozaki, which straddles Aichi and Mie Prefectures. The site will be converted into athletic grounds after 16 billion yen of taxpayer's money was spent reclaiming it for use as farmland. Photo by Yomiuri Shimbun, Tokyo.

mation began four centuries ago when areas near the Edo Castle—the site of today's Imperial Palace—were filled in to serve the court. In modern times industrialization has overtaken wide swaths of wetlands at the expense of a once-flourishing fishing industry. Beginning in 1600, when Tokugawa Ieyasu declared Edo his seat of power, marshes were filled and rivers dredged in the bay area to build one of the largest cities in the world. In the aftermath of World War II, as Japanese migrated to the Tokyo area, the pace of land reclamation soared. Dredging and filling has buried fully one-fifth of the bay's surface, much of it since 1950. Nearly 90 percent of the bay's shoreline has been buried under fill (see fig. 2.18).

The physical environment of Japan—more so than of many other countries—has been modified

REFERENCES

Abe, H. 1992. The symbolism of Mt. Fuji in textbooks in modern Japan. *Geographical Review of Japan* A 65:238–249.

Ajiki, Kazuhiro. 1988. Recent changes in forestry and its regional difference in Tohoku District. *Science Reports of Tohoku University,* ser. 7 (Geography) 38:119–132.

Disaster Prevention Bureau, Earthquake Disaster Countermeasure Division. 1993. *Earthquake Disaster Countermeasures in Japan.* Tokyo: National Land Agency.

Earthquake Engineering Research Institute. 1995. *The Hyogo-Ken Nanbu Earthquake: January 17, 1995.* Oakland, CA: Earthquake Engineering Research Institute.

Esper, P., and E. Tachibana. 1998. Lessons from Kobe Earthquake. In *Geohazards in Engineering Geology,* 105–116. Special Publication no. 15. Tokyo: Geological Society.

Fukutome, K. 1999. Relationship between building damage and tenure of land and houses in the 1995 Hanshin-Awaji Great Earthquake: A case study around Kamisawa Station. *Geographical Review of Japan* A 72:668–690.

Gilman, Theodore J. 1997. Urban Restructuring in Omuta, Japan, and Flint, Michigan: A Comparison. In *The Japanese City,* ed. P.P. Karan and Kristin Stapleton, 176–220. Lexington: Univ. Press of Kentucky.

Karan, P.P., and Abdul S. Abu Dawood. 1990. *International Boundaries of Saudi Arabia.* Delhi: Galaxy.

Kawamura, Takeshi. 1980. Climatological studies. In *Recent Trends of Geographical Study in Japan,* 27–36. *Recent Progress of Natural Sciences in Japan,* vol. 5. Tokyo: Science Council of Japan.

Kumamoto, Takashi. 1999. Seismic hazard maps of Japan and computational differences in models and parameters. *Geographical Review of Japan* B 72:135–161.

Matsuda, Iware. 1987. An urban flood in the Kashio River Basin. *Geographical Reports of Tokyo Metropolitan University* 22:139–152.

Murata, Akihiko. 1987. Secular changes of the Bai-u season in Japan. *Geographical Review of Japan* B 60:179–194.

Nakagawa, Kiyotaka. 1996. Recent trends of urban climatological studies in Japan, with special emphasis on the thermal environments of urban areas. *Geographical Review of Japan* B 69:206–224.

Nakano, Takamasa, Kunio Arai, and Takeshi Mizutani. 1980. Recent characteristics of flood disasters in Japan. *National Geographical Journal of India* 26:1–16.

Nishihara, Jun, and Hiroshi Saito. 2002. Coal mine closure in late 1980s and the reaction of redundant mining workers: The case of the Takashima Coal Mine, Nagasaki Prefecture, Japan. *Human Geography* 54 (2): 1–22.

Nishikawa, Osamu. 1983. Challenge and response in the relationship between typhoon disasters and human action in Japan. *Proceedings of the Department of Humanities, College of Arts and Sciences, University of Tokyo,* series on Human Geography, 78 (8): 43–64.

Normile, Dennis. 1994. Japan holds firm to shaky science. *Science,* June 17, p. 1656.

Ouchi, Shunji. 1996. Studies of process geomorphology in Japan in the first half of the 1990s. *Geographical Review of Japan* B 69:126–133.

Saito, Kyoji. 1999. Development of mountains and alluvial fans in Japan, Taiwan, and the Philippines. *Geographical Review of Japan* B 72:162–172.

Shima, Kazuo. 1999. Japan and whaling. *Social Science Japan* 16 (August): 3–6.

Shitara, Hiroshi. 1978. Fifty years of climatology in Japan. *Science Reports of Tohoku University,* ser. 7 (Geography) 28 (2): 395–430.

Toritani, Hitoshi, and Yousay Hayashi. 1996. Recent studies of local-scale climate in Japan. *Geographical Review of Japan* B 69:194–206.

Umitsu, Masatomo. 1991. Holocene sea-level changes and coastal evolution in Japan. *Quaternary Research* 30:187–196.

———. 1996. Recent studies of the late quaternary landform evolution of riverine coastal plains in Japan. *Geographical Review of Japan* B 69:134–143.

Whitaker, Andrew, et al. 1995. Evolution of seismic design practice in Japan and the United States. In *The Great Hanshin Earthquake Disaster: What Worked and What Didn't?* SEANC Spring Seminar Series, Engineering Implications of January 17, 1995, Hyogoken-Nanbu Earthquake, May 25, 1995. San Francisco: Structural Engineers Association of Northern California.

Yamakawa, Shuji. 1984. Regional and seasonal features of cold fronts in Japan and its surroundings. *Geographical Review of Japan* B 57:154–165.

Yamazaki, Haruo. 1996. Recent progress in tectonic geomorphology in Japan, with special reference to active fault and related tectonic studies. *Geographical Review of Japan* B 69:115–125.

Yamazaki, Kenji. 2000. How farmers adjusted to volcanic disaster: A case study of the Unzen-Fugendake disaster. Paper presented at the International Geographical Congress, Seoul, Korea.

Yoshida, Yasuhiko. 2000. Nuclear safety issue jars Japan to reconsider its policy, program. *Japan Quarterly,* Jan.–Mar., 56–64.

Chapter 3

第三章

The Cultural Heritage

Because of the acidic volcanic soils of the archipelago, fossils of early humans have rarely been preserved in Japan, but the few fossils of early Homo sapiens that are available indicate that the people were short and had flat faces. The characteristics of the fossils are similar to those found in southern China, and thus the mainland of Asia is the area of origin of the Japanese people. The forebears of the dwindling Ainu communities of Hokkaido once occupied northern Honshu, Hokkaido, Sakhalin, and the Kuril Islands and were in fact the original inhabitants of northern Japan.

An elaborate mythology surrounds the origins of Japan and the Japanese. It is said that Izanagi and Izanami, a husband and wife god and goddess, came down from heaven by a bridge, believed to be a rainbow. The two produced a pantheon of gods, but geographic features were also among their offspring, including the Japanese islands, waterfalls, mountains, trees, and wind. It was the wind that completed the creation by blowing away the mists so that the Japanese archipelago was visible for the first time. Amaterasu, the sun goddess, ruler of the heavens, was their eldest daughter and became the center of the Shinto religion. One of her descendants was Jimmu Tenno, who, according to the myth, constructed a palace on the Yamato Plain in 660 BC. Jimmu Tenno is believed to be the first emperor and the founder of the current imperial family. Thus, the country was created by the gods, and the first emperor was a direct descendant of the sun goddess. It was not until modern times, after the national collapse in 1945, that such legends could be subjected to critical comment in print or public speech. The special creation of Japan and the unique ancestry of the imperial family were taught in classrooms all over Japan, and questioning these accounts was never allowed in the ultranationalistic age before the end of World War II.

The Chinese called early residents of the Japanese islands Wa. The name *Nippon* (Japan) came into use later on. Some authors place the origins of the Japanese state in the third century with the development of a cultural core centered in the Yamato lowland; other scholars point to the fifth century, when the Yamato polity established a bureaucracy; or to the seventh century, when it began centralized rule over most of Honshu, Kyushu, and Shikoku.

The Pottery People (Jomon Culture)

During the Jomon period (ca. 10,000 BC–ca. 300 BC), life was based on hunting and gathering. The Jomon culture is, however, distinguishable from the preceding Paleolithic culture, first by the presence of characteristic cord-marked (*jomon*) pottery. The emergence of pottery implies the expansion of the food base for people because cooking and storing food are major functions of pottery. The Jomon pottery gave the period and the culture their names, and it is among the world's oldest known excavated pottery (dated between 10,750 and 10,000 BC). Second, although no evidence proves that the Jomon culture included any forms of agriculture, it was probably not an exclusively hunting and gathering economy. But the people of this culture did not use metals. Based on these characteristics, the Jomon culture is considered by some to be Neolithic.

The Jomon culture innovatively exploited marine and coastal resources. Its people took advantage of the shallow oceans and tidal marshes, which appeared with the high sea levels resulting from the warm climate of the time. The waste material from the use of these marine resources, with other waste and artifacts, accumulated as shell mounds. When gravesites of Jomon people were situated near these shell mounds, the calcium from the shells often preserved human bones well. The shell mounds, therefore, provide rich archaeological evidence of the Jomon period.

A cultural dichotomy, caused by the separation between the southwestern and the northeastern cultures, emerged early in the Jomon period. It persisted at least until the end of the Jomon period, and some think that it persists even today. The geographic areas of these two cultural regions roughly coincided with the distribution of the evergreen broad-leaved forest in the southwest and the deciduous broad-leaved forest in the northeast. Because of the hunting and gathering way of life in the Jomon culture, the inhabitants of the northeastern region may have had some advantages such as more abundant game animals. In the later course of Japanese history, the norm has been the opposite: the southwestern region, which is better suited for wet rice cultivation, has dominated the northeastern region in terms of culture, economy, and politics.

The Jomon people lived in pit houses about 15 to 20 feet (5–6 m) in diameter, and each house likely accommodated a single family. Several pit houses formed a village. The Jomon culture made early contributions to the Japanese culture as a whole. First, the Jomon clay figurines (*dogu*), which mostly represent rotund human females (thus, possibly fertility), demonstrate the Jomon culture's shamanistic customs and view of nature. This view of nature may have been continuous till today, possibly as Shintoism. Note that these figurines should not be confused with the later funerary sculptures (*haniwa*). Second, the Japanese people's taste for marine products may have originated in this period, because the Jomon culture refined techniques of fishing and shellfish gathering. Third, since the Japanese language had probably already separated from the other languages of the Ural-Altaic language family by about 7,000 BC, the Jomon people likely played a pivotal role in the development of the language.

Jomon ruins are found throughout Japan. Among the most striking of recent archaeological finds are the Sannai Maruyama ruins of Aomori city, which is at the far north of Honshu, the largest of Japan's four main islands. They were uncovered when Aomori Prefecture did an archaeological survey before a planned expansion of a local athletic park. The archaeologists found themselves digging right in the center of a huge Jomon village.

The ruins at Sannai Maruyama cover almost 12 acres (5 ha) of ground, and virtually the whole village has been found intact. There are remnants of dugouts, a graveyard, an area where religious ceremonies were held, and even a garbage dump. All together, there are about five hundred houses and some eight hundred earthenware coffins (shaped like large jugs and used to bury children). The Jomon people appear to have revered their children (adults were buried without coffins), and their unique burial patterns have left what could be one of the largest children's mass-burial sites in the world. Jomon sites in northern Kyushu (south of Fukuoka) have large funerary urns used for adults as well as children.

Of special importance are two large mounds uncovered in the northern and southern parts of the village at Sannai Maruyama. The southern mound (262.5 ft [80 m] long, 131.2 ft [40 m] wide, and 9.2 ft [2.8 m] high) is particularly impressive and appears to be both the site of religious ceremonies and a place for disposing of broken earthenware and stoneware. From the artifacts, the archaeologists conclude that Sannai Maruyama was the largest Jomon village in Japan around 3,500 BC. The discovery of *inubie,* a type of millet, that was found in soil taken from the Kitakawa valley, suggests that the Jomon people engaged in managed cultivation. A fist-sized chunk of jade from the Itoigawa area of modern Niigata, 373 miles (600 km) away, was also found. Other products brought from afar include obsidian (a dark natural glass formed by the cooling of lava) from Hokkaido, which was used to make arrowheads, and amber ornaments from Iwate. These artifacts clearly indicate that there was a network of trade and distribution in northern Japan.

The ruins of a Jomon village in Yaze, Tsukiyono town, Gumma Prefecture, in 1992 revealed a line of fifty large poles made from split chestnut wood, each about 24 inches (60 cm) in diameter. The poles were erected in units of six, three to the east, three to the west, defining a "holy place" of 5 to 6 square yards (4 to 5 sq m). These odd structures, which resemble the totem poles of the indigenous inhabitants of the West Coast of North America, were found at Sannai Maruyama as well. Perhaps more important than any trans-Pacific connection, however, is the possibility they raise that the distinctive wooden architecture of the later Horyuji and Todaiji Temples in Nara has its roots not in the Chinese mainland but in the distant Japanese past of the Jomon Period.

YAYOI CULTURE

The Yayoi period (ca. 300 BC–ca. AD 300) is the first period in Japanese prehistory in which people's way of life was based on intensive agriculture. The period was named Yayoi because a pottery belonging to this period was found first in the Yayoi section of Bunkyo Ward, Tokyo. Bronze and iron also began to be used in this period.

The dawn of agriculture (irrigated wet rice cultivation) most likely was influenced by extensive contacts with China and Korea and by Korean migration to Kyushu around the third century BC (the existence of rice in Japan has been traced back 4,000–5,000 years to the Jomon period). Unpopular in Japan, but a logical conclusion, is that the Yayoi were actually Koreans who migrated to Japan bringing their knowledge of wet rice culture. They eventually integrated with the indigenous population. Recent DNA studies show that Koreans and Japanese are virtually indistinguishable. Another argument is that neophytes would not be able to adapt plants to a new environment (rice brought to Japan), nor to learn metallurgy by looking at metal implements. It was most likely a relocation diffusion process, and not a stimulus diffusion. This occurred about the same time as the rise of agriculture in western Europe. It was also about the time of the Phoenician (Poeni) War between the Roman Empire and Carthage in the Mediterranean.

The Yayoi culture was probably first incubated in Kyushu. The culture rapidly spread over southwestern Japan and some coastal areas of northeast Honshu. Agriculture in the northeast probably depended less on rice than on such crops as millet, barley, and beans. The culture did not spread into Hokkaido in the north or the Nansei Islands in the south. In these areas, the Jomon culture progressively continued into the Yayoi and later periods.

During this period, the country was divided into many political units (*kuni*), presided over by regional chieftains. By the late Yayoi period, social stratification had emerged, which was reflected by the size of graves and burial artifacts.

The Yayoi culture is considered by some, especially those who regard wet rice cultivation as the defining cultural trait of Japan, as the beginning of Japanese culture. However, the Yayoi culture shared many traits with the preceding Jomon culture.

Japan's historic time began around the sixth century; there are some, mostly fragmentary, references to Japan in Chinese literature as early as the first century BC, however. Toward the end of the third century, during the late Yayoi period, the first brief but extensive description (about two thousand Chinese characters) of Japanese people and their culture was recorded in Chinese literature. *Wei zhi* (the *Wei Chronicle*), one of the post-Han *Chronicles of the Three Kingdoms*, is a history of the Chinese Wei dynasty (AD 220–265), compiled in the late third century. Its subsection the "Article on the Wa People," commonly known as "Gishi wajinden" in Japanese, describes the Japanese people and their culture around that time.

THE EVOLUTION OF THE YAMATO CULTURAL CORE

Over several centuries there was a gradual technological, social, and economic development from the pottery-making Jomon culture to a metal-using agricultural society (the Yayoi culture). From around AD 300 the physical and cultural landscape was transformed by the appearance of *kofun* (great tombs or large mounds, most of them in the shape of a keyhole) centering on the Yamato region at the eastern end of the Inland Sea (Tsude 1992). Many of these great tombs were built during the Kofun period, spreading from the Yamato region (today's Nara Prefecture) to other parts of Japan. However, the kofun at Saitobaro in Miyazaki are older than those of Yamato Plain. It is believed by some scholars that the custom spread from Kyushu to Yamato. The Japanese have even named one large kofun north of Saitobaro area as belonging to Jimmu, the mythical first emperor of Japan. About the same time, ceremonial bronze bells, bronze mirrors, and bronze weapons were buried in many areas of Japan. This implies that many regional chieftains and their small countries began to be unified under the emerging powerful Yamato rulers and thus, accepting the new Kofun culture, had abandoned the traditional rituals that had employed these bronze items.

The greatest concentration of large kofun is in the Osaka-Nara area, and they are associated with the Yamato rulers, ancestors of the present imperial line. The rulers of Yamato, perhaps a confederation of tribal chieftains, claimed descent from the sun goddess and extended their power westward and eastward from the Nara-Kyoto-Osaka region. By the fifth and sixth centuries, a single kingly line seems to have developed within Yamato.

Throughout these early centuries of the Yayoi and Kofun periods, there were intermittent but close connections between clans in Japan and people in China and Korea. In the mid-sixth century, Japanese society was altered by a new cultural element from the continent, Buddhism. Buddhism was finding its way to Japan through immigrant communities. Gradually Buddhist temples replaced the great tombs as the places of ritual burial for the ruling groups in Japan. When Buddhism was introduced in Japan, the Japanese already had their own system of spiritual beliefs and ritual practices called Shinto, which touched every aspect of Japanese emotional experience and shaped Japanese responses to nature, life, and death. Shinto, Buddhism, Confucianism, and to a lesser extent Taoism and Christianity, have all exerted a profound influence on Japanese culture and the spiritual life of individual Japanese.

Buddhism settled into an easy complementary relationship with Shinto practices, and Japan was transformed in the seventh and eighth centuries from a clan society headed by a great chieftain into an imperial state based on the Tang model of China, ruled by a heavenly sovereign. The change was based on the importation of Buddhism and a whole series of Chinese administrative and legal institutions. Until the establishment of Buddhism, which brought in its wake a clear governmental structure and a code of laws, Japan was a loose confederation of clans in tenuous balance, with the imperial clan precariously at its head. The mechanics of rule and succession were undefined, creating violent conflicts. In addition, each time a new emperor took the throne, the palace was moved to a new site. People at that time apparently believed it was possible to escape natural disasters, calamities, and misfortune simply by abandoning the old palace for a new one.

The sixth century saw the development of the Chinese *ritsuryo* legal system, which included both law and Confucian philosophical concepts. Under this system both land and people became the property of the state, and a centralized bureaucratic apparatus emerged to manage them. A capital city had to be established as well, to house all the offices and functions of the state. This model was exported from China to Japan.

THE NARA AND HEIAN PERIODS

At the beginning of the eighth century, Nara became the capital, built on the contemporary Chinese model. This was the heyday of the early Buddhist sects in Japan, and the splendid temples surviving at Nara are the best remaining examples anywhere of Chinese architecture of the Tang period. The Chinese precedent required a permanent capital, laid out according to an orderly plan. The new capital was built at Nara in 710. All the arts that had made their way from China and Korea had gradually taken root in Japan—architecture, sculpture, painting, calligraphy, music, lacquering, and silk-making—and came into play in creating the temples and palaces of the capital (Barnes 1988).

In 794 the capital was moved to Kyoto (Heian-kyo, the capital of peace and tranquility), which remained the capital of Japan until the emperor moved his court to Tokyo in 1868. The new capital was modeled on Chang'an (modern Xi'an or Sian in China), with a grid pattern of avenues and streets and the great palace to the north of the city. The residences of the aristocracy were close to the Imperial Palace, followed by those of petty officials, artisans, storekeepers, and commoners. The establishment of Kyoto marks the opening of the Heian age (794–1185), a period of remarkable artistic sophistication of the court and metropolitan aristocracy. The elegant Heian life and manners are depicted by the eleventh-century court lady Murasaki Shikibu, in *Genji Monogatari* (*The Tale of Genji*). This masterpiece is the reflection of an exquisite culture already characteristically Japanese, even though the debt to China and Chinese modes may be immense.

The frontier of Japan moved progressively northward during the Nara and early Heian periods as a result of military campaigns (see fig. 3.1) until all of northern Honshu was incorporated by the end of the Heian period (Friday 1997). With the development of the state, a sharp distinction came to be drawn between the inner lands (*kinai*), under direct Japanese control, and the outer lands (*kegai*), outside the zone of administration but located within the Japanese "world" (Batten 1999).

The political ideology in ancient Japan was a modified, self-referential version of the Chinese middle-kingdom ideology (*kai shiso*).

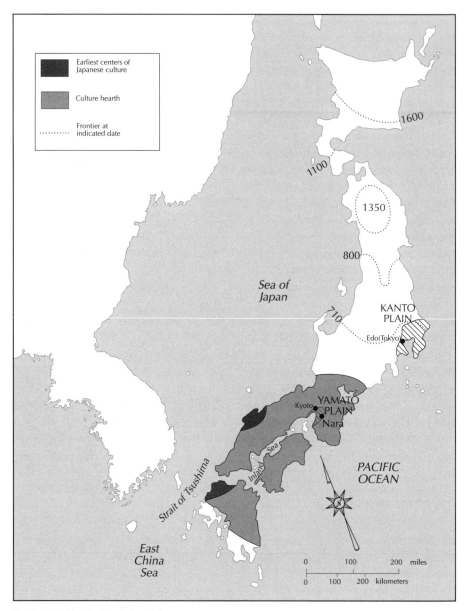

Fig. 3.1. The historical evolution of Japan.

The Shogun, Daimyo, and Samurai Cultures, 1185–1868

By the middle of the twelfth century, effective power in Japan was in the hands of a warrior household, the Taira. Their great rival was another family, the Minamoto. The strife between the two families gave rise to many epics. In 1185 the Minamoto annihilated their enemies, and the leader of the Minamoto, Yoritomo, set up a new system of government, known as the Bakufu (meaning "curtain government" or "ruling from behind the scenes"), at Kamakura, far from the imperial capital of Kyoto. The emperor gave Yoritomo the title *shogun*. The original purpose of the Bakufu was control and administration by the Japanese warrior class, which was now a distinctive entity, one that was rapidly becoming all-powerful in society. The true rule of the country from this time forward, until 1868, would tend to belong to the warrior class. The Kamakura Bakufu lasted until the fourteenth century; a new Bakufu from the Muromachi district of the capital replaced it. A period of feudal disorder and civil war followed, lasting more than 250 years. The period was also marked by economic growth and artistic achievements. The breakdown of the central government gave at least some provincial lords the freedom and incentive to embark on foreign trade on their own, especially with China. At the same time, painting, classical drama, architecture, landscape gardening, ceramics, the tea ceremony, and flower arrangement—a great deal of what is recognized today as Japan's magnificent cultural heritage—blossomed in these stormy years. Here Zen Buddhism, in all its manifestations, played a central part. Japan presented a paradoxical scene of savagery and civilization, of barbarism and beauty, intertwined.

Table 3.1. Japan's shogunates, 1185–1867

Shogunal family	Administrative capital	Dates
Minamoto	Kamakura	1185–1333
Ashikaga	Kyoto (Muromachi district)	1338–1573
Tokugawa	Edo	1603–1867

The one hundred years of the Warring States period, which lasted roughly from 1490 to 1590, saw widespread warfare among provincial warlords. It was a period of continual kill-or-be-killed fighting. Effective central government and internal peace were not finally secured until the early years of the seventeenth century, after Ieyasu founded the Tokugawa Bakufu in Edo (the modern Tokyo), giving the whole country a domestic order that would endure until the coming of Americans in the 1850s. Tokugawa Ieyasu built on the work already performed by two notable men, Oda Nobunaga (1534–82) and Toyotomi Hideyoshi (1537–98). Nobunaga contrived to unify about half the provinces of Japan before his death. Hideyoshi, the son of a foot soldier, was one of Nobunaga's commanders. Within ten years of Nobunaga's death, he made himself master of the whole country, with the help of a wise and cautious ally, Tokugawa Ieyasu. After Hideyoshi's death, Ieyasu made his own position supreme; he was appointed shogun by the emperor.

Ieyasu located the administrative capital at Edo, the present Tokyo, away from the imperial court and nearer the geographic center of the main island. The city became in time the largest in the land. Its castle, the residence of the shoguns, was a massive and extensive piece of masonry and, in an altered form, is today the Imperial Palace. Ieyasu surrounded Edo with fiefs held by members of his own family, the Tokugawa. All strategic points were placed in the hands of chiefs whom he could trust. Officials responsible to the shogun were put over the principal cities, and the main highway between Kyoto and Edo was carefully guarded. Ieyasu skillfully distributed fiefs among members of his family and loyal barons wherever there seemed likely to be disaffection.

Tokugawa Ieyasu, born in Okazaki (Aichi Prefecture) in 1543, led his army into the battle of Sekigahara and won an easy victory in 1600. As a result he emerged as the most powerful warrior leader in Japan, claiming authority over all Japanese *daimyo*. Ieyasu had himself appointed as shogun and placed at the head of the feudalized military system of government that had first been organized by Yoritomo, the founder of the Kamakura shogunate more than four hundred years before. Photo by P.P. Karan, from the shrine at Nikko.

The site of the Battle of Sekigahara, not far from Nagoya in Gifu Prefecture, where the armies of Ieyasu and those loyal to Hideyori fought in 1600 in one of the decisive battles of Japan's history. The two armies met in a narrow valley west of the village of Sekigahara. Aided by treason in the enemy's ranks, Ieyasu won and was henceforth master of the country. Sekigahara retained its strategic importance as a post-station town for the next three hundred years and is still a transportation center. Photo by P.P. Karan.

Osaka Castle, Osaka, was built in 1583 by the national unifier Toyotomi Hideyoshi. Impressive in scale, the castle measures 2 miles (3.2 km) east to west and 1.5 miles (2.4 km) north to south. It was considered impregnable. Hideyoshi's son Hideyori retired with his mother to this strong castle, which his father had built. Ieyasu attacked the castle in 1614 and 1615, and Hideyori and his mother perished, thereby eliminating the most serious potential challenge to the shogunate Ieyasu had established in 1603. Photo by P.P. Karan.

The feudal culture of Japan from the twelfth to the nineteenth century (1185–1868) was dominated by *daimyo,* regional magnates who ranked below Japan's shogun rulers and above other samurai warriors (Shimizu 1988). A daimyo was a samurai who controlled enough land to produce 10,000 *koku* of rice (a koku of grain equaled 5.12 U.S. bushels [0.18 cu m]). He was a rich samurai who had other samurai working for him. Castle towns served as the center of a daimyo's domain (see fig. 3.2). All daimyo were commanded to maintain houses in Edo. Each was to keep some of his family or retainers there part of the time while he visited his feudal domain. Deputy governors under the direct control of Edo were scattered through the country and were still another check on the daimyo.

The martial society of Japan's Middle Ages began about a century after the beginning of Europe's feudal era and lasted well into the Victorian period. The feudal social structure in Japan was similar to Europe's hierarchy of kings, lords, warriors, and vassals, but whereas the Europeans allowed their cultural traditions to lie dormant until the Renaissance, the Japanese daimyo nurtured art forms such as

painting, poetry, drama, and ceremony. The goal of the daimyo was to maintain balance between the arts of combat, or *bu,* and the arts of peace and culture, or *bun.* The embodiment of bu was the sword, which the samurai saw as an object of spiritual significance (Sinclaire 2001). Although mastery of the bu discipline was essential for the daimyo to survive and hold on to land, many regional lords also became patrons and even practitioners of the arts. Literature, painting, and sculpture were all cultivated, but perhaps the most profound of bun-related traditions was the tea ceremony, a disciplined and beautiful event first used to achieve the relaxation of Zen meditation. Another expression of bun was the Noh play, which, like the miracle plays that preceded Elizabethan drama in the West, taught moral lessons in the context of entertainment.

The idea of full-scale warrior government, headed by a shogun detached from the imperial court, was firmly established in the feudal period. The imperial court was enfeebled and reduced to a ritual and legitimating role, but it was not stripped of sovereignty.

Japan had admitted European traders and Chris-

Fig. 3.2. Major domains and castle towns. Based on Nakane and Oishi 1990.

tian missionaries but evicted them and closed its doors after observing what was happening everywhere else in Asia where Europeans were admitted. Introduced into Kyushu in the 1540s, Christianity spread rapidly. Francis Xavier, who landed in Kagoshima in 1549, preached in Hirado, Hakata, Yamaguchi, Kyoto, and Shimabara. Jesuits, Franciscans, and Dominicans strove to convert daimyo and commoners. The expulsion of missionaries in 1587 and the relentless persecution of Christians after 1612 by the early Tokugawa shoguns eventually crushed missionary efforts in Japan. The few remaining Christians who clung to their faith did so secretly.

The policy of excluding foreign influence from Japan began early in the seventeenth century and continued for more than two hundred years. During this time Japan developed into a nation with its own special characteristics—a nation unlike any other in the world. Peace and stability prevailed almost unbroken over this long period of time, which

Samurai premises in Hirosaki. Samurai or warrior elites of premodern Japan became the ruling class of the country from the late twelfth century until the Meiji Restoration of 1868. Photo by P.P. Karan.

A Trappist monastery in Hakodate, Hokkaido. Japan's encounter with Christianity began with the arrival of Jesuit missionaries in 1549. In 1610 there may have been as many as 370,000 Christians in Japan. Tokugawa Ieyasu banned Christianity in 1612. After 1873 most restrictions were lifted. Photo by P.P. Karan.

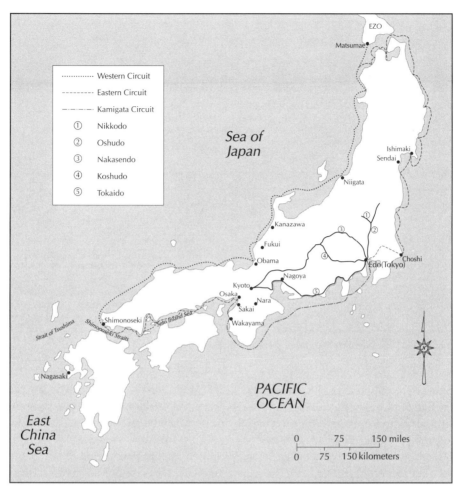

Fig. 3.3. Transportation network in Tokugawa Japan. Based on data from Katsuhisa Moriya.

contributed to the development of the nation. A sea- and land-based transportation network connected various parts of the country with Edo (see fig. 3.3). Since all the daimyo were now under the control of the central government, farmers were not forced to leave the farm to fight for them, and extra taxes to pay for wars were no longer levied. Although peace created the conditions for national development, it was the merchants who provided the driving force that pushed development. For example, the Mitsui family, which operated a sake brewery near the Ise Shrine in the 1620s, had accumulated enough wealth by 1673 to open a shop in Edo to sell cloth. Business was brisk, and the family opened stores in Kyoto and Osaka in the 1680s. By the 1690s, the Mitsui had acquired considerable financial know-how. They became the financial agent for the shogun, the emperor,

and several daimyo. The family had amassed enough capital to finance the draining of marshland for agriculture, land whose production added to the family fortune. Today the Mitsui Company operates department stores all over Japan under the name Mitsukoshi. Likewise, the Sumitomo family of Kyoto sold ironware at the beginning of the seventeenth century. Later they began to trade in copper shipped through the port of Osaka. Like the Mitsui, the Sumitomo became agents for the government, and they began to develop copper mines. Today Sumitomo is a vast industrial and commercial conglomerate. As the examples of Mitsui and Sumitomo illustrate, profit from trade, combined with sound business principles, resulted in the development of new farms and mines that contributed to the prosperity of Japan during the Tokugawa period.

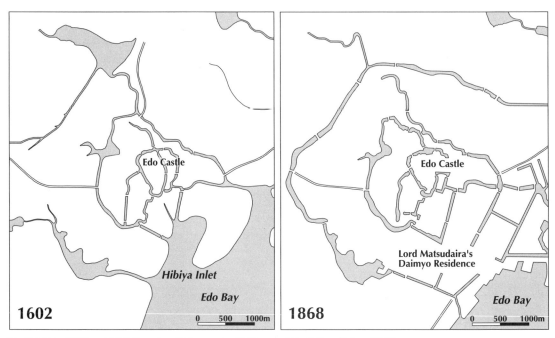

Fig. 3.4. Edo, 1602 and 1868. Based on Matsunosuke Nishiyama, *Edo Culture* (Tokyo, 1997).

By the mid-eighteenth century the teeming garrison city of Edo (Tokyo) began to assume intellectual and cultural primacy over the Kyoto area, which was the cultural pacesetter in Japan. Edo city expanded through reclamation of low-lying marshy areas between 1602 and 1868 (see fig. 3.4). The presence of shogunal court and daimyo residences, temples, shrines, and a large population created a huge demand for goods and services as well as for learning and entertainment. Edo merchants had the wealth and confidence to patronize culture.

More than 80 percent of the population of Tokugawa Japan lived on the land. The Tokugawa shoguns compartmentalized Japanese society into four hereditary status groups: daimyo and samurai, farmers, artisans, and merchants, with outcastes, considered nonpeople, below them. Outcastes were often referred to as *etahinin* (unclean nonpersons). In the Tokugawa status hierarchy, farmers ranked immediately below the samurai in importance. Their valued function in Confucian economic theory was to sustain society through their labor. Daimyo squeezed as much tax from the peasants as possible. By 1640 Japan was closing in upon itself commercially; trade with other countries was restricted to a limited number of sites—the so-called four mouths (*yottsu no kuchi*). Commercial relations with Hol-

land and China were conducted via Nagasaki; with Korea via Tsushima; with the Ryuku Kingdom via Satsuma; and with Ezo (or the Ainu) via Matsumae.

The Tokugawa shogunate survived until 1867, and during this long period of peace and stability a uniquely Japanese cultural style developed. Land surveys to assess the land in terms of rice productivity (*kokudaka*) were completed (measured in kokus, roughly the amount of rice a person consumed in a year). Koku became the basis for setting land taxes, village sizes, and the allotment of daimyo domains, samurai stipends, and feudal obligations. Thus, one characteristic of premodern Japan was that rice production became the standard for everything, as indicated by the expression *komedate* (rice-based calculation). Daimyo had their own domains and castles and were served by samurai vassals. Entrusted by the shoguns with the registers of lands and peoples in their domains, they enjoyed the right to govern the territory and collect the annual land tax.

Chie Nakane and Shinzaburo Oishi (1990) give a very good account of the economy, society, and culture of Japan during the Tokugawa period. John F. Richards (2003) gives an excellent account of the resource management and ecology in Tokugawa Japan. Tsunetoshi Mizoguchi (2001) provides an ex-

During the Tokugawa shogunate (1603–1867), Japanese society was organized into four classes: daimyo and samurai, farmers, merchants, and artisans. Outcastes were outside the four groups. Daimyo lived in castles such as the Kumamoto Castle seen in this photo. Kato Kiyomasa, a daimyo, built it in 1601. It later came under the rule of the Hosokawa family. Photo by P.P. Karan.

cellent detailed geographic account of the spatial organization of Japan during the Tokugawa shogunate. His research, based on data in local gazetteers of the Owari region (Nobi Plain), reveals changes in land use, settlements, and population based on distance from the Nagoya castle. Mizoguchi noted a distinct distance decay function. Villages near the castle had higher koku than those in the periphery. The mean kokudaka per *tan* (a tan equals 0.25 acres or 0.10 hectares) per village, as well as kokudaka per household, increased from the periphery of the region to the core of the Owari region. The land was more intensively utilized in the core, with higher productivity.

Three types of central places existed in Tokugawa Japan: administrative centers of local governors; economic centers, such as market towns and post towns; and places visited often by people from surrounding villages. An elaborate urban network centering on Edo, Kyoto, and Osaka had developed. Edo was the center of the political and economic network, and the city expanded considerably in both population and geographic area (see fig. 3.4 for the geographic expansion). Kyoto was the dominant cultural center, and Osaka was the largest commercial center. Increasing agricultural productivity and the growth of a monetary economy in various regions of Japan encouraged the emergence of market towns at major nodes. About 750 settlements in Japan (not including Hokkaido) had place names connected to a market, such as Yokkaichi, according to Mizoguchi (2001). Post towns had developed on major roads to

provide facilities and services to travelers. Sites frequently visited by rural people living in the local villages also served as central places.

A regional specialization in production had emerged. Perishable vegetables were planted in areas close to the city; root vegetables, such as potatoes, radishes, and carrots, were raised farther away; and products such as tea, persimmons, and sesame were produced in the peripheral area. Tatsushi Inagaki's research (2001) on the Temma vegetable market in Osaka reveals that at the beginning of the eighteenth century some markets were selling products from all over the greater part of western Japan.

JAPAN'S EMERGENCE AS A GREAT POWER, 1868–1914

In 1842 the Treaty of Nanking opened China for trade with Western countries. The United States wanted to have its share of China trade. Japan, of course, lies on the direct route from California to China. In addition, the waters of the North Pacific were the home of thousands of whales, and as many as five hundred American whalers were hunting these waters. The United States wanted Japan to open up for trade, to sell coal, food, and water to American ships, and to provide aid to the crews of ships in distress near Japan.

Eleven years after the opening of China, an American navy commodore, Matthew C. Perry, steamed into Tokyo Bay on July 8, 1853, to deliver a letter to the representative of the emperor from Presi-

Hakodate was one of the first ports opened to foreign trade in 1854, following the arrival of Commodore Matthew Perry. It has been a flourishing seaport since 1741. Photo by P.P. Karan.

dent Millard Fillmore requesting that foreign trade, forbidden since the early seventeenth century, be resumed. After delivering the letter, Perry sailed away with the promise to return within a year for a reply from the Japanese. On February 14, 1854, Perry returned with an armada of eight ships. On March 31, 1854, Japan signed the Treaty of Kanagawa (later renamed Yokohama), which opened two ports (Shimoda and Hakodate) to shipwrecked American sailors and to American trade. By the end of 1856 Britain, Russia, and France had signed similar treaties with Japan. Townsend Harris was appointed the first U.S. consul general at Shimoda.

The alert Japanese were much impressed by the technological superiority of the Americans and realized that Japan needed to modernize to remain independent. In 1868 leaders from the two remote southern domains of Satsuma and Choshu seized the Imperial Palace in Kyoto, declared the restoration of the Meiji emperor, and brought to a sudden end two and a half centuries of rule by the Tokugawa shogunate. Just fourteen years after the Treaty of

Kanagawa, forward-looking Japanese, after overthrowing the Tokugawa government, began reorganizing the Japanese government and society along modern Western lines (McClain 2002). Taking what they considered best from the various Western nations, they patterned their business methods after those of the United States, their legal system after the French, and their navy after the British. But it was Bismarck's Germany that impressed the Japanese most. They built a military machine and an authoritarian government and education system on the model of the German empire.

Osaka-based geographer Toshio Mizuuchi (1999) argues that the successful progress of Japanese modernization after the Meiji Restoration of 1868 and the swift achievement of economic objectives was facilitated by the proper execution of development policies and the establishment of transportation facilities. Five specific policies were key elements in the success of the development and spatial integration of the nation: (1) the policy of river and flood control and water resource management, (2) road construction and

Japan Meets the World

1639	Japan cuts links with the outside world
1853	America demands that Japan open itself to trade
1868	Meiji Restoration
1890	First parliamentary election
1894–95	Sino-Japanese War
1904–5	Russo-Japanese War
1910	Annexation of Korea
1923	Great Tokyo earthquake
1925	Male suffrage
1931	Japanese invasion of Manchuria
1933	Japan leaves League of Nations
1940	Tripartite pact between Japan, Germany, and Italy
1941–45	Pacific War
1945	Atomic bombs dropped on Hiroshima and Nagasaki
1945–52	Occupation of Japan by Allied forces
1946	New American-designed constitution promulgated; female suffrage
1956	Japan joins the United Nations
1992	Japan sends troops to Cambodia for peacekeeping operation
2002	Self-Defense Forces dispatched to East Timor for peacekeeping
2004	Japan sends troops to Iraq to help in reconstruction work

maintenance, (3) harbor construction and maintenance, (4) railway construction, and (5) the policy of city and regional planning.

In an incredibly short time, Japan became a modern, industrialized, military power. In 1894 Japan attacked China, forcing China to pay a large indemnity and to give up Korea (which Japan annexed in 1910) and the island of Formosa (Taiwan). Japan attacked Russia in 1904 and defeated it on land and sea. Japan took the southern half of Sakhalin Island and Russia's railroad and port concessions in southern Manchuria, thereby becoming the dominant power in East Asia. By 1914 Japan was a first-rate power—industrialized, militaristic, and imperialistic. It participated in World War I on the side of the Allies and received Germany's island possessions in the Pacific north of the equator as its reward. Japan gained a military monopoly in East Asia and the western Pacific (Norman 2000). In March 1919 Japanese troops brutally quashed the Samil Independence Movement (the March First Movement), whose members had been demanding Korean independence; at least 7,500 Koreans were massacred and another 30,000 were imprisoned. Emperor Taisho (Yoshihito), the son of one of Emperor Meiji's concubines, reigned during this period. Emperor Taisho did not involve himself, as his father had, with the nation's development, largely because of his ill health, and Crown Prince Hirohito (later emperor) took over as regent in 1921. Emperor Taisho was Japan's first emperor to live with his children but the last permitted to have concubines. Upon the death of Emperor Taisho on December 25, 1926, he was succeeded by Hirohito (Emperor Showa).

THE TRIUMPH OF FASCISM AND WORLD WAR II

In the 1920s Japan stood at a crossroads. It could use its great energies and skills either to develop its own institutions and raise the Japanese standards of living or to become a predatory military state. At the same time liberal democratic trends were being overshadowed and weakened by aggressive nationalism. Japan's quickly built industries had overexpanded during the period of World War I prosperity, and postwar deflation and sharp competition from the former allies brought severe economic stresses.

Three divergent groups competed for the lead-

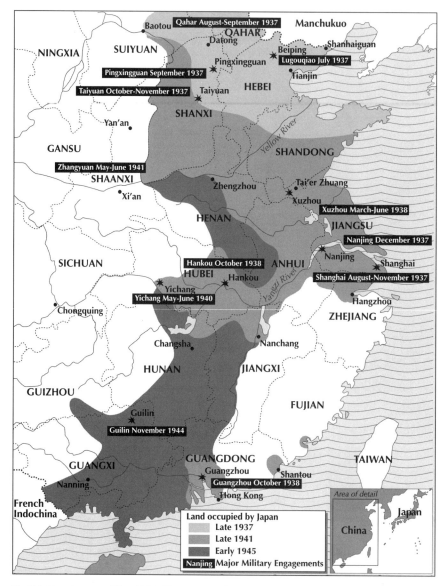

Fig. 3.5. Sino-Japanese War, 1937–45.

ership of Japan in the 1920s. The dominant group was made up of the great industrialists. Seventy-five percent of Japan's industry and capital was concentrated in the hands of five great family conglomerates, called the *zaibatsu*. These industrial giants had such a stranglehold on the Japanese economy that they were able to control the government. The zaibatsu, enjoying this economic and political monopoly, wished to see no fundamental change in Japan. They advocated peaceful economic penetration of Asia (Morikawa 1992).

The liberals constituted the second group, com-prising mostly university professors and students. This group set out to broaden suffrage, which was restricted to the well-to-do; to encourage the more effective unionization of labor; and to diminish the power of the military. In 1925 suffrage was extended and liberal political parties emerged. There were periods of growing democratic incentive. The young Emperor Hirohito, who ascended the throne on December 25, 1926, adopted the name Showa (enlightenment and harmony) for his reign. But the long tradition of passive submission to authority on the part of the masses made liberal reforms difficult.

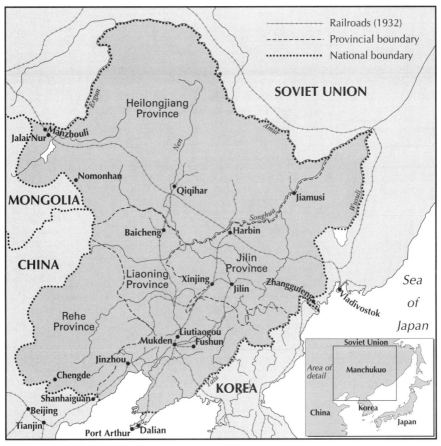

Fig. 3.6. The puppet state of Manchukuo.

The third group, the professional military, was determined to strengthen its own traditional power. In the early 1930s Japan's growing international isolation, resulting from its aggression in China and Manchuria (see figs. 3.5 and 3.6); its war fervor; and its patriotic hysteria combined to undermine the authority of the parties and allow the power of the military to reassert itself. Once in power, the military destroyed all democratic processes of government and civil rights. The zaibatsu were corrupted and won over with lush military contracts. By 1940, with strengthened militaristic and authoritarian tendencies entrenched in Japanese policy, Japan was on the brink of war with the United States. A surprise attack on Pearl Harbor by Japan on the morning of December 7, 1941, started World War II in the Pacific (see figs. 3.7 and 3.8). The attack failed to realize Japan's strategic aims of totally destroying the U.S. Pacific fleet and shattering the American will to fight.

For more than a half century a debate centered on the wartime role of Emperor Hirohito: whether he was the mastermind of the war or merely a puppet. In a new biography of the emperor, American historian Herbert P. Bix (2000), using official records, diaries, and memoirs, provides detailed accounts of Hirohito's intimate involvement in planning Japan's march through China and Southeast Asia—and his postwar maneuvering to distance himself from the war. According to Bix, the emperor approved the plan to attack Pearl Harbor and was involved in early strategic decisions as Japan's army moved across the western Pacific. Hirohito was not implicated in the Tokyo war-crimes trial because the U.S. occupying force decided that he would be useful in maintaining stability. His role, however, turned out to be largely symbolic as a figurehead emperor (Showa: The Japan of Hirohito 1990).

Japanese actions during the Pacific War continue to haunt the country even after more than a half cen-

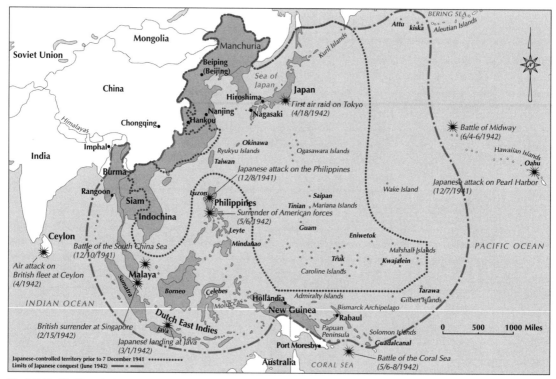

Fig. 3.7. Pacific War, 1941–42.

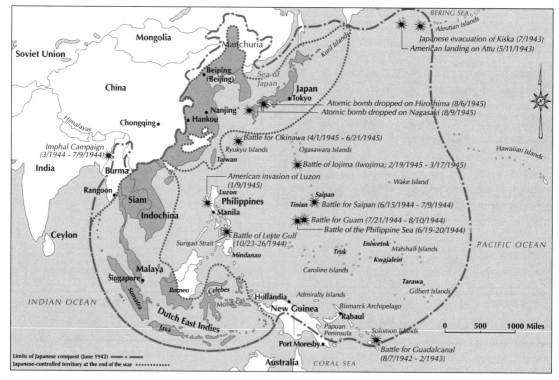

Fig. 3.8. Pacific War, 1942–45.

tury. These include the Nanjing massacre; germ warfare and human experiments by Unit 731 (Williams and Wallace 1989); and the "comfort women" issue, in which Asian and European women were forced to provide sex to Japanese soldiers. In much of China, the Japanese military had a policy of destroying all villages and killing those who might be of help to the other side. It is widely accepted among scholars that after the sudden collapse of the Chinese defense of Nanjing in December 1937, rampaging Japanese soldiers executed thousands of prisoners of war, civilians as well as men suspected of being soldiers, and burned the homes of Chinese (Chang 1997). According to some, as many as 300,000 were killed in Nanjing. Japanese accounts vary from several thousand to 200,000 dead, while some Japanese politicians deny that the massacre ever took place. The Tokyo War Crimes Tribunal concluded that more than 140,000 people were killed during the Japanese military's rampage following the fall of Nanjing in late 1937, making it one of the worst atrocities committed by Japanese forces before and during World War II.

Unit 731, a medical research team of the Japanese Imperial Army, conducted biological experiments on prisoners of war during World War II. Unit 731 killed more than 3,000 Chinese and Russian prisoners of war at its facility in the suburbs of Harbin, Manchuria, in experiments to develop bacteriological weapons (see fig. 3.9). After the end of the war, U.S. intelligence authorities gave Unit 731's top scientists, including its leader, Lt. Gen. Shiro Ishii, immunity from prosecution in return for their data on human experiments. China is building a museum on the site where the experiments, including vivisection and injection of lethal strains of typhus, cholera, and other diseases, were carried out. This is also the location of the ovens in which corpses were burned and the freezer rooms where cold-temperature experiments were conducted.

At Shenyang in northeast China, roughly 1,500 prisoners endured forced labor, subzero temperatures, and, if the allegations are true, a Japanese-administered germ warfare program that used them as guinea pigs. During Japan's brutal fourteen-year occupation of Shenyang and of surrounding Manchuria, beginning on September 18, 1931, untold numbers of Chinese were slain. For many Chinese, the lingering resentment and anger toward Japan is great.

The comfort-women issue involves as many as 200,000 women, mostly from the Korean peninsula but also from elsewhere in Southeast Asia, who were taken to frontline brothels and forced to provide sex to Japanese soldiers. Surviving South Korean and Filipina women, some of whom were as young as ten at the time of the war, have sought compensation, alleging that the Japanese military confined them and forced them into sexual slavery. In 2000 the Tokyo High Court rejected their suit. The suit argued that the government is obliged to compensate the women because sexual slavery violates a 1907 treaty and international rules that protect civilians in militarily occupied territories. The Japanese government argued that international laws stipulate rules to be followed by countries and do not cover individuals demanding compensation, and that Japan had already made war reparations to the Korean government.

Japan's aggression and the atrocities it entailed are treated only cursorily in most Japanese school textbooks. Even recent concessions to textbook reform in this area, such as the mention of the rape and sexual slavery of thousands of Korean and Chinese women, are attacked by conservatives, who cast doubt on the accounts and say these subjects should not be taught to young Japanese. Such pronouncements cause concern in China and Korea.

After Japan's attack on Pearl Harbor in 1941, more than 120,000 Americans of Japanese ancestry, most of them U.S. citizens, were removed from their homes on the West Coast and from parts of Hawaii and taken to internment camps in seven states in the western United States. One of the major camps, at Santa Fe, New Mexico, was operated by the Justice Department and was surrounded by barbed wire. The Santa Fe Camp was largely for Japanese-born men who were professionals and community leaders and therefore considered more of a threat. Some had lived in the United States for decades, but under federal law they could not become citizens. More than 4,500 people passed through the Santa Fe camp. They were neither soldiers nor prisoners of war. Ordered into the detention camps with little or no advance warning, most had to sell their homes and businesses at great loss and without compensation.

In 1982 a congressional commission concluded that the executive order President Roosevelt signed

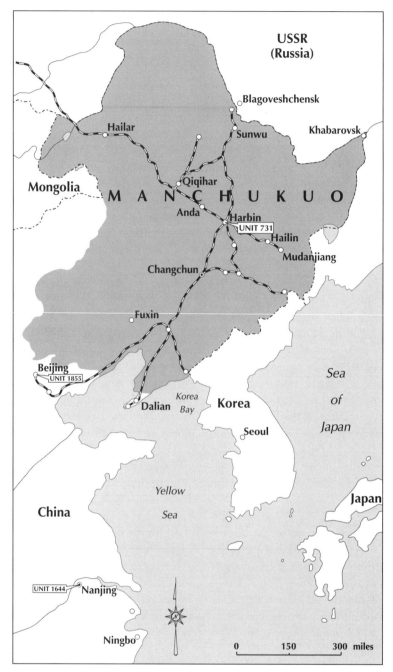

Fig. 3.9. Area of secret germ warfare operations of Unit 731. Based on Williams and Wallace 1989.

to remove Americans of Japanese ancestry to detention camps was not justified by military necessity but was the result of racism, war hysteria, and a failure of political leadership. Six years later, President Ronald Reagan signed a civil liberties law that provided an official government apology, $20,000 each

for surviving inmates, and a $1.25 billion education fund. A plaque was placed at a Santa Fe city park on a hilltop overlooking the site of the internment camp in 1999. But some Bataan veterans in Santa Fe, still bitter after a half century, contrast the internees' treatment to their own. They note that the Santa Fe camp had a farm, a garden, recreational facilities, classes, and a theater. When Japan overran the Philippines and U.S. forces surrendered on the Bataan Peninsula in April 1942, sick and starving soldiers were forced to march 62 miles (100 km) in the hot sun. Denied food and water, they were beaten—and some were killed—if they fell out of line. The cruelty continued in prison camps.

POSTWAR REFORM, RECONSTRUCTION, AND EMERGENCE AS AN ECONOMIC SUPERPOWER

Japan emerged from World War II defeated on sea and land, the shocked victim of history's first two atomic bombs used for military purposes. Japan surrendered on August 15, 1945. With the cessation of hostilities in 1945, all administrative powers of the Japanese government were placed in the hands of General Douglas MacArthur. From September 1945 to April 1952, the Japanese government was officially responsible to the American occupation force. The U.S. government followed a four-point policy for postwar Japan: (1) Japan was to be limited to the four "home" islands and some small ones in the vicinity; (2) Japan was to be completely demilitarized; (3) civil, political, and religious rights and liberties for the Japanese people were to be restored; (4) and Japan's economy was to be developed for its peacetime needs. A democratic constitution was drawn up, and educational and land reform programs were implemented.

During the 1950s and 1960s Japan made an outstanding economic recovery. In rebuilding its ruined industries, Japan adopted the most modern and scientific labor-saving devices. By the mid-1960s Japan was the third-greatest industrial power in the world, outranked only by the United States and the Soviet Union, and its people were enjoying a prosperity and a standard of living such as they had never known before. In the 1980s Japan emerged as an economic superpower in the world. Nagoya-based geographer Mizoguchi (1996) provides an excellent review of geographic research on economic and landscape transformations in modern Japan. At present Japan stands at a crossroads. Unless the economy is freed of regulatory barriers, the bureaucracy reorganized, and the approach to policymaking changed, Japan's aging society and the flight of manufacturing industries to low-wage countries will present major challenges. Between 1990 and 2003, China gained on Japan in terms of its regional position in Asia. World Trade Organization data show that China's share of Asia's overall imports grew from 7.5 percent in 1990 to 17.7 percent in 2001, and its share of exports increased from 8.4 percent in 1990 to 17.8 percent in 2001. In the same period Japan's share declined: its imports went from 33.2 percent in 1990 to 25.4 percent in 2001, and its exports from 38.9 percent in 1990 to 26.9 percent in 2001. Since the turn of the twentieth century, essentially, Japan has tended to hold the chief strategic influence in Asia—first as an aggressive colonial power in Korea and China before World War II, and later as America's chief ally in the region and the world's number two economy. Momentum in this phase appears to be shifting, but it is too soon to arrive at a conclusion.

CULTURAL HERITAGE IN THE TWENTY-FIRST CENTURY

Despite Japan's rich cultural heritage, one could not say that the Japanese have taken great care of their historical heritage sites in the postwar years. For instance, a railway line runs through the former site of Heijo Palace in the ancient capital of Heijokyo in the Nara Basin, while the former site of the residence of Prince Nagaya, an imperial family member in the Nara period (710–94), was destroyed to make way for the construction of a department store.

A Westernized lifestyle and way of thinking, as well as rapid economic growth, have distanced the Japanese people from the history of their own nation. If things continue as they are, Japan can hardly claim to have passed on the cultural heritage of Japan into the twenty-first century. World history is a required subject in the high school history curriculum in Japan, while the study of Japanese history is an elective subject. The tendency among the young Japanese to undervalue Japanese history should be a source of concern. As Japan becomes a more internationalized society in this century, it becomes more important for members of the society to know the history, traditions, and cultural roots of the country. But few young Japanese today are capable of speaking about Japanese history and the heart of Japanese tradition and culture.

Since the end of World War II, history education has been a bone of contention in the ideological conflict that arose during the cold war. Teaching about the *Kojiki* (*Record of Ancient Matters*) and the *Nihon*

Shoki (*Chronicle of Japan*) has often been avoided, since it means exposing students to the theory that Japan is a divine nation, based on the lineage of the imperial family. Amid the postwar ideological conflict over the evaluation of modern and ancient history, negative aspects of the Meiji era were often emphasized, although the period was characterized by a spirit of progressiveness. When it comes to the Edo period (1603–1868), negative aspects such as the exploitation of farmers by their feudal lords and the many peasant uprisings that took place have been highlighted.

What should also be pointed out is that the feudal lords' biannual pilgrimages to Edo, present-day Tokyo, to pay homage to the Tokugawa shogunate, promoted exchanges between Edo and the provinces and improved transportation and communication. At the same time, each region developed its own culture, because ordinary peasants were not allowed to travel outside of the daimyo's domain. This led to regional accents and traditions. Most foreigners who visited Japan between the end of the Edo period and the beginning of the Meiji period praised Japan's culture. In the twenty-first century, learning about the country's cultural heritage should be a priority for Japanese as they advance toward further globalization and internationalization.

RELIGION

The religious beliefs of the Japanese people go back to prehistoric times (Matsui 1998). Indian Buddhism, Chinese Confucianism and Taoism, and later Christianity were introduced into Japan from the outside. All these foreign religious traditions have undergone significant transformations in the process of interaction with native Shinto beliefs.

Japan has a plurality of religious traditions and simultaneous or alternate participation of people in Shinto, Buddhist, and Christian traditions. In recent times, a Japanese may have a birth ceremony in a Shinto shrine, may be married in a Christian wedding chapel, may live according to Confucian social teachings, may hold some Taostic beliefs about "lucky" and "unlucky" phenomena, may participate in folk festivals, and may have his or her funeral conducted by a Buddhist priest.

There is an intimate relationship between a person and the gods and the sacredness of nature (Kaneko 1995, 1997; Matsui 1999). In addition to

the deities, represented in mythology, natural phenomena and emperors and other special human beings were also considered to be sacred or *kami*. Kami and Buddhas are thought to exist in nature and in the lives of human beings.

The family and ancestors have considerable religious significance. Most homes have both a family Shinto altar (*kamidana*) and a Buddhist altar (*butsudan*) for venerating ancestors. Notions of purity and impurity have pervaded Japanese beliefs. At a Shinto shrine it is traditional for a person to rinse her or his hands and mouth ceremonially as symbolic acts of purification before coming into contact with kami. Festivals are the major means of celebration of religion. Aesthetic pursuits such as the tea ceremony and flower arranging also embody religious notions concerning veneration of the forces of nature.

Until 1945 the government controlled religion closely. Complete religious freedom was enacted during the Allied occupation of 1945–52.

A *kamidana*, a Shinto family altar, in the home of the Nomaki family in Kamimura, Nagano Prefecture, central Japan. At the center of this kamidana is a miniature Shinto shrine. Photo by P.P. Karan.

Shinto

Shinto, Japan's indigenous religion, is both a loosely structured set of practices, creeds, and attitudes rooted in local communities and a strictly defined and organized religion at the level of the imperial line and the state. These two basic aspects, which are mixed in a unique fashion, reflect fundamental features of the Japanese national character as it is expressed in sociopolitical structures and psychological attitudes (Littleton 2002).

Shinto practice is circumscribed within the context of sacred space and sacred time. The typical Shinto shrine (*jinja*) is located near the source of a river at the foot of the mountains. Surrounded by a fence, its entrance is marked by a wooden *torii* (gate). The Grand Shrine at Ise stands next to the Isuzu River. The torii consists of a pair of posts topped by two crossbars, one of which extends beyond the uprights. The torii marks the boundary between the impure outer, secular world and the sacred space of the shrine. Shinto shrines range in size and importance from tiny spaces on the roofs of modern high-rise buildings in big cities to the massive Meiji-jingu, which is dedicated to the spirit of Emperor Meiji, and Yasukuni, which honors millions of war dead, including fourteen "Class A" war criminals condemned for their role in World War II.

The Yasukuni Shrine is by far Japan's most controversial religious site, because of its dedication to the 2.5 million soldiers who fell in wars since the mid-1800s. The visits to Yasukuni Shrine by Japanese prime ministers have created strong tensions between Japan and its neighbors, especially China and Korea, over Japan's recognition of its wartime atrocities. They regard Yasukuni as a monument to Japan's twentieth-century militarism. Only three prime ministers have visited the Yasukuni Shrine since 1978, but since the first visit by a sitting prime minister, Yasuhiro Nakasone, in 1985, the question of whether the Japanese leader should appear at the shrine on August 15, the anniversary of Japan's surrender in World War II, has been regarded as something of a nationalist litmus test.

Shinto is associated with a wide variety of art forms, including ritual objects, architecture, sculpture, and painting, in a tradition that dates back to the fifth century. Shinto festivals (*matsuri*) are a means of reactualizing the sacred presence through reenactment of the ancestral rituals and thereby affirming the relationship between the deity and the devotee. Festivals and rituals signify sacred time in the Shinto calendar and provide channels through which humans communicate with the divine realm and maintain their well-being.

At the Shinto shrines the *miko*—the ritual dancers and the givers of offerings—stride across the sacred ground, their archaic red and white costumes flickering in the leafy shade of the trees, then shining bright in the sun. The role of miko comes down from ancient times, when they were shamans revealing the words of the deities who possessed them. Nowadays, they still dance at ceremonies and make offerings, but they spend a lot more time selling good-luck charms and cleaning their shrines. Ritu-

The large granite *torii* (gate) leading to the Yasukuni Shrine on the Kudan Hills on the northwest side of the Imperial Palace grounds in Tokyo. It is dedicated to Japan's national heroes—in particular to the 2.4 million persons who have given their lives for Japan in war since 1853. The shrine was founded in 1869 and represents a potent symbol for nationalism. Among those commemorated in the shrine are General Hideki Tojo and the six other executed Class A war criminals of World War II. Official visits to the shrine by Japanese prime ministers have raised controversy in China and Korea. Photo by P.P. Karan.

als are prominent at shrines as a form of communication between gods and humans. Shinto gives the ritual servant role to females. Girls and young women are seen as pure; older women are often considered dirty and thus barred from sacred spaces. Like the contrasting Shinto colors of red and white—life and death—that they wear, miko serve a dual role of sanctity and practicality.

There are female Shinto priests, but they are much less common than female miko. There are no figures to show how many miko work at Japan's eighty thousand shrines. Although about twenty women graduate from Kokugakuin University as priestesses every year, only one or two actually get jobs, mainly because of the perception that men are more suited to the position. Some miko are high school girls serving part-time when things get busy at the shrines. Others work as miko as a profession for a longer time, but usually not for a whole lifetime. At one of the most important shrines in Ise, Mie Prefecture, miko are called *maijo*, or dancing girls, and their main job is to dance and offer prayers and offerings. Part of the appeal for the job seems to be the chance to experience traditional Japanese culture, including dance, tea ceremony, and flower arranging. At Yushima Shrine in Tokyo's Bunkyo-ku, miko dance at weddings and ceremonies and sell amulets, including a matched set of a headband, a charm, and pencils, to eager students. There is an inner sanctum that is off limits to women, but the miko clean all the rest of the shrine and the offices as well.

According to the Association of Shinto Shrines, there were 25 women among the 404 head priests in Tokyo in 2001. Before World War II, it was virtually unheard of for a Shinto priest to be a woman; the priesthood was usually passed from father to son. But with the lack of interest in religion, and with families growing smaller, shrine priesthoods have had to open up to daughters, to keep the priesthood in the family.

The compound of Yushima Shrine is peaceful, a tiny haven at the top of a hill with huge ginkgoes shading the paths and a little garden of plum trees. An arc of a bridge links the shrine with the offices. Paper lanterns swing in the breeze along with wands of artificial wisteria. Tea and coffee vending machines crowd the cistern where visitors wash their hands and mouth before going farther into the sacred space. The priests and the miko pray for the purification of the world at 9:00 a.m. every day, and the miko make offerings of water, washed rice, salt, and rice wine. On certain days they also offer seasonal fruits and vegetables in the dimness under a heavily carved roof, where guardian beasts freshly painted in blue, gold, or red with glaring golden eyes perch atop pillars, showing dainty pink footpads to worshippers below.

In an increasingly secular Japan, Shinto shrines in large cities are facing difficulty and losing support. Many urban shrines are finding that renting out their land, always a premium in Japan's cities, is the best way to survive. The problem today is the low level of interest in religion. A commonly cited indicator is wedding practices. A generation ago, 70 percent or more Japanese were married with Shinto rites. Today, Christian-style weddings are in fashion, even though few Japanese identify themselves as Christians, and Shinto marriages constitute fewer than 20 percent of the total.

It should be pointed out that a wedding is a fashion celebration in Japan and not a religious ceremony. A ceremony is not even necessary to become married in Japan. The first Shinto wedding in Japan was that of Emperor Taisho. After that it became popular to have a wedding ceremony. Now, young Japanese women like the "look" of a Christian wedding; they like to dress up in that manner as part of their ceremony. It is not really a Christian wedding—it is just a fashion show. Good money is to be made these days by foreign men who look Western: all they have to do is to put on a priest's costume and be ready to read the vows.

There are other indicators of Shinto's decline, from statistics showing fewer shrine visits nationally to a decline in observance of the so-called 7-5-3 rites of passage for children on those birthdays, when the child's family goes to a shrine for prayers. Now shrines are pushing the business angle. Priests in central Tokyo spend days performing purification ceremonies for television studios that hope for success with new plays or sitcoms, or blessing new construction sites to ward off accidents or earthquake damage.

Buddhism

Buddhism was introduced into Japan in 552, according to Japan's earliest chronicles, the *Nihon Shoki*. In the Nara period (710–94) Buddhism was promoted as a state religion. More than 85 percent of the population professes the Buddhist faith. There are more than 75,000 Buddhist temples and nearly 200,000 priests and a rich tradition of Buddhist religious art forms (paintings, sculpture, mandala) in Japan. In the thirteenth century the Zen sect took hold among the ruling military elites and introduced new currents in art. Zen monasteries emerged as both seats of religious discourse and centers for the secular cultural activities for which the Zen monks became increasingly famous: literary studies, poetry, painting, and calligraphy.

A unique feature of Japanese Buddhism is a 750-mile-long pilgrimage to eighty-eight temples in Shikoku (Shimazaki 1977, 1997). Wearing white pants and jacket and a straw hat, and carrying a walking stick with a bell attached, Japanese make pilgrimages to the eighty-eight temples to pray for the souls of dead family members or for cures for their own illnesses, to atone for sins, or to reflect on their past and prepare for an uncertain future in the midst of the solitude that walking alone day after day can provide. Nowadays, the pilgrimage has become more touristy than religious. Only about 1,000 of the 100,000 people who make the trip each year go on foot; the rest travel by car, bus, train, and taxi. Package bus tours do the circuit in less than two weeks, compared with the fifty days on average it takes to walk. Many people visit the temples intermittently, on weekends or holidays, taking a year or more to cover all of them.

The pilgrimage, known in Japanese as *henro,* was started by the priest Kukai, usually known as Kobo Daishi, who was born in Shikoku in 774 and founded the Shingon sect of Buddhism. The walking stick carried by the pilgrims represents Kobo Daishi, so that a pilgrim is said to be never really walking alone. As for the white outfit, in Japanese Buddhism white is the color worn by the dead on their way to paradise. Until sixty years ago, many people did die along the arduous path.

The pilgrimage starts from Naruto in northeast Shikoku and proceeds clockwise (see fig. 3.10). Priests and some other people walk in the reverse direction, from the eighty-eighth temple to the first one, in symbolic hope of meeting Kobo Daishi coming the other way. Most of the temples are along the coast, but some are in the mountains; and the pilgrimage route, marked by signs, is partly paved road and partly steep mountain path (Mori 2001). People living in Shikoku offer the pilgrims fruit, money, and sometimes free meals and lodging as their way of taking part in the religious experience without actually traveling to the temples.

At each temple, pilgrims recite a special sutra and deposit in a box a slip of paper containing their name and address. They also get the name of the temple stamped and written in Japanese calligraphy on a scroll or in a book or both. Those who complete the circuit often come back to temple one to offer thanks and receive a special inscription in their book: "Your wish has been fully accomplished."

One of the major manifestations of Buddhism in the Japanese landscape is the statues of Buddha that dot the country. Since Buddhism's arrival in the sixth century, innumerable statues of Buddha's image have been erected, from the minuscule to the monstrous, and from the secular to the cosmic; they are found from Hokkaido to Okinawa and everywhere in between. One of the latest and most memorable additions to this pantheon of Japanese Buddhist art, completed in 1993, is located in the city of

Visitors at the Sensoji Buddhist temple in the Asakusa district of Tokyo. According to tradition, the statue of Buddha enshrined at Sensoji was found in the nearby Sumida River by two fishermen. Photo by P.P. Karan.

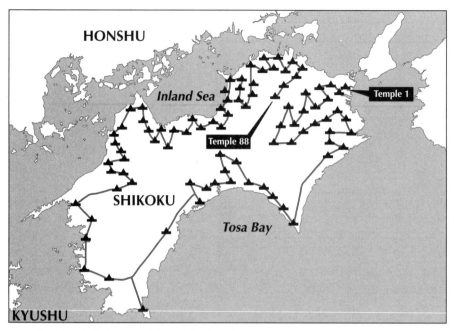

Fig. 3.10. Buddhist pilgrimage route in Shikoku. Based on Shimazaki 1997.

Ushiku, Ibaraki Prefecture. The mammoth Buddha was put together using steel girders overlaid with more than six thousand plates of bronze to give the shell its human form. Three times taller and thirty times larger in volume than the Statue of Liberty, the Ushiku Daibatsu is indeed a colossus of unparalleled proportions.

Christianity

Christianity was first introduced into Japan in the middle of the sixteenth century. The religion was tolerated until the beginning of the seventeenth century, when the Tokugawa shogunate (1600–1868) eventually proscribed it and persecuted its adherents. The Christian community is concentrated in Kyushu, although small Christian groups are also found in other parts of Japan (Oda 1999). Apart from the Nagasaki region, Christianity has yet to make any appreciable impact on rural communities; it draws its strength from urban, professional classes. In 1990 Christians numbered some 1.07 million, or less than 1 percent of the population. There were 436,000 Catholics, with some 800 parishes in 16 dioceses, while Protestants numbered 639,000, with nearly 7,000 churches. The Mormon church is active in Japan, and its members use English conversation lessons and church events as methods for proselytizing

the Japanese (Takemura 2000; Numano 1996). Conversion has been relatively easier in areas where Soto and other sects are dominant; but in areas where the Jodo sect is strong, such as Yamagata and Toyama Prefectures, conversion has been difficult.

Various aspects of traditional Japanese thought and outlook, including polytheism, belief in immanent deities, and the group-oriented ethic differ fundamentally from Christian teaching with its monotheism, its concept of a transcendent God, and its individual ethic. Organized Christianity cannot accommodate itself to traditional thought in Japan as much as Buddhism (also an "imported" religion) has done.

Back in the 1500s Christianity spread rapidly, until a fierce repression began four hundred years ago that sent believers into hiding. As a group, the Hidden Christians, as they were called in Kyushu, survived hundreds of years of torture and executions with their faith intact. The faith that endured centuries of unfathomable repression is now shrinking under more insidious pressures: old age, television, cars, and video games. The extent of the survival crisis facing groups of *kakure kirishitan* or "hiding Christians" is real. Only four hundred families, composed of two thousand individuals, are believed to still practice the old religion in four districts on

Amakusa, in the southern Kyushu part of Kumamoto Prefecture, contains relics of early Christians who lived here. During the seventeenth century many Japanese Christians hid in the area to avoid persecution. Missionaries had their greatest success in this region, and many peasants living in the area were Christians. Photo by P.P. Karan.

Ikitsuki Island in the western corner of the main island of Kyushu, three in the Goto Islands, and two in Sotome. Congregations in the Goto Islands and Sotome are at high risk of extinction due to the old age of their leaders. In Ikitsuki, as elsewhere, surviving believers call themselves "old Christians" to distinguish themselves from other Christians elsewhere in Japan.

REFERENCES

Barnes, G. 1988. *Protohistoric Yamato: Archaeology of the First Japanese State.* Ann Arbor: Univ. of Michigan Press.

Batten, Bruce. 1999. Frontiers and boundaries of pre-modern Japan. *Journal of Historical Geography* 25:166–182.

Bix, Herbert P. 2000. *Hirohito and the Making of Modern Japan.* New York: HarperCollins.

Chang, Iris. 1997. *The Rape of Nanking.* New York: Basic Books.

Friday, K. 1997. Pushing beyond the pale: The Yamato conquest of the Emishi and northern Japan. *Journal of Japanese Studies* 23:1–24.

Inagaki, Tatsushi. 2001. Transformation of vegetable market channels in the Tokugawa period with special reference to Temma Vegetable Market in Osaka. Paper presented at the 11th International Conference of Historical Geographers, Université Laval, Quebec City, Aug. 18.

Kaneko, N. 1995. A review of studies on the spatial structure of mountain religions in Japan. *Humanities Review* 45 (3): 107–117.

———. 1997. The spatial structure of mountain religion: The case of Mt. Iwaki. *Human Geography* 49:311–330.

Littleton, C. Scott. 2002. *Shinto: Origins, Rituals, Festivals, Spirits, Sacred Places.* New York: Oxford Univ. Press.

Matsui, K. 1998. Reexamination of recent studies on the geography of religion in Japan. *Annual Report,* Institute of Geosciences, Univ. of Tsukuba, 24:7–12.

———. 1999. Regional characteristics of Kanamura Betsurai shrine faith. *Tsukuba Studies in Human Geography* 23:39–58.

McClain, James L. 2002. *Japan: A Modern History.* New York: Norton.

Mizoguchi, Tsunetoshi. 1996. Studies in the historical geography of Japan, 1988–1995. *Geographical Review of Japan* B 69:21–41.

———. 2001. Spatial differentiation in the Nobi Core: Villages and towns in Owari Region, 1672–1822. Paper presented at the 11th International Conference of Historical Geographers, Université Laval, Quebec City, Aug. 18.

Mizuuchi, Toshio. 1999. Development policies and spatial integration of Japan from 1868 to 1941. In *Nation, Region, and* the Politics of Geography in East Asia, ed. Toshio Mizuuchi, 30–42. Osaka: Osaka City Univ., Department of Geography.

Mori, Masato. 2001. Contemporary religious meaning of the pilgrimage route. *Human Geography* 53 (2): 75–91.

Morikawa, Hidemasa. 1992. *Zaibatsu: The Rise and Fall of Family Enterprise Groups in Japan.* Tokyo: Univ. of Tokyo Press.

Nakane, Chie, and Shinzaburo Oishi. 1990. *Tokugawa Japan: The Social and Economic Antecedents of Modern Japan.* Trans. Conrad Totman. Tokyo: Univ. of Tokyo Press.

Norman, E. Herbert. 2000. *Japan's Emergence as a Modern State: Political and Economic Problems of the Meiji Period.* Ed. Lawrence T. Woods. Vancouver: Univ. of British Columbia Press.

Numano, J. 1996. Mormonism in modern Japan. *Journal of Mormon Thought* 29:223–235.

Oda, M. 1999. Distribution of Christianity in Japan. *Pennsylvania Geographer* 37 (1): 17–32.

Richards, John F. 2003. Ecological strategies in Tokugawa Japan. In *The Unending Frontier: An Environmental History of the Early Modern World,* 148–192. Berkeley: Univ. of California Press.

Shimazaki, H. 1977. Geographic expression of Buddhist pilgrim places on Shikoku Island, Japan. *Canadian Geographer* 21:116–124.

———. 1997. The Shikoku Pilgrimage: Essential characteristics of a Japanese Buddhist pilgrimage complex. In *Sacred Places, Sacred Spaces: The Geography of Pilgrimages,* ed. Robert H. Stoddard and Alan Morinis, 269–297. Baton Rouge: Department of Geography and Anthropology, Louisiana State Univ.

Shimizu, Yosiaki, ed. 1988. *Japan: The Shaping of Daimyo Culture, 1185–1868.* Washington, DC: National Gallery of Art.

Showa: The Japan of Hirohito. 1990. *Daedalus* 119 (Summer): 1–298.

Sinclaire, Clive. 2001. *Samurai: The Weapons and Spirit of the Japanese Warrior.* Guilford, CT: Lyons Press.

Takemura, Kazuo. 2000. A geographic study on the acceptance of mission of the Church of Jesus Christ of Latter-Day Saints in the provincial cities of Japan. *Geographical Review of Japan* A 73:182–198.

Tsude, H. 1992. The Kofun period and state formation. *Acta Asiatica* 63:64–86.

Williams, Peter, and David Wallace. 1989. *Unit 731: Japan's Secret Biological Warfare in World War II.* New York: Free Press.

Yasuda, Yoshinori. 1978. Prehistoric environment in Japan: A polynological approach. *Science Reports of Tohoku University,* ser. 7 (Geography) 28 (2): 117–281.

Chapter 4

第 四 章

JAPANESE LANDSCAPES

The landscape of Japan is extremely complex and intricately organized. It records the occupancy by a culturally distinct and dynamic society of an archipelago bordering the earth's largest continent and on the brink of an ocean trench 35,000 feet (10,668 m) deep! Great tectonic plates collide in this zone, resulting in earthquakes, tsunamis, volcanoes, and hot springs. The land is indeed alive, and so is the distinctive culture of the people.

Geography spared Japan the tramp of invading armies and the confusion of many intruding aliens with strange cultures and ways. The Korea Strait, which separates the westernmost island, Kyushu, from the nearest part of the Asian mainland, is 100 miles (161 km) wide, and although there are sizable stepping-stone islands within it, it was difficult and dangerous to cross in early times. The barrier strait gave Japan a semi-isolation, placing it within the Chinese culture area and at the same time setting it apart. During certain periods a broad stream of ideas, literature, art, and religion flowed from China to Japan. At other times the flow was shut off from one side or the other, and Japan developed on its own. But whether in isolation or not, Japan was always itself. Thus, the Japanese had more opportunity than most peoples to develop to the fullest their distinctive culture. Everything that came from outside was reshaped to suit Japanese tastes and needs. The mixture of subtlety and sophistication, as well as the delicacy and complexity in this culture, bear testimony in the landscape. The balance between driving ambition and aesthetic sensitivity is clearly evident.

Japan has been inhabited for thousands of years. Northern Kyushu, because of its proximity to the Asian continent, became the site of Japan's first political center. By the fourth century a sovereign court had emerged, which by conquest and alliance even-

tually unified the country as a nation-state. In the seventh century a unified Japan, consisting of Kyushu, Shikoku, and Honshu, was established. Hokkaido was settled by the Japanese between 1600 and 1868 (Kodansha International 1995).

Until the mid-nineteenth century Japan was divided administratively into vernacular regions ruled by daimyo or feudal lords. After the Meiji Restoration (1868) the country was reorganized into prefectures. At present it is divided into forty-seven prefectures (Foreign Press Center 1997). But the Japanese in ordinary conversation often speak of historic regions, corresponding in America, perhaps, to New England or the South. These traditional provinces and circuits, such as Hokuriku, Tosa (Kochi), and Owari and Mikawa (Aichi), still exist among the Japanese (see fig. 4.1).

For nearly two thousand years, an emperor or an empress belonging to the same family as Akihito, the present emperor, has ruled or reigned over Japan. Beginning in the twelfth century, a series of military shoguns seized and exercised real power in the name of the emperor. The shogunate of the Tokugawa family, who governed from 1600 to 1868, sealed Japan off from the rest of the world and left the most definitive imprint on the country.

The ancient landmarks of Japan include old roads, old temples, and old castles. Historic roads such as the Tokaido and the Nakasendo connected Kyoto with Edo (Tokyo), and the Hokurikudo joined Kyoto with Tohoku via the coast of the Sea of Japan side of Japan (formally called Ura Nihon, backside of Japan). Many old stage towns (*shukuba-machi*) developed along these roads. In 1987 there were more than 81,350 Shinto shrines and 77,000 Buddhist temples. Old castles were originally military fortifications designed to provide protection against en-

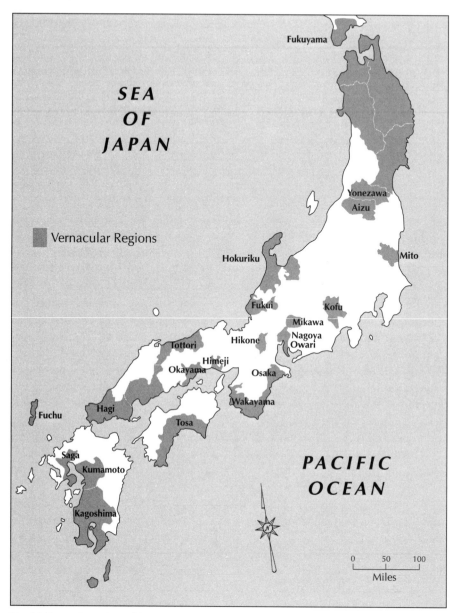

Fig. 4.1. Vernacular regions of Japan.

emy attack. With the rise of feudalism, they became a distinctive architectural form serving as both a palatial residence and a seat of military and political power. The daimyo built castles in the center of their domains. Each castle included residences of the castle lord and his chief retainers. Fortifications such as stone walls were built and moats were dug. Around these castles developed castle towns (*joka machi*), the characteristic form of a Japanese city until the Meiji Restoration of 1868.

Today, however, Japan bears the overwhelming imprint of a bustling, populous, modern society that is finely attuned to severely limited areas of favorable terrain. The legendary Tokaido corridor, which runs from Kyoto to Edo (Tokyo) along the underbelly of Honshu, once a romantic route, is now a megalopolis extending to Osaka and Kobe, similar to the Boston–New York City–Philadelphia–Washington urban belt. Here the landscape is dominated by hillsides with highway cuts, television antennas like a sky full of spiders, factories, tall smokestacks, wide-flung railroad yards, and electric power lines that march across the countryside every which way, with poles and towers carrying as many as twenty cables each. It is a landscape festooned with wire and concrete. On the tops of factories—many of them bright, clean, and modern—signs such as Sony Hi-Fi, Meiji Chocolate, and Kirin Beer shout the temptations that have replaced the complaisant maids of the old inns in stage towns.

Without doubt the Tokaido is one of the world's busiest traffic corridors, for through it run the old road, unrecognizably rerouted and remodeled for car traffic, a new expressway, the Japan Railways' original Tokaido Line, and the bullet-train route. Both rail routes go through the mountains at Hakone in separate four-mile tunnels. The corridor forms one huge, stretched-out city, with little open countryside anywhere along the route.

Although the land of Japan has traditionally been densely settled, and its natural beauty has been overrun in many places, Japan has tried to preserve the natural landscape. Every available plot of ground has been cherished. Forests have been cultivated as carefully as rice fields, and each tree grows in its place because someone intended for it to be there. The people revere the land and protect it. Some spots are famous for their view of a moonrise, others for the turbulence of surf churning around rocky islets. Even Japan's violent aspects—its storm-beaten coasts and fiery volcanoes—are the object of pilgrimages. Honor for nature is so ingrained in the Japanese that they would not fail to pause and contemplate the colors of leaves and blossoms.

Four islands—Kyushu, Shikoku, Honshu, and Hokkaido—constitute 95 percent of Japan's area. Kyushu is separated from Honshu's western headlands by a strait no wider than 0.4 mile (0.6 km). In similar propinquity, the island of Hokkaido nearly touches the northern cape of Honshu. Little Shikoku nestles under western Honshu and thus serves to enclose the scenic and tranquil waters known as the Inland Sea. The nation's total area of 145,825 square miles (377,688 sq km) is just one-twenty-fifth the size of the United States, yet Japan's population, 127 million, is approximately one-half that of the United States! But the Japanese problem of living space is far more constraining than even these figures suggest. Nearly 73 percent of the land is mountainous,

and only about 14 percent is arable. Moreover, because of patchy distribution, the plots of arable land are difficult to connect. Yet on this small lowland total rests most of Japan's population, industry, and agriculture. In 1990 the density per square mile was 128 persons. Comparable figures are 139 in the Netherlands and 125 in Belgium, both flat countries unlike Japan. The density of the Japanese population per unit of area under cultivation is the highest in the world. Since 1950 there has been a strong tendency toward regional concentration. As a result, more than 50 percent of the Japanese live in the densely populated areas surrounding the three major urban centers of Tokyo (the Kanto Plain), Osaka (the Kinki Plain), and Nagoya (the Nobi Plain). The Tokyo Metropolitan Area, in particular, though less than 2 percent in terms of area, has a concentration of nearly 24 percent of the national population. Nationally, about 60 percent of the total population resides in 3 percent of the total land area of the country.

Japan's challenge is basically to organize itself compactly, three-dimensionally, efficiently, and connectedly and to provide a high economic return, a high standard of living, and a long life expectancy. This Japan has done. It now has the highest average life expectancy in the world, the world's largest source of investment capital, and the highest per capita income in Asia. Furthermore, despite its limited land, Japan is the second-largest economic power on the planet!

The Japanese landscape manifests the nature of this accomplishment in the *contrast between old and new landscapes.* Although Japan has a very limited area, the four major islands represent a huge latitudinal stretch: the distance from Kyushu to Hokkaido is comparable in latitudinal extent with that from Florida to Quebec. If the Japanese islands were laid on the Atlantic coast of North America, they would extend from Tallahassee to Montreal.

Visitors often give quite diverse reports on Japan's climate. This is not surprising, in view of the great latitudinal range of the country, as well as its varied terrain and its complexity in terms of elevation. In addition, there are the remarkably sheltered borderlands of the Inland Sea that are so noted for sunny weather and the lowest relative humidity in the nation. At Okayama, for example, more than half of the days in every month are without precipitation. Okayama, about one hundred miles west of Osaka, has 129 days per year with some precipitation, compared with 227 on the Sea of Japan side of Honshu at Niigata.

The thermal range that one might anticipate from the great latitudinal stretch is accentuated by the marked monsoonal factor. Prevailing northwesterly winds spiral outward from continental Asia in winter, and in summer subtropical air masses emanate from warmer latitudes over the Pacific Ocean. So the winters are somewhat colder and the summers are hotter than what is typical for such latitudes. For example, the average January temperatures vary from about 10 degrees Fahrenheit in northern Hokkaido to 45 degrees in southernmost Kyushu. In summer, high temperatures and high humidity make much of Japan sultry, and many people seek respite in the mountains or at the seaside resorts. Most Japanese and their visitors prefer spring and autumn. Flowering plants in profusion adorn the springtime landscapes throughout Japan, and the autumn leaves gloriously color the deciduous trees of northern Honshu and Hokkaido.

Snow falls on Japan from Kyushu to Hokkaido. In Hokkaido, the landscape is snow-covered all winter. Snow cover prevails on the Pacific side of Honshu southward to about 37 degrees latitude and on the Sea of Japan side nearly to Kyushu. In the mountainous western sectors of northern Honshu and Hokkaido, snow may accumulate to a depth of 6 feet (1.8 m) and may persist for more than one hundred days. In addition to the mystical appeal of snow-capped Mount Fuji, the Japanese revel in their seasonal regimes, and winter sports such as skiing and ice skating enjoy great popularity.

Hokkaido represents a newer landscape in human terms; almost all of agricultural Hokkaido was colonized after 1868. The Meiji government placed great emphasis on Hokkaido's development and set up a colonization commission to encourage settlers from other parts of Japan. To advise the colonization commission, the government imported seventy-six foreigners, more than half of whom were Americans. Most influential were Horace Capron, a former U.S. commissioner of agriculture, and William Smith Clark, president of the Massachusetts Agricultural College, who founded what became the University of Hokkaido. Hokkaido today has structures reminiscent of Iowa-style silos and Pennsylvania German barns. Capron helped found Sapporo

and gave it the rigid grid of streets at right angles to one another that is characteristic of midwestern U.S. towns. Of real castles and temples, Hokkaido has only one of the former and few of the latter. Religion lays a light hand on this island, and people prefer to visit the many bright-colored restaurants set out spaciously along the smooth new highways. Hokkaido is noted for its dramatic and unspoiled scenery, which includes active volcanoes, large lakes, and virgin forests. National parks cover four large swatches of the island, preserving lakes (no outboard motors allowed), volcanic areas (vendors are forbidden to boil eggs in the bubbling water), and primeval spruce and fir similar to those in British Columbia. The Hokkaido Development Agency, established in 1950 in the prime minister's office, is charged with formulating and implementing the central government's plan for Hokkaido's development. The rapid pace of development in Hokkaido has sharpened conflict between advocates of environmental preservation and those of development.

So there is this regional contrast between Hokkaido and the rest of Japan, but between the time of Hokkaido's colonization and 2001, Japan's population more than trebled. In 1872 the average population density was 35 persons per square mile. Now it is near 128. In 1868 Hokkaido had only about 160,000 inhabitants. Now there are approximately 5.7 million, but that gives Hokkaido only one-fifth the density of the national average.

Space is one of Hokkaido's major assets, and agriculture is the economic mainstay. Farming in old Japan (from Kyushu to central Japan on Honshu) places a heavy emphasis on rice, and the farmstead there is dominated by the farmhouse. The other farm buildings are really sheds. From an airplane, the farm areas of old Japan are an infinity of small, inundated rice fields resembling verdant mirrors, flashing the sun back to the viewer. Terraced up from the coast, the paddies make a geometry of different hues of green, set against the blue-green of the mountains in the background or, if one looks down from the hillside, against the white-capped aquamarine of the sea. Seen from on high, the paddies form patterns of green that vary according to contour and to whether they are set arbitrarily or as parallelograms. Near villages the paddies, bordered by banks and ditches, make green squares of a checkerboard, alternating with the iron gray roof tiles of the inter-

A dairy farm in Hokkaido. Contrasting with the crowded islands of the rest of Japan, the landscape of Hokkaido is characterized by wide-open spaces. Photo by P.P. Karan.

mixed housing lots. In urban-industrial areas, patches of green rice relieve the eye and give the Japanese landscape its special interdigitated character. Seen from eye level on the ground, the green stems of rice harmonize with the azure of the sky reflected in paddy water.

Hokkaido's farming, in contrast, is relatively extensive (Berque 1977). Despite the high latitude, Hokkaido's main crop is rice; fodder crops for livestock are also raised, as are potatoes, sugar beets, soybeans, and red beans. The fields in Hokkaido are larger and the machinery is bigger than in farms to the south. An individual dairy farm may encompass 75 to 100 acres (30–40 ha), with barns dominating the farmstead. Television commercials in Japan show Marlboro-Country Japanese cowboys pounding leather in Hokkaido; yet most of the cattle are not beef steers but dairy cattle, yielding one-fifth of Japan's milk supply. Dairying makes a good profit, and the government encourages farmers to shift from rice to cows. These illustrations represent the major *contrasts between the old and the new.*

Contrasts in scale are the rule on the Japanese landscape. The areas of low topographic relief are very small in size and are separated by large areas of rough relief. Forests cover about 68 percent of Japan, and their distribution is closely correlated with the mountainous topography. Mountains dominate the terrain of all the main islands: Kyushu, Shikoku, Honshu, and Hokkaido. Indeed, Japan is mostly mountainous and forested, and mostly very sparsely inhabited! This is a stunning aspect of Japan—so populous a nation of such small area, yet with much

of the land nearly devoid of population. The forests, however, are a vital environmental component as regulators of precipitation runoff, as havens for recreation, and as sources of lumber and pulp.

The green of the forests that cover Japan is a green of varying textures. Along the east coast of verdant Kyushu, the forests are all bottle-green conifers, dense enough to make one think that no humans have ever set foot there—until one notices that the trees are in perfectly straight rows. The green of Japan's mountains is mostly the green of tree farms rather than the green of wilderness; the Japanese love of the feel and look of wood in houses has long ago cost the country most of its natural forest. On hillside plantations, the black-green crowns of the mature cypresses make a pattern like the warp and woof of a nubby fabric. Ruler-straight borders separate these trees, ready for harvest, from logged-off patches of mottled-green seedlings and underbrush and the shiny green patches of well-pruned, half-grown trees poking upward like rows of daggers.

The most common Japanese tree is the cedar, generally de-branched in the lower trunk to make it grow straight and knot-free, and rising to a tuft that makes rounded hills look as though they were clothed in green fur. It is the flat green of cedar leaves that colors the mountains north of Kyoto. At mills and sheds in the harmonious little towns of the twisting valleys, men and women scrape the red cortex from the slender young trunks to make naturally fluted columns for the alcoves of *sukiya*-style houses. These houses are simple, austere, and small. During the Edo period (1603–1868) the sukiya style of residential architecture became popular among townspeople. The beauty of sukiya comes from its delicate sensibility, its slender wood elements, the use of natural materials, and the lack of ornaments.

In the lofty, green-canopied cedar forest in the Kii Peninsula, south of Osaka, men climb huge cedars three hundred years old to get seeds. From the seeds will grow more of the big trees, which will be needed two or three centuries hence for pillars in the rebuilding of temples and shrines. Similar cedars that survived recent volcanic eruptions have only small crowns of foliage at their uppermost limbs; they stand like ghosts among the peaks of Unzen National Park, east of Nagasaki. Japan's other evergreens are silver fir, white fir, hemlock, spruce, and several kinds of pine. Patient gardeners dote on pine, plucking some needles before they can grow into branches, leaving others to form green branch-tip clusters. Trunks and boughs are trained into grotesque twists and loops; they can make the pine into a living sculpture. There are even more greens in the landscape: the green of the bamboo's feathers, the dull green oval leaves of the persimmon, the green of palms and weeping willows, the green of tea shrubs shaped like shaggy boulders, and, above the tea, the glossy green leaves of tangerine trees.

Decades ago, all lumbering operations were small, but today's operations include huge ones that are among the world's most modern. The annual timber production in 1999 was approximately 595 million cubic feet (17 million cu m), but this represents only 19 percent of Japan's voracious demand for wood pulp and building construction materials. The importation of wood is critical; most of it is brought from Alaska, British Columbia, Washington, Oregon, the Philippine Islands, and Indonesia. Domestic production has been stagnant because of the steep mountain slopes, depopulation in mountain areas, and the aging of forestry workers. About 80 percent of the lumber is imported even though forest occupies the greater part of the land.

The natural forests of Japan were mainly broad-leaved deciduous hardwoods in the southwest and coniferous trees in the northeast. Reforestation, or new forests, now represents about 40 percent of the total forest area. These replantings are coniferous softwoods, readily observable as great dark green swatches of scientifically managed woodlands. Slightly more than half of Japan's forestland is privately owned; the remainder is under national or municipal ownership. Although the forests of Japan are extensive and productive, less than 1 percent of the nation's labor force is engaged in forestry.

Japan's *coastal component* is an important aspect of its landscape. The length of Japan's coastline is about 21,000 miles (33,796 km). Most of the population is coastal oriented, and the nation's economy depends heavily on importing raw materials and exporting manufactured goods. Japan ranks third in the world in both imports and exports, exceeded only by the United States and Germany. Leading imports include petroleum, foodstuffs, logs and lumber, iron ore, and chemicals.

The shipping of resources and products from one

Lumber coming from overseas is unloaded at the port of Yatsushiro, Kyushu. Nearly two-thirds of Japan's total land area is covered by forests, but the demand for lumber products is so great that Japan must import most of its annual needs. There are a number of factors that limit lumber production. A significant portion of the forest area is on steep slopes, forest roads are undeveloped, the majority of the trees are young, and many forests are in national park areas where lumbering is not permitted. Photo by P.P. Karan.

Japanese port to another is also important. Domestic shipping carries petroleum products, lime, cement, and iron and steel. Once coal was one of the most important items of domestic freight. Coal was carried from the main coal-mining areas in northern Kyushu and Hokkaido to all the industrial areas of Japan. A major heavy industrial area developed near the coalfields of northern Kyushu. Coal reserves are now depleted, and the last coal mine closed in 2002. High-grade coal is now imported. Much oil is imported to meet national energy needs. Now, much of the energy importation is to ports near the industrial centers along the Pacific Ocean. Almost all of Japan's iron ore is obtained from Australia, India, and Brazil.

The importance of raw materials produces ancillary aspects of the landscape. For example, not only is wood imported from British Columbia, but also Canadian log buildings are being franchised now by the Yamaken Company Ltd. in Honshu.

Another important matter that affects the landscape is the *accessibility factor*. This is illustrated vividly by two inlets in Shimane Prefecture, along the Sea of Japan in southwestern Honshu. One inlet is at the port of Hamada, which is absolutely abuzz with marine enterprise. The other inlet, off the beaten path and not easy to get to, is a quiet, secluded, forest-fringed embayment with only a smattering of relict vessels. Hamada (population 49,135) developed during the Edo period (1603–1868) as a port and castle town. Today it is the administrative, commercial, and industrial center of the Iwami region of Shimane. An important fishing port, it has a thriving marine-products processing industry as well as a growing woodworking industry.

The rural *workaday and recreational landscapes* have strong cultural undertones. In 1950 two-thirds of Japan's population was rural and one-third was urban. Today, the rural population is less than 20 percent of the total. This change in five decades has been accomplished by migration from rural to urban areas and by a marked increase in off-farm employment for members of the farm households. The movement from rural to urban areas has involved mainly younger workers, as has off-farm employment. As a result, an aging population has been left to work on the farms. Forty-two percent of the farming population was above the age of sixty-five in 1995. The dwindling farm population (279,000 in 2001)

has led to serious and chronic labor shortages in the agricultural sector. Part-time farmers are numerous, and well over half the labor force is female. The government has aided farmers by establishing price-support programs, especially for rice. Japanese use the term *san chan* (three-person) *agriculture* to refer to their farming system. The three chans are *Oji chan* (grandfather), *Obaa chan* (grandmother), and *Okaa chan* (mother); these are the family members who do most of the work on the farm; the father is employed in a factory or an office in the local area, and he helps these chans on weekends. In the regions with few employment opportunities, such as northern Honshu, the fathers work in metropolitan areas during the agricultural off-season. Some fathers work away for almost a whole year and return home for the New Year holidays (Koganezawa 1987).

Japan's traditional labor-intensive agriculture has been transformed into a highly mechanized and capital-intensive system in less than a generation. Japanese farms are tiny by American standards; the average area of cultivated land per Japanese farm is only 3.5 acres (1.4 ha), and the major crop is rice. Because Japan has an increasingly aging population on the farms, and because the farms are the emotional homes for many persons in need of social security income, supporting the price of rice is in effect a social security payment: it enables these elderly people to remain where they have lifelong social and communal ties. The support for the rice price is thus a far more socially sensitive system than the American practice of moving old folks into nursing-home concentrations, away from their lifelong homes and outside the context of the family. So comparing the price of American-grown rice in the Yazoo Delta of Mississippi or in California's Sacramento Valley with price-supported rice in Japan completely misses the social raison d'être of the price support. It also supports the population in mountain areas where there are no alternatives for employment and helps maintain "food security."

The Japanese recreational landscape, such as *pachinko* parlors, is usually an element of multiple land use. The pachinko parlor is a common feature in most cities and small towns. Pachinko is a kind of pinball game, in which the object is to drop small steel balls into a hole on a vertical board through a maze of nail pegs. The timing of achieving a winning slot has different values and multiplies the num-

Pachinko parlors such as this one in Kumamoto are a common element of the Japanese landscape. Pachinko, a sort of vertical pinball game, is a big business in Japan, with total revenues of about 28 trillion yen ($233 billion) a year, as much as is taken in by Japan's five largest automakers combined. The sour economy, falling land values, and the growing risk aversion of the nation's struggling banks have combined to drive large numbers of mom-and-pop operations out of business, not just in pachinko, but also in the similarly structured tavern and karaoke-bar industries. But for Maruhan Corporation, owner of 121 pachinko parlors from Hokkaido to Kyushu, business is growing by leaps and bounds. As the bubble economy collapsed, Maruhan saw the potential for larger parlors and lined up financing to grab store space in busy central locations as it became available. Maruhan has lured customers with no-smoking sections, free parking, and improved odds of winning cash. Some 70 percent of pachinko parlor owners are of Korean ancestry. Photo by P.P. Karan.

ber of balls that accumulate in trays at the bottom of the machine. Balls can be exchanged for prizes, and each major game center has a wide selection of items. There are ways to exchange prizes for cash. Japan's pachinko industry in 1999 was worth 28 trillion yen, according to figures supplied by Tokyo Plaza Company. Some 18 million Japanese play regularly, representing about one person in eight. Pachinko's color, noise, and speed combine to make it very attractive to the player. The pachinko parlor undergirds the sense of community that is so strong in Japanese life. Thus, the Japanese scene is a strongly social landscape, in contrast to the American scene, which is so markedly economic.

The *travel scene* is very much alive in Japan. The Japanese have loved their land throughout the ages and throughout the realm. The traveler, foreign or domestic, has a magnificent array of attractions. They range from the coral reefs of the Nansei Islands and the live volcano of Sakurajima in far southern Kyushu to Lake Akan and the Ainu land in northeastern Hokkaido. In between are the rugged *ria* coasts of Kyushu; the spectacular karst country (limestone solution topography); the warm resorts in southern Shikoku; many hot springs, spas, and ski slopes; the massive Japan Alps; the ancient capital Nara (before AD 794); the capital Kyoto (794–1868); and the many points of interest in Tokyo. And never neglected is the countryside at cherry blossom time! Japan also abounds with peach, plum, and apple trees. The nation has a love affair with fruit trees at blossom time—and rightly so! A recent survey indicates that approximately 84 percent of Japanese over fourteen years of age enjoy at least one trip a year. The nation has an elaborate transportation system to facilitate travel, and the people do appreciate these many and diverse attractions.

PRIMARY CHARACTERISTICS OF THE JAPANESE LANDSCAPE

Thousands of individual scenes in Japan meet the eye of the observer, but there are recurrent characteristics that represent the distinctive cultural imprint of the Japanese people on their land. The landscape is a vivid portrayal of Japanese ideas and the Japanese value system relating to the organization of space. Identification and comprehension of the characteristics of the Japanese landscape lends understanding of the occupancy patterns and appreciation of the cultural refinements that have evolved on the physical base.

Eight of the characteristics of the Japanese landscape are fundamental:

1. The paucity of idle land
2. The scarcity of level land
3. Compactness
4. Meticulous organization
5. Immaculateness
6. Interdigitation
7. Tiered occupancy
8. Extensive use of underground space

Ten secondary aspects further characterize the Japanese landscape:

1. Gardens with sculptured plants
2. Flowers along thoroughfares
3. Lack of lawns
4. Dearth of roadside shoulders
5. The profusion of aerial utility lines
6. Pervasive vinyl plant covers
7. Walled houses with gates
8. Sacred spaces
9. The waning of traditional architecture
10. Urban theme parks

Together, these eighteen components of the Japanese landscape are related to the limited land, efforts to organize and maximize the land, and endeavors to enhance the aesthetics of the land (Mather, Karan, and Iijima 1998).

The Paucity of Idle Land

Idle land scarcely exists in Japan. The nation has little land for urban or industrial use, and areas for agriculture are extremely limited. Nearly three-fourths of the nation is mountainous, and there are no extensive lowlands. The typical plain of Japan is small, depositional, associated with a river, and deltaic, with its outer end along the sea and with beach ridges and dunes. Rivers, which are often torrents in the mountains, deposit their sediment on the plain as they debouch from mountain valleys. The largest of these lowlands in Japan is the Kanto Plain, on which Tokyo and Yokohama are located. It is only about 6,564 square miles (17,000 sq km) in area—about the size of Connecticut but smaller than Catron County, New Mexico. Volcanic ash known as Kanto loam covers more than half of this plain; the remainder consists

of alluvial areas and the deltas of the rivers Tonegawa, Arakawa, and Tamagawa. Yet on this single Kanto Plain is a population of 38 million—more than the entire population (29 million) of Canada. No wonder that land in Japan is used intensively and that it is sold by the *tsubo* (1 tsubo equals 35.54 sq ft or 3.3 sq m). In Tokyo's Ginza the top price was 44 million yen for one tsubo in 2002.

Housing land prices are highest in Tokyo, where they averaged 318,500 yen (about $28,954) per square meter (1.2 sq yd) in 2001. The lowest housing land prices in 2001 were in Shimane Prefecture, where they averaged 27,500 yen (about $250) per square meter. The discrepancy between land prices in the Tokyo Metropolitan Area and those in other cities increased significantly in the second half of the 1990s. Although residential land prices dropped in the Tokyo Metropolitan Area in the 1990s, they are still too high. As a result it has become increasingly difficult for the average worker to buy a house in Tokyo, or even in the suburbs, more than ninety minutes' commuting time from the central city. Furthermore, serious problems are developing in outlying areas because facilities such as schools and waterworks are unable to cope with the population shifts out of Tokyo.

The differences in land prices are a result of regional imbalances between economic development and population distribution, tax policy, and the limited supply of residential land (Yamada 1992). The government has pursued a policy of population and industrial decentralization in order to balance the use of Japan's limited land resources. To date, however, it has been unable to achieve substantial results.

Land is precious everywhere in Japan, more so in the cities than in the towns, more so in the towns than in the country, more so in old Japan than in Hokkaido, and more so on the limited areas of plains terrain than elsewhere. And nowhere is land more precious than in metropolitan Tokyo and Yokohama. Not only are the urban landscapes of the Tokyo-Yokohama metropolitan area devoid of idle land; they are also used so intensively that they are three-dimensional. The paucity of idle land prevails throughout rural areas as well. Empty lots in America's urban areas may exist for speculative reasons. In Japan, all such lots will be used today even though tomorrow they will be put to a more profitable use. The Japanese do not *zone out* use, as the United States does. They *zone in* multiple types of

A rooftop tennis court in Hakodate, Hokkaido, illustrates the efficient use of space. Making the most of space dominates various aspects of the Japanese landscape and architecture. Photo by P.P. Karan.

use, and thus produce interdigitation on the landscape.

Okujo (rooftops) provide an example of creating functional space atop most large buildings in a country with paucity of space. They are much more than fire escapes or sundecks; they are extensions of the buildings and offer remarkably detailed microcosms of society and environment. The roof of a department store may offer a beer garden, kiddie rides, a bonsai exhibition, tennis and volleyball courts, and a Shinto shrine, all amid a "natural" setting of potted trees and shrubs. Even the least-appointed rooftop garden provides space for meditation, a cigarette, lunch, and a confidential chat. Aside from the rooftop space, the department store (*depaato*) is a mirror of the Japanese society. It is a vivid expression of the prosperity, the cosmopolitanism, and the service quality that are very much part of the country. For the Japanese, the depaato is a place for relaxation, a place to bring the whole family, a place where one gets friendly, quality service—anything but just another building in which to shop.

The polite bow and high-pitched *irasshaimase* (welcome) of the white-gloved girl greeting the depaato customers at the escalator and wiping dust from the hand railing with a dainty cloth, the carefully drilled alertness to detail on the part of employees, and the skill and beauty of the way they wrap packages reflect the immaculate organization of space and culture. A special floor provides shoppers with a row of restaurants to choose from, specializing in everything from Japanese or Chinese cuisine to German, Italian, or French. There are strollers for the kids and even department stores with free nursery service. But the most impressive aspect is the assortment of cultural activities compressed in the relatively small depaato space. On the entertainment floor, tastefully designed exhibitions of temple treasures, ancient works of art, swords, pottery, woodblock prints, and Japanese and foreign paintings are displayed regularly, one after another. These mini art museums in depaato are either free of charge or require only a small entrance fee, and the daily newspapers carry complete listings of what shows are available at different department stores. The keen sensitivity to cultural life that the Japanese depaato shows reflects the important contribution of this small space to society. One hopes that the changing economics of retailing will pass the depaato by and let it remain just as it is.

The Scarcity of Level Land

Little of the land in Japan is level. Mind and land may interplay, and the Japanese are fully aware of their shortage of level land. Because only one-eighth of their territory is level or nearly so and only one-fourth of the nation has slopes of less than 15 degrees, the Japanese have devised many means of maximizing the occupancy of their favorable terrain. This small quantity of level land must contain most of their cities, industries, and agriculture. Moreover, because that terrain is patchy, the many segments must be connected in order to be functionally effective.

Reclaimed land on the Yokohama waterfront with hotel, entertainment, and office buildings. Associated with trade and foreign residents since the last years of the Tokugawa shogunate, Yokohama was a small fishing village in 1859, when it was designated as a foreign trade port city and opened to residency by foreigners. Today it is a major industrial city. Photo by P.P. Karan.

Therefore, the farms are small but intensively worked. Adjacent slopes are terraced for arboriculture and dry crops. Residential areas are compacted, lawns are eliminated, shade trees are absent, sidewalks are rare, and streets are narrow. Industrial areas are finely organized, with space utilized to the maximum. The scarce segments of level land are finely interlaced with roadways and railways. It is an impressive, coordinated, cultural achievement, a striking landscape manifestation of the interplay of culture and physical environment.

The scarcity of land has prompted the Japanese to reclaim land from the sea—to transform shallow coastal waters into land for industrial development and, especially in recent years, for residential housing and urban development. The largest Japanese land-reclamation project in the premodern era was the early-seventeenth-century reclaiming of a vast land area out of Edo Bay (now Tokyo Bay) for the construction of the city. The largest drainage reclamation project of this period was that of Kojima Bay in Okayama Prefecture. After 1950 substantial areas of land were secured for industry by dredge reclamation of coastal areas. Among the many projects under way or near completion in the early 1990s were the Tokyo Bay Frontier Project, a landfill project that includes plans for new urban centers on Ariake and Daiba sites in Tokyo Bay; Port Island and Rokko Island, the artificial islands in Kobe Bay; and the Kansai International Airport, which was completed in 1994 on an artificial island in Osaka Bay.

This scarcity of level land, always an element in the minds of the Japanese, has nurtured an appreciation for quality rather than quantity, for compactness instead of grandiosity. Indeed, it has developed, in the cultural mind, into an acute sensitivity to the principle of reductionism. So the Japanese have not only refined compactness on the landscape but have also become enamored with the bonsai, the delicate bowl on the dining table, the tiny flower print, the small garden representing the universe, and the ultimate poetic form represented by the haiku.

The Japanese are indeed the genius loci for the small place, the guardians of the "inside." Thus, gardens are an inside world, and large parks are a landscape malediction. The urban small plot is a refinement, but the overall pattern of the city is one of interdigitation of land uses. To the Occidental mind, that pattern appears as a lack of zoning, an inchoate and incoherent urban design.

Compactness

Japan is compact in form and compact in spirit. A populous country with a very limited area and much rugged land poses enormous problems of spatial organization. Numerous writers have assumed that Japan's "compact culture" is an environmental response to the problem of too many people on too little land (Lee 1984).

The Japanese landscape mirrors the cultural affinity for smallness (Brown 1993), multiple land uses, and compactness. The people of Japan adore the miniaturization of the bonsai tree, they scale down space in their rock gardens, they are masters of multiple cropping and interculture, and they regard tiny flowers with reverence. But is this just an environmental response?

Japan has approximately quadrupled in population during the past 125 years. In 1870 Japan was not straining for space. Not only was the population density then far lower than it is today, but, significantly, huge new types of space utilization were yet to come. Technological developments such as the automobile were beyond imagination a century ago. In 1870, not only did the Japanese venerate their long-established miniature verse form known as haiku, but they also had the bonsai, their scaled-down garden, their folding fan, their box within a box, their *anesama* doll, their goza mat that could be folded, their *chabudai* (a folding table), and their tiny tea house.

One can conclude, therefore, that compactness as a Japanese cultural characteristic is not simply a modern adjustment to having so many people on so few units of space. Be that as it may, compactness is a fundamental feature of the Japanese culture. It has been an intriguing aspect of the national mind-set on the modern landscape. It is quite apparent that Hokkaido has much more space per person than do Honshu, Shikoku, and Kyushu. The people of Hokkaido have larger houses, more thoroughfare space, and less-crowded urban areas. Yet even in Hokkaido, the Japanese have contracted that space in much more refined and confined terms than Americans would have done in similar circumstances.

The Japanese people experience the greatest space pressures in the huge metropolitan agglomerations, such as Nagoya, Osaka, and Tokyo. Those three metropolitan areas alone contain 43 percent of the national population. This astonishing concentration of human beings in such limited space has been possible only with an extraordinary sense of compactness. Huge apartment buildings stack living unit on living unit, and each of these units has internal space refinements that overwhelm the American mind. Americans are familiar with large apartment complexes, but their individual units are appreciably larger, and they lack the internal niceties of confined space that typify the average Japanese apartment.

And where do the residents shop in Nagoya, Osaka, and Tokyo? Giant shopping cores have been constructed, and neighborhood shopping areas are declining. But until recently, much of the retailing was in residential neighborhoods. Typically, each shop operator was a specialty retailer. Shops were small, varied, and numerous; moreover, they were close by. You simply strolled from your dwelling to the rice store, the fish shop, the fruit store, or the appliance shop. There was no sidewalk, so you proceeded on foot on the narrow street. Pedestrians had no need for a parking space. Your home refrigerator was necessarily small, so your encounters with the shopkeeper and his family were frequent. The relationship was both commercial and social. You and the shop owner lived in the same neighborhood and were members of the same community. With the exception of Shitamachi (the traditional commercial district in Tokyo), all local shopping areas have been declining.

In traditional shopping areas there were a grocery store, a butcher, a sake shop, and a traditional confectioner, but they have all been disappearing with the arrival of supermarkets and convenience stores, or *combini,* as they are known. A friendly "hello" greeted customers in these small shops, rather than the perfunctory "welcome" shouted in large stores. Now brightly lit convenience stores that carry medicines, bath and beauty products, boxed meals, and other sundries, and sell the items at steep discounts, have created a minor revolution in urban life. Japanese can also pay light, gas, and phone bills at these stores. As Japan's economic woes have deepened, urban neighborhood shopping streets are sweeping away musty businesses—old mom-and-pop stores—many of which were handed down from generation to generation. Here decades-old acquaintances of cozy little shopping streets (*shotengai*) are giving way to chain stores like 7-Eleven, fast food outlets, and supermarkets.

Yatai (movable street stalls that sell food and drink) are another expression of compactness. At shrine or temple festivals, in public parks, on side streets near railway stations, in amusement centers, on riversides, and in the alleys of densely populated quarters, yatai are common elements of the landscape. From these popular wooden restaurants-on-wheels, steaming-hot delicacies are served with sake or beer. A yatai is a two- or four-wheeled handcart to which have been added the basic facilities required for serving food and drink. Handles for pulling it slide ingeniously into the body framework when not in use. At the rear, storage compartments rise up to support a solid roof. In these are kept dishes, bottles, food ingredients, sauces, condiments, fuel, and other supplies. Chopsticks, skewers, knives, and cooking

The increasing use of automobiles and the lack of space in urban areas have led to the development of parking structures such as this one in Kita Ward of Tokyo. Photo by P.P. Karan.

utensils are available in a drawer at the front and between the handle shafts. The table for customers is a waist-high wooden surface into which are recessed either a hot plate or a copper-lined receptacle for soup heated from beneath. The compact yatai stalls provide additional functional space and are dear to the hearts of the Japanese, despite changing food fashions and modern innovations.

A gasoline station in Yatsushiro, Kumamoto Prefecture, Kyushu. Gasoline is dispensed to vehicles from pumps hanging down from the ceiling in order to conserve floor space. Photo by P.P. Karan.

Nearly all Japanese now own or use an automobile, and they may park it in a multilevel, steel-girded structure with an elevator, which minimizes the amount of space needed. The community school, too, is contained in a small space. And if you play golf, you may swing a club to your heart's content in the confined space of a small, netted field. Many gas stations in large cities have pumps hanging down from the ceiling—another example of space conservation. All of this exemplifies compactness of landscape where space is at a premium. Statistically, this extreme compactness is manifested in a much higher population-density figure in metropolitan Japan than that which characterizes large American cities.

Compactness and visual aesthetics, stressed in so many areas of Japanese landscape, are especially developed in the *ekiben* (box lunches) sold on trains and at railway stations, where limitations of space and cost require great ingenuity in the designing of containers and the arranging of food. The fact that the ekiben are served cold presents no particular problem, because food is often eaten cold; it is the freshness and quality of the ingredients that are important. Ekiben are generally made from produce of the local region. For Japanese travelers an ekiben is not just a meal but a way to establish a direct physical relationship with the area they happen to be passing through. The fish may have been caught in that bay over there, the greens picked on that mountain, the rice grown in the paddy field just outside the train window. In this sense, travelers are not restricted to merely watching the landscape pass by—they can taste it, too.

Meticulous Organization

The landscapes of the nation are meticulously ordered. The Japanese have a keen sense for organizing the landscape in terms of both time and area. Long ago, farmers practiced *multiple cropping*—they grew only one crop at a time on a plot of land, but they would plant one crop after another in quick succession in order to obtain two or more crops per year from the same piece of land. This, basically, was a meticulous organization of time that affected the landscape seasonally and was also an economic achievement. Also, farmers used to practice *interculture* —the growing of two or more crops at the same time on the same piece of land. This was particularly effective when fast-growing crops such as vegetables could be interplanted with slower-growing tree crops—another type of careful organization of time and space.

These practices of multiple cropping and interculture were refined types of landscape organization, particularly pertinent to an age when most of the population was rural. Today most of the population is urban, but the interdigitation of land uses is fundamentally a refinement of interculture applied to the urban age. Western scholars in the past have been transfixed with Japanese multiple cropping and interculture, but they have not related these concepts of meticulous organization to the modern urban scene.

The Japanese urban focus is on the detailed scene—the small urban area—and on its complex social or neighborhood viability (Bestor 1989; Clammer 1997). This necessitates an interculture or an interdigitation of land uses in order for the neighborhood to function. Informal neighborhood associations have had an important role at various times in Japan's history. *Goningumi* (literally, five-man groups) were established throughout the country during the Edo period. New neighborhood associations called *chonaikai* emerged after 1920. Small groups called *tonarigumi* (neighborhood groups) were also established. Both tonarigumi and chonaikai were abolished by occupation authorities after World War II, but unofficial associations have been revived in many areas. Neighborhood groups called *kumi*, consisting of up to fifteen households bound together by residential proximity, function in the village. Together the members of a kumi plant rice, prepare for festivals and ceremonies, handle funerals, build and repair houses, and often provide capital, credit, and especially labor for one another.

Americans, ever generous with space, have focused on the simplicity of broad urban areas, each set aside as an industrial, wholesale, retail, or residential zone. Their emphasis on the urban landscape is to have functional economic zones; they do not focus on the social concept of the neighborhood.

The meticulous organization that the Japanese apply to the urban neighborhood is, of course, coupled with their cultural predilection for compactness and their fascination with reduction. These characteristics can be seen not only in the small Japanese rock garden, but also in Japanese accomplishments in the development of the small automobile, the small transistor, and the small computer. It is an all-encompassing perspective.

An interdigitated urban landscape in Tokyo's Toshima Ward, devoted to residences, manufacturing, and offices (see the tall retail office building in back). The Japanese regard interdigitation as being well integrated. Photo by P.P. Karan.

Immaculateness

No modern nation is tidier than Japan. The Japanese are quite sensitive to environment in their immediate vicinity but a bit indifferent to the outside world. The clean-tilled fields, the trimmed terrace borders, the weed-free roadsides, the clean city streets, the tidy ditches, the well-swept waterfronts, the neat machine yards, the trim orchards, the uncluttered farmsteads, the clipped hedges, the scrubbed storefronts, the litter-free factory grounds, and the debris-free residential yards set Japan well apart from some other countries' rubbish-laden lands or billboard mania.

Compared to some parts of America, Japan certainly seems immaculate. However, the concept of "inside" is significant here. "Inside" refers to your family and your house or business or, if you are employed by a company, to the company and its grounds. Any place that is not part of anyone's "inside" is neglected. Many public areas are filled with trash unless a government agency has money to pay to clean them up. The slopes of Mount Fuji in August appear to be one huge litter area. Mount Nantai, a sacred peak that is not an "inside" area, has one discarded drink can every foot for the entire trail. At resting shelters, mounds of trash are piled high. But in cities, all areas that are in somebody's "inside" space are immaculate.

There is a dark and somber side to this issue, however, one common to all industrial nations: severe pollution. *Kogai*, or pollution, is a menacing challenge in every major Japanese city. Motor vehicles and industries cast a yellow pall over all population centers. Varying quantities of toxic liquids and solids are released into the streams, lakes, bays, and surrounding seas.

Pollution violates Japan's immaculate beauty. Environmental pollution has accompanied industrialization since the Meiji period. Among the earliest cases were the copper poisoning caused by drainage from the Ashio Copper Mine in Tochigi Prefecture, beginning as early as 1878, and the air pollution created by the Besshi Copper Mine in Ehime Prefecture, Shikoku, first noticed in 1893. The subsequent development of the textile and paper and pulp industries led to water and air pollution, and the use of coal as the major fuel for industry in general contributed to widespread air pollution. The most resented and dramatic offenses have been against human health. The tragedy of Minamata in 1953, a seaside town facing the splendid islets off the western coast of Kyushu, typified the full-scale horror of environmental pollution. Although the scandals of kogai continue, they began to decline as far back as the 1970s. Japan has embarked on a far-reaching, severe, and expensive cleanup program. Behind the government's antipollution effort lies a clear and massive public consensus to restore the immaculate character of the landscape.

Much in contrast to the United States, where labor is often willing to live and die with industrial poison rather than lose jobs, Japanese unions (knowing their members' employment to be guaranteed until recently) often oppose pollution out of the realization that such iniquities as mercury discharge in the long run injure the public, the unionists, and the industry itself. The railway workers' union (rather than management) decided to slow bullet trains from 110 to 62 miles per hour (from 176 to 99.2 km/hr) over a 6-mile (9.7-km) stretch in Nagoya, where residents said the roar of trains at high speed created unbearable noise pollution. Major firms in Japan now put at least 10 percent of their investment into pollution-prevention equipment or devices to maintain the clean landscape.

The obsession with cleanliness in Japan has led to the appearance of a new line of products at stationery stores throughout the country: pens and pencils whose barrels are impregnated with an antiseptic chemical to kill bacteria. Pentel's germ-free pens, decorated with a medical-looking blue cross, are the most successful product. Since the germ-free writing instruments went on sale in 1994, a host of similar antibacterial items have been introduced, including stationery, origami paper, and bicycle handles. Hitachi has even developed an automated teller machine that irons and sanitizes the bills it dispenses.

The Japanese have always been fond of cleanliness. Proper appearance and form are important in Japanese society. Tidiness is also necessary for public health in a country with a population half that of the United States crammed into an area the size of California. Bathing is a ritual in Japan. Shoes are taken off before entering homes. People with colds often wear face masks in the streets and subways, so as not to infect others. Paper money given as a wedding present must be clean and crisp; people actually iron the bills before inserting them in the ceremonial envelopes.

Karaoke bars, where people sing before an audience to recorded background music, give their loyal customers personal microphones that are stored behind the counter for a particular customer's use each time he or she comes in. At some coin laundries, a customer can, before inserting dirty clothes, give the insides of the washing machine a quick shower to wash away any lingering traces of the last customer. Writers in Japanese popular magazines, even as they feature people who are squeamish about germs, also note the emergence of young women who do not care about cleanliness and rarely shower, shampoo, or use makeup; because they need so little care, such people have been called "cactus women."

Interdigitation

The Japanese landscape is remarkably interlaced, interrelated, and interdigitated. Most of the people are crowded onto the nation's scarce flattish land, which amounts to only one-eighth of the entire country, an area about the size of Costa Rica. This means that most of the industrial, commercial, residential, and agricultural land use is concentrated on an extremely limited area. The Japanese response to this areal constriction has been to leave no land vacant even for a short time, and to exclude no major type of land use. This response was not governmentally promulgated. Rather, it evolved as the population increased and with the cultural progression of experience with this extraordinary shortfall of space.

Most of Japan's nearly flat terrain is situated in separate, deltaic plains and in a few small intermontane depressions. Each deltaic plain developed functionally into a regional community, but these communities were separated by mountainous topography. As modernization progressed and Japan moved from feudalism into a truly national state after 1868, social and economic challenges necessitated an effective linkage of these separated deltaic entities and small intermontane depressions. This was accomplished by developing an extraordinary system of interlaced railways and roadways, using many tunnels in the process.

The Japanese landscape that evolved on these bits of nearly flat land has two major features. One is that it is interdigitated, and the other is that the interdigitation pattern is finely textured (Suizu 1984). What could have evolved, but did not, was areal specialization for each plain. Rice could have been grown

mainly on some deltaic plains, vegetables planted on others, and manufacturing developed on still others. It is true that some of these plains have more industrial development than others do and that some have a degree of agricultural specialization. But for the most part, each of the plains is highly diversified, the pattern of diversification is one of interdigitation, and the interdigitation involves small, individual parcels of land—that is, it is finely textured. This pattern seems almost endlessly recurrent.

An illustration of finely textured interdigitation is the Saijo area of Ehime Prefecture, in northern Shikoku. Saijo, on the Inland Sea, developed as a castle town in the Edo period. Electric machinery, papermaking, textile, and dyeing industries utilize its abundant underground water supply. *Nori*, a seaweed, is cultivated in the coastal area. Here a single vista includes both field land and hothouse agriculture, field-crop diversification, industrial and warehouse establishments, and a profusion of roadways and utility lines, besides retailing, recreational, and educational facilities. This segment is divided not into large parcels but into small ones. What does this small parceling denote?

Japan is mainly a nation of mini units. Most of the farms are nearly as small as gardens by American standards. Retailing is done mostly in small shops. Japan does have huge apartment structures, but most of the people live in small houses or in upstairs units above shops or other commercial establishments. Great corporations such as Sony and Nissan flourish, but more than two-thirds of all Japanese industrial workers are employed by companies with fewer than three hundred employees. More than half of all Japanese factories have fewer than ten employees. And on a per capita basis, Japan has almost twice as many wholesalers and retailers as does the United States.

Numerous economic and cultural factors are responsible for Japan's unusually large number of small retailers. Some of these factors are the preference of housewives for shopping in their neighborhoods (especially for everyday goods such as fresh foods), the parking problem and the cost of using automobiles in crowded urban areas, the absence of inexpensive land sites in suburban areas for building large shopping centers, and the Japanese preference for the proximity and individualized service that small neighborhood stores can provide. Nevertheless, in recent years a considerable proportion of sales have been moving to bigger stores.

The landscape reflects the preponderance of minisized units, or fine texturizing. The facts that each type of land use is interdigitated with other types and that there is an absence of unused land awaiting speculative development are striking aspects of the landscape. Land speculation does exist, but Japanese land is remarkably expensive, and the speculative land is invariably utilized in some interim manner, rather than just waiting for a deal to be completed. For example, the Tokyo metropolitan region, home to more than 33 million people (in 2002), includes 88,000 acres (35,612 ha) of farmland held in speculation for building. Even in central Tokyo, farm plots take up roughly 4,500 acres (1,821 ha). It is common to see weekend farmers tending rows of cabbages or vines of table grapes amid towering apartment blocks and industrial structures. Land in agricultural use, even in urban areas, is taxed at a rate of about one-tenth that of regular land. The city farmers continue their land use in the expectation that the price of land will rise as pressure grows for more space for housing.

In 1991 the law was revised to encourage the transfer of speculative farmlands to urban use as well as to conserve green land within urbanized areas. Now the farmland owners in urban promotion areas within the metropolitan boundary have been assigned the residential type of property tax and inheritance tax, unless their farmland is designated a productive green zone and remains as agricultural land for at least thirty years to be taxed as farmland. In December 1999, in the Kanto region (Ibaraki, Saitama, Chiba, Tokyo, and Kanagawa Prefectures) the area of productive green zone was 21,592 acres (8,738 ha), accounting for 42 percent of farmland in all urban promotion areas (51,302 ac, 20,761 ha). As of April 2000, productive green zones covered 1,337 acres (541 ha) in the Tokyo Ward area.

Tiered Occupancy

The land of Japan is set in tiers. Its occupancy has expanded up the lower slopes adjacent to the intensively used lowlands, and the character of this occupancy has resulted in a tiered landscape. The tiered pattern is a series of land-use belts. By the seaside are marine vessels and associated facilities. Behind these are commercial establishments and residential structures. Then come paddy fields and rural residences. Moving up the slopes, the final tier consists of dry-land agriculture on the terraced foothills. This belted, specialized land-use system is one of the fundamental characteristics of the Japanese landscape. How did it develop?

The role of rice in Japanese life and the shift from a primarily rural to a mostly urban society were basic elements in the development of tiered land occupancy. In 1920 more than half of Japan's population was rural and half of the cultivated land was used to grow rice. The areas of dense population were coincident with the alluvial lowlands. This was mainly the consequence of the Japanese farmers' dependence on rice culture. Because "spade agriculture" prevailed then, farms were necessarily small and were concentrated on irrigated alluvial areas. So there were two major field classes, irrigated lowlands and uplands. The former were the more productive, required more labor, and had more homesteads. The uplands, mainly unirrigated, were used for tree crops, with some interculture of vegetables and dry-land cereals.

Before World War II it was believed that farm mechanization could only mean large machines on large farms. But the Japanese devised very small and efficient agricultural implements, and the new devices came into use as the rural-to-urban migration became significant, as off-farm employment increased, and as farmworkers aged. So the two major tiers that were extant in the period of rural population dominance persisted through the transition into an urban-dominated society.

Today less than 10 percent of the labor force works in agriculture, and by 1975 the metropolitan areas of Tokyo, Osaka, and Nagoya housed 40 percent of the nation's population. It is significant that most of Japan's population in the rural-dominated 1920s was on the lowlands, including adjoining mountains, and that in the urban-dominated 1990s it is still primarily on the lowlands. Thus, throughout this period of time, two main tiers have persisted, one heavily and compactly populated, the other one not. The tiered occupancy of today is simply further refined.

Extensive Use of Underground Space

More than in any other country, extensive use of underground space is a dominant feature of the landscape. In Japanese cities underground shopping

A tiered landscape. Nagahama-cho, Ehime Prefecture, western Shikoku. Photo by Cotton Mather.

streets have been constructed, creating new space for retail. They are connected with the basements of multistoried buildings. Nagoya offers a typical example of a city with such underground shopping streets. Underground shopping streets in Nagoya have developed at traffic junctions, such as at Sakae and Nagoya-ekimae (the front area of Nagoya Station), and under public roads, simultaneously with the construction of subway stations. This has provided many people with easy access to underground shopping streets, which showed rapid development after 1957.

At first a group of shops were located along the underground pedestrian passageways that connect subway stations and other means of transport. Then shopping promenades interconnected these areas and the basements of adjacent multistoried buildings, resulting in the increase of underground space for retail. The expansion of underground shopping streets occurred on a large scale in Nagoya and other Japanese cities after 1969.

According to the type of business they contain, underground shopping streets can be classified into two types: one kind has many restaurants, coffee houses, and a wide variety of food stores, and the other features many specialty clothing shops. The shopping streets beneath the front of Nagoya Station belong to the first type, which is a common pattern at other urban railway centers in Japan. In Nagoya as well as the other cities, underground specialty shops are located beneath the central business district. In Nagoya these are at Sakae, which has a long, prosperous history as a central shopping center of the city. Many chain stores are among the shops on underground shopping streets. Because their head offices are in Tokyo, their window displays and selections of merchandise do not reflect local or regional characteristics. This has promoted among the people of various cities in Japan an inclination toward Tokyo-oriented fashion and culture.

This underground shopping mall in central Nagoya near the shinkansen station is one of Japan's largest malls. It connects several smaller malls by hallways and corridors stretching over 5 miles (8 km) with seventy entrances and more than six hundred shops and offers an endless variety of stores, boutiques, pubs, and restaurants. At the underground malls in major metropolitan centers, focused on the station, the worlds of taxi and bus, car and subway, private and trunk line, pedestrian and shopper intersect. And, here, below the ground, the historical street type—varied in architectural scale and texture, and free of vehicles—continues to exist in a transmogrified form. Within the underground shopping complex, urban life and transactions have returned to the personal level, urban life with an emphasis on the pedestrian and the fabric of small shops that—aboveground—has been disappearing from Japan since the 1990s. Photo by P.P. Karan.

Floor space for shops on underground shopping streets is rather small compared with that of shops above ground. Because of the favorable location, rents are high. Underground shops specialize in an assortment of goods that attract young customers. Besides having young people as regular customers, the underground stores' employees are young themselves. The underground shopping streets with these young employees and customers form a community of tradespeople that contrasts with the traditional community of merchants in Japan (Treib 1994).

One of the reasons for the development of underground shopping streets in large cities is that many people use public mass transport, and underground shopping streets have been constructed at its junctions. The development has also been fostered by the improved automobile accessibility brought about by large underground public parking garages connected with the shopping streets.

SECONDARY CHARACTERISTICS OF THE LANDSCAPE

The secondary characteristics of the Japanese landscape are refinements of the immediate environment. These are the characteristics that affect individuals directly in daily life in every region throughout the nation. They define the specific and detailed nature of the *locale*, whereas the primary characteristics pertain to the more generalized traits of the national scene.

Gardens with Sculptured Plants

Japan's public gardens are widely recognized and admired by both Japanese and foreign visitors, but home gardens are the omnipresent and highly distinctive landscape feature of the nation (Nitschke 2003). Public gardens are the idolized representations of the aesthetic concept; home gardens represent economic and spatial compromises with this idolized representation.

Among the salient aspects of public gardens is that they constitute a scaling down of idolized nature; spacious panoramas are compressed into a controlled scale. They are a subjugation of nature. They present nature trimmed, with its form under control; they include a meandering path along which one sees inspiring new perspectives. At their best, they are gardens of meditation.

The typical home garden is in a very confined space, separated from the road or street by a masonry enclosure. It is arranged with meticulous attention to how it will look from the windows of the home. The desire also is to reduce space, to control form by sculpturing or by contorted trimming of the plants. It is a careful endeavor to enhance the aesthetics of the home environment. Moreover, it is very private. In some areas, lacking space for a home garden, people plant trees and shrubs, often in pots, in the narrow strip of ground in front of their home.

The idolized Japanese garden emphasizes nature controlled by the human hand, whereas the English garden conveys studied naturalness and the French garden represents rationality by imposing a geometric order on disorderly nature. A Japanese home garden is an attempt to achieve living perfection in limited space. It consists of three essential elements: rocks, water, and plants. The rocks are the bones of the garden, the water the blood coursing through its veins, and the plants the flesh to give it form. These elements alone are sufficient. Flowers are not an essential component. The compositional beauty derives from blending plants, water, and rocks. The development and interplay of these elements determine the perfection. The home garden expresses the idea of living in harmony with nature, rather than conquering it. All the elements in a garden, including the house, are integral parts of the unified whole.

To achieve the desired effect, each element is precisely located. In these small home gardens, one can appreciate the beauty of nature despite such a density of humanity. Along the west coast of Japan and in areas with heavy snowfall, the garden takes on a different aspect in winter. Every tree branch is tied up to a central pole to help it bear the weight of the heavy snowfalls. Surprisingly, the garden loses little of its charm under these circumstances. So much of its beauty depends on the layout of the individual elements that it can still be appreciated despite a lack of foliage and the presence of rope.

To the Western way of thinking, the intellectualization of nature represented in Japanese home gardens is anathema. In the West people worry that progress is not leaving enough wilderness, yet there is an attempt to sanitize nature and tame it for public parks and gardens. Rationalizing nature to the degree observed in home gardens in front of people's houses is a particularly Japanese phenomenon. The vernacular gardens represent one of the most visual

A home garden with sculptured trees in western Tokyo. Home gardens are designed to enhance the aesthetics of the home environment. Photo by P.P. Karan.

aspects of Japanese culture and landscape, reminding observers of the value system underlying the subtle use of space and methods of scenic composition.

A love of natural form and an eagerness to express it ideally have been primary motives in the development of traditional sculptured plants in home gardens. By pruning branches, pinching off new growth, and wiring the branches and trunk, the home owner–gardener nurtures plants into the desired shape. It is important that plants produce the artistic effect desired in the garden. For home owners, sculptured plants not only duplicate nature but also express personal aesthetics or sensibility by artistic transmutation. They may suggest a scene from nature or even a grotesque character, but in all cases they must appear as a wonder of nature. Evergreens are the most popular sculptured plants. Pines, which symbolize eternity, are especially popular—particularly the fine-needled variety.

In the residences of Zen monks, gardens are designed not so much to produce aesthetic pleasure as to promote a meditative calm. Contemplation of a person's place in the cosmos plays an essential part in Zen, a Buddhist sect that became Japan's most influential religion during the thirteenth century (Tanaka 1984). Accordingly, the gardens in which Zen priests and laymen studied during meditation were symbolic miniature versions of the world of nature. The profundity of nature could best be rendered, Zen gardeners thought, not by ornate and brightly colored plants but by evergreens, dark mosses, and rustic paths, or by a stark design of black rocks on white sand. Such gardens, they believed, preserved some of the mystery and the spirit of a lesson taught by the Buddha, who, when asked to define ultimate reality, silently pointed to a flower.

Another type of vernacular garden is found around teahouses. During the fifteenth and sixteenth centuries, Japan was constantly torn by internal wars. Men found refuge from the strife in the tea ceremony, a ritual of elegant simplicity that developed during this period. Essentially, the tea ceremony was a gathering of friends in a small house, set in a secluded garden; the purpose of meeting was to drink tea and discuss a work of art—often a utensil used in making and serving the tea.

Teahouse gardens are laid out according to a prescribed plan. An entrance path leads to the outer garden and a small shelter where guests gather. After the tea master arrives, the guests proceed to an inner garden. There they perform ritual purification by rinsing their hands and mouth before passing through the low door of the teahouse. Every detail of the teahouse garden must have the correct natural charm. The plantings are as woodslike as possible: no flowers, no majestic views, nothing to startle visitors. The growth is seemingly random and uncontrolled (although, of course, it is carefully planned and tended). The moss that carpets the ground and the inset stepping stones are lightly sprinkled with water to capture the dewy coolness of morning or the freshness that follows a rainfall.

The entrance to the tea garden, that is, a space designed for entry, does not just take visitors physically from the street to the tearoom, but it leads them through a spiritual transition as well. More correctly called *roji,* meaning "dewy path," it offers an environment carefully designed to initiate the kind of mental repose required for the tea ceremony. It compresses into the space between the road and the teahouse the emotional content of a journey from the crowded city to a secluded place.

A series of landmarks and thresholds are designed into a roji. At each of these points, one is encouraged to release the concerns of daily life and progressively enter a "tea" state of mind. The first such point is a roofed gate through a high wall that clearly separates the roji from the outer world. Entering this gate represents the first step from the complexity of the outer world into the "calm of tea." Unless the property is very small, a second, middle gate (*chumon*) divides the inner and outer roji. Passage through the middle gate symbolizes entry into an even deeper state of simplicity. A third threshold is a low stone laver called a *tsukubai.* Here the mouth and hands are washed. The purpose is not hygiene so much as gaining a simple, fresh feeling and a sense of spiritual purification. The last threshold is the entry to the tearoom itself, a tiny door where all must bow to enter, teaching that everyone is equally humble within. Thus, by cleverly controlling the environment, the roji becomes a landscape of entry and a cultural symbol in the Japanese landscape.

Flowers along Thoroughfares

Japan's public space is severely limited, but it is embellished with flowers along the thoroughfares. The role of flowers in the Japanese culture is different from that in the United States. The Japanese place flower arranging much higher in their repertoire of arts. To Americans, a bouquet of flowers is really special; to the Japanese, the delight is in the arrangement of a single blossom. Instead of bunching together masses of blossoms and balancing them with greenery in a vase, the Japanese avoid balance and symmetry. They treat each floral splendor as one to be separately admired—one branch, one color, one luxury of line. That is in the realm of aesthetics.

Then there is the humdrum world, the one in which we all must live. Americans emphasize the sameness of broad, grass-bordered roadways, perhaps interrupted occasionally with deciduous or evergreen trees, but rarely with planted flowers. In Japan thousands flock to see a special variety of plum tree in bloom. And the Japanese have made a national festival out of cherry-blossom time. Cherry-blossom viewings stir deep emotions every spring. Westerners are prone to think that if they have seen one cherry blossom, they have seen them all. But Japanese notice differences between orchards, and between trees in orchards, and between blossoms on trees, and between the petals of the blossoms—differences attributed to the stoniness of the soil or the strength of the sunshine or the chilliness of the breeze—and these differences give them billions of petals over which to exclaim.

In 1909 the city of Tokyo presented cherry trees to Washington, D.C.; they grace the tidal basin, where people flock every spring to experience their beauty.

In Kobe, a wide boulevard called Flower Road, which extends southward from Sannomiya Station, is decorated with flowers of the season. It is common to see beds of flowers planted by the roadside, and sometimes even along a city street, where space is precious and so limited.

Three blocks west of Tokyo Station lies the moat of the Imperial Palace, with huge stones laid in a herringbone pattern. Along this waterfront, with rows of flowers and trees, runs an eight-lane boulevard, behind which stand massive office buildings. These rectangular buildings, along with others on the streets between the moat and the station, make up Marunouchi district, Tokyo's headquarters for banks and corporations. It was here in Edo times that feudal lords from the provinces built their obligatory mansions, to house their hostage families. Emperor Meiji turned the development of the area over to Baron Iwasaki, founder of the Mitsubishi zaibatsu (industrial and financial combine). In this 60-acre (24-ha) district, one of the most valuable swatches of land in the world, narrow strips planted with azaleas and carnations interspersed with intriguing small, modern sculptures line the middle streets. At noon the nearly half million people who work here, among them hundreds of Japan's highest business executives, walk past the blooming flowers.

Lack of Lawns

Americans, on visiting Japan, are quick to observe the lack of lawns. Lawns are absent even in the towns

Flowers along a road at Iyo-shi, Ehime Prefecture. There is no street parking, but there is a profusion of aerial utility lines and a flower-bordered street. Photo by Cotton Mather.

of Hokkaido, where urban space is the least crowded. Lawns are lacking on farmsteads throughout the nation. And there is seemingly no need for lawns in the rest of Japan, even in the cemeteries or the neighborhood Buddhist temples. The landscape certainly reveals that the Japanese do not feel a need for lawns.

Americans are baffled as to why the Japanese are without grass. Our cultural standards are assumed to be the ultimate of rationality. Thus we are unmindful that in most of our regions we plant imported types of grass, that our lawns occupy more land than any single crop, that our 26 million acres of turf grass equals an area larger than the state of Indiana, that most of the water in our cities in the West is used for watering lawns, that our urban householders use far more chemicals than our farmers do, that few of the pesticides used on our lawns have been tested for long-term effects on people, that our compelling preoccupation with lawns is not an American custom but an offshoot from England, that we expend most of our lawn time just cutting the growth that we stimulated with fertilizers, and that the common lawn scene in our country is working on lawns, not enjoying them!

So Americans, after visiting Japan, might well be expected to reduce the monotonous expanse of lawn grass by adding shrubs and rocks, by using more xerophytic plants in their water-thirsty regions, by decreasing their use of chemicals, by maneuvering some time away from lawn work and into lawn leisure, and by asking if our departed family members need grass around their tombstones. More travel to Japan might induce Americans to save much energy, chemicals, and space. But this could devastate employment in our mowing-machine factories and not gain a consensus from our dearly departed. For now, in any case, Americans agree with Senator John James Ingalls's famous pronouncement in 1872 that "grass is the forgiveness of nature—her constant benediction."

Dearth of Roadside Shoulders

The Japanese concept of roads is that they are used for the movement of goods and people. Roadside shoulders do not have this function, so they are rare. Japan's road system reflects the nation's frugality and its limited space. Americans—the world's biggest spenders and borrowers, and custodians of a vast area

for their population—are astounded by the space-saving and money-saving aspects of Japan's road system.

Japan does have added costs in the development of its road system because it has widely scattered, and small, flat-land settlement areas that are separated by mountainous terrain. Most of Japan's areas of dense settlement are along the coast, but the costs of constructing highways there, given the irregular coastlines and rugged headlands, are formidable. Japan's road system is low in both quantity and quality compared with those of other leading industrialized nations.

Japan's national expressways are paved, as are almost all of the general national highways and prefectural roads. The "other" roads, of which one-third were unpaved until 1980, are now paved also, except for the forest access roads. And throughout Japan, all highways and byways are squeezed into rights-of-way that are incredibly narrow by the standards of western Europe and North America.

Japan does rely on railways and coastal shipping more than does, for example, the United States. In 1998 railways carried 4.2 percent of the freight and 27 percent of the passenger traffic; surface vehicles moved 54 percent of the freight and 67 percent of passengers. Coastal shipping was responsible for 41 percent of the freight and 0.3 percent of passenger traffic. Japan has fewer automobiles per capita than the United States, but they are becoming increasingly important in domestic transportation. Could this increasing use of the automobile be a consequence of Japan's affluence or its physical geography, or both?

Japan's space limitations and its frugality are reflected in the almost complete absence of roadside shoulders, even on the national expressways. This is a bane to landscape photographers or those with automotive problems. Japan's admonition to such people is simple: forgo roadside photography and avoid car trouble. The use of highways in Japan, though, is rapidly expanding. The number of passenger cars has more than doubled during the past two decades. Bus and truck traffic, however, has increased far less.

Aomori, on the northern tip of Honshu, is linked by a network of expressways with Kagoshima at the southern end of Kyushu, and the network continues to grow throughout the archipelago. One strikingly modern feature of Japan's expressways is rest stations designed as interludes in highway travel. Service areas, with parking lots, restaurants, shops, gas stations, and restrooms, are situated about every thirty miles. Some rest stations provide faxing and postal service, nursing rooms, bathing facilities (and hot-spring baths on the Chuo Expressway), and vending machines.

Nowhere else in the world are automatic vending machines so widespread. From the bustling urban intersections to the most bucolic rural lane, vending machines are common, dispensing nearly all of life's necessities and many of its frills. In addition to the usual soft drinks and cigarettes, Japan's colorfully turned-out machines dispense jewelry, fresh flowers, frozen beef, rice, whiskey, beer, hamburgers, videocassettes, throwaway cameras, underwear, and batteries. In December 2000 Japan had about 5.6 million of these machines, compared to 7.2 million in the United States, which has double the population. And each Japanese machine produces more in sales volume, on average, than its American counterpart. A total of more than $60 billion in goods was sold through Japanese vending machines in 2000 as compared to $36 billion in the United States. Thus convenience is challenging the tradition of dealing with neighborhood shopkeepers. The popularity of vending machines shows how Japanese are reconciling their age-old devotion to elaborate courtesies with their increasingly harried lives. In a nation where every social encounter—at work, at home, at the store—is still governed by obligation and ritual, many people prefer to drop coins into a machine than to deal with a person.

Seen from the perspective of the high rents, vending machines free up shelf space and run twenty-four hours a day. Along traditional *shotengai,* or shopping streets, small merchants have banks of vending machines in front of their shops. Japanese vending machines also benefit from the country's electronics expertise. Among the latest innovations are solar machines to reduce electricity use; machines that use small elevators to deliver items at chest height; and machines fitted with point-of-sale computers that automatically radio headquarters with details on sales, inventories, and whether the mechanisms are functioning properly. Vending machines have become a ubiquitous element in the roadside landscape.

The Profusion of Aerial Utility Lines

Japan's utility lines are highly visible, and their pattern is extraordinarily complex. They certainly are not buried underground. As in much of the United States, landscape photographers search diligently in urban settings for spots uncluttered by distracting wires and poles. The complexity of the pattern, moreover, is compounded by having lines at many levels and by lines that branch out at many angles from transmission poles along a single street. Indeed, Japan's system evolved by the addition of one more wire or one more cable for every new one needed. Lines were not combined. The consequence in the urban settings has been an amazing and confusing profusion of aerial utility lines.

Two main reasons for the profusion have been propounded. One pertains to Japan's legendary frugality, the other to the nation's "inside" cultural perspective. After all, the system of aerial lines never was organized; it just grew. Modernizing it now would be expensive. Second, when one goes inside a building, one does leave the outside.

The "outside" perspective ranks high in the Occidental world, so its cities favor broad boulevards, grand traffic circles, and heroic monuments and statues. One of the renowned examples of exterior Occidental display is the Champs-Elysées of Paris, leading from the Place de la Concorde to the Arc de Triomphe. The Champs-Elysées is celebrated for its impressive breadth, its tree-lined beauty, and the fountain display at its center. Saint Peter's Church in

Vending machines along a rural highway in Nagano Prefecture. Vending machines are a common feature of both rural and urban landscapes. Photo by P.P. Karan.

Rome boasts a majestic elliptical piazza bounded by quadruple colonnades and a monumental avenue leading to the piazza. Vienna has its imposing Ringstrasse, a magnificent, 150-foot-wide (45.7-meter-wide) boulevard planted with four rows of trees and lined with splendid buildings and huge monuments. Buenos Aires displays its Avenida de Mayo and the Avenida 9 de Julio—the latter reputed to be the world's widest boulevard. Even Washington, D.C., designed by Pierre L'Enfant, has its magnificent mall dominated by the Capitol, the Washington Monument, and the Lincoln Memorial, all flanked by great avenues.

Tokyo and the other Japanese metropolitan centers have nothing similar. The Imperial Palace has an "inside," not a flamboyant "outside," perspective. Indeed, the actual palace is walled and surrounded by moats.

So the streets of Japan have one main characteristic, whether in residential-commercial sectors or in major downtown areas: they are functional. They are thoroughfares, along and across which are utility lines and pedestrian and vehicular traffic. Occidental streets, in comparison, have an "outside," or display, aspect that is of major significance to the cultural psyche.

Pervasive Vinyl Plant Covers

Vinyl plant covers are a strikingly modern element in the agricultural landscape of Japan, and they represent a new economic horizon for Japanese farmers. These plant covers are a response to expanding urbanization, new standards of living, and improved transportation and marketing of agricultural products. The rising standard of living has brought an increased consumption of flowers, fruits, and vegetables. And there is more demand for off-season produce as well as a premium for higher quality.

For example, flowers grown in vinyl-covered greenhouses on the Atsumi Peninsula, south of Nagoya, are shipped in bloom during the off-season months of April and May. Vegetables produced in vinyl greenhouses in southern Kyushu, on the Miyazaki Plain, reach the markets of Osaka, Nagoya, and Tokyo before local produce is available in those areas. Vinyl greenhouses in the Tohoku district of northern Honshu are used for growing rice seedlings. The seedlings are planted in trays, stacked on racks, and later transplanted in the fields by machines.

A street in Hiroshima with a profusion of aerial utility lines. Photo by P.P. Karan.

In southern Shikoku, on the mountain-girded Kochi Plain, vegetables are produced under vinyl cover and shipped off-season by fast, modern transportation to the large metropolitan markets and even north to Hokkaido. In the Yamagata Basin of the Tohoku district—Japan's chief cherry-tree area—fruit is grown under a vinyl canopy to protect it from rain.

The use of vinyl becomes widespread on almost all deltaic and basin lands as the quality of produce is intensified and upgraded. This is particularly evident in and around the suburbs of large cities, where markets are at hand and high land prices dictate extraordinary intensification. Thus, the usurpation of farmland by expanding urbanization is offset by producing more per acre, especially through the use of vinyl.

Urban farmers, such as those in Edogawa ward, eastern Tokyo, who grow crops in vinyl greenhouses have found that their vegetables and flowers are adversely affected by the artificial all-night city lights. There are reports of chrysanthemums blooming at the wrong time, rice ears developing too late, and

Melons grown under vinyl covers near Sakata in Yamagata Prefecture. Vinyl-covered greenhouses are a major feature of the agricultural landscape of Japan. Photo by P.P. Karan.

undeveloped spinach leaves—all owing to artificial city lights along sidewalks and streets. The ward governments have responded by lowering the intensity of outdoor lights. And the vinylization of Japanese agriculture continues to expand.

The number of farm households in Japan decreased from 4.95 million in 1975 to 3.12 million in 2000, and farm households engaged exclusively in farming decreased to 500,000 in 2000; the latter figure included a lot of elderly farmers' households. So part-time farming is the rule now. Although agricultural production per unit area is mounting, Japan is experiencing an increase in food imports. Its virtual food self-sufficiency is mainly in rice, vegetables, and fresh eggs. Wheat, barley, and legumes are the main food imports.

Walled Houses with Gates

The archetypal Japanese home has a walled garden with a locked gate for privacy. Community and family, as opposed to individualism, are exalted in Japanese culture. These values find expression in the walled enclosures that symbolize family solidarity. Within the walls family members are secure—and more closely attached to each other. The Japanese feeling that people are not separate from nature is portrayed in the vernacular garden part of the home. In the United States, single houses standing alone without separate walls around the house lots are an expression of individualism, a value element in the middle-class Anglo-Saxon culture that predominates in the United States. The individualistic American house presents a bold front to the world; in contrast, the Japanese house presents a united front within the walled compound.

The residential life of Japan underwent enormous changes during the twentieth century, when the gulf between the realized and the idealized was huge. In the early part of the century, most of the population was rural, most of the settlement was on flat land, most of the houses were arranged along a single village street, and most of the dwellings looked flimsy. Houses were generally of only one story, with three or four rooms, no attic, no basement, and no continuous foundation. Buildings were framed on wooden poles and roofed with thatch or tile. Whereas the Chinese preferred brick, stone, or clay, the Japanese favored wood. They admired the appearance of weathered wood on the exterior and the rich tones of hand-rubbed interior wood surfaces.

The house had exterior sliding panels, especially on the south side, which could open to the southern breezes of summer and to the sun in winter. Rooms were multifunctional and could easily be adapted for a different use by means of interior sliding panels with translucent panes that permitted the passage of light. Roofs had a pleasing combination of straight and curved lines, and a broad overhang beyond the walls could shield open rooms from rain and yet relate to the differential angles of the winter and summer sun. The house had a fire pit for cooking and heat. Heating was restricted to the specific area where the occupants were; it was not considered a provision for entire-room comfort.

The homes of the wealthy were very different. Their homes had roofs of tile, metal, or composition; they were larger, often two-storied, and were set back from the street behind a wall with a locked gate for privacy. Between the wall and the house was a garden of miniaturized, sculptured plants, meticulously arranged to make it an integral component of the home when the sliding doors were open. The garden had weathered rocks aesthetically placed, and perhaps a pond. These homes, with their walled gardens, were relatively spacious. They represented the ideal in substance and style, and still do.

The traditional walled residences, particularly their entrances, reflect the psychosocial aspect of Japanese society. These entrances consist of three basic elements: a gated wall surrounding the property, an inner court through which one passes, and a special entrance hall called a *genkan* (literally, mysterious gate). The surrounding wall is usually constructed of wood or skillfully finished clay plaster. Significantly, it always extends above eye level. The result of the high wall and the gate is that visibility into the property is either eliminated or strictly controlled. This clear separation of family space and public space reflects the importance of the family in Japanese society. The home and the family (the Japanese word *uchi* is used for both concepts) are the core of Japanese society and, as such, are private and not to be intruded upon lightly. The wall is an expression of this desire for the family to remain apart from society at large.

The entry court, between the outer wall and the house, has a planted garden and a stone path that crosses the court in curves. As a result, the initial focus on entering is never the destination. This deflecting walkway expresses the characteristic Japanese dislike for directness in social interaction. Eyes are cast aside to avoid an offending glance; in speech, points are couched in circular logic. Directness is seen as overly aggressive and simplistic. The genkan's importance can be seen in its size, which may cover 10 percent of the floor area of the house. In a nation where space is precious, size denotes importance. The genkan space is designed for receiving guests with the ritual formality befitting Japanese custom. Entrances rank as a fundamental visual element in the Japanese landscape. They are characterized by the firm control of passage from one space to the next. To the Japanese, the entrance and the way of entering are as important as the destination itself.

Today most of the nation's population resides in a new reality, crowded urban areas where the amount of private space per individual is drastically limited. Epitomizing this is Tokaido Megalopolis, a spectacular urban sprawl of humanity that stretches along southern Honshu from Kobe and Osaka through Kyoto and Nagoya to Yokohama and Tokyo. This amazing agglomeration, 300 miles (483 km) long, is an essentially unplanned urban belt of gigantic dimensions and complexity. The famous French geographer Jean Gottmann was the one who characterized this phenomenon as a megalopolis.

Tokaido Megalopolis embraces most of the nation's residences, all of the central government, the headquarters of most of the large industrial and financial institutions, most of the prestigious universities, and all of the great organizations of publication and communication. This concentration of human beings and their institutions has developed into a world-renowned complex famous for its unparalleled productivity but with stressful social and environmental consequences. Among these are long daily commutes via public transportation from residence to work. Nowhere in the world does the average worker take so long, in such jammed circumstances, for this regular journey.

The adjustments to this new reality are manifold. Mainly they pertain to limitations of space for individuals and families (Mather and Karan 1999). Residential units are compact, children go to parks or commercial playgrounds to play, automobiles are a luxury, and much of daily life transpires in public and semipublic places (Ito 1999). Lacking a guest room in the house, most Japanese do not entertain friends at home but meet them in restaurants or coffee shops. The idealized home for the majority is just a dream, but one that embodies both the space and the style of an elegant and refined tradition.

Sacred Spaces

In Japan small sacred spaces, such as Shinto shrines and Buddhist statues in alleys, streets, or at corners, are a vital part of the landscape. The emphasis here is not on the major shrines and temples but on the sacred spaces and holy places of ordinary folk living in the narrow alleys in various neighborhoods and rural areas. Manifested in a variety of forms, they are ubiquitous. The small, graceful torii (gate) to a neighborhood shrine separates the purified sacred area from the outer world. The essence of Shinto is purity. The formal religion is based on the ritual purging of evil spirits and the invocation of protective gods. The shrine is a purified, and ritually repurified, space.

Tiny statuettes known as *mizuko jizo* are common along the roadsides. These are guardians of babies who have died. Japanese dress up the mizuko figurines like little newborns, with bibs, hand-knit sweaters, booties, and hats against the cold. They pour water over the childlike figurines to quench their thirst. Mizuko jizo, which literally means "bodhisattva of the water-babies," used to refer mostly to miscarriages or stillbirths. After World War II, and especially in recent decades, however, the term has come to be linked more to aborted fetuses stranded on the banks of the river that, according to Japanese Buddhist tradition, separates the worlds of life and death. Women and sometimes men come to stand before these monuments to express their grief, fear, confusion, and hope of forgiveness.

Japan is not sundered by the kinds of debates about abortion that are common in the West. In Japan abortions are entirely legal in the first five months of pregnancy, and they hardly stir a murmur within society. There are no protests at abortion clinics, no debates about banning abortions, and no politicians taking stands on the issue. This state of affairs is also related to the fact that until a few years ago, politicians refused to legalize the pill. Although virtually everyone in Japan believes that abortion is a woman's own business, the silent mourning over abortions in front of mizuko jizo is striking in the sense that many women feel uneasy after exercising their right. And once in a while, groups of gynecologists who perform abortions go to a shrine or a temple to attend a

Statues of mizuko jizo along the street facing a cemetery in Nagoya. Jizo bring solace to the souls of infants who were stillborn or suffered miscarriage or abortion or some other accident that prevented their birth. Every August, Japan's cemeteries come alive during the obon festival, when ancestors who have died are believed to return for a brief visit. Due to shortage of space, cemeteries in big cities are facing a crisis. For people in need of a final resting place, the situation is serious. The space problem is severe in Tokyo, where about one-fifth of the population lives. Tokyo has eight cemeteries, but only four have any openings. In 2000 there were five applicants for each plot, and the winners were chosen by lottery. Most Japanese are cremated; the average grave occupies only about 1 square yard (0.8 sq m). But at Tokyo's publicly operated graveyards, even a memorial plot that size costs up to $18,000. The land pinch has inspired some innovations. Wall tombs are currently being used as a means to alleviate the space dilemma. Photo by P.P. Karan.

special memorial service to purify themselves. Three decades ago, more than a million Japanese women each year turned to abortion. Now Japan has only 300,000 to 400,000 abortions each year. Mizuko jizo are sacred signs in the landscape of a pervasive but silent mourning.

The Waning of Traditional Architecture

The dominant aspect of Japan's human landscape today is its manifest modernness. The nation has precious jewels from its past in various locations, as renowned as those in Nara and Kyoto, but most of the construction in the present landscape is similar to that found throughout the industrial world. Traditional architecture has been diminishing, and the toll on old structures has been hastened by both natural and human-caused disasters (Inoue 1985). In the past half century alone, typhoons, tsunamis, earthquakes, and fires have exacted a dreadful and recurrent cost to the nation of Japan. Indeed, few old societies have so few structures remaining from bygone eras. This loss has been accentuated not only by disasters but also by Japan's unparalleled pace of economic development. The Tokyo-based Association of Minka Commons Advancement promotes the restoration of old traditional farmhouses. Its project, which sometimes includes relocating old houses, is expected to play a big role in the preservation of traditional architecture.

In addition to cost, the declining number of *toryo*, the master carpenters who specialize in the elaborate carving and joining of woods in buildings (homes, teahouses, and temples) without nails or glue, explains the waning of traditional architecture. Toryo techniques date back to 300 BC and began to flourish in the sixth century, when wooden temples became an elite form of architecture. With the widespread use of nails in the nineteenth century, traditional carpentry all but fell into obscurity (Brown 1995). It is estimated that only two hundred master carpenters remain in Japan. The craft of Japanese carpentry stands at a historic low. Few new temples are being built owing to the decline of Buddhism in Japan. Wood is scarcer, too. Large temple columns come from large, ideally Japanese, cypress trees at least 300 years old, and preferably 500 or 600 years old. Most master carpenters today restore old buildings rather than erect new ones. Tools also assume an honorific status in the master carpenter's life. It is said that classically, master carpenters made offerings of oranges, sake, and rice to their tools and vowed each new year to treat their tools better, so that their tools would be kinder to them.

Western-style homes are becoming more popular in Japan, particularly since the Kobe earthquake demonstrated their durability. Whereas American homes typically stand for fifty to seventy years, postwar Japanese houses often survive only about twenty. In Japan there is little market for used houses. Land is the precious commodity—land prices account for 70 percent of a dwelling's cost—and many people routinely tear down houses after one generation and rebuild. "Imported houses" from the United States and Europe are riding a wave of popularity among well-to-do home buyers. Buyers praise the sturdiness of their construction, as well as features such as cathedral ceilings, big windows, and, for the very rich, an occasional two-car garage. In 1995 more than 5,000 homes were packaged and shipped from the United States to Japan, more than triple the number in 1993. And that does not include imported homes from Sweden and log cabins from Canada. That is a tiny share of the 1.5 million houses and apartments built each year in Japan, but it signals a trend toward houses built the American way, with imported raw materials.

Imported houses are popping up even in Tokyo's suburbs, where land prices are among the world's highest. Most families still build at least one traditional Japanese room, with tatami mats, but the rest of the house usually has hardwood floors, large windows, and doors that swing open rather than sliding into the walls. The building of Western-style houses has resulted in a startling spread of what look like upscale American suburbs in the Japanese landscape. Nowhere is that more striking than in Sweden Hills of Hokkaido, where the driveways are packed with Porsches, BMWs, and Jeeps. Design and durability are the major factors in the spread of Western-style houses made with foreign materials. And for people who are ready to move to Japan's more remote northern areas, the energy-efficient Western-style houses also offer a chance for that most prized possession: space.

The capital city of Tokyo, for example, rightfully regards its Imperial Palace with pride, but few primary cities in the world are so overwhelmed by modern edifices and retain so few symbols of the past. It is perhaps not too surprising that an onrushing urban expansion such as that of the Tokaido Megalopolis would obliterate most of yesteryear. But aside from the very modern Hokkaido, it is startling that in the small, outlying centers of old Japan, most of the buildings are modern in age, form, and function.

Traditional historic buildings with unique period features have been disappearing around Japan. The rate of demolition shot up during the "bubble years" from the mid-1980s to the early 1990s, when old structures were torn down to make room for new developments. In most cases there has been opposition from citizens groups and conservation advocates. Japan, unlike Europe or America, has little tradition of balancing modernization with the preservation of historic buildings. Often economics more than aesthetics determines what goes up and what comes down. In March 2000 the historic clubhouse and sports facility annex belonging to Dai-Ichi Kangyo Bank in Himonya, Tokyo, was demolished and the land was sold to the Meguro ward for a park. Featuring arched windows and an elegant balcony, the European-style two-story wooden clubhouse was built in 1937 as a rest house and guest quarters for Dai-Ichi Kangyo.

There are two ways in Japan for buildings to be publicly preserved. One is to have them designated important cultural properties. The other involves a system set up in 1996 by the Cultural Affairs Agency to register buildings as "tangible cultural properties." To attain such status, a building must be at least fifty years old and must boast outstanding exteriors or design techniques. The registration system was introduced because it was felt that too many historical buildings had been demolished in the past because they not quite eligible for designation as important cultural properties. Both systems have built-in tax incentives. But regulations regarding registered buildings are looser than those for designated structures; it is possible to remodel the interior or use a building for enterprises such as a restaurant or a coffee shop and still have it qualify to be registered. The number of registered buildings in Japan stood at 1,872 as of April 2000.

Frank Lloyd Wright's Myonichikan building in Mejiro, Tokyo, built in 1921, was saved from demolition as a result of efforts by people in Japan and the United States, including fashion designer Hanae Mori and professional golfer Ayako Okamoto. Myonichikan (which means "house of hope for the future") housed a radical school for girls. The building survived the Great Kanto earthquake of 1921 as well as the firebombing of Tokyo during World War II.

Urban Theme Parks

Urban theme parks have become a common feature of the Japanese landscape. The Japanese have taken an unremarkable Western idea, the penny arcade, and turned it into a futuristic phenomenon. Joypolis on Tokyo Bay is a good example of the theme parks found in most large urban areas. The gleaming circular doors at Joypolis rumble open for every visitor, giving the waiting crowd a tantalizing glimpse of a manufactured, game-driven future. Inside is a cacophonic world of flickering images and laser signs that emphasize what you are experiencing: "Cutting Edge," "State of the Art," "Stimulating." Many of the theme parks, including Joypolis, have a bank of photo machines that generate frighteningly realistic images of how one would look after a huge weight loss, a sex change, or hair loss. Couples can create photos of a "virtual baby," generated by merging their facial structures, after they have chosen the gender and race.

In Japan there is no concern for political correctness when putting together the software for a virtual maternity ward. And there is a wealthy audience accustomed to limited space and to moving effortlessly from role to role, identity to identity, machine to machine. Hiroshi Nakanishi, a concept designer for urban theme parks, describes it as a breed of fantasy playground that is the entertainment of the future. Japan cannot reproduce the huge theme parks so popular in the United States. Instead, Japan has created an entirely original space, which could also be transplanted to places like the United States. Whereas Disneyland gives the visitor a whole forest, a castle, and a river, the urban theme parks in Japan offer such scenes to visitors through their minds: through sound effects, images, and even smells.

The striking thing is that many aspects of the ultramodern Japanese theme parks have traditional roots. Even many of the New Age machines are based on old-fashioned ideas. The most popular games—in Japan as well as overseas—are killing and sports scenarios. The UFO catcher, a hit product, is a sophisticated variation on the original "goldfish scooping" contest of forty-five years ago. Freezing a frame of the timeless and turning it into an ar-

Field Report

Frank Lloyd Wright's Building in Japan

Wright's concept of a structure with a frame of wood two-by-fours, exemplified by Myonichikan, derived from the so-called prairie style of buildings in his home state of Wisconsin. It is a three-story construction with a total floor space of 12,486 square feet (1,160 sq m). Centered around a large hall, the U-shaped building embraces a courtyard. It is characterized by abundant pale blue and green tuff stone, cream-colored pillars and walls, and geometric window-frame patterns. The overall impression is of a bird that has flown down into a garden from the sky.

Frank Lloyd Wright had a profound knowledge of Japanese culture, and much of Myonichikan's style owes a debt to the symmetrical Hoodo (Phoenix Hall) of Byodoin Hodo Temple in Kyoto, seen on one side of the ten-yen coin. Japanese architect Arata Endo, who worked as Wright's assistant while he was designing the old Imperial Hotel in Tokyo, introduced Wright to Yoshikazu and Motoko Hani, the founders of the school for girls at Myonichikan. Wright undertook the design of the Myonichikan after hearing about the couple's education philosophy, which appeared similar to that of his aunt, who had also founded a radical school. In fact, his aunt's project in Wisconsin provided Wright with his first opportunity to prove his worth as an architect.

Wright's career can basically be divided into three periods. The first was his emergence as a young architect, which lasted until 1910 and was characterized by long, straight-line structures. During the second period, lasting for a quarter century, he perfected his ideas of "organic" architecture as seen in Taliesin, the house and studio he built for himself in Wisconsin in 1925. It was also during this time that Wright came to work in Japan. The third period, beginning in 1936, was characterized by structures such as the Guggenheim Museum and Kaufmann House in Pennsylvania.

Outside the United States, Japan is the only place where Wright's works can be seen. He designed the old Imperial Hotel, part of which was later moved to Meijimura, a museum of historical architecture in Aichi Prefecture, and the old Yamamura residence in Ashiya, Hyogo Prefecture. Wright made twelve designs specifically for Japanese settings, and six were brought to fruition. Sadly, only four remain.

Wright rejected the conventional boxlike structure and came up with a way to harmonize architecture with nature, as seen in his use of well-lit windows, gentle roof angles, and deep eaves. Some of these were clearly influenced by traditional Japanese architecture.

---

cade machine prospers in a society fascinated with games and fantasy, and which has a sense of humor that is a difficult-to-analyze mix of the subtle and the infantile.

Even karaoke, common in bars all over Japan, has its origins in the frustrations of the Japanese working day. It is everyman's and everywoman's chance to be Elvis for the night after a day near the helm of the world's largest bank or the second-largest carmaker. It is a quick escape act in a society in which children grow up under inordinate pressure from the family, the school system, and the office hierarchy.

As a result, Tokyo has more urban theme parks and game arcades than any other city, with at least thirty large facilities such as Joypolis. Outside the cities, the sprawling Japanese fantasylands include full-scale replicas of a Dutch village, Denmark's Tivoli Gardens, a Spanish hacienda, a reconstructed medieval German town in Obihiro, an Anne of Green Gables theme park on the northern island of Hokkaido, and a whole coastline of indoor beaches pounded by manmade waves.

There is intense pressure to devise ever more original machines for the game centers. The Print Club machines have been remarkably successful. One type provides a choice of thirty or more different frames and settings and produces a sheet of 16 to 20 thumbnail photo-stickers. These are swapped among friends and stuck on calling cards, schoolbooks, and mobile phones. Like any megafad in Japan, new versions of Print Club are already outstripping earlier machines, which have spread from the game center to the train station and the shopping arcade. Each new generation of machines attracts another wave of obsessive collectors who want the entire range of formats offered. One of the most successful developments has been a Print Club machine that puts images of celebrities in the photo, so fans appear side-by-side with one of their idols.

Aroma Club, a new machine, may be the next craze. It is an unnerving mix of hippy-hangover and modern technology. These machines quiz users to find the aromatic oil best suited to their mental and physical state. A customer chooses from six categories, including "love," "refreshment," and "beauty"; then the machine asks questions to narrow down the selection. Ultimately, it produces the appropriate oil for the individual's mind and body.

In recent years, food theme parks, featuring famous restaurants and offering popular dishes such as ramen noodles, curry rice, *gyoza* dumplings, and cakes, are emerging as a conspicuous feature of the urban landscape. Many localities have opened food theme parks because they expect them to stimulate the local economy. Jiyugaoka Sweets Forest theme park in the town of Jiyugaoka, Tokyo; Ramen Kaido in Goshogawara, Aomori Prefecture; and Akashi Ramen Port in Akashi, Hyogo Prefecture, are examples of the food theme parks. There were more than thirty large food theme parks in Japan in 2003. Namco Ltd. was responsible for the opening of eight food theme parks, including the Yokohama Curry Museum. A new food theme park has opened in the Ikebukuro district of Tokyo, dedicated to the wonderful world of ice cream. Ice Cream City, operated by Namco, has more than 380 local ice creams using unique ingredients from the different regions of Japan. In addition, Korean shaved ice treat, Turkish *dondurma* (a milky, nougatlike ice cream), and other ice creams from around the world are available. Shin-Yokohama Ramen Museum, which opened in 1994, was the pioneer food theme park. By recreating a 1958 townscape, the museum has attracted annually an average of about 1.5 million people, who enjoy eating ramen specialties from many parts of the country while immersing themselves in nostalgic environs. Food theme parks have assumed the status of a new kind of inexpensive leisure activity.

REFERENCES

Berque, Augustine. 1977. L'évolution de la Societé Japonaise à Hokkaido. *Science Reports of Tohoku University* (Geography) 27 (1): 1–12.

Bestor, Theodore C. 1989. *Neighborhood Tokyo*. Stanford, CA.: Stanford Univ. Press.

Brown, Azby. 1993. *Small Spaces*. Tokyo: Kodansha.

———. 1995. *The Genius of Japanese Carpentry: The Secrets of a Craft*. Tokyo: Kodansha.

Clammer, John. 1997. *Contemporary Urban Japan*. Oxford: Blackwell.

Foreign Press Center. 1997. *Japan: Eyes on the Country, Views of 47 Prefectures*. Tokyo: Foreign Press Center.

Inoue, M. 1985. *Space in Japanese Architecture*. New York: Weatherhill.

Ito, T. 1999. The areal characteristics of the residential landscape and its formative process in Sendai, Japan. *Geographical Review of Japan* A 72:357–380.

Kodansha International. 1995. *Japan: Profile of a Nation*. Tokyo: Kodansha.

Koganezawa, Takaaki. 1987. Recent changing patterns of "dekasegi" seasonal migration in South Yokote Basin, northern Japan. *Geographical Reports of Tokyo Metropolitan University* 22:85–98.

Lee, O-Younge. 1984. *The Compact Culture: The Japanese Tradition of "Smaller Is Better."* Tokyo: Kodansha.

Mather, Cotton, and P.P. Karan. 1999. Urban landscapes of Japan. In *Urban Growth and Development in Asia*, ed. Graham P. Chapman, Ashok K. Dutt, and Robert W. Bradnock, 1:402–415. Brookfield, VT.: Ashgate.

Mather, Cotton, P.P. Karan, and Shigeru Iijima. 1998. *Japanese Landscapes: Where Land and Culture Merge*. Lexington: Univ. Press of Kentucky.

Nitschke, Gunter. 2003. *Japanese Gardens*. Cologne: Taschen.

Suizu, Ichiro. 1984. The codes of Japanese landscapes. *Geographical Review of Japan* B 57:1–21.

Tanaka, Hiroshi. 1984. Landscape expression of the evolution of Buddhism in Japan. *Canadian Geographer* 28:240–257.

Treib, Marc. 1994. Osaka: Underground in Umeda. In *Streets: Critical Perspectives on Public Space,* ed. Zeynep Celik, Diane Favro, and Richard Ingersoll, 35–44. Berkeley: Univ. of California Press.

Yamada, Hirohisa. 1992. Regional differences in the land price decline in three metropolitan areas, Japan. *Science Reports of Tohoku University* (Geography) 42 (1): 21–37.

Chapter 5

第 五 章

REGIONAL REALITY

EAST AND WEST, CENTER AND PERIPHERY, OMOTE-NIHON AND URA-NIHON

Often Japan is described as a homogeneous island nation, but in reality it consists of distinctive constituent regions, each with a unique character. On a broader scale there are differences between eastern and western Japan (Nakamura 1980), between the seat of political and economic power in central Honshu and the outlying peripheral areas (Sugimoto 1997, 56–62), and between the Pacific Ocean front of Japan (Omote Nihon) and the back (Ura Nihon). These regional differences are widely recognized in Japan, and there is a particular consciousness associated with each geographic area (Yagasaki 1997). Kyoto, the capital of Japan for over ten centuries, represents western Japan; Tokyo represents eastern Japan. In the past, hunting and fishing played a significant role in the east, and farming was more important in the west. Today there are subtle differences in the language and culture of the people inhabiting the two areas. For example, food tastes differ: people of eastern Japan use heavily colored, strong soy sauce; in western Japan a lighter-colored and weaker flavoring is preferred. The soba noodles of the east are saltier than the udon noodles of the west. Western Japan records more cancer deaths; eastern Japan, more deaths by stroke. Traditional methods of pain relief such as acupuncture and massage are more popular in the west than in the east.

The economic, political, and cultural power in Japan lies in Honshu and is centered on three major urban complexes: Tokyo-Yokohama, Osaka-Kyoto-Kobe, and the Chukyo Metropolitan Area, whose focus is Nagoya. The shinkansen (bullet train) line and expressways connecting these urban complexes have ensured the status of this region as the nucleus of the nation. The area contains nearly half of the population of the country, and its per capita income is higher than that of the outlying areas. The regional differences between the core and the periphery are vividly expressed in the cultural landscapes and human geography of Japan.

People of Japan have long recognized a traditional regional division between the two halves of the country, the "face" fronting the Pacific Ocean, and the "back" toward the Sea of Japan. The Pacific side, known as Omote Nihon, is more developed than Ura Nihon, which borders the Sea of Japan. For several centuries the nation's western side was its front door to the world. In this area between the Japan Alps and the Sea of Japan, the Japanese absorbed culture and commerce from China through Korea. In the late 1800s, Japan promoted development on the Pacific side of the country. As mainland Asia's economy expands, Japan's back may again assume a dominant role.

On the basis of physical, cultural, economic, and historical factors, Japan is divided into nine regions. These are Hokkaido, Tohoku, Kanto, Chubu, Kinki, Chugoku, Shikoku, Kyushu, and the Nansei (Ryukyu) Islands (see fig. 5.1). Over the centuries human influence in each area has accentuated the regional distinctiveness. Throughout Japanese history these regions have maintained their identity and local distinctive character. For example, the people of Hokkaido, who remained outside the jurisdiction of Japanese central government until its incorporation in the second half of the nineteenth century, exhibit a relaxed and open-minded attitude. Likewise, the independent Ryukyu Kingdom endured in Okinawa for four hundred years before it was absorbed by Japan. Ryukyu had a close economic relationship with China, maintained an autonomous culture, and had only limited identity with Japan. From the establish-

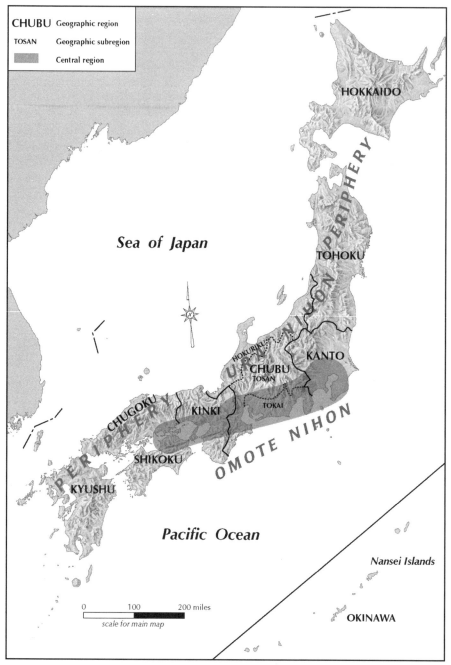

Fig. 5.1. Geographic regions.

ment of the imperial rule in the seventh century, the Kinki region expanded its hegemony over the other regions, placing them under its control. From the end of the twelfth century to the middle of the nineteenth, the seat of power shifted to the Kanto, but Kinki remained the seat of imperial power and a dynamic hub of economic activity. The cultural characteristics of the Kinki region are distinctively different from those of the Kanto: Osaka, the center of commercial activity during the feudal period, retains a merchant lifestyle, with emphasis on practicality, informality, and pragmatism; whereas Tokyo, the heart of Kanto, retains marks of a warrior culture, with significantly more formality and hierarchy.

HOKKAIDO

Hokkaido, northernmost of Japan's main islands, is the nation's last frontier. Here stretch the virgin forests and open wilderness that give the island its unique character. Geographically, it is a cold and sparsely populated region of mountains and hills (see fig. 5.2), developed only since the Meiji times. Several mountain ranges cross Hokkaido, separated by a series of basin areas. To the west of these mountains lies the Ishikari Plain. To the southwest of the plain is the long Oshima Peninsula, which is the area closest to Honshu and the first part of the island

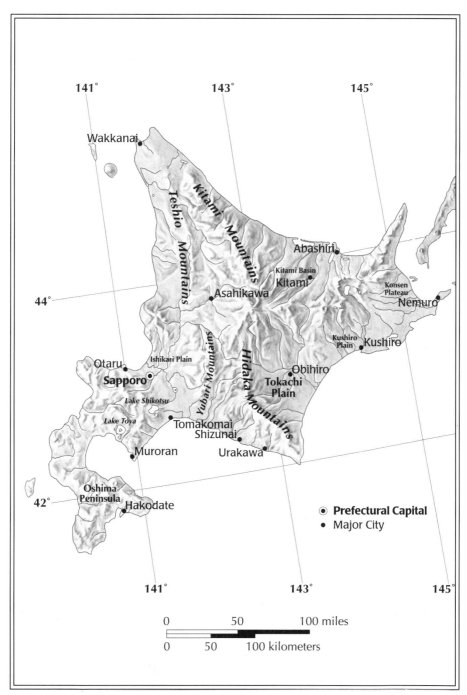

Fig. 5.2. Hokkaido.

settled by the Japanese. The climate is colder and drier than the rest of Japan. Hokkaido forms about one-fifth of the total area (32,247 sq mi or 83,520 sq km) of the country but is home to only one-twentieth (5,667,024) of the nation's population.

Hokkaido was inhabited by the Ainu (Watanabe 1973; Endo 1994) until Japanese settlements were established in the southwest corner during the Edo period (1600–1868). The development of Hokkaido began during the Meiji period (1868–1912). People were encouraged by the government to settle in Hokkaido. The early settlers had to struggle against a harsh environment, but they persevered, and now the results of their pioneering efforts are visible in the well-developed agriculture, forestry, and fisheries. About 10 percent of the area is cultivated, the most important crops being rice, oats, and wheat. The region has large dairy farms, and vegetable farming is important.

The Ishikari Plain (Ishikari Heiya) is the most productive farming area in Hokkaido. It occupies a tectonic depression. The most distinctive geomorphological character of this area is the vast extent of marshy alluvial and deltaic plains. During the past seventy years, all the poorly drained, low-lying plains have been reclaimed as paddy rice fields. Along with the reclamation, the meandering course of the Ishikari River has been contained to prevent floods and protect the agricultural development of the region. Wetlands along the Ishikari have been converted to agricultural use, providing fertile land for rice, vegetable, and dairy farming. The establishment of Sapporo in 1869 and the subsequent arrival of a colonist militia (*tondenhei*) contributed to the agricultural development of the region. The Meiji government established the Hokkaido Colonization Office in 1869 in Sapporo. In 1873 the government adopted a plan in which former samurai in the northern prefecture on Honshu (many of whom had been unemployed since the Meiji Restoration of 1868) were encouraged to settle in Hokkaido. By 1882 more than 2,400 people had been resettled. Around 1890 Japan intensified its presence in Hokkaido by recruiting some 40,000 people, commoners as well as samurai, to settle in the area. With increased population, the tondenhei system of settlement was abandoned in 1904.

The rural landscape of Hokkaido, which has large farms, pastures, and barns, is unique within Japan. The urban centers reflect modern layout and structure. Much of Hokkaido's mountainous interior comprises national parkland. With more than 70 percent of the area under forest, lumbering is a key industry, and Hokkaido is responsible for a quarter of the nation's annual lumber production. Kushiro is a major center of lumber and fishing industries. In the Muroran area there is a major coalfield, which is the basis of an important iron and steel industry. In recent years biotechnology industries have developed in Hokkaido. Manufacturing is largely concen-

A Hokkaido farmhouse on the Ishikari Plain. The main crop is rice; grain, vegetable, and dairy farming are also important. Fishing and forestry have long played an important part in Hokkaido's economy. They also form the basis for much of Hokkaido's industrial activity, including the food-processing and the pulp and paper industries. Photo by P.P. Karan.

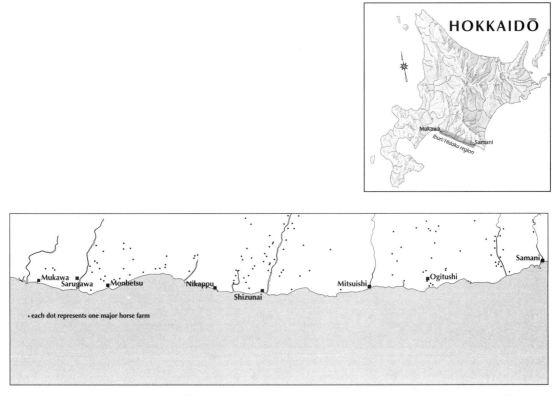

Fig. 5.3. Major horse farms in Hokkaido, 2000. Based on data from Japan Bloodstock Information System and JS Company, Shizunai.

trated in the Muroran-Sapporo-Asahikawa corridor. Among major towns, Muroran, Tomakomai, Kushiro, and Hakodate are relatively specialized in manufacturing activity, whereas Sapporo, Asahikawa, Obihiro, and Kitami have diversified manufacturing output.

A distinctive activity in Hokkaido is thoroughbred horse-breeding farms, which are concentrated in the Iburi and Hidaka regions (see fig. 5.3). The farms, much smaller and less manicured than those in the Bluegrass of central Kentucky, rarely include training facilities. Although many of the breeding operations are modeled after Kentucky horse farms—a farm near Lexington's sister city of Shizunai was christened Lex Stud by its owners—they look more like Wisconsin dairy farms than like any of Kentucky's blue-ribbon horse operations. Most of Japan's horse farms are small, family-run operations. Shadai Farm, Japan's biggest at 1,680 acres (680 ha), is divided into four locations in Hokkaido. Shadai's facilities are superior, but it cannot escape the long, cold winters. Because of the space shortage, training facilities are another problem. The Japan Racing Association began construction of a massive new 3,500-acre (1,416-ha) training facility for yearlings in the Hidaka region in 1991.

Japanese thoroughbred breeders such as Terya Yoshida have been buying high-priced Kentucky horses for decades in an effort to improve his own bloodstock. Because the Japanese bought the best horses, now they are able to sell their foals on the international market. Thoroughbred racing is one of the most popular sports in Japan, where fans wagered $24 billion on races in 1995. Total U.S. betting on thoroughbreds was less than one-half that, at $10.4 billion. Japan's breeding industry is the third-largest in the world, after those of the United States and Australia.

Shizunai, the center of the thoroughbred horse industry, with a population of 23,652, has more than three hundred family-run horse farms. Work on the farms varies with the changing seasons of breeding, birthing, weaning, and auctioning. Nearly 33,000 people are employed directly or indirectly in horse breeding and related businesses in Shizunai and the surrounding Hidaka region.

Hokkaido has three large wetlands, near Kushiro,

One of Japan's largest horse farms, near Tomakomai, Hokkaido. Most of Japan's thoroughbred horse farms are located between the Hidaka Mountains and the narrow coastal area. Photo by Cotton Mather.

Lake Kutcharo, and Lake Utonai. Portions of the wetlands have been reclaimed and turned into factory and residential sites, garbage disposal lots, and other developments. However, a multitude of plants and creatures inhabit the wetlands in a complex ecological system. The Kushiro Marsh, some 45,196 acres (18,290 ha) in area, provides a safe nesting habitat for the rare Japanese red-crowned crane. The present size of the marsh represents less than two-thirds of its original size. Although 66,375 acres (26,861 ha) of wetland in this area were designated as a national park in 1987, nothing protects the periphery from developers of homes and leisure facilities, or from the local paper industry's desire to fell more trees. All of this activity in the periphery affects the water table and the ecological integrity of the adjacent wetlands. National parkland in Japan is classified into three different categories, two of which permit development (in varying degrees). Only 16,037 acres (6,490 ha) of the Kushiro National Park lie in the area where development is prohibited. Only 19,091 acres (7,726 ha) have been registered by Japan under the Ramsar Convention on Wetlands of International Importance. Between 1980 and 1985 nearly 7,413

acres (3,000 ha) of Kushiro Marsh were lost to development, posing a threat to the splendid giant cranes that depend on it for their existence.

The modern settlement and colonization of Hokkaido has also led to the disappearance of the unique culture developed by the Ainu. By the end of the fourteenth century, the Ainu, an indigenous people, had developed a culture based on hunting and fishing. They built communities called *kotan* along the rivers. They sailed to Kamchatka and the far reaches of the Amur River to barter bear fur and deer skins for other commodities. Extensive contact between the Ainu in Hokkaido and people in Honshu started in the twelfth century, giving rise to increasingly serious conflicts. After the 1669 Battle of Shakushain—believed to be one of the largest Ainu uprisings against the Japanese—the Ainu and their land were placed under the virtual control of the Matsumaehan, a feudal clan in northern Japan. Their lifestyle and living conditions then began to crumble, as a result of overfishing, overhunting, and exploitation by Japanese traders (Siddle 1996; Walker 2001).

During the Meiji era, the Ainu people were brought under the control of the central government.

The thoroughbred sales pavilion at Shizunai, the center of the horse industry in Japan. Photo by P.P. Karan.

In the 1890s many Japanese were migrating to the north to settle in Hokkaido, and an 1899 law required the Ainu to abandon their hunting and fishing rights in exchange for farmland. Since that time rapid assimilation of Ainu into Japanese society and intermarriage have reduced the number of pure-blooded Ainu to about twenty-five thousand, or less than 0.5 percent of the Hokkaido population. The Ainu maintain that the 1899 law impugns their dignity, and the Hokkaido Ainu Association has sought to replace the law. The Ainu also protested the building of the Nibutani Dam to supply nonpotable water to an industrial complex scheduled to be built east of Tomakomai. It submerged an Ainu *chinomishiri,* or holy site. The Ainu took the matter to court, and the court ruled in favor of the Ainu. The Japanese District Court held that expropriation of indigenous lands on the island of Hokkaido to provide for construction of the dam without consideration of the impact on the local indigenous community, the Ainu people, was in violation of Japan's obligations under Article 27 of the International Covenant on Civil and Political Rights.

Hokkaido was hit hardest by the economic troubles facing Japan in the 1990s. A record number of Japanese companies in Hokkaido, including the main bank, Hokkaido Takushoku, went bankrupt. The bank's failure triggered a string of bankruptcies across the island. Hokkaido's unemployment rate is well above the average Japanese rate of 3.9 percent. Traditional industries on the island once relied on natural resources, but many of the old firms have

The Northern Horse Park near Chitose, south of Sapporo, attracts a large number of visitors. Photo by P.P. Karan.

faded away. Although some timber and paper factories are still operating, coal mines closed in the early 1990s (Cutler 1999). Agriculture is now the region's main industry, and dairy farming is its most competitive business. With one-fifth of Japan's arable land, Hokkaido is the country's food basket. The shelves in Tokyo's supermarkets are incomplete without a selection of Hokkaido Camembert. Yet Hokkaido's northern location means the region suffers from severe weather. Snow blankets the farms for half the year. Although the weather attracts skiers, around which a tourist industry has been built, there are no other large, growing industries to provide work: less than 2 percent of Japan's manufacturing industry is based in Hokkaido.

Poor communication with the rest of Japan has been blamed for the region's woes. Despite a tunnel between Hokkaido and northern Honshu, connections to the country's industrial heartland are poor. During the years of rapid economic growth, the government built transport links west of Tokyo, to Osaka and beyond. Air travel is expensive with overregulated airlines. The investment promotion division of the Hokkaido government tries to attract business to the prefecture. Biotechnology and information technology industries have established themselves in Hokkaido and are acting as pioneers in recent development. These industries are attracted by the support systems such as research institutes, various types of incentives and subsidies, vast open spaces, and a living environment rich in nature.

With little private investment, some 30 percent of Hokkaido's economy depends on government spending, much of which is devoted to public works. This mainly benefits the building industry, which in the past has soaked up workers unable to find other jobs. When the government started to cut spending, the effects on Hokkaido's economy were severe. Spending on public works will help Hokkaido in the short run. But it will take time to wean Hokkaido from government handouts.

In recent years the visits of Russian sailors to Otaru may have been the vanguard of new economic opportunities for Hokkaido and Russia. Nearly 30,000 Russian sailors come into Otaru each year. Twenty years ago, there were virtually none. The impact is striking. Near the Otaru harbor, Russian flags fly outside stores. Sailors hang out in front of convenience stores, and a troupe of Russian dancers performs daily at a local hotel. Otaru, population 154,000, is one of the several ports in Hokkaido that have felt the effects of the nation's deepening ties with Russia during the 1990s. Just 485 miles (780 km) across the Sea of Japan from the major Russian port of Vladivostok, Otaru is within easy sailing distance of eastern Russia—a mineral-rich area that resource-poor Japan has long eyed as a potential gold mine of trade. In 1998 the Russian governor of Sakhalin signed an agreement of friendship and cooperation with the governor of Hokkaido. For Otaru, this has meant an explosion of trade. The number of Russian ships entering the port of Otaru in 1991 was 370; by 1999 it had jumped to 945. The Russians come bearing seafood—crab, shrimp, and sea urchin—caught in Russian waters to be sold in Hokkaido. They buy Japanese goods, everything from used cars to disposable diapers, to take back to Russia. Otaru and other ports in Hokkaido could use the business. Like the rest of Hokkaido, Otaru has suffered severely from the recession and the collapse of the Hokkaido Takushoku Bank, the island's largest financial institution.

Wakkanai, the air and sea listening post during the cold war, is evolving into a modern-day commercial bridge between Russia and Japan. In 2003 Wakkanai was Japan's top port for Russian fishing boats, registering thirty-three hundred port calls. Wakkanai has developed as a staging ground for oil and gas investments in Sakhalin. More and more construction equipment, materials, and workers are transported from Wakkanai across the Soya Strait to Sakhalin to build a liquefied natural gas plant. As with most towns on Japan's far edges, Wakkanai's young people have been leaving and its population is aging. Since 1975 the population has ebbed by one-third, to forty-three thousand in 2004. Wakkanai plans to resurrect its old Sakhalin supply role to enhance the local economy.

Tohoku

Encompassing the entire northern part of the island of Honshu, the region of Tohoku consists of six prefectures—Aomori, Iwate, Miyagi, Akita, Yamagata, and Fukushima. The area is largely mountainous (see fig. 5.4). The frontier of Japanese settlement passed through present-day Tohoku between the seventh and the ninth centuries. Remote from centers of Japanese culture and political life, much of Tohoku has

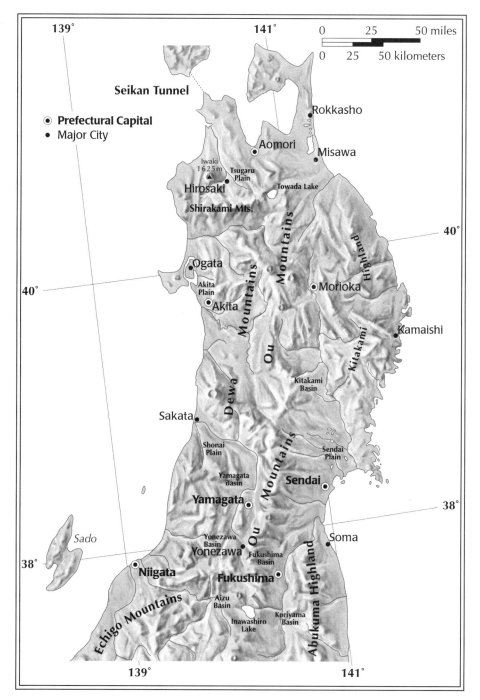

Fig. 5.4. Tohoku region.

retained its rustic character and is relatively little developed (Itakura 1982). The main area of settlement is in the wide intermontane valley between the Ou and the Kitakami Ranges, in other smaller mountain basins, and along the Pacific and Sea of Japan coastal plains. The climate is highly seasonal, with short summers and long winters. The region, comprising an area of 25,835 square miles (66,912 sq km) has about 10 million people, nearly 8 percent of the nation's population.

Intensively occupied land in the basin at the base of Mount Iwaki, about 25 miles (40.2 km) south of Aomori city in Tohoku. The region is largely mountainous, and most towns and cities are along the coasts and in the center of several basins. The area is primarily agricultural. Photo by Cotton Mather.

During the Edo period, development took place in some of the feudal domains. Cottage industries developed in castle towns such as Morioka (ironware), Yonezawa (silk weaving), and Soma (pottery). After the Meiji Restoration (1868) the development of Tohoku was not emphasized. Following World War II, improvement in agriculture in Tohoku was emphasized to increase food production. Tohoku has now become an important rice-producing area. The southern part of the Tsugaru Plain, around Hirosaki, is Japan's leading area for apple production. Many Tohoku farmers migrate to Kanto and other regions of Japan during the long winters to supplement their incomes when there is little agricultural activity in the area.

Sendai is a castle town that developed on a terrace of the Hirose River. The central business district of Sendai was occupied by residences of the middle-class retainers in the feudal period. High-class retainers' quarters were in the northeast close to the river. The *tera-machi* (temple quarter) and the *ashigaru-machi* (foot soldiers' quarters) bordered the northern fringe of the castle town. Many temples, graveyards, and shrines were placed on the highest river terrace from west to east. These temples' quarters served as a barrier zone for the castle town in the feudal period. The Sendai railroad station was constructed in 1877 when the Tohoku railroad line was extended from Tokyo. The area around the station has developed into a flourishing shopping and business district. North Sendai Station was opened in 1929 as the first station from Sendai on the Senzan line connecting Sendai and Yamagata.

South of Sendai lies the Joban coalfield. The Joban-Koriyama area is recovering from the decline of its traditional coal-mining industry. A new port has been constructed in Sendai to encourage the development of new industries. Akita, on the west coast, has petroleum refining and metallurgical industries. There are minor industrial areas in larger cities. Tohoku is not favored with large coastal industrial regions. Its dominant role traditionally has been as a food-producing region. Hundreds of illuminated stalks of rice are taken in procession through the streets of Akita during the Akita Kanto festival in August each year.

Faced with a declining population, local residents in several areas of Tohoku have established "farm villages" as part of the regional plan to promote tourism. The program was founded by the Ministry of Agriculture and Forestry in 1971 to encourage regional promotion by using agricultural resources in tourism (Nakayama 2000).

The harbor at Aomori city. Since the establishment of harbor facilities in 1624, Aomori has been an important shipping and fishing center. Its role as a terminal for ferries between Honshu and Hokkaido declined in 1988 when the Seikan tunnel between Aomori and Hakodate was opened. Photo by P.P. Karan.

Winter as well as summer tourism is an important element in the economy of the Tohoku region. Many ski resorts are found in this area of Japan. Photo by P.P. Karan.

Field Report

Snowboarding in Japan

Japan is home to more than six hundred ski resorts, and about 80 percent of them welcome snowboarders. Most of these are located in the Tohoku, Hokkaido, and Chubu regions. If not for the snowboard boom in the 1990s, the ski industry in Japan would be in serious trouble. Snowboarders account for 35 to 40 percent of the business at resorts nationwide, but in some places the figure is closer to 90 percent.

Although the number of skiers has dropped over the past decade, the snowboarding ranks continue to swell. According to the Snowboard Federation of Japan, an industry watchdog, there were about 1.5 million snowboarders in Japan in 2000, an 87 percent increase since 1997. Zao Onsen in Yamagata Prefecture, one of the nation's oldest and most popular ski resorts, has built a snowboard park with jumps and a boarder-cross course and started hosting several snowboard competitions in 2001. It averages about a million visitors each year.

From the famous *juhyo* (snow monsters) near the peak to the sulfuric hot springs steaming up the village below, Zao is truly a one-of-a-kind experience. The small inns near the springs and the narrow cobblestone streets offer a welcome contrast to the massive hotels that dominate most big resorts. It is a most culturally rewarding snowboard experience. Nothing can compare to riding the snow until your legs turn to jelly, then soaking the pain away in an outdoor hot-spring bath as the slopes loom overhead.

The Siberian air masses sweeping over the Sea of Japan give Hokkaido an early start of the season and also make it a powder lover's paradise. Japan's northernmost island is simply one of the best snowboard destinations in the world, host to national and international competitions. Niseko Hirafu, near Sapporo, is very snowboard-friendly, with half-pipes, jumps, and natural quarter-pipes as well as a refreshingly open attitude toward freestyle acrobatics.

For people living in Osaka and Tokyo, nothing beats Niigata Prefecture for convenience, but many other people favor the region's slopes over those in Hokkaido, based on variety and quality alone. Yuzawa, the town used as the setting for Nobel Laureate Yasunori Kawabata's novel *Snow Country*, feeds into several resorts and is just over an hour away from Tokyo by shinkansen. The area's most popular resort is Naeba, a sprawling complex of hotels and condominiums that plays host to 2 million skiers and snowboarders in the winter and tens of thousands of music fans in the summer, when the Fuji Rock Festival invades the slopes.

GALA Yuzawa, built by Japan Railway East, is the only resort in Japan with its own shinkansen station. GALA Yuzawa Station, just two minutes past Echigo Yuzawa, is also the gondola terminal. If one can get the gear on before boarding the train, one can be tearing down the slopes less than 90 minutes after leaving Tokyo. The hardest part of any trip to the slopes in Japan is the trip to the slopes. Aside from Yuzawa, most destinations require a train or two and a shuttle bus.

Recession and diversification of leisure pursuits have led to the closure or suspension of services at several ski hills in Tohoku. The early 1990s was the peak period for the ski sector. At the Tengendai Kogen ski resort in Yonezawa, Yamagata Prefecture, the number of skiers, which totaled about 300,000 in 1991, fell to around 50,000 in 2001. Accumulated losses for the area's economy snowballed to 600 million yen. In 2001 the East Japan Railway Company (JR East) withdrew its investment from the prefecture-operated Tazawako ski hill in Akita Prefecture, and pulled out of the Hachimantai Resort in Iwate Prefecture in 2002, citing decline in the number of customers as the reason. Following JR East's withdrawal, private companies and organizations have continued the operations of the two ski hills, but the main concern of whether a recovery of customers will occur continues. Hachimantai Resort opened in 1979, three years before the Tohoku bullet train services reached Morioka. Customer numbers peaked in 1991, when about 300,000 skiers visited the resort. The number plunged to 160,000 in 2001.

Distance and time have also kept skiers away. It takes about two and a half hours to travel from Tokyo to Morioka by bullet train, with a further hour or so by car to reach Hachimantai Resort. The Tohoku operators also lose out to cheaper ski tours by plane to Hokkaido. Among the ski hills that have closed between 1999 and 2001 are Nishine and Sawauchi (Iwate Prefecture), Kazuno (Akita Prefecture), Kitakata (Fukushima Prefecture), and Nagaoka and Sumon (Niigata Prefecture).

KANTO

Located in east central Honshu (see fig. 5.5), the Kanto region consists of Tokyo, Chiba, Saitama, Kanagawa, Gumma, Ibaraki, and Tochigi Prefectures (fig. 5.6), with an area of 12,504 square miles (32,385 sq km). Kanto began to develop when the Tokugawa family made it the base of their power. They raised their mighty castle at Edo, present-day Tokyo. After the Meiji Restoration (1868), Kanto became the center of Japanese politics, economy, and culture. Now the most densely settled region in Japan, it is home to 38 million people, about 30 percent of the nation's population.

In terms of landforms, Kanto may be divided into mountains, diluvial upland terraces, and alluvial plains (fig. 5.7). The plains occupy more than half of the Kanto region. The western two-thirds is low diluvial upland. The eastern third contains alluvial areas and deltas of the rivers Tonegawa, Arakawa, and Tamagawa. There are numerous lakes and swampy areas. The mountains are composed of alternations of gravel, sand, and clay beds, with a cover of volcanic ash called Kanto Loam. The terraces are made up of gravel or sand and clay covered by a thick layer of Kanto Loam. The alluvial plain consists of very thick and unconsolidated marine clay covered by alluvial deposits. Divides between the major streams in the center and the east are generally tongues of diluvial terraces extending toward the center from the west. The center and the eastern part of the plain are particularly flat and subject to flooding. Many of the rivers flow between levees and dikes. The Tone River, which flows through the Kanto, was diverted eastward to its present course into the Pacific Ocean during the Edo period (1600–1868) because of frequent floods in Saitama Prefecture and downtown Edo (Tokyo). A number of dams have been built on the upper reaches of the Tone River for flood control and water-power development. The Tama River used to be the principal source of domestic and industrial water for Tokyo. Water is now diverted from the Tone River to Tokyo by the Great Tone Dam at Gyoda to meet the increasing demands of the urban area.

The lower portion of the Arakawa River floodplain, which includes Saitama Prefecture, was developed as farmland to supply rice to Tokyo in the seventeenth century. During the past fifty years, the urban expansion of Tokyo has resulted in crowded housing in the area. Land subsidence and water pollution, which have been sharply increasing with the change from farming to an urban area, have emerged

A view of the Tokyo skyline from Shinjuku, an urban node in the western part of the city. The Kanto Plain is one of the most urbanized regions of Japan. This is Japan's most heavily populated region and is the political, economic, and cultural center of the nation. Photo by P.P. Karan.

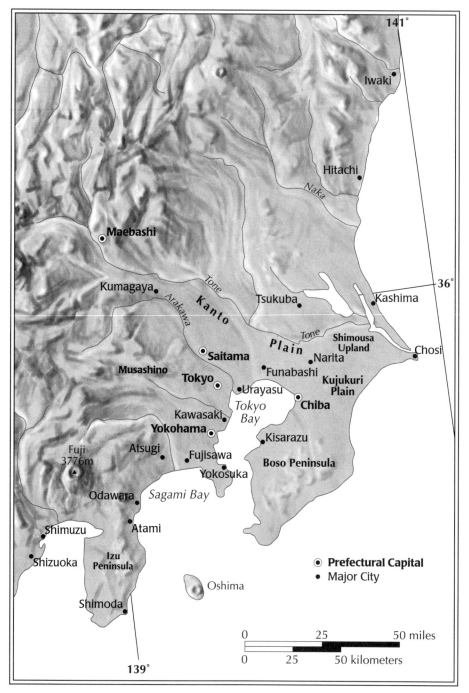

Fig. 5.5. Kanto region.

as important environmental problems in this part of Kanto, in addition to floods. The Arakawa River forks at Iwabuchi. One of the channels, the Sumida, was the original waterway of the Arakawa until 1928. The other channel (a floodway) was excavated over a period of seventeen years, beginning in 1911, to drain floodwater directly from the upper stream to the sea. When flooding occurs in the upper drainage, the water does not flow along the Sumida, but is diverted to the floodway. This floodway has successfully drained the floodwaters, and no floodwater has overflowed its embankments. The Arakawa flood-

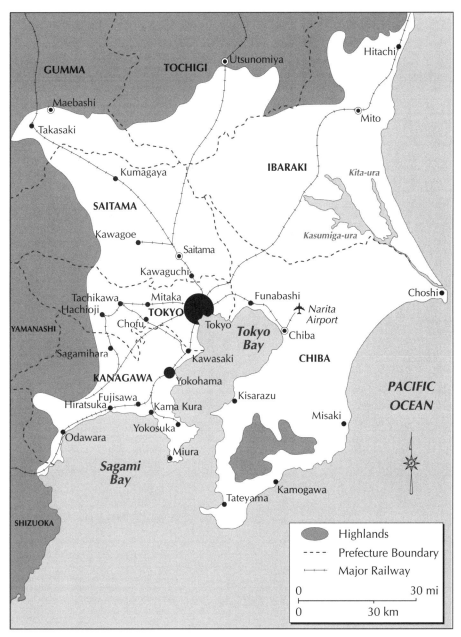

Fig. 5.6. Kanto Plain: Prefectures, major centers, and railroads.

way has two types of beds: low, narrow ones and high flow beds, which are immersed only when floodwaters are unusually high. The high flow beds of the Arakawa are utilized not only for flow control but also for other purposes, such as parks, golf links, and athletic fields.

Land subsidence was observed in the Tokyo urban area as early as the nineteenth century and accelerated in the 1960s, reaching a level exceeding 13 feet (4 m) in many places. Factories and residential areas have greatly increased the demand for water, most of which was supplied from groundwater in the 1970s. Because of the lowering of the groundwater level, the ground has sunk more than 3.9 inches (100 mm) per year in some places. With strict regulation of groundwater pumping, land subsidence has declined in the Naka River basin of Saitama.

Population growth has been rapid in the region

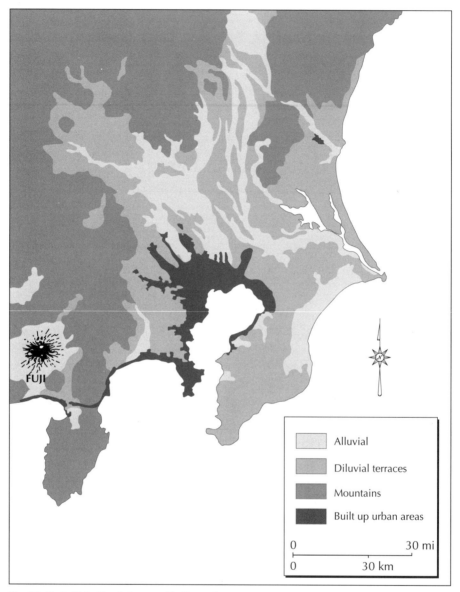

Fig. 5.7. Kanto Plain: Terrain types and built-up urban areas.

since the 1970s, particularly in the upper and middle parts, where residential districts are concentrated. The ratio of land area in rural use has been declining steadily since 1964. Urban land uses now encompass more than 70 percent of the Kanto region. The region is undergoing rapid change as land is reclaimed in Tokyo Bay and as the hills are turned into residential areas for the swelling Tokyo Metropolitan Area, which includes Tokyo, Yokohama, Kawasaki, and their suburbs. The Tokyo-Yokohama urban area in the center of the Kanto region is Japan's leading commercial and industrial area. Yokohama's Chinatown attracts some 16 million visitors each year—almost the same number as visit Tokyo Disneyland, Japan's most popular tourist attraction. Chinatown's origin dates back to the mid-nineteenth century, when Chinese immigrants began to settle in the area after the port of Yokohama was fully opened to foreign trade in 1859. Japan's new wave of Chinese immigrants is a breed apart from their Chinatown cousins. Not only do the majority of the 252,164 registered Chinese (the 1999 figure) now live outside the traditional eth-

Yokohama Bay Bridge and the port of Yokohama. Automobiles are waiting to be loaded for export. The Tokyo-Yokohama district in the center of the Kanto region is Japan's leading commercial and industrial area. Photo by P.P. Karan.

nic communities, but many also speak a different dialect, work outside the traditional fields, and are more interested in cultivating their own culture. Most of Tokyo's Chinese immigrants have settled in Shinjuku and Nakano Wards.

When Tokyo and Yokohama ran out of the essential commodity of space, they turned toward the sea. Landfills have been adding new dimensions to both Tokyo and Yokohama for almost four hundred years. Although it is difficult to imagine, even the Ginza was an unwholesome, snake-infested marsh before reclamation began during the Edo period. Land reclamation by refuse disposal has a long history in Japan. Since the Edo era in the middle of the seventeenth century, more than 9,884 acres (4,000 ha) of land have been reclaimed in the Kanto region. The Tokyo Waterfront project and Yokohama's Hakkeijima are notable examples of land development in the bay. Hakkeijima is 59 acres (24 ha) in

size, built at a cost of 55 billion yen. The city government leases 17 acres (7 ha) to the private sector, which operates the amusement complex known as Sea Paradise. Sea Paradise includes facilities for international conferences and hotels.

Although Kanto is one of the most urbanized areas in Japan, agriculture plays a significant (though declining) role in the region. Rice is an important crop on the alluvial lowlands and the coastal plain. Other crops, such as barley, vegetables, and fruit, are common on the diluvial uplands. Intensive raising of vegetables and flowers, poultry, and dairy cattle has spread to the Boso and Miura Peninsulas. Summer cabbage, fruits, and vegetables are grown in Gumma prefecture. Hideya Ishii (1985) has described the land-use changes and the transformation of the eastern part of the Kanto region in Ibaraki Prefecture into a major agricultural area producing vegetables.

A large residence fronted by a rice field and a garden in the eastern part of the Kanto Plain. In spite of its urban character, the Kanto Plain is a significant producer of farm products. Photo by Cotton Mather.

The expansion of Tokyo and its suburbs as well as the other cities has covered most of the arable land of Kanto. The increased urban development in the rural-urban fringe has led to the breakdown of the traditional rural community and its replacement with an urban value system. T. Waldichuk and H. Whitney (1997) have highlighted the conflicting attitudes toward urban development and agricultural activities in the rural-urban fringe of Tokyo.

Coastal fishing in the Pacific and in Tokyo Bay has declined because of vastly increased catches by deep-sea fishing trawlers and because of increased pollution and land reclamation in Tokyo Bay. Warm and cold currents converge just offshore from Choshi in the part of Kanto that juts out into the Pacific Ocean, making it one of the best fishing grounds in Japan. The hundreds of fishing boats docked at Choshi bear witness to this fact, as do the dozens of dolphins and whale species that populate these waters for much of the year.

CHUBU

The Chubu region, with an area of 25,783 square miles (66,777 sq km) and a population of 21.2 million, comprises Niigata, Toyama, Ishikawa, Fukui, Yamanashi, Nagano, Gifu, Shizuoka, and Aichi Prefectures in central Honshu (see fig. 5.8). The region is steeped in history and noted for its mountainous terrain. The Chubu region produced three men—Oda Nobunaga (1534–82), Toyotomi Hideyoshi (1537–98), and Tokugawa Ieyasu (1543–1616)—who had an indelible impact on the formation of premodern Japan. Oda Nobunaga was a military genius known for his extraordinary foresight. No mere warrior, Nobunaga devoted himself tirelessly to encouraging commerce and culture. Hideyoshi, who was the son of a poor farming family, in 1590 completed the work of national reunification begun by Oda Nobunaga. Ieyasu, the first shogun or generalissimo of the Tokugawa shogunate, ushered in a 265-year period of peace in Japan starting in 1600.

The mountains of Chubu form the backbone of Japan, with conspicuous knots of highland in central Honshu. Here the Japan Alps, which rise to over 10,000 feet (3,050 m), form the highest terrain in the country, although the highest single peak, Mount Fuji (12,388 ft or 3,776 m) is a dormant volcano unrelated to the fold mountains of the alps. Complex folding and faulting have resulted in an intricate mosaic of mountains, which alternate with small pockets of intensively cultivated lowland. In the mountains short, fast-flowing torrents, fed by meltwater in the spring and heavy rains in the summer, have carved a landscape that is everywhere characterized by steep and sharply angled slopes. Narrow, severely eroded ridges predominate.

Chubu is geographically divided into three districts: the Hokuriku on the Sea of Japan side, the Central Highlands or Tosan, and the Tokai district on the Pacific seaboard. This largely mountainous region is dominated by the Japan Alps and contains numerous volcanoes, including Mount Fuji (Fujisan). Some of Japan's longest rivers, the Shinanogawa, the Kisogawa, and the Tenryugawa, flow through the Chubu region.

Because of the central location of Chubu, the region has served as a corridor linking the Kinki and the Kanto regions. Highways such as the Tokaido and the Nakasendo connected Kyoto with Edo (Tokyo), and the Hokurikudo joined Kyoto with Tohoku. During the Edo period (1600–1868) many stage towns (*shukuba-machi*) developed along these roads. Today, the corridor-link function of the region remains important, with fast trains along the Tokaido and the Tokaido-Sanyo lines, and with the Nagoya-Kobe and Nagoya-Tokyo Expressways.

The Hokuriku area along the Sea of Japan receives heavy snowfall in winter and has high temperatures in summer. This area is Japan's principal single-crop rice-production area. Many of the fields in the lower course of the Shinano River on the Niigata Plain were formerly swampy and poorly drained. Irrigation and drainage channels were constructed and pumps were installed, resulting in high yields of rice. Both hydroelectric and nuclear power plants are located here. Japan's worst nuclear power accident took place at the plant in the town of Mihama in Fukui Prefecture in 1991. An estimated twenty tons of radioactive water leaked from the plant, contaminating the water in the steam generator. Several other small accidents at nuclear plants have fed a growing antinuclear movement. The accidents embarrass the government and have forced it to reduce somewhat its plans to substantially increase nuclear power capacity.

Kanazawa, a regional center in Hokuriku, is a famous castle town (McClain 1982). The city is keeping its historical image but also pressing forward to

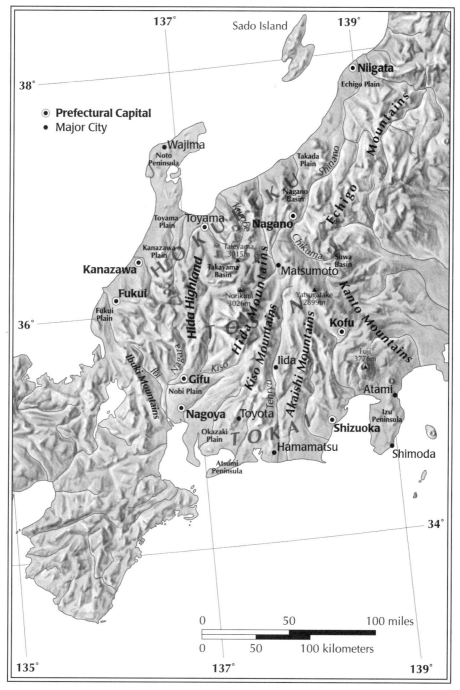

Fig. 5.8. Chubu region.

meet the changes and demands of the twenty-first century. Kanazawa has preserved some of its Edo-period neighborhoods, where old homes line narrow, winding streets, and the Kenrokuen, the private garden of the lord of the Kaga domain. To enhance the potential of Hokuriku, Kanazawa city and Ishikawa Prefecture are advocating cooperation with surrounding areas in the promotion of plans for a connected horizontal axis (Ishikawa–Toyama–Gifu–Aichi) and a connected vertical axis (Ishikawa–Fukui–Gifu–Nagano–Yamanashi) of development through central Japan.

Field Report

Japanese Tarai Bune, a Cultural Icon on Sado Island

Japan could arguably be called the most modern society in the world. Yet within this land of bullet trains and cutting-edge electronics there are bastions of old Japan that hark back to its isolationist past. While ancient temples rest in the shadow of high-rises and kimono-clad grandmothers ride on subways, an even older Japan still exists where the traditional is simply a way of life. From one of those enclaves of traditionalism, Sado Island, comes the strange little *tarai bune* or tub boat.

To most Japanese, Sado Island's tarai bune are a curiosity—like Dutch wooden shoes, more comical than quaint. These small, barrel-shaped craft, once common in western Japan, are now found only on one corner of Sado. In the small city of Ogi, tourists can book rides in tub boats paddled by young women in costume. But in six local villages out of sight of the tourist buses, men and women take to the sea before dawn in tub boats, gathering shellfish and seaweed with bamboo spears. Most tarai bune are propelled with a paddle, though in one village they have outboard motors.

The origins of the tub boat are unclear. Some believe that it was invented by cutting miso barrels in half (hence the local name of *hangiri* or half barrel). Others believe the boats developed from the wooden tubs used to feed animals or carry fish.

The simple, inexpensive tarai bune survives because of its convenience and its ability to navigate close to shore where the finest seaweed and shellfish are gathered. About one hundred tub boats still work along the coast of Sado Island.

Heavy-chemical industries are important in Hokuriku. Toyama and Takaoka have chemical fertilizer, synthetic fiber, and aluminum industries. Petroleum refining and the petrochemical industries are important in Niigata. Among the traditional products of the region are lacquered ware in Wajima and silk weaving in Ojiya and Fukui.

The Central Highlands (Tosan) consist of three mountain ranges extending north to south, the Hida Mountains (also called the Northern Alps), the Kiso Mountains (Central Alps), and the Akaishi Mountains (Southern Alps), with several peaks over 10,000 feet (3,050 m). Nestled among the mountains are important basins such as the Takayama, Nagano, Matsumoto, Suwa, and Kofu Basins. The weather in the mountains is often cloudy, so that one can go an entire day seeing no farther than 164 feet (50 m). On a clear day, though, one can witness the Creation. The rising sun lifts entire ranges out of darkness, the peaks dividing light and shadow like prisms separating colors. Above the layer of morning clouds the vertebrae of ranges—the Northern Alps and the Central and Southern Alps—form archipelagos that range nearly as far as the prominent cone of Fuji.

Nestled in the mountains are small towns and villages that have developed into major centers of tourism (Kamiya 1993), such as Takayama in the Hida region, which has lofty peaks encircling it. The Takayama Basin is set deep within the mountains of Gifu Prefecture. Rice is cultivated along the Miyagawa, and fruits and vegetables are grown along the highland slopes. The mountains have been good to Takayama, a castle town that began in 1586, although they never yielded good crops, forcing people of the area in earlier times to resort to making noodles and cakes—the staple foods—from chestnuts rather than the usual grains. The mountains could not supply arable farmland, but they were a treasure trove of trees, and their inhabitants were workers in wood. In the eighth century, every year 100 to 150 men were called to the court of Nara to build the capital's shrines, temples, and palaces. Today Takayama is a world of wood. Every second shop seems to specialize in it, exquisitely crafted into one type of article or another. The atmosphere reflects the colors—weathered and polished grays, tans, browns, and blacks of wood, thatch, tools, tatami, folk crafts, and firewood. Isolation has helped to protect the tradition and culture of Takayama. The development of railroads and highways has brought changes. The city would like to attract more high-tech industries like Hitachi's factory, which produces television tuners and video-recorder parts. Tourism is important, currently supporting 30 percent of the working population. The Sanmachi district, which was the center of the old town, is a major tourist attraction in Takayama. It is lined with well-preserved stores selling traditional wares, restaurants, and sake breweries, which can be identified by a ball made of cedar leaves hanging outside. Some of the buildings date back more than one hundred years. The Sanmachi area also hosts more than half of the twenty-three remaining fireproof *yatai-gura* or old storehouses.

Takayama is preserved by nature. Settled deep in the *yuki-guni,* or snow country, it often gets a foot of snow a day in the winter. Perhaps that's why the spirit of tradition lives on, not only in its aesthetics, but also in the simple nod, smile, and "konnichiwa" greeting of an elderly pedestrian. (Rural Japan has cornered the market on jovial old folks.) Although modernization has set in, this town's nickname of "Little Kyoto" is a nod to its resemblance to Japan's most traditional city. Its walkable downtown includes an old government house, which was used to tax citizens, entertain leaders, and torture criminals. Towns such as Takayama in Hokuriku conjure up a pair of words: *graceful* and *tranquil.* Nearly oblivious to the dilemmas of modern times, they foster a feeling of serenity. The simplicity of a circling water wheel or a rest on a bench on the cusp of a mountain range

stirs thoughts of tranquility. Balls hung outside of sake breweries and rows of dangling persimmons also mark years—and lives—gone by.

Noto Peninsula in Ishikawa Prefecture, a hook of land projecting into the Sea of Japan, has retained a magical, unspoiled quality that is hard to find elsewhere in Japan. Thanks to its inaccessibility, there are swaths of hilly woodland—not regimented plantings for timber production but lush jumbles of all sorts of trees and plant life. On the coast breathtakingly narrow cliff-top roads lead past charming fishing villages, whose only concession to twenty-first-century life might be some odd vending machines. Often there is no sound apart from the buzzing of insects and the swish of the waves. Of course, progress means Noto's pristine environment probably will not last forever. A new airport was built in Wajima in 2003. There are also plans on the table for a nuclear power station in the area.

The city of Wajima on the northern coast is famed for its beautiful lacquerware, an industry that thrived there because of the dust-free, humid climate. Approximately 2,750 local people are still involved in the laborious, time-consuming process of producing lacquerware. But Noto is dominated by its coastline, and as can be seen from a visit to Wajima's famous morning market, a large proportion of the people still rely on the sea for at least a part of their livelihood. However, they are by no means all fishers. A number of people produce salt by hand from the seawater. A little closer to Wajima is another of the area's most famous attractions, the *senmaida*. The name literally means "thousand rice fields," and it is

A farm and rice field in the Azusa River valley, Matsumoto, Nagano Prefecture. Agriculture is important in the narrow mountain valleys of the Chubu region. Photo by P.P. Karan.

a picturesque hillside overlooking the sea, covered with tiny terraced rice plots that glint like mirrors when filled with water in the spring. There are two thousand of them in all, and they are owned by nine families, each family working its own tiny plots. Therein lies a problem. The plots are so small that machines can't be used—everything has to be done by hand. The youngest of the current owners is now pushing sixty, and many members of the next generation have moved away, so that the task of preserving this historic piece of scenery is becoming increasingly difficult. Volunteers have been brought in to help out, but because they are not experts, the yield tends to fall off in the areas they cultivate. Another local tradition is the making of *ishiru*, a surprisingly delicious fish sauce. It is used in place of soy sauce to add a spicy note to pickled vegetables and *nabe* dishes.

Nagano Basin consists mainly of alluvial fans and the floodplain of the river Chikumagawa. This long narrow basin is known for the cultivation of rice, apples, and apricots. Nagano, the major city in the basin, developed as a market and one of the post-station towns on the old historic road. Today it is a commercial center for electric machinery, food-processing, publishing, and printing industries.

The Matsumoto Basin is one of three basins along the western edge of the Fossa Magna, a tectonic zone crossing the central part of Honshu (the other two basins are Suwa Basin and Kofu Basin) (Okuno 1987). It is flanked by the Hida (the Northern Japan Alps) and Chikuma Mountains and forms a long slender area with a north-to-south axis. The area of the basin is about 185 square miles (480 sq km); it is about 31 miles (50 km) long and roughly 6 miles (10 km) in average width. The altitude ranges from 1,706 feet (520 m) to about 2,625 feet (800 m) above sea level. The city of Matsumoto lies around 1,936 feet (590 m) above sea level and is ranked the highest city in Japan. It has a population of more than one hundred thousand. The basin consists of piedmont alluvial fans below the fault scarp and river terraces. The Hida Range to the west of the basin rises very abruptly, and many rivers flowing into the basin from Hida have built alluvial fans. The Chikuma Mountains on the east have a plateau-like flat top, and the piedmont is markedly straight in contrast to the western margin of the basin. The floor of the Matsumoto Basin is filled with thick gravel beds;

drillings made in the center of the basin so far indicate that the basal rocks are situated more than 565 feet (200 m) below the basin surface.

The area is known for horseradish (*wasabi*) and rice. The city of Matsumoto has one of the best-preserved feudal castles in Japan. Suwa is a graben basin, spread around Suwa Lake in Nagano Prefecture. The basin is noted for the production of raw silk and precision instruments. The city of Suwa developed as a castle town. The traditional silk-reeling industry was replaced after World War II by precision instruments, miso (bean paste), and woodworking industries.

Kofu Basin lies in central Yamanashi Prefecture, bounded by the fault scarps of the Akaishi and Misaka Mountains. The basin is made of piedmont alluvial plains of the upper reaches of the Fujikawa. Rice is grown on the floodplain, and grapes and peaches are grown on the slopes. Kofu developed as a castle town and post-station town during the Edo period. Food processing, textiles, wine, and crystal ware are major industries.

Karen Wigen (1995) has investigated changes in the historical and economic geography of Ina Basin (south of Matsumoto) between 1750 and 1920. During the eighteenth century the basin, with its regional center at Iida, was producing silk and cotton textiles, lacquered bowls, tobacco, and dried persimmons for the distant national markets. In the late nineteenth century, as Japan entered the modern era of international trade and development, the old economic network ruptured, and the population declined in mountain regions. The geographic transformation of the Ina Basin between the Tokugawa and Taisho eras is replicated in different forms in various parts of Japan.

The mountain villages of Tosan have been losing population rapidly since the 1950s. In some areas attempts are being made to counteract depopulation by pioneering grassroots resort development. Doo-Chul Kim (2000) has recorded how this kind of tourism development has led to an increase in visitors and related increases in employment and income in mountain villages in Nagano Prefecture. The construction of a highway network in the mountains of central Japan has made many remote areas accessible, and new freeways have had a significant impact on commercial development in Tosan (Hashimoto 1999).

Field Report

Nozawa Onsen, Skis, and Hot Springs

Nozawa Onsen is a resort tucked into the mountains of Nagano Prefecture, about four hours from Tokyo. It is a village of narrow, winding streets. Long before the broad flanks of the adjacent Mount Kenashi, a 5,400-foot (1,646-m) peak, were developed for skiing, Nozawa was popular for the curative properties of its natural hot springs (hydrogen sulfide springs with water temperature of 104–194° F) and culinary delicacies.

The village's maze of streets are lined with all manner of inns and shops. Nozawa has a population of less than 5,000 but accommodates 20,000 visitors, guaranteeing a variety of amusements and a range of lodgings, from ancient *ryokan,* or traditional Japanese inns, to modern hotels and less formal *minshuku,* the Japanese equivalent of a pension. The quaint communal bathhouses, called *sotoyu,* with steamy baths fed by natural hot springs that bubble up from every crevice in the village; the constant trickle or roar of water, tumbling through the culverts that lie beneath or alongside every street; and prodigious quantities of snow that blow into the area make Nozawa very popular.

The most interesting hot spring is Ogama. It spills out at the near-boiling temperature of 190 degrees at the top of the village, just below the ancient Shinto shrine. Since it's much too hot for bathing, this spring has been turned into a sort of communal cooking pot for the use of villagers. They bring baskets of eggs or big bamboo trays of vegetables to simmer in the steaming pools, as skiers tread through the rising banks of mist on their way to a nearby lift. Beside the spring is a row of shops selling boiled eggs and an array of pickled vegetables, one of the specialties for which the village is famous in Japan.

During the ski season, which lasts from early December until mid-April, Nozawa is alive with the rattle of ski gear and the clunk of heavy ski boots on the streets. At many ski resorts in the United States and Japan, the town is a good way from the slopes, but at Nozawa the first lifts start where the streets end. Nozawa gets over 10 feet (3 m) of snow a year, and the wide trails are well groomed. In stages chairs lift skiers to the top of Mount Kenashi, which provides a spectacular view of the Japan Alps on a clear day, and of the Sea of Japan a few miles to the west.

After a day at the slopes, Nozawa's streets start filling up with Japanese clip-clopping in plastic or wooden sandals to one of the thirteen communal baths. The baths are social places. Although men and women are segregated, their voices mingle in convivial swirls of laughter, teasing, and chatter, above and around the tin walls that usually separate the sexes. Many of the better inns at Nozawa have their own very private sets of spring-fed indoor baths. The baths are perfect for easing the aches and pains of a day of skiing and an ideal way to get ready for the excellent meal the innkeeper serves.

The rustic country cuisine usually consists of eight to twelve dishes. It is likely to begin with a whole chilled, cooked trout; a bowl of pickled lotus root; crunchy flakes of mountain potatoes; and a bowl of soft and creamy sesame tofu bathed in soy sauce. Next, there is a hot dish known as *oden.* It consists of a ceramic pot filled with a boiling broth in which there are squares of *konnyaku,* a translucent root vegetable; slices of daikon, a big radish; seaweed; tofu; a boiled egg; and discs of fried lotus root stuffed with fish. The oden is followed by a local version of *shumai,* a steamed Chinese dumpling stuffed with ground meat; a type of local broccoli in sesame sauce; a rich, warm bowl of miso soup in which wild mushrooms float; and some light, fluffy Nozawa rice, with more pickles on the side. Dessert is tangerine gelatin served in a tangerine skin. No meal is served without plenty of Nozawa-na, probably the village's most famous specialty. It is pickled broccoli, a thin-stemmed, leafy form of the vegetable that is often boiled in the Ogama hot spring before being packed in vinegar.

Nozawa's streets fill up at night with young Japanese visitors, strolling amid the sound of crashing watercourses, browsing through candy shops looking for gifts to take home, or stopping for a beer.

Throughout the Tosan district there are a number of ski resorts and hot springs, making this region one of the major tourist areas in the country (Shirasaka 1984). The Japanese have taken to skiing with the kind of enthusiasm they used to reserve for exporting video recorders, but in recent years the sport has been declining because of the economic slowdown. Modern ski resorts in Tosan are indistinguishable from their American counterparts, except for the language and the fact that cafés serve bowls of noodles and green tea instead of chili and hot chocolate.

Nagano Prefecture, in the center of Tosan, is a major fruit-producing area in Japan after Aomori, Ehime, and Yamanashi. Nagano is a microcosm of Japanese agriculture because it displays all agricultural sectors: rice, vegetables, livestock, and fruits. Among the fruits, Nagano ranks second in apple production after Aomori and is important for grapes, peaches, and pears. It also produces significant amounts of apricots and walnuts. Fruit production is concentrated in three main regions. The largest of these, the Nagano Basin, is centered around the cities of Nagano, Suzaka, Nakano, and Obuse and produces mainly apples, peaches, and grapes. The other two regions are a grape-producing region in the center of the prefecture near the cities of Matsumoto and Shiojiri and a southern region, near Iida city, that produces Japanese pears. Except for apricots and persimmons, which were put under cultivation before the Meiji period, most fruit crops, starting with apples, began to be cultivated in 1879. That is when the agricultural experiment station that had been established in Nagano Prefecture to encourage commercial agriculture started to import young shoots from America and elsewhere and distribute these to progressive farmers, mainly farmers of samurai families who were now jobless. The hillsides were not in use and could be used for fruit growing. However, fruit crops spread very little at that time and did not begin to develop until after the great depression. Nagano Basin experienced a boom in fruit orchards in the 1950s. The production of apples dispersed rapidly, and grapes and peaches were introduced in the 1960s. The cultivation of asparagus and *enokidake* (a delicate kind of mushroom) increased, and the Nagano region evolved into a region of diversified commercial agriculture centering on fruit production.

With the opening of Japan to trade, the export of silkworm eggs prospered, and by 1880, along with the rapid increase in the exports of raw silk, sericulture developed rapidly. In 1870 the Meiji government decided to establish a modern filature factory and invited French government employee Paul Brunat (1840–1908) to oversee the project. The Tomioka Filature Plant in Tomioka, Gumma Prefecture, was established in 1872 as a government-operated factory for modern raw silk production. Edmond Bastion, an engineer at the Yokosuka Seitetsusho, predecessor of the Yokosuka Naval Arsenal, designed the Tomioka facility. The plant started operations in October 1872 and had a staff of 300 to 550 female workers. It was established as a pilot factory to produce high-quality raw silk by incorporating modern engineering. The government took this step to improve the quality of silk after the reputation of Japanese silk took a beating in the international market. Since the last days of the Tokugawa shogunate in the mid-nineteenth century, the rising demand for raw silk had brought about increased production, resulting in cruder finished products. The Tomioka plant was sold to the Mitsui zaibatsu in 1893, then transferred to the Hara Gomei Company, and eventually absorbed in 1938 by the Katakura Silk Reeling and Spinning Company, which is now known as Katakura Industry. The filature ceased operations in March 1987.

In the 1870s dry fields were increasingly converted to plantings of mulberry; and the cultivation of earlier commercial crops like cotton, along with subsistence food crops such as barley, wheat, and soybeans, decreased. The city of Suzaka, in the northern part of Nagano Prefecture, was home to a flourishing silk industry a century ago. The period from World War I to the great depression of 1929 was the peak for sericulture, and the great majority of agricultural households engaged heavily in it as a major supplementary source of income. Some of the old silk warehouses are still owned by small businesses in Suzaka; others were donated or purchased by the city and are used as museums. Industry also shifted entirely in the direction of silk reeling, which used silk fibers as a raw material, and all of the major factories in the Nagano Basin were involved in silk reeling. During the depression the price of raw silk and thus of cocoons collapsed, and sericulture declined rapidly. This situation stimulated the diversification of agriculture; fruit trees first and then crops like vegetables, hops, and tobacco were planted to replace the mulberry groves. With the food crises of World War II, the mulberry fields disappeared even more rapidly, and the cultivation of grains increased.

The Tokai region lies along the Pacific coast between the Kanto and the Kinki regions. The Tokai area has a mild climate, and mandarin oranges, green tea, and vegetables are important products grown here. Since the Meiji period the area has undergone heavy industrialization. Hamamatsu has pharmaceutical, musical instrument, and motorcycle industries.

The paper and pulp industries dominate Fuji and Fujinomiya. Food-processing industries are important in Shimoda, Yaizu, and Shizuoka. Shimizu, on Suruga Bay, has petroleum and aluminum refining industries. Today, Tokai is renowned as Japan's major manufacturing area. It has the headquarters of Toyota Motor Corporation (the world's fourth-ranking automaker in terms of number of cars rolling off the assembly lines) and the Toyota group's companies and factories.

On the Izu Peninsula, inns and hot springs coexist with snack bars and crowded beaches. The 35-

Field Report

Lost in Time: Tsumago, Kiso Valley

It is spring in the Kiso Valley, and fresh cold water is gurgling everywhere down the mountain slopes to the broad river rushing through a maze of bleached boulders. Smoke rises from the traditional wooden houses of Tsumago, a former post town on the Nakasendo, the "Road through the Mountains." The Nakasendo, of which the Kiso Valley portion is one small segment, was one of the two main routes between Tokyo (Edo) and Kyoto. Many chose this way because along the Tokaido—the main route, still followed by the bullet train today—rivers that had to be forded were often flooded and impassable. All manner of travelers, from pilgrims to government officials and samurai, made their way through deep forests and over the mountain passes. Progress was difficult, so post towns developed every five or ten miles along the path, where travelers could refresh themselves and change horses.

Today Tsumago looks little different than it must have appeared a hundred years ago. A preservationist movement started locally more than thirty years ago, in part to prevent further depopulation of the village, and in 1969 the Japanese government awarded Tsumago a special landmark designation. Telephone and electric lines were buried underground, cars and traffic were banned on the main street during daylight hours, and subsidies were provided for restoring many of the old buildings. The concept has spread through Japan, resulting in many more towns so designated, but it started in Tsumago.

In Tsumago, the Wakihonjin, or annex to the Honjin, was the official inn for the highest level of daimyo traveling from their home provinces to Edo. Here in the family/sitting/dining room, each family member would have a place designated according to her or his status. The annex housed important members of the daimyo's party and still belongs to the Hayashi family, who trace their ancestors to the 1580s. The Meiji emperor is said to have stopped in 1880 to rest for fifteen minutes and have a cup of tea at the Wakihonjin.

Many of the old inns and houses along the road have been converted to minshuku, modern versions of the ryokan, or traditional Japanese inns, serving breakfast and dinner. Shops sell finely crafted household utensils and succulent sweets from the famous Kiso chestnuts, such as those at Sawadaya, filled with slightly sweetened chestnut paste.

Narai is near the northern entrance to the Kiso Road and has a more serious, businesslike ambience compared to Tsumago. Narai has the highest elevation of Kiso's eleven post towns, at 2,300 feet (701 m). Here shops still make the traditional bentwood boxes used mainly for *bento*, lunch boxes for the traditional Japanese-style packed meals. The Kiso Valley is probably the nearest real escape from the bustling Tokyo.

Rural and urban land use on the Nobi Plain near Toyota City, east of Nagoya. Photo by P.P. Karan.

mile-long (56-kilometer-long) peninsula begins about 65 miles (105 km) south of Tokyo. Its wrinkled western coast, jutting southward into the Pacific, is an array of dramatic cliffs and fishing villages nestled in coves. The mountains, which once hid political exiles, are dotted with natural hot springs that have been channeled into soothing baths at traditional inns. Izu is also well known for its excellent seafood and, in the wooded interior, pheasant and wild boar. Over it all towers the graceful symbol of Japan: the perfect cone of Mount Fuji, just a few miles across Suruga Bay.

Izu, like much of the Japanese countryside, can be irritatingly commercial, overbuilt, and jammed with people, particularly on the more popular east coast, which has miles of sandy beaches and some golf courses. The towns are often clogged with souvenir shops and snack bars. Neon-lighted motels carry names like L'Auberge des Blue Marlins and stand near beaches that can become packed with sun-worshippers. In short, Izu has some of the best and the worst of the Japanese countryside. It exemplifies the jarring experience that people undergo when they try to square the nation's sophisticated aesthetic heritage and splendid natural setting with the poorly situated power lines, industrial plants, and tacky commercial strips that mar parts of the country.

At the southeast tip of Izu Peninsula is the heavily commercialized resort of Shimoda. This is where the United States established its first consulate, in 1856, after Commodore Matthew Perry forcibly opened Japan with his imposing black ships. The one enduring memory of that episode seems to be the tragic fate that befell Tojin Okichi, a woman the Japanese offered as a mistress to Townsend Harris, the first American consul. As the story goes, Harris, a New Yorker who had helped found what became City College, returned Okichi after three days. She became dissolute, wandered for years, and eventually drowned herself, a result, according to legend, of the humiliation she suffered at the hands of the barbarian. Her memory is preserved at one temple, Hofuku-ji, with placards depicting the sacrifice she made for her country.

To the west, on the Nobi Plain along the Pacific coast, is one of the most densely populated and industrialized areas in Chubu. The Chukyo industrial region, centered on the city of Nagoya, extends east to Toyobashi in Aichi Prefecture, north to southern Gifu, and west to northern Mie Prefecture. The major industries are chemical fibers in Gifu and Okazaki, automobiles in Toyota, petroleum refining and petrochemicals in Yokkaichi, and steel and machinery in Nagoya. There is considerable agricultural development on the Okazaki Plain, with emphasis on vegetable growing for the Nagoya market.

Nagoya is a blue-collar city. Since auto manufacturing, shipbuilding, plastics, and machinery are a few of its main industries, on some levels it is fair to say that Nagoya's average worker would have as much in common with his or her peer in Cleveland as in Tokyo. Nagoya is Japan's fourth-largest city and boasts a port that is ranked at the top in terms of both volume and value of cargo handled. That does not mean that Nagoya lacks cultural destinations. There is the stately Nagoya Castle, which was built

A view of the Nobi Plain. Rivers Kiso, Nagara, and Ibi (from right to left) flow across the plain into the Ise Bay. The Kiso enters the plain near the city of Inuyama. The Nagara flows through the cities of Mino and Gifu. Numerous farming settlements (called waju) in the delta of the three great rivers of the Nobi Plain are protected by circular embankments. Photo courtesy of *Asahi Shimbun.*

The Motoyama section of Nagoya city. Nagoya is the political, cultural, and financial center of the Pacific coastal area between Tokyo and Osaka, and the center of the Chukyo industrial region. In the seventeenth century Nagoya became the base of the Owari domain. The daimyo family of the Owari domain was one of the most honored branches of the Tokugawa family. Today Nagoya is primarily a business and industrial city. Photo by P.P. Karan.

in 1612 and restored after World War II. Nagoya's aquarium features a stunning array of marine wildlife, from grinning beluga whales to king sea crabs the size of golden retrievers. Nagoya is also the birthplace of pachinko, the famous Japanese upright pinball machine game, and Ichiiro, the nation's best baseball player and resident idol. But above all, a population of 2.1 million people makes Nagoya a prime example of Japanese industry, urban planning, and urban experience.

When one leaves Nagoya, things change as quickly as the train cars move across the rails. The bulk of the Japanese population lives in urban areas, which means that although cities live up to their sardinesque reputation, once the city is out of sight, the country catches up fast. As the Chuo rail line leaves Nagoya's cluster of high-rises and towers and heads north, the buildings shrivel. Soon they are spread out, diffused among natural features of the land, and accompanied by yards and gardens. A glance later, forests, greenhouses, and rice fields dominate the scenery. Concrete and steel are just a memory.

Mino, the area comprising Gifu Prefecture, is the home of a variety of traditional and vibrant crafts. Mino silk textiles are mentioned in a document dating back to twelve hundred years ago. Mino *washi* paper has been manufactured for more than thirteen centuries. Mino ceramics reach their culmination in highly stylized Shino and Oribe wares. The cutlcry of Scki, following the tradition of the Japanese swords of Seki, is just as famous. But perhaps the best known of these traditions in the Mino region is the unique cormorant fishing technique. Over

thirteen hundred years, fishers on the Nagara River have perfected a technique in which they use trained cormorants to catch fish.

More recently, automobiles, aircraft, industrial machinery, and electric appliances make up the prefecture's industrial base. Gifu has recognized that the growth of information technology is indispensable for industry to progress. In recognition of that, Gifu is building Softopia Japan, a base for global research and development in information technology software. There are also hopes that a similar base, the VR Techno Center, now under construction, will be able to promote advanced technology research to meet the needs of the twenty-first century.

The waters of the Kiso, Nagara, and Ibi Rivers drain into the sea west of Nagoya. Because water levels are different in the three rivers, water often used to flow from one of them into another, flooding large areas, rather than into the sea. The only way to stop the flood was to separate the three rivers. The Tokugawa shogunate ordered the samurai of the Satsuma Clan (now Kagoshima Prefecture) to begin flood control work on the three rivers. The work began in 1754, but the rivers were not completely separated. When Japan was opened to the outside world at the beginning of the Meiji era, advanced technology began to enter Japan. A Dutch engineer, Johannes de Rijke, worked between 1887 and 1912 to separate the three rivers. It was during this period that the rivers were given the forms they have today. The basic work for flood control, such as strengthening dikes and digging out the river beds, continues today to protect the low-lying waju or polder lands. The Kiso

Field Report
Gifu's "Rag Trade Quarter"

Gifu has earned a name as one of the nation's three foremost centers for apparel makers, alongside Tokyo and Osaka. Its reputation stems from postwar years, when repatriates returning from Manchuria set up stalls in the firebombed area outside the city's railway station and sold secondhand and surplus military uniforms. Starting around 1948, used-clothing stocks were augmented with the production and marketing of ready-to-wear clothes. In those days, people were still short of clothes, so they sold well, and soon Gifu's ready-to-wear industry was a byword up and down the country.

Today, about nine hundred wholesale stores line the meandering alleys (collectively known as the "rag trade quarter") near Gifu Station. The stores, many of which deal in women's clothing, are feeling the pinch of recession. Some proprietors who are retiring and cannot find any successors have been forced to close. Nevertheless, the area has long been host to sewing companies and accessory outlets, so it has the potential to cater to the quality end of the market.

A new store, Rep Mart, which opened in 2000, expects to revive the reputation of the quarter as a paradise for wholesale ready-to-wear bargains. Rep Mart is a wholesaler making its core pitch to fashion-conscious youth. To ensure that its stock sells, the store's owner keeps clothing manufacturers right up to the minute on what's "in" and what's "out" in Tokyo and Osaka fashions. The manufacturers produce the fashions most in demand and supply them to Rep Mart. The Gifu Fashion Industry Association admits that some people are looking to Rep Mart to help spark a revival of Gifu's apparel industry.

The bulk of customers in the rag trade quarter's stores are themselves clothing store owners from the countryside. The recession has left most of them focusing on clothes for older women rather than trying to cover all age ranges.

Sansen National Park, at the mouth of the three rivers, demonstrates the flood control and water management in the area.

The Chubu region (Hokuriku, Tosan, and Tokai) has launched an intensive drive to become the country's most influential region internationally by means of a number of major projects that are intended to improve its industrial and cultural infrastructure. Projects on transportation, industrial technology, and urban development are planned. Chubu International Airport Construction Promotion Council has been established for the purpose of arranging an early opening of the Chubu International Airport, which is under construction off the coast just 18.6 miles (30 km) south of Nagoya. The 311-mile (500-km) Chuo Linear Express (a magnetically levitated train that will provide a one-hour connection between Tokyo and Osaka via Nagoya) and the second Tomei and Meishin expressways are among the other transportation projects under consideration as keys to further development of the region. Although Chubu holds its own against other regions of Japan in economic development, there is concern about the lack of labor in the region. In the 1990s the job opportunity ratio in Aichi was 1.28, compared with the national ratio of 0.88. The figure translated into 128 jobs for every 100 job seekers. The region has started attracting foreign workers from other Asian countries and from Peru, Brazil, and Iran. The major industrial firms and their subcontractors, national and local government agencies, local chambers of commerce, and private-sector lobbying groups have worked together to develop an innovative, dynamic economy, particularly in the Tokai industrial region around Nagoya (Edgington 1999).

KINKI

The soul of Japan dwells in the Kinki region (also known as Kansai). This is Japan's heartland—where the nation began, where the people defined who they are. With an area of 12,767 square miles (33,075 sq

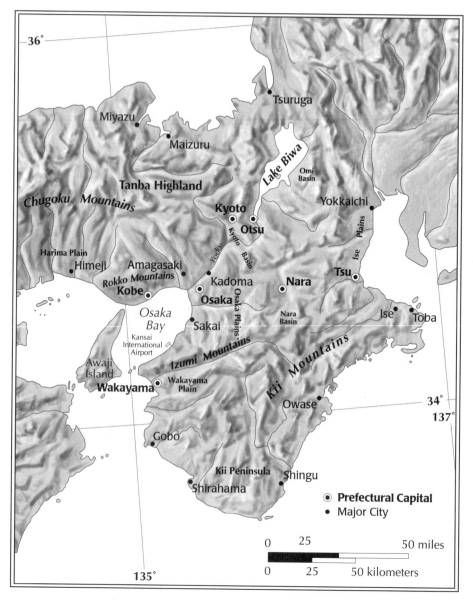

Fig. 5.9. Kinki region.

km), it comprises Osaka, Hyogo, Kyoto, Shiga, Mie, Wakayama, and Nara Prefectures (see fig. 5.9). To the east of Osaka, the Yamato clan took root and gave birth to the people called Japanese. Venerable Kyoto, where they honed their culture and arts, lies to the north.

It is a mountainous region with a population of 22.47 million, concentrated in many small basins and coastal plains on the Inland Sea, Osaka Bay, and Kii Peninsula. The northern part of Kinki faces the Sea of Japan and is colder than the rest, with snowfall in the winter. It is an area characterized by seasonal out-migration of workers to the Kyoto-Osaka-Kobe urban region (Nakamura 2000). The southern Kii Peninsula receives heavy precipitation and is relatively warm in winter. Osaka, Ise, and Harima Plains (Himeji), and Nara, Kyoto, and Omi Basins constitute major areas of level land. The Omi is a tectonic basin; part of the basin was filled with fresh water, forming Lake Biwa. The water of Lake Biwa drains through an outlet at the southern end of the lake, through Seta, Uji, and Yodo Rivers, and on to Osaka

A view of the area near Namba, Osaka. The Osaka Metropolitan Area dominates the Kansai region. Kansai is the traditional heartland of Japan— a densely populated industrial region with major developments along the coast of the Inland Sea and on the Osaka Plain. Photo by P.P. Karan.

Bay in the Setouchi (Inland Sea). The volume of out-flow is controlled by gates at Seta for flood control and irrigation. The mountains surrounding the Omi Basin have steep fault scarps. The alluvial plain surrounding Lake Biwa is narrow on the western side but wider in the east. Fan deposits from debris flow are found on the western side. On the eastern and northern sides, wide deltas expand along the lower courses of the longer rivers.

The alluvial plain has had a long history of cultivation with paddy fields; the boundaries of the fields were established more than a thousand years ago. They are in a rectangular grid pattern called the *jori* system whose lines cross every 2,146 feet (654 m). This system originated from patterns in early China.

The whole region is interlaced with a clean, efficient rail network that connects major urban centers. With some 14 million people in Osaka-Kyoto, it's hard to tell where Osaka leaves off and Kyoto or other cities begin. Osaka has always been the economic center of the Kansai. In this City of a Thousand Bridges (actually there are only 906 bridges or *bashi*), canals branch off from the Yodo River (Yodogawa). The Yodo ties Osaka to Kyoto. For eleven centuries (794–1868), Kyoto sat as the Imperial Capital—its written characters mean simply "Capital City."

The Kii Peninsula exemplifies Japan's religious roots and striking natural landscape, with the wilderness of its forests, waterfalls, and rushing rivers. At the center of the peninsula is Koyasan, a small plateau resting atop some steep slopes rising from the heavily wooded interior of the Kii peninsula and surrounded by a cluster of slightly taller peaks. A temple complex, one of the most sacred in Japan, occupies this relatively flat, elevated area, which is often shrouded in mountain fogs. For most Japanese it is also shrouded in the mists of legend and myth, associated as it is with a powerful religious sect, influential priests, religious wars, and some of the country's greatest warriors and rulers. Koyasan is the headquarters of the Shingon sect of Buddhism, which was founded with an imperial blessing on the 3,000-foot (914-m) peak in 816. Koyasan's central place in Japanese history and culture is evident in the famous necropolis, where some of the best-known figures in the country's legends are buried. It remains an active destination for religious pilgrims. Monks with shaved heads and wearing robes stroll the streets and the Buddhist monasteries. South of Koyasan lie more rounded mountains and canyons sculptured by several rivers, dotted with pleasant and isolated *onsen*, or natural hot-spring resorts. To the east, along the Ise Bay, lie an agricultural area that produces some of Japan's finest green tea and the city of Ise, home to the holiest Shinto shrine.

Over the centuries, Ise has remained a magnet for pilgrims. Every year more than 6 million people visit the shrine. Here, the sun goddess Amaterasu is revered as the ancestral goddess of the imperial family and guardian deity of the nation. Her shrine is no opulent palace, but a humble, unpainted structure made of cypress wood with reed-thatched roofs, reflecting the Japanese love of simplicity. Following ancient rites, in 1993 white-robed priests symboli-

Field Report

Kinki or Kansai

The terms *Kansai* and *Kinki* have generally the same meaning, but the people of Osaka seem to prefer *Kansai*. An overwhelming majority of Osaka residents refer to the region as Kansai rather than Kinki in daily conversation. In 1997 NHK radio and television replaced *Kinki* with *Kansai* in all the titles of its programs broadcast in the Kinki region; *Ohayo Kinki* was changed to *Ohayo Kansai, Kinki Plaza* became *Kansai Square,* and *Weekend Kinki* became *Weekend Kansai.*

Historically, Kinki referred to five provinces surrounding Kyoto when it was the capital of the country: Yamashiro, Yamato, Kawachi, Izumi, and Settsu. Kansai referred to strategically important outposts in ancient times: Suzuka in Mie Prefecture, Fuwa in Gifu Prefecture, and Arachi in Fukui Prefecture.

Recently the two terms have taken on new meanings. *Kansai* is used today in reference to an area that includes Osaka, Kyoto, Nara, Hyogo, Wakayama, and Shiga Prefectures, while *Kinki* defines a wider area, covering all those prefectures plus Mie and parts of Fukui Prefectures.

So why are the people of Osaka averse to the name *Kinki*? The reason is that it conjures up the image of an administrative district. The names of government offices, for instance, often begin with the word *Kinki,* such as the Kinki Local Finance Branch Bureau and the Kinki Regional Bureau of International Trade and Industry. The phrase *Kinki region* is also commonly included in the names of administrative offices. Thus, it is only natural for Osaka residents, who detest government authority, to prefer the term *Kansai.*

Kansai connotes culture and lifestyle. This is illustrated by such terms as *Kansaiben* (Kansai dialect) and *Kansaifu-aji* (Kansai-style taste). A growing number of large-scale projects have the word *Kansai* incorporated into their names, such as the Kansai International Airport and Kansai Science City. According to the Osaka office of Teikoku Data Bank, a private research organization, many businesses have dropped *Kinki* from their names. Kinki National Credit Company, for example, changed its name to Kansai Matsushita Credit Service.

A group of Kansai business and civic leaders have been meeting regularly to discuss Kansai's future in the twenty-first century. They have been working hard to boost the region's image, and as one idea in their "Kansai Charter," the group proposed establishing new entities such as Kansai-shu (province), Kansai-ken (block) and Kansai provincial assembly. Although the people of Tokyo are attached to the name *Kanto,* the feelings that Osaka residents have for the Kansai region are said to be much stronger.

cally transported the sun goddess Amaterasu through towering cypress trees to her new home at the Grand Shrine of Ise. Every twenty years a new shrine is built nearby and the sun goddess is moved from her old sanctum and resettled in the new one. The old shrine is then burned. The ritual in 1993 was the sixty-first recorded divine "house moving."

The Kyoto-Nara area was the political and cultural center of Japan in ancient times, but it lost its political significance after the capital was moved to Tokyo in 1868. Osaka developed as a center of commerce and industry during the Edo period (1600–1868). Today the Osaka-Kobe area is the center for industry and commerce in western Japan. This area, called Hanshin industrial region, is dominated by chemical and heavy industries. A port for trade with China during the seventh and eighth centuries, Osaka developed around the Osaka Castle built in the late sixteenth century by Toyotomi Hideyoshi, the national unifier. Osaka served as the entrepôt for goods, especially tax rice, for the entire nation during the Edo period. Osaka is the third-largest city in Japan, after Tokyo and Yokohama.

This heartland of Japan is a vast conurbation of some 22 million people, who live and work within an hour or so of the center of Osaka. Unlike the beehive of bureaucracy and international business that Tokyo has become, the three principal cities of the region—Osaka, Kobe, and Kyoto—are noted for their many small and medium-sized manufacturers and their networks of merchants. Several of these firms have grown to become household and even global names: Matsushita, Sumitomo, Kawasaki, Sanyo, Nintendo, Kyocera, Suntory, Nomura, and Nippon Life are among them.

In view of the Kansai region's history of entrepreneurial imagination, it is considered the engine room of Japan. The world's first futures contract—for ice—was developed by Osaka merchants some 250 years ago. The small but innovative Osaka Securities Exchange continues to handle 80 percent of the country's trading in derivatives, a business considered too tricky for Tokyo. Out of the 74 new Japan industries begun since the end of World War II that have been identified by the Nomura Research Institute, Kansai has produced an astonishing 59. They involve karaoke, video games, instant noodles, and the like.

At about $610 billion (80 trillion yen), Kansai's gross regional product is slightly larger than that of Canada. Its broad mix of textiles, chemicals, shipbuilding, steel, and engineering represents 16 percent of the Japanese gross domestic product (GDP), down from 20 percent two decades ago. The rustbelt around Osaka Bay—from the Mitsubishi shipyards in the west to the blast furnaces of Kobe Steel in the east and the former Hitachi Zosen yards to the south—is testament to the region's metal-bashing past. The textile mills scattered through Senshu farther south are a reminder of what North Carolina was like decades ago. Some trace the region's slide to the political climate twenty years ago. Both Osaka and Kyoto Prefectures had left-wing governors during the 1970s. Both were fiercely anti-Tokyo because of the ruling Liberal Democratic Party's venal ways, and both refused to go cap-in-hand to the central government for handouts.

To this day Kansai gets back as public spending only one-quarter of what it contributes in taxes to the central government. The taxpayer has picked up some of the bill for repairing damage done by the Kobe earthquake in 1995, but road building in the region has not kept pace with road building in the rest of the country. The slowdown has taken its toll on Kansai's business.

Over the years, local giants such as Sumitomo, Itochu, Marubeni, and Nomura Securities have largely uprooted and left. Most have moved their headquarters to Tokyo or at least now do most of their decision making there. This has been to the detriment of local business. For instance, with few around to set the pace, Kansai has been slow to grasp the significance of the new information-based industries. Only one major software company, Capecom, has made Osaka its home.

Although the recession sweeping Japan since the 1990s has hurt Kansai, so have several problems peculiar to the region. First, Kansai has been hit harder than other parts of Japan by the collapse of eastern Asia's currencies: Asia accounts for more than 70 percent of the trade flowing in and out of the ports of Osaka and Kobe. Second, the increase in consumption tax in 1997 savaged Kansai's huge appliance industry. Third, the recent completion of the world's largest suspension bridge—between Akashi, near Kobe, and Awaji Island in Osaka Bay—spells the end of Kansai's few remaining public-works programs.

Kansai's recovery will depend upon finding homegrown solutions for its problems. Hopeful business and political leaders in the area point to three new research-and-development centers being established by the private sector in partnership with local government to alleviate the region's paucity of high-tech innovation. They want to see the grimy jobs lost in steel, shipbuilding, chemicals, and textiles replaced with something better. The region's problems are structural and would exist even if the rest of Japan were thriving, but of course the current national recession is making the region's troubles even worse. Yet in Kansai, the economic forces sweeping Japan are providing a stimulus for change.

Osaka: The Hub of Kansai

Osaka and Tokyo are frequently compared. The two cities lie about 370 miles (600 km) apart, the former in western Japan and the latter in eastern Japan, but their differences are greater than the physical distance suggests. It is widely held, for example, that large corporations are based in Tokyo, whereas small companies dominate the business of Osaka. People often comment that Tokyoites are indifferent to others, whereas Osakans are frank and sociable. The language of Tokyoites is considered polite, that of Osakans crude. Tokyoites are aloof, Osakans pushy.

Fig. 5.10. Underworld syndicates. Based on data from the *Daily Yomiuri* (Tokyo), 2000.

Tokyoites live a sophisticated life; Osakans are flashy. And so on. But what is Osaka really like?

Osaka has a lingering image problem, caused mostly by the fact that it lies in a shadow cast by the national capital, Tokyo. Osaka has thrived as a port and leading center for more than 2,000 years, and the Kansai area has for most of that time been the center of Japan's political, economic, and cultural life. But ever since Tokyo was established as the nation's capital, more than 135 years ago, Osaka has been losing ground. The trend has been accelerated in recent years with the rise of one of the most powerful political and governmental bureaucracies in the world, forcing anyone doing business in Japan to look to the nation's capital. Half of the time Osaka businessmen are in Tokyo negotiating over budgets or trying to get a waiver on some regulation, because all the power lies in Tokyo. Although Osaka was the founding place for Japan's leading trading and manufacturing companies, many have relocated their headquarters to Tokyo, where the action is.

Osakans emphasize their distinctive identity. The culture of Osaka took its basic shape from commercial development (McClain and Osamu 1999). In subtle ways this city, with its glistening canals, wide thoroughfares lined with yellow ginkgo trees, and its bustling crowds of shoppers, even feels different from Tokyo. Osaka people say that because the city is dominated by its business culture, the crowds are noisier, the shoppers are more impatient and price-conscious, and even the organized-crime syndicates are tougher than elsewhere in Japan (see fig. 5.10). Osaka people are also known for their talkativeness. No wonder Osaka was the birthplace of such narrative arts as *manzai* (fast-talking comedy duos) and *rakugo,* or storytelling (Yamaguchi 2002).

Osaka Castle, built by Toyotomi Hideyoshi (1536–98), together with the surrounding park and garden, is the focal point for this ancient city. To the northwest of the park, across the Hiranogawa, lie the skyscrapers of Osaka's business district, creating a startling contrast of old and new. The space between Midosuji and Sakaisuji Streets, on the banks of Dotombori, the canal that cuts east to west

Field Report
Airin, an Osaka Neighborhood, and Yakuza

On the surface, most Japanese view their country as a classless society prizing harmony and consensus among its many contending forces. Once in a while, however, stresses, conflicts, and antisocial behavior are exposed underneath the placid exterior.

In 1990 police officers battled more than a thousand rock-throwing rioters in Airin, an Osaka neighborhood. Several buildings, including the railway depot, were burned, and about two hundred people were injured in the worst rioting in Japan in nearly twenty-five years. The area is quiet now, but violence may recur because little has been done about the police harassment and corruption that is at the heart of the grievances of the neighborhood.

Most of Japan's major cities have neighborhoods of grizzled laborers and derelicts living in ten-dollar-a-night flophouses, with grimy back streets that reek of urine and alcohol. But the 1990 riots made Airin a new symbol of the grim underside of Japan's economic boom. Airin is one of the highest-crime districts in Japan, a place where organized gangs flourish and police power is everywhere. In Airin, crime syndicates, known as *yakuza*, have forty-five known storefront offices, from which they run gambling operations, extortion schemes, and businesses that supply laborers to construction companies in Osaka.

Airin residents say the police never arrest the gangsters themselves when they carry out periodic crackdowns on gangster-run gambling operations, because the police are making money off the crimes they are supposed to control. The Airin neighborhood has been a troubled area for decades. The Osaka government has established myriad social welfare programs for the derelicts and laborers in the neighborhood. Almost all the ramshackle wooden buildings were razed, re-placed by multistory hotels with televisions and air conditioning. And in an effort to push the yakuza out of the labor business, a government center was set up where companies could come to recruit people for construction work in the city's development boom.

As the Japanese economy has grown, the day laborers' living standard has risen, but they are still doing the kind of jobs other people don't like to do. These workers don't really know how to control their budgets, and they tend to spend everything they earn on gambling or alcohol. They have no families, and they feel isolated, deserted, and alienated from society.

Despite the government programs, there is no sign of declining yakuza influence. There are more than 88,000 gangsters in Japan, belonging to 3,305 gangs, and their aggregate income has skyrocketed to more than $10 billion a year. Osaka is the center of Japanese organized crime, which is dominated by the Yamaguchi syndicate. Gang warfare ebbs and flows, but tempers smolder steadily in Airin.

The gang crime syndicates such as the Yamaguchi-gumi (based in Kobe) and the Kyokutokai (based in Tokyo) earn money through protection rackets, control over street vendors, and other activities. Gangland battles flare up as one group attempts to expand its activities into the territory of others (see fig. 5.11). The 1992 Antigang Law has failed to put down the violent rivalry. Many of Japan's yakuza gangs obtain funds by just charging exorbitant prices for goods and services they sell. Citizens often pay the asked amount because of the potential for violence if they refuse. Certain gang groups have turned to stock investments and running companies for new revenues. These gang members sport business cards and operate offices with their gang insignia proudly displayed.

through southern Osaka, is the distinctive Namba entertainment retail district. A second entertainment and business district is found in north Osaka around the terminal station at Umeda. Both have more than three hundred years of history and are often the setting for songs, plays, and novels. Shin-Umeda City is a complex to the northwest of Osaka Station that opened in 1993. Down the Okawa River on the coast is Osaka's port, Tenpozan. Another distinguishing factor is the role that underground malls play. Many of the city's restaurants, retail shops, and amusement spots are located underground.

Osaka's commercial prosperity led to the emergence of Ryotei, a restaurant with impeccable cuisine. It is also from Osaka that such cheap fare as *okonomiyaki* (a savory pancake of flour, eggs, and water smothered to taste in vegetables, meat, and fish) and *takoyaki* (balls of flour, eggs, and water stuffed with vegetables and chunks of octopus meat) got its start. It is fitting that Osaka is famous for this kind of traditional fast food, whereas Kyoto, the old cultural and imperial capital fifty miles away, developed a much more exquisite and delicate cuisine that can take hours to present and eat.

Although Osaka is trying to lure businesses and people back from Tokyo by proclaiming itself as a less expensive, more livable environment, many worry that it is becoming more and more like Tokyo every year. The new Kansai International Airport is a cherished centerpiece of the drive to revitalize Kansai.

A major boost to the economy of the Osaka region in the long run should come from the new Kansai International Airport (Jain 1995), built on a 1,300-acre (526-ha) artificial island in Osaka Bay. It was completed in 1994 after nearly seven years of construction. It is Japan's first twenty-four-hour airport, allowing leeway on arrival and departure times for flights connecting with locations in different time zones in Europe and North America. Out of deference to local residents, the airports at Tokyo are closed from 11 p.m. to 7 a.m., and the old Osaka airport is closed from 9 p.m. to 7 a.m. The new Kansai airport is able to avoid this problem by routing all takeoffs and landings over the sea—well away from the residents of Osaka, Kobe, and the surrounding communities. Built at a cost of $17 billion, it is the most expensive airport in the world. To cover the cost, the airport charges the highest rents, food prices, and landing fees in the world.

The airport is involved in a nasty conflict between central government bureaucrats and the local business community. The question is, Who should pay for running it? The locals say the central government should pay, since the project is expected to attract a great deal of commerce, and thus tax revenues. The government—especially the Finance Ministry—has insisted that the users must bear the costs. Despite this dispute, there is at least one thing everyone agrees on: it is Japan's most elegant architectural wonder, despite the fact that the airport is sinking much faster

Fig. 5.11. Gangland battle sites. Based on data from the *Daily Yomiuri* (Tokyo), 2000.

than expected. It was originally estimated that it would settle no more than 11.5 meters (38 ft) over fifty years. The airport had already sunk that much by December 1999. Sinkage is worst around the island's center, where the main airport facilities are situated. Of the airport's seventeen monitoring sites, five, including the terminal and part of its main runway, have reached or exceeded their fifty-year sinking projection. The airport officials say the sinkage is expected to slow and that it will not compromise the airport's future.

In 1992 a special law was enacted for the development of Osaka Bay. The law is designed to ensure systematic development of business, academic, housing, and leisure facilities in the area, while giving full consideration to environmental protection. In addition to boosting the local economy, the development plan of Osaka Bay is expected to become a model of well-balanced development of national lands and serve as a first step toward decentralization of power and cooperation among local governments. The centralization of government functions in Tokyo has been under fire for decades. The experiment with decentralization of power and cooperation among seven prefectures in Osaka Bay and the surrounding area is most appropriate, because the region includes many areas of historic, cultural, and economic importance. It also contains major cities known for their independent spirit, such as Kyoto, Osaka, and Kobe. The prefectural governors are required to work out development policies in consultation with local organizations such as the Osaka Bay Area Development Organization, which comprises local governments, businesses, and academic institutions. This means that the governors will seek a broad regional view for growth and development beyond the narrow boundaries of a single prefecture.

Kobe

Kobe ranks second in importance as a port, after Yokohama. It is one of the largest container ports in the world. Overlooking Osaka Bay and sheltered on the north by the Rokko Mountains, Kobe has developed as a major urban area. Only limited space is available for development, and residential areas have been built on the steep slopes at the foot of the mountains. Kobe is forging ahead with futuristic blueprints for the development of its once-grimy waterfront. The plan for transforming the Kobe waterfront is

simple. Carve up a few mountains, dump them in the bay, and put up on the resulting land some of the most sophisticated office and residential buildings in the world. Kobe insulated itself from the bursting of the bubble economy of the 1980s by resisting the temptation to count on collecting inflated rents to recoup money spent on massive projects. So, although Kobe's real estate prices have fallen along with those of other urban areas, contracts for the city's massive Rokko Island project remained viable in the 1990s. Kobe's biggest problem is the land shortage that makes building huge islands in the sea seem sensible. During World War II Kobe was laid to waste by firebombs and was hurriedly rebuilt afterward in a hodgepodge of cul de sacs, winding alleys, and tiny homes and shops. Kobe began planning for transforming the heavily industrialized city in the 1970s, when it became clear that the steel and shipbuilding industries were destined to decline. Kobe built an 8.75-mile (14.1-km) conveyor belt to transport to the bay earth and stones from mountains flattened for inland suburbs. Port Island, a 1,076-acre (435-ha) reclamation project finished in 1981, was created to provide land for housing, government offices, and modernized port facilities. About 40 percent of Kobe's revenue still comes from activities related to shipping. Kobe's next big project—1,432-acre (580-ha) Rokko Island, which opened in 1992—includes a water amusement park, moderate-income and luxury housing, a five-star hotel, and a shopping center.

Nara

Nara, located in a basin, was the site of the Yamato Court, which unified Japan between the fourth and the seventh centuries (see fig. 5.12). The city of Nara was the country's capital between 710 and 794. Nara has a population of 300,000, but since the boundaries of the city enclose 81 square miles (210 sq km), it embraces rice fields, orchards, small mountains, and part of a national park as well as temples, shrines, and dwellings. The gentle hills of Yamato surrounding Nara today are the setting where a thousand years of Japanese art and literature were produced. Vermillion-pillared, tile-roofed temples rose by the score within the orderly grid of streets. The new imperial capital, planned along the lines of the Chinese capital at Chang'an (modern Xi'an), blossomed twelve hundred years ago into a metropolis of 200,000 in-

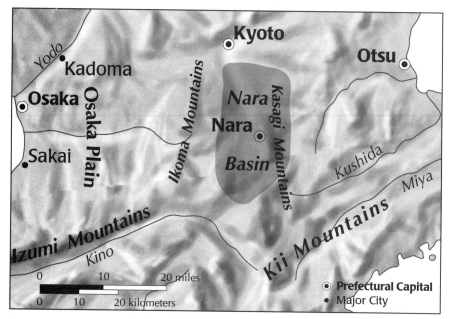

Fig. 5.12. Nara Basin.

habitants, of whom perhaps 20,000 formed an elite society centered on the imperial court. Among Nara's most impressive structures is the great temple of Todaiji, completed in the mid-eighth century. The dedication of the Great Buddha image, 71 feet (21.6 m) high, established Buddhism as the state religion over the Shinto faith. Todaiji's Great Buddha Hall, though rebuilt in 1700 to only two-thirds its original size, remains the largest wooden building in the world. But it is not, in the end, the monumental Nara that is most appealing.

Nearly 15 million tourists visit Nara each year. Probably most of its inhabitants rely, directly or indirectly, on tourism for a living. In the narrow, quiet streets and lanes away from the Todaiji Temple, crowded with tour buses, the hundreds of schoolgirls in identical navy blue uniforms and white socks, the souvenir shops selling pagodas and miniature Great Buddhas, Nara is a small town quietly going about its own small business.

Although Nara's history is ancient, the town as we know it today took shape during the sixteenth century; the layout and names of districts and streets were probably fixed when the Tokugawa shogunate established an administrative office here in the first half of the seventeenth century. Although doubtless rebuilt many times since then, the old houses with their smoky gray, cracked walls, tiled roofs, and rus-

tic fences of unstained and aged wood (these seem to be typical, maybe unique, to Nara) recall an earlier time more poignantly than Kyoto's perfect, and thus somehow exclusive, house fronts. The ancient capital region of Nara is more than the sum of its many great and small temples, graceful pagodas, and parks. It is, more than anything else, a sense of quietness that pervades the narrow street, the gravel-covered precincts of a small temple surrounded by rice paddies and persimmon orchards, shifting sunlight on a worn and mossy stone Buddha.

Today the problem of how to reconcile the thirteen-hundred-year history of the city with a modern appetite for growth is gripping Nara. Visitors expect the city to remain old and traditional. Some of the residents expect modernization and growth. Some fear that Nara will be ruined by a chaotic mixture of contemporary buildings and traditional architecture. Nara Machi, an area dominated by more than thirty temples and a row of old stores and houses, has been labeled a preservation district, and residents receive subsidies to help maintain the wooden front entrances to their homes. New modern buildings are coming in a development zone around JR Nara Station that may ruin the city's skyline.

The designation of several locations in Nara as World Heritage Sites has elated local residents but also has raised the issue of how to strike a balance between preservation and progress. The Todaiji, Kofukuji, Gangoji, Toshodaiji, and Yakushiji Temples; the Kasuga shrine and its surrounding forest; and the ruins of the Heijo Imperial Palace were officially designated World Heritage Sites in 1998. They joined Nara's Horyuji Temple, which was chosen in 1993. As more high-rise buildings are built in downtown Nara, the view of Mount Wakakusa, with the pagoda of Yakushiji Temple jutting up from below, is being altered. Despite the presence of recognized historical sites, the Nara prefectural government has acted contrary to the wishes of preservationists. It raised the height limit for buildings to 102 feet (31 m) in 1972 and again to 131 feet (40 m) in 1986. A further easing of the height restriction to 148 feet (45 m) was made in 1998 in the interest of "revitalizing" the local economy. Citizens' protests against a proposed 98-foot (30-m) government office building in a scenic district in 1992 went unheeded. The building was completed in 1996. Among other concerns environmentalists have expressed is the worry about air pollution and its effect on the cultural sites, all of which are made of wood.

Kyoto

Serene and contemplative, Kyoto is the heart of Japanese Buddhism, the site of hundreds of Shinto shrines, and an irrepressible fountainhead of art and artisanship. For more than a thousand years, from AD 794 to 1868, Kyoto was the imperial seat of government. It was called Heiankyo, the capital of peace and tranquility. Living up to its name centuries later, it came through World War II unscathed. Though no longer the capital, Kyoto still reflects the peculiar aura that surrounded the throne from time immemorial. Lacking a harbor and surrounding open land, Kyoto was slow in developing industries. It has electrical, machinery, and chemical plants. But Kyoto is primarily a cultural and educational center. The city has been divided into three districts for planning purposes, and new developments are rapidly transforming Kyoto. The Kyoto municipal government designated its northern section as a preservation area, its central zone as a redevelopment area, and its southern area as a development section.

Public opinion is divided over two major development projects in the southern section—the JR Kyoto Station and Kyoto Hotel. The city must now choose which way to go: modernization or preservation. In addition to functioning as a key railway station, the Kyoto Station Building also serves as a complex offering public space, a hotel and convention hall, a shopping center, an auditorium, and a parking lot. Everything is housed in a 197-foot-high, 1,542-foot-wide (60 m by 470 m) box-shaped building. Some people are worried that Kyoto's traditional landscape is damaged by the new complex. The "cityscape dispute" between the municipal government and Kyoto residents began in 1964 with the construction of Kyoto Tower, which stands in front of the JR Kyoto Station. Many citizens were against the construction of the 427-foot-high (130-meter-high) tower because they felt it would spoil the view of Kofuku Temple's five-storied pagoda.

The city went ahead with the project, and a series of high-rise apartments and office buildings were constructed in the 1980s. The building rush triggered land price inflation and prompted residents to move out, leading to the creation of what are called "hollow" districts. The Kyoto municipal office has given consent to the construction of buildings up to 148 feet (45 m) tall in the development area.

The conversion of Kyoto Hotel into a 197-foot-high (60-meter-high) structure was another major issue. The Kyoto Buddhist Association opposed this development. It feels that the construction of high-rise buildings will dull people's five senses, particularly the sense of aesthetics. Most business leaders and city officials believe that high-rises will lead to prosperity and revitalize the local economy. Many people feel that the new Kansai airport, which opened in 1994, will spur development in Kyoto, Nara, and Osaka; and all construction projects in the area are being built with the new airport in mind. What should Kyoto preserve? What is necessary to Kyoto? These are questions that the people of Kyoto and Japan must consider seriously.

There is relatively little flatland for urban development in Kyoto. As a result development has been taking place on mountain sides and tops; Mount Hiei, to the west, has been completely developed, changing the appearance and landscape of the mountain. Until the 1980s Mount Hiei provided an important natural backdrop for the old capital city of Kyoto. In addition, it has been the site of many shrines and temples, such as Enryakuji Temple, and the focus of the Daimonji fire festival. Mount Hiei has had a sacred image throughout the ages. However, during the postwar period of high economic growth, golf courses, hotels, and roadways were built on the mountain, along with leisure and other recreation facilities. A large housing development project called *Hieidaira* was developed as a mountaintop city.

In Kyoto, the objects of conservation and the objects of development functionally overlap, so that no matter which predominates—conservation or development—any decision is bound to have major repercussions on the very foundations of the city. Despite its undisputed historical significance, Kyoto must contend with problems of urbanization, development, and cultural preservation.

Chugoku

The entire western tip of Honshu comprises the Chugoku region (fig. 5.13). It consists of Hiroshima, Okayama, Shimane, Tottori, and Yamaguchi Prefectures, with an area of about 12,000 square miles (31,790 sq km) and a population of 7.72 million. It is a mountainous region with many small coastal plains and basins. The Sea of Japan side of the region is called Sanin, and the area facing the Inland Sea is known as Sanyo.

Communications between the Sanin and Sanyo areas of Chugoku are poor. Economically, Sanin is among the least developed parts of the country. Shimane Prefecture in Sanin ranks thirty-sixth among Japan's forty-seven prefectures in terms of per capita income. In per capita national tax payments, it ranked forty-third in 2000. Despite its poverty and relative isolation, Shimane ranked number one at that time in new public-works construction projects financed by the national government. It had more museums and art galleries per capita than all but one other prefecture. This peripheral area had strong leverage in the political world in the late 1980s, because it was represented by the most powerful members of the Liberal Democratic Party in the lower house of the Diet, including Takeshita Noboru. Because of their remoteness, Shimane and neighboring Tottori have remained predominantly agricultural.

In recent years the beef cattle industry has been growing in the Chugoku region. The growth of the cattle industry is due to the rise of calf prices since the 1980s. Most of the people engaged in the cattle industry are part-time operators with principal employment in other sectors such as fishing. Effective use of common pastures, increasing use of labor-saving measures, and investment of private capital are major factors that have prompted the expansion of the beef cattle industry in the area. The cattle industry contributes additional income and provides an efficient use of abandoned land rented from friends and relatives. However, the industry faces an uncertain future because of insecure procurement of pastureland, an unstable fodder price, and casual land rental agreements with friends and relatives (Oro 2000).

The Tottori Plain, formed by the floodplain of the river Sendaigawa, is a rice-producing area; pears are cultivated on the surrounding foothills and along the coastal sand dunes. Other industries include fishing, forestry, and food processing.

Shimane Prefecture contains two large lakes, Nakaumi and Shinjiko, the fifth- and sixth-largest

Most of the Chugoku region is mountainous with few areas of level land between the mountains. The Chugoku Expressway runs through the central mountains and has numerous tunnels. The settlements tend to be concentrated in small basins and on coastal plains. Photo by P.P. Karan.

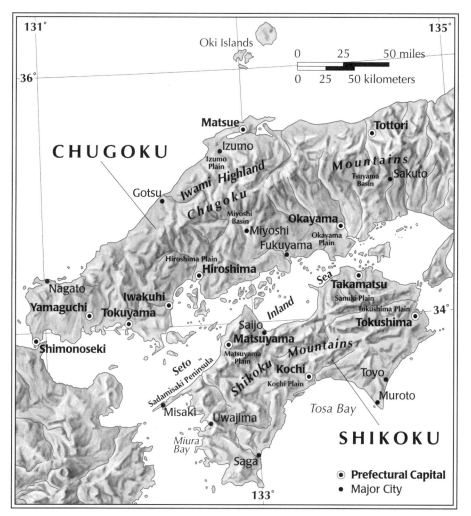

Fig. 5.13. Chugoku and Shikoku regions.

in Japan. A bridge spans the Ohashigawa, connecting the two lakes near Matsue, the prefectural capital. This is the only place in Japan where people can fish for large sea bass, which swim upstream from Nakaumi to Shinjiko; they fish from a bridge in the entertainment district of a prefectural capital city. Both lakes contain a mixture of salt water from the Sea of Japan and freshwater from the river because of the ebb and flow of the tides. The quiet atmosphere of the area has attracted many writers, including Lafcadio Hearn (known in Japan as Yakumo Koizumi) and acclaimed authors of the Meiji era such as Naoya Shiga. Land reclamation has been completed at four sites, totaling about 2,100 acres (850 ha) at Nakaumi Lake, and there is a proposal to reclaim the Honjo area in the northwestern part of the lake. The Honjo site measures about 4,200 acres (1,700 ha), or about a quarter of the area of Nakaumi Lake. The Honjo reclamation project is designed to create more farmland. Considering the present state of agriculture in Japan, the question is whether to create new farmland through large public-works projects that may damage or threaten the natural environment. The Honjo reclamation site is in the area of the lake that is closest to the sea, and fish lay their eggs and grow to maturity in the seaweed that grows in its shallow waters. If the area is reclaimed, Shinjiko and Nakaumi Lakes will lose their hatching grounds. More than 30 percent of three species of wild white ducks (about 26,000) winter at the Honjo site and dive for food in Nakaumi Lake. They eat *hototogisukai* clams, which are harmful to short-

The city of Tsuyama in northern Okayama Prefecture. Cities such as Tsuyama in the mountainous Chugoku region specialize in the production of local textiles, handmade paper, and paper goods. Photo by P.P. Karan.

Along the south coast of Chugoku there are a number of densely populated delta plains with large urban centers such as Hiroshima, located on the river Otagawa. On August 6, 1945, the world's first atomic bomb was dropped on the city, destroying 90 percent of the urban area and killing about 140,000 people, according to a 1977 estimate. Now completely rebuilt, Hiroshima is a major center of machinery and automobile industries. Photo by P.P. Karan.

necked clams and corbiculae. Ducks also help purify the water by preventing deoxidation in summer. One hopes that there will not be so many large public-works projects that the ecological balance of the Sanin region is damaged. Partly in response to protests from environmental groups, in August 2000 the land reclamation project planned for a section of Nakaumi Lagoon in Shimane Prefecture was cancelled.

Sanyo, comprising Hiroshima, Okayama, and Yamaguchi Prefectures, has a modern industrial economy. Its strategic location between western Honshu, Kyushu, and Shikoku led to its early development. Industrial areas have developed along the Inland Sea coast. While agriculture, fishing, and forestry have declined in recent years, industrial growth has been rapid in the coastal cities. Major industries include shipbuilding, chemicals, steel, machinery, automobiles, textiles, petrochemicals, and food processing. The waters off the coast were once among Japan's richest fishing areas, but catches have declined because of industrial pollution and overfishing. The most heavily populated areas are along the Inland Sea, around the cities of Hiroshima, Okayama, and Shimonoseki.

Hiroshima is the regional center of Chugoku. Three stages can be recognized in Hiroshima's urban history: in the first stage (1867–1945) it was a military city, in the second stage (1945–78) it was the atom-bombed city characterized by major rebuilding, and in the third stage (1979–present) it is developing into a postindustrial city. Hiroshima, a castle town in the Edo era, grew rapidly during the Meiji period as a military base. From Hiroshima soldiers sailed to Korea and China. Nearly 42 percent of the city's area was occupied by the military, and urban planning was controlled by the armed forces. The presence of the military fostered the war industries, and the military-related economy prospered in the city. Hiroshima soon developed into a major urban center in western Japan; and it became the Special Capital in 1889 when the emperor came to Hiroshima and summoned the Imperial Congress to work out the strategy for the Japan-China War. Large numbers of poor farmers from surrounding villages moved to Hiroshima seeking work, and the social and physical structure of the city came to be differentiated functionally. At the same time the surrounding villages and small towns were absorbed into Hiroshima administratively, and the seashores of Hiroshima Bay were developed for military and industrial purposes.

Slum areas where poor Korean migrants lived developed in various parts of the city. There were 127 cheap hotels for day laborers in Hiroshima in 1927. In one of these communities the population increased from 889 in 1871 to 6,037 in 1944. Koreans migrated to Japan voluntarily in the beginning, then were brought to Japan by recruiters, and finally were brought compulsorily by the Japanese military. There were 17,477 Koreans working at the military factories and shipyards of Hiroshima in 1937.

Hiroshima had an area of 27 square miles (70 sq km) and a population of 336,483 in 1944 just before the atomic bomb explosion in 1945. More than 70,000 citizens were killed immediately by the explosion, and another 70,000 died within five years. The dead included at least ten American prisoners of war held by the Japanese. Between 1945 and 1978 Hiroshima recovered from the ruins caused by the atomic bomb. The Declaration of Complete Recovery from the ruins was announced by the local government in 1978 after the clearance of areas destroyed by the explosion was finished. The living victims of the atomic bomb (the Hibakushas) were the most outstanding contributors in the rebuilding of Hiroshima. Lands occupied by the military were returned to the people of Hiroshima.

Between 1979 and 2000 Hiroshima developed as one of the megacities of Japan. With an area of 286 square miles (740 sq km) and a population of 1.08 million in 1992, Hiroshima has become a major industrial city. Automobile, shipbuilding, and steel industries dominate the manufacturing (secondary) sector. But the tertiary sector (service) is also very significant, employing 71 percent of the labor force. In the 1990s the globalization and postindustrialization of Hiroshima's economy was accelerated.

About 75 miles northeast of Hiroshima is the city of Kurashiki. It was the hub of a lucrative spinning industry in the early twentieth century. This once-humming factory town, run by the wealthy Ohara clan, is now focused on arts and crafts. The Ohara family endowed many of the schools and hospitals in the area, and nearly all of the museums and cultural institutions that make Kurashiki an important art center in Chugoku. The historic district of Kurashiki, along a canal, was built during the Edo period; it comprises *yashiki,* or sumptuous houses, and *kura,* or warehouses. Barges laden with grain and other goods used to be floated down the town's canal to the Inland Sea. Today the old company town thrives on art.

SHIKOKU

Shikoku, the smallest of Japan's four main islands, is 7,262 square miles (18,808 sq km) in area with a population of 4.18 million. It consists of Kagawa, Tokushima, Ehime, and Kochi Prefectures. The island is largely mountainous, so its agricultural area is limited (see fig. 5.13). The northern half of the island has a long narrow plain along the Inland Sea; the southern half has a wider plain facing the Pacific Ocean. Three newly constructed bridges linking Shikoku to Honshu are expected to bring new industries and tourists to the island (Funk 1993). The 37-mile (60-km) Shimanami Sea Road between Onomichi in Honshu and Imabari in Ehime Prefecture, with ten suspension bridges, has proved very popular with the tourists since its opening in 1999. The previous two bridge links—the Kobe-Awaji-Naruto Expressway and the Seto Chuo Expressway—have been financial disasters because of much lower than expected vehicle usage and the resulting meager toll revenues.

Tokushima, the regional center in eastern Shikoku, known as Awa in feudal times, was a strong economic power from the Edo period through the Meiji era, owing to its production of indigo. Following World War II, however, Tokushima fell behind in urban-

Field Report

Hiroshima, Ground Zero—Fifty-five Years Later

The shimmering heat and clear skies over Hiroshima in the summer of 1945 determined that it, as opposed to other targets such as Niigata, was chosen as the city on which the first atomic bomb was to be dropped. Thus, on August 6, at 8.15 a.m., the bomb exploded next to Aioi Bridge over Hiroshima Prefectural Industrial Promotions Hall, the remains of which have become the central feature of Peace Memorial Park. Hiroshima had played an important part in the war, both as a manufacturing center and as a point of embarkation for troops being posted overseas. Its importance wasn't surprising, given its historical association with armed conflicts.

In both the Sino-Japanese and the Russo-Japanese Wars, it had a significant role, and in the Sino-Japanese War, it even served as the emperor's military headquarters for a brief period. But finally it was not Hiroshima's role in the war effort that determined its fate but the relentless blue skies and sunshine, which made it an easy target for the crew of the Enola Gay as they flew through the brilliant summer morning.

The immediate effects of the explosion came in two waves; first the radiant heat, then the shock. The radiant heat was such that everything burnable within a 0.62-mile (1-km) radius was reduced to ashes; even the roof tiles of the houses were blistered by its intensity. The shock wave that followed leveled most of what remained. The longer-term effects of the bomb were as grim if not as dramatic: cancer, unhealing burns, and radiation sickness added to the usual impairments of bombardment; and the costs in terms of bereavement, disorientation, and despair are impossible to calculate.

Hiroshima today looks very much like any other Japanese city in many respects. But, by virtue of the farsighted actions of one of Hiroshima's postwar mayors, something of the city's past has been preserved: the A-Bomb Dome. The remains of the Hiroshima Prefectural Industrial Promotions Hall stand as a warning against atomic war. It is fitting that, amid Hiroshima's urban modernness—parking towers, baseball stadium, and department stores—there should be such a stark reminder of an event that leveled the city.

Nearly 40 million people have come since 1955 to see the A-Bomb Dome and the Hiroshima Peace Memorial Museum, which bear testimony to one of the greatest horrors of the twentieth century. Many visitors are struck by the absence of suggestions that the bombing brought an end to Japan's war of aggression in Asia. The museum does include references to the fact that Hiroshima was a major military supply center, however. Hiroshima has rejected the demands of some citizens and victims groups that the museum include an exhibition on Japan's "aggressive role" in World War II alongside the gruesome displays of the suffering and devastation caused by the bomb.

The dispute is only one of several signs of continuing difficulties faced by Japan in articulating its sense of responsibility for the war. A related issue has been the mixed feelings over the historical question of the responsibility of Emperor Hirohito, who died in January 1989. In recent years, while expanding its economic influence in Asia, Japan has increasingly been willing to issue statements of regret or apology to China and South Korea, both of which were invaded and plundered by Japanese troops. At the same time, China and South Korea continue to criticize the sanitized versions of the war appearing in Japanese school textbooks, and to assail statements by some Japanese political leaders that the issue of whether Japan was the actual aggressor is for future historians to decide.

The Hiroshima peace groups regularly use the anniversary of the Hiroshima bombings to issue statements deploring Japan's increased military spending, the supposed presence of nuclear weapons aboard American ships in Japan, and Japan's reliance on nuclear energy. The right-wing groups, in turn, charge that the peace groups use Hiroshima to advance a left-wing agenda that includes the abolition of the emperor system in Japan.

Naruto Bridge, one of the new bridges across the Inland Sea, linking Honshu and Shikoku, built to promote development on Shikoku. Photo by Todd Stradford.

ization and industrialization because of geographic constraints such as distance from Honshu. Recent transportation projects have provided direct connections between the Tokushima and Kinki regions. Tokushima aims to become the base of the Shikoku, Kinki, and Chugoku regional cooperation network. Takamatsu is striving to reinvigorate existing industries and stimulate the growth of new industries through the Kagawa Technopolis Plan. It has created Kagawa Intelligent Park, a technology information and culture multicenter on the 79-acre (32-ha) site of the former airport. Matsuyama, Ehime's capital, is on the west end of the island. Famous for its citizens' active practice and enjoyment of haiku, it is the economic center of Shikoku. Matsuyama is positioning itself as a center for new forms of international trade and exchange in the Shikoku and Inland Sea economic area. Kochi, in southern Shikoku, is concentrating on the development of the prefecture's technical skills and knowledge-based industries around Kochi University of Technology by promoting cooperation among the industrial, academic, and government sectors.

In the Kochi Plain, facing the Pacific Ocean, a warm climate allows two rice crops in some areas, but government regulations now limit the practice. In the Matsuyama Plain, located in central Ehime Prefecture, rice is cultivated in the lowlands and mandarin oranges in the surrounding hills. Many of the industries in Shikoku, such as the textile manufacturers, are moving overseas. Manufacturers of traditional products have been expanding their business in China and other Asian countries. Materials as well as labor are cheaper in China, so industries such as the Asahi Senshoku Company, an Ehime towel manufacturer, are able to operate at lower cost overseas. Asahi Senshoku established in 1991 a $2.1 million subsidiary in Dalian, China. The subsidiary, Dalian Asahi Senshoku Company, exports towels to Japan, and its annual sales are reaching $8.5 million.

The Kusubashi Mon-ori Company, another Ehime Prefecture towel company, began in 1988 to invest in Raja Uchino Company in Bangkok, Thailand. Towel manufacturers in Ehime Prefecture will stop manufacturing in Shikoku within a few years. The industry will survive by establishing joint companies or subsidiaries in Asian countries. Shifting the production base to foreign countries has weakened the island's industrial base.

Miura Bay, in western Shikoku, is a major area of the Japanese pearl industry. In the late 1990s the best-quality pearls, *akoya* pearls, accounted for 80 percent of the Japanese market and for 65 percent of all cultured pearls sold in the United States. A disease in 2000 killed 70 percent of the akoya oysters, and production plunged, resulting in a string of bankruptcies and reported suicides among Japan's beleaguered pearl producers. No area has been as hard hit as Ehime Prefecture, center of the oyster plague. Its warm and shallow bays on the western shore of Shikoku were the source of up to 80 percent of all Japanese pearl oyster production until the shellfish began to die en masse.

Agricultural land in eastern Ehime Prefecture, Shikoku, near Saijo. Vinyl "tunnel" agriculture dominates the rural landscape. Photo by Cotton Mather.

Like much of the Japanese economy, the pearl industry is highly regulated, and producers are allowed to either cultivate pearls or raise baby oysters, but not both. Twice a year, the oyster breeders sell their young shellfish to pearl cultivators. The cultivators seed an oyster with a bead made from the thick shell of a freshwater mussel. Then they wait a year or two for the oyster to coat the irritant with lustrous nacre before harvesting the pearls. Since the epidemic began, 15 percent of the licensed pearl cultivators and 23 percent of the oyster breeders have gone out of business.

For the Japanese pearl industry to endure, it must produce a high-quality product. The pearl cultivators in western Shikoku have begun experimenting with new breeds of oysters, new cultivating techniques for the fragile akoyas, and new breeding grounds. Many in the pearl industry fear that a virus is not the only cause of the akoyas' woes. Even before the disease appeared, some producers believed that the oyster had been weakened by overbreeding, overcrowding, and pollution. Others point their fingers at the fish farmers who raise *fugu*, a poisonous but tasty Japanese blowfish, for contaminating the seas with chemicals used to fight *fugu* parasites. Global warming is seen as the scariest threat of all. The waters off Ehime have been 1.5 degrees warmer than the average figured over the past fifteen years. Higher temperatures make shellfish more susceptible to disease. Akoya farmers will have to wait the epidemic out, trying to improve environmental conditions, and leave the oysters to try to overcome the disease naturally.

KYUSHU

Kyushu, including the southern Nansei Islands, consists of Fukuoka, Nagasaki, Oita, Kumamoto, Miyazaki, Saga, Kagoshima, and Okinawa Prefectures. The region has an area of 17,000 square miles (44,420 sq km) and a population of 14.79 million. Kyushu has a mountainous interior with many small coastal plains, volcanoes, and hot springs (see fig. 5.14). The climate is subtropical with heavy precipitation.

Northern Kyushu, with the regional capital of Fukuoka, is one of the major areas of industrial activity in Japan. Kitakyushu was the site of Japan's first Western-style steel mill, built in 1901 by the government-operated Yawata Iron and Steel Works (now Nippon Steel, a private corporation). Kitakyushu was proud of its slogan: "Kemuri wa hanei no shirushi" (Smoke is the symbol of prosperity). The industrial area based at Kitakyushu grew rapidly after 1901, because of its proximity to Chikuho coalfield and the availability of iron ore resources imported from China. Its importance declined after World War II, when these imports ceased. Other factors contributing to the industrial decline were the switch from coal to oil as an energy source and a shift in the industrial structure away from the dominance of heavy

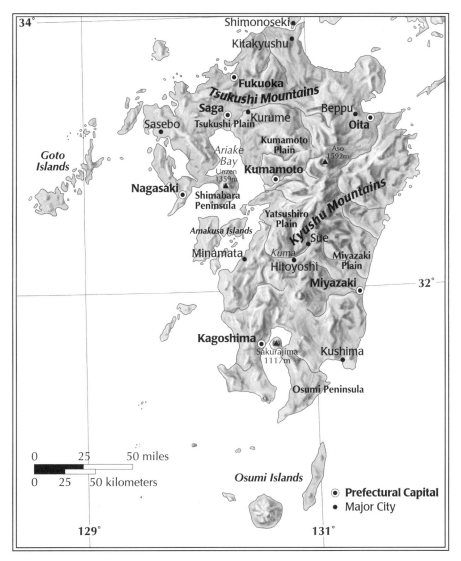

Fig. 5.14. Kyushu.

industries such as iron, steel, and cement. In recent years, iron and coal have been imported from Australia and other countries. At present Kyushu's steel, chemical, machinery, ceramics, food-processing, and electric-appliance industries are concentrated along the 19-mile (31-km) coastline of Kitakyushu from Moji to Tobata. Increasingly information-intensive high-technology industries are replacing the traditional manufacturing muscle.

Once Kyushu's biggest city, Kitakyushu built its fortunes on steel. Despite the decline in the industry, the Yawata steelworks remains at the heart of Kitakyushu's economy, and Nippon Steel, Yawata's parent company, is still one of the world's biggest steel companies. The wealth of coal in the area attracted other energy-intensive companies as well, such as those producing chemicals and glass. In 1950 Kitakyushu's companies accounted for 5 percent of Japan's output. In its heyday in the 1970s, the Yawata works alone employed 46,000 people. Now it employs 8,000, and some of the land is used for a theme park. Kitakyushu contributes just 0.7 percent of the country's GDP.

Southern Kyushu is relatively less developed and agricultural. Historically, the eastward extension of Japanese civilization began from southern Kyushu

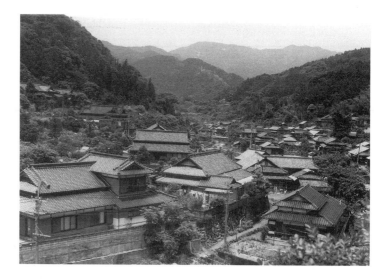

Sakamoto-mura, a settlement in one of the narrow mountain valleys of Kyushu, southeast of Kumamoto. Photo by P.P. Karan.

and later set the foundations of the Yamato Court in the Nara Basin of the Kinki region. Reflecting its close proximity to the Asian mainland, Kyushu was the principal gateway through which outside influences entered Japan from very early times. In 1549 Christianity was introduced in Japan with the arrival of Saint Francis Xavier at Kagoshima. When Japan adopted a policy of seclusion from the rest of the world between 1639 and 1853, the island of Dejima in Nagasaki Bay was the only port through which Western foreign influences trickled into the country. Nagasaki maintains a strong cosmopolitan atmosphere, resulting from its long contact with the outside world. After massive destruction caused by the atomic bomb that was dropped on it at the end of World War II, Nagasaki has been completely rehabilitated to its former status as Kyushu's leading shipbuilding port and center of Catholicism.

Kumamoto Plain in western Kyushu extends from the diluvial uplands on the slopes of Asosan, where fruits and vegetables are grown, to the alluvial lowlands that border Shimabara Bay, where rice is the major crop. The city of Kumamoto has emerged as a principal center of the semiconductor industry. Kyushu, sometimes called Silicon Island for its concentration of companies similar to those in California's Silicon Valley around San Jose, is quiet and clean. The semiconductor industry has been attracted to this area by the relatively dust-free environment (ten particles to a cubic foot [0.03 cu m] of air), the land availability, the local government policies, the labor supply, and excellent transport facilities for the ship-

ment of raw silicon chips to markets in China, South Korea, and Southeast Asia. Kyushu now produces 40 percent of Japan's integrated circuits—one-tenth of the world's market. In the past decade hundreds of corporations, Japanese and foreign, have set up factories here, tapping the island's reservoir of cheap land and well-educated workers and counting on its proximity to the rising economies of Asia to pull them into new global markets.

Tsukushi Plain, located in Fukuoka and Saga Prefectures, borders the Ariake Bay. It consists of the floodplain and delta of the river Chikugogawa and has extensive alluvial fans. It is an important rice-producing area in Kyushu. Kurume, the major city on the plain, is a center for the rubber industry in Japan.

Along the Miyazaki coastal plain in eastern Kyushu, vegetables, sweet potatoes, and mandarin oranges are grown on upland terraces, and rice on the lowlands. Plastic tunnels serve as greenhouses for sweet potatoes and other crops in Kagoshima and Miyazaki Prefectures. Japan places a premium on Kyushu's stretches of level land for agriculture.

Kyushu's most enduring challenge is what the Japanese call *kaso*—or depopulation (Miyaguchi 1992). A large percentage of the island's high school graduates still leave their native towns and villages for work off the island. But local governments are now encouraging their return to Kyushu's technopolis centers such as Kumamoto. Kyushans refer to return migrants as "U-turn" persons—a growing number of young and middle-aged professionals who eschew

Field Report
Nagasaki, Cradle of Modern Japan

I arrived in Nagasaki expecting to be infected by the sadness of war, as if it were hanging in the air like residual radiation. But the only living things that weep in modern Nagasaki are the willows that line its narrow rivers; the only painful groans come from the old streetcars as they limp through the city center, from the suburbs to the sea.

After the atomic bomb exploded above 171 Matsuyamamachi at 11:02 a.m. on August 9, 1945, it was believed that nothing would grow in the city for seventy years. Fifty years later Nagasaki has risen like a phoenix from the ashes and stands as a tribute to the resilience of the human spirit. Its schools, factories, stations, and even its medical college have been rebuilt exactly where they were prior to the bombing.

Nagasaki appears to have evolved like any other Japanese city, almost as if the great catastrophe, the unforgettable fire, had never happened. However, underneath its appearance as an ordinary modern city—conveyed by the high-rise hotels, the pachinko parlors, and the wide avenues—lies a quiet dignity, the stubborn pride of the survivor. It is indomitable, having enjoyed the best of times and endured the worst of them.

Unlike the flat delta that is Hiroshima, Nagasaki is made up of a series of valleys converging on a narrow strip of seashore by the port. The bomb, intended for the giant Mitsubishi shipyard, drifted up the Urakami Valley and exploded in midair close to Japan's largest Roman Catholic church. Nearly 75,000 people were killed outright, and another 75,000 were wounded, many of them dying later of their injuries or from radiation sickness. Urakami Valley, like Nagasaki, certainly had its share of war plants. But in contrast to Hiroshima, which had long been a military headquarters, Nagasaki was used to being identified as Japan's gateway to the West.

It was founded in 1570 by a local lord eager for Portuguese arms and other Western goods. He even let the Jesuits rule for a while. Western goods and religion flowed into Japan through Nagasaki. Then, in 1636, came a reaction. Christians were persecuted. Travel abroad was forbidden on pain of death. The Tokugawa shoguns (a dynasty of military commanders who ruled Japan from 1600 to 1868) allowed only Dutch and Chinese to stay as merchants in Nagasaki, under harsh restrictions. All other Japanese ports were closed to foreign trade. The island of Dejima in Nagasaki Bay was the country's only port open to foreign trade.

The Jesuits' influence is evident even today in the form of Kasutera sponge cake, a southern-European sweet (from Bizcocho Castella in Spain and Pao de Lo in Portugal) that Nagasaki has nurtured. Kasutera is a damp, rich, sweet sponge cake with a light, delicate texture. It is made from flour, eggs, malt syrup, and a mixture of finely granulated and large-crystal sugar.

During the next two centuries, Nagasaki was the narrow door through which some Western knowledge reached Japan. In 1854, U.S. Commodore Matthew Perry and his black ships forced open Japan's door. Some years later the shogun was overthrown, and under Emperor Meiji Japan rushed to catch up with the West. Merchants from Europe and America thronged Nagasaki's streets, and the city came into its own. For most Japanese, it was an exotic blend of East and West. Buildings constructed by foreign traders and missionaries in their own inimitable styles are grouped around the old harbor in the southern part of the city, an area that escaped the fury of the bomb.

Every year in August, when the oleanders bloom, citizens of Nagasaki bow their heads in prayer to pay homage to the war dead and to recall Emperor Hirohito's August 14, 1945, broadcast announcing his decision to surrender. Nowhere are memories more poignant than in Nagasaki. But Nagasaki is also strong and obstinate, like the palms that grace its gardens; it is cheerful and elegant, like the hydrangea, the city flower.

The 3,503-foot (1,068-m) Kammon Bridge linking Honshu and Kyushu at Shimonoseki. Kyushu and Honshu are also connected by two undersea rail tunnels and a highway tunnel. Photo by P.P. Karan.

the higher salaries and prestige of jobs in Tokyo and Osaka in favor of the more relaxed ways of their native Kyushu.

Kyushu has fared better than the rest of Japan since the burst of the economic bubble in 1989. This is partly because land prices never rose as much on the island as in Osaka or Tokyo, so they have not fallen as far. The cheaper land—and the cheaper labor—has drawn many companies. Toyota and Nissan, the country's biggest carmakers, built factories on Kyushu in 1992. All the big electronics companies also have plants in Kyushu. Tourism is booming in Kyushu. Theme parks, such as Huis ten Bosch, a replica of a Dutch town, and Space World, set up with America's space agency, are a big draw. In 1995, 416,000 foreigners visited Kyushu, double the number of eight years earlier.

Yet if Kyushu as a whole is doing well, some areas are doing far better than others. Fukuoka, with a population of over 1 million, is the biggest city and is where most of the companies have their regional headquarters. A highway completed in 1996 gives Fukuoka a rapid link to the rest of the island. One of Japan's biggest shopping centers, Canal City, opened in 1996 in Fukuoka. In the first six months 10 million people went to gaze at its water displays, shop at its boutiques, stay at its hotel, or go to its theaters. Department stores have risen everywhere. In 1995 about 800,000 square feet (75,000 sq m) of new office space was built in Fukuoka, compared with about 5.9 million square feet (550,000 sq m) for the whole

of the Kansai region, Japan's business heartland around Osaka. A similar amount of office space was built in 1996.

Thirty-eight miles (60 km) away is Kitakyushu, Kyushu's second-largest city. The most conspicuous features of Kitakyushu are the city's oil storage tanks and its smoking factory chimneys. From the top floor of the city government's office, the view is of two steel factories, an electric power company, and a very functional port. Just as Fukuoka is the model of a modern service-driven economy (service companies account for four-fifths of its output), Kitakyushu epitomizes old Japan—the industries that thrust the country into the modern era but whose competitive edge has been eroded by rivals abroad. But even in Kitakyushu things are getting better. Once a byword for pollution, the city has cleaned itself up. Fish have returned to its rivers. An energetic local government is striving for change. It is trying to attract conferences and sell technological know-how abroad. An offshore airport is being built, and the port will be deepened; change is afoot.

Kyushu's proximity to East Asia has contributed to an increase in trade, tourism, and educational exchanges with Asian countries. By 2000 more than 46 percent of Kyushu's gross trade was with Asia and 73 percent of Kyushu's overseas business investments were within Asia. Nearly 91 percent of the foreign visitors were from the Asian region. Kyushu's historic links with Asia have created many potential economic opportunities.

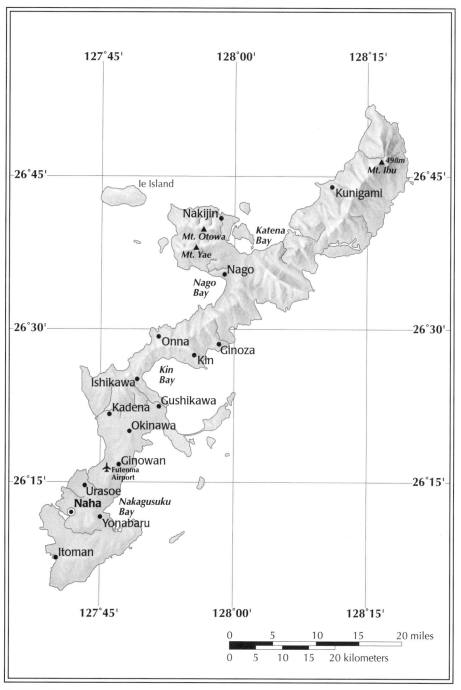

Fig. 5.15. Okinawa.

OKINAWA AND THE NANSEI (RYUKYU) ISLANDS

South of Kyushu lies a chain of more than 150 islands generally referred to the Ryukyu Islands. Okinawa is by far the largest in terms of size, population (1.34 million in 2002), and economic development (Tamamori and James 1995). Geographically, these islands are semitropical and tropical, with steep mountain slopes, thick vegetation, and beautiful sandy beaches (see fig. 5.15). Coral reefs, including rare blue coral, ring the islands, making the Ryukyus

A tourist hotel in Okinawa. Tourism and military bases are major elements in the economy of the island. Photo by P.P. Karan.

an attractive location for divers, snorkelers, and beachgoers from the Japanese mainland (Takahashi and Koba 1977). Much of the large-scale tourist development in Okinawa is dominated by enterprises based outside of Okinawa Prefecture (Uezu 2001).

The Ryukyu Islands developed outside the framework of the Japanese state for much of their history. Various smaller kingdoms gave rise to the Ryukyu Kingdom in the fourteenth century. This small kingdom was notable for its role in trading between Northeast Asia and Southeast Asia; for its cultural elegance, noted by many foreign observers; and for its peaceful inhabitants, who are said to have possessed no weapons at all. The Ryukyu Kingdom paid tribute both to China (since the fourteenth century) and Japan (since the seventeenth century, when the Satsuma invaded) for most of its existence and has a unique cultural tradition reflecting both these and indigenous influences. After the Meiji Restoration (1868), Japan claimed formal sovereignty over the Ryukyus in 1879, but it was not recognized by China until the conclusion of the Sino-Japanese War in 1895. During World War II Okinawa was the site of some of the bloodiest battles. The islands were administered by the United States from 1945 to 1972, when they were returned to Japan. More than fifty thousand American military personnel and their families still live on Okinawa.

Okinawa's postwar history is largely dominated by the presence of U.S. forces and bases (Taylor 2000). After World War II Okinawa was devastated, with an estimated 25 percent of its people killed and 85 percent of the buildings on the island destroyed. The United States rebuilt the infrastructure and the economy, at the same time seizing Okinawan lands for the construction of its military bases. During the U.S. occupation period, Okinawa was largely left out of the economic boom that propelled the rest of Japan to remarkable heights. Although the economy did grow, the growth was mainly in the service sector, where Okinawa's economy is still disproportionately weighted today. After reversion, Japan instituted "catch-up" development policies to try to boost Okinawa up to mainland levels. These efforts came mainly in the form of huge public-works projects and, since the 1980s, the development of Okinawa as a tropical resort destination for Japanese tourists, who now number more than 3 million per year. As a result, Okinawa's economy went from being base-dependent to being tourist- and public-works-dependent. The Japanese development policies did create wealth, but they also had great environmental consequences, resulting in the death of an estimated 90 percent of Okinawa's coral reefs. Wealthy compared to most countries in the world—Okinawa's per capita income is roughly equal to that of France—it remains poor compared to the rest of Japan, with the lowest per capita income, one of the highest numbers of hours worked per week, and the highest unemployment rate of any of Japan's prefectures. Gavan McCormack (1999) has noted the contradictions of ecological and economic development in Okinawa.

Table 5.1. Okinawa timeline

1609	Japanese warlords annex island kingdom of Ryukyu.
1879	Ryukyu renamed Okinawa and incorporated into modern Japan.
1945	In the last months of World War II, U.S. forces attack and seize the island.
1955	American soldier rapes and murders a six-year-old girl.
1959	U.S. fighter jet crashes into elementary school, killing 128.
1972	United States returns Okinawa to Japan.
1995	U.S. soldiers rape schoolgirl, and opposition to American bases flares up.
1999	Governor calls for moving Futenma Base from Ginowan to Nago, but Nago does not want it either.
2000	U.S. marine arrested for reportedly molesting young girl; American airman's car allegedly hits Okinawan pedestrian.
2000	Benefiting perhaps from Japan's desire to soothe the feelings of islanders, Okinawa hosts the G-8 summit.

Politically, many Okinawans are resentful of how Japan abandoned Okinawa to a foreign power at the close of the war. The debate has centered, superficially, on a series of clashes between local people and American forces. But the context for these controversies is Okinawa's sense that it is once again Japan's political pawn, that little has changed since the islands were forcibly brought under Japanese control in 1879. That sense was reinforced when evidence emerged that Emperor Hirohito—never a popular figure on the only Japanese island to suffer invasion—invited the United States to continue the occupation of Okinawa long after the four main islands returned to Japanese sovereignty.

For most Okinawans, born long after soldiers battled each other with flamethrowers and destroyers blew up after hitting mines in the bay, the import of the emperor's message seems remote. But older people say it is unthinkable that the emperor would have invited a foreign nation to permanently occupy one of Japan's four main islands to the north. They feel, correctly, that they are bearing the burden of the U.S.-Japan Security Agreement for the whole of Japan. Many Americans in Okinawa, even those on the receiving end of the anger, say they understand the way Okinawans feel.

Okinawa lacks political muscle in the central government. No Okinawan has served in the cabinet. The governor is usually involved in simmering disputes with the mainland about the future fate of the bases and the relocation of the Futenma heliport, and the two parties are now effectively not on speaking terms. Thus, a large part of the problem rests in Okinawa's lack of autonomy. This has even sparked a fairly small independence movement, which believes that Okinawa should be a separate country or at least have a special political status different from that of the other prefectures.

Aside from the U.S. bases and the controversy surrounding them, Okinawa has another dimension—its distinct cultural *champuru* (mixture). Okinawa's cultural landscape differs in many ways from the Japanese mainland. Houses are generally built of concrete instead of wood, to withstand the powerful typhoons that have played a large role in the region's history. Okinawans bury their dead in large concrete or stone tombs, found virtually everywhere on the island. The American influence has produced a plethora of fast food franchises, more than in any other part of Japan. The lack of railroads on the island has fueled Okinawans' love affair with the automobile, by far the most prevalent form of transportation for most people on the island.

Although historically Japan wished to integrate the Okinawans into the mainstream of Japanese culture, in Okinawa there is increasing realization of the side effects of such cultural assimilation. There is an inherent feeling among the Okinawans that the Japanese are trying to undermine their cultural vibrancy. Previously the cultural flow went one way, from the Japanese mainland to Okinawa. But now Okinawans are beginning to reverse the trend. Despite efforts by the mainland to assimilate Okinawa, and the presence of U.S. forces for more than fifty years, Okinawa has strongly maintained aspects of its traditional culture. In fact, maybe in response to U.S. efforts to encourage Okinawan independence before its reversion to Japan, or as a reaction against occupation, Okinawan culture has positively flourished. Nowhere else in Japan is traditional folk music as popular and revered as in Okinawa, where it sometimes seems that half the population plays the *sanshin,* an Okinawan samisen, a banjolike instrument made from snakeskin. Okinawan music has also successfully blended with modern sounds, creating a traditional-modern fusion now popular all over Japan. Many famous Japanese singers and groups are from Okinawa. *Aisa,* traditional Okinawan drumming and dancing, is popular, and Okinawan festivals both small and large occur year-round. Textiles, fabrics, and pottery are also distinctive. Okinawa cuisine is different from the mainland's and is another point of Okinawa pride, as is the consumption of *awamori,* an exceptionally potent type of sake, consumed voraciously by most Okinawan men.

Okinawans have experienced several cultural inroads. In fact, Okinawa's diversity contrasts sharply with the world notion of Japan's homogeneity. Okinawa is a meeting point of different national and ethnic cultures. Located closer to Shanghai, Manila, and Seoul than Tokyo, Okinawa's food is a mixture of Japanese, Chinese, and Southeast Asian cooking, as attested by a stir-fried noodle dish called *somen champuru.* The cultural mix stems not just from forced assimilation or cultural domination, however. Okinawans are extremely proud of their motto "Ichariba-chode" (Everyone we meet is a friend). Okinawa's location has also been a tremendous burden, leading some to refer to it as the "Pawn of the Pacific." Its strategic military location has made it subject to a military occupation with no clear end in sight. Even if the United States removes its bases, as many Okinawans hope will eventually occur, there is fear that the Japanese Self-Defense Forces may then move in.

REFERENCES

Cutler, Suzanne. 1999. *Managing Decline: Japan's Coal Industry Restructuring and Community Response.* Honolulu: Univ. of Hawaii Press.

Edgington, David W. 1999. Firms, government, and innovation in the Chukyo region of Japan. *Urban Studies* 36 (2): 305–339.

Endo, M. 1994. The mobility of household members of the Ainu in Takashima district of Hokkaido, Japan, 1834–1871. *Geographical Review of Japan* A 67:79–100.

Funk, C. 1993. Types of tourist development in Japan: Examined in Ehime Prefecture. *Faculty Bulletin, Humanities and Social Sciences* (Kobe Gakuin Univ.) 6:147–162.

Hashimoto, K. 1999. Impact of a new freeway network upon commercial behaviour and locations in Nagano Prefecture. *Revue de Géographie Alpine* 87 (1): 189–200.

Ishii, Hideya. 1985. Land use and development characteristics of Namekata District, Kanto region. Tsukuba Studies in *Human Geography* 9:49–63.

Itakura, Katsutaka. 1982. On the structure of economy and society in Tohoku. *Science Reports of Tohoku University,* ser. 7 (Geography) 32 (2): 71–87.

Jain, Purnendu C. 1995. Decentralization in Japan's political economy: Kansai International Airport. *Social Science Japan* 5 (November): 30–31.

Kamiya, H. 1993. Development of tourism in highland villages: A case study of Kaidamura, Nagano Prefecture. *Human Geography* 45:68–82.

Kim, Doo-Chul. 2000. Regional process of dependency and changes of endogenous self-organizations in a depopulated area: A case study of Namiai village, Nagano Prefecture, Japan. *Human Geography* 52 (2): 28–49.

McClain, James L. 1982. *Kanazawa: A Castle Town in Seventeenth Century Japan.* New Haven, CT: Yale Univ. Press.

McClain, James L., and Wakita Osamu, eds. 1999. *Osaka: The Merchants' Capital of Early Modern Japan.* Ithaca, NY: Cornell Univ. Press.

McCormack, Gavan. 1999. From the sea that divides to the sea that links: Contradictions of ecological and economic development in Okinawa. *Capitalism, Nature, Socialism* 10 (1): 3–39.

Miyaguchi, T. 1992. Socio-economic change of isolated mountain villages and vitalization of depopulated areas in Japan: A case study of Momiki village of central Kyushu. *Regional Views* (Komazawa Univ.) 5:3–21.

Nakamura, Kazuo. 1980. Eastern and western Japan. In *Geography of Japan,* ed. Association of Japanese Geographers, 184–196. Tokyo: Teiko-Shoin.

Nakamura, Shusaku. 2000. Migration behavior and seasonal migrant workers: The case of Kudoyama area, Hamasaka town, Hyogo Prefecture. *Human Geography* 52 (2): 1–18

Nakayama, Akinori. 2000. Tourism development and regional promotion in "Shizenkyuyousen": A study of Nakatsugawa district in Iide town, Yamagata Prefecture. *Human Geography* 52 (4): 52–64.

Okuno, Takashi. 1987. A consideration of the socio-economic regionality of the Matsumoto Basin. *Geographical Reports of Tokyo Metropolitan University* 22:153–168.

Oro, Kouhie. 2000. The development of beef cattle breeding in Chiburi-Jima Island, Shimane Prefecture. *Human Geography* 52 (6): 43–63.

Shirasaka, Shigeru. 1984. Skiing grounds and ski settlements in Japan. *Geographical Review of Japan* B 57:68–86.

Siddle, Richard. 1996. *Race, Resistance, and the Ainu of Japan.* London: Routledge.

Sugimoto, Yoshio. 1997. *An Introduction to Japanese Society.* Cambridge: Cambridge Univ. Press.

Takahashi, Tatsuo, and Motoharu Koba. 1977. Emerged Holocene coral reefs around Kume Island, Ryukyus. *Science Reports of Tohoku University* (Geography) 27 (2): 149–162.

Tamamori, Terunobu, and John C. James. 1995. *A Minute Guide to Okinawa: Society and Economy.* Naha, Japan: Bank of the Ryukyus International Foundation.

Taylor, Jonathan Solomon. 2000. Okinawa on the eve of the G-8 Summit. *Geographical Review* 90 (1): 123–130.

Uezu, Kaoru. 2001. Land transactions by enterprises and their characteristic impacts on tourism development in Onna-son, Okinawa Prefecture. *Human Geography* 53 (5): 57–70.

Waldichuk, T., and H. Whitney. 1997. Inhabitants' attitudes toward agricultural activities and urban development in an urbanizing Konjuka area in the rural-urban fringe of Tokyo. *Geographical Review of Japan* B 70:32–40.

Walker, Brett L. 2001. *The Conquest of the Ainu: Ecology and Culture in Japanese Expansion, 1590–1800.* Berkeley: Univ. of California Press.

Watanabe, H. 1973. *The Ainu Ecosystem: Environment and Group Structure.* American Ethnological Society Monograph 54. Seattle: Univ. of Washington Press.

Wigen, Karen. 1995. *The Making of the Japanese Periphery, 1750– 1920.* Berkeley: Univ. of California Press.

Yagasaki, Noritaka. 1997. *Japan: Geographical Perspectives on an Island Nation.* 3rd ed. Tokyo: Teikoku-Shoin.

Yamaguchi, Susumu. 2002. Street performers and street artists in Minami, Osaka. *Human Geography* 54 (2): 65–81.

Chapter 6

第六章

DEMOGRAPHIC AND SOCIAL CHALLENGES

Japan faces a number of demographic challenges as it enters the twenty-first century—falling birthrates, an aging society, shortage of labor—and social problems involving homelessness, minority groups, gender discrimination, and social welfare services. In this chapter the geographic dimension of these challenges and Japan's approach to them are analyzed. It is clear that these problems will affect Japan's domestic policy and international competitiveness.

Japan's population of 126.9 million (in 2000) is ninth largest in the world after China (1.2 billion), India (1.02 billion), the United States (284 million), Indonesia (210 million), Brazil (170 million), Russia (150 million), Pakistan (130 million), and Bangladesh (128 million). Japan accounts for 2.1 percent of the world population. Its population density in 2000 was 340 persons per square kilometer (0.4 sq mi) (as compared to 28 in the United States), making Japan the fourth-most-densely populated country. But because Japan's land is largely mountainous, its population density in terms of habitable land is far higher.

Since World War II the pace of socioeconomic and demographic change in Japan has been extraordinarily rapid. For example, between 1950 and 1980, real per capita income, often used as a measure of an area's general level of development, increased more than sevenfold, and the proportion of people living in urban places increased from 37 percent to 77 percent. Very rapid declines in fertility and mortality

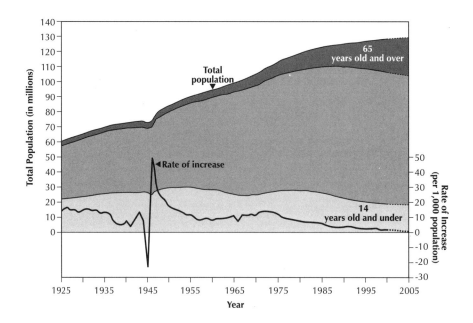

Fig. 6.1. Growth of population, 1925–2005. Based on data from the Management and Coordination Agency, Tokyo.

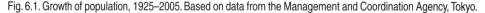

Table 6.1. Growth of population, age structure, and population density, 1870–2000

Year	Population (1,000)	0–14 years (% of population)	15–64 years (% of population)	65 and over (% of population)	Average annual rate of increase (%)	Population density (per km²)
1870	34,896	28.1	65.2	6.7		91
1880	36,649	31.9	61.7	6.4	0.7	96
1890	39,902	32.8	60.8	6.3	0.8	105
1900	43,847	33.9	60.7	5.4	1.1	115
1910	49,184	36.0	58.8	5.2	1.1	129
1920	55,963	36.5	58.3	5.3	1.2	147
1930	64,450	36.6	58.7	4.8	1.5	169
1940	73,114	36.1	59.2	4.7	1.1	191
1950	84,115	35.4	59.6	4.9	1.5	226
1960	94,302	30.2	64.1	5.7	0.9	253
1970	104,665	24.0	68.9	7.1	1.1	281
1980	117,060	23.5	67.3	9.1	0.9	314
1990	123,611	18.2	69.5	12.0	0.4	332
1997	126,166	15.3	69.0	15.7	0.2	338
2000	126,910	14.7	68.1	17.2	0.2	340

Source: Statistics Bureau, Ministry of Public Management, Home Affairs, Posts, and Telecommunications, Government of Japan.

occurred as well. Between 1947 and 1997, the total fertility rate (the number of births a woman would have if she experienced current age-specific birthrates throughout her reproductive age span), fell from 4.5 to 1.5 children per woman, and life expectancy increased from 50 to 77 years for males and from 54 to 84 years for females. As a consequence of the changes in fertility and mortality, Japan's population aged rapidly. The proportion of the population age 65 and over increased from 5 percent in 1950 to 15.7 percent in 1997 and is projected to increase to 20 percent by 2006. The population is expected to reach 128 million in 2010 and to decrease thereafter.

During the latter half of the Tokugawa shogunate, from the eighteenth century to the middle of the nineteenth, the population of Japan remained stable at around 30 million. Along with modernization and economic development after the Meiji Restoration in 1968, the population began to increase, reaching 55.9 million in 1920, when Japan's first census was taken. The population reached 60 million in 1926 and exceeded 100 million in 1967 (see fig. 6.1). After the early 1970s, the average annual rate of growth declined rapidly. During the years 1995–97 it was as low as 0.24 percent, compared with about 1 percent during the 1960s and the first

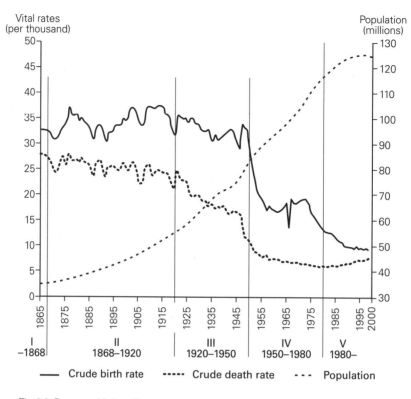

Fig. 6.2. Demographic transition.

half of the 1970s. The population increased 1.1 percent or 1.34 million between the censuses of 1995 and 2000.

The course of demographic transition in Japan can be divided into five phases: (1) premodern Japan, before 1868, with high birthrates and death rates and a stable population; (2) from 1868 to 1920, when the population began to grow more rapidly, from 34.8 million to 55.9 million; (3) 1920 to 1950, when, as a result of a rapidly declining death rate and slowly declining birthrate, the population increased from 56 million in 1920 to 84 million in 1950; (4) 1950 to 1980, characterized by a major decline in birthrate and a continued decline in the death rate; and (5) the period since 1980, characterized by both low birthrates and low death rates (see fig. 6.2).

Within the framework of demographic transition theory, the population of Japan during the preindustrial period (before 1868), comprising the first stage of the demographic transition, remained stable at 30 million because of the balance of high death rates and high birthrates. The excess of births over deaths, if any, was almost always either small or negligible. In the second stage (1868–1920), with the shift from a feudal to a modern society, the population began to increase rapidly: from 40 million in 1887 to 50 million in 1911, and 55.9 million in 1920. Mortality declined rapidly through the broadly perceived development process, which included industrialization and urbanization. The rapid decline in mortality without a concomitant decline in fertility resulted in rapid rates of population growth. In the third stage of demographic transition (1920–50) the birthrate (per 1,000) declined from 36.2 in 1920 to 28.1 in 1950, and the death rate (per 1,000) went down from 25.4 to 20.9 during the same period, resulting in moderate growth of the population, from 55.9 to 83.5 million. During the fourth stage of demographic transition (1950–80), the birthrate declined rapidly to 13.6 and the death rate to 6.2 in 1980, resulting in a slower growth of population. The fifth stage (1980–present), characterized by rapid declines in the birthrate to 9.5 in 1997 and a continued low death rate, resulted in slow population growth from 116 million in 1980 to 126 million in 1997. The age-specific fertility rate per woman (or

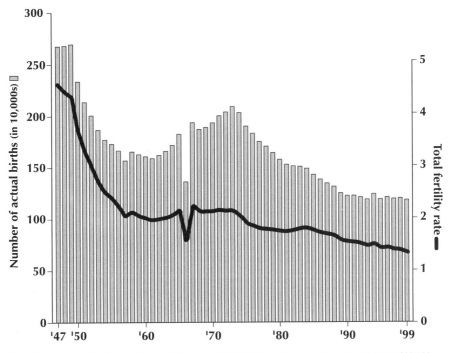

Fig. 6.3. Number of births and total fertility rate, 1947–99. Based on data from the Ministry of Health, Labor, and Welfare, Tokyo.

average number of children one woman gives birth to throughout her life) was 1.43 in 1996 (see fig. 6.3). To maintain the current population, this rate must be 2.1, but in recent years it has continued to decline. In 1997 it was 1.39, and in 1999 it declined to 1.34, the lowest ever recorded.

FALLING BIRTHRATES

Declining birthrates are a feature of all modern industrial societies, including the other rapidly developing nations in the Asia-Pacific region where work opportunities are opening up for women and social security systems are taking the place of children in caring for aging people. But no other country in the world has experienced the steady and rapid drop in birthrate that Japan has seen over the past twenty years (Hodge and Ogawa 1991). The declining birthrate has resulted in decreasing enrollments in elementary and secondary schools, and some schools have been closed (see fig. 6.4).

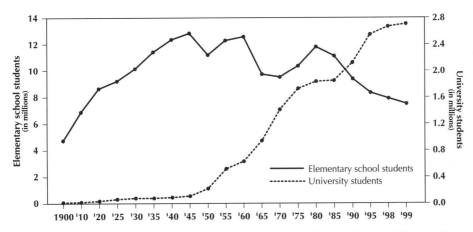

Fig. 6.4. Elementary school and university enrollment, 1900–1999. Based on data from the Ministry of Education, Science, Sports, and Culture, Tokyo (since 2003 Ministry of Education, Culture, Sports, Science, and Technology).

A mother with a baby in Yatsushiro, Kyushu. Japan's birthrate is among the lowest in the world. As a result the country's population is not increasing. The census of 2000 recorded a population of 126.91 million as of October 1, 2000. This was a 1.1 percent increase of 1.35 million from the previous census, taken in 1995. A declining rate of population increase has continued since 1980, and the decline over the previous five years was the greatest in any similar postwar period. Japan's population is smaller than that of Bangladesh, making it the world's ninth-most-populous nation as opposed to the eighth place it held in the previous census. Photo by Cotton Mather.

The causes of the drop in the birthrate, not to mention the concerns it has provoked, offer a lesson in how increasing wealth has not brought increasing happiness among the Japanese. Today two-thirds of the men and one-third of the women do not marry until their thirties. The average age at which Japanese marry for the first time has been rising for both men and women; in 1999 it was 28.7 and 26.8, respectively. Only in Sweden do people marry later, but unlike Sweden and other places, Japan is a country where unmarried couples almost never live together.

Young women are more interested in careers, education, and the attractions of a single lifestyle. They complain about living in a tiny apartment as a married woman, about the drudgery of marriage to a demanding husband who does not help at home, and about the near impossibility of mixing work and motherhood. To increase the number of births in Japan, it will be necessary to improve working conditions for women so they can get married and have children without facing the attendant difficulties. In addition, society as a whole must reconsider its attitude toward family and lifestyles.

Measures to halt the decline in the birthrate were initiated in 1990 after the fertility rate hit a low of 1.57 in 1989. The previous low was 1.58, recorded in 1966, by the Chinese calendar a Hinoe Uma year. According to folklore, women born in a Hinoe Uma year have a wild disposition and are shunned as brides; thus, the number of births dropped drasti-

Two mothers take a group of preschool children for a stroll through a neighborhood in Arakawa Ward of Tokyo. The number of preschool and elementary school students in Japan increased continuously from 1900 to 1945, and after World War II the number rose and fell alternately, but since 1980 the trend has been a continuous decline due to falling birthrates. As a result many schools are closing in Japan. Photo by P.P. Karan.

cally that year. The fertility rate was estimated at 1.24 in 2002.

Based on the concept that marriage and childbirth are personal-choice issues, the government has adopted an indirect approach to persuade people to have more children: it has been attempting to alter society so that both men and women can participate equally. In 1994, the government launched its Angel Plan, aimed at making child-rearing and work compatible. Under the plan, the government implemented a five-year program to create a better environment in which to rear children by investing 1.2 trillion yen to improve nursery schools and related programs. These efforts have not been able to halt the declining birthrate.

Even if a woman wants to have a child, working and other social conditions often make it difficult for her to do so. A task force panel looking at ways to reverse the declining birthrate reported in 1998 that part of the problem was that "workplaces place priority on work." The panel reported that it was difficult for women to both work and bring up a child because most housework in Japan is still done by women. As a result of this report, the government drew up its New Angel Plan in December 1999, with the targets of providing more child-care services, enhancing employment conditions for women, and improving housing for families with children.

Despite the various programs the government has come up with, the slide in the birthrate continues, raising questions about the effectiveness of the government measures. There are signs of change in Japanese companies' child-rearing leave systems, but essentially the work-comes-first mentality remains firmly entrenched. Many companies consider maternity leave for the first child acceptable but are inclined to view periods of leave for subsequent children as detrimental to a worker's job performance.

The National Institute for Population and Social Security Research linked the decline in total fertility rate to the increase in the number of unmarried people. Young Japanese now want to raise children in comfortable circumstances, because that is the lifestyle to which they have grown accustomed. Unmarried young people living with their parents have been termed "parasite singles." It is difficult for them to marry and give up the comfortable standard of living they are enjoying under their parents' roof.

A prevailing social anxiety is considered another reason for the decline in the number of children. Whatever the case, a sense of crisis about the future decline of Japan's population is shaking the political and business worlds. In April 2000 the Japan Federation of Employers' Associations (Nikkeiren) and the Japanese Trade Union Confederation (Rengo) released a joint statement that economic growth would be limited because the rapid decrease in birthrate would cause the domestic market to contract and increase the pressure on people of working age.

Aging Society

Japan's transformation into an advanced industrial nation has been accompanied by changes in the age structure of the population, as a result of declines in

An couple in their nineties in front of their home in Oshima, an island in the western Inland Sea, with a visitor from the University of Minnesota. The man served in the Imperial Army during the Meiji era and at the time of this photo still continued to grow rice and *mikan*. In 2004 the Japanese were healthier and lived longer than people in most of the industrialized nations; indeed, Japan has achieved the world's highest longevity rates. It is estimated that by the year 2020 one-fourth of all Japanese will be older than 65. The proportion of population age 65 or older, which was 12 percent in 1990, had risen to 16.6 percent in 2000 and was projected to be 20.3 percent in 2010 and 24.5 percent in 2020. This would make Japan the "grayest" of all the advanced industrial nations. An aging population presents challenges to the nation's domestic social policy and international competitiveness in the twenty-first century. Photo by P.P. Karan.

Field Report

Japan Wants More Babies

Japan is worried. Twenty-five years ago, its government could rely on the average Japanese woman to produce 2.13 children during her childbearing years. In 1990 the figure was down to 1.66 per woman. And the Ministry of Health, Labor, and Welfare is warning the people that, "just as was the case in the last days of ancient Rome, the decrease in the number of children is a sign of declining civilization" (*Asahi Shimbun*, July 3, 1987).

In 1988 the government suggested a new national holiday to be called Conjugal Day. It would be celebrated by husbands and wives enjoying each other. The idea got nowhere. Japanese women are not in favor of increased propagation, and neither are their husbands—not, at least, with their mates. Toshiki Kaifu, the prime minister in 1990, exhorted his countrymen to take their full annual vacations—from ten days to two weeks—but most Japanese workers prefer not to. In their table of values, spending time at work has a higher priority than fooling around with "the little woman." As a result the government has appealed to the people's sense of patriotism, warning that if they don't increase their reproduction rate, there will be no Japanese one thousand years from now. The government warns more persuasively of a shrinking tax base and skyrocketing demands for government services, especially for the elderly. The people aren't buying that threat either. Not now anyway. They may opt for more leisure time in the future, but not for a rising birthrate. Many are convinced their country is already overpopulated.

Indeed, women generally see the government's drive to combat the low birthrate as a test of their freedom. Many Japanese women postpone marriage or choose to have only one or two children, if they have any at all. Women complain about the high cost of education, the lack of day care, the scarcity of decent or affordable housing, and the physical and emotional burdens of raising children when their husbands are away at work from early morning until toward midnight when they stagger home on the last subway train.

Japanese humorists note that even so eligible a bachelor as Crown Prince Naruhito, the son of the emperor of Japan, had trouble finding a bride—and future empress—because few women of high social standing were willing to surrender their freedom to the imperial family.

Japan has started a program of family subsidies for each preschool child and also increased subsidies for day care programs. The government plans longer hours for twenty-three thousand government-supported day care centers, with some to stay open until ten o'clock in the evening. Local governments are going further by offering their own subsidies and campaigns. Yamaguchi Prefecture in rural western Japan has launched Operation Stork, with television commercials and postcards bearing slogans like "Get a brother or sister for your child."

Most public surveys show that the Japanese are unmoved by such steps. The government has responded by showing some appreciation of the complex nature of the problem, and it has suggested steps to improve housing, encourage maternity leaves, and permit men to come home earlier from work. But few think that these ideas will materialize soon. Not the least of the problem is the view that husbands in Japan work long hours and weekends not simply because of job pressures but because they enjoy the companionship of male colleagues more than what many now commonly call "home service."

Feminists in Japan say men's attitudes are changing but deep-rooted cultural traditions die hard. Feminists view the low birthrate as reflecting a "silent resistance by women" to the male-dominated system.

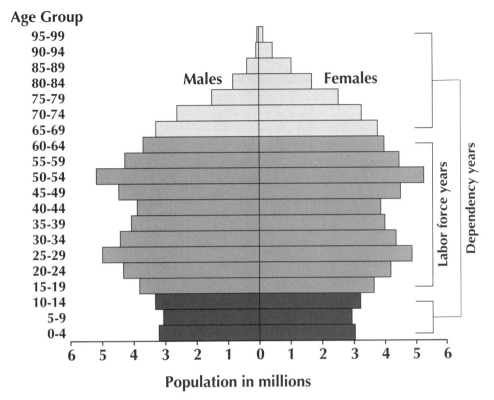

Age Group

Fig. 6.5. Population pyramid, 2000. Based on the National Census.

both birth and death rates (see fig. 6.5). Japan is not an old country, yet. Only 16 percent of its people are over age 65, a proportion comparable to that in most European nations. But the situation is changing rapidly. The average Japanese woman lives 83.6 years, and the average man 77. Meanwhile, women are having fewer babies than ever. So by 2035, it is estimated that more than 30 percent of Japanese will be 65 years or older. Forecasts like these have prompted middle-aged Japanese to turn conservative politically and to

A resident of a nursing home in Tokyo talks with officials of the home. The graying of Japan is a worry for the twenty-first century. The conservative habits of an aging population clinging to their savings have a lot to do with Japan's difficulty in restructuring its economy. Photo by Unryu Suganuma.

try to hang on to their financial assets. Concerned that state-supported pensions will dry up, consumers are clinging to their savings as never before and as a result deepening Japan's recession.

In places like Kiryu, a textile manufacturing town of 120,000 people sixty miles north of Tokyo, one can get a sense of things to come. About one in five people in the town is over 65, partly because competition from China and South Korea has hurt the textile industry and sent young people seeking jobs elsewhere. The town's commercial district is filled with clinics, dentists' offices, and companies offering services for the homebound elderly. Nighttime is quiet, with only a handful of teenagers hanging out in the main shopping area.

Since 1980 population growth is the lowest ever recorded. Because of the low birthrate, the average family size is shrinking, and there is a shortage of young people entering the workforce. In addition, because the Japanese have the longest average life span in the world, the percentage of elderly in the population is increasing rapidly. In 2000 the elderly population (65 years and over) numbered more than 20 million, or 16 percent of the nation's population, the highest level ever in Japan in both absolute numbers and percentage. The percentage, which was 7.1 percent in 1970, more than doubled to 15.7 in 1997. The aging of the population is expected to proceed at a rapid rate and may exceed 20 percent of the population in 2006. The number of children (0–14 years) has gradually declined; this group accounted for 14.3 percent of the population in 2000. At the same time the elderly population made up 18.4 percent. The working age group (15–64 years) has continued to shrink; it numbered 86 million, or 68 percent of the population, in 2000. As a result, the dependency ratio (the ratio of children and the elderly to the working population) is expected to increase in the future (see fig. 6.5). It is estimated that by 2025 some 26 percent will be in the over-65 category. Japan will then have a higher proportion of elderly people than any other country in the world, including even Germany and Sweden. And although today there are still 5 people working and contributing to national pension schemes for every person collecting an old-age pension, by 2025 there are likely to be only 2 workers per pensioner.

Demographic trends like those noted above threaten to wreck havoc with Japan's economy (Martin 1989). They will put the brakes on economic growth and corporate profits and will likely contribute to higher inflation and a weakening of the yen. But the effects on corporate Japan will not be uniformly negative. There will be winners as well as losers. Makers of baby products are likely to be hurt, for example, while those catering to the needs of the elderly are likely to benefit. The private sector is beginning to see benefits in catering to the elderly. Take real estate, for example. Japanese developers are targeting the elderly as valued customers by building homes designed to accommodate them. Features include single-level layouts, handrails in the bathrooms and along staircases, wider hallways for the wheelchair-bound, and automatic lights along walkways. A company called Mitsui Homes offers a "Long Life" model incorporating wall panels that can easily be dismantled and put up again elsewhere so that rooms can be altered with the owner's changing needs.

Modifications extend beyond housing matters to everyday products ranging from toiletries to appliances. Does failing eyesight make it difficult for senior citizens to tell a bottle of shampoo from a rinse? Toiletry maker Kao has the answer: mold ridges into the plastic containers so they can feel the difference. Can't make out whether the CD player is turned on? Electronics giant Sony makes a model that signals this by sound. For easier identification, other manufacturers are producing gadgets with switches that flick up and down, instead of flat control panels. The company TempStaff, better known for dispatching office personnel, offers workers to help senior citizens with household chores and check on their health. For those who want to travel, a Tokyo firm called Life Commons provides a trained traveling companion. The services extend to sports. Manna Country Club in Chiba, east of Tokyo, has built a second golf course with the elderly in mind. Among the attractions: eight health-check stations equipped with machines that allow golfers to measure their heart rate and blood pressure every couple of holes. In case of emergency they can call for a doctor from the telephones installed in each booth. And there is no extra charge; players pay the same fee as they would on the unadorned greens.

The major fiscal implications of the aging society are clear. Either the pension contributions that working people make will have to rise from the current 17 percent of salary to around 30 percent by 2025, or pensioners will have to accept far lower benefits. As in most cases, the outcome is bound to include adjustments in both directions. The government believes it would be political suicide to allow pension contributions to rise above 30 percent. It has devised a schedule for increasing contributions gradually over the next three decades to a maximum of 29.6 percent. The premiums rose to 17.4 percent in 1997 and will go up by 2.5 percentage points every five years. The government has managed to sell this idea to employers, who pay half of the pension contributions. Normally, the Liberal Democratic Party (LDP), the main force in Japan's coalition government, would do anything to avoid antagonizing its supporters in big business. Although the union-backed socialists (who call themselves Social Democrats) have had no objections to getting employers to pitch in more, they have fought hard to prevent benefits from being scaled back or deferred. The political parties have struck a deal to raise the mandatory retirement age from 60 to 65, starting early in the twenty-first century.

Because of years of rising payments, interest rates near zero, and falling stock prices, faith in the Japanese pension system is so weak that a staggering 37 percent of self-employed workers do not pay their premiums, which could leave them without any pension. Japan's pension situation is one of the worst cases among industrial nations because of the size of the deficits and the graying of the population. Many other countries have had an influx of younger immigrants, who have been replenishing tax rolls and pension plans, but Japan has not. Raising investment returns on Japan's Government Pension Investment Fund (31.6 trillion yen, or about $283 billion) to keep the national pension system from collapsing is a major challenge. Through new investment techniques, such as indexing, and through breaking with Japanese custom by rewarding better-performing (not better-connected) investment managers, Japan is hoping to increase returns and reassure the public.

Japanese women are facing more serious consequences as Japan heads toward an aging society. Since women live longer than men in Japan, the number of elderly widows living alone is rising rapidly. The population of women 65 or older reached about 8.92 million in 1990, while men in the same age group numbered 6.01 million, a difference of 2.91 million. It was estimated that there would be 3.34 million more elderly women than men by the year 2000; by 2025 the figure will rise to 4.6 million. In addition, the percentage of women 65 or older living alone will rise sharply from the 1.47 percent recorded in 1990 to about 19.5 percent in 2010 and 21.8 percent in 2025. According to official figures, about 20 percent of all elderly women will be living alone by the turn of the century. In contrast, the percentage of elderly men living alone in the year 2025 will be about 12.3 percent.

The number of bedridden elderly women is also higher than the number of bedridden elderly men, and this trend is not likely to change in the coming decades. By the year 2025, there will be about 1.45 million bedridden elderly women in Japan. In addition, the number of senile elderly women is expected to increase sharply—reaching 2.21 million by 2025 and accounting for about 11.69 percent of elderly women. The main reason for the steep increase in the number of senile women is that the population of "very old" women (85 or older) is expected to grow rapidly. In the next thirty years, that group is expected to show more rapid growth than any other age group among the elderly. As a result, Japanese health professionals have started formulating measures to provide services in the future for the senile, bedridden elderly women living alone.

Welfare services and nursing homes for the elderly are relatively limited in Japan (Sugiura 2000, 2002; Miyazawa 1999). Based on a study in Gifu Prefecture, Yuko Tahara and Hiroo Kamiya (2002) have shown that elderly people in Japan tend to stay put in their small towns or rural communities because of their emotional attachment to the home place. Most of the time women—generally women in their forties—are the ones who care for their bedridden, senile parents. In 1990 one out of every fifteen women in their 40s was taking care of an elderly parent or other relative. But by 2025, the percentage is likely to rise to about 45.63 percent. This means that one in every two women will be in charge of looking after elderly people. Of course, the women who will be in their forties in 2025 probably will have entered the workforce, because of shortages in the labor market. As a result, it does not seem likely that one out of two of them will have the time to take care of bedridden or senile parents.

CARE OF THE ELDERLY

The household structure in Japan has changed in the direction of relatively fewer stem households and relatively more nuclear households. Between 1960 and 1990, the proportion of parents over 65 living with their children fell from 87 percent to 50 percent, but it was still much higher than in other advanced industrial countries. In Japan, older persons are also less likely to be institutionalized. The proportion of persons over 65 who were institutionalized was only 1.6 percent in Japan in 1985, but it was 5 percent in the United States in 1987. However, hospital stays of elderly persons are about ten times longer in Japan than in the United States. The unusually high incidence of coresidence in Japan partly reflects the persistence of Confucian moral teachings about filial obligations to parents. These prescriptions, which are reinforced by a "shame culture" characterized by deep sensitivity to social approval, emphasize obligations between individuals in direct lineal descent within stem families.

Customarily, the first in line for this duty involving living arrangements is the eldest son. In such households, it is usually the son's wife who plays the role of principal caregiver for her parents-in-law if they need care (Ogawa, Retherford, and Saito 2003). Reinforcing Confucian tradition are legal requirements for familial support of the elderly that still exist in Japan.

Because women are the primary caregivers for elderly persons, changes in the status of women have also had an impact on care of the elderly (Campbell and Brody 1985). The educational attainment of women has been rising in Japan over the past few decades. In 1960 only 2.5 percent of women were enrolled in a university, compared with 13 percent of the men. In 1997 these figures had risen to 26 percent and 43 percent respectively. There also has been a major shift in female employment, away from farming and unpaid family work to paid employment outside the home. In 1997 women made up 40.6 percent of the work force. These changes in women's education and work outside the home have tended to weaken obligations to elderly parents.

Legal changes have also weakened these obligations. In 1948 the Civil Code was revised to reflect more closely a philosophy of individual rights suited to the requirements of a modern economy. The new Civil Code, which replaced the old Meiji Civil Code, did away with primogeniture inheritance and the legal power of family heads. These code revisions have contributed to further changes in gender roles in modern Japan.

Another factor tending to weaken obligations to care for elderly parents is increased public support for the aged in the form of pensions and medical insurance coverage. In 1961 the government established a universal pension and health care system. Japan's recent pension replacement rates (ratio of pension to previous earnings, taking into account how long the recipient paid into the system before retiring) are now comparable to those in other industrial nations. Although Japan's outlays for social security are still low compared with those in other

This woman in Tokyo's Shinjuku Ward is one of many who take care of their aging parents at home. The struggle to care for aging parents is increasingly preoccupying Japan. There is a belief that the elderly want to live at home with their children and that Japan can resolve the elderly-care problem through filial duty and a massive plan for home nursing care. Photo by P.P. Karan.

A nursing home on Oshima Island, south of Iwakuni, in the Inland Sea. Japan, with the world's most rapidly growing elderly population, has 1.2 million people bedridden, and half of that number have been bedridden for three years or more. Hospitals are overburdened with seniors who stay for months, and nursing homes are in short supply. The monthly cost of a nursing home is $2,860, of which the individual pays $286. Photo by P.P. Karan.

advanced industrial nations (less than half of those in many western European nations and the United States), they have grown substantially over time. Social security expenditures amounted to 19.1 percent of the national budget in 1998.

The support of the elderly within families is increasingly based on personal needs and motives rather than blind conformity to traditional norms and values (Campbell and Campbell 2003; Liang 2003). Coresidence patterns and supporting norms and values nevertheless have changed slowly during the postwar period, compared with the rapidity of underlying socioeconomic and demographic change.

The bulk of Japan's very old population (over 85) is in the Pacific Corridor from Tokyo to Kyushu (see fig. 6.6). Within this belt, Kyushu has one of the largest populations of hundred-year-olds in Japan. The locals attribute this to hard work, healthy diets including plenty of fresh vegetables, and *mokosu*—a dialect term for a state of mind hovering somewhere between the merely stubborn and the devoutly cantankerous.

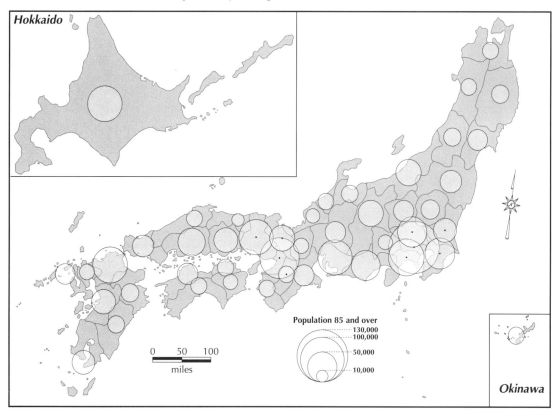

Fig. 6.6. Population age 85 and over, by prefecture. Based on data from the Ministry of Health, Labor, and Welfare, Tokyo.

Field Report

A Grave Concern—Japan Short of Burial Space

Every August, Japan's cemeteries come alive during the Festival of the Dead, when ancestors who have died are believed to return for a brief visit. But with the living crammed into just about every nook and cranny in large metropolitan areas, the ancient festival is forcing many to face a harsh fact of life: for those in need of a final resting place, the situation is, well, quite grave.

During August, tens of millions of Japanese visit their family plots for the Obon festival, one of the most important celebrations on the Japanese calendar. Many of the country's businesses close down for the festival. But Obon's centerpieces—the cemeteries—are in the throes of a serious crisis. The problem is space, particularly in the greater Tokyo area, where one-fifth of the Japanese live.

Tokyo has eight city-operated cemeteries, but only four have any openings. In the year 2000 there were five applicants for each plot, and the winners were chosen by lottery. Temples, which have traditionally handled most of the burden, are running out of space as well. For example, at Daiyoji, one of the more than seventy Buddhist temples in Tokyo's eastern cemetery district, the chances of getting a plot are nil.

Most Japanese are cremated; the average grave occupies only one square yard. But at Tokyo's publicly operated cemeteries, even a memorial plot that size costs on the average up to $18,000. The land pinch has inspired some innovations. There are now tiny grave-boxes that look like coin-operated lockers, or computer-operated machinery that brings memorials up from space-saving underground storage whenever a relative comes to visit. According to a recent book, *Graves: What Will You Do?* the cremated remains of as many as 1 million Tokyoites are being kept at home by families who, for various reasons, are unable to make suitable arrangements.

Japan's funeral industry is worth nearly $15 billion. A rough estimate of the annual cost of funeral services is $7 billion, with another $3 billion spent on ceremonial gifts. The gravestone and cemetery plot segment of the industry takes in $3 billion a year, and the *butsudan* (a small, family Buddhist altar) industry grosses $2 billion.

The funeral industry is supported by the practice whereby people attending the funeral present the grieving family with condolence gifts of money. Approximately half the cost of the funeral is covered by these gifts, called *koden.* When older folks die, about half the people attending their funerals are the colleagues and business associates of the deceased's children. As Japanese society ages, it is increasingly likely that the chief mourner—usually the eldest son—will himself have retired, so there will be fewer people at the funeral. The drop in the birthrate also means the deceased will have fewer children in the future. In forty years, the average money received in condolence gifts could be half what it is today.

During Japan's period of rapid economic growth, a good funeral was considered to be one that cost a lot of money. But now there is backlash against high funeral costs, which until recently were rising faster than consumer costs. Social trends are also changing. In Japanese funerals prior to the mid-1980s, the dead were hidden from view. Increasingly, however, viewing death is no longer regarded as taboo. This change is incompatible with the future expansion of the funeral business. The prosperity of the funeral business has always been supported by the Japanese view of death as taboo. People were content to leave decisions about funeral costs and details entirely in the hands of funeral directors. Now more and more people are asking for simple funerals that reflect the character of the person who passed away. In the future more and more consumers will make the decisions about the arrangements and their cost.

A Chiba-based funeral home has set up an online system allowing people to worship their ancestors via the Internet, sparing them the trouble of visiting the grave in person. The funeral home Joko arranges for the Buddhist monk to read sutras aloud at a box-shaped gravestone

(continued on the following page)

Field Report: *A Grave Concern—Japan Short of Burial Space* (continued)

that contains the ancestor's remains. Images and sounds from the ceremony are transmitted in real time to personal computers and Internet telephones through high-speed asymmetrical digi-

tal subscriber lines. The service, the first of its kind in Japan, helps relatives worship together without physically leaving their homes to attend the ancestral graves.

Since April 1, 2000, when a new elder-care system was started, about a million people chose some of the options offered—help with bathing or eating, or simply conversation—and are paying 10 percent of the cost. About 1.2 million elderly are bedridden, and half of this number have been so for three years or more. Hospitals are overburdened with seniors who stay for months, and nursing homes are in short supply. The struggle to take care of aging parents is one that is increasingly preoccupying Japan. All the tensions in the Japanese society between its modern, Western face and its patriarchal foundations play out in the effort to set up a long-term care program. The struggle is to reconcile the needs of modern Japan—with more women working outside the

home and fewer elderly living with their children—with the belief that the elderly want to live at home and that Japan can bring this about through filial duty and a massive plan for nursing care. The program puts Japan ahead of most other industrialized countries in dealing with long-term care for the aged, but it is criticized for its continuing reliance on female relatives to shoulder the bulk of the burden.

POPULATION DISTRIBUTION AND MIGRATION PATTERNS

The uneven geographic distribution of population in Japan is related largely to regional differences in the level of development (see fig. 6.7). Since early times, a major proportion of the country's popula-

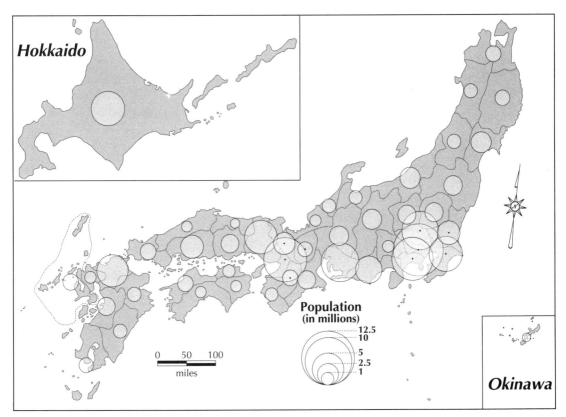

Fig. 6.7. Distribution of population, 2000. Based on the National Census.

Table 6.6. Area, population distribution, density, and per capita income, 2000

Prefecture	Capital city	Population (in thousands)	Area (km²)	Density (km²)	Per capita income in yen (1,000)
Hokkaido	Sapporo	5,695	83,452	73.1	2,809
Aomori	Aomori	1,475	9,606	157.8	2,491
Iwate	Morioka	1,414	15,278	94.0	2,578
Miyagi	Sendai	2,360	7,285	321.4	2,798
Akita	Akita	1,196	11,611	103.8	2,599
Yamagata	Yamagata	1,250	9,323	134.6	2,638
Fukushima	Fukushima	2,135	13,782	155.9	2,778
Ibaraki	Mito	3,002	6,094	490.5	2,995
Tochigi	Utsunomiya	2,012	6,408	311.7	3,203
Gumma	Maebashi	2,030	6,363	316.4	3,098
Saitama	Urawa	6,929	3,797	1,791.8	3,365
Chiba	Chiba	5,920	5,156	1,132.4	3,267
Tokyo	Tokyo	11,837	2,187	5,408.6	4,255
Kanagawa	Yokohama	8,443	2,414	3,425.6	3,355
Niigata	Niigata	2,490	12,582	198.7	2,905
Toyama	Toyama	1,125	4,246	266.1	3,063
Ishikawa	Kanazawa	1,186	4,185	281.5	3,037
Fukui	Fukui	831	4,188	197.9	2,841
Yamanashi	Kofu	893	4,465	198.2	2,912
Nagano	Nagano	2,223	13,585	162.7	3,032
Gifu	Gifu	2,118	10,598	199.2	2,948
Shizuoka	Shizuoka	3,776	7,779	483.3	3,120
Aichi	Nagoya	7,008	5,151	1,349.0	3,572
Mie	Tsu	1,864	5,714	321.5	2,934
Shiga	Otsu	1,333	4,017	324.2	3,337
Kyoto	Kyoto	2,633	4,612	571.4	3,086
Osaka	Osaka	8,801	1,892	4,562.4	3,257
Hyogo	Kobe	5,484	8,387	652.5	3,046
Nara	Nara	1,449	3,691	392.0	2,649
Wakayama	Wakayama	1,074	4,724	232.6	2,521
Tottori	Tottori	614	3,507	177.2	2,638
Shimane	Matsue	764	6,707	115.4	2,403

(continued on the following page)

Table 6.2. Area, population distribution, density, and per capita income, 2000 *(continued)*

Prefecture	Capital city	Population (in thousands)	Area (km²)	Density (km²)	Per capita income in yen (1,000)
Okayama	Okayama	1,959	7,110	275.8	2,916
Hiroshima	Hiroshima	2,883	8,475	340.4	3,036
Yamaguchi	Yamaguchi	1,538	6,110	254.1	2,771
Tokushima	Tokushima	830	4,144	202.6	2,702
Kagawa	Takamatsu	1,029	1,875	553.5	2,822
Ehime	Matsuyama	1,497	5,675	269.3	2,589
Kochi	Kochi	810	7,104	114.6	2,442
Fukuoka	Fukuoka	5,000	4,968	1,002.8	2,702
Saga	Saga	884	2,429	364.3	2,549
Nagasaki	Nagasaki	1,525	4,091	375.8	2,572
Kumamoto	Kumamoto	1,865	7,402	253.6	2,507
Oita	Oita	1,226	6,337	194.0	2,698
Miyazaki	Miyazaki	1,176	7,734	154.7	2,214
Kagoshima	Kagoshima	1,788	9,186	197.1	2,277
Okinawa	Naha	1,312	2,265	567.4	2,149

Source: Statistics Bureau, Ministry of Public Management, Home Affairs, Posts, and Telecommunications, Government of Japan.

tion has resided on coastal plains, inland basins, and flatlands along river valleys, which are suitable for agricultural and fishing activities. In the past, the western part of the country, particularly the more developed Kinki region, was more densely populated than the eastern part. During the Meiji Restoration, the promotion of developmental activities in Hokkaido resulted in new settlements and consequently in an increase in population in the northeastern part of the country.

Industrial development since 1872 has led to the concentration of population in a few urban areas, while many rural areas have experienced population declines. During Japan's post–World War II recovery and the period of high economic growth since 1960, employment shifted from primary industries to secondary and tertiary industries. These shifts in employment were accompanied by a massive concentration of the population in urban areas (Kaki-uchi and Hasegawa 1979). The population of three large urban regions—Tokyo, Osaka, and Nagoya—increased from 30 million in 1955 to 47 million in 1975 and 56 million in 2001.

The southern part of the Kanto region, which includes the metropolitan Tokyo Prefecture, has had the largest share of Japan's population since 1950. It has 8.7 percent of the total land area of the country but nearly 25 percent of the national population. The second-largest concentration of population is in the western part of the Kinki region (about 14 percent of the country's population), which includes the metropolitan Osaka and Kyoto Prefectures. The Tokai region, with Nagoya city, has the third-largest metropolitan area, with 12 percent of the nation's population. Thus, more than half of the country's population is concentrated in the densely populated areas in and around the cities of Tokyo, Osaka, and Nagoya. The population densities of these areas are

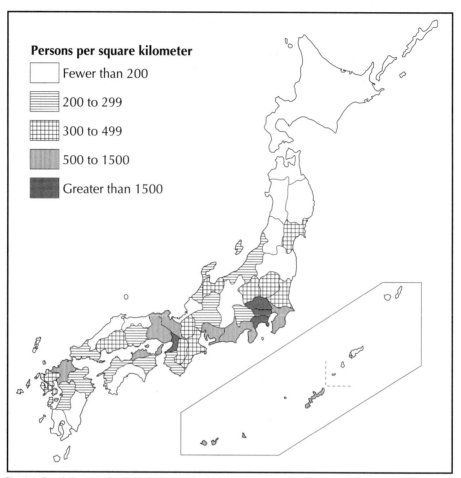

Fig. 6.8. Population density, 2000. Based on the National Census.

very much higher than average; in 2000 there were 5,409 persons per square kilometer in Tokyo, 4,562 in Osaka, and 1,349 in Nagoya (see fig. 6.8). These areas face a number of problems related to overcrowding, such as environmental pollution and housing shortages.

Since 1950 some nonmetropolitan regions such as Tohoku, Hokuriku, Tosan, Shikoku, and Kyushu have experienced a decrease in the absolute numbers of their population as well as in their share of national population. The continuing flow of people from nonmetropolitan into metropolitan areas, particularly to the three major metropolitan areas of Tokyo, Osaka, and Nagoya, has been conspicuous since the early 1950s (Gauthier, Tanaka, and Smith 1992; Ogawa 1986). The Minami-Kanto (south Kanto) region receives about 55 percent of its migrants from northeast Japan (the Hokkaido, Tohoku,

Kita-Kanto or North Kanto, Hokuriku, and Tosan regions). The Nishi-Kinki (west Kinki) region receives its migrants from western Japan, especially from east Kinki, Choguku, and Shikoku. The Kyushu region sends out one-third of its migrants to the Minami-Kanto region and another one-third to Nishi-Kinki region. The Tokai region (Nagoya Metropolitan Area) receives about 30 percent of its migrants from Kyushu and another 24 percent from Minami-Kanto.

There are two major focal points serving as the destinations for migrants—the Tokyo and Osaka Metropolitan Areas. Tokyo has a nationwide attracting influence, whereas the influence of Osaka is limited largely to western Japan. The Nagoya Metropolitan Area, situated between Tokyo and Osaka, serves as a destination only for local migrants.

Japanese rural regions and communities have

Field Report

Foreign Brides in Japan

In the snowcapped rugged mountain regions of northern Japan, rural, rice-growing towns are shrinking as young men and women abandon the rigors of farm life for the anonymous freedom of Japan's giant cities.

Japanese custom affords no such freedom to the family's oldest son, however. According to rural tradition, the eldest male must stay to care for his aging parents and inherit the family land. The situation has led to a shortage of eligible women in rural villages. More women are working now and don't want to stay in the village or rural town. For example, the village of Shirataka in Yamagata Prefecture has seen most of its young women leave. In 1998 Shirataka had only 127 babies. At this rate, Shirataka would have to close its schools soon. The very existence of this rural town is in jeopardy.

So Shirataka and dozens of other rural settlements throughout Yamagata Prefecture have encouraged families to spend more than $25,000 each to import brides from China, South Korea, Thailand, and the Philippines. In 1997 the Japanese Justice Ministry issued 274,000 residency visas for foreign spouses of Japanese citizens, an increase of 39 percent in five years. But of more

than one thousand marriages arranged for Japanese men and foreign women in Yamagata Prefecture, only a few are happy.

The women who come from Asian countries are attracted by the relative prosperity of Japan (Ueda 1993), by far the most prosperous economy in the region even after a decade of crippling recession. Many women feel guilty about walking out of their bad marriages because of the large amount of money their husbands' families paid to bring them to Japan. The money they earn in Japan helps ease the poverty of relatives back home, and if their husbands divorced them, most of the women would be forced to leave Japan—possibly without their children.

Even if a man and a woman are compatible, Japanese xenophobia sometimes gets in the way. Communities in rural Japan, where families have often lived together for five or six generations, are not especially welcoming to outsiders, even to Japanese who grew up in other parts of the country. These foreign wives don't speak the language and get married to a stranger with no information and no love. So it is a very stressful situation.

changed remarkably since the 1950s, as a result of the outflow of labor from rural areas brought about by rapid economic growth. Many farm laborers have begun to work in the urban industrial sector. Part-time farmers have increased in number, and the worker-peasant phenomenon has become widespread. As economic conditions in the rural areas have stagnated, farmers have made efforts to get more stable off-farm employment, such as working in the public sector or for large companies. Such nonfarm occupations have become so important for farmers that they are a detriment to efficient farm management.

The overwhelming concentration of population in the Tokyo Metropolitan Area and the declining population in the countryside have prompted the government to begin relocation of certain administrative functions from Tokyo to other regions. In re-

cent years, attempts to revitalize industries such as biotechnology and semiconductors in Kyushu have had some success in attracting young people back to depopulated rural areas from the big cities. A return migration from major metropolitan areas to depopulated regions has been recorded in recent years (Esaki, Arai, and Kawaguchi 1999, 2000).

LITERACY, EDUCATION, AND CIVILITY

With the recognition that education, science, and technology are important cornerstones for socioeconomic development, Japan's expenditure on education has increased since the Meiji era. In the post–World War II period, investment in research and development in science and technology increased substantially. The number of both schoolchildren and university students increased continually

Students at a high school in Toshima Ward of Tokyo enjoy lunch, which they cooked in the school's kitchen. The percentage of students who went to high school exceeded 50 percent in 1954 and continued increasing until recent years, when it leveled off at about 95 percent for both male and female students. Photo by P.P. Karan.

from 1900 to 1945. But owing to falling birthrates the number of schoolchildren has declined. For example, the number of lower secondary school students (age 12–15 years) in 1998 decreased to 4.38 million, down by 26.3 percent from 6.08 million in 1987. By 2000 the high school enrollment had leveled off at 95 percent of the high-school-age population. University enrollment has continued to increase since 1945, and in 1998 more than 2.6 million students were enrolled in Japanese universities (see fig. 6.4).

The struggle for education is a grim one in Japan. The competition to get into a good senior high school and then into a leading college is far more rigorous than in the United States. The reason for the intensity of the struggle is that where one receives one's education, along with family status, means literally everything in job determination. If a student cannot enter a good college, and if he or she does not occupy a special social position (and only a few do), he or she cannot look forward to getting a satisfactory job. Consequently, the Japanese student is more serious and industrious than the American. In senior high schools, students will work themselves to a high degree of tension preparing for the college entrance examination. Failing the entrance examination is a common cause of suicide. Such intense striving for education is responsible for the 98 percent literacy rate in Japan—the highest in the world.

In Japan the pressure to excel starts with the exam to enter first grade in one of the most competitive elementary schools. Students enter cram schools to prepare for entrance exams. Cram schools have been a hotly debated facet of Japanese education for years, and the burden is spreading to younger and younger children in order to gain an edge in an increasingly competitive society. At about age three, children in some families begin a string of cram schools and exams that will play a crucial role in determining whether they retire from first-rate jobs sixty years later. To be a tiny tot in many Japanese families is not to play leisurely on swings and seesaws, but to spend hours at classroom desks, memorizing stories, learning homonyms, making calendars, taking achievement tests, and walking on balance beams—all before four years of age. The phenomenon of competing to get into a good preschool, and competing once there, may not be entirely new to an American with young children, but it is carried to greater lengths in Japan.

Many parents are deeply troubled by the *shiken jigoku,* or examination hell. But if they try to spare their sons and daughters the ordeal of cram school and exams, they may be sentencing them to second-rate futures. Good schools make a difference everywhere in the world. But the advantage of a good school is hugely magnified in Japan. The best jobs go almost exclusively to those who have just graduated from prestigious universities; companies and ministries almost never hire midcareer professionals. But to get into a first-rate university, one should go to a top high school, and to enter a prominent high school, one should study at a good elementary school—a worry of many of the parents of Japan's

Parents in Japan invest time and interest in the education of their children. With fathers commuting to work from suburban homes and absent for many hours each day, the job of getting the children ready for the schooling that will determine their life paths falls to the mother and wife. The "education mama" (*kyoiku mama*), as mothers are termed, bears the responsibility of seeing to it that her children secure entrance into prestigious schools that will provide launching pads for future success. Examinations and preparation for them are the focus of education from early life through entrance into colleges and universities. Photo by P.P. Karan.

1.3 million first-graders-to-be. The sad fact is that the salary and prestige that a Japanese executive has in his sixties may have less to do with his job performance in his forties or fifties and more to do with whether he went to cram school and was a good test-taker as a four- or five-year old.

Successful cram schools, or *jukus,* which range from national chains to small classes in an apartment, may charge more than nine thousand dollars a year for essentially two and a half hours of instruction each week. Often exclusive, they sometimes have no listings in the phone book. Application is by recommendation only, and gaining admission is extremely difficult. Although many Japanese experts say stimulus for young children is generally good, they also warn that cram schools could end up smothering a child's ability to think independently. The system is criticized for depriving children of the joy of youth and for turning out mechanical thinkers. Broadly speaking, Japanese students learn to obey, not to question. Japan's educational system is now struggling to reshape itself, starting with the youngest pupils. Parents and educators alike say they want to nurture more individuality and independent thinking.

Much of Japanese society, good and bad, seems rooted in school practices; in some ways the Japanese economic miracle was won in the nation's classrooms. They offer discipline, orderly classes, safe corridors, and rigorous training in basics like reading and mathematics. Schools not only teach students academics but also train them to fit into society.

A father plays violin with his daughter at home in Nagoya. Parents emphasize music and arts education for their children. Photo by P.P. Karan.

Schools begin to inculcate the values that dominate Japanese society, such as the emphasis on team and hierarchy. Beginning in junior high school, for instance, everyone is cast as *senpai* or elder, or as *kohai* or junior. Pressure from teachers and parents to study is intense. Particularly great is the pressure from the "education mama"—the devoted housewife—whose mission in life is to wheedle her children to spend time studying.

The academic pressure in most cases pays off. Japan's educational system produces students who perform far better on international examinations than Americans do, and Japanese students are indisputably among the best in the world in solving mathematical equations. Despite a recent decline in the quality of education, Japan excels in international comparisons, even though government spending on education accounts for a smaller proportion of its gross national product than in the United States. The lower spending is partly attributed to spartan physical conditions: students do all the window-cleaning and floor-waxing themselves. Japan's educational system served the nation admirably over the last century, in building an industrial society with a labor force skilled in science and engineering. Youngsters are well behaved, studious, and law abiding; Japan's low crime rates are well known and widely envied around the world. But what is even more striking than the lack of crime is the overwhelming civility: graffiti and vandalism are rare, and school sports teams not only bow to each other before a game but also rush over to the opposing team's stand after the game to pay their respects.

MINORITY GROUPS IN JAPAN

About 4 percent of the Japanese population consists of minorities, who suffer discrimination resulting from psychological and cultural factors. The minorities include burakumin, Koreans, Ainu, and Okinawans, representing respectively indigenous, foreign, aboriginal, and conquered minority population groups (Weiner 1997).

There are in Japan 2 to 3 million former outcastes, called burakumin. Nearly 40 percent of the burakumin, as well as the bulk of the Koreans, live in the Kinki region. The Shinto association of pollution with death was linked long ago with the Buddhist teaching against the killing of animals. Those who were engaged in work dealing with the dead and the slaughtering of animals were considered polluted and called burakumin. Contacts with these people were shunned, and a pattern of residential segregation of burakumin has emerged in major communities. Despite occupational changes, their outcaste status continues as long as they live in the segregated areas known as *buraku*. Some burakumin try to hide their outcaste

A group of Ainu in Shiraoi, Hokkaido, performs a dance. The Ainu population has continued to decline. In 1986 the total number of people identifying themselves as Ainu was about twenty-four thousand. Photo by P.P. Karan.

Field Report

Little Korea in Chiba City

Sakaecho, in Chiba city's Chu Ward, was once a typically bustling neighborhood that could have been anywhere in urban Japan. No more: today it is a Little Korea. A community of Koreans, sustained since prewar days, has converted the district into a vibrant center of culture and commerce.

Some of the ethnic Koreans who call Sakaecho home have roots in Japan stretching back many years; others took residence during the boom years of the asset-inflated economy or even more recently, since its collapse. The popular old name for this area was Humming Road, but its assortment of Korean *yakiniku* (barbecue) restaurants and specialty goods stores has earned it a second nickname, Kimchi Road. An elderly Korean lady manages a yakiniku restaurant on Kimchi Road. She came to Japan at age six with her mother, father, and younger sister. The family was following her father, who was assigned to work in a Hokkaido coal mine. In 1943 the whole family fled to Mobara in Chiba Prefecture, where they had relatives, to escape the harsh working conditions in the mine. After World War II the lady began operating restaurants. Some of the customers tossed their leftover pork bones in the restaurant doorway after finishing their meals, she recalled. Often strangers would stand outside, hissing at her and taunting: "Koreans stink of garlic."

In the restaurant's early days, patronage was equally divided between Japanese and Koreans. But now nearly 90 percent of her customers are Japanese. The restaurant touts its fare as "the real taste of Seoul," and the lady owner regularly travels to her homeland to buy up the hot peppers and Korean vegetables featured in the menu.

Sakaecho was once nothing out of the ordinary, located as it was between two Chiba train stations—one owned by the Japanese National Railways (JNR), the other by Keisei Electric Railway Company. But in 1963 JNR opened a new Chiba Station, and four years later Keisei followed suit. A ghostly hush fell on the once busy local streets.

When vacant floor space became a common sight in Sakaecho's once-thriving commercial area, Koreans hastened to fill the void. Even before the war, Korean-run bars, restaurants, and rag and bone merchants had been attracted to the area. Around 1990, before the collapse of the asset-inflated economy, a wave of new comers from South Korea (many of them without valid visas) opened up "snack" nightclubs, yakiniku restaurants, and Korean dry goods shops—all in this inexpensive abandoned railway district.

A survey of South Korean–run businesses carried out by the principal regional office of Mindan, the Korean Residents Union in Japan, reported that Sakaecho in 2000 had some 30 yakiniku restaurants and 150 snack nightclubs, employing nearly two thousand South Koreans. Also, down the Kimchi Road there are beauty salons catering to Korean nightclub workers, a twenty-four-hour Korean supermarket, and stores that stock Korean television and movie videos. Sakaecho is Japan's one genuine Korean community.

identity from their friends by getting off at bus stops or train stations some distance from their buraku homes. Japan's elaborate system of family registers—a permanent, official record of each person's ancestry—makes it almost impossible for a burakumin to conceal her or his origins and, therefore, to work for a major company or marry outside the caste.

Discrimination against burakumin persists in many aspects of social life. Parents routinely investigate the background of their children's prospective marriage partners. A pending marriage between a burakumin and a person of nonburaku origin may be broken up by strong objections from the latter's family. There has been an increase in the number of incidents of harassment against burakumin. There is no law in Japan prohibiting incitement to discrimination, and there are no effective ways to cope with such incidents.

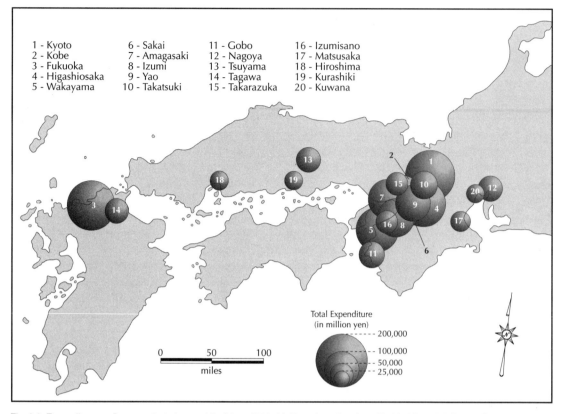

1 - Kyoto
2 - Kobe
3 - Fukuoka
4 - Higashiosaka
5 - Wakayama

6 - Sakai
7 - Amagasaki
8 - Izumi
9 - Yao
10 - Takatsuki

11 - Gobo
12 - Nagoya
13 - Tsuyama
14 - Tagawa
15 - Takarazuka

16 - Izumisano
17 - Matsusaka
18 - Hiroshima
19 - Kurashiki
20 - Kuwana

Total Expenditure
(in million yen)

- - - - - 200,000
- - 100,000
- - 50,000
- - 25,000

Fig. 6.9. Expenditure on Dowa projects by municipalities, 1969–91. Based on data from Toshio Mizuuchi, Osaka City University.

Yet Japan is also remarkable for the progress it has made. Today almost two-thirds of the burakumin say in opinion polls that they have never encountered discrimination. About 75 percent of them now marry nonburakumin. The E-word—*eta,* or "much filth," the traditional word for burakumin—has been banished from discourse, so that virtually no Japanese ever uses it. Osaka geographer Toshio Mizuuchi has described the efforts to improve the living conditions of burakumin (Mizuuchi 1998).

About 5 percent of the burakumin are on welfare, seven times the national average. Burakumin community leaders say they worry not only about the impact of discrimination but also about the dependency of the burakumin on welfare and about social problems such as alcohol and drug abuse, school dropout, and children born out of wedlock. The burakumin group has a profile somewhat like that of welfare recipients in the United States.

In 1922 the Buraku Liberation Movement began with the formation of the Suiheisha in Kyoto. It denounced all kinds of discrimination against

burakumin and strove to improve their living standards. In 1953 the national government began to give small subsidies to the local governments for improvement of buraku areas. In 1960 a law was enacted to establish a council to develop programs for the same purpose. This law and other similar legislation have provided funds for improvements of buraku areas, educational scholarships for burakumin, and aid to small buraku businesses. The distribution of expenditure on burakumin welfare under *dowa* projects (see fig. 6.9) reflects the concentration of the burakumin population in Kansai and northern Kyushu (Lee and De Vos 1981).

The presence of a large Korean ethnic minority, which also faces social discrimination, is mainly a legacy of Japanese colonialism. During World War II Koreans were brought to Japan as forced laborers. In 2000 there were more than 635,000 Koreans living in Japan. Most of these are Japanese-born second- and third-generation Koreans, but they are legally aliens, since birth in Japan does not assure Japanese citizenship unless one parent is a Japanese national. There has been recent improvement in their legal status. Since 1993 they have not had to be fingerprinted as aliens. Some local authorities, though not yet the central government, now employ Koreans. On naturalization, Koreans no longer have to take Japanese names; those who did so in the past can revert to using their Korean names. Korean schools in Japan are allowed to compete in sporting contests with Japanese schools.

The Korean population is highly concentrated in the Kansai region, which includes the cities Osaka, Kyoto, and Kobe. These people are descendants of Koreans brought to Japan during wartime to work in the heavy engineering and chemical industries of the Kansai region and the coal mining areas of southwest Japan. The distribution of the Korean population reflects the timing of the Koreans' arrival and the circumstances of their insertion into the Japanese labor force. More than 80 percent of Koreans marry Japanese; their children are thus automatically Japanese. Members of the Korean-speaking older generations are dying out. Young ethnic Koreans tend to speak only Japanese and have few links with their ancestral country.

Overseas Migration of Japanese

In the early part of the twentieth century, there were several waves of international migration of Japanese to California, Hawaii, and Canada to work as laborers, a practice known as *dekasegi*. Noritaka Yagasaki (1982) provides an excellent account of the pre–World War II Japanese migrants engaged in floriculture and truck farming in California. As anti-Japanese exclusion movements developed in the United States and Canada in the 1920s and 1930s, there were streams of Japanese migration to Brazil (Ninomiya 1994), Peru, and other Latin American countries. There were also significant migrations to Japanese colonial territories in southern Sakhalin, Taiwan, Korea, and northern China. These migrations came to an end before the outbreak of World War II, when North American and Latin American countries closed their doors to migration from Asia for political reasons. By 1940 about a half million Japanese migrants and their descendants were estimated to be living in the two American continents.

With the end of overseas migration to North America and Latin America, a considerable volume of migrants went to Manchuria, with the establishment of Manchukuo in northern China, to alleviate the population pressure in Japan and to provide some relief from the economic depression that had become widespread in the 1930s. Between 1929 and 1937, the number of Japanese migrants who were settled in the northeast region of China increased from 814,000 to nearly 1.8 million. At the same time, there was a considerable influx of Koreans and Chinese into Japan during the war.

Short-term population movements were large during and immediately after World War II. Between 1942 and 1945, about 4 million people left Japan, including military forces and civilian migrants, for the "new land development" campaign in Manchukuo. About 400,000 Koreans were imported into Japan, by force in most cases, to meet the labor shortage resulting from mass overseas mobilization. With the termination of World War II, the Japanese population stationed or settled in the former colonies, or in militarily occupied areas, returned to Japan, and their influx continued for two years after the war. Nearly 5.7 million Japanese came back to Japan, and 1.2 million Koreans and Chinese returned to their countries.

After World War II, a small volume of Japanese migrants began to flow to the United States, Canada, and some Latin American countries, chiefly Brazil, Argentina, and Paraguay (see fig. 6.10). These migrations reflected the economic difficulties and population pressure felt in Japan immediately after the war. Overseas migration of Japanese exceeded 15,000 migrants at its peak in 1958; it then began to dwindle in response to increasing economic prosperity. In 2000 the number of Japanese citizens with permanent residence abroad was nearly 790,000; of this nearly 36 percent were living in the United States, and 12 percent in Brazil. People of Japanese descent settled abroad numbered about 1.4 million, with 670,000 in the United States, 1,300,000 in Brazil, and 80,000 in Peru.

In the hope of dealing with the war-ravaged domestic economy and Japan's 6 million civilians and military personnel repatriated from former Japanese colonies and occupied territories in Asia, the Japanese government made attempts to encourage emigration. Japan considered Central and South American countries the most suitable destinations for Japanese settlers, because there had been a history of Japanese emigration to those regions be-

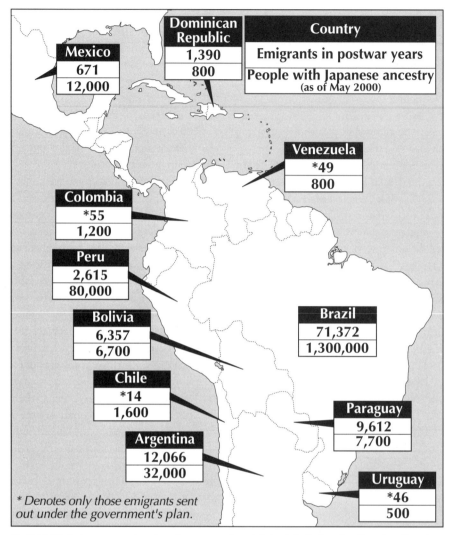

Country		
Emigrants in postwar years		
People with Japanese ancestry (as of May 2000)		

Mexico
671
12,000

Dominican Republic
1,390
800

Venezuela
*49
800

Colombia
*55
1,200

Peru
2,615
80,000

Bolivia
6,357
6,700

Brazil
71,372
1,300,000

Chile
*14
1,600

Paraguay
9,612
7,700

Argentina
12,066
32,000

Uruguay
*46
500

Denotes only those emigrants sent out under the government's plan.

Fig. 6.10. Ethnic Japanese and postwar Japanese emigrants living in Latin America. Based on *Encyclopedia of Japanese Descendants in the Americas* (Lanham, MD: Alta Mira Press, 2000).

A Japanese emigrant in Aichi Prefecture who has returned to Japan. Latin America, particularly Brazil, was the favorite destination for Japanese emigrants, and they began to go there in 1908. Before World War II about 190,000 Japanese emigrated to Brazil. The majority of them worked on coffee plantations, and some later became large-scale landowners or business operators. Emigration to Brazil resumed in 1952, with the number of Japanese emigrants shipped out under the government plan totaling 54,000 by 1993. Currently, about 1.3 million Brazilians of Japanese ancestry live in Brazil. About 80 percent of the emigrants live in Sao Paulo and, as a group, wield a powerful influence on local politics and the local economy. Recently, Brazilians of Japanese descent have been returning to Japan—primarily to seek employment—in sharply increasing numbers. As of 1998, about 220,000 Brazilian nationals were living in Japan, the majority of them of Japanese descent. Photo by P.P. Karan.

Field Report:

San Francisco's Japantown

San Francisco's Japantown is the oldest Japanese-American community in the United States. Once a thriving city-within-a-city with hundreds of businesses as well as newspapers and schools of its own, it has now been pared down to a mere four blocks of sushi restaurants, grocery stores, and a shopping mall with a concrete pagoda.

Most of Japantown's residents are in their seventies and eighties, their children long gone to the suburbs. In place of those children, a fresh generation of Korean immigrants is setting up shop, transforming the cultural landscape. Japantown's precarious future mirrors changing immigration patterns in San Francisco. While the large Chinatown continues to boom and Hispanic neighborhoods of the Mission district gain in strength and vibrancy, ethnic identity is dimming in older enclaves like the Italian neighborhood of North Beach. But none has dried up as quickly as Japantown, which, along with similar districts in Los Angeles and San Jose, is one of the country's last three remaining Japanese neighborhoods.

Japantown's struggle for survival is not new. The community has fought through two similar crises in the past. The first came during World War II, when the U.S. government ordered Japanese-Americans into internment camps after the bombing of Pearl Harbor. Hundreds of families moved out of their homes with only what they could carry, returning later to find their homes taken over by strangers. After the war, Japantown had shrunk from a thirty-block neighborhood to just fifteen blocks. The second crisis came in the 1970s, when San Francisco's urban renewal program forced Japantown families out of their homes as part of a citywide effort to renovate older buildings and redevelop. That push led many younger Japanese-American families to pull up stakes for the suburbs, which offered more space and better schools. By the end of 1999, Japantown had dwindled to the meager four blocks that survive today.

Seeing that Japantown faces a real threat of extinction, its community leaders have jumped into action. With the support of the city's Redevelopment Agency, they have targeted community outreach and have made fresh efforts to revitalize Japantown's aging infrastructure as the first steps toward making it a viable community again. Construction work to renovate the Peace Plaza and Buchanan Mall in the center of Japantown was started in 1999, and plans to add gardens and stone fountains were under way.

But Japantown needs more than a simple sprucing up. With few new Japanese immigrants, and young Japanese-Americans increasingly estranged from Japanese culture, the real challenge lies in making Japantown relevant again.

fore the war. Thus, the social infrastructure set up by the original Japanese settlers and subsequent generations was already in place. Another plus was that anti-Japanese sentiment was relatively low in these countries. Some of the emigrants turned out to be successful and assumed leadership roles in their new homes, but many were forced into a daily struggle for survival on previously uninhabited land (Kikumura-Yano 2002). In most Latin American countries, Japanese settlers faced unfavorable conditions and a lack of infrastructure, and the Japanese government often failed to address the complaints of the colonists (Horst and Asagiri 2000).

In 1951 the Brazilian government agreed to accept 5,000 Japanese families into the Amazon region. An emigration ship, the *Santos Maru,* left Kobe for Brazil in December 1951, carrying the first group of Japanese to emigrate under the plan. The Japanese government created the Federation of Japan Overseas Associations under the guidance of the Foreign Ministry and set up a special government corporation to extend soft loans for emigration with funds borrowed from U.S. banks. Under its ten-year emigration program, the Foreign Ministry planned to send out 426,000 emigrants.

The Foreign Ministry was responsible for the

emigration program, but since the government-run emigration schemes centered on agricultural projects overseas, the Agriculture and Forestry Ministry also got involved. The Japanese emigrants suffered from the interministry struggle for leadership. The complex distribution of authority considerably hindered the development of infrastructure needed to improve the land earmarked for emigrants. The first group of Japanese emigrants to the Amazon region in the postwar era arrived in their settlements in 1953. Less than a month after their arrival, however, many of the emigrant families began deserting their assigned settlements.

The new settlements were often beset with adverse conditions. The soil was sometimes infertile and unsuitable for farming, or even if the land was arable, there often were no roads to transport products or no markets nearby. Furthermore, in some settlements, the dwellings and the health and sanitary conditions were substandard. In most cases

emigrants were settled on plots of land provided by the Brazilian government without prior inspection or sufficient research into the suitability and condition of the settlements. However, the wave of settlement desertions was blamed (by ministries in Japan) on the screening process for Japanese emigrants and on the character of the settlers.

About 6,000 Japanese emigrated to the Amazon region in the postwar era. In 2000 about 13,000 people of Japanese descent lived in the region. They were located in three settlements: Guama, Quinari, and Bela Vista. Guama lies on the banks of a tributary of the Amazon River near Belem. Quinari is situated deep in the Amazon region, and Bela Vista lies across from the city of Manaus on the upper reaches of the river (see fig. 6.11).

FOREIGN WORKERS IN JAPAN

An insular nation (in more than geography) that prizes ethnic and cultural homogeneity, Japan has

Fig. 6.11. Postwar Japanese settlements in the Amazon region. Based on *Encyclopedia of Japanese Descendants in the Americas*, 2000.

long kept its foreign workers at arm's length (Selleck 2001; Komei 2001). But with a daunting demographic hump on the horizon, Japan is changing its approach. By 2010 Japan's baby boomers will start retiring, so Japan must start importing foreign workers to keep the world's second-largest economy on track and its pension systems from collapsing. Foreign workers were attracted to Japan during the economic boom of the 1980s that led to severe shortages of labor, especially in construction and service industries. In the 1990s between 95,000 and 112,000 foreign workers entered Japan each year for the first time for work. In addition, each year in the 1990s between 30,000 and 65,000 foreigners who entered Japan as tourists or on student visas were working illegally, mainly in retail, restaurant, and service industries. At the end of 2000 the number of foreign residents in Japan was 1.68 million, of which 38 percent were from Korea, 20 percent from China, 15 percent from Brazil, and smaller percentages from the Philippines, the United States, Peru, Thailand, the United Kingdom, Indonesia, and Vietnam. Most of the Brazilians are descendants of Japanese who had sought opportunity in South America earlier in the twentieth century and started returning to Japan in the 1980s (Tsuda 1999). Foreign residents have the right to live in Japan, but not necessarily to work.

In 2000 the government started offering permanent visas to Brazilian migrants, largely of Japanese descent, turning them into immigrants. Japan's Brazilian population was estimated at 254,000 in 2001, with a major concentration in the Hamamatsu area, giving Japan a foretaste of cultural diversity. A number of private Brazilian schools have mushroomed in this area, where the visitor can hear the sound of Brazilian Portuguese. These schools prepare students for life in Brazil, not their future in Japan. The children of immigrants do not study Japanese language, laws, or customs. Of Japan's 35,000 school-age Brazilians, only 7,000 attend public schools. There are two Brazilian television channels and four Brazilian weekly newspapers. But all is not smooth for the new immigrants in a society that prizes conformity. Japanese cities with large Brazilian minorities have reported social problems, from cultural clashes to school absenteeism to crime. Immigrants fail to take seriously the municipal recycling system and the ban on picking apples from trees on the city's boulevard. The key to success for Brazilian immigrants lies in embracing Japanese culture, customs, and language and in integrating into the community to create a new generation.

Known as *nikkeijin,* these second- and third-generation descendants of Japanese immigrants to Latin America are already changing society. Envisioned as a labor source that would not threaten the country's monoculture, nikkeijin proved to be as foreign as their passports. In many industrial cities Latinos make up a sizable portion of the population. The boutiques, butcher shops, travel agencies, video-rental shops, and music stores in the Brazilian Plaza mall all cater to Latin immigrants. The traditional bento, or Japanese lunchboxes, in these areas come stuffed with New World fare, like braised beef, Brazilian rice, salad, and sausage. At carnival time every summer, immigrants parade through town dressed in feathers and G-strings to a pounding samba beat.

The Chinese form the second-largest group of

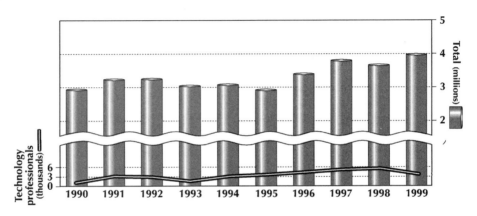

Fig. 6.12. Number of foreign nationals entering Japan, 1990–99. Based on data from the Ministry of Justice, Tokyo.

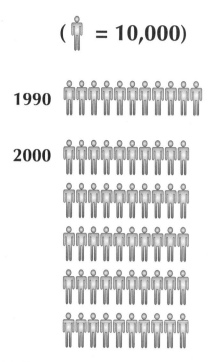

Fig. 6.13. Undocumented aliens. Based on data from the Ministry of Justice, Tokyo.

illegally to find work (Morita and Sassen 1994). In recent years Chinese are entering illegally at a fast pace, aided by a formidable linkup between Chinese smugglers and the Japanese underworld, or yakuza (Kaplan 1986; Seymour 1996). These migrants often turn to crime. Many of them have borrowed money ($20,000 to $25,000) to pay for being smuggled into Japan, and if they cannot earn money easily to repay the loan, they tend to turn to crime. Although Chinese make up only 17 percent of the foreigners living in Japan, they committed 41 percent of the crimes by foreigners in 1996. Chinese gangs called Snakehead in Fujian Province in China, presumably with the protection of the local police and military, organize the expeditions and enforce payment, and they have agents in Japan to ease the passage of illegal migrants into Japanese society. Snakeheads smuggle Chinese into Japan under a "three-pronged system" known as *sanpo*, providing the entrants with illegal entry, housing, and employment. Much of the work of receiving the smuggled

foreign residents (335,000 in 2000) after the Koreans. Nearly 25,000 of these are descendants of Chinese brought to work in Japan during World War II, and some are persons associated with the strong commercial links between Japan, China, Taiwan, and Hong Kong, but the majority are students and trainees in Japan. In contrast to the Koreans, the Chinese are concentrated in Tokyo, and to a lesser extent in Yokohama and Kobe. The Chinese communities in the port cities of Yokohama and Kobe are of much longer standing, but Tokyo provides a wider opportunity for unskilled and skilled work (Shimizu 1995).

The number of foreign nationals entering Japan is larger than the number of registered foreign nationals resident in Japan (see fig. 6.12). Many of the Asians come to Japan on tourist visas and remain illegally while the immigration authorities look the other way. Most of the illegal workers come from China, the Philippines, Bangladesh, Nepal, Pakistan, and Iran (Shelby 1989). The number of illegal foreign workers was estimated at more than 40,000 in 1998, a decline from 64,000 in 1993. The number of undocumented aliens was reportedly much higher (see fig. 6.13).

Each year a flood of workers sneak into Japan

An illegal worker from Nepal in a restaurant in Nagoya. A shortage of workers is forcing Japan to rethink its attitude toward outsiders. Japan once had little room for foreigners, who worked as waiters, dug ditches, or worked in factories. Now as Japan is aging rapidly and facing a severe labor shortage, it is becoming increasingly reliant on foreign workers to fill the job gap. They come from Iran, Spain, China, Bangladesh, Brazil, Ghana, Pakistan, and Nepal. Although many of Japan's nonimmigrants are not in the country legally, authorities turn a blind eye because the economy needs them. The foreign workers are making Japanese society more multicultural. Photo by P.P. Karan.

Chinese seems to be done by Japanese gangs, possibly with Chinese accomplices. Many of the illegal Chinese migrants settle in the Airin district (Nishinariku) of Osaka. Until 1997 the illegal migrants usually went to the Kanto region. But now, with rising unemployment due to the prolonged business slump, the illegal aliens are settling in Airin, Japan's largest community of day laborers.

Many illegal Chinese immigrants meet a need in Japan, working at construction sites, or cleaning toilets, or taking menial jobs that Japanese themselves do not want. Nevertheless, because the number of illegal Chinese immigrants is surging, some Japanese worry that this is the beginning of a long-term trend. If Japan's economy continues to flounder, the problem could get worse.

A recent study warns that Japan must bring in 600,000 foreign workers a year just to maintain current levels of economic output (Papademetrion and Hamilton 2000). Despite restrictive policies, the immigrants are arriving—and transforming Japan into a more multicultural society. Immigration is such political dynamite that the government has largely ignored the changes that are sweeping the country. Although foreigners are quietly pouring in, the Japanese government has stuck to its nearly blanket ban on permanent immigration. That is because admitting that foreign workers are a positive force—and officially letting them in—would challenge familiar notions that Japan is a closed, homogeneous society. Thousands of undocumented aliens live at the edges of the law, without health insurance or other benefits, fearing a knock at the door by police or immigration officials. Many Japanese support their struggle and want the government to lift its laws against immigration. Skirting the more fundamental debate about opening up the society, the government has quietly used legal loopholes to fill the yawning labor gap. Japan has recruited foreigners for work-study schemes and training programs designed to perpetuate the myth of temporariness. In fact, many graduates of these programs stay in Japan and enter an illegal labor pool, which has grown to some 500,000. That tally does not include a swelling population of Latinos with Japanese ancestry, or the many thousands of foreign brides imported to marry Japanese farmers. See the Field Report "Foreign Brides in Japan," above.

Japan accepts foreign brides for farmers, but foreign workers for factories are generally not allowed to immigrate. Industrial policy lags behind policies affecting the farmers. Since the 1980s, Japan has exported low-end manufacturing plants overseas, has outfitted remaining factories with advanced robotics, and has expanded recruitment among women and the elderly. But by the late 1980s labor had grown so scarce that the shortage threatened all major industries. Businesses began clamoring for help. The Japanese government response was to open the door to foreigners, but only those with Japanese blood. The nikkeijin have stampeded in.

Across Japan, ethnic enclaves are cropping up. There is a Chinatown in Yokohama, a community of Koreans in Osaka, and a large Shanghai-Chinese settlement in Tokyo's Shinjuku Ward. In nearby Ikebukuro immigrants cluster to work, play, dine—and also worship. Down one alley near the train station, a five-story walk-up hosts a Ghanian-owned sportswear store, an Indian restaurant, an Irish pub, a halal food and Indian video shop, and a mosque where the faithful prostrate themselves toward Mecca six times a day. Nearly 18,000 foreigners live in the industrial city of Hamamatsu, and many of them work in the city's factories.

In Japan's oldest ethnic enclaves, a distinctly American pattern has emerged: old immigrants assimilate into mainstream society, to be replaced by newcomers. Take Osaka's handmade shoe industry. Once dominated by Koreans brought to Japan before World War II, it later attracted workers from South Korea. Today the city's leather factories lure workers from China.

More than twenty years have passed since the asset-inflated economic years of the late 1980s unleashed a sudden onslaught of foreign workers in Japan from Asia and Latin America (Nagayama 1993). In 2000 they made up 1 percent of the nation's working population. Nearly 126,000 foreigners hold temporary work permits in Japan, and about 60 percent of them are from Asian countries. These people are working in sectors that require special skills or knowledge. Foreigners without such skills are not granted work permits in Japan. But many unskilled foreigners work in Japan illegally. It is estimated that more than 250,000 foreign workers whose visas have expired continue to reside and work in Japan. This figure is below the peak 1993 estimate of 300,000, but it remains fairly high. The illegal foreign workers do jobs that most Japanese would do last, the so-called 3K jobs—*kitsui* (hard), *kitanai* (dirty), and *kiken* (dangerous). Japanese, particularly in rural areas, are generally opposed to accepting unskilled foreign workers. There is more willingness to accept them in cities, notably in metropolitan regions where the unskilled labor offsets a shortage of such workers.

Japan has no immigration quota for foreigners in quest of permanent residency. With the declining-population scenario becoming reality, some industries are calling on the central government to begin accepting immigrants and open Japan's labor market, which has often been criticized as closed. Foreign workers can aid Japanese companies not only by making up for a future labor shortage but also by helping create a more diverse and dynamic corporate environment in the current trend of globalization. For now, foreign workers (both skilled and unskilled) are needed mainly to secure a labor force, considering the dwindling overall working population. In the long term, it is inevitable that many companies will diversify their employment practices and create a management force that utilizes workers' different skills regardless of their nationalities.

Although it is the government that must review Japan's laws relating to immigration, Japanese society also must step up efforts to break down barriers—inside and outside of the corporate world—and accommodate foreigners. If Japan fails to take such a positive attitude in the twenty-first century, it will lose dynamism and competitiveness in the long term. A sudden influx of foreign workers may come as a shock to people in Japanese society who have little experience living with foreigners. Therefore, Japan needs to make preparations at an early stage, while allowing the number of foreign workers to increase slowly. Foreign workers as members of the community will place a demand upon services such as education and health. It will be necessary to make facilities such as schools and hospitals more foreign-friendly. The government will also need to work to create housing-assistance mechanisms, language institutes, and social support systems for foreign workers.

Some foreign nationals are now seen as vital in order for Japan to keep pace with the global information technology (IT) revolution. The personnel shortage in Japan's engineering and programming sectors was estimated at 12,400 as of February 1999, despite the nation's high unemployment rate, which is a result of a mismatch between supply and demand in the overall labor market (there is an oversupply of workers in obsolete sectors and a shortage in growth sectors). The dwindling number of computer science students in Japan makes it harder for the nation to deal with the increasing demand for IT specialists. The shortage has prompted Japan to recruit engineers and researchers from abroad—for example, from emerging IT countries such as India and China—as part of a basic strategy to revive the nation's technological competitiveness in the transition from the machinery age to the information age. To realize this goal, however, Japan must overcome many of the obstacles noted above. In addition, Japan is at a disadvantage in attracting foreign engineers because of competition from English-speaking and more immigration-friendly countries like the United States. Also, without a long-term national policy to attract young talented people of its own to IT fields in universities, government, and businesses, Japan will continue to lose competitiveness as it has been doing since the burst of the bubble economy.

Japan's prospects as an advanced nation of the twenty-first century depend upon how well it can rise above the barriers of nationalism to welcome foreigners into its midst. Universities must do the same in order to become truly autonomous and internationally competitive in the pursuit of knowledge.

THE STATUS OF WOMEN

The wedding of Masako Owada, a successful career woman, to the Crown Prince in 1993 sparked debate about the role of women in Japanese society. Many acknowledge that Japanese women have made great strides over the past decade but point out that they still face enormous obstacles and pressures both in the workplace and in society in general, so that it is difficult for them to pursue careers (Brinton 1993).

In Japan the privileges of manhood are deeply entrenched, and there are few areas where this is clearer than in the workplace. Despite the passage of a landmark antidiscrimination law in 1995, many Japanese companies maintain separate personnel management tracks for men and women. Men are hired with the general assumption that they will build a career with the company, but women are still typically categorized in one of two ways: *ippan shoku* (miscellaneous workers or office ladies) and *sogo shoku* (career employees). The miscellaneous workers, still legion in every Japanese ministry and large company despite a ten-year recession, are typically women in their twenties who, dressed in company uniforms or in smart clothing of their own, smilingly direct visitors to their appointments and serve tea to guests. Some of them may be involved in clerical work, sales work, or accounting work, but what they generally do not do is rise above this lowly status and enter career tracks largely reserved for men. For women who choose to remain in the workplace, the challenge to be respected on the basis of their competence instead of being valued primarily for their ability to embellish their surroundings remains almost as great now as it was earlier (Iwao 1993).

Bound by tradition, women struggle to take on responsibility at work while society still expects them to leave their jobs for family life. The quality and conditions of women's jobs remain poor, making women a useful and inexpensive source of labor. Many companies still have policies that reflect prewar attitudes that women mainly want to get married and will quit when they reach marriageable age. In fact, many companies expect women to leave once they are married. Many Japanese still think women should choose between marriage and a career. Those who venture outside the house usually are given the lowest-paid, least significant work, often wearing office uniforms with aprons to run errands and pour tea for their bosses and male colleagues. On average, they earn half of what men do. Women are still barred from many jobs that require them to work past ten o'clock in the evening.

Although Japanese women are among the most educated and affluent in the world, their primary role continues to be that of housewife and mother; they are expected to wake early with the children and stay up late to provide food, bath, and bed for their husbands arriving from work and after-hours entertaining (Nagai 2000).

There are signs of change, however. Women have been creeping into the professional career ranks in Japan in recent years, but their numbers are still small, and many women complain that everything from social mores to the lack of day care to the tax code conspires to keep things that way (Yumiko 2000). In 1998 only 1.2 percent of corporate department heads in Japan were women. In lesser categories, such as section head, the lowest managerial title, where women hold 7.8 percent of the positions, there have

A hostess in a bar in Yatsushiro, Kumamoto Prefecture. Clubs like this one are common in Japan's cities, catering to the country's freewheeling males. Hostess bars have proliferated to entertain men in Japan. Indeed, many Japanese companies pick up the tab for their male employees' evenings on the town visiting hostess bars. Japanese sociologists say that the prevalence of the clubs is a result of a complex cultural history, reinforced by the crowding and sprawl of large cities. For centuries, while Japan was under feudal rule, regional warlords were required by the shogun to have their families reside in the capital, while the lords themselves traveled back and forth to their domains on lengthy pilgrimages. With lords separated from their spouses for long stretches, a culture of geisha and concubines flourished, and along with it, so did the idea that paying for the company of women was normal. In urban Japan, where houses are tiny and long commutes the norm, men stay out on the town, typically with their co-workers. Photo by P.P. Karan.

been small gains. Nevertheless, in 1998 women earned only 64 percent as much as men among salaried workers, and 51 percent as much as men when part-time jobs were taken into account.

Television networks now have female co-anchors who report the news, instead of simply smiling demurely at the male anchor, as used to be the case. A woman recently served as the Speaker in the Diet,

Field Report

Ume Tsuda: A Pioneer in Women's Education

On a fine day toward the end of 1871, the steamship *America* left Yokohama harbor, bound for San Francisco. On board was a large delegation of officials of the new Meiji government—and five Japanese girls. Two of the girls were fourteen, one was eleven, and one was eight. The smallest was Ume Tsuda, six years old.

These girls were on a mission. They were going abroad to acquire "high female culture." At a solemn audience, the Empress Meiji herself had presented each of them with a document: "When in time, schools for girls are established, you, having finished your studies, shall be examples to your countrywomen. Bear this in mind and apply yourself to your studies day and night." The girls' samurai families had all been on the wrong side of the political upheaval of the Meiji Restoration. How, then, did the girls come to be so privileged? The Meiji government, following Japanese tradition, was attempting to bring former opposition families into their fold. These families thus now saw a chance for their daughters to better their fortunes. Ume's father, Sen Tsuda, himself a pioneer of vocational education, had high hopes for his daughter.

The two oldest girls returned home within months. The younger children, with less say in the matter, stayed. Charles Lanman, secretary of the Japanese chargés d'affaires in Washington, and his wife took Ume and helped her fulfill her mission. In 1882 Ume was sent home to Japan, and she taught English at a school established by her father for poor girls. Later she taught at a school for the wives and daughters of the aristocracy that developed under the patronage of the empress. Finally, in 1900, she opened the Women's Institute of English Studies, later to become Tsuda College. Rebuilt after the great earthquake of 1923, and a full university since 1948, it has more than fulfilled her hopes, producing many high-achieving women, including diplomats, civil servants, professors, and politicians. The women's college in the quiet woodlands of western Tokyo celebrated the one-hundredth anniversary of its founding in June 2000. It is a monument to the dream of a pioneer educator who dedicated her life to empowering Japanese women.

Ume Tsuda (1864–1929), the resourceful little girl who became the most eminent Japanese woman of her time, is buried on the campus, by a grove of plum trees.

and several women have been appointed as cabinet ministers. At the local level, too, the number of women politicians is rising, although women still make up less than 1 percent of local legislatures. A few women, then, have made it into top government jobs and the executive ranks of department stores, clothing and car companies, and banks, although they are rare enough to be major news stories.

The number of working women recently edged above the number of housewives, although many housewives work part time and most join the workforce only after their children enter junior high school. In Japan's tightly structured and hierarchical work world, a part-time worker is hired only for low-level jobs. Nonetheless, day care centers are flourishing in an effort to keep up with the demand.

For years the ideal for women espoused by parents and in schools, novels, and movies has been to become "good wives and wise mothers." Some younger women continue to adhere to the notion that a woman should be married by age twenty-five lest she become Kurismasu Kay-kee, or Christmas cake, which is stale and unappealing after the twenty-fifth. There are also many people who believe that without the hard-working housewife, Japan's postwar economic success story could not have been written. Much of a mother's sense of personal accomplishment is tied to the educational achievements of her children, and she expends great effort helping them.

While men still dominate much of the center of Japanese society, women have been waging a "quiet revolution," using both the traditional and the changing social structure to create new spaces to pursue newly defined interests. The one-time inevitable institutions of marriage and family are now considered options. Although some women professionals are successfully challenging the male-controlled workplace, many are experiencing conflicts stemming from traditional women's roles, the paucity of role models, and male chauvinism.

There are evidences that the status of Japanese women is changing. Consider the following: in 1975 only one in eight Japanese women went to a four-year college, a prerequisite for the better jobs; by 1996 the proportion was almost one in four. Women are also marrying later. Their average age at marriage is now approaching 28 among college graduates. More than half of those between 25 and 29 are still single, compared with less than one-third in 1970.

Although women tend to get laid off first in recessions, more women are working. In 1975, 32 percent of the workforce was composed of women; the figure now is about 40 percent. In big companies, women have 1 in 25 managerial positions, compared with 1 in 40 in 1984. At least one court is assisting the trend. In November 1996, twelve female bank employees won 100 million yen ($890,000) in compensation and were promoted by court order after they successfully sued the Shiba Credit Association. It was the first time a company had been held liable in a promotion-related sex discrimination suit. About two dozen other sexual harassment (*sekuhara*) suits are pending.

The Tokyo Securities Exchange accepted its first woman floor trader in 1996. The first woman in more than a thousand years to perform the Knife Ceremony, a hallowed Shinto sushi ritual, did so in 1996. And, however improbably, women have started a sumo (wrestling) circuit as well.

It may appear as if Japanese women are treading the path marked out by Western feminists thirty years ago. Not so. Japanese feminism is different, having a less combative tone and a greater emphasis on protecting motherhood. Japanese women are less determined to break down traditional sex roles. A 1996 survey, for example, found that 37 percent of Japanese women strongly believed that a home and children were what women really wanted; 7 percent of American women agreed. This outlook may have something to do with the attractiveness of women's role as wife and mother in Japanese society.

The result of this ambivalence on the part of Japa-

nese women, and of a 1986 law designed to encourage equal opportunity, has been the two career tracks that big companies have established for women: one (which most choose) for those who do not want to be part of management, and one for those who do. In principle, this makes it possible for women to compete with men on an equal basis. In practice, men are not allowed to get on the noncareer track, and women find it difficult to stay on the management track. Given the frequent transfers, long hours, and lack of domestic help, moving up the corporate ladder all but requires a stay-at-home spouse. Corporate practice has done nothing to adapt to the woman who wants to reach the top and also to bring up a family. Typically, a woman will leave her job after her first child is born and later resume a part-time career or pursue hobbies or community work (Kamiya and Ikeya 1994).

The *oyaji* girl—a professional in her twenties who works hard and plays hard—has been the clearest beneficiary of the new latitude for women. But not everyone wants to be like her, or at any rate to remain like her in an unmarried state. Many women, particularly mothers, are happy to stay out of the corporate rat race. Married women tend to prefer *onna tengoku*, women's heaven (a mix of part-time work, bringing up children, hobbies, and commu-

A working mother with her child in Sapporo. These women accept a multirole ideology of "new women": they adhere to the primacy of the wife-mother role but also believe that women should be able to play other roles and have careers on an equal basis with men. Photo by P.P. Karan.

nity work), to the restricted life they would have as a *sarariwoman.*

The fact is that equality with men is not a particularly appealing prospect to most Japanese women right now. Educated young women, those most likely to lead a revolution, tend to see their male peers as dull corporate drones. Women, meanwhile, with comparatively freer schedules, have more time to cultivate their interests. As a result there is a growing perception gap between the sexes. A comic book series called *Sweet Spot,* which pokes fun at workaholic men and salutes the leisurely attitudes of young female workers, is a best seller.

Indeed, although a 1985 law bans sex discrimination and requires Japanese companies to offer females the same opportunities available to men, few women choose to apply for career-track jobs (Imamura 1996). Being a housewife is nothing to be ashamed of in Japan, because most husbands leave their salaries and children entirely in the hands of their wives. Women have wide-ranging responsibilities. It was not always thus. Traditionally, wives and children obeyed the father as ruler of the roost. But postwar economic growth toppled fathers from that lofty post by imposing longer work hours that kept them away from home.

SOCIAL WELFARE AND THE HOMELESS

The sight of poor people sleeping on street corners is nothing unusual in big American cities. The Japanese, by contrast, are justly proud of their record in keeping urban blight and visible poverty at bay. But things are changing. Ueno Park in Tokyo, home to some of Japan's finest museums, is now also home to hundreds of homeless men, who carefully line up their shoes before entering their tents. Despite a controversial expulsion in 1996, the homeless have reoccupied many of the bustling hallways in Shinjuku railway station in central Tokyo. Now many take shelter in the Shinjuku Park overlooking the Tokyo Government Metropolitan Office complex. Homeless residents in Shinjuku are mostly men in their late forties and fifties. The plight of the homeless and attacks on them by young people in Kawasaki's Fujima Park were reported in the *New York Times* ("For Japan's New Homeless, There is Disdain and Danger," December 17, 2003). The homeless build shelters from cardboard and live in public parks in major cities of Japan—Tokyo, Osaka, and Nagoya. In order to get people out

A young female worker in Tokyo dressed in a kimono for an evening in town. The kimono of Japan speaks the most eloquent language of weave, thread, dye, and drape. The elegant beauty and wealth of these garments needs no elaboration. Young female workers generally tend to buy expensive clothes. Photo by P.P. Karan.

of the public parks for good, Tokyo's local government started a program in 2004 that provides homeless people with an apartment for two years at a nominal rent. With a stable residential address, former homeless people have a better chance of finding a job. Nearly 1,800 homeless people have taken advantage of this program in Tokyo. With respect to their Japanese culture, which emphasizes honor and Confucian values, local authorities are struggling to find a solution to the homeless problem. The major concentration of homeless in Osaka is in the Airin district in Nishinari-ku. They are orderly, stay in designated areas, and do everything under the watchful eye of the police.

The problem is tiny by comparison with America's. The best estimates are that Tokyo has 5,000 to 6,000

A group of homeless people find shelter in Shinjuku Park in central Tokyo. The decade-long economic slump has created a growing underclass of homeless in Japan. Makeshift shanties erected by the homeless in parks and public areas in Tokyo, Osaka, Nagoya, and even rural areas are common. Photo by P.P. Karan.

homeless people and that Osaka, the hub of Kansai's rapidly rusting manufacturing belt, has about 14,000 (see fig. 6.14), compared with 50,000 living in shelters or on the streets in New York. Most of the homeless in Japan are hard-to-employ men for whom the slowdown in building and the concomitant collapse of the market for casual labor have meant destitution. Some homeless people have mental problems, but for far more the greatest affliction is the lack of hope or the warmth of human contact. Their plight highlights the shortcomings of the traditional Japanese way of dealing with poverty. Japan has tried to avoid making state assistance the first resort of poor people. The initial line of defense is work, then the family, and only then does the state step in with cash. The system has cracks, and it is possible to fall through them. The government's response to homelessness has been discussed by Tom Gill (2001, 2002).

In contrast to America's homeless population, which has high rates of alcoholism, drug abuse, and mental illness, a large proportion of the homeless in Japan had steady jobs and stable lives until their companies went bankrupt or they were put out of work for some other reasons (see fig. 6.15).

The poor in Japan are obliged to get help from their families, and a poor person who is physically able to work is not eligible for help—whether or not the person actually has a job. From some perspectives, this system has worked brilliantly. The country's already strong family ties have been strengthened, and the main safety net is the family rather than the government. The number of Japanese in the basic welfare program has declined sharply over the past half century, as people have become better off and have built up savings. In 1996 only 0.7 percent of the population received benefits—compared with the 4.8 percent of Americans who get grants from Aid to Families with Dependent Children or the 9.7 percent who receive food stamps. About 2.3 percent of Americans receive grants through the Supplemental Security Income program, which serves the elderly, blind, and disabled.

To be sure, Japan's welfare system operates in a very different milieu from that in the United States. Only 1 percent of Japanese births are to unwed mothers. That compares with a percentage that keeps climbing in the United States and has now reached 30 percent. Japan has a far lower percentage of drug addicts than the United States has, a much lower unemployment rate, a much more egalitarian dis-

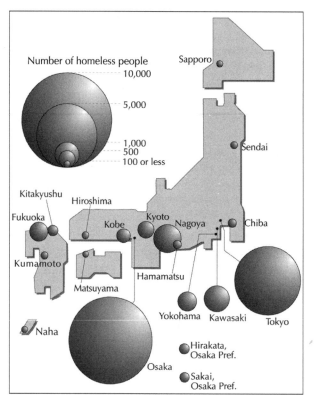

Fig. 6.14. Homeless people in major urban areas, 2000. Based on data from *Japan Times* (Tokyo) archives.

Fig. 6.15. Causes of homelessness.

tribution of wealth, a greater sense of family obligation, and an abiding sense of shame that colors almost every aspect of life. Many people who are eligible for welfare do not apply, because of this sense of shame. Some scholars say that the system in Japan almost never breeds dependence, and they suggest that the Japanese approach has emphasized the work ethic and the importance of family ties.

Japanese welfare caseworkers rigorously check applicants and drop by their homes regularly to make sure that they do not have banned luxuries like cars or air conditioners; fraud is extremely rare. A welfare worker has a caseload of sixty in Japan, and there is time for regular, unscheduled visits to recipients' homes. The caseworkers have great discretion in handling cases, as well as considerable moral authority in advising recipients about what they should do. The welfare system has broad public support. In fact, instead of grumbling about welfare mothers in Cadillacs, as people do in the United States, Japanese people often carp about how the authorities are too harsh on the poor.

In 2000 the monthly unemployment rate in Japan was around 4.7 percent—high by Japanese standards, but enviable by most other countries in Europe and North America. Larger companies still try not to sack people, and service industries such as gasoline stations and shops are overstaffed. In addition, by men's agreement, it is women in menial jobs who are fired first when the crunch comes. That protects household finances, since in Japan men almost always earn more than their wives.

Typically, a government-appointed neighborhood official known as a welfare commissioner (there are more than two hundred thousand of these) identifies a household in difficulty. The family's situation is investigated. If an elderly couple has working children, for example, the welfare commissioner may ask the children to chip in to the family budget. If the children are reluctant, the matter may be taken up with their employer. The system is intrusive, but it forms an important part of the principle behind Japanese welfare policy: family first. However, the fragmentation of the traditional family is beginning to cause some problems. By Western standards, Japanese marriage is stable; the divorce rate is one-third of the U.S. rate. All the same, some estimates suggest that the number of single-parent families has risen by half since 1970. These households make up a dis-

proportionate share of the poor. In 1994, 103 single-parent families in every thousand received public assistance, ten times the rate for Japan as a whole, and over twice the rate for the elderly, who constitute almost half of the poor.

Because able-bodied people are normally excluded on the ground that they could find work if they wanted to, the largest group of recipients is the elderly, amounting to 44 percent of households getting aid. Many of these are bedridden widows. Households with a sick or handicapped person account for another 41 percent; about 9 percent are single mothers, mothers who are divorced or widowed, rather than never married (as in the United States). Most single mothers in Japan do not receive benefits, because they have parents or other family members who can support them. Because of this, single mothers are likely to live with their parents, and thus the children grow up under supervision of several adults.

When work and the traditional family networks fail, the state steps in. According to the welfare ministry, about 1 percent of Japanese receive public assistance; these are the official poor. In America and the European Union, by contrast, about 15 percent are considered poor. For those Japanese who cannot work, such as the handicapped or the elderly, or who work but do not make enough to get by, there is direct assistance. The guaranteed minimum for a city family of three is 157,274 yen a month (about $1,400), with the central government paying three-quarters and local government the rest. The number of people using the system is small and dwindling. In 1985 some 20 Japanese per 1,000 received public assistance; a decade later, the proportion had dropped by one-third. Japan has no food stamps and relies principally on a single program of cash grants.

Japan does have two elements of a social welfare program that far surpass anything in the United States: universal medical care and comprehensive day care. Everyone has access to doctors and hospitals at affordable prices, with the services free for the poor. And the neighborhood nurseries throughout Japan provide excellent care for children from six months old to school-age, if mothers work, for a modest fee that is waived for low-income families.

The bad news is that more than a few people slip off the safety net, and there is often nothing to save them. To be eligible for welfare, Japanese must prove both that they are unable to work and that they have a fixed address—conditions the homeless cannot fulfill. For them there are no permanent shelters and little sympathy.

THE GAP BETWEEN RICH AND POOR

The gap between rich and poor Japanese is widening, spurred by economic and social changes. People are living longer and accumulating more wealth. Increasingly, pay is being set by performance rather than seniority. Lifetime employment is crumbling. Women, once relegated to the home, are trooping to office jobs. Tax laws have been changed to let the rich keep more of their money, and loopholes once exploited by the middle class are closing.

Whereas once everyone seemed to be treated more or less the same, merchants and marketers are focusing on the affluent. And it is paying off even during Japan's recession. Luxury cars are selling at a brisk pace, while overall car sales have slumped. Private banking services offered to the wealthy are also proliferating.

Increasing income stratification raises potentially troubling questions for Japan, where sameness, or the perception of it, contributes greatly to social harmony. Japanese concede that greater income disparity is inevitable as the economy becomes more competitive. But they fear that differences between the rich and poor will lead to more theft, more petty crime in general, and a host of other social problems. Already job losses and other economic hardships have added to the ranks of the homeless.

The disparities that exist now are less pronounced than they are in the United States and Britain. In the average big Japanese company, the chief executive makes about 35.7 million yen, or roughly $350,000, whereas the Labor Ministry puts the average salaried employee's pay at 5.5 million yen, or roughly $56,000. But that situation is changing.

The government points out that the leading cause of Japan's widening income disparity is aging. Income and wealth differences are generally more pronounced among the elderly, as some have saved and invested better than others. Research by private economists and academics suggests that the phenomenon is driven by government policy as well as by changes in the private sector. Japan has used one of the world's most progressive tax codes as a social leveler. The highest income tax rate has been cut from 65 percent to 50 percent and will be reduced further. At the same time, the government would like to begin taxing people of lower income levels, who have previously been exempted. And it is seeking to eliminate some of the special tax breaks used by one-third of Japanese wage earners to avoid income taxes. The government is also considering reducing Japan's exorbitant inheritance taxes, which have been the prime mechanism for leveling incomes. The private sector, including such companies as Sony Computer Entertainment, the firm that created the phenomenally successful Play Station video game, pays its employees on the basis of performance. There are none of the traditional noncash allowances for housing and transportation that are common in Japan.

REFERENCES

Brinton, Mary C. 1993. *Women and the Economic Miracle: Gender and Work in Postwar Japan.* Berkeley: Univ. of California Press.

Campbell, John, and Ruth Campbell. 2003. Adapting to long-term-care insurance: Where to live? *Social Science Japan* 27 (November): 3–5.

Campbell, Ruth, and E.M. Brody. 1985. Women's changing roles and help to the elderly: Attitudes of women in the United States and Japan. *Gerontologist* 25:584–592.

Esaki, Y., Y. Arai, and T. Kawaguchi. 1999. Return migration from major metropolitan areas to Nagano Prefecture. *Geographical Review of Japan* A 72:645–667.

———. 2000. Return migration in Japan: A comparative analysis of migrants returned to Nagano and Miyazaki Prefectures. *Human Geography* 52 (2): 80–92.

Gauthier, Howard L., K. Tanaka, and W.R. Smith. 1992. A time series analysis of regional income inequalities and migration in Japan, 1955–1985. *Geographical Analysis* 24:283–298.

Gill, Tom. 2001. Homelessness: A slowly dawning recognition. *Social Science Japan* 21 (September): 17–20.

———. 2002. Government responses to homelessness: The view from ground level. *Social Science Japan* 23 (April): 24–28.

Hodge, R.W., and Naohiro Ogawa. 1991. *Fertility Change in Contemporary Japan.* Chicago: Univ. of Chicago Press.

Horst, Oscar H., and Katsuhiro Asagiri. 2000. The odyssey of Japanese colonists in the Dominican Republic. *Geographical Review* 90 (3): 335–358.

Imamura, Anne E., ed. 1996. *Re-Imaging Japanese Women.* Berkeley: Univ. of California Press.

Iwao, Sumiko. 1993. *The Japanese Woman: Traditional Myth and Changing Reality.* New York: Free Press.

Kakiuchi, George, and Masami Hasegawa. 1979. Recent trends in rural to urban migration in Japan: The problem of depopulation. *Science Reports of Tohoku University,* ser. 7 (Geography) 29 (1): 47–61.

Kamiya, Hiroo, and Enko Ikeya. 1994. Women's participation in labor force in Japan: Trends and regional patterns. *Geographical Review of Japan* B 67:15–35.

Kaplan, David E. 1986. *Yakuza: The Explosive Account of Japan's Underworld.* Reading, MA: Addison-Wesley.

Kikumura-Yano, Akemi. 2002. *Encyclopedia of Japanese Descendants in the Americas.* Lanham, MD.: Alta Mira Press.

Komei, Hiroshi. 2001. *Foreign Migrants in Contemporary Japan.* Melbourne: Trans Pacific Press.

Lee, Changsoo, and George De Vos. 1981. *Koreans in Japan: Ethnic Conflict and Accommodation.* Berkeley: Univ. of California Press.

Liang, Jersey. 2003. Changes in health and well-being among older Japanese. *Social Science Japan* 27 (November): 6–8.

Lutzeler, Ralph. 1995. The regional structure of social problems in Japan. *Geographical Review of Japan* B 68:46–52.

Martin, I.G. 1989. The graying of Japan. *Population Bulletin* 44:1–42.

Miyakoshi, T. 1999. Trade off between pension and jobs for the elderly: Theoretical and empirical observations from Japan. *Asian Economic Journal* 13 (1): 93–107.

Miyazawa, Hiroshi. 1999. Inter-municipality inequality in elderly nursing home services: The case of Tokyo. *Science Reports of Tohoku University*, ser. 7 (Geography) 49 (1): 23–35.

Mizuuchi, Toshio. 1998. *Power Struggles, Public Supports: Renovating Japanese Minority Community.* Osaka: Osaka City Univ., Research Center for Human Rights.

Morita, K., and S. Sassen. 1994. The new illegal immigration in Japan, 1980–1992. *International Migration Review* 28 (1): 153–163.

Nagai, Akiko. 2000. Combating modern Japanese myths: The challenges for young working housewives in Japan. *Social Science Japan* 18 (April): 10–11.

Nagayama, T. 1993. New developments in population movement and the issue of foreign workers in Japan. Special issue, "Japan and International Migration," *International Migration* 31 (2–3): 423–433.

Ninomiya, M. 1994. Eighty-five years of Japanese emigration to Brazil and the recent "dekasegi" phenomenon. *Journal of Behavioral and Social Sciences* 4:119–130.

Ogawa, Naohiro. 1986. Internal migration in Japanese postwar development. NUPRI Research Paper Series, no. 33, Nihon Univ. Population Research Institute, Tokyo.

Ogawa, Naohiro, Robert D. Retherford, and Yasuhiko Saito. 2003. Caring for the elderly and holding down a job: How are women coping in Japan? *Asia-Pacific Population and Policy* 65 (April): 1–4.

Onishi, Norimitsu. 2003. For Japan's New Homeless, There's Disdain and Danger. *New York Times.*

Papademetrion, Demetrios, and Kimberly Hamilton. 2000. *Reinventing Japan: Immigration's Role in Shaping Japan's Future.* Washington, DC: Carnegie Endowment for Peace.

Selleck, Yoko. 2001. *Migrant Labour in Japan.* Houndmills, Hampshire, UK: Pelgrave.

Seymour, C. 1996. *Yakuza Dairy: Doing Time in the Japanese Underworld.* New York: Atlantic Monthly Press.

Shelby, M. 1989. Human rights and undocumented immigrant workers in Japan. *Stanford Journal of International Law* 26:325–369.

Shimizu, Masata. 1995. Residential relocation and friendship associations of overstay foreign workers in Tokyo. *Geographical Review of Japan* B 68:166–184.

Sugiura, Shin'ichiro. 2000. Regional framework of welfare services for the elderly in the Higashi Hiroshima Area, Japan. *Geographical Review of Japan* A 73:95–123.

———. 2002. The spatial distribution of nursing homes for the elderly in Japan: A geographical analysis of construction policies in the 1990s towards the establishment of long-term care insurance. *Human Geography* 54 (1):1–23.

Tahara, Yuko, and Hiroo Kamiya. 2002. Attachment of the elderly to their home places fostered by their insideness: A case study of Kamioka town, Gifu Prefecture. *Human Geography* 54 (3): 1–22.

Tsuda, T. 1999. The motivation to migrate: The ethnic and sociocultural constitution of the Japanese-Brazilian return migration system. *Economic Development and Cultural Change* 48 (1): 1–31.

Ueda, Takahiko. 1993. Foreign brides adapt to rural life. *Japan Times,* January 8, 3.

Weiner, Michael, ed. 1997. *Japan's Minorities.* London: Routledge.

Yagasaki, Noritaka. 1982. Ethnic cooperativism and immigrant agriculture: A study of Japanese floriculture and truck farming in California. Ph.D. diss., Univ. of California, Berkeley.

Yumiko, Ehara. 2000. Feminism's growing pains. *Japan Quarterly* (July–Sept): 41–48.

Chapter 7

第 七 章

Rural Landscape, Settlements, and Agriculture

The nature of Japanese agriculture, farm villages, and the countryside has changed radically during the past half century. Rice continues to be a staple crop, but truck gardening for the urban market has grown in importance. Quality- and labor-intensive production is much more significant. Apples, grapes, strawberries, and other fruits are produced in increasing amounts for the metropolitan markets and as seasonal expensive gifts to support the labor-intensive production methods. There is concern for the competitive ability of Japanese agriculture in an open market. The farm lobby pressures the government to maintain agricultural support programs (Mulgan 2000).

The farm village has also changed with government subsidies to encourage efficient tillage and higher individual productivity. Greater use of farm machinery has replaced the traditional tillage practices, such as the common seedbeds and rice planting described by Ellen Churchill Semple (1912) in her classic study of Japanese agriculture at the beginning of the twentieth century. Large-scale outmigration from farm villages has influenced rural life and the countryside. The construction of roads to remote areas has brought most of rural Japan within reach of metropolitan areas or large towns. And part-time farming is now well entrenched within the postindustrial agricultural structure of Japan (Yamamoto 2000).

The Rural Landscape

The rural landscape of Japan reflects the interaction of space and culture over a long period of time. Geographic space has been a luxury in the country. Under the circumstances, agricultural land use is of primary importance; any other use, such as open

Truck farming near Nagasaki, Kyushu. Production of vegetables for the urban market has become important in the urbanized central zone of intensive farming along the Pacific coast of Japan. Photo by P.P. Karan.

A *jori* field pattern in northern Kyushu. The rectangular pattern of land division, or jori system, was introduced in Japan at the time of the Great Taika Reform in AD 645. This system can be seen in rice fields, road networks, place names, and settlements. The areas dominated by the jori system are old rice lands that were under the control of the Yamato court. The jori system is dominant in the core area of Yamato culture, which stretches from Kinki to northern Kyushu. Photo by P.P. Karan.

space or recreation, has a lower priority. The task of intensifying land use and increasing crop yields began over eleven centuries ago with the creation of a grid system—essentially an extension of the grid plan of the capital city. The rivers of the Yamato lowland, the cultural core of early Japan, were canalized to flow along *jo* and *ri* lines, perpendicular to one another, and the jori system was imposed on the landscape (Hall 1932; Kinda 1986). There are similarities to the range and township system of land division in the United States.[1] In certain areas, such as around Okayama, the main axes of the jori system conformed to those of the valleys and not to the cardinal directions.

The paddy field, the common feature of the rural landscape of Japan, is the culmination of centuries of effort. Leveling, reworking of the soil and subsoil, construction of clay hardpans, dike and wall building—all represent attention to the ultimate use potentials of each plot of land, and these efforts have produced a landscape of compact units and cellular forms. In most parts of the country, a single row of soybeans rises above each dike, marking field borders. In the Inland Sea area, taro or eggplant is planted

on the dike, and soybeans alternate with *koaliang* (a type of grain). Paddy fields are drained for winter dry crops and are ridged if draining is difficult. A common cool-season combination is interrowed wheat and broad beans, two rows of each alternating mile after mile. The Japanese farmer has a highly developed feeling for the interchangeability and the interrelationship of crops and semiseasons. The farmers also have developed strategies for saving space. A farmer will plant squash on the very edge of a ditch and build a bamboo-covered rack above the flowing water for the spreading plant. Another farmer will stack rice or wheat straw on a frame over a ditch, taking care that the shadow falls not upon growing plants but on a village roadway. Orchards descend from hillsides and stand in rows along the south sides of roads, giving shade to the traveler but not denying sunlight to the cucumber plants below. Paddy-bank orcharding includes peaches, pears, and persimmons, and an occasional orange tree is carefully wrapped in straw all winter.

Hills and house lots are also intensively used in the same way as the level fields. Often vegetable gardens surround the old village temple. Hillside orchards are rarely clear-cropped. Late autumn radishes may precede winter wheat or may be intercropped with wheat in the spring, and sweet potatoes are the most common floor crop in summer. In some areas grapevines are planted in orchards. The rural landscape of Japan vividly reflects the farmer's effort to

---

[1] The "range and township system" refers to the division of territory in surveys of U.S. public land, where a township consisted of 36 sections or 36 square miles. A *range* was one of the north–south rows of sections. The result of applying this system was a rectangular pattern of fields in public lands in the Midwest and the West.

A village near Wakamatsu, Fukushima Prefecture. Houses are clustered near the hillside, with cultivated fields occupying the flat lower areas. The share of agriculture, forestry, and fishery income in national income has declined from 30 percent in 1946 to 17 percent in 1954, continuing downward to 11 percent in 1960. By 2003, it had slumped to less than 1 percent. Photo by P.P. Karan.

employ every technique to make the most effective use of the land or give a greater yield. As one moves from the cultural heartland of Kansai to the peripheral regions of the north, the tightness and compactness of the rural landscape loosens. The Japanese farmer compresses space to its ultimate intensity, just as a haiku poem compresses a universe of meaning into seventeen syllables.

RURAL SETTLEMENTS

A village, or *mura,* comprising clustered houses is the dominant form of rural settlement in Japan. Separate farmhouses scattered in the field are found only in Hokkaido (Davis 1934). Dispersed settlements are also found in mountainous regions of central Honshu. Agriculture in Japan has been associated with much communal activity, especially for the allocation and organization of irrigation facilities, which has favored the development of clustered rural settlements. Most Japanese villages are a loose agglomeration of houses separated by small fields and connected by winding, narrow lanes.

There are five types of villages in Japan, based on their origin or historical method of formation (Hall 1931). Jori settlements are nucleated villages laid out on a rectangular or grid pattern under a system of land division that was followed in the seventh and eighth centuries. Tracts of land were divided into squares measuring one *cho,* or 358 feet (109 m), to a side. Villages, roads, canals, and fields in the Kyoto-Nara-Osaka region retain the dimensions of the ancient jori system. Japanese geographer Akihiro Kinda (1986) has published several excellent studies on the development of the jori grid pattern, which is dominant on the alluvial plains of Kinki, along the Inland Sea, and in northern Kyushu (see fig. 7.1). The density and distribution of jori settlements decrease with distance from the ancient Kinki core area.

Goshi settlements were developed by country gentlemen (*inaka no shinshi*) from manorial estates in the outer domains of the empire, away from the Kanto and Kinki heartlands of Japan. The low-ranking samurai who lived in the countryside supported themselves from these holdings.

Shinden villages developed on new lands reclaimed by feudal lords during the Tokugawa shogunate. The opening of new lands to cultivation and the conversion of dry fields to paddy during the Edo period (1603–1868) marked one of the most active periods of land reclamation in Japan. Shinden referred to reclaiming new lands for paddy. The Tokugawa shogunate and the daimyo encouraged land reclamation to increase the base for their major source of revenue, the annual land tax. Toshio Kikuchi (1986) has investigated the shinden villages established on newly reclaimed lands. The regional pattern of the development of shinden villages in relation to geomorphology has been noted by Toshio Fukuda (1986); and T. Miura (1985) has documented the development of shinden villages in Akita. At the end of the Tokugawa period (1603–1867) there were about 8 million acres of arable land and 70,000 villages; of these totals, 2.8 million acres were reclaimed land and 15,000 villages were shinden settlements. There were three periods of major shinden reclamation, from 1630 to 1676,

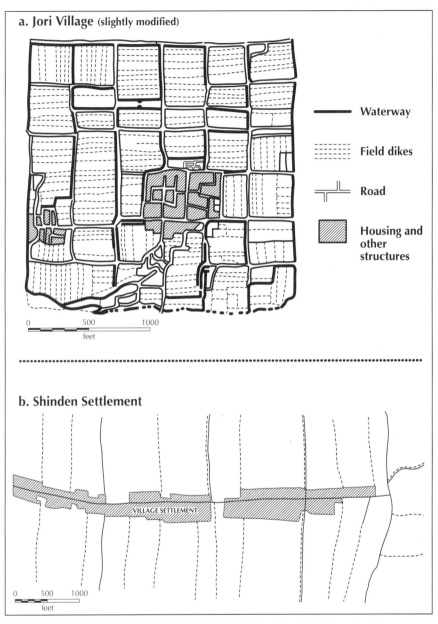

Fig. 7.1. Jori and shinden settlement patterns. Based on Sasaki 1984.

from 1696 to 1746, and from 1804 to 1867. During the first period, the reclamation activity was dominant in central Japan from Kanto to Chugoku and in the northern parts of Shikoku and Kyushu. In the second phase, reclamation activity was confined largely to the Kinki region. During the third period, reclamation activity extended to southern Kyushu and southern Shikoku. The frontier of reclamation was pushed further out in each of the three periods.

In all these areas, the reclamation activity was concentrated on tidal lands, since the deltas were already reclaimed before the Tokugawa period. After the Meiji Restoration (1868), reclamation activity moved to the lagoons, lakes, and deltas in the Tohoku region of northeastern Japan.

The increase in shinden reclamation during the Tokugawa period is attributed to the growing population, advances in civil engineering, and the accu-

LAND USE AND RECENT CHANGES
IN AGRICULTURE

The importance of agriculture in the Japanese economy has been declining since 1955. In that year 23 percent of the gross domestic product came from agriculture and related sectors; by 1980 the percentage was 2.4, and in 1999 it declined to 1.1. In the meantime, Japan's share of world imports of agricultural, forestry, and marine products has increased. Historical, cultural, and social factors are important influences on the way agricultural policies have developed in Japan. Rice, the traditional basis of the Japanese diet, is of religious and symbolic importance to the Japanese people and therefore has dominated Japan's agriculture. Religious and social factors have also influenced developments in the livestock industries. Before the middle of the nineteenth century, livestock products were not widely consumed in Japan because of religious prohibitions. Since the 1950s Westernization of Japanese tastes and lifestyles, as well as higher incomes, has increased the demand for animal protein and caused an expansion of the livestock sector.

An important historical influence on Japan's agricultural sector was the land reform program introduced after World War II (Dore 1966, 1984; Sum 1979). This gave tenant farmers ownership over the small plots of land they farmed. Reforms also imposed ceilings on land ownership. As a result, the distribution of farms according to the cultivated area has been almost unchanged over the past five decades. In 1950, for example, about 73 percent of Japanese farm families had less than 2.5 acres (1 ha) of cultivated land, whereas in 2000 the proportion was still about 67 percent. Mary McDonald (1997) has investigated changes in the agricultural land holdings during the half century after the land reform.

Agriculture in Japan is largely confined to alluvial lowlands and diluvial uplands, which together make up nearly 13 percent of the total area of the country (see fig. 7.2). There are small areas of cultivated land in most of the mountains, but most of the hilly and mountainous areas are covered with forests. Intensive farming practices are common because of the limited cultivated land area. In the early 1960s, total cropped area exceeded 20 million acres (8 million ha), while the total arable land area was nearly 15 million acres (6 million ha). Since the

Farming on the reclaimed land of Hachirogata Lagoon in the eastern part of Oga Peninsula, northwestern Akita Prefecture. The Hachirogata Lagoon was the second-largest lake in Japan (after Lake Biwa) before land reclamation projects (from 1957 through 1966) converted practically all the lagoon area into land. It is an important agricultural area with large-scale farming using modern machinery. Because of falling rice prices, this farmer is now growing soybeans. Photo by P.P. Karan.

mulation of capital by merchants and feudal lords. The population of Japan at the beginning of the Tokugawa period was about 20 million; it increased to 32 million in the middle period and to 34 million at the end of the shogunate. The shinden were populated by transplanting farmers from older settlements (*honden*). The increasing population in the honden prompted the reclamation projects. In most cases shinden settlements are found in the land outside of the honden areas. For example, Tsugaru Plain in northeastern Japan has 836 settlements; among them 709 are shinden that were reclaimed by the feudal lords of the Hirosaki domain. Wealthy merchants in Osaka reclaimed 48 large shinden on the tidelands of Osaka Bay.

Tondenhei settlements were developed by colonist militiamen, soldiers recruited to open up and defend new farmland in Hokkaido. The tondenhei were pioneer settlements in Hokkaido laid out in grids according to the jori pattern.

The *echigo* type of settlement, which has a shoe-string form (*Reihensiedlung*), is found in the Niigata Plain. These settlements are located on higher, flood-free ancient dunes and active or abandoned levees (Sasaki 1984).

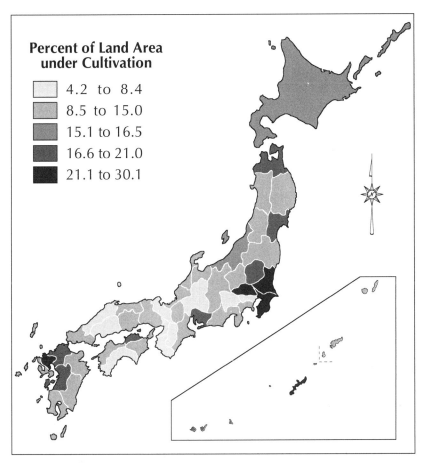

Fig. 7.2. Distribution of cultivated land by prefectures, 2000. Based on data from the Ministry of Agriculture, Forestry, and Fisheries, Tokyo.

1960s both the cropped area and the arable land area have declined. In 1995 total cropped area stood at 12.3 million acres (4.92 million ha) and total arable land had decreased to 12.6 million acres (5.04 million ha). By 1997 the total cropped area had contracted to 11.8 million acres (4.72 million ha) and the total arable land to 12.37 million acres (4.95 million ha). The total cropped area has usually exceeded the total arable land, because of double cropping, but in recent years the rate of double cropping has also declined. The total cropped area is now lower than the total arable land because some of the arable land is no longer used for farming. In 1999 workers employed in agriculture numbered 3.15 million, or 4.6 percent of all employed persons in Japan. Nearly 55 percent of the cultivated area was in paddy land (see fig. 7.3). Japan's self-sufficiency in grain is only 29 percent, and for food-

stuffs on a caloric basis it is about 42 percent. Among the industrial countries, Japan's dependence on foreign countries for agricultural products is relatively high.

Table 7.1. Land use, 2000

Use	In 100 km²	% of total area
Agricultural land	504	13.1
Forests	2,538	67.2
Built-up area	174	4.7
Roads	123	3.3
Water area	133	3.5
Other uses	306	8.2

Source: Director-General's Secretariat, National Land Agency, Tokyo.

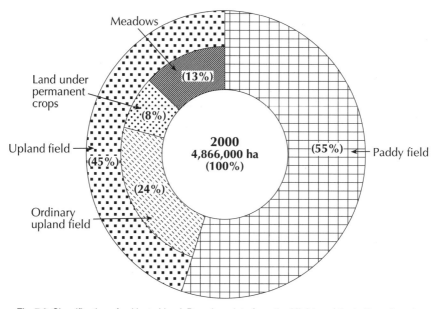

Fig. 7.3. Classification of cultivated land. Based on data from the Ministry of Agriculture, Forestry, and Fisheries, Tokyo.

The striking transformation in Japanese agriculture and rural areas in terms of land use, employment structure, and rural landscape are related to (1) the increased application of technology (Oshiro 1982), (2) changes in the rural socioeconomic environment, particularly in transportation, and (3) the impacts of urbanization and industrialization (Yamamoto and Tabayashi 1989). The technological revolution in Japan has led to the mechanization of agricultural production and a rapid increase in knowledge-intensive agriculture. The development of agricultural infrastructure has transformed the traditional rural landscape. Increased transportation facilities have led to the expansion of metropolitan markets to distant farming regions, as trucks are now generally used to bring produce to the market. With increasing use of private automobiles, farm families' opportunities for off-farm employment have greatly increased. Expanding cities and an increase in the number of urban residents have created a larger demand for a variety of agricultural products, which in turn has promoted the consolidation and intensification of farm production. The increase in leisure time that has accompanied urban growth has raised the demand for rural areas to function also as recreational areas.

Urbanization and industrialization have led to the intensification of agriculture even as the abandonment of farmland as a trend toward farming as a secondary occupation has accelerated (Isoda, Kim, and Matsuoka 1998). Conversion of farmland to nonagricultural use led to diversification in the use of rural space, with increasing demand for residential, commercial, industrial, and recreational uses. Since the 1970s traditional farming in which only a small part of the farm produce was sold in the market has declined, and commercial farming has increased. As farming has become commercial, both mechanization and the scale of operations have generally increased (Moore 1990).

The number of farm households has declined continuously, going from 6.2 million in 1950 to 5.4 million in 1970, or 19.3 percent of all households. By 2000 the number of households engaged in farming had declined to 2.4 million, or 5.6 percent of all households. Of these nearly 13 percent were exclusively engaged in agriculture, and another 13 percent had significant income from farming. About 51 percent received a larger proportion of their income from sources other than farming (see fig. 7.4). There has been only a moderate decrease in the number of farm households, despite a swift decline in the number of agricultural workers. As the figures above indicate, only a small proportion of farm households

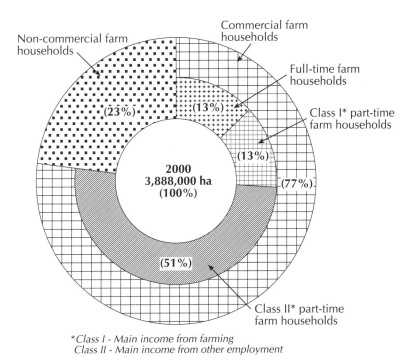

Fig. 7.4. Full-time and part-time farm households. Based on data from the Ministry of Agriculture, Forestry, and Fisheries, Tokyo.

obtain their income fully from farming. Regionally, the basic pattern is a low proportion of full-time farmers in central Japan and a high proportion in eastern and southwestern Japan (see fig. 7.5). Another feature of Japanese agriculture is that the average age of farmworkers has been rising. The average age of the core workforce in agriculture is over fifty-five, and the shortage of agricultural workers is expected to increase as more farmers in their sixties begin to retire. Overall, the farm household population has declined from 37.7 million in 1950 to 26.3 million in 1970 and 14.8 million in 1998.

The shift in employment from agriculture to nonagricultural industries, the drop in the birthrate, and the increasing tendency toward nuclear families have caused the decline in farm households. In addition the number of younger farmers is dropping. The low level of income is the main reason for the continuing decline of the number of new workers in farming. Per capita productivity in agriculture is roughly one-fourth that of manufacturers. One reason for the low productivity may be the government's policy of keeping prices low for agricultural products. The average area of tillage for rice cultivation in Japan is 1.7 acres (0.7 ha). Expansion of this size is needed for Japan's rice cultivators to compete internationally. A sweeping redistribution of land largely eliminated tenancy by 1949 and resulted in 90 percent of the cultivated land being farmed by owners. Land reforms of 1946 were most successful in bringing about basic changes in Japan. In less than a generation, Japan's traditional labor-intensive agriculture has been transformed into a highly mechanized capital-intensive farming system. Yet agriculture faces several problems. First, production costs, especially for rice, are very high, and Japanese agriculture requires heavy subsidies. Most farms are too small for maximum use of land and capital. Therefore, small-scale, relatively unproductive farms still predominate. Second, much of Japan's food supply is imported, and the country's self-sufficiency in food continues to decrease. This is partly because of the high value of the yen, which makes it less expensive to import food than to grow it domestically. Third, urbanization and industrialization, coupled with steep land prices, are steadily reducing the amount of land available for farming (Tanaka 1982). Finally, there is a chronic shortage of agricultural labor due

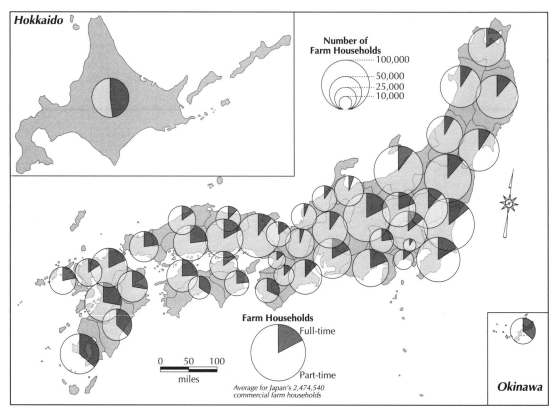

Fig. 7.5. Distribution of full-time and part-time farm households by prefectures. Based on data from the Ministry of Agriculture, Forestry, and Fisheries, Tokyo.

to the gradual decrease in the number of farm households and the shrinking size of farming communities.

Based on the intensity of agricultural land use, Japan may be divided into two major agricultural regions: (1) a central zone of intensive farming extending from Kanto along the Pacific coast to the Tokai and Kinki regions and extending on both sides of the Inland Sea up to Kyushu, and (2) an outer ring of less intensive agriculture (Himiyama and Kiyotaka 1988). The second region can be subdivided into three distinctive areas: Hokkaido, Tohoku, and western Honshu along the Sea of Japan (see fig. 7.6).

The central zone of intensive agriculture is characterized by highly intensive production of vegetables, fruits, flowers, meat, and dairy products to meet the large urban market of the cities of the Japanese urban belt. Many of the crops are grown under vinyl covers. Stall-fed livestock and factory-type poultry operations are common in this region. Along the Inland Sea truck farming is very significant. The area is characterized by wide diversity of agricultural products. Kanto-Tosan accounts for 17.2 percent of

the national rice output, and Yamanashi and Nagano produce more than one-third of Japan's grapes. Nagano is also second in apple production; Chiba produces well over two-thirds of the peanuts, and 40 percent of the green tea comes from Shizuoka. There are major concentrations of *mikan* (tangerine) production in Ehime, Wakayama, Shizuoka, and Kyushu. The development of the mikan cultivation in Shizuoka Prefecture has been investigated by Shozo Yamamoto, Yoichi Asano, and George H. Kakiuchi (1969).

The area around the town of Katsunuma, in the center of Yamanashi Prefecture, has emerged as a major wine-making region in Japan. Although the area is proud of its thirteen-hundred-year history of grape cultivation, grapes did not begin to be grown for wine-making until the beginning of the Meiji period (1868–1912). Now the Katsunuma area produces nearly 40 percent of Japan's domestic wine. Most of the grapes grown in the area are varieties such as *koshu,* which is equally appropriate for eating fresh or for making wine. In order to grow the

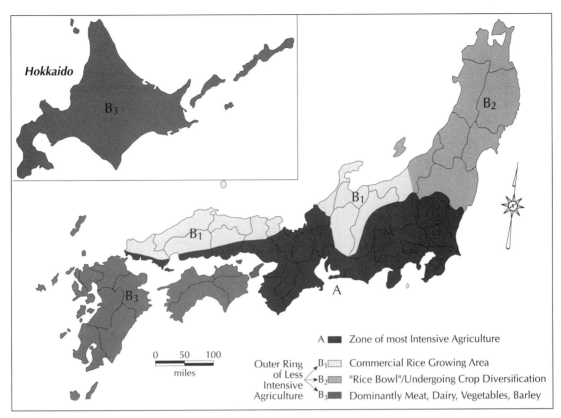

Fig. 7.6. Agricultural zones.

most attractive, full clusters of grapes for sale as fresh fruit, as well as to increase the number of clusters each vine produces, most growers use trellises for grape cultivation. But in the vineyards of Katsunuma, eighty-three local wineries' grapes are grown using hedge cultivation, which produces grapes with full flavor—ideal for use in making wines. Since 1991 Katsunuma wineries have cultivated their own grapes, growing Cabernet Sauvignon, Chardonnay, and other varieties for wine-making. However, Japan's strict Agricultural Land Law prevents a winery—which falls in the category of "manufacturer"—from renting or buying farmland; this limits the efficiency of the operation and the size of the harvest. This hurdle was overcome in April 2003, when the Katsunuma region was designated a Special Zone for Structural Reform, which permits more flexible application of agricultural land-use laws and allows wineries to lease agricultural land to cultivate grapes.

In the outer ring of less intensive farming, Hokkaido is distinctive for its production of meat, dairy products, and root vegetables. Here farms are larger and the farm landscape is different from that in the rest of the country. Hokkaido is the biggest dairy-farming region, with 28.3 percent of the dairy cattle and 24 percent of the raw milk production in Japan. In 2000 Hokkaido supplied nearly 80 percent of the nation's demand for butter and other processed dairy products. Nearly one-third of all farms specializing in dairy production are located in Hokkaido; Chiba and Iwate are also dairy-producing areas. Hokkaido also produces more than three-quarters of the entire potato crop grown in Japan.

Tohoku is the major rice-producing area, with 27 percent of the national rice output. Farmers in Tohoku are diversifying production with a new emphasis on soybeans, livestock, and dairy production in the upland area. Apples and other fruits are important in Aomori and in mountain valleys. Western Honshu along the Sea of Japan is an important producer of rice. Southern Shikoku is also a rice-growing region, and southern Kyushu is emerging as a significant area of livestock and meat production, along with rice farming. Beef cattle farms in Kyushu are concen-

A farmer growing tomatoes in a greenhouse near Yatsushiro, Kyushu. Recently, onions, eggplant, and other vegetables have been actively cultivated in the vinyl-covered greenhouses. For farmers these winter crops can be more profitable than rice. Photo by Cotton Mather.

Cultivation of strawberries and other produce in vinyl greenhouses for the Tokyo market has become important in Shizuoka Prefecture during the past two decades. Photo by P.P. Karan.

Agriculture in the Ishikari Plain of Hokkaido. The average cultivated acreage per farm in Hokkaido is about 27 acres (11 ha), nearly ten times the size of farms in the rest of Japan. The primary crops are red beans, soybeans, potatoes, and sugar beets. Photo by P.P. Karan.

A dairy farm north of Kushiro in Hokkaido. The dairy industry is relatively new, since milk and dairy products did not enter the Japanese diet until well into the twentieth century. The dairy industry commenced rapid growth in the 1960s under the umbrella of government protection during a period of growing demand. Hokkaido Dairy Cooperative, named Snow Brand Milk Products in 1950, is Japan's largest dairy product company. As imported dairy products have increased in recent years, Hokkaido's dairy farmers are facing keen competition to reduce production costs and increase the quality of products. Photo by P.P. Karan.

trated in Miyazaki, Kagoshima, Nagasaki, and Kumamoto Prefectures. This area accounts for nearly 60 percent of all beef cattle farms in Japan.

Nearly 78 percent of agricultural gross income per commercial farm household came from crops in 2000, and 20 percent came from livestock farming (see fig. 7.7). Among the crops, rice accounted for 29 percent of the income, followed by vegetables, 23 percent; fruits and nuts, 10 percent; and industrial crops, 5 percent; the rest came from other crops such as wheat and barley and from sericulture. In 1996, on a regional basis, farmers in Hokuriku (71.7 percent), Tohoku (48 percent), Chugoku (40.3 percent), and Kinki (35.9 percent) derived the bulk of their agricultural income from rice sales. Rice was the most important source of income in the Hokuriku prefectures of Toyama (87.3 percent) and Niigata (72.6 percent) and the Tohoku prefectures of Akita (69.6 percent) and Yamagata (50.5 percent).

Livestock and livestock products accounted for 32.8 percent of farm household income in Hokkaido and 27.2 percent in Kyushu; fruit farming produced 71.3 percent of household income in Yamanashi, 59.5 percent in Wakayama, 45.4 percent in Ehime, and 29.1 percent in Aomori. Regional variations in farm income dependence on specific agricultural products generate keen interest among local farmers in policy issues affecting the particular farm product. For example, farmers in Hokuriku and Tohoku, where the bulk of the income comes from rice, are particularly interested in rice issues such as producer prices, set-aside subsidies, and rice imports.

Significant changes in the structure of Japanese agriculture were put in place during the postwar oc-

A farm in Suemura, about 50 miles (80.5 km) south of Kumamoto, raising beef cattle. The cattle are stall-fed, and grazing, which is relatively rare, occurs in small pens. This reflects the fact that grazing land is limited and the desire of the farmer to produce animals with as little sinew as possible in order to achieve a high level of feed conversion. Photo by P.P. Karan.

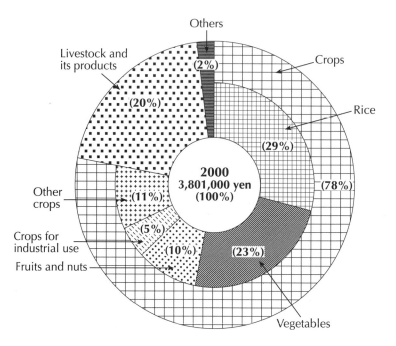

Fig. 7.7. Agricultural gross income per commercial farm household. Based on data from the Ministry of Agriculture, Forestry, and Fisheries, Tokyo.

cupation nearly a half century ago. Agrarian land reforms were imposed by the U.S.-led occupation as part of the effort to democratize Japan. Prior to the postwar reform, lands leased by tenant farmers comprised nearly one-half of the total land under cultivation. And rents were not only high (as high as 91.7 percent of the total yield for paddy fields), but they were to be paid in kind, rice for paddy fields. Under the circumstances, tenant farmers could hardly afford to accumulate capital for improving farming. The wealth that piled up as rents in the hands of the noncultivating landowners was not invested in the development of agriculture but flowed instead to more profitable nonagricultural activities. In this manner, in striking contrast to the remarkable progress of manufacturing industry since the Meiji Restoration, Japanese agriculture remained inevitably backward in its major aspects. A large number of tenant farmers in the 1920s organized themselves against the landowners, demanding reduction of rents and established rights of cultivation. Following the years of economic depression and a decade of wartime economy, the urgent need to secure food production strengthened the position of people who were directly cultivating the land.

With the end of hostilities, a legislative measure for land reform was promulgated in November 1946 in accordance with a directive of the supreme commander for the Allied Powers. A drastic land reform was considered one of the prerequisites for democratization of Occupied Japan. Noncultivating resident landowners were allowed to hold tenant land of one cho, or 2.4 acres (about 1 ha), on the main islands except Hokkaido, and noncultivating nonresident owners were absolutely disallowed to own any farmland. For the transfer of the leased land from owners to cultivators, the government pursued the policy of buying it from the owner and reselling it to the cultivator. As a result by 1950 most of the Japanese farmers became owner-cultivators (*jisakuno*), and big landowners completely disappeared.

Under the reforms, 4.82 million acres (1.93 million ha) of land (or about 80 percent of all tenant-farmed land) were sold at very low prices to the farmers who had worked the land. The vast majority of Japanese farmers then owned the land they worked, and owner-farmers were motivated to intensify their farming efforts. The agrarian land reforms also contributed to the pattern of small land holdings, as the average farm size was reduced to 2.5

acres (1 ha). The Agricultural Cooperative Law was enacted in 1947 to enable these owner-farmers to band together economically, and this was the start of Japan's giant agricultural cooperatives.

Japan's acceptance of the Uruguay Round Agricultural Agreement liberalized trade in agricultural products. When the agreement came into force in 1995, Japan was faced with the need to bring its own laws and regulations into line with the Agricultural Agreement. As a result the Food Control Law, which governed the production and sale of the two staple grains, rice and wheat, was repealed. A new Staple Food Stabilization Law deregulated the Japanese rice market. The law stripped the agricultural cooperatives of their monopoly control over the rice market and gave market forces a greater role. Because the government had controlled rice production and distribution for so long, the deregulation of the rice market is having a major impact on both agricultural production and the Japanese food market. Production, distribution, stockpiling, imports, and other aspects are in transition, but it is clear that there can be no turning back from the fundamental shift to a freer market in agriculture. Todd Stradford (1994), in his excellent study of the agricultural sector of Kochi Prefecture, has noted the impact of the government's economic and political decisions on farming, which are visibly evident in the agricultural landscape.

Rice has long been a battleground between the United States and Japan in the competition over trade and market access. U.S. pressure on Japan to import more American rice has boosted U.S. rice sales to Japan from $31 million in 1995 to $144 million in 1999. But although U.S. farmers and trading companies have carved out dominant market shares in Japan in corn, wheat, and soybeans, Japanese politicians and farmers have managed to keep rice imports to only a fraction of domestic consumption. This is because of rice farming's special place in Japanese history and culture—and the political clout wielded by rice farmers as a core constituency of Japan's ruling Liberal Democratic Party (Jones 1989; George 1991). Time—and changing Japanese tastes—may take care of the problem. Younger Japanese are eating less rice and more bread. Whereas rice accounted for 47 percent of calories and 26 percent of protein in the early 1960s, these shares declined to just 23 percent and 12 percent in 2001. And Japanese farmers, under pressure from the government, are slowly switching to other crops.

In recent years Japanese farmers have been adopting value-added crops and economies of scale to succeed in the nation's changing agricultural economy. Vegetable farmers on the Nobeyama upland in Minamisaku-gun, Nagano Prefecture, for example, are earning healthy incomes of 20 to 30 million yen ($280,000) per year. Total produce shipments from the region average 25 billion yen ($280 million) a year. Thanks to technological innovations in lettuce cultivation and online marketing strategies, this formerly depressed, remote mountain region is now home to some of the most prosperous farming villages in the nation. For more than thirty years, farm-

Paddy fields in Tsukushi Plain, near Saga, Kyushu. Rice is an important crop in the alluvial lowlands of Japan. A farmer is planting rice seedlings using modern machinery. Japanese consumers have moved away from the traditional diet of rice and fish to a meal with more vegetables, meat, and salad. As a result rice consumption has declined. Starting in 1971, the government devised financial incentives to encourage farmers to reduce their rice output and switch to other crops. Photo by P.P. Karan.

Planting of rice seedlings is still done by hand in some areas. Here two women are planting rice seedlings in Tsugaru Plain, near Hirosaki, in the Tohoku region. Photo by P.P. Karan.

ers in Nakano, Nagano Prefecture, prospered as a fruit-growing region (mainly grapes and apples), but in the 1980s local farmers also began cultivating enoki mushrooms and asparagus. As a result, the region is among the most prosperous farming areas in the nation, and passing on the family farm is not the problem it is in other regions.

In the Mikawa region of Aichi Prefecture, historically a flourishing agricultural area, greenhouse farmers earn between 59 million and 100 million yen ($940,000) per year. In this region, agriculture still wins out over secondary and tertiary industries. During the bubble economy, a labor shortage sent businesses in the area in search of part-time workers.

Farming on the steep mountain slopes in Kamimura, a village in southern Nagano Prefecture near Iida. Farmers grow buckwheat and millet, which are sold at relatively high prices to specialty restaurants in Tokyo for the preparation of soba. Photo by P.P. Karan.

Field Report

Apple Growers of Aomori

It is July. This is the time for wrapping apples on the trees, a traditional Japanese practice that is a tribute to the time-consuming fastidiousness of the farmers and the passion for quality among the Japanese. Farm women wearing sunbonnets teeter on ladders under the trees and fold and twist tiny baby-blue papers around each of the dangling apples. The women are in a hurry because the rising summer sun will soon tan the pale skins of the young fruit if they are not covered. To get a good-looking apple, Japanese farmers must wrap the fruit with splashes of blue, purple, green, and yellow paper that hang like origami from the gangly trees blanketing this northern region of Japan.

Much of the fruit in Japan, from grapes to pears to peaches to apples, is individually wrapped. Originally devised as a way to keep out worms, wrapping now has become the means by which farmers naturally paint their apples. Apples that would be red if unwrapped turn a shade of pink, and green apples take on a red sheen when wrapped. To get an even brighter color, shortly before the harvest, farmers put an aluminum sheet on the ground to capture the reflection from the sun. This turns the bottoms of the apples red.

Farmers acknowledge that wrapped apples, which contain less sugar, do not taste as good to most palates as unwrapped Japanese apples. But they look prettier, and they last longer in storage. Distributors and cooperatives smooth over this taste deficiency by staggering their shipment schedules so that wrapped and unwrapped apples spend as little time as possible in direct competition with each other. The consumers do not have a choice of wrapped and unwrapped apples at the same time.

Wrapping also underscores the inefficiencies of family farms. In the old days, when there was no foreign competition, it did not matter so much that Japanese apple farmers were inefficient. Retail prices of up to $7 for a fine apple covered a lot of inefficiency. In 1995 Japan allowed the import of about 14,000 tons of American apples, a fraction of the 1 million tons Japan produces each year. American apples have made only a tiny dent in the Japanese market, because the Japanese like their apples the way they have been sold to them for years: overpriced and perfectly colored. Farmers in Japan contend that American products simply cannot meet Japanese standards of quality, which depend on wrapping of apples. Indeed, the best apples are wrapped and unwrapped twice while they are still on the tree to achieve a delicate color.

An apple orchard at the base of the mountains along the Iwaki River in the Tsugaru Plain, Aomori Prefecture. This area produces approximately one-half of all the apples grown in Japan. Apples bring a higher return to the farmers in Aomori than rice. Each fruit is covered with paper to protect its surface and give it a perfect color. Photo by P.P. Karan.

Agriculture seemed to be the most popular part-time job for many. While the hourly wage in the general market was 600 yen ($5.65), greenhouse farmers in the area were paying up to 1,000 yen ($9.40) per hour. In the past, the agricultural sector provided a part-time labor force for secondary and tertiary industries, but now agriculture is winning out over other industries in the struggle to attract workers.

Declining Rice Farming and Increasing Diversity of the Rural Economy

Japan has been a rice-growing society for more than two thousand years, and rice is the major crop on Japan's cultivated land (see fig. 7.7). Rice planting and harvest rituals are crucial elements of the nation's culture, traditions, and the indigenous religion, Shinto. Rice is so symbolic of Japanese agriculture that one of the emperor's important annual duties on behalf of the nation remains the planting of seedlings in the imperial rice paddy.

Rice is grown widely in Japan, from Hokkaido to Okinawa. The wide range of latitudes and the high average temperature in summer, combined with the development of rice varieties adapted to low temperatures and the use of special techniques in the north, have made it possible to grow rice throughout Japan (see fig. 7.8). The distribution of major rice-growing areas has been influenced by three fac-

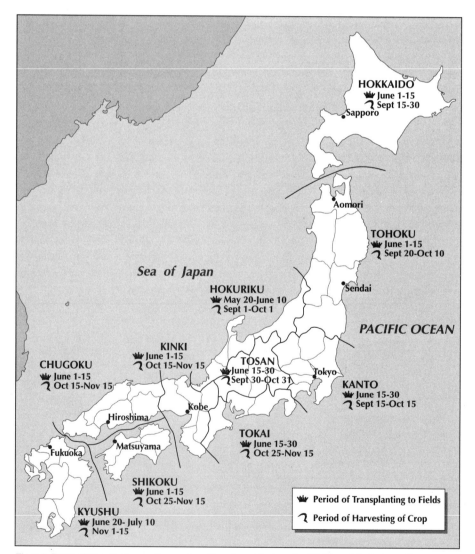

Fig. 7.8. Dates of rice planting and harvesting. Based on data from the Ministry of Agriculture, Forestry, and Fisheries, Tokyo.

tors: the size of the alluvial plains, the availability of water and irrigation systems (Tabayashi 1987; Latz 1989), and government policy. Principal rice-growing areas are located in Niigata, Kitakami Plain, Ishikari Plain, western Kanto, Nobi Plain, and Tsukushi Plain, and to a lesser extent in the inland basins. *Koshihikari* and *sasanishiki,* both grown in the northeast, are among the most popular types of Japanese rice and command high prices. In 2000 rice was grown on more than 4.2 million acres (1.7 million ha), and the production totaled 12.9 short tons (11.8 million metric tons) (see table 7.2).

In addition to environmental factors, such as cool temperatures experienced in some years in northern Japanese rice fields, damage by typhoons to rice fields in southern Japan, and local flooding resulting from heavy rainfall at the end of the summer rainy season, rice farming in Japan faces critical problems for several reasons: (1) rice farming is increasingly becoming a part-time occupation, (2) the rural population is getting older, (3) the scale of operation is small, (4) the gap between the price of rice in Japan and abroad is increasing, and (5) there is pressure on Japan to open its rice market. Under the World Trade Organization agreement, Japan provides market access to imported rice equal to 7–8 percent of base period (1986–88) consumption.

As the productive capacity of the paddy fields in Japan exceeds the demand for rice, the rice fields are being converted for cultivation of alternative crops. However, many rice fields do not have separate irrigation and drainage systems, and in some areas this is an important constraint to the use of rice fields for other purposes. In spite of substantial govern-

A full-time farmer in Kumamoto Prefecture, who grows rice, vegetables, and fruits. The number of full-time farmers has declined because farm holdings in Japan (except in Hokkaido) average less than 3.7 acres (1.5 ha). The small size of the farms, together with the rising costs of production, have contributed to the creation of an agricultural sector increasingly dominated by part-time farmers. Photo by P.P. Karan.

ment farm subsidies and price support, rice farming cannot compete with other economic activities, and income from farming is lower than nonagricultural earnings. Despite full mechanization of rice farming, production costs are higher because of exorbitant land prices and the high cost of farm labor.

Table 7.2. Rice in Japan

	1960	1985	1995	1999	2000
Production (million tons)	12.85	14.57	13.40	11.40	11.80
Area harvested (million hectares)	6.00	2.34	2.11	1.78	1.77
Yield (tons per hectare)	5.0	6.2	6.3	6.4	6.7
Rice imports (thousand tons)	–	19.6	28.9	664	–
Number of people producing rice (millions)	11.96	–	3.26	–	–

Source: Abstract of Statistics on Agriculture, Forestry, and Fisheries in Japan, Ministry of Agriculture, Forestry, and Fisheries, Government of Japan, Tokyo, 1985, 1997, 2000.

In the decades following World War II, Japan made remarkable progress in breeding rice for cold-tolerance and yield; in controlling diseases, pests, and weeds by chemicals; and in modernizing such tasks as tilling, transplanting, applying fertilizers and other chemicals, harvesting, and threshing/drying. Rice yields average 5.5 short tons per 2.5 acres (5 metric tons per ha), and the labor required has decreased to five hundred hours per 2.5 acres (1 ha). The increasing labor efficiency has allowed farmers to leave their villages to work in urban industries. Young people are generally not interested in rice cultivation, which is carried out mainly by older people.

Since the 1960s the area in Japan under rice farming has been declining. Less than 41 percent of the agricultural land is devoted to rice today. To be sure, there are still "rice bowls" like Niigata, Akita, and Miyagi Prefectures in northern Honshu, where this proportion rises above 70 percent, but they are the exception rather than the rule. On the southern island of Kyushu, only around one-third of flat agricultural land is devoted to rice. In Hokkaido, the northernmost island, that fraction falls to one-eighth. Rice is even less important when it comes to farming-family income. According to the Ministry of Agriculture, Forestry, and Fisheries, rice farming yields only one-tenth of the national total income for farming families—one-third of the figure for 1960. Government pensions provide twice as much income to farming families as does rice. With rice production declining, producer rice prices (ten times world levels) remaining static, imports beginning to enter Japan, and the national budget in a chronic deficit, there is every prospect for further decline in the already limited attractiveness and importance of rice to Japanese farmers.

According to the Ministry of Agriculture, Forestry, and Fisheries, farmers' total net income from rice production stood at 2.66 trillion yen in 1996, but two years later that figure had plummeted by nearly 20 percent, to 2.16 trillion yen. In Hokkaido, average family incomes for farmers involved in relatively large-scale cultivation—24.7–37.1 acres (10–15 ha)—amounted to 6.76 million yen in 1996 but fell to 5.82 million in 1998, marking a decrease of almost 1 million yen. For farmers who rely exclusively on rice farming for their livelihood, the outlook is grim.

Rice production across the nation has basically been strong ever since 1994, while the per capita rice consumption has been declining, thereby contributing to the glut and fueling price reductions. Per capita consumption for 1999 (132 lb or 59.9 kg milled rice) was only about 60 percent of 1965 levels, and the Food Agency reports that there is no end in sight for the trend of sagging consumption. A relaxation of the regulatory regime governing rice sales is another factor in the lowering of prices; this change has encouraged more supermarket chains and other large-scale retailers to enter the rice market themselves. In fact, they have become such influential market players that they now largely determine the grain's price. Reduced production cost, increased productivity through the application of advanced technology, and multipurpose use of rice fields in agriculture are important for sustaining rice cultivation in Japan.

Table 7.3. Comparison of rice productivity, 1987

	Japan	Thailand	United States
Average planted area per farm (ha)	0.8	5.3	114.0
Unpolished rice yield (t/ha)	5.3	1.5	4.9
Labor hours (hour/ha)	481	600	20
Labor productivity (kg/hour)	11.0	2.5	245.0
Wages ($/hour)	6.91	0.18	5.82
Labor cost per ton ($t)	627	72	24
Total cost per ton ($t)	2,158	132	199

Source: Based on data from Kome Sangyo no Kokusai Hikaku [International Comparison of Rice Industry], ed. Tadashi Kamegai and Tadao Hotta (Tokyo, 1990).

Field Report
Itadakimas, *Let's Eat*

Summer bridges two seasons. Warm days of summer linger, but thoughts turn to autumn harvests. Growing grains is an involved process, a real-time drama starring Man and Nature. Now with the rice crop near completion, the farmers and the markets wait with anticipation for the final act.

Rice has a rather long growing season. Small seedlings are planted in the wet of spring. In water-filled paddies, the muddy earth grabs hold of their roots as well as the feet of the farmer. By midsummer the fields are swaying seas of green. In early autumn, the heads of rice have fattened toward maturity. In the sparkle of morning dew, the ripening grains glimmer like precious gems. And what could be more precious than this grain for the Japanese.

The visits of the Japanese, no longer predominantly a rural people, to the countryside are now nostalgic journeys. Interest in the eye-pleasing terraced rice paddies is booming. Their beauty and ecologically balanced control of mountain and rainwater have found favor with artists and environmentalists. Country villages are offering workshops that actually get city folk into the paddy fields. Growing rice is hard work, whether done by hand or by machine. The strong work ethic needed to succeed has been transferred into Japan's modern cities, where the "power of rice" keeps the machinery humming.

Rice is the center of traditional Japanese meals. The ever-present bowl offers a neutral nucleus around which numerous side dishes congregate. Nowadays these side dishes can be anything from raw fish to beefsteak, fried tempura to vinegary vegetables, cold tofu to steaming Chinese dumplings. However, times were not always so good. After the war one was lucky to have some salted pickles to help get the plain rice down. Many families had to eat sweet potatoes in place of rice, which was then scarce or unaffordable.

A bowl of pure white rice is aesthetically pleasing. Nonetheless, most people prefer to mix it with whatever else is on the table. A favorite "bachelor" meal is sautéed tofu and vegetables served over rice in a big bowl. Rice covered with fish, meat, chicken, or eggs, a popular meal-in-a-bowl called *donburi*, is served everywhere in Japan.

Traditionally soybeans are grown around the edges of the rice paddies and have been called the "meat of the fields." Though most are left to dry for later use in making miso, some soybeans are harvested to eat green. Mixed with sushi-style newly harvested rice, this is an emerging dish to help one cross the seasonal bridge.

If Japanese farmers no longer farm so much rice, what do they do? They grow more and more vegetables, soybeans, tea, tobacco, and fruit, particularly mandarin oranges and even, since the mid-1980s, kiwifruit. Cattle-raising and poultry have also become more important since the mid-1960s, despite a rising tide of meat imports (Nagasaka 1991). Increasingly, Japanese farmers have been turning to nonfarming sources for supplementary income (Nagashima 1972). The average Japanese farmer is now nearly sixty-five years old, so pensions are naturally becoming more important. So is wage income from industry. In the early postwar years, seasonally migrant Japanese farmers (the so-called dekasegi) commuted between their homes and big cities like Tokyo and Osaka to work in factories and service jobs. This pattern is still important in the "snow country" of the Tohoku and Hokuriku regions (Okahashi 1996), which still sends almost fifty thousand dekasegi a year to Japan's major metropolitan areas. Since the early 1970s, however, industry has been coming to the farmers. This pattern was influenced by the strong regional policies of former prime minister (1972–74) and Liberal Democratic Party (LDP) strongman Kakuei Tanaka, himself a native of Hokuriku's Niigata Prefecture.

Gifu Prefecture—astride the Tokaido Shinkansen line in the countryside between Tokyo and Kyoto—now has 43 percent of its workforce in industry, compared to only 28 percent in Tokyo itself. Consumer

A tobacco field near Minamata, Kyushu. Tobacco has become an important cash crop for Japanese farmers. American-brand cigarettes such as Marlboro are popular in Japan. Japan's biggest tobacco maker, Japan Tobacco Inc., bought the overseas operations of RJR Nabisco. Photo by Cotton Mather.

electronics and precision machinery both are much more important than rice for Gifu's citizens. Indeed, less than 5 percent of Gifu's workforce is primarily on the land, although many residents have a small orchard or vegetable patch that provides extra pocket money.

This pattern is also pronounced in rural Kyushu, now known as Silicon Island. Kyushu currently produces half of Japan's integrated circuits—mostly in gleaming, state-of-the-art facilities miles away from any city. Toyota and Honda Motors also have their newest auto plants in rural Kyushu, employing workers who thirty years ago might have grown rice but do so no longer.

Construction and government service are also, together with old-age stipends and factory jobs, important parts of the emerging political economy of the Japanese countryside. Since the late 1960s, there

has been a huge expansion of public-works construction, especially high-speed railways, in the Japanese countryside. That has helped ease diversification away from the rice, especially for men. Local government white-collar work has also expanded, providing still more employment opportunities, particularly for women.

Japan is currently developing some of the most successful agribusiness in the world. Yamamoto Dendrobiums in Okayama Prefecture, for example, accounts for 70 percent of the world's market in dendrobium, any of numerous species of the orchid genus. Hazama Farm in Miyashiro, Miyagi Prefecture, is a world-class large-scale beef cattle operation with eighteen hundred head of breeding stock. Raising cattle is an extensive enterprise; breeding, in contrast, requires relatively little space. In the United States, many farmers raise a small number of feeder

Tea is an important product of Shizuoka Prefecture in the Tokai region of Japan. In the Makinohara upland area of Shizuoka, the temperate climate and well-drained soils create favorable physical conditions for producing high-quality tea. Photo by P.P. Karan.

Field Report

Make Mine Green

When the Japanese want to indicate that something is nothing out of the ordinary, they will say it is *nichijo sahanji*, as commonplace as tea and rice. Better than anything else, this saying reflects the intrinsic role played by *cha*, or green tea, in the life of this island nation. Japan's ubiquitous brew, green tea is served from Hokkaido to Okinawa, in sushi shops and school cafeterias, boardrooms and bullet trains. It now even comes canned, hot or cold, in the omnipresent vending machines. Indisputably the national drink, it is drunk after almost every meal, its soothing, slightly astringent taste the perfect complement to the flavors of Japanese cuisine.

It has not always been this way, however. In fact cha, or more politely *ocha*, became the drink of the average Japanese only as recently as the late Edo or early Meiji period—that is, in the latter half of the nineteenth century—when the introduction of machinery facilitated cultivation and processing and lowered prices.

No one knows exactly when tea arrived in Japan, but credit for its introduction is usually given to a Buddhist priest named Eisai, who, in 1191, brought back seeds from the Chinese mainland, where the plant was prized for its medicinal properties. These were planted in Uji, then a small village to the southeast of Kyoto, and tea and town flourished. Today Uji is a fair-sized city. Along with Shizuoka, it is one of Japan's two most famous tea-growing centers. Green tea is grown mainly in Japan and China. Once backbreaking tasks, tea picking and processing are now performed by a battery of machines, which can sort, stream, dry, chop, and even rub the leaves. In Japan, Shizuoka is the main production center for these ingenious devices, many of which are exported to China.

The quest for a perfect cup of ocha, however, still makes for some painstaking manual work. Long ago the Japanese discovered that shading the tea bushes slowed transpiration and produced a sweeter leaf. Although *senchu*, the most common type of green tea, is grown in direct sunlight, the higher grades of green tea, such as *gyokuro* and *tencha*, are all produced by means of shading the plants. In the past this was accomplished by constructing a reed roof over the bushes around the tenth of April. After ten days, the reed roofs were covered with straw. To intensify the shade even further, the sides were enclosed as well, blocking out 95 percent of the light. The bushes were then left like this for another ten days. Today, this same shading method, which is apparently unique to Japan, is still followed, but a double-decker arrangement of black nylon mesh has replaced the traditional reed and straw.

Bancha (low-grade tea), *hojicha* (roasted bancha), *genmaicha* (tea with brown rice added), *sencha, gyokuro, matcha* (very bitter powdered green tea) . . . today there is a type of tea to suit every taste and occasion. In spite of this variety, however, the drink's popularity shows signs of waning. Japan's older generation of office workers and bureaucrats still pace their day with cigarettes and cups of ocha, but younger Japanese seem to increasingly prefer their caffeine in coffee form. Perhaps the very availability of tea—its nichijo sahanji factor—has lessened its appeal.

calves on their own lots. The feeder calves are then sold and pooled together in huge feedlots. Hazama's breeding herd is on a scale unparalleled anywhere in the world. Hazama achieved this scale by applying swine reproduction technology to beef cattle. Ingenious use of technology and the scale of the operation have enabled Hazama's business to thrive even after the liberalization of the Japanese beef market.

The Japanese countryside of the 2000s thus presents a patchwork of employment and income patterns, the hallmark of which is diversity. Despite the regional crop and livestock specialization, the diversity is the countryside's most important safety net, and the source of intense politicization. Virtually nowhere does one find complete dependence on any one source of livelihood, least of all on rice.

Subsidies and the Future of Japanese Agriculture

What are the prospects for survival for Japanese farmers? Because of the system of price control, by which the government determines the price of rice each year, and because of various rice farming subsidies, farming families are well rewarded for their hard work. But there is more money going into Japanese agriculture than it generates, and this imbalance is worsening, with ever-increasing land prices, wages, and prices for capital goods on the one hand and stagnating prices for produce on the other.

Rice prices in Japan have been regulated by the national government for many years. Although free marketing of a certain portion of the rice crop has been allowed since 1969, farmers must sell most of their rice crop to the government through giant agricultural cooperatives (Zenchu) at a price set by the government. The rice is then distributed to authorized retailers, who sell it to consumers at a lower price, also established by the government. Thus, rice prices in Japan have been determined by political considerations, not by free market forces. Both prices are kept artificially high, and the result is that Japanese pay about eight times more than the world price for rice. The giant agricultural cooperatives—the government-sanctioned monopolies that profit from the huge subsidies of about $5 billion annually—prefer to maintain the status quo. Rice subsidy is a welfare program for the cooperatives. The subsidies and tax breaks for rice are more than most part-time farmers can resist. As a result, Japan is covered with tiny, inefficient rice farms (more than 80 percent are only a few acres) that have been producing far more than the country can consume.

In the 1980s rice, the import of which was prohibited, became a symbol of Japan's closed market. In 1993 Japan dropped its resistance to rice import by a small opening of its rice market; it imported 4 percent of its rice in 1995, increasing the percentage to 8 percent by 2001. The government's decision to begin an opening in the rice market is in effect a recognition that Japan's future depends more on its globally competitive automobile and electronic companies than on its uncompetitive farmers. Limited rice import in some sense also signifies the end of decades of Japanese history during which farmers have wielded power far out of proportion to their numbers. That power resulted in policies that favored farmers at the expense of urban consumers, most notably protection from foreign products that kept the price of rice far higher in Japan than elsewhere in the world. Farmers were favored because they were a pillar of support of the Liberal Democratic Party, which governed Japan for thirty-eight years until it was voted out of office in the summer of 1993 as corruption scandals spiraled around its leaders.

As Japan became urbanized in the past three decades, electoral districts did not change fast enough, leaving farmers overrepresented in the parliament (Diet). And the farmers often act with a single voice because of the role of powerful agricultural cooperatives, which have a wide influence over the business and political life of farming villages. The farmers are still a political force to be reckoned with. But there has been erosion of the farm bloc influence due to the shrinking of farm households from 6 million in 1960 to less than 3 million in 1992 as farmers abandon a business that is often unprofitable despite government subsidies. What is more, most farmers now till the soil only part-time and earn the majority of their income from jobs in factories and stores.

Wet, cool weather destroyed much of the 1993 rice crop in Japan. To cope with the bad harvest, retailers were required to package or blend domestic rice with imported varieties. This was a stunner in a country that has maintained a "not one grain" policy against imported rice. The problem is the traditional leeriness about imported products that bedevils many foreign companies trying to sell to the Japanese. This is compounded by the seriousness with which the Japanese take rice. People in Japan pride themselves on being able to distinguish among high-grade brands of rice the way wine connoisseurs distinguish among vintages. Nevertheless, California-grown rice proved highly popular during the first days of spring 1994 foreign rice sales, because it is short-grain like Japanese rice and closely resembles it in flavor and texture. But Chinese and Thai rice often remained unsold, after unfavorable publicity.

It is most likely that Japanese policymakers are going to stick to the current support system, allowing only marginal, step-by-step changes. For Japanese policymakers the key item on the agenda is to define a position for a rural economy in the process of postindustrialization. Theoretically, there is a future for Japanese agriculture in producing food of good quality for a reasonable price. Japanese farmers have skills, technology, and initiative. They lack a proper infrastructure (parcels of land grouped together) with a proper scale of management. Without this capital, technological progress does not work, for there are no benefits of scale—not even in the sense of relieving the workload. Some of the newly developed machinery is dedicated to such relief, but a rice harvester is not cost-effective for farmers with less than 49 acres (20 ha), for instance. A farming policy that is stuck in the mud of spiraling price support combined with fiscal privileges and investment subsidies does not give much optimism for the future.

Despite billions of dollars in subsidies and protective rice tariffs as high as 490 percent, through which a farmer can earn fifty thousand dollars a year from three acres, young rural dwellers are migrating to the cities, abandoning the farms. In Fukushima Prefecture, north of Kuriyama, one can see some of the region's 40,000 acres of recently abandoned farmland. Cattails grow in abandoned paddy fields, weeds grow in old tobacco patches on hillsides, and mulberry orchards have been left to grow wild as silkworm businesses have collapsed. Fukushima Prefecture once had Japan's largest tobacco crop and its second-largest production of silkworms. With government support for tobacco being phased out, the value of tobacco produced in the area has dropped 75 percent since 1975, the mulberry leaf production has been wiped out, and the production of rice has dropped by one-third. The only growth has been in truck farming; production of vegetables has doubled, largely for the urban market. Since 1980 the number of people in Miharu,

an agricultural community of 20,000 (north of Kriyama), making most of their money from farming has dropped 56 percent, to 1,635. In the 15- to 59-year age group, the drop has been more rapid: 83 percent, to 455. The only segment that has grown is that of farmers over 70, numbering 633 in 2003. Farming is in retreat.

Japan should develop an agricultural policy for the twenty-first century. Three major items should be included. First, remove old regulations that bind domestic agriculture, allow the market mechanism to work, and establish agricultural structures that correspond to the new age. Second, recognize the values inherent in agriculture itself and in rural communities, and provide the necessary protection. Third, maintain domestic production so that the self-sufficiency rate of food does not fall any further. Above all, the development and introduction of high value-added crops is the main challenge for the future.

URBAN AGRICULTURE IN JAPAN

The great cities of Japan are spreading rapidly over the agricultural land around them. The growing demand in the cities for fresh vegetables and the lower tax for land in farm use have supported the development of a distinctive type of extremely intensive agriculture within the general framework of paddy rice cultivation. Because of its close economic and geographic ties with cities, this type of agriculture is referred to as urban agriculture.

In southern Japan, where winters are mild, several succeeding crops of vegetables are often planted

Rural areas in Japan have been facing continued depopulation for the past five decades. An abandoned farm can be seen here near Hitoyoshi city, Kyushu. Photo by P.P. Karan.

Field Report

Japan's Unstable Staple

Although rice is bound up with Japan's most ancient mythology; although rice and sake, the wine fermented from it, are offered to Shinto gods; and although pounded rice cake, *mochi,* is a common offering in Buddhist temples, meat and dairy products have replaced rice as the mainstay of the Japanese diet.

In a 1993 study that reflects the continued Westernization of this traditional non-Western Asian society, Japan's Ministry of Agriculture, Forestry, and Fisheries reported that meat and dairy together replaced rice as the chief cash crops of Japanese farmers in 1991. The ministry predicts the dominance of meat and dairy and the decline of rice in the coming years. The report reflects a fundamental change in the Japanese diet. It is a transformation visible each day at noon in every Japanese city, as tens of millions of people turn away from the traditional lunch of rice balls wrapped in seaweed to form long lines in front of places like McDonald's and Kentucky Fried Chicken, which now rank as the number one and number two most popular restaurants in Japan.

The surge in meat and dairy products in 1991 figures came after the government liberalized meat imports. Farm interests have warned that permitting meat imports from the United States, Australia, and elsewhere would destroy the high-cost domestic meat industry. Instead, the government study showed, lower-priced imports increased overall demand and turned out to be a boon for Japan's meat producers.

One reason for rice's fall from its traditional number-one position is that farmers, foreseeing an eventual end to the import ban, are moving out of rice production into other cash crops. Not only meat and dairy but also fruits and vegetables, mushrooms, and other crops are on the increase, while rice production remains flat.

Per capita rice consumption has decreased dramatically in Japan since the early 1960s. In 1960, according to the Ministry of Agriculture, Forestry, and Fisheries, the people of Japan got 48 percent of their caloric intake from rice. Today, the figure is about 28 percent. Meats, dairy products, and vegetables, meanwhile, have all increased in share of average caloric intake. Far more than other non-Western nations, Japan has switched to Westernized menus.

Virtually every Japanese home has a *denki-gama,* or electric rice cooker, and most housewives still make a full pot of rice in it every morning. But more and more, the rice is a supplement to meals of meat and vegetables, bread and marga-

(continued on the following page)

Drying seaweed in a fishing village in southern Hokkaido. The Japanese use seaweed in their diet more than any other people. The cold water around Hokkaido is well known for the production of Kombu, a seaweed variety. Photo by P.P. Karan.

Field Report: *Japan's Unstable Staple* *(continued)*

rine that would look familiar on an American table. The traditional Japanese breakfast—rice with seaweed-pickled vegetables and soybean-paste soup—has been replaced almost everywhere by something called a "morning set": toast, cereal, scrambled eggs, and tossed salad (a breakfast item people in Japan think they learned from America). This is so common that some hotels now actually advertise that they offer a Japanese breakfast in addition to the expected Western version.

The sharp decline in rice consumption has sparked a countermovement, as rice interests adopt Western promotional ideas to sell their product. National agricultural groups have built big campaigns around a popular book by a food writer, Sonoko Suzuki, which bears the irresistible title *Get Slim by Eating Rice*. Rice sellers have also worked their product into the menus of the fast food chains. McDonald's has introduced seaweed-wrapped rice balls and curried rice in its Japanese stores, alongside its burgers. This way the Japanese continue to enjoy their sacred food, which ties them both to their land and to their gods, in a Western-style fast food chain restaurant.

The Japanese food-service business has been making concentrated efforts to get more rice on their menus. MOS Burger Food Services, the parent company of the fast food chain MosBurger, is a pioneer in this field. MOS was established in 1972 in an attempt to create a healthy, delicious hamburger that was more pleasing to the Japanese palate. In 1986 the company created the "rice burger," a burger made with buns of compressed rice instead of bread and topped with a chicken patty flavored with soy sauce. After twelve years of popularity, the rice burger had a boost to even greater favor in autumn 1998. The rice buns now include five grains (rice, wheat, and various types

of millet), and there are two variations—the *yakiniku* rice burger and the *gomoku kimpira* rice burger—both of which are soon to be joined by a shrimp rice burger.

The yakiniku rice burger is topped with thin slices of beef on a bed of lettuce, and the kimpira burger is filled with five kinds of vegetables, including carrots, burdock root, and bamboo shoots. The kimpira burger no longer contains bacon, thus making it a vegetarian dish—a kind of novelty among fast food restaurants.

While other hamburger franchises reduce prices, pass out coupons, and tempt younger customers with attractive prizes, MOS remains devoted to good and nutritious food. It uses mineral-rich vegetables grown by its own network of designated farmers, imports its beef from special farms in Australia, and gives top priority to freshness. In fact, every hamburger is made to order, so a meal at MOS can sometimes involve a long and patient wait while the cook grills the patty, heats the bun, and deep fries the potatoes. MOS now has 1,505 outlets all over Japan and continues to grow slowly but surely, which means that it must be doing something right.

Despite the decreased rice consumption, most Japanese still consider rice to be a necessary accompaniment to a proper meal. Not only MOS rice burgers, but hot rice bentos, packed sushi, precooked rice, and ready-to-east convenience-store rice balls are all hot items in the food-service business. In fact they may be helping Japanese get back to the rice-centered diet.

Some experts on Japan argue that this ancient society is highly resistant to change; others maintain that Japan is becoming more like Western industrialized countries all the time. Dietary habits of younger Japanese support the latter view.

---

instead of the usual winter grain crop, or a single vegetable crop may be squeezed in between the rice harvest and the late autumn sowing of winter grains. Some vegetables even compete with rice in summer. The land harvested approximates three times the area

of cultivated land, and production per unit area may be twice as high as in other districts where ordinary double cropping of paddy land predominates.

Urban agriculture is characterized by multiple cropping and year-round land use. Seldom is a field

Urban agriculture in Nagoya. Since the land is taxed based on its use, with a lower rate for agricultural use, many people continue to raise crops on small plots of land surrounded by urban development. The land is sold for development when the price of land rises beyond the level expected by the owner. Since such land is held out of the urban land market for a long time, it reduces the supply of land for sale and increases the land price. High land prices in Japan are attributed to the tax laws that favor agricultural use. Photo by P.P. Karan.

idle for longer than a week or two at a time, for the harvest of one crop is followed almost immediately by the planting of another. Each farmer devotes most of the land to rice in summer and then plants part of it to wheat or barley, which provides one winter crop, and part to vegetables, resulting in several winter crops. The patterns of land use are a reflection of the farmers' desire to plant these various crops, rather than of variations in soil, the supply of irrigation water, drainage, or other physical conditions.

The rather widespread summer planting of high-value vegetables such as tomatoes and eggplant on

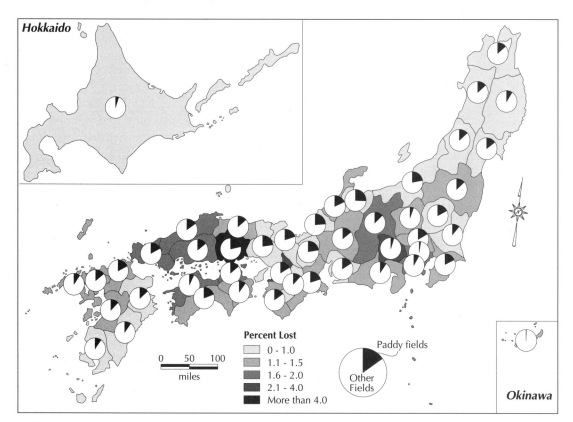

Fig. 7.9. Loss of cultivated land by prefectures, 2000. Based on data from the Ministry of Agriculture, Forestry, and Fisheries, Tokyo.

Field Report

An Urban Farm in Tokyo

The Okada family lives in Kitano, Mitaka city, about 40 to 50 minutes by train and bus from the center of Tokyo. There are still around sixty families running farms in the area, but most of them earn their living by other means. On a 140,000-square-foot (13,000-sq-m) field across the road from their home, the Okadas grow about thirty different kinds of vegetables throughout the year: lettuce in the spring; cucumbers, tomatoes, eggplant, corn, green soybeans, and kidney beans in the summer; and daikon (giant white radish), turnips, cauliflower, broccoli, and spinach during the autumn and winter. Their crops enjoy an excellent reputation and have won a number of awards.

The Okadas seldom use artificial fertilizers, relying instead on compost made from dead leaves, a traditional method of fertilization that ensures the flavor and safety of their crops. Ichio Okada's 79-year-old mother, Toshi, still helps out in the field, but his wife, 46-year-old Masae, works as his number-one partner. Their eldest son, 24-year-old Yuichi, graduated from an agricultural college two years ago and immediately started working alongside his parents. He will eventually take over the farm from his parents.

The other Okada children are 22-year-old Masao, who is studying economics at a university, and 20-year-old Toshikazu, who studies medical administration at a vocational training school. They help on the farm when an extra hand is needed or whenever they have some free time, but most of the work is done by Ichio, Masae, Yuichi, and Toshi.

A farmer's day starts early. In the summer, the Okadas rise at four or five o'clock in the morning and do their chores before breakfast. They harvest crops until lunch, take a break until around three in the afternoon, and then work until eight at night getting the harvested crops ready for shipment. The workload is lighter in the winter: they generally work from eight or nine in the morning until sunset, caring for their winter crop and making compost. They take no regular holidays.

"My ancestors began cultivating this field during the Edo era," explains Ichio. "When I took over, my mother said to me: 'We are not giving you this farm—we are entrusting it to you. It has been passed down from generation to generation, and you will pass it on to your children, so take care of it!'"

The Okadas love their work. In fact, the husband and wife take only one trip away from the farm each year; they drive to Niigata, where Masae's family grows rice—and bring back a load of straw for their compost heap! "My wife and I are always at home or in the field," says Ichio, "so there is no need to set aside special time on weekends to talk with the kids or go somewhere together. We are together most of the time."

And yet the Okada family will have to face a crisis in the not-too-distant future. "The biggest problem with farming in the city is inheritance. Land prices are much, much higher than they used to be, so we can't pay the inheritance tax on the money we earn from the farm," says Ichio. "When my father died in 1994, we had to offer part of the farm as the inheritance tax. We still have not calculated exactly how much we have to offer. If the ownership of the farm is passed on several times in this way, it will be impossible to continue growing crops under the same conditions as before—and that's going to be sad," he explains.

This fertile patch of ground has been passed on from generation to generation since the Edo era. The question now is, How many more generations of Okadas will be entrusted with it?

land that otherwise would be in rice illustrates departure from the usual Japanese summer cropping scheme. But winter crop patterns, with the emphasis on multiple cropping of vegetables, most clearly characterize urban agriculture in southern Japan. Such multiple cropping exemplifies an intensiveness of agricultural land use seldom equaled even in other Asian cultures.

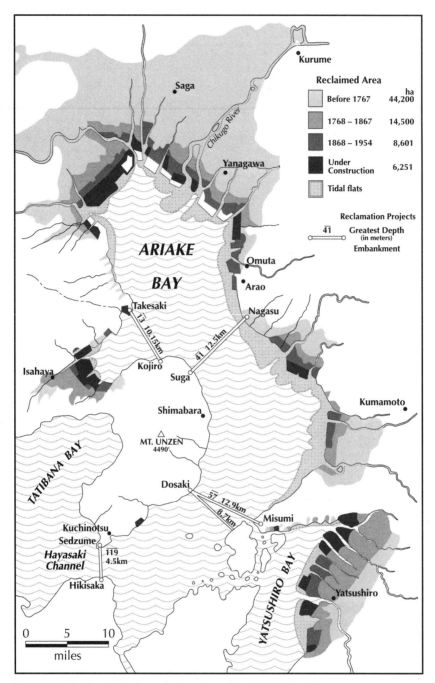

Fig. 7.10. Ariake Bay land reclamation. Based on a map by Reiji Okazaki.

Urban agriculture seems to be one answer to city growth in Japan. The higher production per unit of area associated with it helps offset the loss of farm land (see fig. 7.9) accompanying the spread of the cities over agricultural land in the Japanese megalopolis.

LAND RECLAMATION FOR AGRICULTURE

Reclamation of land for intensive agricultural use has reached its peak in Japan. Since the end of the sixteenth century, considerable parts of bay heads along shallow embayments have been reclaimed for use as paddy fields. Filled lands along Kojima Bay, Osaka

Fig. 7.11. Nakaumi reclamation project, Shimane Prefecture. Based on a map by the Shimane Prefectural Government.

Bay, and Ise Bay have been remarkably expanded by general application of highly developed technologies. Land reclamation in Ariake Bay in Kyushu (fig. 7.10) epitomizes and illustrates this aspect of Japanese farming.

In recent years arguments have been made to cancel several of the state-run reclamation projects for agricultural use. The project to reclaim part of Nakaumi Lagoon in Shimane Prefecture is one of these (fig. 7.11). The plan to reclaim Nakaumi Lagoon to create agricultural land was launched in 1963. The initial plan was to reclaim a total of 6,279 acres (2,541 ha) at five sites. Major construction work, including a floodgate to convert lagoon water into freshwater, was finished by 1981. Although reclamation at four of the five sites has been completed, work at the Honjo site—the largest of the five, at 4,174 acres (1,689 ha)—has been postponed because of strong local opposition.

The Shimane prefectural government gained the agreement of three concerned localities and asked the Ministry of Agriculture, Forestry, and Fisheries in March 1996 to reclaim all of the remaining site for farming. The ministry's expert panel presented three alternatives in 2000: full reclamation, partial reclamation, and cancellation of the project. The Shimane governor proposed a fourth option to freeze the project.

Although conventional wisdom holds that public-works projects, once started, are like unstoppable juggernauts, the government—cowering under accusations of pork-barrel spending—began reviewing major projects in 2000. Furthermore, the public need has shifted from construction projects to welfare and information-related projects. The review of public-works projects by the Liberal Democratic Party government was partly a response to opposition criticism in the lower house election of June 2000 that the LDP was trying to entice the public with the economic benefits of such projects. This criticism led to the party's suffering major setbacks in urban constituencies. The 2000 election results may have accelerated the move to cancel the Nakaumi project, which is seen as a symbol of large-scale public-works projects.

According to a Management and Coordination Agency survey, 109 of a total of 8,207 projects planned by the Ministry of Agriculture, Forestry, and Fisheries, the former Ministry of Construction, and the Ministry of Transport (now the Ministry of Land, Infrastructure, and Transport), plus three other government agencies, were cancelled or suspended in 1998. Among the state-run reclamation projects, the government decided in 1997 to cancel projects in Yokaku Bay in Kumamoto Prefecture and in the Ariake Sea in Saga Prefecture, despite having invested more than 20 billion yen in the two projects. The reclamation project in Nagasaki Prefecture's Isahaya Bay, which the government aimed to complete in 2006, started in 2002.

Maintaining the Vitality of Rural Communities

The importance of maintaining the vitality of rural communities is frequently noted in the discussion of Japan's future economy and society. In 1986, for example, the Agricultural Policy Council made specific mention of the need to ensure income opportunities for and the vitality of rural communities when considering future agricultural policies. In view of the small contribution made by agriculture and other primary industries to the economy of most prefectures, agricultural policies may not be the appropriate means of maintaining the vitality of rural communities. Regional development policies involving projects to develop rural infrastructure rather than agricultural industries may contribute to maintaining the vitality of rural communities by creating nonfarm job opportunities and providing the opportunity for people to continue living in their rural communities. A guarantee of stable employment in the nonagricultural sector in rural areas would be the key to maintaining the vitality of rural communities. Many rural prefectures are attempting to foster development by providing subsidy and land development assistance to manufacturing and service firms willing to locate in their regions.

Some young Japanese are quitting their jobs in the big cities to take up farming in the countryside (Hagiwara 2000). This move may be nothing out of the ordinary for young Japanese today, now that the lifetime employment and seniority systems that once contributed to securing employee loyalty have begun to fade away. Another influence is young people's lack of interest in working for a firm that represents the typical Japanese corporate economy and culture. A trend of moving to the country has been observed in certain agricultural areas, such as Hokkaido, Nagano, and Gumma Prefectures, where workers in their twenties are giving up their big-city jobs and turning to the soil. This trend has major implications for reviving the vitality of rural areas of Japan. Most people who relocate to rural areas are joining producers' corporations to become farmers with the hope of obtaining a more secure livelihood.

The producers' corporations were first established as a means of bringing in large-scale management to make production more efficient. But they also serve to revive rural areas. The corporations began to attract people to farms by introducing them to the rural work environment, while making farms more efficient through better management. As of January 1999 there were 5,587 such corporations, which have the support of the Ministry of Agriculture, Forestry, and Fisheries. Young would-be farmers find the salaries and social insurance benefits that the corporations provide their employees, just as any other private corporation would do, especially attractive. The system also guarantees young workers a secure transition to an agricultural career; not only are they salaried farmers, but they also have the opportunity to start their own farms after a few years of training. An increasing number of such corporations have been established in recent years (about 300 to 400 are formed each year) to entice new blood into rural areas (Saito 2000).

Asahi Ainou Agricultural Producers' Cooperative in Asahi, Chiba Prefecture, is one such corporation, co-owned by about fifty farms in the prefecture. The corporation manages their production cycle by purchasing feed for livestock and selling their product. Over the past five years, the cooperative has taken on about ten young people with no farming background.

Zenkoku Shinki Shunou Gaido Center, a nationwide organization that offers assistance to people wanting to return to rural areas and enter farming, holds workshops in various locations, including Tokyo and Osaka. Most of the workshop participants seek positions in agricultural producers' corporations. A decision to join a corporation is a more practical choice than other farm jobs for people in their twenties and thirties because it offers them opportunities to do tasks other than farming, such as product development and marketing through the Internet. However, there are also many young workers who have left agricultural corporations because they cannot adjust to the heavy workload and the few days off. To find replacements for these people, weeklong farming workshops are organized in agricultural training schools in locations such as Nagano, Ibaraki, and Hokkaido, as well as in prefectural agricultural universities across Japan.

References

Davis, Darrell Haug. 1934. Types of occupance patterns in Hokkaido. *Annals of the Association of American Geographers* 24 (4): 201–223.

Dore, Ronald P. 1966. *Land Reform in Japan*. London: Oxford Univ. Press.

———. 1984. *Land Reform in Japan.* 2nd ed. London: Athlore Press.

Fukuda, Toshio. 1986. *Kinsei shinden to sono genryu* [Shinden in the Edo Era and Their Origin]. Tokyo: Kokan Shoin.

George, A. 1991. The politics of interest representation in the Japanese Diet: The case of agriculture. *Pacific Affairs* 64: 506–528.

Hagiwara, Shogo. 2000. Farming: New trend for young urbanites. *Daily Yomiuri* (Tokyo), August 8.

Hall, Robert H. 1931. Some rural settlement forms in Japan. *Geographical Review* 21 (1): 93–123.

———. 1932. The Yamato Basin, Japan. *Annals of the Association of American Geographers* 22 (4): 243–292.

Himiyama, Yukio, and Jitsu Kiyotaka. 1988. Recent achievements in land use studies in Japan. *Geographical Review of Japan* B 61:99–110.

Isoda, Yuzuru, Doo-Chul Kim, and Keigo Matsuoka. 1998. The geography of changes in agricultural land use in the Sendai Metropolitan Area, Japan; An examination of the topographic characteristics using the Geographic Information System. *Science Reports of Tohoku University*, ser. 7 (Geography) 48 (1–2): 35–64.

Jones, R.S. 1989. Political economy of Japan's agricultural policies. *World Economy* 12:29–38.

Kikuchi, Toshio. 1986. *Zuku shinden Kkaihatsu-Jjirei Hhen* [The Development of Shinden, Case Studies]. Tokyo: Kokon Shoin.

Kinda, Akihiro. 1986. The Jori Plan in Ancient and Medieval Japan. *Geographical Review of Japan* B 59:1–20.

Latz, Gil. 1989. Agricultural development in Japan: The land improvement district in concept and practice. Univ. of Chicago Geography Research Paper, no. 225.

McDonald, Mary. 1997. Agricultural landholding in Japan: Fifty years after the land reform. *Geoforum* 28 (1): 55–78.

Miura, T. 1985. On the chronological characteristics of the development of shinden in the feudal Akita Province. In *Chiiki no tankyu* [Researches of Regions]. Department of Geography, Rissho Univ., Tokyo.

Moore, R.H. 1990. *Japanese Agriculture: Patterns of Rural Development.* Boulder, CO: Westview.

Mulgan, Aurelia George. 2000. *The Politics of Agriculture in Japan.* London: Routledge.

Nagasaka, Masanobu. 1991. Formation of production areas in the Japanese broiler chicken industry. *Geographical Review of Japan* B 64:50–68.

Nagashima, H. 1972. Non-agricultural land use by farmers in Soka city. *Human Geography* 24:38–58.

Okahashi, Hidenori. 1996. Development of mountain village studies in postwar Japan: Depopulation, peripheralization, and village renaissance. *Geographical Review of Japan* B 69:60–69.

Oshiro, Kenji. 1982. Mechanization of paddy cultivation in Japan and its effects on farm households. *Science Reports of Tohoku University*, ser. 7 (Geography) 32 (1):1–13.

Saito, Taisei. 2000. Young attracted to natural lifestyle of farms. *Asahi Evening News,* October 30.

Sasaki, Hiroshi. 1984. Transformation of the echigo type settlement pattern in Japan. *Annual Report, Institute of Geoscience,* Univ. of Tsukuba, 10:21–24.

Semple, Ellen Churchill. 1912. Influence of geographic conditions upon Japanese agriculture. *Geographical Journal* 60 (6): 590–607.

Stradford, Todd. 1994. Changes in the agricultural landscape of Kochi Prefecture, Japan, 1987 to 1990. Ph.D. diss., Univ. of Oklahoma, Norman.

Sum, Kong-sut. 1979. Peasant movement and land reform in Japan. *Science Reports of Tohoku University*, ser. 7 (Geography) 29 (1): 41–45.

Tabayashi, Akira. 1987. Irrigation systems in Japan. *Geographical Review of Japan* B 60:41–65.

Tanaka, K. 1982. Changes in the land ownership and land use of former farms in Nakano-ku and Musashino-shi, Tokyo. *Geographical Review of Japan* 55:453–471.

Yamamoto, Shozo. 2000. Recent changes in Japanese agriculture and rural areas: One view of research. *Geographical Review of Japan* A 73:147–160.

Yamamoto, Shozo, Yoichi Asano, and George H. Kakiuchi. 1969. Areal functional organization in agriculture: An example from Japan. *Science Reports of Tokyo Kyoiku Daigaku* [Tokyo Univ. of Education], sec. C (Geography, Geology, and Mineralogy), 10 (97–98): 165–209.

Yamamoto, Shozo, and Akira Tabayashi. 1989. The structure of rural space in Japan—the impact of urbanization and off-farm employment on the transformation of Japan's rural landscape and economy. *Science Reports of the Institute of Geosciences,* Univ. of Tsukuba, sec. A, 10:1–22.

Chapter 8

第 八 章

Urban Settlements

Because Japanese cities have grown at different times (over several centuries), in different geographic regions, and in varied economic settings, they reflect diverse characteristics. Specific features of site and topography influence the form of the city. However, despite intraregional and interregional variations, recurrent national patterns of urbanization are, in their particular characteristics, a reflection of the social values and economic life of the country (Scholler 1984). During the past twenty-five years, as a result of the increasing trend toward globalization of the world economy and the important role that Japan plays in it, contemporary large Japanese cities and urban areas have emerged as places where the many separate and superimposed social, technological, institutional, and economic networks that link them with each other intersect with wider interconnected groups of global networks. In the future, the complex interactions of global networks will increasingly influence the shape of urban life and urban development in Japanese cities (Fujita and Hill 1993).

Japan is one of the most highly urbanized countries in the world. The high level of urbanization has occurred mostly in the past fifty years and is expected to continue, although at a reduced rate (see table 8.1). However, the large city is not something new for Japan. There is a long tradition of urban life. During

Table 8.1. Urban population in Japan, 1920–2000

Year	National population (in millions)	Urban population (in millions) (%)	DID population (in millions) (%)	Percent of land area in DID
1920	55.9	10.1 (18)		
1930	64.4	15.4 (24)		
1940	71.9	27.6 (38)		
1950	83.2	31.4 (37)		
1960	93.4	58.6 (63)	40.8 (43.7)	1.03
1970	103.7	74.2 (72)	55.5 (53.5)	1.71
1980	117.1	88.9 (76)	69.9 (59.7)	2.65
1990	123.6	94.4 (77)	78.1 (63.2)	3.11
1995	125.5	98.0 (78)	81.2 (64.7)	3.24
2000	126.9	99.8 (79)	82.8 (65.2)	3.30

Source: Japan Statistical Yearbook 2004 (Tokyo: Statistical Survey Department, Statistics Bureau, Ministry of Public Management, Home Affairs, Posts, and Telecommunications, 2004).
Note: In 1960 Japan established Densely Inhabited Districts (DIDs) in the population census. Because of the expansion of city area by absorption of neighboring *machi* (towns) and *mura* (villages) and amalgamation into new *shi* (cities), the old definition of urban and rural areas had become unsatisfactory. A DID is defined as a group of contiguous census-enumeration districts with a high population density (4,000 inhabitants or more per square kilometer) within the boundary of a shi, a *ku* (ward), a *machi*, or a mura constituting an agglomeration of 5,000 inhabitants or more. DIDs are actually built-up urban areas that should rightfully be called urban.

the eighteenth century Tokyo, with an estimated 1 million inhabitants, was the largest city in the world, and in 1700 Osaka was probably third in the world urban hierarchy after Tokyo and London. Again today, with approximately 39 million people, the Tokyo Metropolitan Area, as opposed to the city of Tokyo, is the largest in the world (Masai 1990).

Early Historic Cities: Nara, Heiankyo (Kyoto), and Kamakura

The development of cities in Japan can be traced back to the Nara (710–94) and Heian (794–1185) periods, when the first permanent capitals of Heijokyo (now Nara) and Heiankyo (now Kyoto) were established. Both of these old cities of Japan illustrate the detailed town planning in early Japan. Nara was built on a river plain crossed by the Sahogawa and the Akishinogawa. Empress Gemmei moved her court there in 710. The city was laid out on a grid pattern of square blocks modeled on the pattern of Chang'an, the capital city of China during the Chinese Tang dynasty (618–907). Major streets intersected so as to form 72 large blocks—8 rows of blocks running north to south and 9 rows running east to west. Each large block was subdivided into 16 smaller blocks. Later 12 additional large blocks were added on the northeast side of the city and 3 partial blocks on the northwest. After the capital was moved from Nara in 784 by Emperor Kammu, the city continued as an important center and attracted pilgrims to its many Buddhist temples.

Heiankyo (literally "capital of peace and tran-quility") was the original name of Kyoto, the capital of Japan from 794 to 1868. Heiankyo was located between the rivers Kamogawa and Katsuragawa. This city was also patterned after Chang'an, the capital of Tang China. The course of the Kamogawa was shifted to flow around the city, and canals were dug parallel to the major north-south avenues. The new capital city measured about 2.8 miles (4.5 km) east to west and 3.2 miles (5.2 km) north to south. With the exception of the state-sponsored Toji and Saiji, constructed near the gate Rajomon, no temples were allowed within Heiankyo. Among other reasons, the capital was moved to Heiankyo to eliminate the excessive political power of the Nara Buddhist priests. The residence of the emperor and imperial government offices were located in an area called the *daidairi* (outer palace grounds) in the northernmost part of the city. Also located there was the hall called the *daigokuden,* from which, initially, the emperor governed the country. The palace of the emperor stood at the right center of the daidairi within the *dairi* (inner palace grounds). Directly south of the daidairi was a large park, Shinsen'en.

Heiankyo was divided by the broad avenue Suzaku Oji (276 ft or 84 m wide) into two districts, Sakyo to the east and Ukyo to the west. In each of these districts was an office called the Kyoshiki. Together the officials in the two Kyoshiki administered the affairs of the capital city. Each main district was subdivided into large square sectors called *bo* by streets running east to west and avenues running

Todaiji Temple in Nara, the capital of Japan from 710 to 794. Nara was built in 710 and was patterned after the Tang dynasty capital of Chang'an (modern Xi'an). The original city had a population of 200,000. Todaiji (the Great Eastern Temple) is the headquarters of the Kegon Buddhist sect. It is world famous for its Great Buddha, one of the largest bronze images in the world. Photo by P.P. Karan.

A view of the busy commercial and transportation district of Umeda, Osaka. Once a small village, Umeda became the gateway to Osaka after Osaka Station was opened in 1874. Today Umeda is one of Osaka's three busiest districts, the others being Namba and Tennoji to the south. A large transportation terminal, Umeda has many high-rise buildings, department stores, underground shopping centers, and entertainment facilities. Osaka is the third-largest city in Japan after Tokyo and Yokohama. It is the financial center of western Japan. Photo by P.P. Karan.

north to south. The Shijo Oji area was the center of industry and commerce in the city. The Ukyo quarter was a damp lowland, and the city developed toward the east, straddling the Kamogawa, with its population center near the west bank of the river. During the Onin War (1467–77) more than half of the city was destroyed, but it was rebuilt in the sixteenth century. The palace was moved to the present site in the north central section of modern Kyoto in the eighteenth century, but the present buildings, now known as the Kyoto Imperial Palace, date from the nineteenth century.

During the Nara and Heian periods, Japan fully emulated the elements of Chinese city planning and succeeded in creating a reasonable approximation of the city after a Chinese model, complete with detailed administrative areas and an impressive capital that demonstrated the transcendent magnificence of the emperor. Although the Chinese influences never died out completely, the Japanese created indigenous urban architecture, style, and institutions later on that bore only a slight resemblance to the Chinese prototypes.

At the start of the Heian period, Kyoto had a population of at least 100,000. Soon other cities were built, primarily for political and military purposes, although some, such as Naniwa (now Osaka), also were developed to serve the needs of travelers. In the seventh and eighth centuries Osaka, now the third-largest city in Japan after Tokyo and Yokohama, was a port for trade with China and the site of several imperial residences. In 1583 Toyotomi Hideyoshi, the

national unifier, built Osaka Castle. In the Edo period (1603–1868) Osaka served as the entrepôt for goods, especially rice, for the entire nation and was called Japan's kitchen.

By the thirteenth century, Kamakura, seat of the Kamakura shogunate (1192–1333), had a population of more than 10,000. Kamakura, overlooking Sagami Bay, was a small seaside village when it was selected as the seat of the shogunate. The feudal bureaucracy that was created by the shogun to oversee the vassals made Kamakura the center of political power in the nation. As a capital city it offered two major advantages: it was far removed from the intrigues and refined influences of the imperial court in Kyoto, and it was a natural stronghold. Bordered by Sagami Bay to the south, Kamakura was protected on the other three sides by an unbroken crescent of hills. Easily defensible passes were cut through these hills at strategic points to enable overland travel to and from the town without jeopardizing its security. The leaders of the Kamakura shogunate began to patronize Buddhist temples. The vigorous urban culture of Kamakura—which stood in clear contrast to the cultivated delicacy of the aristocratic city culture evolved by the courtiers of Kyoto—sprang up in large measure from the affinity that developed between the warrior leaders and the Zen monks.

After the fall of the Kamakura shoguns early in the fourteenth century, a new shogunal government was established by the Ashikaga family in Kyoto, but Kamakura remained the center of administration of

The seated bronze image of the Buddha Amitabha in Kamakura dates from the mid-thirteenth century. This 37.4-foot-high (11.4-meter-high) Buddha has been in the open since the temple building that housed it was destroyed in 1495. Kamakura city, 28 miles (45.1 km) southwest of Tokyo, became the seat of the Kamakura shogunate, the first military government in Japan, in the twelfth century. Kamakura remained the political center of the country until the fall of the shogunate in 1333. Photo by P.P. Karan.

the Kanto region until the civil wars that preceded the rise of the Tokugawa family in the sixteenth century.

ORIGINS AND DEVELOPMENT OF CITIES IN FEUDAL JAPAN

As the central authority of the military government declined in the fifteenth and sixteenth centuries, towns increasingly evolved around castles built by regional warlords (daimyo) to defend their petty fiefdoms. The castles of the local fiefs, surrounded by the living quarters of a large group of professional warriors, the samurai, became propitious centers for the development of cities (see fig. 8.1). These towns offered the advantages of a strategic market, a degree of protection in a period of internecine warfare, and opportunities for amusement and entertainment. Thus most of the first large cities and towns of Japan had their origins as strategic political-economic centers of small feudal semi-independent territories. Artisans and traders flocked to these castle towns, and in several instances a town became so specialized because of some feature of trade or manufacture that it acquired national fame. So firmly established did these specializations become that even now certain Japanese cities have maintained

their reputation for specific trades. During the Edo period (1603–1868) the castle towns continued to grow in size and stability. The castle town of Edo (now Tokyo) had a population of more than 1 million by the mid-eighteenth century.

The castle town (joka machi), which formed the administrative center of a daimyo domain, became the characteristic form of the Japanese city from the mid-sixteenth century until the Meiji Restoration of 1868. The antecedents of joka machi can be traced to the turbulent fourteenth and fifteenth centuries, when local magnates built wooden fortresses, often situated on bluffs and protected by walls or moats, to secure control over the surrounding territories. Full-fledged urban communities emerged in the sixteenth century with the enforced resettlement of the samurai around their lord's castle and the joining of market and castle in a single location.

Initially, castle towns were small, consisting of the castle complex and surrounding dwellings. The growing authority of the daimyo was increasingly mirrored in their imposing city plans. The relatively few daimyo who survived the internecine warfare of the sixteenth century converted their cities from defensive outposts to administrative and commercial headquarters for mobilizing the area's resources. Af-

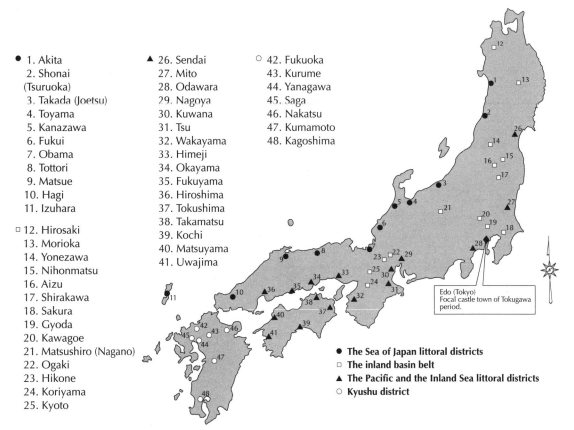

● 1. Akita	▲ 26. Sendai	○ 42. Fukuoka
2. Shonai (Tsuruoka)	27. Mito	43. Kurume
3. Takada (Joetsu)	28. Odawara	44. Yanagawa
4. Toyama	29. Nagoya	45. Saga
5. Kanazawa	30. Kuwana	46. Nakatsu
6. Fukui	31. Tsu	47. Kumamoto
7. Obama	32. Wakayama	48. Kagoshima
8. Tottori	33. Himeji	
9. Matsue	34. Okayama	
10. Hagi	35. Fukuyama	
11. Izuhara	36. Hiroshima	
	37. Tokushima	
□ 12. Hirosaki	38. Takamatsu	
13. Morioka	39. Kochi	
14. Yonezawa	40. Matsuyama	
15. Nihonmatsu	41. Uwajima	
16. Aizu		
17. Shirakawa		
18. Sakura		
19. Gyoda		
20. Kawagoe		
21. Matsushiro (Nagano)		
22. Ogaki		
23. Hikone		
24. Koriyama		
25. Kyoto		

Edo (Tokyo)
Focal castle town of Tokugawa period.

● The Sea of Japan littoral districts
□ The inland basin belt
▲ The Pacific and the Inland Sea littoral districts
○ Kyushu district

Fig. 8.1. Tokugawa period castle towns (with fiefs exceeding 100,000 *koku* of rice). Based on Fujioka 1980.

The moat surrounding the Imperial Palace, formerly Edo Castle, in Tokyo. After nearly a century of warfare, Toyotomi Hideyoshi partially united the country and dispatched Tokugawa Ieyasu to Kanto in 1590 as lord of Edo Castle. After Hideyoshi's death, Ieyasu completed the unification of Japan and established the Tokugawa shogunate in Edo in 1603. He built a castle town at Edo with a samurai residential district on the castle's western side. To the east marshland was reclaimed, and a commercial and industrial area taking advantage of river and canal transportation came into being. As the city flourished, merchants and artisans flocked to Edo, and the population reached 1 million by 1720, making Edo the largest city in the world at that time. The Nihombashi, the bridge first built in 1603, was the starting point for Tokaido and other highways leading out of the capital. The bridge served as the symbolic center of Japan during the Edo period (1603–1868). Photo by P.P. Karan.

ter the advent of the Tokugawa rule in 1600, separate branch-castle settlements were abolished by the rule "one domain, one castle." The number of joka machi then stabilized at between 200 and 250. The preoccupation of the Japanese society of that time with social distinctions was reflected in the segregation of elite residences, the correspondence of the lot's size and proximity to the castle with the samurai resident's rank, and the designation of urban commoners' wards. The common people of the towns —those who were not nobles, samurai, or priests— were called *chonin*. Although some of the chonin were wealthy merchants, the vast majority were poor artisans, peddlers, and day laborers. The function of the chonin was to serve the needs of the administration and of the samurai who staffed it. They were always subordinate to the samurai authorities. Guilds, groups, and other associations of townsmen existed for control purposes rather than for self-government. The highly structured residential and social patterns of the castle town began to disappear abruptly after the abolition of the feudal domains in 1871.

The castle towns of Japan monopolized local and regional military and administrative functions and prevailed in commerce and crafts as well (Hall 1934; Trewartha 1934). Almost all of the large concentrations of population were in joka machi, which generally contained about one-tenth of a domain's population, including all or most of the samurai. By the early eighteenth century, most castle towns had reached their peak populations.

Other types of city origins in feudal Japan are post-station towns (shukuba machi), religious towns (*monzen machi*), port towns (*minato machi*), and market centers (*ichiba machi*). Post-station towns developed along the five radial roads (*gokaido*), which extended from the shogunate capital of Edo. These towns catered to the needs of travelers along the major roadways. The daimyo and their retainers stopped at special inns in the shukuba machi as they traveled back and forth fulfilling their obligation of alternate-year residence (*sankin kotai*) in Edo. Alternate-year residence in Edo was a device developed by the shogun to maintain control over the more than 260 daimyo who were autonomous feudal rulers of four-fifths of Japan. The daimyo had to maintain residential estates in Edo, where their wives and children were permanently detained by the shogunate. Shukuba machi facilitated the national integration of Japan through an efficient regulation of movement across the country. The influx of people from neighboring villages to post towns resulted in an increase of the population of those centers, leaving wide hinterlands such as Kanagawa and Hodogaya with relatively sparse populations. In post towns the majority of the population were merchants and workers in inns and hotels. Ordinary trades dealing with cloth and foodstuffs, for example, also increased, as well as handicrafts.

Monzen machi, or religious towns, developed near popular temples or shrines. Establishments catering to the pilgrims sprang up along the roads leading to the shrine or temple. Inns and related facilities emerged near these centers, such as Ise, Zenkoji (at Nagano), Kambara, Suwa Shrines, and Mishima. Nara is one of the major monzen machi of Japan,

Fukuoka in 1949. The city developed as a port town in the seventh century when Hakata port (now Hakata Ward) became important for travel and trade with China. It reached its prosperity during the fifteenth and sixteenth centuries as a result of trade with Ming dynasty China (1368–1644). In 1601 a castle was constructed in the western part of Hakata, and the area surrounding the castle was named Fukuoka. In 1889 Hakata and the castle town of Fukuoka merged to form the city of Fukuoka. Photo by Wilford A. Bladen.

Jozankei Hot Spring, southwest of Sapporo, developed as an onsen machi. Situated on the upper reaches of the river Toyohiragawa, it is in Shikotsu-Toya National Park. A Zen priest named Jozan is said to have opened the spa in 1866. There are many hotels along the hot spring. The Japanese take special pleasure in mineral and hot-spring bathing, and towns developed at important hot springs. Photo by P.P. Karan.

since the town developed under the protection of the great temples. During the centuries of unrest, the merchants and country folk gathered about the great temples. Unlike the castle, which usually occupied a somewhat central position in the town, the temples and shrines most commonly were on the periphery. Temples and shrines played a major role in the economy of these towns, influencing their growth and form.

Trading centers that developed along seaports are known as minato machi or port towns. Many towns such as Hakata (now part of Fukuoka), Sakai (in Osaka Prefecture), Nagasaki, and Hyogo (now Kobe) flourished as minato machi. Under the seclusion policy of the Tokugawa shogunate, when overseas trade was almost entirely forbidden, domestic trade continued at the port towns of Osaka, Shimonoseki, and Niigata on the major sea routes. Many of these free ports were under the control of the merchants who inhabited them.

Another group of Japanese towns developed as ichiba machi or market centers. These market towns established a link with urban life for the merchants of nearby villages and served as their trading places. Most of these towns grew up where some unusual opportunity for trade existed, such as the intersection of two or more important roads. Mikkaichi, meaning "Third Day Market" (in Toyama Prefecture), Yokkaichi, "Fourth Day Market" (in Mie Prefecture), and Futsukaichi, "Second Day Market" in northern Kyushu are examples of the old market towns. The market towns held one-day fairs or out-door markets and were named after the date of the first opening during the thirty-day lunar month.

A number of towns developed as *onsen machi* (hot-spring towns or spas); hot springs have been major popular attractions for the Japanese people since ancient times. Many of these towns have now developed into large resort complexes. Koji Kanda (2001) has analyzed the development process of a spa resort in southern Wakayama Prefecture. The town of Tamayu, Shimane Prefecture, is based on Tamatsukuri onsen, one of the best-known hot-spring spas in western Honshu. The development of Matsuyama, western Ehime Prefecture, Shikoku, is in part based on Dogo onsen, one of Japan's oldest spas. Beppu, a major spa town in Kyushu, receives nearly 12 million visitors annually. Atami, Shizuoka Prefecture, developed as a resort town around numerous hot springs in the area. Takarazuka, known for its hot springs since the eighth century, is now a residential satellite of Osaka and Kobe. Noboribetsu in Hokkaido is an example of a spa town that has developed in recent times. These spa towns have many hotels, Japanese-style inns, restaurants, and recreational facilities.

Riding the tide of the surging postwar economy, Izu Peninsula capitalized on its proximity to Tokyo and its bountiful hot-spring resources to promote tourism in the region. It reached a peak in 1988 when 73.5 million people visited Izu, flocking to such famous hot-spring resort towns as Atami, Ito, and Shuzenji. When Izu's onsen towns were hit by a number of earthquakes in 1989, the number of visitors dropped dramatically. The decline continued as the bubble economy collapsed. In 1998 the number of visitors declined to 52 million, just 70.7 percent of the peak year. Izu has led Japan's onsen industry and serves as a model for other onsen.

Sakurajima onsen in southern Kyushu is tucked up against the base of the fuming volcano and cupped in a cove of jagged rock. Laden with minerals and bubbling at temperatures that sometimes test a body's limits, the pool at Sakurajima steams like a brew cooked up by the earth. These hot springs are more than just baths. Each soothes the visitor with its own particular blend of curative and restorative powers. The people of Japan have long enjoyed the country's onsen. The springs, forced to the surface by underground volcanic activity, are seen as sort of a trade-off for Japan's location over an earthquake zone. But perhaps what is most enjoyable about onsen machi is that no two ever seem to be the same. Since they are shaped largely by forces of nature, these onsen machi can be found nestled in the folds of mountain ranges, alongside or even in streams and rivers, or washed by the cold waters of oceans and bays. The Sakurajima area is also home to one of Japan's most unusual onsen—the *sunaburo* (sand baths) of Ibusuki. Here visitors put on a cotton robe and lie down on the beach and relax while women in bonnets shovel hot sand over them. The sand, infused with the water of underground springs, soon reaches up to the neck, and it feels wonderful.

With few exceptions, Japan's modern cities have grown from one of these origins. Many cities had more than one function in feudal times. For example, Shizuoka and Nagoya were both joka machi and shukuba machi. Osaka was both a joka machi and an ichiba machi. In general, towns that had strong locational advantages in feudal days have retained their site advantage in modern times and have become the great industrial and commercial cities. Castle towns such as Osaka, Tokyo, Nagoya, and Hiroshima have not only maintained their locational advantages but have improved their positions as centers of commerce and industry.

Although the city in Japan has ancient roots, the contemporary geographic framework of Japan's urban pattern was established during the feudal period. After 1868 many castle towns became prefectural or regional capitals and added educational, cultural, and service functions, which brought about the func-

tional transformation of historic cities. Smaller castle towns became centers of light industries such as food processing, textiles, brewing, and farm implements. The larger castle towns attracted heavier industries, such as metals and shipbuilding, and became foci of transportation networks.

There were 452 castle towns in feudal Japan according to Professor Kenjiro Fujioka (1959, 1980) of Kyoto University (see table 8.2). Of these 113 developed as cities, 174 as towns, and 165 as villages.

Most of the old castle towns in Japan are now major urban centers situated on the main lines of modern transportation. Among them, most of the industrial cities are located on the coast. Some of the castle towns that flourished in the past but are not prosperous now owe their decline to locations in the mountain basins that are away from the main lines of transportation.

Castle-port cities such as Osaka, Niigata, Shimonoseki, and Nagoya have continued their administrative-political functions and have added important manufacturing and service functions. Japan's railroads follow the old feudal highway network, and former stage towns such as Sendai, Kawasaki, Hamamatsu, and Nagano have now become railroad centers with manufacturing and commercial functions. Many religious centers as well as resort towns have grown in importance during modern times along with the surging economy.

The form and structure of Japanese cities have been influenced by their historical roots and traditions, harmonizing the modern and historical urban landscapes. The municipal or administrative center—the core of the city—has been converted from the old castle of the late feudal period. Streets of these old cities resemble labyrinths; their purpose was to protect the central castle or the daimyo's residence. In the case of castle towns, these labyrinths were T-shaped; the samurai lived close to the castle, and the merchants lived along the main streets. Temples were on the margins of cities to protect the castle. The moats surrounding the castle were very deep, and often there were two or three rows of moats.

CITY GROWTH IN THE MODERN PERIOD (1868–2000)

The period of about 130 years from the beginning of modernization in the early years of the Meiji era to the present can be divided into four stages (see

Table 8.2. Feudal domains and castle towns (fiefs exceeding 100,000 *koku* of rice), 1813

Regions	Castle Towns	Feudal Lord	Fiefdom
Sea of Japan side	Akita	Satake	Kubota
	Shonai (Tsuruoka)	Sakai	Shonai
	Takada (Joetsu)	Sakakibara	Takada (Echigo)
	Toyama	Maeda	Toyama (Etchu)
	Kanazawa	Maeda	Kanazawa (Kaga)
	Fukui	Matsudaira	Fukui
	Obama	Sakai	Obama (Wakasa)
	Tottori	Ikeda	Tottori
	Matsue	Matsudaira	Matsue
	Hagi	Mori	Hagi (Nagato)
	Izuhara	Sou	Izuhara (Tsushima)
Inland basin belt	Hirosaki	Tsugaru	Hirosaki
	Morioka	Nambu	Morioka
	Yonezawa	Uesugi	Yonezawa
	Nihonmatsu	Niwa	Nihonmatsu
	Aizu (Aizuwakamatsu)	Gamo	Aizu
	Shirakawa	Matsudaira	Shirakawa
	Sakura	Hotta	Sakura (Shimoosa)
	Gyoda	Abe	Oshi (Musashi)
	Kawagoe	Matsudaira	Kawagoe
	Matsushiro (Nagano)	Sanada	Matsushiro (Shinano)
	Ogaki	Toda	Ogaki (Mino)
	Hikone	Ii	Hikone
	Koriyama (Yamatokoriyama)	Matsudaira	Koriyama
	Yodo (Kyoto)	Inaba	Yodo
Pacific Coast and Inland Sea	Sendai	Date	Osaki
	Mito	Tokugawa	Mito (Hitachi)
	Odawara	Okubo	Odawara (Sagami)
	Nagoya	Tokugawa	Nagoya (Owari)
	Kuwana	Matsudaira	Kuwana
	Tsu	Todo	Tsu (Ise, Mie)
	Wakayama	Tokugawa	Wakayama (Kii)
	Himeji	Sakai	Himeji
	Okayama	Ikeda	Okayama
	Fukuyama	Abe	Fukuyama
	Hiroshima	Asano	Hiroshima
	Tokushima	Hachisuka	Tokushima
	Takamatsu	Matsudaira	Takamatsu
	Kochi	Yamauchi	Kochi (Tosa)
	Matsuyama	Matsudaira	Matsuyama
	Uwajima	Date	Uwajima (Iyo)
Kyushu	Fukuoka	Kuroda	Fukuoka
	Kurume	Arima	Kurume
	Yanagawa	Tachibana	Yanagawa
	Saga	Nabeshima	Saga (Hizen)
	Nakatsu	Okudaira	Nakatsu (Buzen, Oita)
	Kumamoto	Hosokawa	Kumamoto (Higo)
	Kagoshima	Shimazu	Kagoshima

Source: Fujioka 1980.

fig. 8.2), based on levels of urbanization and the growth of urban centers (*Japanese Cities* 1970; Ito and Watanabe 1980). The first stage covered a period of more than 60 years from the Meiji era to 1930. The modern growth of Japanese cities is linked to changes that occurred in the nation's economic structure beginning in the late Meiji period (1868–1912). The shift in economic activity from agriculture, mining, forestry, and fishing to manufacturing encouraged large sectors of the workforce to leave the rural areas, small towns, and villages for the industrial activity of the large cities. During the Meiji period the percentage of the population living in cities of 50,000 or more grew from less than 8 percent to more than 16 percent. The proportion of the population living in cities of any size increased from 10 percent in 1868 to 24 percent in 1930. This change was accompanied by a decline in employment in the primary rural sector from more than 80 percent to about 50 percent.

During the second stage (1930–50) urban growth rose remarkably, from 24 to 37 percent, with the continued decline of the labor force in the primary sector to 41 percent, reflecting the steady advance of urbanization. A significant aspect of urbanization in

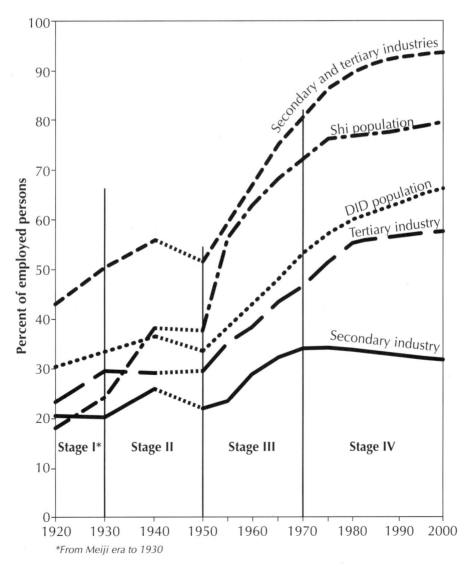

Fig. 8.2. Stages of urban growth, 1920–2000.

Japan during this period was the development of metropolitan areas; this trend has continued to the present. In 1920 there were only 16 cities with 100,000 or more inhabitants; and the combined population of these cities constituted 12.2 percent of the total national population. Among these cities, only Tokyo and Osaka had a population of more than 1 million each, and these two cities accounted for 6.2 percent of the nation's population. By 1940 the number of cities with populations of more than 100,000 had increased to 45, and their combined population constituted 29.4 percent of Japan's population. In 1940 there were four cities with more than 1 million—Tokyo, Osaka, Kyoto, and Nagoya—and their combined populations accounted for 17.2 percent of the national population.

During World War II American B-29 bombers dropped thousands of napalm-filled firebombs on Tokyo, leaving almost nothing standing in an area larger than 16 square miles (41 sq km). In the spring and summer of 1945, similarly devastating raids on more than 60 Japanese cities occurred before the atomic bombing of Hiroshima and Nagasaki brought World War II to an end. The bombing of war industries located in dense residential areas resulted in widespread incineration of Japanese cities. Although the incendiary campaign did more urban damage and killed more people than the atomic bombings of Hiroshima and Nagasaki, it has received much less attention.

There was major urban reconstruction after World War II. Although the number of cities with 100,000 or more inhabitants had increased to 64 in 1950, the proportion of people living in these cities to the total national population declined to 25.7 percent. Also, the proportion of the population living in cities of more than 1 million declined to 11.4 percent. In fact, in terms of absolute numbers, the population of Tokyo decreased from 6.8 million in 1940 to 5.4 million in 1950 and that of Osaka from 3.3 million to 2 million during the same period. This was largely due to the evacuation of many residents from the larger cities during the Pacific War.

During the third stage (1950–70) the pace of urbanization intensified and the growth of cities accelerated with high economic growth. In 1950, only 37 percent of the population lived in urban areas; by 1970 this figure had increased to 72 percent. During this period the labor force in the primary sector declined from 41 percent to less than 21 percent, and there was a massive migration of people from rural to urban areas. From about the middle of the 1950s, as economic recovery brought increasing industrialization and millions of new jobs were created, the movement toward the urban areas accelerated rapidly. By 1960 the number of "million cities" had increased to six, with the addition of Yokohama and Kobe, and the populations of Tokyo and Osaka had increased to 8.3 million and 3 million, respectively. The number of cities with 100,000 or more people increased to 150 in 1970, and their combined populations made up more than 50 percent of the total national population. This shift away from a rural-based population is indicated by the fact that as many as twenty-five of the rural prefectures lost population during the first decade of high economic growth. The concentration of population in Tokyo, Osaka, Nagoya, Kyoto, and Kobe was particularly noteworthy. Accompanying this growth was a rapid expansion of urban zones into the surrounding areas. The pace of city growth began to slow in the 1960s; migration into the greater Tokyo area reached a peak in 1962. A similar peak in growth was also experienced in the 1960s by major cities like the Kyoto-Osaka-Kobe area and Nagoya.

The fourth stage is the period following 1970 during which urban population attained a high level of more than 75 percent. The labor force engaged in the primary sector dropped to a low level of 10 percent or less. The oil crisis of 1973 weakened the process of urbanization, as did the declines in the conversion of land to urban use in the metropolitan areas and in the pace of subsequent land-use changes to urban functions. But by 1975 four more cities—Kitakyushu, Sapporo, Kawasaki, and Fukuoka—joined the "million cities" group, and the population of the ten "million cities" equaled 20.8 percent of the country's population. This figure dropped slightly to 19.9 percent in 1980, mainly because of a decline in the populations of Tokyo and Osaka. In 1980 Yokohama, with a population of 2.8 million, was the second-largest city in Japan, while Osaka was third (Karan and Stapleton 1997). In 1990 there were 209 cities with a population of 100,000; more than 72 million people lived in these cities. The population of the eleven cities that were "million cities" in 1990 are given in table 8.3. Except for

Sapporo, all the "million cities" are located in the Japanese Megalopolis (see fig. 8.3).

The period between 1970 and 2000 was marked by the technological and industrial transformation of the nation as it evolved into a postindustrial information-based society. By 1990 the population of the Tokyo Metropolitan Area (Tokyo and its surrounding seven prefectures) had reached close to 39 million, a concentration of 32 percent of the nation's population in the Kanto Plain and adjacent areas. The cities of Tokyo, Osaka, Nagoya, Kobe, and Kitakyushu were losing population, but all the other "million cities" were growing. Particularly significant is the growth of population on the outskirts of major cities (Kuroda 1990; Kuroda and Tsuya, 1989). In 1990 the built-up urban areas constituting the Densely Inhabited Districts (DID) contained 78 million inhabitants: 63.2 percent of the population on 3.11 percent of the total area of the country. In 1995 the DIDs contained 81 million people (64.7 percent of the population living on 3.24 percent of the national area). The density of population in the DIDs

Table 8.3. Population of the "million cities," 1995 and 2003

City	Population 1995	% change over 1990 population	Estimated 2003 population
Tokyo (23 wards)	7,967,614	-2.4	8,289,000
Yokohama	3,307,136	2.7	3,503,000
Osaka	2,602,421	-0.8	2,620,000
Nagoya	2,152,184	-0.1	2,188,000
Sapporo	1,757,025	5.1	1,849,000
Kyoto	1,463,822	0.2	1,467,000
Kobe	1,423,792	-3.6	1,512,000
Fukuoka	1,284,795	3.9	1,371,000
Kawasaki	1,202,820	2.5	1,283,000
Hiroshima	1,108,888	2.1	1,136,000
Kitakyushu	1,019,598	-0.7	1,003,000

Sources: Japan Statistical Yearbook 2004 (Tokyo: Statistics Bureau, Ministry of Public Management, Home Affairs, Posts, and Telecommunications, Government of Japan, 2004); and *Monthly Statistics of Japan,* March 2003.

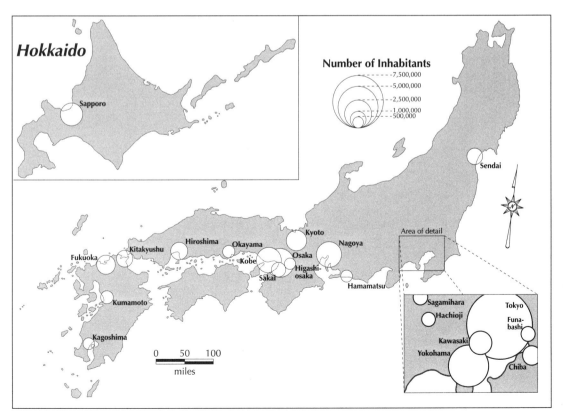

Fig. 8.3. Major cities of Japan.

in 1995 was 6,630 per square kilometer, a decline from the high figure of 10,263 in 1965 that was due to increasing suburban development and dispersal of the urban population. The population of inner wards of all the major cities began to decline during this period. This trend is most evident in Tokyo, Osaka, and Nagasaki (see fig. 8.4). A study by Takano (1993) revealed that the inner area of Japanese cities is characterized by a higher elderly population and more one-person households, a decline in blue-collar workers, the dispersion of commercial facilities, and the centralization of professional workers.

THE JAPANESE MEGALOPOLIS

The axis of the greatest concentration of cities in Japan extends from Kanto to Kinki and along the Inland Sea to northwest Kyushu (see fig. 8.5). This belt forms the Japanese Megalopolis, with six great metropolitan areas: Tokyo, Yokohama, Nagoya, Kyoto, Osaka, and Kobe. It extends along the Inland Sea to

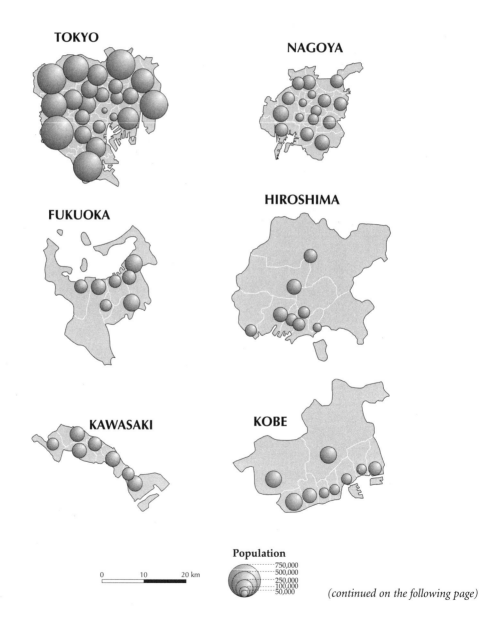

TOKYO

NAGOYA

FUKUOKA

HIROSHIMA

KAWASAKI

KOBE

0   10   20 km

Population
750,000
500,000
250,000
100,000
50,000

(continued on the following page)

Fig. 8.4. Population of cities by wards, 2000. Based on the National Census.

include cities such as Himeji, Okayama, Fukuyama, and Hiroshima and across the Inland Sea to take in the cities of Tokushima, Takamatsu, Niihama, Imabari, and Matsuyama on Shikoku and Kita-kyushu, Fukuoka, and Nagasaki on Kyushu, along with the constellation of their suburbs and satellites (Harris and Edmonds 1982; Kiuchi 1963). The Japa-

nese Megalopolis, similar to the urbanized northeast-ern seaboard of the United States, represents a new order in the organization of space. It is characterized by increasing dominance of the service sector of the labor force and the advent of the postindustrial, in-formational, and transactional era. The megalopolis resulted from the coalescence, recently achieved, of a

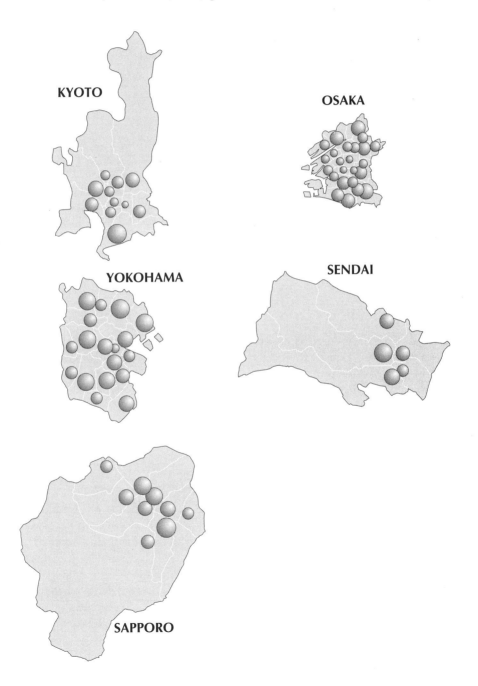

Fig. 8.4. *(Continued)*

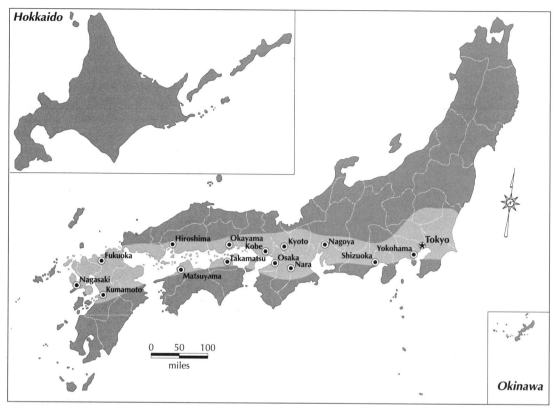

Fig. 8.5. The Japanese megalopolis.

chain of metropolitan areas, each of which grew around a substantial urban nucleus. Urban geographic studies in Japan and the complex network of interconnectivity between major cities of the megalopolis have been analyzed by Kazutoshi Abe (1996, 2000).

The Japanese Megalopolis is an extraordinarily interesting geographic region, where many of the features of the postindustrial civilization of the early twenty-first century are taking shape. By its size and mass, the Japanese Megalopolis is both an exceptional and a unique region. It is exceptional because nowhere else in Japan can one find another concentration of population, of industrial and commercial facilities, of financial wealth and cultural activities, comparable to it.

Compared with other parts of the country, the Japanese Megalopolis is a unique combination of exceptional population numbers and density, history, wealth, physical diversity, and dynamism. When Japan took its census in 1990, the megalopolis was home to 78 million people, or 63 percent of the nation's population. Nearly two-thirds of all Japanese live here, occupying about 3 percent of the country's land. Residential densities in the region exceed 6,600 persons per square kilometer (Masai 1994). In some of the old urban cores, population densities are lower, but they generally exceed 11,000 per square kilometer in Tokyo.

Historically, the region has been the major center of population and economic activity in Japan since the feudal period. The historic Kinki district, where Japan emerged as a cohesive state in the late fifth century, lies in this urbanized belt. It has been the gateway for virtually all of Japan's trade, and during the Meiji era it served as the launching pad for much of the nation's economic development and modernization. Today, along with the population, the Japanese Megalopolis has a disproportionately large share of the nation's wealth, personal income, commerce, and industry.

The cities of the Japanese Megalopolis have undergone drastic changes since the 1960s. There has been major suburbanization of the population, extension of the commuter zones, and dispersal of the retail and industrial activities within the metropolitan areas. In the Tokyo, Nagoya, and Osaka Metropolitan Areas, the decentralization of population has resulted in population decline in central parts of cities and increase at the periphery of the built-up areas. Rising real incomes along with huge increases in land values both force and allow people to seek housing on lower-valued suburban land. Perhaps high housing costs in the inner city are more responsible than any other factor for suburbanization. There is enormous pressure on residential land owners to sell their urban land and even greater economic pressure for land to be developed in the suburbs for housing. As a result of the suburbanization process, automobile use has risen and more money has been spent on improving the transportation system. The higher cost of commuting is borne partly by employers who subsidize workers' transportation costs.

In Tokyo, Nagoya, and Osaka many factories moved away from the core industrial areas. Factories relocated in suburban areas draw workers from the central city as well as from local communities. The decentralization of metropolitan functions involves not only housing and industrial facilities but also retail businesses. Metropolitan retail functions have rapidly developed in suburban areas. At the initial stage of decentralization, higher-order retail functions tended to remain in the central business district (CBD), while the lower-order retail functions moved to the suburbs. Large retail shops such as supermarkets, which sell general foods and daily necessities, played an important role in the decentralization of retail functions into suburban areas. Supermarkets, which have rapidly increased in number since the 1970s, spread from central cities to suburbs and satellite cities in response to the population increase in the suburban areas. Supermarkets are also changing from food- and clothing-oriented retail to diversified shopping centers.

Central Tokyo has attracted industries with large investments and administrative-information industries. Peripheral areas, by contrast, contain resource-oriented industries. The number of central managerial functions and corporate headquarters has rapidly increased in central cities. Tokyo and Osaka have attracted the majority of the central managerial functions, especially financial and insurance businesses. The high rent charged for urban space in Japan has

intensified urban land use. As buildings in cities have become taller, urban underground space has expanded. The vertical distribution of urban activities in the high-rise buildings in the central parts of the cities exhibits a pattern in which amusement and retail activities are concentrated on lower floors and residential, cultural, and administrative functions tend to occupy higher floors. The use of underground spaces is one of the major changes in Japanese urban cores. Underground space complements the CBD ground-floor space, which has become popular for retail use with the development of subways and urban expressways.

As metropolitan growth has continued, several subcenters have formed within the metropolitan area. The urban structure of most cities of the megalopolis has acquired a multiple-nuclei pattern. Despite the relative decline of the central city, the Japanese metropolitan areas do not have "severe" inner-city problems. Toshio Mizuuchi (1986) has pointed out the spatial inequality in the living environment of the modern Japanese cities, particularly the inequality seen in the residential districts of minority groups.

Will the trend of decentralization in Japan continue in the twenty-first century? Japan will likely follow the patterns of urban development of other developed countries, such as the United States, where rural depopulation, a high concentration of population in large cities, and suburbanization characterize metropolitan areas.

Physically, all cities of the megalopolis are built either on alluvial plains or on both alluvial plains and the hills or terraces bordering the plains. The size of the cities and the size of the plains on which they are located are in close agreement. Tokyo, the largest city, is on the large Kanto Plain, Osaka is on the Osaka Plain, Nagoya is on the Nobi Plain, Hiroshima is on the delta of the Otagawa, and Fukuoka is on Hakata Bay. All the great cities except Kyoto are on the seacoast, and the megalopolis occupies a narrow belt along the seacoast between Tokyo and Fukuoka. The region has an intricate shoreline of estuaries, deltas, capes and bays, tidal marshes, and many picturesque islands.

Today, the Japanese Megalopolis is a region of immense population concentration along the major railroads that follow the coastal belt. But automobile-era dispersal and decentralization is beginning to occur. Here, on 3 percent of the nation's land, most of Japan's labor force commutes between home and work by rail. The megalopolis accounts for most of the country's rail and vehicle mileage. Daily activities in the megalopolis consume the bulk of the energy used in Japan and generate an equally large share of all the nation's garbage, rubbish, waste gases, and other pollutants. The magnitude and complexity of this urbanized belt of Japan is overwhelming. Although the modern features of Japanese cities—factories, smokestacks, wide streets, and noisy, motorized forms of transport—are similar to the features of Western cities, in most Japanese cities the ancient forms and structures are still recognizable despite rapid development.

Between the metropolitan built-up areas from Tokyo to Nagasaki, the Japanese Megalopolis contains hundreds of villages. Some of the most productive farming in the country thrives on the suburban edges of Tokyo, Osaka, Nagoya, Kyoto, Kobe, Hiroshima, and Nagasaki. However, only a very small percentage of the people living in the villages are full-time farmers. Instead, the vast majority of them are part-time farmers who are supported by urban-type jobs and who in every other respect are urban. Consumer electronics, precision machinery, integrated circuits, construction, and government service are important parts of the economy of the Japanese countryside in the megalopolis. Part-time farming provides extra pocket money.

Recent trends in the megalopolis are enabling some employees to work at home. Telecommuting is spreading rapidly in Japan, especially among electronics manufacturers. Among them, IBM Japan Ltd. has one of the most active approaches, experimenting with a mix of telecommuting and flextime policies to free employees from the drudgery of the daily commute. According to the Japan Telework Association, in 2000 there were about 2.46 million "teleworkers"—people who work at home or visit clients without going into the office. This is three times the 1996 figure of 810,000, and it is expected to rise to 4.45 million in 2005. As telecommuting takes hold in the workplace, the concept of commuting may be changed forever in the nation.

Fundamentally, the Japanese Megalopolis is a vast, interlocking urban network of job trips, shopping and service trips, and social or recreational trips linking dwellings, nonresidential buildings, and recreational and farmland open space. The network is dramatized vividly from the air on a dark winter morning: as the lights come on, you know that millions of people are rising to begin their day. In a short time, the buildings, roads, and rail lines come alive with hundreds of millions of points of light, and millions of moving lights mark the streams of traffic from home to work. People converge from a multitude of dwelling places and diverge again into several million workplaces. The pattern of commuting is incredibly immense in the large metropolitan areas. But beyond those high-intensity areas, the interconnected networks of the Japanese Megalopolis branch out to the farthest edges of the region, linking the congested urban or industrial clusters that make up this great conurbation on the Pacific belt of Japan.

The past twenty-five years have witnessed remarkable changes in the economic, social, and geographic makeup of the cities in the Japanese Megalopolis and in their political and cultural dynamics. Comprehensive strategies blending urban, industrial, and telecommunication policies have been employed to create new futuristic cities and urban spaces (Edgington 1989). In the 1970s a large new town for scientific research and development was developed outside Tokyo at a place called Tsukuba, and in the 1980s Kansai Science City was established near Osaka (Castells and Hall 1994). Several other towns and cities were also designated as "technopoles" for the development of high-technology industry (Masser 1990). Japan's Ministry of Posts and Telecommunications developed the Teletopia program to assist public information services in sixty-three model cities. The Ministry of Construction has developed its Intelligent City program to encourage the hardwiring of cities with fiber-optic systems and advanced urban management networks (Terasaka et al. 1988). These efforts represent the most important national approach to urban and regional development in Japan based on technology.

Cities such as Tokyo, Yokohama, Osaka, Kobe, Kyoto, Hiroshima, Fukuoka, and Nagasaki are emerging as electronic hubs for telecommunications and telematics networks (services and infrastructures that link computer and digital media equipment). Cities of the megalopolis have become powerhouses of communications whose traffic floods across global telecommunications networks. Thus has begun a process of transformation from

Field Report

Sounds of the Megalopolis

Metropolitan din in the megalopolis fails to still delicate village sounds. Construction clangor and traffic roar merge with the cries of street vendors in this major conurbation, one of the largest in the world. On a street corner by night a noodle man raises his small bugle and a thin wail is heard plaintively against the rhythmic crash of a pile driver. From somewhere nearby comes the screech of a bicycle brake and the gruff roar of a racing cement-truck engine. A sudden, startling instant of silence, and then from around a dim corner ticks the barely audible clock-clock of wooden clogs against a pavement.

By night and day, the life of the world's largest megalopolis is echoed in its sounds. Some of them are piercing and raucous, some of them so delicate and faint that they seem almost imagined. But all of them are reflections of the different paces, tastes, and moods of the region. There are times when the cities of the megalopolis are a blare, a roar, and a howl caught up in the madhouse futility of trying to shout louder and louder so as to make oneself heard.

The construction booms by day and by night. The chatter of riveting guns competes around the clock with the pounding of the pile drivers and the whines and creaks and rumbles of construction machinery. Around each excavation huge trucks circle like a line of elephants, and their motors raise a throaty, insistent roar that blends into the general clangor.

Sometimes above the noise of the building, and sometimes merging with it, the sounds of the streets in the central business sections of the cities assert themselves—the bellow of streetcar horns, the huge, crashing rattle of the elevated trains, and the whistles and sirens and perpetual metropolitan hum that seems to come from nowhere but exists as a separate entity. But there are also a flute and a mellow temple bell and the clacking of a wooden clapper and the soft trickle of water in a fountain. The blatant noises of the great urban centers are everywhere, but nowhere have they been able to still entirely the muted sounds of the village.

The cities of the Japanese megalopolis are not neatly regimented like most of the cities of the West—a place to work, a place to shop, a place to sleep. Here everything is everyplace. It is an intertwined chain of settlements. Next to the fine house of a merchant is a tinsmith's shop, and next to that a temple, and next to that more houses, and then a couple of coffee shops and perhaps an eel restaurant, and then a stall where apprentices are repairing straw floor mats. Around the corner a man sells scrolls in a tiny store overshadowed but not quite dominated by a new insurance building.

Morning office workers who will in an hour be swallowed by the subway's din wake to the horn of the seller of bean curds and greens. Later the man who sells sweet beans and pickles comes around with his bell. When the children are out of school, the stuntmen appear banging the drums. The wandering storyteller flaps his clapper, and the children rush out to listen to his cliffhanger stories and buy his candy.

Music, too, has its place in the sounds and life of the megalopolis. It may not be true that there is more music played in the Japanese Megalopolis than in other urbanized areas of the world. But because houses are small and streets are narrow and walls are thin, the sounds of music seem to be much more a part of the megalopolis. From a restaurant pour the sounds of a ballad. Next door, in a five-story coffee house, a band of musicians who look like teenagers bray the "Tokyo Calpyso." Around the corner, the door to another coffee house opens, and for a moment the night is gentle with Mozart.

an industrial, manufacturing-dominated urban society to one increasingly dominated by information, high-technology manufacturing, service, and leisure industries, forcing changes in urban labor markets and urban socioeconomic dynamics. A complex interaction between technologies and the social, economic, cultural, and political changes is under way in the cities (Gottman 1991). At stake here are industrial innovation and trade policies that are crucially affected by the spatial and social development of telecommunications infrastructures and services, stimulating Japan, as well as Europe and the United States, to construct information superhighway policies with which to boost their economic positions and their strength in the export markets for hardware, software, and support services. These policies have important implications for the Japanese Megalopolis, because cities here are the centerpieces of the national and increasingly international telematics marketplace. Contemporary city economics of the megalopolis can be understood only through their relations to global economic and technological changes.

Increasing shifts toward liberalization and the growth of investment markets have led to a remarkable boom in financial services fueling the growth of larger cities of the megalopolis, which are placed at the hub of global electronics and financial networks. As a result economic activity involving processing and adding value to knowledge and information is now becoming a dominant aspect of the economies of many cities in the megalopolis, transforming them into "post-industrial information cities" (Hepworth 1987). The world financial and corporate capitals, including Tokyo and Osaka (Sassen 2001), have emerged as key command-and-control centers where the best jobs are located. Tokyo and Osaka remain the economic powerhouses of the Japanese Megalopolis. Centralization is occurring here as well as decentralization. In particular, headquarters and control functions are centralizing further into the elite group of command centers such as Tokyo, Osaka, and Nagoya. At the same time the movement of routine service functions away from larger cities is leading to new processes of urbanization in smaller cities. Certain cities such as Hiroshima, Kumamoto, and Fukuoka have managed to specialize in advanced manufacturing, research and development, or high-technology services. Some have strengthened their roles as centers for consumption, leisure, and tourism services both for their region and for the national hinterland. At the same time many older industrial cities with weak service bases, such as Kitakyushu, are competing to sustain their socioeconomic fabric.

The urban landscape of cities in the megalopolis is being reshaped by global economic forces. Derelict or decaying old industrial spaces are being reborn in many cities as postmodern urban developments that are foci of global consumption and culture. Office complexes, business and technology parks, and shopping malls are transforming the urban areas. Core cities are turning into extended urban regions, which blend into the wider megalopolis. In some cities and regions of the megalopolis, new processes of innovation and manufacturing growth are making an important impact on the urban economy. In Osaka and Tokyo, the Teleports form the centerpieces of massive land-reclamation and property development projects (Itoh 1988). Tokyo's Teleport Town is built on reclaimed land in Tokyo Bay. New urban settlements are planned for completion in the twenty-first century on the Ariake and Daiba sites that will include blocks of high-technology "intelligent buildings," sports and leisure activities, and international conference centers.

A range of new industrial spaces, linked into the global market, involves key sectors such as semiconductors, electronics, biotechnology, and environmental technologies. Examples of such localized production complexes are spread all across the megalopolis in gleaming, state-of-the-art facilities; major clusters are on Kyushu (Silicon Island) and in Osaka, Nagoya, and the Tokyo Metropolitan Area. Within these spaces, continuous intellectual and knowledge inputs are far more important than in the previous era of production in the megalopolis. Research and development are ongoing activities, as short product cycles require constant improvements in products. This means that links with academic research institutes and universities, good global transport, and telecommunication infrastructures are important to new emerging high-tech industries in the megalopolis.

Nagoya, including the Tokai area, is renowned as one of Japan's largest manufacturing centers (Eyre 1982). It is the headquarters of Toyota Motor Corporation—the world's third-largest automaker in terms of cars rolling off the assembly line—and of the Toyota group's companies and factories. Beginning in the year 2000, three prominent regional projects in Nagoya will influence this section of the megalopolis. One that particularly captured attention was JR Central Towers, a vast multipurpose building in Nagoya. Standing 804 feet (245 m) tall and boasting a total floor area of 492,000 square yards (410,000 sq m), JR Central Towers is among Japan's largest freestanding high-rises. Its diverse amenities, which include an office wing and an observation deck, a hotel, a department store, and a restaurant area, opened, in gradual succession, between December 1999 and May 2000. The multipurpose tower block cost Central Japan Railway Company (JR Tokai)—the Tokaido Shinkansen operator—some 200 billion yen to build. This imposing edifice has already become the architectural symbol of the Tokai section of the megalopolis.

In 2000 the Central Towers attracted some 30 million visitors, far exceeding the 17.5 million guests who flocked to Tokyo Disneyland during fiscal 1998. The Central Towers is blessed with an extremely convenient location, sitting above Nagoya Station, a vital terminus for bullet trains, JR lines, subways, and private railways alike. Nagoya's most popular quarter used to be Sakae, 1.6 miles (2.5 km) east of Nagoya Station. Completion of this brand new landmark has reversed the flow, with crowds converging now around the Central Towers. This monument to Nagoya's penchant for doing things on a grand scale has lured visitors from Kyoto, Nagano, and Shizuoka Prefectures—indeed, from more than 62 miles (100 km) away. The Central Towers is taking its toll on existing businesses. Take the department store: JR Tokai and Takashimaya Company had first-year sales of 60 billion yen in 2000. This is equivalent to one-seventh of the annual sales by the city's other four existing department stores. So as individual consumption remains sluggish, the sales of preexisting stores have plummeted as a consequence of the new Takashimaya outlet. And in 2000 two prominent hotels—one of them the Nagoya Miyako Hotel—closed their doors.

The second project that has drawn attention to the Nagoya and Tokai section of the megalopolis is the construction of a site for the 2005 World Exposition, since it has been decided to hold the exposition in that area. The proposed expo location underwent substantial modification after the presence of the nesting goshawk (a bird species protected under Japanese law) was confirmed in the vicinity of the original venue. Then, in early 2000, the Paris-based Bureau International des Expositions denounced the Japanese organizers' development plans for destroying

the surrounding woodland. The organizers—bending to the views of citizens' and environmental groups—agreed to a radical reduction in the scale of the site. Instead of swallowing up 141 acres (57 ha) of Kaisho no Mori forest, just one-fifth (28.17 acres [11.4 ha]) of the woodland will be used. The expo, bearing an environmental theme, will now be held from March through September 2005 and is expected to attract 15 to 18 million visitors.

The third project in the Tokai section of the megalopolis is the construction of the Central Japan International Airport off the Ise Bay shore opposite Tokoname city. The project had been pending for more than three decades when in August 2000 the settlement of a long-standing claim for compensation to the local fishing industry was reached. Work is progressing at top speed so that the new airport will be up and running by the expo's opening day.

The simultaneous progress of these three projects reflects a sense of vibrancy in the Tokai section of the megalopolis, which was long regarded as lagging behind the two leading metropolises of Tokyo and Osaka. Although the expo planners and the airport project managers have yet to solve the problems of fund-raising and profitability, they have overcome the initial challenges entailed in implementing their plans. The expo will present an opportunity for participating companies to show off their latest environmentally friendly technologies. And the new airport's growth potential will be enhanced if it can attract a steady supply of international flights by cutting costs and reducing the fixed landing fee. Perhaps the biggest challenge facing the Tokai section of the megalopolis will be to harmonize the positive spin-offs of these large-scale projects with the interests of the local manufacturing industry that continues to underpin the region's economy. Nagoya has demonstrated that well-integrated national, prefectural, and municipal development planning; supportive public policies; and corporate commitment can maintain a vibrant regional economy (Jacobs 2001).

The Kansai region of the megalopolis is dominated by the Osaka Metropolitan Area, an urbanized district that includes numerous cities, towns, and villages within a 31-mile (50-kilometer) radius of Osaka city (see fig. 8.6) and Osaka Prefecture; this area has a population of 21.5 million and a workforce of about 10 million (Edgington 2000). As of 1994,

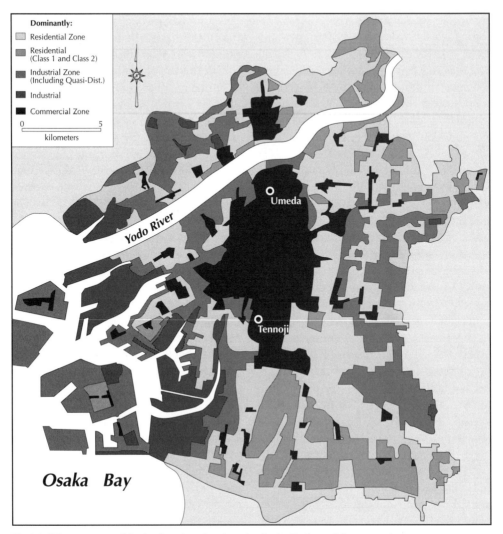

Fig. 8.6. Urban structure of Osaka. Based on data from the Osaka Prefectural Government.

the gross domestic product of the Kansai region of the megalopolis was 92 trillion yen (about $830 billion), equivalent to about 2 percent of the world gross national product and comparable in size to the economy of Canada. Located at the center of western Japan, Osaka is also a rail hub; the many commuter lines that converge on the city are connected together by the JR Kanjosen, which rings the city (Yamashita 1987). Osaka has thrived as a port and trading center for 2,000 years, and the Kansai area has for most of that time been the center of Japan's political, economic, and cultural life. But ever since Tokyo was established as the nation's capital, more than 130 years ago, Osaka has been losing ground. The city has a lingering image problem because it

lies in the shadow cast by the more noted Tokyo, about 320 miles (515 km) away. The trend accelerated in recent years with the rise of one of the most powerful political and governmental bureaucracies in the world, forcing anyone doing business in Japan to look at the nation's capital. Although Osaka was the founding place for Japan's leading trading and manufacturing companies, many have relocated their headquarters to Tokyo to be where the power and decision making are concentrated. More than 33 percent of the large corporate headquarters are based in Tokyo; Osaka and adjoining cities have only about 13 percent of them.

Recently Osaka has begun to fight back against the dominance of Tokyo with several construction projects and regional development initiatives to prepare Osaka and Kansai for the twenty-first century. These are the construction of the Kansai International Airport and the Kansai Science City. The completion of the Kansai International Airport in 1994 is changing the region's economy. The Kansai Science City is western Japan's equivalent of Tsukuba Science City, 37 miles (60 km) north of Tokyo. Osaka is transforming itself into a cultural and information trendsetter in the twenty-first century. Innovations and new ideas will be the basis of its future development.

Kyoto, despite its undisputed historical significance, like most cities of the megalopolis, contends with the problems of urbanization (see fig. 8.7). Since the 1960s people and some businesses have moved away from the core area to the outer ring areas or outside the city, altering the structure of the urban area. The core area has experienced a decline in population. The recent completion of the futuristic Kyoto Station is one example of the city's efforts to attract visitors and industry. But Kyoto temples and shrines also vie for a slice of the economic pie. Harmonizing conservation and development is a continual challenge for Kyoto. The city's many legacies from over twelve hundred years of history are national assets. Its traditional culture and landscapes have survived, and they contribute to this area's identity in the megalopolis. Most Kyoto residents still enjoy a visual quality of life rare in the Japanese megalopolis. Of all the

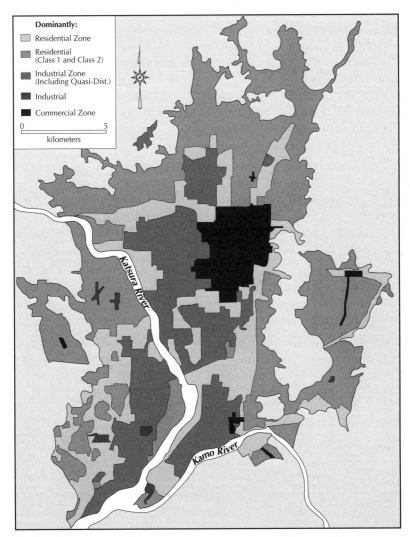

Fig. 8.7. Urban structure of Kyoto. Based on data from the Kyoto Prefectural Government.

Japanese cities, Kyoto, with its rivers, commercial canals, irrigation channels, artesian wells, and garden ponds, is perhaps the most aquatic of Japan's inland cities, though these features harmonize with the surrounding city so discreetly and seductively that one would hardly notice its aquatic character. The founding site, surrounded by mountains at the northern extremity of a fault basin, conforms to the Chinese principles of geomancy. Kyoto's exquisite temples, garden sanctuaries, elegant backstreets, rippling streams, and gurgling brooks artfully blend into the city's landscape.

January 2005 marked the tenth anniversary of the Great Hanshin earthquake, which claimed more than six thousand lives in Kobe city (see fig. 8.8). The years since the quake have seen remarkable progress in the effort to rebuild devastated areas of the city. An event that symbolizes this reemergence is the nighttime pageant of lights that illuminates the historic *ijinkan* district of Western-style houses in central Kobe for fifteen days in December. The spectacle attracts more than 5 million visitors and has become the biggest event Kobe has ever hosted. With people milling around the streets until late in the night, Kobe appears to have regained the glimmer it was once famous for. The return of the bright lights attempts to turn one the nation's biggest disasters into a distant memory. The Kobe quake has reminded people that no place in the Japanese megalopolis is immune to earthquakes and that disaster preparedness programs must learn from Kobe's experience.

Hiroshima, a castle town, developed as one of the largest military cities in pre–World War II Japan (see fig. 8.9). It was a port town from which soldiers were shipped to Korea and China. Nearly 42 percent of the land in central Hiroshima was occupied by military facilities. The military-related economy prospered in the city, providing jobs for people who came from surrounding villages and towns. The physical and social structure of Hiroshima became differentiated functionally. Koreans migrated to Japan voluntarily at first but later on were brought by coercion to work as laborers in the machinery factories and shipyards of Hiroshima. The city had an area of 27 square miles (70 sq km) and a population of 336,483 in 1944, just before the atomic bomb was dropped on August 6, 1945. The period 1945 to 1978

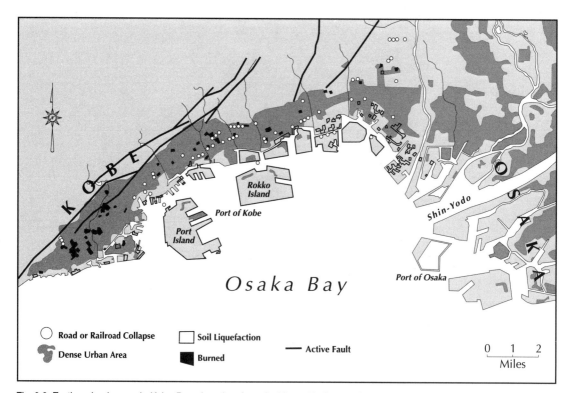

Fig. 8.8. Earthquake damage in Kobe. Based on data from the Hyogo Prefectural Government.

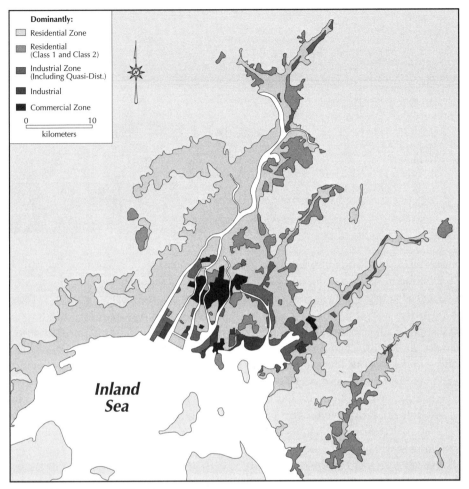

Fig. 8.9. Urban structure of Hiroshima.

was characterized by recovery from the bombing. In 1978 final clearance of the areas destroyed by the bomb was completed by the local government, and Hiroshima was born again with the slogan Peace City.

During the 1980s period of high economic growth, Hiroshima developed into one of the megacities of the Japanese Megalopolis, with an area of 286 square miles (740 sq km) and a population of more than 1 million (Morikawa 1995). Automobile, shipbuilding, and steel industries developed in the area. At the same time, service industries grew rapidly, employing 71 percent of the labor force. The globalization and postindustrialization of Hiroshima's economy have accelerated in recent years.

The northern Kyushu region of the megalopolis has fared better than the rest of the urbanized belt in the 1990s. This is partly because land prices never rose as much in Kyushu as in Osaka or Tokyo. The

relatively cheaper land—and cheaper labor—has drawn many companies. Toyota and Nissan, the country's biggest carmakers, built factories in 1992. All the big electronic companies also have plants in Kyushu. One-tenth of the world's semiconductors are made in the area. With one-tenth of the country's population, this part of the megalopolis accounts for about 12 percent of its gross domestic product. Its economy is about the size of the economies of Indonesia, Thailand, and Malaysia combined.

Fukuoka, with a population of more than 1 million, is the largest city in the Kyushu section of the megalopolis. This is where companies have their regional headquarters. One of Japan's biggest shopping centers, Canal City, opened here in April 1996. Offices are being built in Fukuoka at a rapid pace. In 1995 about 800,000 square feet (75,000 sq m) of new office space was built in the city, compared with about

Rapid urbanization has resulted in conversion of agricultural land to urban use throughout the megalopolis. The expanding urban fringe of Kitakyushu, seen in this picture, is absorbing rural lands at a fast pace. Photo by P.P. Karan.

592,000 square feet (55,000 sq m) for the whole of the Kansai region of the megalopolis, around Osaka. A similar amount of office space was to be added in 1996.

About forty miles to the east in Kitakyushu, the second-largest city in the Kyushu section of the megalopolis, the most conspicuous features are oil-storage tanks and smoking factory chimneys. Fukuoka is the model of a modern, service-driven economy (service companies account for four-fifths of output), whereas Kitakyushu epitomizes old Japan—the industries that thrust the country into the modern era but whose competitive edge has been eroded by rivals abroad. Once Kyushu's biggest city, Kitakyushu built its fortunes on steel. At the heart of the economy is the Yawata steelworks, a factory that was founded in 1901 and became one of the world's largest steel companies. Because of the wealth of coal in the area, other energy-intensive companies, such as those producing chemicals and glass, were also located there. In 1950 Kitakyushu's companies accounted for 5 percent of Japanese output. In its heyday in the 1970s, the Yawata works alone employed 46,000 people. Now it employs 8,000, and some of its land is used for a theme park. Kitakyushu contributes just 0.7 percent of the country's gross domestic output.

But even in Kitakyushu the economy is improving. Once a byword for pollution, the city has cleaned itself up. Fish have returned to its rivers. An energetic local government is striving for change, trying to attract conferences and sell technological know-how abroad. An offshore airport is being built; the port will be deepened. It is too soon to say whether all these efforts will bear fruit, but beneath the bald statistics, change is afoot in the western end of the Japanese Megalopolis.

With Japan's internationalization there has been an influx of foreign labor migrants into the cities of the megalopolis, adding another dimension of change to the urban centers of the region. Attracted by the economic prosperity and shortage of labor, particularly of young workers in construction and manufacturing, the foreign population in Japanese cities has been rapidly increasing. These international migrants are changing the social geography of cities and towns in the megalopolis.

The economic and social shifts in the Japanese Megalopolis have led to a growing concern to address the environmental dimensions of the cities. The number of citizens' complaints concerning environmental pollution is greatest in the megalopolis. There is a need to address the legacies of pollution and dereliction from the industrial era as well as the side effects of burgeoning traffic congestion. The urge to compete as an attractive business environment is joining with wider social awareness to force environmental issues to the forefront of urban development policy. Concern centers on the need for an environmentally sustainable urban future.

To a large degree the environmental problems that now characterize Japanese cities have arisen because during the last twenty-five years Japanese have superimposed a vast industrial or urban economy upon an already very intensive agricultural base, in a country possessing an unusually low proportion of flatland. The exceptional congestion, arising from the juxtaposition of tightly concentrated industrial plants with no-less-crowded residential areas, has led to some of the most severe environmental stress in the urban areas. Land shortage may be regarded as the root cause of many of these problems. Demand for urban land greatly outstrips the supply, and in consequence, land prices are high. High land prices in large cities of the megalopolis have resulted in the widening of commuting zones around these cities. The excessive overcrowding of Japanese commuter trains is also partly due to high land prices: the construction of additional railway tracks to relieve pressure during rush hours would involve purchase of expensive urban land.

Among the environmental issues, air pollution caused by emissions from vehicles remains a serious problem in larger cities of the Japanese Megalopolis. In May 1996 patients suffering from air pollution diseases filed suit in the Tokyo District Court against the central government, the Tokyo metropolitan government, the Metropolitan Expressway Public Corporation, and seven companies that manufacture diesel vehicles. The victims demanded a ban on the emission of pollutants as well as compensation. This was the first lawsuit on Tokyo's air pollution, which is getting worse every year, and the first lawsuit nationally that focused on traffic pollution from vehicle exhausts and placed the responsibility for such pollution on the vehicle manufacturers—Toyota, Nissan, Mitsubishi, Hino, Isuzu, Nissan Diesel, and Mazda. A ruling in 1995 recognized the central government and the expressway public corporation, which constructs and manages roads, as responsible for air pollution. According to research in 1994 by the Tokyo Council for Air Pollution Monitoring Movement, the average concentration of nitrogen dioxide in Tokyo was 0.068 parts per million, far exceeding the government's standard of 0.060 ppm. In Tokyo and in the other cities of the megalopolis, 70 percent of the nitrogen dioxide in the atmosphere is discharged by vehicles. Nitrogen oxides are a principal contributor to the photochemical smog, which first became a public concern in Tokyo in July 1970. Since then it has appeared in all the major cities of the megalopolis.

In 1988 the central government canceled the designation of Tokyo as a polluted area, thereby ceasing to recognize patients suffering from the effects of environmental pollution. There are now 500,000 to 600,000 patients in Tokyo suffering from air pollution diseases who are not recognized as such. The number of recognized patients based on the metropolitan government's regulation between 1988 and 1994 increased threefold. In major lawsuits regarding pollution-related diseases, the rights of the victims to compensation has been established, and enterprises must accept financial responsibility for damages they inflict on the community. Even so, when environmental goals conflict with "stable" growth in the Japanese cities, the latter generally prevails.

URBAN DEVELOPMENT AND HISTORICAL PRESERVATION IN THE MEGALOPOLIS

Rapid urban development has transformed the central core of many cities in the megalopolis. For example, the landmark Marunouchi Building near Tokyo Central Station was torn down as part of the redevelopment project. Actions like this will result in erasing the remaining traces of prewar Tokyo and other cities—not to mention the heritage of the Edo period and the Meiji era. An urban development policy that emphasizes coexistence with history is required (Asano 1999). In the case of Tokyo and other urban centers of the megalopolis, this means coexisting not only with temples, shrines, and historic landmarks from the Edo period but also with the more modern heritage from the Meiji, Taisho, and early Showa periods.

Until recently, however, Japan's efforts at historical preservation were directed overwhelmingly at architecture dating to the Edo period and earlier. Those few structures remaining from the Nara period (710–94) are all designated national treasures. It was not until the 1960s that the preservation of Meiji architecture received any attention at all. As Japan approached the fiftieth anniversary of World War II, there emerged a sense of the need to assign prewar architecture a permanent place in the nation's architectural heritage. Around that time, Japan's Agency for Cultural Affairs announced a policy of considering structures completed at least fifty years earlier—in other words, prewar architecture—as important cultural properties. At the same time, the agency demonstrated its determination to substantially extend the concept of cultural property to encompass not only architectural monuments in the conventional sense but also monuments of civil engineering, industrial facilities, and other large-scale compound structures. As part of the cultural heritage embodying the progress of Japan's modernization, these are sometimes described as *kindaika isan,* or modernization heritage. The designation of Hiroshima's Atomic Bomb Dome as a national historic site—and its subsequent inclusion on the UNESCO World Heritage list—can be seen as part of this trend.

As of April 1998, there were forty-nine areas designated by the Agency for Cultural Affairs as historical preservation districts under a program begun in 1976. They range in location from the city of Hakodate in Hokkaido to the island of Taketomijima in Okinawa. A significant trend that has emerged in recent years in Japan is a new emphasis on finding a practical use for the properties that are protected. One notable example of this application in Tokyo is the simultaneous preservation and revitalization of a site that includes the head office of the Dai-Ichi Mutual Life Insurance Company (Daiichi Seimei Kan) on Hibiya-dori, right across the moat from the Imperial Palace, and the adjoining Norin Chukin Bank Yurakucho Building. The Daiichi Seimei Kan, famous as the building that housed the offices of the supreme commander for the Allied Powers—the general headquarters of the post–World War II Allied Occupation—was completed in 1938, making it the last major prewar edifice in Japan. The Norin Chukin Bank building is a well-known structure in an or-

thodox classical style, distinguished by its precise architectural proportions and Ionic columns. The notion of coexistence of preservation and development is gaining momentum in Japan. It is a welcome development because it helps preserve a city's historical continuity and gives it character. For large cities of the megalopolis, this approach opens up a whole new world of possibilities for redevelopment geared to enhancing urban functions while preserving large-scale monuments of modern architecture.

The Kunitachi municipal government in Tokyo is trying to save the Kunitachi Station building on the Chuo Line of the East Japan Railway from demolition. The station, built in 1926, and the Daigaku Dori (street) leading to Hitotsubashi University are regarded as symbols of the city. The building has walls that hide its structural pillars and has intrinsic value as a cultural asset.

THE STRUCTURE OF THE TOKYO METROPOLITAN REGION

The Tokyo Metropolitan Area, called Shutoken, comprises the region within a 93-mile (150-km) radius of central Tokyo (fig. 8.10). It extends into the surrounding Saitama, Chiba, Kanagawa, Ibaraki, Tochigi, Gumma, and Yamanashi Prefectures. The

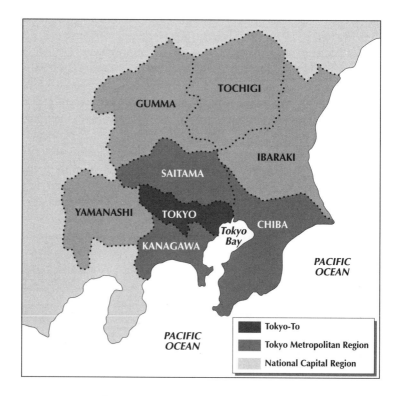

Fig. 8.10. Tokyo Metropolitan Area.

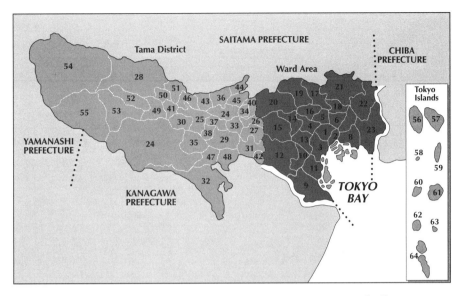

Fig. 8.11. Tokyo city wards.

Wards		Tama District: cities, towns and villages			
1 Chiyoda	13 Shibuya	24 Hachioji	35 Hino	46 Musashimurayama
2 Chuo	14 Nakano	25 Tachikawa	36 Higashimurayama	47 Tama
3 Minato	15 Suginami	26 Musashino	37 Kokubunji	48 Inagi
4 Shinjuku	16 Toshima	27 Mitaka	38 Kunitachi	49 Akigawa
5 Bunkyo	17 Kita	28 Ome	39 Tanashi	50 Hamura
6 Taito	18 Arakawa	29 Fuchu	40 Hoya	51 Mizuho
7 Sumida	19 Itabashi	30 Akishima	41 Fussa	52 Hinode
8 Koto	20 Nerima	31 Chofu	42 Komae	53 Itsukaichi
9 Shingawa	21 Adachi	32 Machida	43 Higashiyamato	54 Hinohara
10 Meguro	22 Katsushika	33 Koganei	44 Kiyose	55 Okutama
11 Ota	23 Edogawa	34 Kodaira	45 Higashikurume	
12 Setagaya				

Islands: towns and villages

56 Oshima	59 Kozushima	62 Hachijo
57 Toshima	60 Miyake	63 Aogashima
58 Niijima	61 Mikurajima	64 Ogasawara

suburbanization of Tokyo and other major metropolitan areas has been investigated by Kohei Okamoto (1997). The Tokyo Metropolitan Area is the economic, political, and cultural center of the nation. Yasuo Masai (1990) provides an excellent account of the growth of Tokyo from a feudal city to a world city.

Urban Tokyo, including the Tama district, had a population of 12 million in 2003, of which nearly 8 million lived in 23 wards of central Tokyo (see fig. 8.11). The city grew around Edo Castle, the present site of the Imperial Palace, with a samurai residential district on the castle's western side (see fig. 8.12). To the east marshland was reclaimed and a commercial and industrial area developed, taking advantage of river and canal transportation. The city grew rapidly as merchants and artisans moved to Edo. Jinnai Hidenobu (1995) provides a very good description of the form of Tokyo and its roots in the land, culture, and traditions of Edo. The population reached 1 million in 1720. At the Meiji Restoration Edo was renamed Tokyo, and the imperial family moved to Edo Castle in 1869. Tokyo grew steadily as the political, commercial, and financial center of the country (Center for Urban Studies 1988). The residential structure of Tokyo in the Taisho era as it became industrialized is described by Ken'ichi Ueno (1985). In 1923 an earthquake destroyed most of the city, and again during World War II it was destroyed by bombing.

After the war, during the period of economic re-

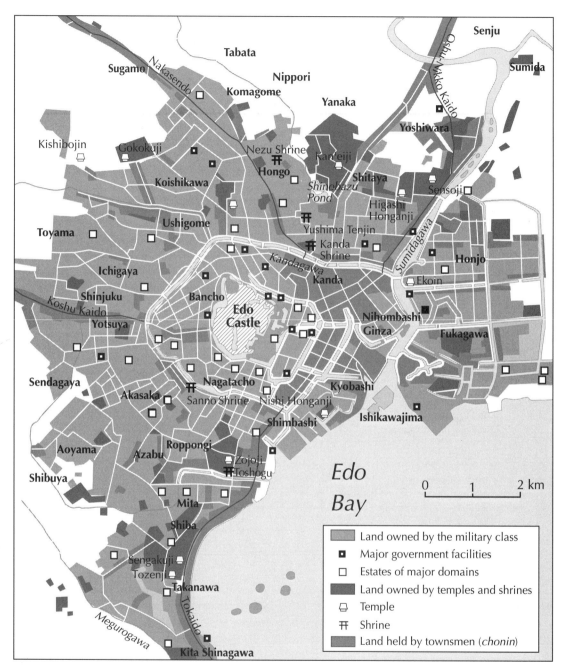

Fig. 8.12. Early-nineteenth-century Tokyo. Based on Masai 1990.

covery, most of the large Japanese corporations selected Tokyo as the center for their business operations. The population of Tokyo increased from 6.3 million in 1950 to 9.7 million in 1960 and by 1965 reached 10.9 million, resulting in serious housing shortages, environmental problems, and skyrocketing land prices. In the 1980s the Tokyo Metropolitan Area emerged as a world financial center along with London and New York, and specialized financial business and other high-order functions became concentrated in the metropolis. Tokyo's transformation into a world city influenced the steep rise of residential and commercial land prices in the late 1980s. The rapidly spiraling land prices since the

Arakawa Ward Office, Tokyo. Arakawa is one of the twenty-three municipal wards of Tokyo; it has a population of about 184,000. Photo by P.P. Karan.

mid-1980s have put home ownership beyond the means of most Tokyoites. Hirohisa Yamada (1992) has analyzed the regional differences in land prices in the three major metropolitan areas of Tokyo, Osaka, and Nagoya.

Along the Tokyo Bay waterfront, land has been reclaimed for a number of development projects. In Yokohama, a new center with hotels, parks, a convention center, housing, and attractive commercial buildings has been developed as part of the Minato Mirai 21 project on reclaimed land. It is designed to attract business from the Tokyo area. Japan's tallest building, the seventy-story, 971-foot-tall (296-meter-tall) Landmark Tower, is in the Minato Mirai center of Yokohama; it opened in 1993. During its 134-year history, Yokohama has usually been a place verging on its future. An insignificant village with ninety households, Yokohama was established as the first treaty port in 1859 under the Japan-U.S. Treaty of Amity and Commerce. Though devastated by wars and earthquakes, Yokohama has developed into one of the world's great ports and is Japan's second-largest city, with a population of 3.5 million.

At the other side of Tokyo Bay, on a bustling plot of landfill, is Tokyo Disneyland. With 16.7 million visitors in 1998, each spending on average about one hundred dollars, the park, less than ten miles from downtown Tokyo, has surpassed the original Magic Kingdoms in the United States in attendance (the Magic Kingdom at Walt Disney World, Florida, had 15.6 million visitors in 1998; Disneyland, Anaheim, California, had 13.7 million).

Globalization and Urban Restructuring of Tokyo

Increasing integration of the Japanese economy with the global economy has impacted Tokyo's urban structure by making it a command-and-control center for the multinational corporations and a center of global finance. As the Japanese capital extended its business reach to overseas countries through export, merger, and investment, Tokyo assumed command-and-control functions to coordinate its global business. Tokyo's financial market expanded rapidly in the late 1980s, and it became a world financial center along with New York and London. The rapid expansion of the money market, coupled with the increase in the demand for office buildings (due to the expansion of foreign financial institutions and the professional service industries), brought increased speculation in stocks and land. After the burst of the asset bubble, Japanese banks found themselves saddled with a huge number of bad loans, and the foreign financial institutions started moving to Hong Kong and Singapore, resulting in the "financial hollowing" of the Tokyo market. During the 1990s, although Tokyo maintained its dominant position domestically, it lost ground to international competitors because of its closed financial system. The collapse of the Japanese asset bubble made evident the weaknesses of Tokyo—a "closed global city" heavily influenced by imperfect competition with leftovers of a national protectionist policy.

A transformation of Tokyo, termed "urban restructuring," was brought about by a cluster of poli-

Field Report

Magic Kingdom on Tokyo Bay

Tokyo Disneyland offers a major contrast with the financial train wreck outside Paris known as Euro Disneyland, which opened in 1992 with soaring expectations. In 1993 Euro Disneyland reported a $905 million loss. Back in Japan, a market that Disney entered a decade ago with misgivings, it is a different story entirely. The Oriental Land Company, the owner of Tokyo Disneyland, enjoyed a pretax profit of $202 million in 1993. And that was in the middle of the worst recession in Japan since the end of World War II. Tokyo Disneyland celebrated its twentieth anniversary on April 15, 2003. The Tokyo Disney Resort, comprising Disneyland and the adjacent DisneySea (which opened in 2001), had 24.82 million visitors in 2002, with consolidated revenue of 331.7 billion yen ($2.8 billion).

A look at these two overseas parks offers some harsh lessons in the vexing uncertainty of translating American icons into other cultures, and in how important timing can be for such overseas projects. As different as Japan is from the West, the twenty-year-old Tokyo theme park is an enormous success. Increasingly, it is drawing affluent young people from all over Asia. Cinderella does not wear a kimono here, and Winnie the Pooh has not forsaken his beloved honey for sushi. Except for some subtle changes, Tokyo Disneyland is a near replica of the American original. Almost all the signs are in English, with occasional lines of Japanese and, now that other Asians are coming here, Chinese. Various versions of the Stars and Stripes flutter atop reproductions of American-style buildings.

It is so sanitized and precise in its depiction of an unthreatening, fantasy America that, in an odd sort of way, the park has become totally Japanese. Indeed, the park is reminiscent of the traditional Japanese garden, which reproduces a tightly confined version of nature that is supposed to be more satisfying and perfect than the real thing.

The Walt Disney Company studied the Japanese and European sites extensively, and yet it failed to anticipate the enthusiasm in Tokyo and the difficulties in France that explain the contrast between the fortunes of the Japanese and European theme parks. When Oriental Land first brought the idea of building a Magic Kingdom in Japan to Disney executives two decades ago, it was a hard sell. After some persuading, Disney finally decided to go ahead with the project in Tokyo. But it took a cautious course and rejected a chance to buy an interest in the park. That decision has cost the company hundreds of millions of dollars. Disney has control over many aspects of the Tokyo park's design and operations, but it collects royalties only from the park's intake—about 10 percent of the revenue from admissions and rides and 5 percent on the sale of food, drinks, and souvenirs. To make things worse, Disney also hurt itself by cashing in $700 million in 1988 for twenty years' worth of anticipated future royalties.

Who would have thought a people whose history is a tapestry of samurai warriors, rice farmers, and Buddhism would take so quickly to Mark Twain, the Old West, and Peter Pan? And who would have thought that Europeans would be so much less enamored of the Disney retinue?

Tokyo Disneyland has also benefited from superb timing—one of the reasons that Euro Disneyland has done so poorly. The European Magic Kingdom opened in the midst of a deep recession in 1992, whereas the Tokyo park opened in 1983, early in one of the most economically vibrant decades in Japan. The 1980s was a decade of great economic affluence and an era when Japanese society started to feel a part of world culture. Tokyo Disneyland really became a symbol, for many people, of Japan's entry into world culture. When people looked for a model of an affluent society at that time, they looked to the United States. It was as natural for Japanese to enjoy Disneyland as it was for Japanese to go to McDonald's. As it happened, McDonald's was establishing itself around the same time as Japan's largest fast food chain.

cies that led to the conversion of urban space and urban functions into new forms. The closure and relocation of manufacturing firms, the expansion of the service industry, the concentration of globally linked economic functions, the proposal to develop a multipolar urban structure to create several subcenters to accommodate different business needs, the greater utilization of private capital in public construction and infrastructure projects, and the rapid movement toward an information society led to the process of urban restructuring and the flourishing of several urban redevelopment projects, including the massive Tokyo Waterfront Sub-Center Development project (Rinkai Funu-Toshin). Urban restructuring has produced significant economic and social impacts. Horizontal and vertical expansion and renewal of old business locations have increased the space available for global control functions, such as financial institutions and headquarters of multinational companies, in the central area and in new sites such as Tokyo Waterfront. The control-supporting functions both inside and outside big corporations and regional control functions have relocated to subcenters and suburban areas. The research and development divisions of high-tech industries have located in suburban areas. The basic pattern of change has been to remove old and unnecessary functions from central districts and to make space available for new global control functions.

One outcome of restructuring is that the number of foreign residents has increased considerably during the past fifteen years. Most of them are mi-grant laborers from East Asian countries. Males are employed as manual workers in construction industries or as cleaners and waiters, while the females work as hostesses, dancers, and maids. Although the number of foreign residents is still small in comparison with their numbers in other world cities, their impact is significant in Japanese cities. The expansion of business space into traditional urban neighborhoods has caused conflict in the central districts and inner areas. The rapid increase in land prices has deepened the split between urban residents in Tokyo. For those who could pursue the exchange value of space, it meant a considerable increase in the value of fixed assets. For ordinary citizens, who make use of space only for housing, the rise in land prices increased the costs of living such as rent or property tax, forcing a lot of people to move out of central Tokyo.

The waterfront development illustrates the crucial role of the state in the strategy of global city formulation. In addition, the alliance between the Japanese government and the national business community was a major driving force behind the urban restructuring of Tokyo. Tokyo waterfront development spreads over reclaimed islands in Tokyo Bay. The site is only 4 miles (6.4 km) from the city center and has good access to both international and domestic airports. It was planned as one of three subcenters for urban development, along with the area around Tokyo Central Station and the former Shiodome fleet station. But the main project was the Waterfront Sub-Center. The development is divided

Tokyo Bay City, a part of the Tokyo Waterfront Sub-Center, is situated on 1,092 acres (442 ha) of reclaimed land. This waterfront development comprises a variety of commercial and business enterprises as well as residential areas. The global and informational requirements of the times have been anticipated, and the waterfront urban subcenter is an attempt to reorient the structure of Tokyo by moving functions away from the nucleus. Photo by P.P. Karan.

into four areas: the Aomi area, with business and commercial facilities associated with Tokyo's Teleport Town; the Ariake-Minami area, with international convention facilities; the Ariake-Kita area, featuring housing with rich amenities adjacent to Ariake Seaside Park; and the Daiba area along the seaside, with a combined commercial and leisure zone and with high-rise municipal housing. The objectives were to build an ideal city subcenter where environmental concern and future technology would strike a balance among working, living, and leisure space; the development was expected to adjust to the global society and the information society through facilities for information exchange and international conventions. The Tokyo Waterfront Sub-Center is an example of an entrepreneurial center in which the Tokyo Metropolitan Government (TMG) took a proactive stance to promote development in order to hook up to the global economy. The TMG had planned a very unique exhibition called Tokyo Frontier on the waterfront site to highlight how a futuristic city may be built with the aid of technology to improve urban life. As the general economic situation deteriorated in the 1990s, the Tokyo Frontier exhibition ran into trouble and was called off in 1995.

Functional Areas of Tokyo

Tokyo is different from other cities of the world (Cybriwsky 1998). It is one of the few great cities left that has not been reduced to blandness by sociological and economic segregation regulations that decree zones for residential districts, shopping, small industries, and offices. In Tokyo and other Japanese cities, various functions are all mixed up together in a great savory stew, and every part of town, almost every street, has in it all the stuff of life, not merely an antiseptically zoned part of it. The sights of the city mix in a huge Brueghel picture everywhere: a merchant's mansion with a tinsmith shop in its shadow, and next door a tiny restaurant where eel is broiled and sauced, a policeman's booth a few steps away, a half-dozen bars around the corner, then an insurance office, a grocery, and a secondhand bookstore.

Geographically, Tokyo consists of a series of densely built subcenters or districts, each centered on a train or subway station (see fig. 8.13). Among these are (1) Shinjuku, with an emphasis on administration and business, (2) Shibuya, the information and fashion hub (Cybriwsky 1988), (3) Ikebukuro, (4) Ueno-Asakusa, the traditional cultural center, (5) Kinshicho-Kameido industrial and cultural subcenter, (6) Osaki, with its advanced technological information, and (7) Tokyo Waterfront Sub-Center. Each of these districts retains its distinctive character; others have evolved into commuter service centers. Despite the mixed land use, a number of distinctive functional areas can be identified in the city (Takahashi 1985). These urban subcenters, forming a multiple-nuclei pattern, are spaced in a 4-mile (6.4-km) radius from Tokyo Central Station. The subcenters consist of department stores, markets, amusement and cultural facilities, restaurants, banks, and high-rise office and apartment buildings.

Shinjuku, one of the major urban subcenters of Tokyo. During the Edo period (1603–1868), Shinjuku was a post-station town on Koshu Kaido (highway). It developed rapidly in the 1920s. Photo by P.P. Karan.

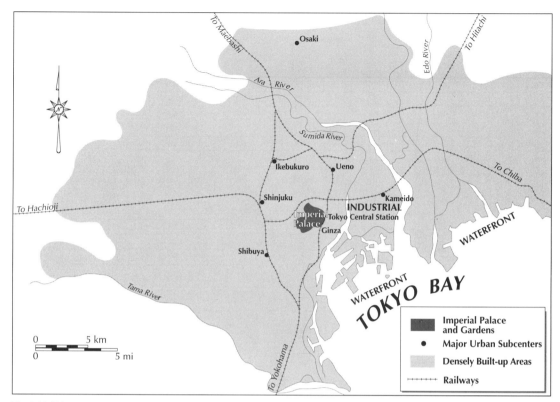

Fig. 8.13. Tokyo urban subcenters.

Central Business District On the eastern side of the Tokyo Central Station is Nihonbashi, the commercial district, lined with department stores, shops, and restaurants (see fig. 8.14). This commercial area extends south toward Ginza, famous for elegant and expensive shops. To the west of the station is Marunouchi, headquarters of major Japanese banks and financial institutions. About one hundred years ago the Marunouchi area was sold off by the government and developed as a business area. It was an area of mainly redbrick buildings. After World War II and during the period of rapid economic growth, the area was rebuilt with the present-day buildings. A new wave of rebuilding has started here. In 1998

A large apartment complex in Oji, Toshima Ward, Tokyo. Housing in Japan has changed dramatically in the past century as a result of rapid urbanization, population pressures, changes in family and social relationships, and the influence of Western architecture. In large cities multi-unit dwellings have become the norm, although a majority of people aspire to own their homes. In addition to the publicly subsidized *danchi* apartments, private developers have built a large number of mid- to high-rise apartment buildings since the 1960s. Individual units are for sale or rent in the privately built complexes. The average cost of a house in Tokyo in 1999 was about 56 million yen, and the average floor space was about 1,216 feet (113 sq m). Photo by P.P. Karan.

Mitsubishi Real Estate, which owns a substantial part of the land in the Marunouchi area, announced plans for the demolition and rebuilding of the Marunouchi Building, the oldest office block in the area. The old Marunouchi Building, like many of the imposing office blocks nearby, was constructed at a time when

there was a strict height limit of 101.7 feet (31 m). From the roof of this relatively low-level building, which is to be devoted entirely to shops and restaurants, will project a thirty-six-floor skyscraper containing space that is to be let out as offices. Banking on the Marunouchi financial district's potential as a

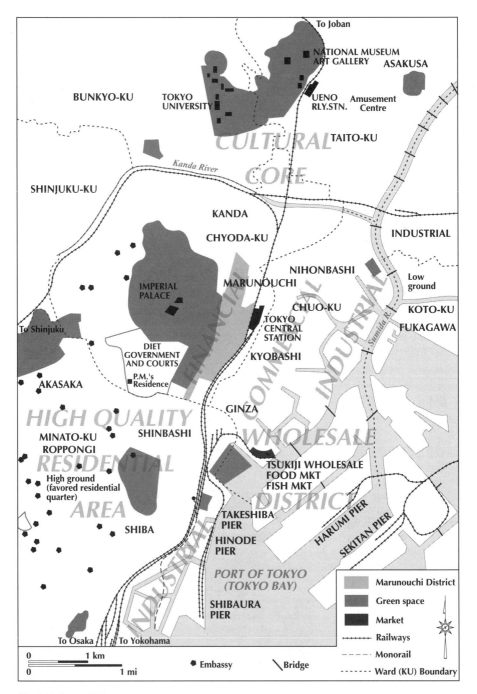

Fig. 8.14. Central Tokyo.

Ginza shopping and entertainment district, southeast of the Imperial Palace, Tokyo, in the evening. Ginza centers on a 0.68-mile (1.1-km) section of Chuo Dori (street). The district takes its name (meaning "silver mint") from a mint for casting silver coins that was built in this area in 1612 by the Tokugawa shogunate. The completion of the railway between Yokohama and nearby Shimbashi in 1872, and the proximity of Ginza to Tsukiji, where foreigners resided, led to the rapid assimilation of Western culture, and Ginza emerged as a fashionable shopping center. The highest land price in Japan (11.68 million yen per square meter) was recorded in Chuo Dori in Ginza. Photo by P.P. Karan.

place for grown-ups to shop, Naka-dori Avenue in the district is attracting development projects that mix business with pleasure. Tomorrow Land, Zucca, Comme des Garcons, Issey Miyake's Pleats Please, Hermes, Prada, and Giorgio Armani are among the fashion stores that have recently opened in the Marunouchi to provide a relaxing shopping experience for busy working people. Many of the stores have been attracted by the area's history and cultural connections. Because of the area's proximity to Tokyo Central Station, it seems likely that Marunouchi will turn out to be another retailing area.

Along about seven o'clock every evening, Ginza sedately ends one life and ecstatically leaps into another, into a neon nighttime delirium. Then about midnight the dancing lights and the high laughter stop; Ginza's wild screeching in pleasure suddenly dims and disappears. Located in East Ginza is the classic Kabuki-za theater. The site, once known as *kabikicho,* was an area with a handful of prestigious government-authorized theaters in the Edo period. It has been a center of Japan's theatrical circle for about four hundred years.

The old Tokyo Central Station building is a symbol of the Taisho era (1912–26) culture, which makes it an oasis among the skyscrapers surrounding the area. In 1914, when the station was first built, only one side existed, much to the delight of Mitsubishi, the major landowner and developer of the Marunouchi district; Mitsubishi later developed the area into a commercial node. The Yaesu side of the station was not completed until after the 1923 earthquake. The designer

of the original Tokyo Central Station, Tatsuno Kingo (1854–1919), was a pioneer Western-style architect of the Meiji period. The station's redbrick building had three stories when it was completed in 1914, but its third floor and domes were destroyed in a 1945 air raid. The station was renovated into its present two-story structure in 1947. It is planned to completely restore the building to its majestic prewar visage, which will take five to six years.

Between the Ginza shopping streets and the Kasumigaseki government office district lies Hibiya Park, the first Western-style garden in Japan. It offers a quiet haven away from the surrounding busy central city. Nearly one hundred years old, the park has been the scene of numerous historic incidents. In September 1905, citizens frustrated with the Portsmouth Treaty that ended the Russo-Japanese War staged a riot in Hibiya Park and clashed with military troops. In 1960 the chairman of the Japan Socialist Party was assassinated by a seventeen-year-old ultra-rightist during a speech at the park.

Back in 1602, Hibiya and the surrounding area of the central district formed an inlet in Edo Bay, now called Tokyo Bay. The outer garden of the Imperial Palace was a delta area with many tidal inlets. By 1603 the Hibiya inlet was reclaimed, and Edo's coastline began to extend into the harbor as the city continued to expand. From the mid-seventeenth century to the late eighteenth century, the site of the present Hibiya Park was the residence of a daimyo, Lord Matsudaira of Hizen Province, now known as Nagasaki Prefecture. Many daimyo residences in the

The redbrick building of Tokyo Station, designed by Tatsuno Kingo, a leading Meiji- and Taisho-era architect, was partially completed in 1914. Its third floor and domes were destroyed in a 1945 air raid. The station was renovated in 1947; there is a plan to completely restore the old station building, which was a symbol of the Taisho era (1912–26) culture. The renovation will make it an oasis among the surrounding skyscrapers. The bullet trains link all the major cities of the megalopolis from Tokyo to northern Kyushu, welding all the metropolitan areas into a higher order of urban structure. Commuters living within a distance of 44–62 miles (70–100 km) from their workplace in the megalopolis are now increasingly using the bullet trains. Photo by P.P. Karan.

city were turned into military drill grounds after the Meiji Restoration in 1868, when the newly established central government replaced the daimyo and officially changed the name of the national capital from Edo to Tokyo. Lord Matsudaira's residence on the reclaimed Hibiya land became a drill ground of the Imperial Japanese Army in 1884. In 1889 the government decided to construct an urban park on the site. The park was gifted with American dogwood trees sent in 1915 from the United States in return for cherry trees sent by Japan for planting along the Potomac River in Washington, D.C.

The inner-city wards of Arakawa, Taito, Kita and Sumida, adjacent to the central business district, are characterized by economic stress resulting from the shrinkage of manufacturing, high unemployment, and low levels of investment to develop the area commerce (Nakabayashi 1987). These areas have poor physical environment and housing conditions with a larger concentration of tenement houses, an increasing elderly population, and the subsequent loss of economic vitality. However, the inner-city problem in Tokyo is not as severe as in American cities.

Cultural Core   The Ueno district, with many big museums, art galleries, bookshops, temples, and the zoo, along with Tokyo University, forms a major cultural core. It has been a popular area for outings and excursions since the Edo period. In addition, it has developed into a major shopping district. To the east of Ueno is the oldest temple in Tokyo, Asakusa Kannon (Sensoji), in the heart of the Shitamachi area,

where there are many shops selling traditional handicrafts. To the south of Ueno is Kanda, renowned for its bookshops and universities, and Akihabara, famous for its discount stores selling electronic and electric appliances.

This area includes part of Shitamachi, the small area in the northeastern part of Edo that was set aside as a place for merchants and craftsmen to pursue their trades in support of the samurai class, who lived in other sections of Edo. Merchants' shops lined the main streets, with one-story tenement houses behind them. These and other buildings were connected by narrow alleys. Living quarters usually included a small area, big enough for about 4.5 tatami mats (about 40 square feet or 3.7 square meters), and a separate entryway that opened onto the street and doubled as a kitchen. Lavatories and running water (or wells) were shared. With such small living quarters, there was an almost complete lack of privacy, and as a result, Shitamachi people were friendly and helpful toward each other. The flavor of Shitamachi is being lost in the frenzy of Tokyo's urban renewal. The Shitamachi area still remains a commercial and entertainment district.

Information Core   Various media and allied industries are concentrated in Shibuya, Akasaka, and Roppongi, where Tokyo Broadcasting Company (TBS), Asahi National Broadcasting Company, and Japan Broadcasting Company (NHK) are located. The high concentration of information industries and services in Shibuya has made this area a "media

Field Report

Akihabara: The World's Most Famous Electronic Toy Town

An electronic-gadget mecca since the 1960s, Tokyo's Akihabara district glares with neon and bright signs that beckon from shops piled high with boom boxes, electronic goods, and appliances. Teams of young women dressed in space suits jabber promotional slogans in squeaky voices, while others in miniskirts sing along to karaoke machines, trying to entice passersby into their shops.

Akihabara started after World War II as an open-air market located between Ogawamachi and Kanda-Sudocho in Tokyo. At first all the stores sold textiles and everyday goods. But one incident turned most of the stores into electrical shops almost overnight. One shop began stocking secondhand vacuum tubes, a basic radio part, for students of a nearby electrical engineering school, today's Tokyo Denki University. These became an instant hit with the students, who used them to make and repair radios, then the main source of entertainment in Japan. This prompted other shops in the market to stock vacuum tubes and other electronic parts. By 1950, of the 120 shops in the district, about 50 specialized in electronics.

In 1948 the Allied Occupation's GHQ ordered all open-air shop owners off the streets to enable roads to be built. The Tokyo metropolitan government, with the help of the now-defunct Japanese National Railway, prepared new accommodations for the shops under the elevated railway tracks of Akihabara Station. From this beginning the district developed into a distinctive electronics retail area.

The Japanese spend about 6 trillion yen on consumer electronics each year, 5 percent of it in Akihabara. About 110,000 people shop in the district each weekday and 350,000 on weekends. After three decades of thriving business, Akihabara is now facing a slowdown. The economic slump and the lack of new products have cut into sales, forcing the enterprises of Akihabara to search for new ways to maintain the district's allure. Instead of the usual signs like Panasonic, Sony, and Sanyo, one prominent building in the district displays a huge picture of "Sonic the Hedgehog," a video game. Many home electronic shops are deserted by all but their sales staff, who stand idle in front of banks of screens and stereos. But in Sega Hi-Tech Land, groups of workers take a break from the office to crowd around computer games and bet on miniature horse races.

Reeling from the double punch of a stagnant economy and the challenge of discount chain stores, Tokyo's internationally famed electronics district is trying to diversify before the lights become too dim. Minami Musen, which started in the 1950s as a wholesaler of electric appliances, has removed all appliances from its shop and has started selling designer goods, wristwatches, jewelry, furs, and other luxury items at discounts that make airport duty-free shop owners turn pale. Many large stores have started specializing. For example, Laox's computer-kan now boasts the world's largest single computer retail shop in both sales and the volume and variety of stock.

About 40 percent of the district's weekend shoppers are foreigners. To cater to this huge group of customers, many stores employ foreigners as shop clerks. Nearly 30 percent of the foreign shoppers are residents in Japan, and 70 percent are tourists from China, South Korea, and Taiwan who want to take advanced high-tech equipment back home. Also, ethnic Japanese from Latin America often visit Akihabara shops to stock up on electronic goods before leaving for home. Growing purchases by foreign shoppers have helped offset an overall sales decline.

Although Asians and Latin Americans with Japanese ancestry make up the majority of Akihabara's foreign shoppers, some stores, such as Nishikawa Musen, are popular among shoppers from Russia and eastern Europe. For Russian customers, the shops stock radios that can receive the frequencies of Russian shortwave radio broadcasts as well as electric appliances for export to the former Communist bloc.

town." The offices of various television and information service businesses are called, together, the fashionable Small Office Home Office, or SOHO. This area is often referred to as Shibuya Alley after the Silicon Alley of Manhattan. Furthermore, multimedia-allied industries have located also in Ochano-mizu, Kanda, and Akihabara, forming the Ochanomizu Triangle, and the animated cartoon industries concentrated in Musashino terrace areas such as Kokubunji and Koganei form the Musashino Plateau. With the development of the information and cultural amusement industries, urban redevelopment projects related to cultural recreational facilities such as movie theaters or concert halls have become common.

Shibuya has also emerged as an area where teenage fashions and consumer trends are born before spreading to the far reaches of the Japanese archipelago and to Taipei, Seoul, and Shanghai. Shibuya became known as a mecca for young women in the 1970s, as Japan grew into a rich country and department stores opened up. Back then, the women were college students. As Japan grew richer, younger and younger girls began coming to Shibuya, so that it is now more a place for junior high school girls. Shibuya has also traditionally been a place where men had liaisons with geisha who worked in expensive restaurants, or with lovers in the area's inns. That tradition survives in the many so-called love hotels and sex businesses that dot a part of Shibuya.

Wholesale Food District   In the south, near the Port of Tokyo, lies the wholesale food and fish market. Tsukiji is the principal fish market (Bestor 2001).

Thousands of wholesalers and retailers use the market each day. The Tsukiji district awakes at five every morning, when fish brokers start the day's bidding. It takes less than ten seconds for a fish to find a buyer. Huge frozen tunas are carted out one after another. Forty thousand retailers visit the market each day to buy 2,600 tons of fish and 1,600 tons of vegetables.

The market reflects the sweeping changes affecting Japanese society. Foreign workers are rapidly increasing in number. About three hundred foreigners work at the market, the majority of them Chinese. But there are also many Bangladeshis and Iranians. The increase in foreign workers started in 1988, replacing young Japanese who hate the jobs described with three Ks—*kitsui* (hard), *kitanai* (dirty), and *kiken* (dangerous); foreigners now constitute an important part of the wholesale fish market's workforce.

The wholesale market moved to Tsukiji from Nihombashi after the Great Earthquake in 1923. It started trading fish and vegetables as the Central Wholesale Market in 1935. For nearly sixty-five years, except for the time when food was rationed during and after World War II, the market has been "Tokyo's kitchen." The development of a truck transportation network has expanded the quantity of merchandise so much that the 54.4-acre (22-ha) market is now too small. A multistory market building is being planned by the local government.

Port District   South of the commercial and business district lies the Port of Tokyo, with several wharves and terminals. The port has faced major restructuring since the late 1970s. One source of change

The Tsukiji wholesale fish market occupies 56 acres (22.7 ha) on the edge of Tokyo Bay. It ranks first among the fish markets of the world, handling more than four hundred types of seafood imported from sixty countries on six continents. Tsukiji is a small community where all work together toward the common goal of moving the fish as quickly as possible from the sea to the sushi bar or the supermarket. Photo by P.P. Karan.

Manufacturing industries are concentrated along the banks of the Sumida River in Tokyo Metropolitan Area, with numerous plants making a wide variety of consumer goods. The industrial belt continues along the coast toward the lower reaches of the Tama River in Kawasaki and farther on to Yokohama. Photo by P.P. Karan.

has been industrial restructuring. The port was essentially an industrial port surrounded by shipbuilding and repair firms, the petrochemical industry, warehouses, and energy production sites like the gas works. As the Japanese industrial structure changed, these sites became obsolete, while the growing service-sector industry needs demanded more space. The changes in transport technology and distribution have also affected the port. Containerization of shipments and the changing pattern of distribution of goods required new port facilities, and the port area expanded, which resulted in creating unused property and vacant land on the old obsolete facilities. The Port Authority of Tokyo envisions land uses such as offices, housing, and leisure facilities for this vacant property.

Major projects are under way to develop the waterfront area. The 1,106-acre (448-ha) Teleport Town development in Tokyo Bay, begun in 1987, is intended to provide homes for 60,000 people, offices for 110,000 workers, and leisure facilities for the entire city. Financing problems brought about by the fall in real estate prices in 1992 and difficulty finding tenants have delayed the project's schedule.

Manufacturing District The manufacturing area extends along the Sumida River into Shitamachi. Concrete warehouses and factories with rusting metal roofs line the river. Industrial areas now extend into Kawasaki and Yokohama, forming the Keihin Industrial District of Japan. Large plants along the waterfront are devoted to manufacturing of electric machinery, precision apparatus, and fertilizers;

iron and steel; and petroleum refining. Publishing and printing businesses are concentrated in the city.

Residential Areas Residential areas are generally mixed with business or commercial use in Japanese cities. In the 1950s the city expanded beyond the wards into the neighboring prefectures. Large housing complexes developed east and north of the city. Akasaka-Aoyama, Shibuya, and Meguro have expensive residential districts. Since 1965 large-scale development of new towns in peripheral areas, such as Tama New Town, west of Tokyo, and Tsukuba city, northeast of Tokyo, has relieved the congestion in Tokyo.

About two miles from the Imperial Palace, a large residential complex tower, called Roppongi Hills, with offices, shops, restaurants, and theaters, opened in 2003. For decades fear of earthquakes made Tokyo a sprawling city, but now earthquake mitigation techniques seem to be assuring people that living in a skyscraper is just as safe, and more pleasant than the long train commute each day. Paris, New York, and central Tokyo all have large daytime populations, but the proportion of full-time residents compared to daytime residents is 73 percent in Paris, 44 percent in New York, and 18 percent in central Tokyo. Residential developments with a host of multiple uses, such as in Roppongi Hills, is the path of Tokyo's future growth.

Housing in Tokyo is still the most expensive in the world, despite a continued drop in land prices in the 1990s. A standard single-family detached home in Tokyo's Suginami-ku costs the most, at 114.5 million yen in 1999 ($1.05 million at the June 2004 exchange rate). A similar home in the western industrial city of Osaka was valued at 83.7 million yen (about $770,000). House prices 12 to 18 miles from the center of Tokyo are the same as in the heart of the major city of Osaka, and prices 35 miles out are still equivalent to those in central Nagoya. The most expensive housing outside of Japan, valued at 101 million yen (about $927,000), was in London in 2000, according to the Japanese Association of Real Estate Appraisal Survey of Global Land Prices.

Looking at the ownership of dwellings, as of 1998, 52 percent of dwellings were detached housing owned by the residents, 36 percent were rented dwellings in apartment complexes, 8 percent were owned dwellings in apartment complexes, and 4 percent were rented detached houses. The proportion of dwellings owned (60 percent) is lower than that in the United States (66 percent), but it is high in comparison to France (53 percent) and Germany (38 percent). Ownership rates may be relatively high, but the average total floor space of a dwelling was 982.7 square feet (91.3 sq m) in 2000, which falls just short of the average for Europe. The floor space of detached houses in Tokyo was 1,614.6 square feet (150 sq m), as compared to 190 in New York. In the twenty-five years between 1973 and 1998, the average dwelling space per person increased by a factor of 1.7.

Open Space Tokyo has only about a 10 percent allocation of open space. Most of it is found in gardens and parks. One of Tokyo's finest gardens, deep in the urban folds of Iidabasi, is the Koishikawa Korakoen Teien, situated next to Tokyo Dome. Despite a ring of encroaching roads, office blocks, and occasional announcements over the Dome's public-address system, there are parts of the garden that seem almost soundproofed, immune to Tokyo's perpetual, audible growth. Leveled for purposes of road, canal, and office construction, the garden is not only a cultural time capsule but also a geographic slice of what was once the much larger, undulating Koishikawa plateau. Construction of the garden at the main residence of Yorifusa Tokugawa, the founder of the Mito Tokugawa family, began in 1629. Koishikawa Korakoen is a classic example of the Japanese stroll garden; it was intended for leisurely walking. The contemporary Japanese term for gardens of this style, *kaiyushiki teien* (excursion-style garden) highlights

their function as high-brow, Edo period amusement parks. As visitors follow paths through the garden, scenic spots from China and Japan and literary scenes based on Heian period classics unfold. A bridge in the garden recreates Tsuten-bashi, a bridge that crosses a maple-lined gorge at Tofukuji Temple, in Arashiyama on the outskirts of Kyoto. The facsimile bridge spans the Oikawa River, the garden's modest stream. Two small hills, grassy knolls covered with dwarf bamboo that resemble Shilla tombs, represent Mount Lu, a Buddhist pilgrimage site in China. Rice paddies are a unique feature rarely seen within a formal garden arrangement. These were created by Itsukuni Mito to show his daughter-in-law the realities and hardships faced by peasant farmers. The paddies still serve an instructive purpose: Bunkyo-ku elementary school children come here each May and September to plant and harvest the rice.

THE URBAN DEVELOPMENT CHALLENGE

What development challenges are facing Japanese cities as they enter the twenty-first century? Several major tasks include realigning the urban structure, upgrading living environments, achieving better disaster-proofing, supplying housing in good residential districts, and improving infrastructure.

In order to achieve those goals, there are two urgent problems that Japan must tackle. The first is the problem of residential redevelopment, which includes redevelopment to maintain a residential population in the inner-city area and rebuilding wooden houses and apartment buildings. The second urgent problem is disaster preparedness.

Many cities have poured tremendous energy into relatively easy-to-develop suburbs but have done little about the old and congested industrial and residential districts of their inner cities. For example, Kobe became famous for the massive development project that began in the 1950s with slicing off part of the Rokko Mountains behind the port and using the earth to reclaim lands in the bay. There Kobe built a small offshore "city" that included homes, hotels, an international conference hall, and a hospital; on the site of the former mountain, Kobe started a new suburban residential development. The city's densely populated inner core was neglected. Lack of inner-city development projects is a weakness of all Japan's major cities.

Dealing with the decline in the inner-city resi-

Field Report

Entertainment Districts in Japanese Cities

Get off at the train station in any major Japanese city and walk for a while, and you will invariably stumble upon the entertainment district of the city (Sugiyama 1999). Single bright red paper lanterns hang outside the doors of the neighborhood yakitori bars, where salarymen drink beer or sake and consume delicious skewered barbecued chicken. A number of red lanterns often mark an *izakaya,* or Japanese bar, which serves a variety of different types of food and drink. Specialized Japanese restaurants are everywhere, serving popular Japanese foods: sushi and sashimi (raw fish); ramen, soba, or *udon* (noodle dishes and soups); shabu-shabu (thinly sliced beef boiled and dipped in sauces); *yakiniku* (Korean-style barbecued meats); *tonkatsu* (deep-fried pork cutlet); or local delicacies such as *okonomiyaki* (a pancake filled with eggs, vegetables, meat, and seafood), *takoyaki* (fried octopus), or *gyutan* (beef tongue). Alongside the restaurants are a variety of drinking establishments: "snack bars" with expensive drinks and gracious hostesses to pour them; cheaper "shot" bars, discos, and clubs; and a range of adult-oriented entertainment, which Japan has in abundance. These bars are mainly for the purposes of heavy drinking, socializing, and facilitating companionship. Most likely, the drinks in the patrons' hands will be beer, especially Japanese beer produced by the Big Four Japanese beer companies: Kirin, Asahi, Suntory, and Sapporo. Also available are a number of drinks made from fermented rice—traditional sake, or rice wine, and the increasingly popular *shochu,* rice alcohol mixed into a tall cocktail.

The entertainment district is a staple of the Japanese city. Typically, it is an area of between a few blocks and a few square miles (2–3 sq km), including some major thoroughfares and many smaller streets and alleys lined with businesses. This is where the young and old of Japan come out at night to play. Along with the bars and restaurants are pachinko parlors, where people spend hours putting money into the machines in the hopes of striking it rich, and video game arcades, with noisy virtual reality games.

Each major Japanese city has a famous entertainment district. Sapporo in Hokkaido has the famed Susukino, Sendai has the Kokobuncho, Osaka the Minami district, and Tokyo, as one might expect, has more than one. Unlike entertainment districts elsewhere, Japan's tend to be vertical as well as horizontal. Large skyscrapers may have as many as twenty bars and restaurants in one building, and these districts as a whole often have hundreds of nightspots for Japan's evening playtime. Neon is omnipresent, and in some places large video screens flash overhead, invariably provoking comparisons with scenes from the movie *Blade Runner.* Streets are well lit, with some closed to automobile traffic, and on an average night are filled with people from sunset to the early hours of the morning. Young men and women line the sidewalks at busy intersections, some handing out flyers for new bars while older bar masters and *mamasan* beckon to passersby in the street with the ever-present cry of "irrasyaimase!" (welcome).

Drinking plays an important social role in Japan, and many office workers retreat to the bar after work. This is where the real discussions of business roles, corporate strategy, and office politics take place. Women also increasingly frequent these areas, going out in groups of two or more for a night on the town. Entertainment can be expensive in Japan, and drinks are priced quite a bit higher than most Americans are used to. However, all but the seediest of these spots are quite safe, even late at night. Entire families and children of all ages can be seen wandering past the display cases in restaurant windows, while drunk salarymen lurch along the street and scantily clad women stand outside "show clubs" that charge entrance fees of up to one hundred dollars.

As the nation's capital, largest city, and cultural center, Tokyo has the most famous and larg-

(continued on the following page)

Field Report: *Entertainment Districts in Japanese Cities* (continued)

est entertainment districts in Japan. There are so many that they have become specialized for different age groups and styles. Harajuku is for the young and trendy. In Harajuku's Yoyogi Park, various styles of rock bands line the park on Sundays, showing an amazing ability to mimic American music. Shibuya is for the somewhat older but still trendy youths and has large discos and clubs. Shinjuku's infamous Kabuki-cho is full of sleazy bars and adult nightspots and is the best place to see yakuza (members of Japanese organized crime) in Japan. Roppongi, near Tokyo's center, houses the government offices and most of the foreign embassies and is also the main "foreign" or *gaijin* district of Tokyo. It boasts hundreds of bars and nightclubs; this is the central location for Japanese interested in getting better acquainted with foreigners, and vice versa. On any given night, a bar in Roppongi might be filled with German businessmen, South American hostesses, expatriate English teachers, U.S. servicemen from the nearby Yokosuka base, Japanese salarymen, and young Japanese looking for a good time. Many young Japanese can only afford to visit places like this once a month or so and are determined to make the most of their infrequent nights out. As a result, the mood is often that of a desperate singles bar, with new romances blossoming all around.

Japan's entertainment districts thus play vital social and economic functions. Socially, they allow office workers to unwind after their long workday and loosen up before they catch the last train back to their homes in the suburbs. The fact that the districts have also fostered a new generation of Japanese who are tired of their traditional social roles and seek fun and freedom is surely related to Japan's very late average age for marriage—now one of the latest in the world. Economically, the entertainment districts are at the center of Japan's tremendously vital entertainment service sector. The sheer number of places to go and the high cost of real estate in these areas does not seem to deter new businesses from opening. Generally not mentioned in traditional travel guidebooks on Japan, these are the places to go if you want to see the real social life of modern Japan.

dent population has been an issue for Japanese cities since the 1970s. Authorities in large cities have tried to turn back this "hollowing" of the inner city by rezoning predominantly old residential areas, which allows multilevel buildings in areas formerly reserved for only one- or two-story buildings, and through a "bonus housing system," which permits a larger building volume for buildings combining residences and offices. This sort of housing redevelopment traditionally has been handled as a local problem, but in the middle of the 1980s, the central government tried to restore residential neighborhoods by rezoning areas of central Tokyo as "exclusive residential districts." Under this program, height restrictions that had kept buildings to a maximum of three stories were lifted and high-rise housing projects were encouraged. Unfortunately, the program did not lead to the increase in residential space envisioned. Developers were more interested in meeting the demand for offices elsewhere in the city.

During the five years from 1985 to 1990, the population of Tokyo's seven central wards declined by 9 percent. Recovery of residential areas has thus become an urgent challenge for the central wards. In 1992 the government revised the City Planning Law and increased the number of zoning areas from eight to twelve. The traditional zoning designations included residential, commercial, industrial, and the like. The revisions added new types of residential zones and allowed for "exclusive high-rise residential districts" that would bring residential spaces back to downtown areas.

Redevelopment of wood-built houses and apartment buildings is another problem. Tokyo, for example, has about 800,000 of them and is pushing redevelopment in densely populated areas as a means of improving living standards and disaster preparedness.

Japanese cities, which have been engines for the nation's rapid economic growth, are not only cramped but also have had their share of major disasters, with earthquakes occurring frequently. Many redevelopment programs are at least in part attempts

Field Report

Mitaka, a Suburban Community

If you had visited Mitaka a century ago, you would have had to travel the eight miles from central Tokyo by rickshaw or by foot along a dirt road. Once there, you would have found gently terraced rows of rice paddies and other crop fields and rolling swaths of pine forest broken here and there by wooden farmhouses with thick thatched roofs. You would have walked among farmers in cotton breeches and wide-brimmed straw hats, stooping step by step to plant or harvest their vegetables and rice. If you had looked to the east, toward Tokyo, a concentration of buildings 1 mile (1.6 km) away would have identified the nearest markets and entertainment quarters. And if you had looked toward Kyoto, to the southwest, you would have seen Mount Fuji gleaming on the horizon, a hard four-day journey away.

If you visit Mitaka today, an hour's ride by train from Tokyo Central Station, the only reminder of the fields, forests, and farmhouses you will see is the neat garden plots—about the size of the service box on a tennis court—behind the wooden walls and tiled roofs of the town's oldest and wealthiest families. Mount Fuji may still be seen—on a pollution-free day—but only from the few choice spots where you can look over or around the high-rise apartment buildings. In a

century of mind-boggling change in Japan, Mitaka has been changed from a farmer's wilderness to one of the commuter "bed towns" (as the Japanese say) that encircle Tokyo. And yet, if you live for a while in Mitaka, you will find the old Japan and the new Japan coexisting—not always peacefully, but successfully—as a modern Japanese-style suburb.

The busiest place in Mitaka, where the day really begins and almost ends, is the railway station. At seven o'clock on weekday mornings in Mitaka and thousands of other suburbs in the Japanese Megalopolis, the sarariman (businessmen) are rising. In the more traditional homes, the wives have already been up for a half hour, preparing the morning rice, miso soup, seaweed, pickles, eggs, salad, and green tea. In the most Westernized homes, the wives are struggling out of bed with their husbands, getting ready to rouse the children and to make coffee, toast, and fried eggs. About seven thirty, men in dark suits begin to emerge from the gray concrete apartment buildings that line the street, forming a briefcase-bobbing trickle toward the railway station.

Most of the markets are still closed, sleeping behind their gray aluminum shutters, but here and there white-haired women in white caps,

(continued on the following page)

A suburban home in Mitaka, a western Tokyo suburban town. Photo by P.P. Karan.

Field Report: *Mitaka, a Suburban Community* (continued)

aprons, and black rubber boots are vigorously sweeping and hosing down the areas in front of their shops. The trickle of businessmen has now become a stream moving leisurely toward the station. Although no traffic can be seen, a red traffic light momentarily dams the stream. When the light turns green, the people move again. At Mitaka Station some people scatter to make change and buy tickets, but most simply hurry past the ticket-takers, who glance at their monthly passes. On the platform the commuters arrange themselves in relatively neat lines in spaces painted to show the location of doors. After five minutes the Tokyo-bound train glides in, and newspapers are folded, books are put away, briefcases are clutched. The doors spring open, and the great crush begins. Commuters surge into the already packed train. They are scrunched and squished together like slices of bread at the bottom of a shopping bag.

In Mitaka, as in most of Japan, school begins at eight thirty, and around eight o'clock a second stream begins its trickle through the streets as children walk to their schools. This stream is markedly brighter than its commuter counterpart. Children in school uniforms—blue shorts or skirts, white shirts, and blue caps—and

others in a rainbow of regular shirts, shorts, and skirts walk hand-in-hand. Many carry black backpacks that are wider than the backs they ride on. A few mothers walk with the group, joking with one another and with the children.

As soon as the morning sun has warmed its way through the clouds, on every balcony of every sun-side apartment are festooned futons set out to air, so that from a distance an apartment building resembles a huge checkerboard quilt. A condominium unit with a floor area of 753.5 square feet (70 sq m) in Mitaka was valued at 40 million yen in 1999 ($367,000 at the 2004 exchange rate). A quiet lane leads to the neighborhood shrine. Up a flight of steps and between stone lanterns whose crowns resemble temples, through the orange goalpost-shaped torii, past two lionlike shrine guardians, and up another flight of steps is the red-roofed shrine, surrounded by pines, oaks, and thin, leafy ginkgoes.

Close by, a group of Mitaka folks are playing baseball, and some men with Gucci golf bags are hooking and slicing into the green nets of the Mitaka Golf Range. No space goes unused. At the gas station, the gas is contained in three tanks suspended about 30 feet (9.1 m) in the air, with hoses that hang down to car level.

to prepare the cities for possible misfortune. In Tokyo's case, the Metropolitan Government takes the lead in designating places of shelter and building escape roads, and it also redevelops areas into what are called "disaster prevention shelter bases." The Kobe earthquake of January 1995 drove home the need for preparedness. Roads, railways, and other lifelines collapsed, houses and buildings crumbled, and fires raged for days. In all, 6,200 lives were lost and 420,000 households were affected. About 32 percent of greater Kobe was partially destroyed, and more than 50 percent of its central areas was obliterated. Kobe, which was considered a low-risk area, had set its building code only to resist earthquakes of an intensity of 5, which was one of the reasons the damage was so great. The Kobe earthquake registered 7 on the Japanese scale of intensity.

The majority of the burned or collapsed buildings were low wooden buildings, but 19 percent of the housing structures with six stories or more were affected as well. The chief victims of the Kobe quake were the poor and elderly who lived in low-rent, dilapidated housing demolished by tremors or fires. Fifty-three percent of those killed by the quake were aged sixty or over. The mass transit railway linking the small offshore city area built on reclaimed land in Osaka Bay with the mainland was destroyed. The vitality of a city depends on social and public services—transportation, electricity, gas, water supply and sewage, communication, and medical services. The Kobe earthquake showed how the lives of citizens can be crippled by the breakdown of these services. No emergency relief centers or contingency disaster plan existed. The inadequacy of municipal welfare programs for the elderly became apparent in the relief effort. Japanese cities, Kobe included, now have to revise their earthquake-resistance standards, and redevelopment projects are being reviewed in terms of these new perspectives on disaster preparedness.

What shape should urban redevelopment take in Japan? First, it seems as if every city in Japan has adopted a cookie-cutter redevelopment program based on the 1968 Urban Planning Law. That regulation is concerned more with projects to develop urban districts with basic infrastructure projects such as roads, parks, and sewage systems than with regulation of land use (Shibata 2002). In the postwar period, the highest priority of urban planning was to boost urban functions that would facilitate development of the basic manufacturing industries as catalysts for economic growth. Japan's urban planning policy has been a means of "state development" centered on basic infrastructure improvements. With the decentralization of power in 2000, urban planning has been removed from the central government, and the greater part of the decision-making authority has passed to the basic unit of local government. Now, explorations are under way to institute a more community-led mode of urban planning in which local residents can participate. A partial convergence between *toshi keikaku* (urban planning) and *machizukuri* (town building) is being realized (Harada 1996; Nakai 2002). Cities need to be more innovative and must take advantage of local strengths.

Second, urban redevelopment in the twenty-first century needs to put more emphasis on cultural perspectives, emphasizing the distinctive local or regional personality. Japanese urban planning in this regard has been inadequate. Third, Japanese cities must prepare for the coming "gray society." Some housing projects for the elderly are going up in Tokyo and other cities, but urban development must adapt the cities themselves to the needs and concerns of elderly people—for example, by constructing more parks and by replacing steps with slopes.

Finally, in addition to being economic spheres, Japanese cities must become amenity-equipped sustainable communities that can maintain vital functions and lifelines in emergencies. Every city in Japan needs to formulate urban policies incorporating several important concerns. Large-scale urban development projects that entail destruction of the natural environment, especially the razing of forests and the building of artificial islands, should be avoided. Forests, agricultural lands, riverbeds, and coastlines should be preserved as open space or parks. In 1988, in order to bring more land into the housing market, the government increased taxes on the farmland within the areas designated for "urban promotion" to a level equal to those on residential land. The result was a reduction of urban farmland, which was the only open space left in the larger Japanese cities. Open space is a critical problem in Japanese cities; for example, the ratio of parks to inhabitants is 10.8 square feet (1 sq m) per capita in Tokyo compared with 247.6 square feet (23 sq m) in London and 129.2 square feet (12 sq m) in New York. For open space, cities in Japan have relied on areas devastated by industrial activity, such as gravel pits in the Tama Valley or reclamation sites around Tokyo Bay, which have been reconstructed for recreation at public expense. The urban agricultural land should be kept green as urban farms or wooded public parks.

MOVING JAPAN'S CAPITAL

The overwhelming concentration of functions and services in Tokyo has led to the suggestion that the capital be moved out of the overcrowded, overpriced, earthquake-prone city. Although momentum is growing in the Diet for a long-debated government relocation plan, it is also running up against one of the nation's most formidable obstacles—Tokyo City Hall. But the National Land Agency is selecting a site. Once a site has been selected, a "Parliament city" for 100,000 people will be built from the ground up, covering an area of 4,942 acres (2,000 ha). The second phase involves the construction of satellite cities, with populations ranging from 30,000 to 100,000. The entire project will cost at least $105 billion, but the price tag could be as high as $350 billion. It will be a huge economic boon for the chosen site.

One of the sites is directly north of Tokyo in an area spanning Tochigi and Fukushima Prefectures, which was rated highly by the commission because of the ease of transportation to Tokyo. The second candidate is west of Tokyo, a section of Gifu and Aichi Prefectures that was deemed least likely to be destroyed by earthquakes, landslides, typhoons, floods, and other natural disasters that frequently afflict this volcanic archipelago. The panel conditionally recommended a third region near Japan's ancient capitals, an area that would include Nara, Kyoto, and Shiga Prefectures, provided a high-speed transportation system is completed there as planned. But the selection of the site is a political decision of such historical import that there is no telling what the final outcome might be.

The new-capital project has the potential to serve as a lever that will help Japan create the society that it desires in the twenty-first century. To realize this goal, four major objectives should be incorporated. First, the new capital city should be environmentally friendly. Second, it should be both an international core city with an intellectual ambience and a center of international information. To prevent the nation's new capital from becoming a dull political city, it is important to construct an international metropolis. Third, the city must provide a comfortable living environment and advanced information resources. Also, homes built in the new capital should include cooling and heating equipment, hot water, and parking spaces, and they should become models for Japanese housing in the twenty-first century. Fourth, the new capital should be designed to promote culture and citizen participation. It is important to consider using the new capital as a laboratory for the flexible engineering that will build the future and provide Japanese youth in the twenty-first century with a chance to participate.

In the meantime, the government is considering a plan to relocate some agencies affiliated with the central government from Tokyo to other locations. The Small and Medium Enterprise Agency may be moved to either Aichi or Osaka Prefecture; the Cultural Affairs Agency to either Nara or Kyoto Prefecture; the Forestry Agency to Akita, Nagano, or Gifu Prefecture; the Meteorological Agency to Okinawa Prefecture; and the Fisheries Agency to Hokkaido. The Natural Resources and Energy Agency may be transferred to either Aomori or Fukui Prefecture.

REFERENCES

Abe, Kazutoshi. 1996. Urban geography in postwar Japan. *Geographical Review of Japan* B 69:70–82.

———. 2000. The Japanese urban system from the standpoint of large private firms' head offices and branch offices, 1995. *Geographical Review of Japan* B 73:62–84.

Asano, D. 1999. The conservation of historic environments in Japan. *Built Environment* 25 (3): 236–243.

Bestor, Theodore C. 2001. Tsukiji, Tokyo's pantry. *Japan Quarterly* 48 (1): 31–41.

Castells, Manuel, and Peter Hall. 1994. *Technopoles of the World.* London: Routledge.

Center for Urban Studies. 1988. *Tokyo: Urban Growth and Planning, 1868–1988.* Tokyo: Metropolitan Univ.

Cybriwsky, Roman. 1988. Shibuya Center, Tokyo. *Geographical Review* 78 (1): 48–61.

———. 1998. *Tokyo: The Shogun's City at the Twenty-first Century.* Chichester, UK: Wiley.

Edgington, David W. 1989. New strategies for technology development in Japanese cities and regions. *Town Planning Review* 60 (1): 1–27.

———. 2000. Osaka: City profile. *Cities* 17 (4): 305–318.

Eyre, John D. 1982. *Nagoya: The Changing Geography of a Japanese Regional Metropolis.* Studies in Geography, no. 17. Chapel Hill: Univ. of North Carolina.

Fujioka, Kenjiro. 1959. Feudal traditions in the forms and zone structures in Japanese cities. In *Proceedings of the IGU Regional Conference in Japan 1957,* 317–319. Tokyo.

———. 1980. The changing face of Japanese Jokamachi (castle towns) since the Meiji period. In *Geography of Japan,* 146–160. Tokyo: Teikoku-Shoin.

Fujita, Kuniko, and Richard Hill. 1993. *Japanese Cities in World Economy.* Philadelphia: Temple Univ. Press.

Gottman, Jean. 1991. The dynamics of city networks in an expanding world. *Ekistics* 58:277–281.

Hall, Robert B. 1934. The cities of Japan: Notes and distribution and inherited forms. *Annals of the Association of American Geographers* 24:175–200.

Harada, Sumitaka. 1996. Urban land law in Japan. *Social Science Japan* 6:30–31.

Harris, Chauncy D., and Richard L. Edmonds. 1982. Urban geography in Japan: A survey of recent literature. *Urban Geography* 3:1–21.

Hepworth, M. 1987. The information city. *Cities,* August, 253–262.

Hidenobu, Jinnai. 1995. *Tokyo: A Spatial Anthropology.* Berkeley: Univ. of California Press.

Ito, Tatsuo, and Yoshio Watanabe. 1980. Recent trends in urban geography of Japan. In *Recent Trends of Geographical Study in Japan,* 89–98. Tokyo: Science Council of Japan.

Itoh, S. 1988. Urban development by teleport. In *Teleports and Regional Development,* ed. K. Duncan and J. Ayers, 235–241. North Holland, Netherlands: Elsevier.

Jacobs, A. 2001. Planning for a vibrant central city: The case of Nagoya. *International Review of Comparative Public Policy* 12:21–59.

Japanese Cities: A Geographical Approach. 1970. Tokyo: Association of Japanese Geographers. Special Publication no. 2.

Kanda, Koji. 2001. The development process of the Nanki-Shirahama Spa Resort and images of other places: A consideration of the production of tourism space in the modern period. *Human Geography* 53 (5): 24–45.

Karan, P.P., and Kristin Stapleton. 1997. *The Japanese City.* Lexington: Univ. Press of Kentucky.

Kiuchi, Shinzo. 1963. Recent trends in urban geography in Japan. *Annals of the Association of American Geographers* 53:93–102.

Kuroda, Toshio. 1990. Urbanization and population distribution policies in Japan. *Regional Development Dialogue* 11:112–129.

Kuroda, Toshio, and N. Tsuya. 1989. *Urbanization and Counterurbanization in Japan: A National Case Study.* London: Edward Arnold.

Masai, Yasuo. 1990. Tokyo: From a feudal million city to a global supercity. *Geographical Review of Japan* 63:1–16.

———. 1994. Metropolitization in densely populated Asia: The case of Tokyo. In *The Asian City: Processes of Development, Characteristics, and Planning,* ed. Ashok K. Dutt, Frank J. Costa, Surinder Aggarwal, and Allen G. Noble, 119–126. Dordrecht: Kluwer.

Masser, I. 1990. Technology and regional development policy: A review of Japan's Technopolis Programme. *Regional Studies* 24:41–53.

Mizuuchi, Toshio. 1986. Awareness of spatial inequality in the living environment of the modern Japanese city. In *Japanese Contributions to the History of Geographical Thought (3),* 27–38. Fukuoka, Japan: Institute of Geography, Faculty of Letters, Kyushu Univ.

Morikawa, Hiroshi. 1995. Changing regional urban systems in Hiroshima Prefecture. *Geographical Review of Japan* B 68:1–22.

Nakabayashi, Itsuki. 1987. Socio-economic and living conditions of Tokyo's inner-city. *Geographical Reports of Tokyo Metropolitan University* 22:111–128.

Nakai, Norihiro. 2002. Toshi keikaku and machi-zukuri. *Social Science Japan* (April): 17–19.

Okamoto, Kohei. 1997. Suburbanization of Tokyo and the daily lives of suburban people. In *The Japanese City,* ed. P.P. Karan and Kristin Stapleton, 79–105. Lexington: Univ. Press of Kentucky.

Sassen, S. 2001. *The Global City: New York, London, Tokyo.* Princeton, NJ: Princeton Univ. Press.

Scholler, Peter. 1984. Urban values: A review of Japanese and German attitudes. *Urban Geography* 5:43–48.

Shibata, Byron. 2002. Land-use law in the United States and Japan: A fundamental overview and comparative analysis. *Washington University Journal of Law and Policy* 10:161–266.

Sugiyama, K. 1999. The amusement quarter in the night constructed as social space: A case study of the Ekimae district in Toyama city. *Human Geography* 51 (4): 396–409.

Takahashi, N. 1985. Structuralization of the Tokyo Metropolitan Region. *Science Reports, Institute of Geoscience,* Univ. of Tsukuba, sec. A, Geographical Sciences, 6:29–46.

Takano, Takehiko. 1993. Change of inner city's inhabitants and its implication in urban residential structure: A comparative study of four regional capital cities in Japan. *Science Reports of Tohoku University,* ser. 7 (Geography) 43 (2): 91–118

Terasaka, A., Y. Wakabayashi, I. Nakabayashi, and K. Abe. 1988. The transformation of regional systems in an information-oriented society. *Geographical Review of Japan* B 61:159–173.

Trewartha, Glenn T. 1934. Japanese cities: Distribution and morphology. *Geographical Review* 24:404–417.

Ueno, Ken'ichi. 1985. Residential structure of Tokyo in the 1910s (the Taisho era). *Geographical Review of Japan* B 58:24–48.

Yamada, Hirohisa. 1992. Regional differences in the land price decline in three metropolitan areas, Japan. *Science Reports of Tohoku University* (Geography) 42:21–37.

Yamashita, M. 1987. Characteristics of spatial land use in Osaka's CBD. *Human Geography* 39:54–69.

Chapter 9

第 九 章

THE POLITICAL CHALLENGE

Japan's political system is one of the most controversial areas in contemporary research. The basic nature of the system is hotly contested. There are three main models: (1) some scholars, such as Edwin Reischauer, have argued that Japan is an advanced democratic system characterized by unity derived from its Confucian past and strongly influenced by the West; (2) some say that Japan is politically different from the United States but similar to many European countries: and (3) others claim that Japan has a unique political system—one that sets it apart from other countries—and that in many ways it is undemocratic. The discussion of how Japan's political system works involves the question of where power actually lies within the system. An issue that is debated is whether consensus in Japan is real consensus or perhaps agreement enforced by particular groups.

THE POLITICAL CULTURE

Until World War II, parliamentary democracy was undermined by Japan's constitution, according to which the cabinet stood above the Diet (the name of the Japanese parliament) and could ignore it on most issues. Since the end of the war, one political party has held power almost continuously. Then in July 1993, its fall prompted a period of flux: there have been seven prime ministers during the ten-year period 1993–2003. Each has wobbled atop squabbling multiparty coalitions. A strong government, one that would remain in place for a decade or so, has so far proved elusive.

As a result, Japan's democracy has suffered. Continuous rule by a big party and chaotic rule by many small ones share one characteristic: they deprive the electorate of the chance to choose between clear sets of policies. This political climate has stifled the views of ordinary Japanese and has produced governments incapable of tackling vested interests and politicians captive to the lobbies that supply the cash that buys the votes. Electoral corruption, in turn, lowers the standing of politicians, with the result that the real power is wielded by bureaucrats. Politicians are beholden to the bureaucrats (Curtis 1988), who grant the favors that keep money coming from big businesses. In short, Japan's political system favors insiders (notably big firms and the well-organized farm lobby), who get government preferences, often to the detriment of less-well-connected outsiders (small firms, foreign firms, and consumers).

A two-party system, with elections that express the popular will and so confer a popular mandate, would be of some help to build a stronger democracy in Japan. But pluralism has never taken root because of modern Japan's antidemocratic origins. The United States tried to impose liberalism on Japan after World War II, but within a decade Japan's antidemocratic tendencies had reasserted themselves. Even today the shadow of the Meiji past is visible in the political culture. Like the Meiji government, today's senior civil servants regard fiscal or foreign policy as a technical matter for experts to decide, not as the subject of democratic discussion. The bureaucrats who head each ministry are called *vice ministers,* a term coined in Meiji times to underscore their importance relative to the politicians. Public policy depended on fine drafting by bureaucrats and nonverbal communications by politicians. In making decisions, both groups considered emotional factors such as personal relationships and the "atmosphere" surrounding the matter. Rationalism—whereby a conclusion is reached based on logic after clarification of the points at issue—did not have a firm foundation in Japanese political culture. This point was seen in Japan's inadequate military and diplomatic strategies when it fought against the United States in World War II. The Meiji government was more interested in industrial might than in pluralism and accountability. As a result, schools taught pupils what to think, not how to think; universities mostly trained people to serve industrialization as scientists and civil servants. When it came to drafting a constitution, the Meiji reformers chose authoritarian Germany as the model.

History naturally shapes a country's ideas; but it is extreme to argue that modern Japan is captive to the events of the past century. Germany's past authoritarianism has given way to exemplary democracy. The historical explanation for Japan's weak pluralism does not stop here.

Another school of thought sees its roots in American postwar occupation policies. By making the major postwar decisions itself, America prevented the Japanese from debating the matter of how their country should be rebuilt. It was this kind of postwar debate that launched West Germany on the democratic road; the country's basic body of law was conceived and written by German jurists. Because it was their own, not imposed from outside, the country embraced it with a passion.

The Japanese were not allowed to do the same. The United States occupied Japan from 1945 to 1952, and for these seven years Japanese politicians were puppets of the occupation force. In 1945 Prince Fumimaro Konoe, who had been prime minister during 1937–39 and 1940–41 (and grandfather of one of today's reformers, Morihiro Hosokawa), tried to revise Japan's constitution in a way that would appease America's liberal ideas; he committed suicide after occupation authorities withdrew their support of his constitutional reforms and indicted him as a war criminal.

The United States ensured that Japan would remain only half sovereign even after the occupation ended. This was achieved partly by means of the new constitution that the Americans drafted. Its ninth article required that Japan renounce the use of force abroad; it therefore made Japan dependent on America's armed forces. In 1951 Japan's dependency was formalized in the two countries' security treaty, which gave the United States nearly sovereign rights over its military bases on Japanese territory. The treaty empowered America to veto a third power's

The reformist Morihiro Hosokawa, formerly governor of Kumamoto Prefecture, was elected prime minister of Japan in July 1993, which ended thirty-eight years of Liberal Democratic Party rule in the country. For his outstanding contributions to the advancement of regions and localities in Japan, he was awarded the John Wesley Powell Medal in 1999 at the University of Kentucky by the New Mexico Geographical Society, the oldest geographical society in the earliest settled part of North America. Photo by Lee P. Thomas.

military presence in Japan, and even to intervene in Japanese affairs to stem domestic disorder. Again, the Japanese had no say in this. The treaty's contents were secret until after it was signed, making public debate impossible.

In the postoccupation years, some Japanese politicians have resented the slight to Japan's sovereignty imposed by the constitution's pacifist clause and have tried to revise it (Green 1995). As with electoral reforms, the Japanese lack the parliamentary strength to achieve this. A half century later, Japan has potentially one of the strongest armies in the world. But the constitution still has not been revised; the military buildup has been made possible by tortuous interpretation of the constitution.

Like the legacy of the Meiji period, the effects of the American occupation can still be observed. Sophistry over the pacifist clause in Japan's constitution adds to the vagueness of political discussion in Japan. If war broke out in the Korean peninsula, for example, Japan could not help to control it, since the constitution forbids the use of force beyond its own borders. Foreign crises often strengthen the leaders of democracies, but Japan's politicians are not very assertive in such situations. But, again like the Meiji legacy, the American occupation's influence does not seem insurmountable. Although defense dependency discourages the emergence of strong political leadership, strong leadership is not impossible. Given a hard shove, Japan's political culture could change.

Japan has had already a taste of this, when the 1993 election toppled the Liberal Democratic Party from government. The prime minister who emerged from the 1993 election, Morihiro Hosokawa, enjoyed the closest thing Japan had seen to a popular mandate (until the election of Junichiro Koizumi in 2001). His opinion poll ratings rose to around 70 percent, three times as high as those of his predecessor. Hosokawa's popularity yielded a lasting result: he and his allies used it to push electoral reform through parliament (Christensen 1994). This achievement guarantees that Japan's old political culture will suffer further setbacks and that eventually political reforms will follow.

The Current Political System

Japan's current political system is largely a creation of the postwar U.S. occupation. Occupation reforms are found in the Japanese constitution, which was written mainly by U.S. government advisers. Remnants of the prewar Japanese political system—largely based on the British parliamentary system—and the Meiji era traditions are other sources influencing the political system. Before the Meiji period, Japan was a feudal nation ruled by lords. There was no democratic tradition. The Meiji reformers in the mid-nineteenth century were also not interested in democracy. Their objective was to build a strong Japan—both economically and politically. They did adopt some Western democratic practices, but the underlying ideology of democracy—government by the people —was absent.

During the Meiji period sovereignty resided in the emperor, not in the people. This system was based on German monarchic constitutionalism. The ministries and the military were responsible to the emperor, who was considered divine. The emperor did not actually rule, and had not since the twelfth century, but all authority was still derived from the emperor. Although sovereignty was assigned to the emperor, the system prevented him from really making any decisions. State Shintoism reinforced the worship of the emperor—as a religious and national

figure. So the main use of the emperor was to spur patriotism and obedience to authority. Thus, symbolic power was in the person of the emperor, but actual power was in the ministries and in the military.

In the ministers in the Meiji government, characteristics can be seen that demonstrate the political heritage of the country: (1) little experience with the concepts and practices of democracy; (2) a strong sense of unity, which translated into a strong sense of nationalism; (3) a willingness to learn from the West, especially in terms of how to gain economic and political power; and (4) group leadership. Real power was in the hands of the court ministers—who later became the bureaucracy. The bureaucracy preceded the Diet, the constitution, and the political parties. It was the heritage of the samurai—nobility and ancient officials. There was a sense of elitism about the bureaucrats, but also a feeling of duty to rule their country. A British-style parliament, called the Diet, was introduced, but it did not have as much power as the bureaucracy.

In the 1920s and 1930s the military began to exert more power in the political system, and antimilitary politicians were arrested. This period was highlighted by struggles between various groups. Eventually, the dominance of the military led to World War II.

The new post–World War II constitution, promulgated in 1946, changed the status of the emperor. The constitution defines the emperor as "the symbol of the State," but the sovereign power rests with the people of Japan. This was a major change. Also state Shinto was abolished, and the emperor issued a statement saying he was not "divine." Older people often continue to have great reverence for the emperor, and sometimes right-wing politicians in Japan use this for political purposes, calling for the restoration of sovereignty to the emperor. Besides taking sovereignty away from the emperor, the new constitution strengthened the Diet. According to the constitution, it is the sole lawmaking organ of the state. A crucial difference between this system and the U.S. system is that the legislature in Japan (the Diet) does not write the laws. The bureaucracy writes the laws, and the Diet approves them.

The Diet has two Houses—the House of Representatives and the House of Councillors. Both of these are elected. The lower house, or House of Representatives, consists of 480 members now, elected

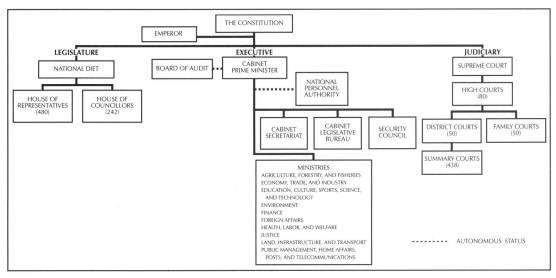

Fig. 9.1. Structure of the national government.

for four-year terms. The House of Councillors has 242 members, elected for six-year terms. The cabinet, the head of which is the prime minister, holds executive power. The highest judiciary is the Supreme Court, whose members are appointed by the cabinet (see fig. 9.1).

Internal Administrative Divisions

For administrative purposes, Japan is divided into 47 jurisdictions: 43 prefectures (*ken*), 3 urban prefectures (*fu*), and one district (*do,* Hokkaido). Large cities are subdivided into wards (ku) and further split into precincts (machi or cho) or subdistricts (*shicho*) and counties (*gun*). Each of the 47 local jurisdictions elects a governor and an assembly by popular vote every four years. The governor is responsible for the administration of the jurisdiction (see fig. 9.2).

Cities (shi) are self-governing units administered independently of the larger jurisdictions within which they are located. City governments are headed by mayors elected for four years by popular vote. The wards (ku) of larger cities also elect their own assemblies, which select ward superintendents. In order to attain shi status, a jurisdiction must have at least thirty thousand inhabitants, 60 percent of whom should be engaged in urban occupations.

The terms *machi* and *cho* designate self-governing towns outside the cities as well as precincts of urban wards. Like the cities, each machi and cho has its own elected mayor and assembly. Villages (mura) are the smallest self-governing units in rural areas. They consist of a number of hamlets (buraku) containing several thousand people connected by a formal vil-

Nagoya City Hall. The mayors of Japanese cities are elected by popular vote every four years. The mayor is responsible for all activities supported through local taxation or grants from the national government. Photo by P.P. Karan.

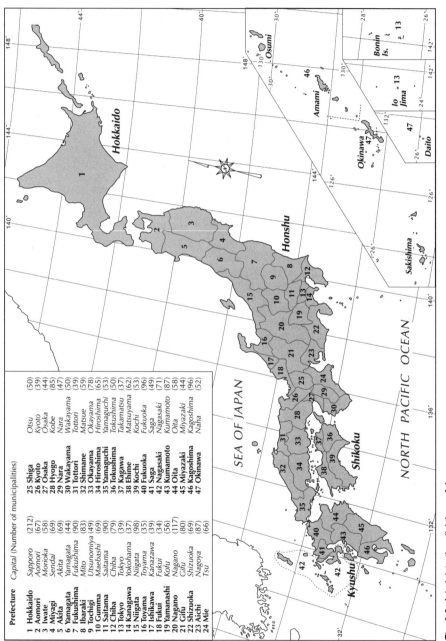

Fig. 9.2. Administrative divisions of Japan.

lage administration, headed by elected mayors or councils.

The present pattern of local jurisdictions in Japan has evolved from approximately 260 domains (*han*) and local administrative units in the pre-Meiji period. In 1871 the Meiji government instituted a nationwide administrative system of 72 prefectures with prefectural governors appointed by the central government. Further amalgamations reduced the number of prefectures to 47.

Both administratively and financially, local governments in Japan depend greatly on the national government (Takahasi and Ida 1987). The national ministries have the power to intervene in local gov-

ernment affairs. There is a high level of standardization in policy and organization among the different local governments. Since local tax revenues are insufficient to support prefectural and city governments, these jurisdictions look to the central government for support. Traditionally, Japan's 47 prefectural governments have maintained close ties with the central ministries (see fig. 9.3). These ties have preserved some of the features of prewar society in modern Japan: uniform, centrally administered policies and their implementation at the local or regional level. Japan's current economic problems have brought frustrations with the top-down rule. Local governments have started clamoring for local/re-

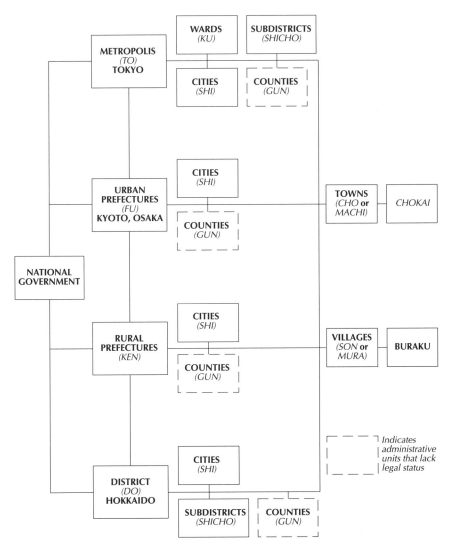

Fig. 9.3. Structure of the local government.

gional-based decision making. In Nagano prefecture citizens' groups oppose a dam that the construction ministry wants to build against the wishes of local residents. The governor of Mie Prefecture has opposed the construction of a nuclear power plant that the government and the utility company, Chubu Electric, have been trying to build for three decades. In Chiba Prefecture the governor wants to cancel a land reclamation project that would provide space for new factories because there are plenty of empty factory sites available in Chiba, due to the weak economy. Once the pliant tool of the central bureaucracy, the governors of Japan's prefectures are starting to assert local autonomy.

Political Parties and the Electoral System

Racked by scandals and controlled by one party from 1955 to 1993 and another from 1996 onward, Japan's weak political system contrasts sharply with its strong economic system. Although Japan adopted the formal structure of democracy—constitutional government, universal suffrage, multiple political parties—the way the political system operates in practice is often far removed from the ideals of liberal democratic government. The weakest link in the chain is the party system, which enjoys little popular respect and has consistently failed to implement badly needed reform.

The Liberal Democratic Party (LDP) has been the dominant political party in Japan since the end of the war. A conservative party, it governed Japan for thirty-eight years before being defeated in 1993. In the early 1990s the LDP was plagued with numerous scandals and reports of corruption, which were responsible for its defeat in 1993. In addition, the LDP refused to pass political reform bills that were up for vote in the Diet. The party won back the majority in the Diet in the 1996 elections.

In the early 1950s, in order to prevent the Japanese left from impeding economic growth, the private sector got together with conservative politicians and government bureaucrats to shape the political system in their favor. The result was the formation of the Liberal Democratic Party in 1955, by a merger of conservative forces. In return for keeping the left out of power, corporate Japan agreed to fund the new party on a massive scale and give it whatever other support it needed. In turn the LDP offered to provide voters with economic prosperity. For forty years, until 1993, there had seemed to be no real alternative to the LDP, which was supported by business and the bureaucracy and preached economic expansion and alliance with the United States.

In the early 1990s, there was a major upheaval in the political arena. The public was becoming disillusioned with a rash of corruption cases, and politicians felt it was urgent that they address the task of doing away with money politics. They committed themselves to accomplishing a wide range of reforms, including revamping of the electoral system. In 1992 Morihiro Hosokawa formed the Japan New Party, vowing to clean up the political system. The LDP's failure to carry political reforms prompted other members to leave the party in June 1993 and form Shinseito (Japan Renewal Party) and New Party Sakigake (Pioneers).

After the LDP failed to pass a package of political reform bills, Japanese voters punished the party in the elections of 1993; since then there have been several successive governments in Japan. From August 1993 until April 1994, Hosokawa's Japan New Party, or Nihon Shinto, was in power. Hosokawa was a former LDP member who served two terms in the upper house of the Diet, then two terms as governor of Kumamoto Prefecture in Kyushu. He is the direct descendant of feudal lords who ruled Kumamoto for more than two hundred years. Hosokawa, like other critics, blamed centralization for the political system's endemic corruption, as businesses lean on parliament members to lean on the bureaucracy for contracts and necessary approvals. His proposed solution was to decentralize power from the central government in Tokyo to the prefectures. Hosokawa succeeded in passing a political reform package in 1994, but, undermined by a corruption scandal, his government collapsed. Tsutomu Hata, who was backed by the governing coalition, replaced him. When the Social Democratic Party of Japan left the coalition, Hata's government fell in June 1994. He was replaced by Social Democratic Party leader Tomiichi Murayama as prime minister.

Many Japanese favor political reforms, especially changes in the electoral system, which discourages mass participation and preserves the status quo. The medium-sized multimember constituency system makes political campaigning extremely expensive and discourages the development of new parties. Many traditional forms of political campaigning,

An official election campaign in Japan lasts for a brief period of twelve days. Candidates post their pictures on official wooden boards that have poster space for all the candidates together. Candidates stump in the streets and sound trucks announce their candidacy. By law sound trucks can be used no more than twelve hours a day and only one at a time by any one candidate's support group. Photo by P.P. Karan.

such as door-to-door campaigning, signature drives, parades, and candidate-produced literature, are not allowed. Candidates send out government-produced postcards, place posters on official signboards, and make television and radio announcements. In order to get around the campaign laws, politicians spend most of their time doing favors for constituents, attending weddings and funerals, and generally trying to secure as much patronage as possible for their home districts.

When the electoral boundaries were drawn up after the war, Japan was primarily rural. Now Japan is primarily urban, but the seats have not been adequately redistributed. Even though the courts have encouraged redistribution, they have no power to enforce their will, and so urban Japan is underrepresented by at least sixty seats. This helps explain the political delicacy of the rice import issue and also why urban salaried employees end up paying most of the taxes in Japan.

There were two main problems with the electoral system for the House of Representatives in the Diet. Japan was divided into electoral districts with multiple seats, giving several districts more than one representative, but each voter could vote for only one candidate. There might be fifteen people on the ballot, and the five with the most votes would win. Thus, a person could be elected with maybe 20 percent of the vote or so, and people from within the same party were often running against each other. Since candidates from the same political party espouse the party's policy, ideological differences became irrelevant, and candidates were led to engage in pork-barrel politics. Voting by multimember districts with single votes was a notable characteristic of Japanese elections. Some Japanese want a two-party system like that of the United States and support a single-member plurality system. Others advocate a proportional representation system to keep proportionality between popular support and party strength. In a proportional representation system, voters cast their vote for the political party of their choice. The party that wins then selects the person to represent the area in the Diet.

The second major problem was that the number of seats per district did not keep up with changes in the population. As people migrated from rural areas to urban centers, the number of seats per district did not change accordingly. As a result, rural areas were overrepresented in the Diet. Politicians therefore often catered to rural interests.

At the beginning of 1994, the Diet created a new electoral system. Under this system 300 seats were single-member district seats, where the representatives are elected in a "winner-take-all" system as in the United States. The remaining 200 seats were based on a regional proportional representation system—the voters just vote for a political party, and the party chooses the representative. For election purposes the country is divided into eleven areas: Kinki (33 proportional representation [PR] and 47 single members), Kyushu (23 PR and 38 single), Minami-Kanto (23 PR and 32 single), Tokai (23 PR and 34 single), Kita-Kanto (21 PR and 31 single), Tokyo (19 PR and 25 single), Tohoku (16 PR and 26 single), Chugoku (13 PR and 21 single), Hokushinetsu (13 PR and 20 single), Hokkaido (9 PR and 13 single), and Shikoku (7 PR and 13 single). This system was the result of compromise between the Liberal Democratic Party, which supported a single-member district, and the opposing parties, which supported a proportional representation system. The 1996 elections in Japan were held under this new system (Sano and Nakaya 2000).

In February 2000 the Diet enacted a bill to reduce the number of proportional representation seats in the House to 180, keeping the 300 seats allocated to single-seat constituencies. So the new law has reduced the number of lower-house seats to 480. The general election held in June 2000 elected 480 members.

Equal Value for Every Vote

In a democratic state, the equality of voting rights is taken for granted; this is a basic principle. There is no question that every vote should have the same value, or equal value, regardless of who casts it or where it is cast. In Japan's case, however, there are wide disparities in vote value between urban and rural constituencies. Obviously, this reflects flaws in the regional seat distribution that the Japanese Diet has not been able to correct. In the election for the House of Councillors in July 1998, the value of a vote in Tokyo had 4.98 times less value than a vote in the sparsely populated prefecture of Tottori. The Supreme Court of Japan ruled in September 2000 that the disparity is within tolerable bounds and therefore constitutional, thus effectively endorsing the election system. Five dissenting justices, however, saw "considerable inequalities" in the differences in the value of a vote and concluded that the election system was unconstitutional. Since 1964 voters in urban constituencies have filed ten suits seeking fairer distribution of Diet seats. The partial redistricting carried out in 1994 left fundamental problems unaddressed. As a result, some sparsely populated prefectures still have more seats than densely populated ones.

POLITICAL CHANGES IN 1993: CAUSES AND CONSEQUENCES

The change in Japanese party politics in 1993 was significant because it ended the LDP's one-party rule and resulted in revision of the 1947 electoral law, replacing the old electoral system with a hybrid of a single-member plurality and a proportional representation system. The mounting public pressure for political reform played an important role in this change.

In the October 1996 general elections under the new system intended to nurture a two-party system, representatives were selected for 300 single-member seats and 200 proportional representative seats in the 500-seat lower house. The Liberal Democratic Party came out as the clear winner, with 239 seats in Japan's House of Representatives. But the party narrowly missed capturing a majority of seats. It surpassed its pre-election seat count of 211 but was unable to get outright control of the lower house, being 12 seats short of a 251-seat majority. The LDP won 169 single-member and 70 proportional representative seats.

Shinshinto (the New Frontier Party) came in second but failed to strengthen its position in the lower house. It won 156 seats (96 single-member and 60 proportional), 4 seats less than its pre-election 160, weakening the power of the party.

Minshuto (the Democratic Party of Japan) was third with 52 seats (17 single and 35 proportional),

Table 9.1. Area, population, and new apportionment of electoral seats in the lower house, 1993

Area	Population	Proportional representation part[a]	Electoral districts	Total seats
Kinki	20,414,233	33 (30 in 2000)		80
Osaka	8,734,516		19	
Hyogo	5,405,040		12	
Kyoto	2,602,460		6	
Nara	1,375,481		4	
Shiga	1,222,411		3	
Wakayama	1,074,325		3	
Kyushu	14,518,257	23 (21 in 2000)		61
Fukuoka	4,811,050		11	
Kumamoto	1,840,326		5	
Kagoshima	1,797,824		5	
Nagasaki	1,562,959		4	
Oita	1,236,942		4	
Okinawa	1,222,398		3	
Miyazaki	1,168,907		3	
Saga	877,851		3	
Minami-Kanto	14,388,786	23 (21 in 2000)		55
Kanagawa	7,980,391		17	
Chiba	5,555,429		12	
Yamanashi	852,966		3	
Tokyo	11,855,563	19 (17 in 2000)		44
Tokyo	11,855,563		25	
Kita-Kanto	13,152,134	21 (20 in 2000)		52
Saitama	6,405,319		14	
Ibaraki	2,845,382		7	
Gumma	1,966,265		5	
Tochigi	1,935,168		5	
Tokai	14,220,526	23 (21 in 2000)		57
Aichi	6,690,603		15	
Shizuoka	3,670,840		9	
Gifu	2,066,569		5	
Mie	1,792,514		5	
Tohoku	9,738,285	16 (14 in 2000)		42
Miyagi	2,248,558		6	
Fukushima	2,104,058		5	
Aomori	1,482,873		4	
Iwate	1,416,928		4	
Yamagata	1,258,390		4	
Akita	1,227,478		3	
Chugoku	7,745,083	13 (11 in 2000)		34
Hiroshima	2,849,847		7	
Okayama	1,925,877		5	
Yamaguchi	1,572,616		4	
Shimane	781,021		3	
Tottori	615,722		2	
Hokushinetsu	7,739,584	13 (11 in 2000)		33
Niigata	2,474,583		6	
Nagano	2,156,627		5	
Ishikawa	1,164,628		3	
Toyama	1,120,161		3	
Fukui	823,585		3	
Hokkaido	5,643,647	9 (8 in 2000)		22
Hokkaido	5,643,647		13	
Shikoku	4,195,069	7 (6 in 2000)		20
Ehime	1,515,025		4	
Kagawa	1,023,412		3	
Tokushima	831,598		3	
Kochi	825,034		3	
Total	123,611,167	200 (180 in 2000)	300	500 (480 in 2000)

Sources: *Asahi Shimbun* archives, Tokyo; *Daily Yomiuri* (Tokyo), June 27, 2000. [a]Reduced to 180 in 2000.

maintaining its pre-election 52 seats. The Japanese Communist Party captured 26 seats (2 single and 24 proportional), 11 more than it won in the previous election. Independents claimed 9 single-member seats. Sakigake earned 2, 7 less than before.

In the June 2000 and November 2003 general elections, several major political parties contested for seats in Japan's lower house, running on the following platforms:

The Liberal Democratic Party's major policy is to seek full-fledged economic recovery through budget and tax reforms and maintain social security benefits. In 2000 it won 233 seats in the lower house (177 in single-seat districts and 56 in proportional representation). The LDP lost 37 seats in the 2000 election. In the 2003 election the LDP won 237 seats but retained control of the government through alliances with other parties. The party retains strength in rural areas, which are dependent on public spending, but the electoral reforms will increasingly tip the balance away from rural areas and yield more voters for the opposition Democratic Party of Japan. The Liberal Democratic Party–led coalition, which includes Komeito and Hoshuto, has 275 seats in the Diet after the 2003 election, down from the 287 it had before.

New Komeito (the Clean Government Party) advocates restructuring of the fiscal framework, use of consumption tax revenue for social security, having the government share half of the financial burden for the basic pension, and nursing care for the elderly. The party won 31 seats (7 in single-seat districts and 24 in proportional representation) and lost 11 seats in the 2000 election. The Komeito party won 34 seats in the 2003 election.

Hoshuto (the New Conservative Party) advocates fiscal restructuring after economic recovery, using revenue from the consumption tax for basic social security, and simplifying corporate and income taxes. The party won only 7 seats in single-seat districts and lost 11 seats in the 2000 election. In the 2003 election it was able to win only 4 seats.

Minshuto (the Democratic Party of Japan) advocates measures to reconcile economic recovery and fiscal restructuring, channel consumption tax revenue to finance pensions, and lower the minimum taxable income, which is now about 3.8 million yen (about $35,000) for a couple with two children. Minshuto gained 32 seats in the 2000 election, for a total strength of 127. In the 2003 election, it picked up 177 of the 480 seats in the lower house. The Democratic Party's generally younger and more dynamic candidates are making inroads among younger urban voters. The party, which portrays itself as offering a break from the pork-barrel politics of the Liberal Democratic Party, campaigned on a reformist agenda.

The Japanese Communist Party (JCP) places priority on social welfare and people's lives in budgetary allocations to facilitate economic recovery and fiscal restructuring, and it opposes increases in the consumption tax. In 2000 the party won 20 seats and lost 6 of the seats it had held in the pre-election house. The JCP was able to win only 9 seats in 2003.

Jiyuto (the Liberal Party) wants to reform the economic structure to achieve self-sustaining economic recovery, review income and resident (local) tax systems, and allocate all revenue from the consumption tax for social welfare expenditures. Jiyuto won 22 seats in 2000. It merged with Minshuto in 2003.

The Social Democratic Party (SDP) advocates fiscal restructuring, national debate on the use of consumption tax revenue for the basic pension system, and creation of a welfare system in which civilians can actively design plans and choose the quality of services and personal costs for welfare services. It won 19 seats in the 2000 elections, but only 6 seats in 2003.

In the general election of 2000, the ruling coalition of the Liberal Democratic Party, New Komeito, and Hoshuto placed priority on economic recovery in election campaign pledges. The ruling coalition won a total of 271 seats in the lower house; but the fact that the coalition parties lost 59 seats from their pre-election strength indicates that the electorate passed harsh judgment on their administration for failure to achieve economic recovery. The economy grew 0.5 percent in real terms in fiscal 1999—the first positive growth in three years. How Japan can achieve an economic growth rate of 2 percent—

Table 9.2. Party strength in the lower house, June 2000 and November 2003 elections

Political party	Total seats		Single-seat districts 2000 (300 seats)	Proportional representation 2000 (180 seats)	Pre-2000 election strength
	2000	2003			
LDP[a]	233	237	177	56	270
Minshuto	127	177	80	47	95
New Komeito[a]	31	34	7	24	42
Jiyuto	22	-	4	18	18
JCP	20	9	0	20	26
SDP	19	6	4	15	14
Hoshuto[a]	7	4	7	0	18
Mushozoku no Kai	5	1	5	0	4
Jiyu Ringo	1	1	1	0	1
Reformers' Network Party	0	-	0	-	5
Independents	15	-	15	-	4
Others	-	11	-	-	-
Total	480	480	300	180	497
Vacancies (in 1996)					3[b]

Sources: Daily Yomiuri (Tokyo), June 27, 2000; and Kyodo News Service.
[a]Ruling parties.
[b]The lower house had 500 seats before the 2000 elections. The number was reduced to 480 in 2000.

which is seen as a realistic target—is a major question for the political parties. The ruling coalition parties pledged to expand deregulation to create new industries, to revise or establish laws to promote development of an information technology–oriented society. The voters dismissed their campaign pledges as cosmetic—aimed only at winning the election. The opposition parties, meanwhile, have focused on the importance of carrying out fiscal structural reforms. Minshuto (Democratic Party of Japan) made major gains, but the biggest opposition party did not achieve a mandate.

Foreign policy and security issues were not mentioned in the election campaign, although most Japanese realize that in the twenty-first century a reunified Korean Peninsula may present a diplomatic challenge, and the relationship with China will become even more delicate as China's navy transforms itself from a coastal force into an oceanic force. The parties have not debated the revised (1960) Japan-U.S. security treaty, which was forty years old on June 23, 2000, and the 1997 agreement on the new guidelines for Japan-U.S. Defense Cooperation, which need to be implemented with increased efficiency.

For that purpose, the issue of the host-nation budget, under which the Japanese government bears part of the costs of stationing U.S. forces in Japan, needs to be settled in a way that does not damage the mutual confidence existing between the two countries. It is also a matter of urgency to deal with the issue of constructing an alternative facility for the U.S. Futenma Air Station in Okinawa Prefecture and to solve an environmental pollution problem caused by the U.S. Naval Air Facility in Atsugi, Kanagawa Prefecture.

In the campaign the reform plan for the civil service system was not discussed. The civil service system enabled Japan to get a fresh start in the postwar era. But after a half century the system is showing signs of institutional fatigue, such as the profusion of corruption cases and the widespread practice by bureaucrats of "descending from the heavens" (amakudari) into special quasi-governmental organizations that pay exorbitant salaries. The practice of amakudari is based on a pyramid structure. At the top of the pyramid are career bureaucrats who pass the Class 1 examination and are guaranteed to move up the ladder. While the top candidates from

Bridge construction across an inlet in Sado Island, off the coast of Niigata in the Sea of Japan. This sparsely populated island is the site of several construction projects similar to those in other parts of the country. Close links exist between the corporate world, particularly the construction industry, and the government. Contracts for infrastructure development are the mainstay of the construction industry, which is one of the major sources of funds for the political parties—in particular the Liberal Democratic Party. The LDP has governed the country for most of the time since the end of World War II. Photo by P.P. Karan.

each age cohort that joins the bureaucracy each year can aspire to the top post of vice minister, the remaining members of the class are usually forced into early retirement in their mid-fifties. But they are promised cushy second careers in quasi-governmental organizations upon retirement from their ministries and agencies. In order to correct the abuses of the amakudari system, career patterns in the civil service must be revised. But few politicians were talking about the changes in the election campaign. The public's distrust of the bureaucracy requires changes to increase openness and transparency and to place more emphasis on ability and achievement.

Another major problem in Japanese politics is the link between contractors and politicians. In Japan local legislators or their relatives sit on the boards of construction companies that receive public-works orders from prefectural governments. During 1999, in 25 of the nation's 47 prefectures, more than 10 percent of assembly members or their kin served as directors for the contractors. In some cases, orders awarded to builders increased sharply after their directors or family members became legislators. There is evidence of questionable ties between the construction industry, local assembly members, and governments in the mostly rural prefectures (Woodall 1996). Public-works orders are a major source of income for construction companies in these areas. In Aomori, Gumma, Wakayama, Kagawa, Saga, and Nagasaki Prefectures, 20 percent or more of assembly members or their relatives are linked to public-works contractors.

The coalition government was returned to power in the June 2000 election for the lower house of parliament, but the voters slashed its presence in the House of Councillors and deprived the LDP of an outright majority. The Democratic Party of Japan, which attacked the LDP free-spending policies in its campaign, made substantial gains. Prime Minister Yoshiro Mori was reconfirmed by the Diet as Japan's prime minister, but he soon faced a more confident opposition and criticism because of a new scandal involving a former construction minister, Eiichi Nakao, accused of taking 30 million yen ($284,000) in bribes from a construction company in exchange for helping it to win public-works contracts. The scandal ensnared some key Liberal Democrats. In April 2001 Junichiro Koizumi became prime minister, presenting himself as a new kind of iconoclastic leader for Japan and promising the painful changes necessary to clear the way for a brighter economic future. Koizumi was reelected in 2003. The pace of his economic reforms has been slow, and Japan's economy in early 2004 remained mired in a slump. He lost an important battle to slash pork-barrel spending by reducing highway-building projects; construction-friendly members of his own Liberal Democratic party prevailed instead. However, there are signs of business expansion in some sectors, and the jobless rate dropped to its lowest level in two and a half years in December 2003.

A close examination of the June 2000 and November 2003 election results reveals three small signs of change in the political ideals of Japanese voters.

Field Report

Japan Goes to the Polls

It is 8 a.m. on June 16, 2000, and the candidate's campaign car sets out through the winding residential streets of Motoyama in Nagoya with loudspeakers on the roof, ready to blare out the campaign message. With national elections set for June 25, 2000, candidates for the Japanese parliament are campaigning with a mix of courtesy and aggressiveness. The campaign is not issue-oriented, and strict campaign rules limit election activities. Television advertising is severely limited. Stumping in the streets and blaring the candidate's name is permitted for twelve hours a day. The law limits the campaign period to twelve days before the election, and a candidate cannot knock on private doors or call on factories, stores, or restaurants to ask for votes. These restrictions work to the disadvantage of newcomers.

Of the 1,404 candidates jostling for 480 seats in the lower house general elections, 177 are "hereditary candidates" running on the basis of family connections. Thirty-five are competing for the first time. Political dynasties are not unique to Japan; think of Bush, Gore, and Kennedy in the United States. Nevertheless, the sheer number of hereditary politicians in Japan is beyond comparison.

After shaking hands with passersby in a narrow alley in Nagoya's Motoyama neighborhood, the candidate, dressed in a suit and wearing a sash proclaiming his name, bows in the street toward the people inside the shop windows. Handshaking is uncommon in Japan, where the traditional greeting is the bow, which this candidate likes to use as a campaign tool.

Candidates in Japan cannot hand out campaign posters to supporters or plaster them around town. Each candidate can hang a limited number of posters. Posters go on official wooden boards that have poster space for all the candidates together.

For reasons of etiquette, negative campaigning is less frequent than in the United States.

The first is declining support for the LDP's rural-oriented politics. As long as the LDP sticks to a governing style that involves spending money at its support base in farming and rural areas, it is unlikely to ever win a majority in the House of Representatives. As Japan enters the twenty-first century, the LDP needs to change the way it deals with rural areas. The second sign of change is an increase in support for Minshuto (the Democratic Party of Japan) in urban areas. Japanese city-dwellers voted for Minshuto as a protest against the LDP. Third, there is declining support for parties with strong religious leanings, such as New Komeito.

The primary causes of the conflict of interest between Japanese cities and rural areas are the economic recession and globalization. During the bubble economy, there was no conflict because both sides enjoyed the benefits of unprecedented economic growth. But when the bubble burst and the pressures of globalization became obvious, the harmonious relationship broke down. A growing number of companies began to rely on cheap overseas labor, rather than migrant workers from the countryside, to produce goods. Rural areas have found themselves left behind, unable to cope with the changes brought about by globalization. The LDP, whose support base is in rural areas, was forced to secure votes by funding pork-barrel public-works projects. The fact that the electoral district of a former prime minister has the largest number of construction firms per capita in Japan, and prides itself on its unshakable local support for the LDP, is eloquent testimony to this approach. City-dwellers suffering the effects of the recession have come to bitterly resent the way the government pours their hard-earned tax money into rural areas. The LDP losses in urban areas are a direct reflection of this discontent.

In addition, the 2003 election highlighted four significant changes taking place in Japan. First, the campaign message of youthful change and "reform" brought up by Koizumi is well on its way to establishing a new "popularity politics" in which media savvy and fashionable appeal are as important as good-old-boy networks or specific policies in coming to power. Second, the Japanese voters appear for the first time to be moving closer to a two-party system. The rise of the Minshuto party as a credible alternative to the LDP dates back to 2000. Third, and perhaps of greatest long-term significance, is the issue of "constitutional change" that candidates discussed in the election campaign. The LDP and the rising nationalist factions were talking about reform, about Japan's role in the world, about defense against countries such as North Korea. The major postwar taboos about changing the constitution are loosening. Finally, an election issue of particular interest among the electorate was pension reform. The current "pay as you go" system, which finances the pensions of the current generation of retirees with mandatory contributions from those now working, operated well enough when Japan had a pyramid-shaped distribution of population by age, but it is obvious that the same system cannot continue to function in a society where the elderly population is ballooning and the birthrate continues to drop. Nonetheless, candidates running for election avoided discussing the issue in earnest, leaving the Japanese—especially the young—deeply mistrustful of the system.

In the upper house parliamentary elections held on July 11, 2004, the governing coalition led by Prime Minister Junichiro Koizumi's Liberal Democratic party held its majority. But voters displeased with recent coalition government policies on pension reforms and the country's participation in a multinational force in Iraq favored the opposition Democratic Party with a significant number of seats, though not enough to change the real balance of power.

As Japan continues its quest for a cleaner, more open political future, the people register three common states of mind: (1) a revulsion against corrupt politicians, (2) a skepticism that real change will occur, and (3) a sense that the public is powerless. Opaque politics has stifled the views of ordinary Japanese and produced governments incapable of tackling vested interests. Until Japan's political system changes, attempts to tackle its economic woes will remain tied in knots.

THE NATIONAL FLAG AND THE ANTHEM: SYMBOLS TO UNITE THAT DIVIDE

In 1999 Japan's parliament overwhelmingly confirmed the rising-sun Hinomaru flag and a hymn to the emperor as the official symbols representing the Japanese people and the state. Legalization of the flag, a red circle symbolizing the sun on a white field, is less controversial than the anthem, which appears to grant almost holy status to the emperor for the first time since the defeat of imperial Japan in 1945. The formal name of the anthem, "Kimigayo," is translated "His Majesty's Reign," and the verse in translation venerates the emperor, who was officially a holy figure enshrined as a god in the Shinto religion until the Japanese defeat. In translation, the anthem reads,

> Thousands of years of happy reign be thine,
> Rule on, my lord, till what are pebbles now
> By age united to mighty rocks shall grow
> Whose venerable sides the moss doth line.

There is nothing unusual about giving legal recognition to a national flag or anthem by an act of parliament. Many countries do that; some even put such recognition in their constitution. More often than not, universal acceptance of national symbols is a matter of tradition and custom. The Hinomaru and "Kimigayo" have been Japan's de facto national symbols since the 1950s; they are seen and heard at diplomatic ceremonies and sporting events. Many Japanese support the Hinomaru and "Kimigayo." But the painful fact is that there is also considerable public opposition to an act that supposedly unifies the nation. The parliament's action in making the flag and the anthem official ignored the feelings of a large segment of the public who are not comfortable with these symbols. Teachers in particular have strongly opposed the anthem, contending that it evokes the 1930s and early 1940s, when Japanese troops conquered much of China and Southeast Asia. The song was composed when the emperor was the absolute monarch. Many people feel that the anthem is a paean to the emperor and therefore incompatible with the spirit of the postwar constitution. Opponents of the Hinomaru and "Kimigayo" view them as symbols of Japan's militaristic past; and they consider the government's action inappropriate because it establishes symbols that still evoke strong feelings among those who suffered under the boots of the Imperial Japanese Army and its political allies. The feelings are not limited to war victims overseas. In Japan, pitched battles have been waged at many schools over the treatment of the flag and the anthem. The flag and the national anthem have been lightning rods for controversy throughout the postwar era.

Japan's Defense Policy

Tucked away near Roppongi Crossing, the neon-lit center of Tokyo's nightlife, is a drab building that houses the headquarters of Japan's armed forces. Its air of unkempt insignificance reflects the army's low status in pacifist Japan. Yet the armed forces control more than 150 combat aircraft, 140 ships, and 250,000 uniformed personnel. And during the 2001 financial year, more than $45 billion (4.94 trillion yen) was spent on keeping this force in readiness to fight. If a war breaks out, the military would almost certainly break one of Japan's most fundamental laws: that force may be used only for self-defense inside the country's borders.

Article 9 of the constitution commits Japan to pacifism, allowing Japan's forces to parry blows from outside but not to root out trouble at the source. So the armed forces could shoot down incoming missiles but not, legally at any rate, attack the bases from which they were being launched. And though, as a sovereign power, Japan claims the right of collective self-defense with other states, it paradoxically claims that exercising such a right would be unconstitutional. The question of collective self-defense has tied the country into constitutional knots. The cornerstone of Japan's nonaggressive defense policy is that it can rely on the United States for its defense. But the presence of American forces in Japan worries extreme constitutionalists. The Social Democratic Party (formerly the Socialist Party of Japan)—part of the government in 1993–94—maintains that any attack launched from Japanese soil, even by American forces, would be illegal. Some politicians such as Ichiro Ozawa (of the Liberal Party, which merged with the Democratic Party of Japan) would like to cut through the constitutional tangle by scrapping Article 9 altogether. The governing party is expected to propose revisions to Japan's constitution by 2005, and the prime minister wants the Self-Defense Forces to become a full-fledged military.

Because of uncertainty in the Korean peninsula, Japan and the United States in their 1996 joint declaration on security reconfirmed the importance of the Japan-U.S. security treaty and the presence of U.S. forces in Japan for peace and stability in Asia and the Pacific region (Stokes and Shinn 1998). Following North Korea's admission in 2002 that it has been enriching uranium that can be used to make nuclear weapons, Japan, South Korea, and the United States have worked together to persuade North Korea to scrap its nuclear program. To create a basis for more effective and credible Japan-U.S. cooperation, it is necessary to resolve issues such as the "sympathy budget"—through which Japan offers host-nation fiscal contributions toward the stationing of U.S. forces in Japan—as well as the relocation of functions of the U.S. air station in Futenma, Okinawa Prefecture, as early as possible. In 1998 Japan formally approved a plan to start joint research with the United States on theater missile defense (TMD) systems. The TMD systems are intended to protect the United States and its allies within a 1,864-mile (3,000-km) radius from incoming ballistic missiles by detecting them with satellites and shooting them down with missiles or by other means.

Territorial Disputes with Russia, China, and Korea

Although more than a half century has elapsed since the end of World War II, Japan and Russia still have not concluded a formal peace treaty. The key issue in treaty negotiations has been a dispute over four islands—Iturup, Kunashir, Shikotan-to, and the Habomai group—located just to the northeast of Hokkaido. The strategic, political, and emotional importance of the islands, which have a total land area of some 193 square miles (500 sq km), far exceeds their economic worth, although they are surrounded by rich fishing grounds and have some mineral resources. Czarist Russia and the Soviet Union (until the end of World War II) recognized the islands as Japanese. The Soviet Union unilaterally broke its neutrality pact with Japan three days after the atomic bombing of Hiroshima and attacked Japan one week before Japan surrendered in 1945. The Soviets retook the southern half of Sakhalin, which had been lost in the Russo-Japanese War, and grabbed the entire island chain north of Hokkiado for good measure. Because of the occupation of Japanese territory by Russian forces, there is no peace treaty between Japan and Russia. The Japanese refer to the islands as the Northern Territories, regarding them as part of Japan's "inherent" territory. The antagonism on both sides has deepened and the respec-

A billboard in Hokkaido proclaims Etorofu (Iturup) and Kunashir, at the southern end of the Kuril Island chain, and the smaller Shikotan-to and Habomai Islands, as Japanese territory. These islands, northeast of Hokkaido, were seized by Russia in the last days of World War II. Public and media opinion remains strong in Japan regarding these islands, known as the Northern Territories. Strains in Japan-Russia relations have deep historical roots going back to the competition of the Japanese and Russian empires for dominance in northeast Asia. The territorial dispute over the Northern Territories remains a stumbling block in Japan's efforts to establish bilateral relations on a stable basis. Photo by P.P. Karan.

tive positions of Japan and Russia have solidified during the last five decades.

The Kuril Islands became the frontier between Japan and Russia in the eighteenth century, during Russia's great expansion to the Pacific Ocean. The first formal delimitation of boundaries between the two countries was made in the 1855 Treaty of Shimoda, by which the Kuril Islands north of Iturup were recognized as Russian and those from Iturup south as Japanese—the boundary, the Japanese government contends, that should obtain today. Competition over Sakhalin Island remained unresolved until Japan renounced its claims in exchange for the northern and central Kuril Islands in the 1875 Treaty of St. Petersburg. The strategic value of the relinquished islands quickly became apparent to Russia, which saw its access to the Pacific dominated by Japan, whose imperialist ambitions increasingly conflicted with its own. The Russians have never forgotten their disastrous naval losses and the humiliation of their defeat in the Russo-Japanese War of 1904–5; the settlement of that conflict included the cession of the southern half of Sakhalin to Japan (see fig. 9.4).

The present dispute springs from the controversial Yalta Agreement of February 11, 1945, which Russia claims awarded the Kuril Islands to the Soviet Union. Japan does not consider the disputed islands part of the Kuril Islands (Morris-Suzuki 1999). The official Japanese position is that the Kuril Islands include only those islands acquired by Russia in 1855. Iturup and Kunashir are not part of the Kurils. They

never belonged to any country but Japan and, like Shikotan-to and the Habomai Islands, have traditionally been considered extensions of Hokkaido; they are part of Japan's inherent territory. The conflicting claims are facilitated by the fact that in the Yalta Agreement there is no description of what constituted the Kuril Islands. After breaking its 1941 neutrality pact with Japan to join in the final days of the Pacific War, the Soviet Union moved quickly to make good its irredentist aims. The Russian occupation of the four islands was conducted as an invasion and met with initial Japanese resistance in the north. In the postwar era, the Soviet Union incorporated the islands into the Soviet administrative structure, isolated them almost completely from non-Russian contact, and expelled all of the Japanese who had not escaped earlier. (There were 16,500 Japanese inhabitants before the Russian invasion.)

Some of the people who used to live on these four islands now live in Nemuro, in northeastern Hokkaido, on a peninsula that is the easternmost bit of land still controlled by Japan. On a clear day, some of the disputed islands emerge through the haze as splotches of brown on the horizon of ocean, teasing the memories of former inhabitants.

Although outsiders might have a hard time figuring out why anybody would want a set of tiny, windswept islands that could use a few billion dollars worth of infrastructure investment, Japan and Russia are doggedly resistant to compromise on their territorial claims. So the islands remain one of the unsolved legacies of World War II. As the dispute

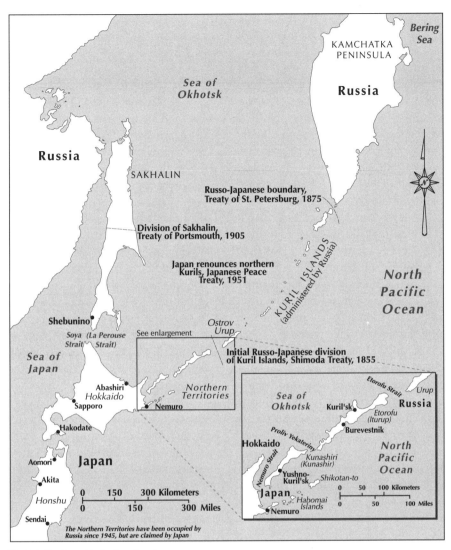

Fig. 9.4. Northern Territories dispute.

continues, nearly ten thousand elderly Japanese refugees from the Northern Territories bide their time in Nemuro and in nearby towns. The movement to restore the islands is strong among Japanese born in the Northern Territories, but support for the movement is weak among others (Nakamura 2000).

Scholars doubt that Russia will be much inclined to compromise, partly because democracy makes it difficult for politicians to ignore nationalist sentiment against giving up territory. Moreover, the Russian military argues that it needs the islands to defend the Russian Far East and to protect Russian ballistic missile submarines in the Sea of Okhotsk. Russia considers the Kurils vital to its position as a Pacific power. The islands screen the eastern Russian littoral, contain passages into the Pacific, and provide excellent forward bases.

Outsiders do not seem enormously sympathetic to Japan, perhaps partly because other countries also lost territory in World War II but do not make an issue of it. Germany, for instance, lost eastern regions to Poland and Russia. Moreover, Japan controlled the Northern Territories for a relatively brief period. The islands were traditionally inhabited by Ainu, an indigenous people who also live in northern Japan and in parts of the Russian Far East, and Japanese settlers arrived there only in the late nineteenth century.

Many of the former residents visit the islands in

an exchange program. Every year about 420 Japanese—mostly former residents of the islands and their families—are allowed to travel without visas to their former lands, while the same number of Russians come to Nemuro for a visit. But the exchanges have done little to ease the animosities, partly because Russia still seizes Japanese fishing boats that stray into what it regards as Russian waters. In any case the Japanese describe the return visits to their native islands as a melancholy experience, for there are almost no signs left of the Japanese presence. Homes, buildings, shrines, and signs have all been destroyed, replaced by dilapidated buildings that, in Communist fashion, look old and weary. However, under strict Russian environmental protection measures, which include a ban on industrial activities in many parts of the disputed islands, the Northern Territories are brimming with wildlife such as sea otters, tufted puffins, and big owls—animals rarely seen in nearby Hokkaido. Fishing is one of the biggest threats to the islands' coastal and marine wildlife, and fishing nets have not been used in this area.

In the meantime, with the economy of the disputed islands in shambles, Russians on these stormy, volcanic islands are debating a radical survival plan—leasing their territory to Japan. Kunashir's port—the very heart of the most populous island—is an unbroken vision of decay, with rusting trawlers, derelict cars, and wrecked machinery littering the coast. A fish processing plant, once the island's economic hub, stands silent following its bankruptcy in 1998. The port stirs to life only when Russian fishing boats return from Japan, just a few miles across the rough seas. The boats return after selling loads of sea urchins, and bring back food and clothes for the island's thinly stocked stores. The cars greeting the boats are secondhand used Japanese models, as are almost all vehicles on the island. Against this bleak economic backdrop, some Russians on two of the four disputed islands have signed petitions to lease their land to Japan for up to 99 years in exchange for investment and economic assistance. The frustrated residents on Shikotan-to, the poorest island, reached their breaking point on October 14, 1998, when their electric power station exploded, leaving them in darkness. Almost all adults on Shikotan-to signed a petition calling for the island to be leased to Japan. More than 80 percent of the islands' food, and nearly all of the cars and electronics, come from Japan. The Russians

know their feeble economy would crumble without the Japanese, but many worry that if the Japanese took over, Russians would become second-class citizens.

In an exercise of green diplomacy, environmentalists have proposed a cross-border park linking Shiretoko National Park on Hokkaido with a series of land and marine reserves on the four disputed islands. A cross-border park would unite two radically different environments. A pave-and-dam ethic characterizes the landscape on the Japanese side. The Russian side has largely been left alone without major modification of landscape by human activities. The disputed islands have become reservoirs for several bird species on the verge of extinction in Hokkaido, including Blakiston's fish owl, Steller's sea eagle, the tufted puffin, and the red-crowned crane. There are old forests where there has been no cutting. For the past two decades, the Kuriliski Nature Reserve has protected about 60 percent of the three contested islands. Cross-border cooperation could contribute to building of stocks of species for reintroduction into Hokkaido. Along the Russia-Alaska border, the Beringia Heritage International Park has led to frequent international exchanges among native communities, and joint monitoring of polar bears and walruses. A cross-border peace park and promotion of Kuril tourism could transform the Russia-Japan border area's stagnating economy and promote regional peace and stability. However, Russia's suspicion of outsiders and bureaucratic corruption, along with Japan's reluctance to compromise its position on the islands, present formidable hurdles to this kind of cross-border environmental project.

A second territorial dispute involves a tiny chain of islands in the East China Sea (Suganuma 1997, 2000). The Japanese call them the Senkaku Islands (see fig. 9.5). The Chinese refer to them as the Tiaoyutai (Diaoyu) Islands. They are uninhabited and consist of five tiny rock islands and three reefs 125 miles (200 km) northeast of Taiwan, 250 miles (400 km) east of China, and 180 miles (288 km) west of Okinawa. Japan has long asserted sovereignty over the Senkaku Islands, but since they were returned by the United States to Japanese control along with nearby Okinawa in 1971, the nation has never taken steps to press its claim. China and Taiwan have also long asserted sovereignty. The seabed around the island group is thought to be rich in oil reserves and maritime resources. In 1996 the Japanese govern-

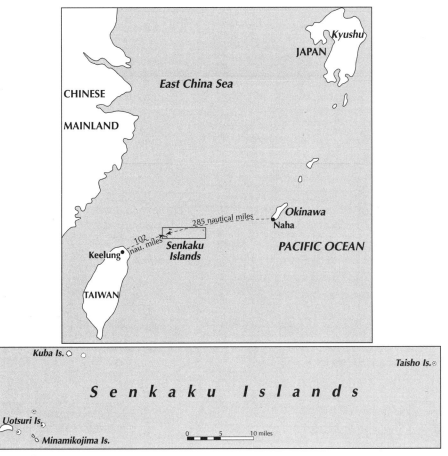

Fig. 9.5. Senkaku Islands dispute.

ment approved an exclusive economic-zone status for the islands and erected a lighthouse on one of them.

A number of factors account for the dispute. The most obvious is the potential economic resource. Both Japan and China covet the energy resources of the area. The strategic location of the Senkaku Islands and the troubled relations between China and Japan in modern times have also contributed to the dispute. Extensive Chinese records refer to the islands by name since the middle of the sixteenth century and suggest that China regarded the islands as Chinese at least since then. The irredentist territorial claims serve as a powerful force generating patriotism and nationalism in China. Japan's claim is more recent: it says that it discovered the islands in 1884, and it has claimed them since 1895. Japan does not want to give up the islands because it developed Senkaku over a period of years. Tensions over own-

ership of the islands have surfaced from time to time since the 1970s. In January 2004 the Japan Coast Guard blocked two fishing vessels carrying twenty Chinese activists attempting to land on the Senkaku Islands. The Chinese, including soldiers and white-collar workers, were planning to set up a monument asserting Chinese sovereignty. Japan has succeeded in barring several attempts by activists from mainland China, Hong Kong, and Taiwan from landing on the contested islands.

Take Shima, an uninhabited island in the Sea of Japan, is the focus of a dispute between Japan and the Republic of Korea (see fig. 9.6). Located just south of the 38th parallel and approximately equidistant from Honshu and the Korean peninsula, the island is called Tok-do by the Koreans. Small (0.09 sq mi [0.23 sq km], one-fifteenth the size of New York's Central Park) and barren, the island is little more than a cluster of reefs. It was occupied by Japan dur-

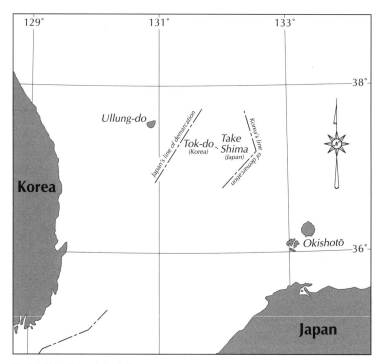

Fig. 9.6. Take Shima Island dispute.

ing the Russo-Japanese War (1904–5) and was incorporated into Shimane Prefecture in 1905. The Republic of Korea claimed the island after World War II. Efforts to resolve the dispute have not been successful. The island represents the interaction of Korea's deep sense of victimization at the hands of Japan and Japan's equally deep attachment to its island extremities. In January 2004 South Korea released postage stamps featuring the disputed island, an action that unleashed a flood of anti-Japanese sentiment.

The hunger for energy in the region may make it difficult to manage and resolve the territorial disputes because of interstate competition to control possible petroleum and mineral deposits in the seabeds near disputed islands—the Senkaku or Diaoyu Islands and Take Shima or Tok-do. The area around the islands has rich squid, crab, and mackerel fishing grounds. Rich fisheries and dreams of offshore oil and gas discoveries strengthen Japan's resolve to defend the islands.

JAPAN, ASIA, AND THE UNITED STATES: GEOPOLITICAL ASPECTS

As Japan begins its quest for leadership in Asia, it nervously glances back at the World War II era bru-

talities that it has never properly acknowledged. Candor on war crimes always came grudgingly to Japanese leaders. Education ministers airbrushed unpleasant facts out of Japanese textbooks, while foreign ministry officials drafted ambiguous "apologies" for top leaders to read on visits to countries ravaged by Japanese troops. In just six weeks, Japanese forces murdered between 100,000 and 300,000 people in Nanjing and raped 20,000. Two million Vietnamese starved to death under Japanese occupation. Hundreds of thousands of Koreans, Filipinos, and Indonesians were dragged into slavery. Japanese citizens, most of whom have no personal responsibility for war crimes, must honestly come to terms with their country's recent history and thus with how Japan is perceived throughout Asia. More than a half century after the war, it's right for Japan to resume an active role in Asia and the world. But first it must honorably face up to the unspeakable crimes of a long-unspoken past.

Because economic power tends to translate into military power, China's economic boom is a major concern for Japan. With the rise of an increasingly powerful and assertive China, and with the spread of Japanese investments all over China (Suganuma

1998), Japan has a greater regional economic interest to protect. Japan's only reliable partner for deterring China and keeping the peace around Asia is the United States. Japan alone cannot handle China, and Japan alone cannot protect its own sea-lanes.

Japan normalized relations with China in 1972. Since then history has been a major factor shaping their relationship, which has been characterized by a duality of economic and political cooperation and mutual fears of economic and strategic competition. A strong China and a weak Japan defined the landscape of East Asia for a long time until the Meiji Restoration, but this situation reversed during the past hundred years. As China has reemerged as a major power in Asia, Japanese view China as a potential threat. China, for its part, having lost wars to the great powers in the modern era, even now perceives itself to be behind the industrialized nations in terms of economic development. This mixture of pride and psychological complex has warped the way China and Japan perceive each other.

Chinese and Japanese are often misled by the things they have in common on the surface, such as Oriental facial features, the use of Chinese characters for writing, and eating rice as the main staple of their diets. These similarities tend to lead them to unconsciously interpret the culture, thought patterns, and actions of the other country according to their own standards. In reality, Japan's culture came into its own and took an independent turn from that of China during the Kamakura Period, roughly eight centuries ago. The two countries have many stark differences, among them that Japan is a nation closely oriented to the sea, while China is a state anchored on a huge continent.

Chinese suspicion and distrust, on the one hand, and Japanese war guilt mixed with an element of superiority complex, on the other, have prevented the development of a close relationship. China has used war guilt to manipulate the relationship quite effectively. Japan's principal concern has been stability in China and fostering beneficial economic growth. Yet Japan's inability to honestly confront its past remains a major source of friction in China and elsewhere in East Asia (Harris 1994). This has been displayed during many controversies, particularly those over the issue of "comfort women" and Japanese school textbooks' depiction of the Pacific War. The two nations could overcome their past if Japan would remember the lessons of its invasion and ensuing war with China, and if China would stop repeatedly referring to them.

American Military Bases in Japan

American military bases in Japan form the bedrock of the political relationship between Japan and the United States, but they have also been a source of irritation in the relations (see fig. 9.7). As of 1990 there were 105 U.S. military bases in Japan, occupying a total of 125 square miles (323.7 sq km). The largest concentration of bases and personnel by far is on the small island of Okinawa. The most important U.S. military bases include Kadena Air Base on Okinawa, the largest U.S. air base in the Pacific. Other bases are air bases at Yokota, Atsugi, Iwakuni, and Futenma; naval bases at Yokosuka and Sasebo; the maneuver area at Fuji; and communications bases at Sobe, Misawa, Tokachibuto, and Iojima. The Fifth Air Force, which is responsible for air defense of Japan and South Korea, is stationed at Yokota. The Seventh Fleet maintains two supply and repair bases at Yokosuka and Sasebo. Army headquarters are in Zama, navy headquarters in Yokosuka. A large number of U.S. Marines are deployed primarily in Okinawa, where there are large Marine encampments in the southern part of the island and training areas and camps in the northern part. The commander of the U.S. armed forces in Japan represents the three branches of the military and coordinates their activities. Under the terms of the host-nation accord, Japan pays for (1) Japanese working at U.S. base facilities, (2) electricity, heating, and water used at U.S. base facilities and related areas, and (3) relocation of military training grounds of U.S. forces that is carried out upon Japan's request. These expenditures amounted to 157 billion yen (about $15 billion) in fiscal 2000.

Low-altitude flying drills by planes stationed at the Misawa Naval Air Facility in Aomori Prefecture have been criticized by the governments of cities on the flyover route as well as by environmentalists. The F-16 fighters regularly thunder over the Shirakami Mountains, where endangered golden eagles breed. Environmental groups are worried because studies have proved that excessive noise adversely affects wild animals' reproductive systems. Some three thousand residents near the Yokota Air Base in Tokyo's western suburbs, most of them living in Fussa, have com-

Fig. 9.7. Principal U.S. military bases.

plained of noise pollution and have sought a ban on flights at the base between 9 p.m. and 7 a.m.

People living in the vicinity of the U.S. Atsugi Naval Air Facility, Kanagawa Prefecture, also suffer from noise pollution. In a landmark noise-pollution case, the Yokohama District Court in October 2002 ordered the Japanese government to pay about 2.75 billion yen in compensation to 4,935 residents around the Atsugi military base in Kanagawa Prefecture. The ruling follows the outcome of similar suits over U.S. bases in Yokota (Tokyo) and Kadena (Okinawa) and a Japanese base in Ishikawa Prefecture.

Major U.S. Military Bases in Japan

The Kanto Plain Base Complex

Yokota Air Base: COMUS/JAPAN headquarters; Fifth Air Force headquarters, 374th Airlift Wing; logistics/transport hub.

Yokosuka Naval Base: Seventh Fleet Flagship (USS *Blue Ridge*), commander, Seventh Fleet; USS *Kitty Hawk* Carrier Battle Group; commander, Carrier Striking Force Seventh Fleet; ten surface combatants (cruisers, destroyers, frigates); commander, U.S. Naval Forces, Japan; commander, Submarine Group 7; ship repair facility, Yokosuka.

Atsugi Air Base: commander, Fleet Air Western Pacific; Carrier Air Wing Five (USS *Kitty Hawk* Air Wing); Light Helicopter Anti-Submarine Squadron 51.

Kamiseya Communications Facility: commander, Patrol Wing One; headquarters, Seventh Fleet Maritime Patrol Aircraft Task Force; headquarters, Fifth Fleet Maritime Patrol Aircraft Task Force.

Yokohama: headquarters, Military Sealift Command, Far East; Yokohama Military Port; Sagami Army Depot.

Zama: headquarters, U.S. Army, Japan Ninth Theater Army Area; Command (TAACOM); 1 (U.S.) Corps (Forward) Liaison Detachment; Seventeenth Army Support Group (ASG); Army Medical Department Activity Japan (MEDDACJAPAN).

Camp Fuji: USMC live firing area.

Sasebo, Northern Kyushu

Sasebo Naval Base: Amphibious Ready Group (ARG) Bravo, 4 amphibious ships, 2 minesweepers.

Misawa, Aomori Prefecture, Tohoku

Misawa Air Base: Thirty-fifth Fighter Wing (USAF), 36 F-16 aircraft; Fleet Electronic Reconnaissance Detachment (Navy), 2EP-3 aircraft; Misawa Air Patrol Group (Navy), 6–7 P-3C aircraft.

Iwakuni, Yamaguchi Prefecture

Iwakuni Marine Corps Air Station: Marine Air Group 12 (MAG 12), USMC F/A-18, EA 6b, and C-130 aircraft.

The Okinawa Base Complex

Camp Zukeran (206 ac or 83.4 ha): Marine Corps Base Camp S.D. Butler; headquarters, Marine Corps bases, Okinawa; First Marine Aircraft Wing Headquarters; Twelfth Marine Regiment (Artillery).

Camp Courtney: headquarters, Third Marine Expeditionary Force; headquarters, Third Marine Division; headquarters, Thirty-first Marine Expeditionary Unit.

Camp McTureous: USMC housing facility.

Camp Kuwae: U.S. Naval Hospital; most of Camp Kuwae (245 ac or 99.1 ha) will be returned by March 2008, after the Naval Hospital is relocated to Camp Zukeran.

Tengan Pier: U.S. Navy ordnance handling facility.

Futenma Marine Corps Air Station: Marine Air Group 36 (MAG 36). This facility will be returned to Japan within the next few years, after adequate replacement facilities are completed and operational.

(continued on the following page)

Major U.S. Military Bases in Japan (continued)

Kadena Air Base: Eighteenth Wing; 54 F-15 aircraft; E-3 AWACS; KC-135 aerial; refueling aircraft; 353 Special Operations Group C-130 aircraft; Okinawa Air Patrol Group (Navy).

Kadena Ammunition Storage Area: USAF and USMC ammunition storage facility.

Kadena Oil Storage Facility.

Camp Shields: USAF and Navy barracks; construction equipment repair facility.

Yomitan Auxiliary Airfield (471 ac or 190.6 ha): returned to Japan, March 2001.

Torii Station: First Battalion, First Special Forces Group, U.S. Army (Airborne); Tenth Army Area Support Group; communication site.

Senaha Communication Station (151 ac or 61.1 ha): except for the microwave tower portion (0.3 ac or 0.12 ha), most of the land was returned to Japan in March 2001 after the facilities were relocated to Torii Communication Station.

Sobe Communication Site: U.S. Navy communications facility (132 ac or 53.4 ha), returned to Japan in March 2001 after support facilities relocated to Camp Hansen.

Makiminato Service Area: USMC logistics base; Third Force Service Support Group. Land adjacent to Route 58 (8 ac or 3.2 ha) will be returned to Japan to widen the highway.

Naha Military Port: U.S. Army Logistics Command facility (140 ac or 56.7 ha); embarkation point for combat loading of III MEF equipment. The return of Naha Military Port, agreed upon many years ago, has been delayed by the lack of a suitable alternative in Okinawa.

Camp Schwab: Fourth Marine Regiment (Infantry); live firing and amphibious training exercises.

Henoko Ordnance Depot: USMC ammunition storage, adjacent to Camp Schwab.

Gimbaru Training Area: USMC training facility (149 ac or 60.3 ha); helicopter operations and amphibious training exercises. Land to be returned to Japan after facilities are relocated to Kin Blue Beach and Camp Hansen.

Kin Blue Beach: USMC training facility; ship-to-shore movement training.

Kin Red Beach: USMC training facility; embarkation training.

White Beach: commander, Amphibious Group One (U.S. Navy), Seventh Fleet Commander of Amphibious Ready Groups permanently stationed in Japan and deploying from the United States.

Awase Communication Site: U.S. Navy communications facility.

Northern Training Area (9,852 ac or 3,987 ha): major portion returned in March 2003.

Aha Training Area: USMC training facility (1,185 ac or 480 ha) and water area (19,509 ac or 7,895 ha) surrounded by the Northern Training Area. Returned to Japan.

Ie Jima Auxiliary Airfield: USMC training facility; AV-8 Harrier aircraft take-off and landing exercises, and parachute training.

Okuma Rest Center: USAF recreation facility.

Source: "Report on the Security Relationship between the United States and Japan, March 1, 1995, Submitted in Compliance with Section 1325 of FY 95 Defense Authorization Act and the Special Action Committee on Okinawa (SACO) Final Report," December 2, 1996.

The U.S. presence in Japan remains for a number of reasons. Ostensibly, the main reason is the U.S.-Japan Security Treaty and the lack of offensive capability of Japan's Self-Defense Forces. The instability of the secretive communist regime of North Korea and its potential aggression is a frequently cited rationale. Japanese fears of North Korea were exacerbated by North Korea's launch of a rocket over Japan in the fall of 1998. Containing China was also a cold-war-era justification for the U.S. presence. The United States has used its bases in Japan for other purposes, however. During the Vietnam war, Okinawa was the primary port for servicemen and supplies headed off to the frontlines. Troops can also be (and have been) deployed to the Persian Gulf region from Okinawa. Therefore, for U.S. military strategists, the bases in Japan and particularly in Okinawa remain important for U.S. military activities beyond the Pacific region (Hosokawa 1998).

Most of the U.S. bases were either preexisting Japanese military bases taken over after 1945 or new bases that were constructed during the Korean War (1950–53). Initially the rents for use of the bases and subsidies to surrounding areas were minimal, and local residents were sometimes even forcibly removed and relocated. Now, however, U.S. military rents are well above average for those tracts of land. Popular opposition and resentment against the bases is based more upon an ideological pacifism, which is a legacy of Japan's constitution and war experience, and against social effects of the bases, especially in Okinawa. Resentment is strongest in Okinawa and centers around a host of social problems: accidents involving injury to Japanese citizens and property for which the United States paid no compensation, the noise caused by U.S. aircraft, environmental problems blamed on the bases, and, especially, violent crimes committed by U.S. servicemen.

Public hostility to the American military presence surged in 1995 after three American servicemen were arrested, and later convicted, for kidnapping and gang raping a sixth-grade girl in Okinawa. During the years since the reversion of Okinawa's administration from the United States, 4,716 criminal cases such as sexual crimes and murders involving U.S. servicemen have been reported (an average of 205 cases per year). The rates of violent crime by servicemen on Okinawa exceed the rates of crimes by U.S. troops at home or in other foreign areas. More than 110 women have been sexually assaulted by U.S. servicemen since 1990, and these are just the cases that the Okinawa Prefectural Police have become aware of. Presumably, additional women who have suffered such assaults remain silent.

Okinawa has in effect borne a huge burden for Japan since the end of the war (Pollard 2002). First the Battle of Okinawa decimated its population. Then the construction of the bases took some of Okinawa's most fertile land away from its people. After Okinawa reverted to Japan in 1972, the bases remained, covering about 20 percent of the island's land area. The bases are also located in the middle of urban areas, creating densely packed suburban sprawl in central and southern Okinawa, and horrendous traffic congestion. The bases are impossible to ignore, causing Okinawa citizens daily inconveniences from the noise of low-flying aircraft and from traffic accidents. Recently ultralow flight exercises by U.S. military planes have been increasing, bringing further dangers in many parts of Japan.

The 1996 Japan-U.S. Special Action Committee on Okinawa (SACO) was established to alleviate the burden of having so many U.S. military bases on Okinawa Prefecture. The SACO agreement specifies eleven measures to be taken to return land on which U.S. military facilities are located. These include the return of the Northern and Aha Training Areas and the Sobe Communications Site and efforts to hasten the return of land at Naha Bay. If all the measures stipulated in the agreement were carried out, the area occupied by the military bases would be reduced by 20 percent. By the end of 2003 only the Aha Training Area was closed down and returned; most of the land at Senaha Communication Station was also returned. The Gimbaru Training Area was to be returned by the end of 1997, but negotiations with local people have run into difficulties and the issue remains unresolved. One reason behind the delay is that the local economy and businesses rely heavily on the existence of U.S. military bases. Concern about the possible economic impact has divided local opinion and has delayed reaching an agreement. No progress has been made since Japan and the United States decided on a replacement site for the Futenma Air Station—the focus of the SACO agreement—because they cannot agree on a fifteen-year limit on the use of the heliport as requested by the prefectural and Nago governments (Appel 1999). The

SACO agreement also includes items such as noise reduction and improvement in the Status of Forces Agreement between Japan and the United States. Restrictions on aircraft noise at Kadena Air Base and Futenma Air Station and on night flights at Futenma Air Station have been implemented.

Although many Okinawans are angry about the U.S. bases, their anger is directed as much against Tokyo as it is against Washington, or maybe more. They realize that the presence of so many bases on their small island is now the responsibility of the Japanese government, which shows little inclination to relocate these facilities to the Japanese mainland. Not all Okinawans are upset about the bases, however. Some receive large rents from tracts of land they own, and many Okinawans work on the bases, which pay excellent wages compared to other jobs in the area. The multiplier effect of American spending in Okinawa also has to be considered. As Japan's poorest prefecture, Okinawa has few viable economic options in the short term, and a sudden removal of the bases would be devastating to the regional economy, which is already heavily dependent on the Japanese mainland.

Nonetheless, anger from the rape incident has spread from Okinawa to the rest of Japan and has fueled increasing Japanese citizen disapproval with the current situation. The United States and Japan announced a plan in 1996 to coordinate the American military presence in Okinawa and in particular to close a heliport at the Futenma Air Station within seven years after Japan had built an equivalent heliport somewhere else. No other prefecture in Japan has offered an alternate site. A proposal to build a large floating heliport off Okinawa's east coast has been temporarily stalled by local residents' objections, largely over environmental concerns, and has created a rupture between Okinawa's government and the national government. Somewhat relieved, the United States has sat back and left the relocation problem to the Japanese. Meanwhile, the U.S. administration has reiterated its commitment to keeping its military forces intact in Japan for the foreseeable future.

In 1995 the United States announced (under the "Nye initiative") that it would keep one hundred thousand American troops in East Asia for the foreseeable future; for years, the emphasis has been on the importance of defending against the threat of military attack. In the 1980s, the United States pointed to the Soviet threat; in the 1990s, there was a continuing threat from North Korea. The United States does not want to invoke (at least not in public) a threat from China as a rationale for the U.S. forces in Japan and South Korea. As the challenge of a nuclear North Korean threat rises, the United States has shifted emphasis to the need for American troops to preserve "stability" and the "balance of power" in East Asia. South Korea has accepted this idea and the need for U.S. troops to protect South Korea from its powerful neighbors, Japan, Russia, and China. For the United States to sell this "balance of power" justification in East Asia will require some delicate work. It means persuading China that the U.S. troops help prevent the rise of a militarized Japan, convincing Japan that the American troops protect it against rising China, and telling other Asian countries that the U.S. forces protect them against China and Japan. At the moment, such arguments have enough plausibility to be accepted in East Asia. Over the long run, they may prove a tough sell. If China seems threatening, the U.S. forces will no doubt be begged to stay. If not, Asia may eventually wish them farewell.

Despite the controversy surrounding the military bases, Japan and the United States are bound by common values related to democracy, an open economic system, and human rights. The U.S.-Japan security relationship has contributed to political stability in the region (Vogel 2002).

JAPAN AND RUSSIA

A century after the Russo-Japanese War, the two perennial adversaries are now embarking on an era of economic cooperation despite an outstanding territorial dispute. Their bilateral trade increased about 25 percent in 2003. For the first time, Japanese power companies took deliveries of Russian oil and committed themselves to buying Russian gas. Oil and gas investment has flowed in such volumes in 2003 that it has roughly doubled Japan's total foreign direct investment in Russia to about $1 billion. Mitsui holds 25 percent, and the Mitsubishi Corporation holds 20 percent, of the Sakhalin Energy Investment Company, a joint natural gas venture operated by Royal Dutch Shell. By 2006 there will be a lot of natural gas coming out of Sakhalin to Japan. Behind the new business investment is the growing realization that each country has things the other wants. Besides

Japan's desire for Siberian oil and Russia's interest in Japanese investment, each is looking for an ally in the neighborhood to keep China in check. Russia's shrinking population in the east and a lot of Chinese across the border present a potential demographic geopolitical concern for the Russians. Lately, the mutual desire for trade, oil and gas integration, and geopolitical concerns of a rising China have pushed the territorial dispute to the back burner.

JAPAN AND LATIN AMERICA

Japan's relationship with Latin America has been described as "strong in blood but weak in business" (Kagami 2001). The approximately 1.3 million people of Japanese origin in Latin America constitute the largest Japanese population outside Japan. About 200,000, mostly from Brazil and Peru, have come to Japan as dekasegi after the 1990 Law on Immigration Control permitted foreigners of Japanese descent (nikkeijin) to reside and work in Japan. Upon their return to the home country, the dekasegi can play an important role as a bridge between Japan and Latin America through technology and cultural transfer. Japan can strengthen its relationship with Latin America through increasing imports from the region and by directing more foreign investment into the area.

As Japan enters the twenty-first century, the question arises whether in the light of its history the nation will forever remain on the sidelines in military and security affairs, or whether it will assume a larger role. The present prime minister, Junichiro Koizumi, wants a more assertive Japan, ready to take its place among the world's great powers. Both public and elite opinion in Japan remains supportive of expanding its role in the world.

REFERENCES

Appel, R. 1999. Floating fiasco: The environmental and social impacts of the Nago Heliport. *Journal of Environment and Development* 8 (2): 170–182.

Christensen, Raymond V. 1994. Electoral reform in Japan: How it was enacted and changes it may bring. *Asian Survey* 34:589–605.

Curtis, G.L. 1988. *The Japanese Way of Politics.* New York: Columbia Univ. Press.

Green, Michael. 1995. *Arming Japan: Alliance Politics, Defense Production and the Postwar Search for Autonomy.* New York: Columbia Univ. Press.

Harris, Sheldon H. 1994. *Factories of Death: Japanese Secret Biological Warfare, 1932–1945, and the American Cover-Up.* New York: Routledge.

Hosokawa, Morihiro. 1998. Are U.S. troops in Japan needed? Restoring the alliance. *Foreign Affairs*, July–August.

Kagami, Mitsuhiro. 2001. Japan and Latin America. *Japanese Economy* 29 (3): 21–47.

Morris-Suzuki, T. 1999. Lines in the snow: Imagining the Russo-Japanese frontier. *Pacific Affairs* 72 (1): 57–77.

Nakamura, Naohiro. 2000. The weakening movement for restoring the Northern Territories by former islanders and their descendants. *Human Geography* 52 (5): 90–106.

Pollard, Vincent K. 2002. Designing a peaceful Okinawa: Local opportunities and regional obstacles. *Social Science Japan* 23 (April): 29–35.

Sano, Hiroshi, and Tomoki Nakaya. 2000. Electoral bias of single-member constituency system under a multiple party system: Case study of the 1996 Japanese general elections for the House of Representatives. *Geographical Review of Japan* A 73:559–577.

Stokes, Bruce, and James J. Shinn, eds. 1998. *The Tests of War and the Strains of Peace: The U.S.-Japan Security Relationship.* New York: Council on Foreign Relations.

Suganuma, Unryu. 1997. Diaoyu or Senkaku Islands under Pax Sinica: Chinese national defense during the Ming times. *American Journal of Chinese Studies* 4 (1): 73–86.

———. 1998. Geostrategic considerations of Japanese ODA to China, 1979–1994. *Geographical Review of Japan* B 71:121–143.

———. 2000. *Sovereign Rights and Territorial Space in Sino-Japanese Relations: Irredentism and the Diaoyu/Senkaku Islands.* Honolulu: Association for Asian Studies and Univ. of Hawaii Press.

Takahasi, N., and Y. Ida. 1987. Regional characteristics of local government finance in Japan. *Annual Report, Institute of Geoscience,* Univ. of Tsukuba, 13:30–36.

Vogel, Steven K., ed. 2002. *U.S.-Japan Relations in a Changing World.* Washington, DC: Brookings Institution Press.

Woodall, Brian. 1996. *Japan under Construction: Corruption, Politics, and Public Works.* Berkeley: Univ. of California Press.

Chapter 10

第 十 章

The Economic Challenge

Japan has the second-largest market economy in the world, with an aggregate output of more than $4.8 trillion. The per capita gross national product (GNP) was $38,000 in 1997, as compared to $29,000 in the United States. However, once corrections are made for Japan's high cost of housing and of various goods, the effective per capita GNP in terms of purchasing power parity was $24,400 in 1997. With its large productivity and volume of exports, Japan is one of the three centers of world economic power, alongside the United States and the European Union. In the 1990s Japan's economy and fiscal system began to face serious problems (Ito 1992). What changes need to be made to revitalize the nation's economy and fiscal system to prepare for the twenty-first century?

At the end of World War II, Japan's economy was in ruins. During the Allied Occupation several economic reforms were instituted that laid the foundation for growth after 1950. In 1950 Japan's economy got a big boost from an unwelcome source, the Korean War. Japan became an invaluable base for the United States in the Korean conflict, supplying harbors, airfields, food, repair services, cotton goods, electronics, steel, and ships for the military. The military expenditures of the United States and other nations involved in the Korean War, totaling $4 billion, stimulated the Japanese economy to a growth that continued for the next four decades. By October 1950, production in certain industries had risen to the level of prewar days. By 1955 Japanese production overall was equal to prewar production, and the growth of several new industries was yet to come. The economy grew at an annual rate of 8 percent between 1953 and 1973. The growth continued during the 1970s and 1980s at a slower pace (Allen 1981).

Rapid growth was also encouraged by indirect government assistance in the form of tax breaks, trea-sury investments and loans, and the Ministry of International Trade and Industry's policy of administrative guidance. The high-ranking bureaucrats were a major source of policy innovation and seem to have had a fairly free hand in controlling and regulating the economy (Komiya 1990). Increased consumer spending and rapid export penetration into the U.S. market, as well as the close nexus in Japan among banks, corporations, and the government are additional factors that helped foster rapid economic growth (Flath 2000). Bank-oriented financial control minimized pressures toward "short-term objectives" in corporate decision making. It also provided support to sustain other features of the Japanese economic system, such as lifetime employment practices.

Since the years of postwar reconstruction, Japan's development policy has assisted in transforming and adjusting its economy to changing economic circumstances. During the high growth era from the mid-1950s to the early 1970s, the government selected key industries for preferential treatment, promoting them in a supportive domestic economic environment. Usually this meant that foreign competitors were excluded from the Japanese market (Drysdale 1995). When access was permitted, it was restricted to industries in which Japanese firms had a strong foothold.

Following the dislocation to Japan's manufacturing sector caused by the first oil price shock in 1973, the emphasis of industrial policy shifted from helping potential "winner" industries expand to assisting structurally depressed industries, such as steel, food processing, shipbuilding, and coal mining. This emphasis has been most pronounced since early 1985, when the yen started appreciating rapidly. In addition, the economic policy became geared toward reducing the trade tensions generated by Japan's massive current-account surpluses. The trade surplus resulted from Japan's underimporting by setting up informal and invisible barriers, and its overexporting through aggressive tactics. The practices devised to restrict imports included establishing unreasonable product standards and certification procedures, obstructionist customs inspections, inadequate protection of intellectual property rights, favoring local suppliers in government procurements, administrative guidance by the national government, collusion among Japanese firms against outsiders, ingrained trade practices and Japan's traditional distribution system (Ito 1997), and the manipulation of cultural traits to ward off imports. As bilateral imbalances widened, there were trade conflicts between the United States and Japan in 1969–72, 1976–78, and from 1981 onward. The Japanese government asked industries to voluntarily reduce their exports of textiles (1955), steel (1972), television sets (1977), automobiles (1981), and semiconductors (1986).

JAPAN'S FOREIGN DIRECT INVESTMENT

A major feature of the world economy since the 1960s has been the rapid expansion of foreign direct investment (FDI) (Dunning 1998). Strong world economic performance, changes in policies concerning FDI in developing countries, the substantial realignment of the exchange rates of major currencies, and technological developments in transportation and communication services have all contributed to unprecedented growth in FDI, particularly since the mid-1980s. The United States, Japan, Germany, the United Kingdom, and other developed nations have been the main investing countries. Among these nations, the increase of Japanese FDI has been particularly high since the mid-1980s. With the notable exception of Japan, the leading investing countries are also major recipients of FDI.

Japan's role as a foreign investor has been extraordinary. After 1965, total investment flows began to gather momentum, rising from $227 million in 1966 to a peak of $3.943 million by 1973. The investment boom slackened because of the oil crisis of 1973 but resumed again in 1978. After receding slightly in 1982, it rose steadily until 1985, and between 1986 and 1989 it surged ahead at a rapid pace. From near insignificance in the 1950s, Japan emerged with about 17 percent of the world's stock of foreign direct investment in the late 1980s. By 1989 Japan was the single largest source of FDI, with outflows amounting to $67 billion, compared with $40 billion from the United States and $35 billion from the United Kingdom. A number of factors contributed to the high investment rates in the 1980s, among them Japan's increasing trade surplus; the 1980 deregulation of exchange controls, which paved the way for banks, financial security companies, and institutional investors such as life insurance firms to invest abroad; and the 46 percent appreciation of the yen between 1985 and 1987. Japan's foreign investment growth has been negative in the 1990s as a result of the bursting of the "bubble" at the end of 1989 and the resulting pessimistic economic forecast.

Southeast Asia was an important destination of Japanese foreign direct investment (Karan and Jasparro 2000). Some FDI in natural resource sectors was undertaken in Southeast Asia in the 1960s to secure a stable supply of raw materials for manufacturing in Japan. Examples of such FDI include petroleum drilling in Indonesia, iron ore mining in Malaysia, and copper mining in the Philippines. Beginning in 1970, Japanese FDI began to increase owing to a concentration in the newly industrializing economies (NIEs) of Taiwan, South Korea, Hong Kong, and recently China, in manufacturing activities such as textiles and consumer electronics. Both internal factors in Japan and external factors in the Asian NIEs played a role in promoting Japanese FDI. An increase in the price of Japanese products, particularly labor-intensive products, resulting from rising wages and appreciation of the yen, led Japanese producers to shift their production to countries where it could be carried out at a lower cost. The abundance of quality low-wage labor, FDI promotion policies such as export processing zones, and preferential taxes attracted Japanese FDI to Asian NIEs. One of the objectives behind the active FDI by Japanese firms was to secure an export base, and the developing Asian NIEs served as an attractive export base for Japanese firms because of the provisions of the Generalized System of Trade Preferences.

In 1989 the share of Asia in overall Japanese FDI was 12.2 percent. The Asian NIEs, Southeast Asia, and China accounted for most of Japanese FDI in 1989. The largest recipients in Southeast Asia were Thailand, Malaysia, Indonesia, and Singapore, in reported value of FDI. Between 1990 and 1995 Malay-

Toyota Motor Manufacturing Company, Georgetown, Kentucky, represents one of the major Japanese investments in the United States since the 1980s. Photo by P.P. Karan.

sia, Indonesia, and Thailand continued to attract the most FDI in Southeast Asia, ranking third, fifth, and seventh in the world, respectively, based on cumulative FDI. The rapid appreciation of the yen after 1985 deteriorated the competitiveness of Japanese products and prompted Japanese producers to shift their production overseas. Rising wages due to the shortage of labor and rising land prices in Japan provided additional incentives for overseas production.

Japanese firms hoped to meet three main objectives by moving production overseas. One was to shift to Southeast Asian countries the production of products to be exported to developed countries. A second goal was to substitute local production in Asian countries for exports to those countries. Third, a number of firms set up production bases in Southeast Asia to supply products to the Japanese market. One of the characteristics of the Japanese FDI in Southeast Asia is the high share of small and medium-sized firms, a large portion of which supply components to large Japanese-owned assembly firms. The bulk of the Japanese investments in Southeast Asia have been in the manufacturing sector, but in Indonesia, the Philippines, and Malaysia substantial investments have been made by the Japanese in natural resource development—mainly logging and mining. Investment in finance, insurance, and banking services was dominant in Singapore.

The Japanese and the NIEs' investments have led to the emergence of an Asia-Pacific growth region that links Japanese–Singaporean–Taiwanese–South Korean capital with Chinese, Malaysian, Indonesian,

and Thai labor. The cross-investment among a large number of Asian-Pacific countries has produced new regional linkages and interdependence, which recalls patterns of integration that have evolved in Europe. The Asia-Pacific regional interdependence has been driven by investments and markets rather than political forces. The distinguishing feature of Japanese firms in Asia is that joint ventures between indigenous and Japanese partners are more common than in North America and Europe.

The United States accounted for 48.2 percent of Japan's overall FDI in 1989, but in the 1990s, as a result of the fall in Japan's stock and land prices, FDIs were drastically reduced. The bulk of the Japanese investments in the United States are concentrated in manufacturing, particularly in electric machinery and transport equipment. The Japanese automobile industry has made major investments in the United States and Canada; there are several major Japanese automobile assembly facilities, as well as some 270 automotive parts suppliers. Honda was the first to produce in the United States in 1982. By 1989 all others (Nissan, Toyota, Mazda, and Mitsubishi) had factories located in rural sites in the Midwest and the South. The increasing threat of U.S. import barriers precipitated a massive onrush of Japanese manufacturing FDI in the period 1978 to 1984. Besides the desire to have a production presence in the United States to ensure market access, a number of Japanese firms, particularly in areas such as chemicals, optical goods, and electronics, have acquired U.S. corporations to obtain a direct channel to sought-after technology. The United States offers many attractions to foreign investors, such as a large and growing market, few bureaucratic restrictions and regulations that impede corporate activity, an excellent social infrastructure, low energy costs, and an educated labor force. Most state and local governments have welcomed Japanese investment and have solicited Japanese firms (Karan 2001).

By the end of the 1980s, Europe accounted for 21 percent of Japanese FDI. The United Kingdom was the favored FDI destination, followed by the Netherlands, Luxembourg, Germany, and France. Switzerland and Spain also received Japanese FDI. Relatively lower wages, favorable public investment incentives, and an absence of strong local rivals in automobiles and electronics explain the attraction of Britain to Japanese FDI. There the Japanese have selected peripheral regions such as Wales, Scotland, and northeast England for locating firms. France offered a central location and a large internal market. Germany offered a good industrial relations record, high labor skills, and centrality. Spain, which has a large reservoir of cheap labor, had a relatively large Japanese production presence because of its high import barriers. Machinery, electronics, and transport equipment dominate the FDI. As in the United States, Japanese firms have invested in Europe partly because of trade restrictive measures.

Historically, much of Japan's foreign investment has been induced by the need to avert potential market losses resulting from host country protectionist policies or by the desire to secure overseas raw materials, as well as other factors such as relative exchange rates and industry restructuring (Farrell 2002). By setting up overseas plants, Japanese firms are able to retain much of their market share. Investments in low-wage countries in Asia and Latin America have helped in retaining the general export competitiveness of Japan's products. The FDI has served Japan well.

JAPAN'S ECONOMY, 1990–2004

Throughout the 1980s the Japanese economy grew at a faster rate than that of most industrialized countries. Concomitant with this spurt in growth was an extraordinary rise in stock and land prices. Japan was beset by a speculative mania, which grossly inflated its asset values. In May 1989, when the asset price inflation began to be very worrying, the government tightened its monetary policy. Between 1981 and 1989 the increase in asset values was around fivefold. Then at the end of 1989, the "bubble" burst: the stock market tumbled more than 63 percent between December 1989 and August 1992 (Wood 1992; Mikuni and Murphy 2002, 145–170). Land values also declined.

In the years following the collapse of the asset price bubble at the end of 1989, the Japanese economy grew at a rate, on average, of just about 1.5 percent a year. The economy's performance in the 1990s as compared with its performance in the 1980s was particularly disappointing. This weak performance resulted in an unemployment rate of just over 5.0 percent in 2001 (see fig. 10.1). The figure for 2003

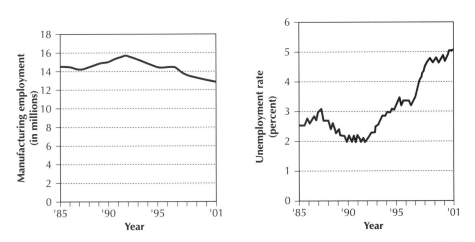

Fig. 10.1. Manufacturing employment and unemployment rate. Based on data from *Japan Times* (Tokyo) archives, 2000.

Economic Models of the Three Large World Economies: Japan, the United States, and Germany

The Japanese model

Positive aspects: Loyalty and high skill levels; public services, especially education, of high quality; close relations between banks and other firms; corporate cross-shareholdings that shelter managers from impatient shareholders, allowing them to take a long-term view of investment. This, it was argued, gave Japan an advantage over American capitalism, which was obsessed with short-term profit.

Negative aspects: These "virtues" are now seen as vices that lie at the root of Japan's economic problems; firms sheltered from the full force of the market feel little pressure to use capital efficiently.

The American model

Positive aspects: Flexible labor and product markets; low taxes; fierce competition; and shareholder capitalism, which puts pressure on managers to maximize profits.

Negative aspects: Wide income inequalities; low welfare benefits; poor quality of "public goods," such as primary and secondary education; low investment and very low savings rates.

The German model

Positive aspects: A generous welfare state and narrow wage dispersion, which breed social harmony; close relations between firms and banks, which encourage high investment.

Negative aspects: Overly powerful trade unions, high taxes, overgenerous jobless benefits, and widespread labor and product market restrictions, which have led to persistently high unemployment.

was 5.3 percent, 0.3 percentage point up from 2001. The economic crisis is manifested in the form of a self-reinforcing mixture of very slow growth, severe banking-sector problems, rising fiscal deficits and public debt, the failure of asset prices to recover from their collapse in the early 1990s, and a profound lack of confidence on the part of both consumers and businesses.

Why has Japan been subject to a protracted slowing of growth, instead of experiencing the sharp decline and quick recovery observed elsewhere? Has the failure to solve the problems in the banking sector prolonged the economic difficulties? Are structural rigidities in the Japanese economy impeding economic revival?

Major declines in domestic demand and investment have prolonged the slow growth of the Japanese economy. In the bubble years there was rapid growth of domestic demand. Private consumption increased rapidly during the second half of the 1980s. There was also a marked rise in investment. The collapse of the asset price bubble in 1990 was followed by a sharp contraction of domestic demand and a severe decline in investment. In contrast to the decline in private investment, public investment has increased relatively rapidly in the 1990s as the government has repeatedly attempted to revive the stalling economy. However, the returns on public investment have declined. The weak returns have been attributed to limited control by the central authorities over project implementation, weak incentives for local governments to achieve cost effectiveness, and the tendency at times to use public investment for distributional objectives.

Structural impediments to the recovery of demand and the working of market mechanisms in the Japanese economy are also important in explaining the prolonged slowdown of growth. Labor market arrangements, product market regulations, and other features of the functioning of economic institutions and their interrelationships, such as the relationship between banks and corporations, have also affected economic performance.

In July 2001 Japan's trade surplus was half the size it was in July 2000, and though its surplus with the United States increased in July, it was mainly because Japan's shrinking economy bought 14 percent less from America than before. Economists foresaw a 0.6 percent growth in the Japanese economy in fiscal year 2003 (Belson 2002). Shock waves from the terror attacks in the United States also impacted the Japanese economy. When the air service across the

Pacific was suspended for up to five days following terrorist attacks in September 2001, consumers saw immediate effects: the wholesale price of Boston tuna doubled, for example, and California strawberries vanished from the supermarkets. Aircraft carried 40 percent of Japan's trade with the United States in 2000—11,000 parcels and 360,000 pieces of mail daily, or $76 billion worth of goods a year. Japanese industry, whose early adoption of just-in-time inventory methods gave it a big edge in efficiency in the 1980s, also found itself immediately suffering from the air shutdown. With no semiconductors or car parts crossing the ocean by air, factories on both sides of the Pacific had to halt production lines.

Accounting Practices and Economic Woes: Japan's Bank Crisis

The weaknesses stemming from the bad-loan problems and the slow process of loan-loss recognition and disposal have been major items in the discussion of the banking crisis. The collapse of the Hokkaido Takushoku Bank and Yamaichi Securities highlighted the depth of the banking crisis in Japan. The difficulties in the banking sector were sparked by the collapse of the asset price bubble. Since banks directly own a significant portion of the total value of listed equities, the direct impact on a bank's balance sheets was severe in Japan. More important, the decline in property prices sharply reduced the quality of banks' loan portfolios. A distinctive aspect of the banking crisis in Japan has been the opaque accounting practices that masked the true size of problem loans for many years, and official statements regarding problem loans have lacked credibility in markets. The lack of transparency in recognizing the scale of the problems in the banking sector has undermined confidence among businesses and the public at large, with deleterious effects on domestic demand. When the problem of nonperforming loans emerged in the early 1990s, both banks and the government tried to conceal the fragility of the balance sheets, thereby aggravating the economic setback. The management of the bank-centered financial system in postwar Japan has been independent of external control. A vacuum of governance in bank management developed, and it needs to be filled (Horiuchi 2000).

The Financial Supervisory Agency and the Bank of Japan classify loans into four agency-defined cat-

egories: healthy, doubtful, highly risky, and irrecoverable, and they are referred to using the numbers 1 through 4. Category 2 loans are considered to be in the gray area. Banks usually set aside a portion of their profits or internal reserves as a certain percentage of their bad loans to be used for possible loan-losses. This accounting practice allows banks to reclassify irrecoverable loans as category 1 or healthy loans. Some banks have classified loans to troubled nonbank finance affiliates and real estate companies as either healthy or gray loans. Loose accounting procedures were employed to turn corporate losses into profits. The Long-Term Credit Bank of Japan Ltd., the country's tenth-largest lender, for instance, had covered up the enormity of its bad debts. Banks had implemented a policy of disguising their losses. Since April 1999 the Ministry of Finance has required corporations to report earnings and assets for all the subsidiaries they control. That is important, because loose rules for classifying subsidiaries allowed companies to extend loan guarantees or shift money-losing stocks to units they effectively controlled, without disclosing those liabilities to shareholders.

If accounting standards are relics in Japan, so too are accountants. The auditors are virtually indistinguishable from the companies whose books they probe and from the regulators who oversee them. All three see their mission as promoting corporate interests, rather than providing accurate information to shareholders. Unlike accountants in other countries, Japanese accountants are not required to warn shareholders that their companies are in trouble. Some executives worry that Japan simply does not have enough accountants to bring companies up to international standards. Japan has only 12,000 certified public accountants to audit 3,422 public companies, an average of 3.5 auditors for each business. For comparison, in the United States there are 330,000 certified accountants to audit 12,500 public companies, an average of 26.4 auditors per company. This lack of accounting personnel has become even more apparent as Japan seeks to deregulate its banks, securities houses, and insurance firms—a series of reforms begun in April 1998. Nowhere have Japan's accounting inadequacies been more apparent than in banking. In March 1998 the Long-Term Credit Bank of Japan (LTCB) said its equity capital equaled $5.96 billion, or 10 percent of its assets. That's well above the 8 percent ratio required by the Bank for

International Settlements for banks that operate across borders. Yet a little more than eight months later, Japan's new bank watchdog, the Financial Supervisory Agency, valued all the LTCB's assets at market price, declared the bank insolvent, and put it under government control.

Even after new accounting rules are introduced, obstacles to reform remain. The problem lies not only in the rules, but also in whether they are being properly enforced. It may take years to undo the perception that auditors are more loyal to their corporate clients than to upholding accounting principles. Change comes slowly in Japan. But if Tokyo wants to compete with the financial hubs of New York and London for investors, it cannot afford to wait too long before opening its books. As economic activities transcend national borders, transparency and fairness are more important than ever in responding to the demands of international accounting standards and disclosure.

ESSENTIALS FOR FUTURE ECONOMIC PERFORMANCE

Japan's economic performance in the years ahead will depend significantly on (1) growth in personal consumption, (2) strengthening regional economies, (3) encouraging entrepreneurship, and (4) transparency of the public sector. In addition, steps toward deregulating segments of the economy will have to be combined with efforts to increase transparency and reduce nontariff barriers to trade.

Increasing Consumer Spending

Personal consumption accounts for about 60 percent of Japan's gross domestic product, and so it holds the key to the country's economic health. In 1999 government-issued gift coupons handed out across the nation to boost public consumption did not have the expected big effect. The coupons, worth 20,000 yen ($183.50 at the 2004 exchange rate) per set, were distributed to some 35 million people across the nation. The majority of the coupons were used for daily necessities and hardly went beyond the confines of regular spending. Fears of global economic slowdown; an unrelenting stream of large-scale bankruptcies, leaving record liabilities; and ongoing corporate downsizing continued to weigh heavily on the consumer mind in 2003. People were not spending because they were worried about the future of their

jobs, their income was falling, or they wanted to save money for their retirement. The government, meanwhile, has failed to adequately address the root of some of these fears, such as the state of the public pension program. The lack of consumer confidence is crippling economic activity. Bearish public sentiment, which is not readily apparent from economic statistics, is one of the major factors preventing the economy from being effectively stimulated. It is time for the government to restore public confidence in the future through presenting medium- and long-term goals with specific economic outlooks for the years to come. Bold measures that depart from existing approaches are required to encourage people to spend more money.

Strengthening Regional Economies

Regional economies within Japan have become heavily dependent on the government's public-works budget. Few regions have distinctive or unique features that allow them to prosper without such public outlays. The central government distributes about 70 percent of its tax revenues to local governments, and it uses this fiscal power to control them. Local governments devote much of their efforts to currying favor with Tokyo and coming up with funding requests that will be easy to approve. Requests that truly match local needs are not likely to get approval from the central government, where bureaucrats prefer to authorize expenditure on items that are standard, expenditures that are common in every region. So regions lose their individuality and tend to become uniform as far as budget is concerned. This is a change from the past. During the Edo period (1603–1868), though the feudal lords were required to demonstrate loyalty to the shogun through regular attendance at his court, each of the regions had its own distinctive systems, industries, and culture, creating an interesting mosaic. Local cultures and local industries in the recent past have generally languished.

At present central government approval is required for every outlay. Unless power is decentralized, there is little hope for revival of the enfeebled local economies. A serious program of decentralization is needed, to make the regions autonomous over their own economy. This must start with a reform of the fiscal system, which will be no easy task. Unless local autonomy is restored, it will be difficult to accomplish real reform in establishing local and regional development policies. In the existing system of allocating public-works appropriations, the percentages going to particular agencies and regions have become fixed. Budgetary arrangements that will allow local governments to act on their own initiative should replace the existing system.

In 2003 the Japanese government introduced a program of Special Zones for Structural Reform in which deregulation is carried out at the local level in response to local needs and conditions, with the hope that local deregulation will eventually translate into nationwide reform. In Special Zones exceptions are made to existing nationwide regulations, to promote local development based on ideas and plans that originate from local government agencies and private companies. By the end of 2003, 164 Special Zones for Structural Reform were established in different regions based on proposals from regional governments and private companies. A special feature of the Special Zones is respect for the spirit of self-help and self-reliance of local communities. The first step in the process of establishing a Special Zone is for a local municipality or private-sector company to submit to the government an idea for a project that draws on the local characteristics of the region concerned, or a proposal for a specific type of deregulation aimed at encouraging local revitalization. After review and evaluation, a set of exceptions to regulations is created. The program of Special Zones can be a catalyst for the revitalization of Japan by creating new opportunities for deregulation.

Encouraging Entrepreneurship

Lack of entrepreneurial spirit is another major problem. Japanese society as a whole is reluctant to support new businesses, and partly for this reason, starting a business involves both hardship and risk. Entrepreneurs wishing to start something new are likely to run into both opposition from existing business groups and intervention by the government. In the current economic environment it is hard to make a profit, and even if an entrepreneur succeeds, nearly 65 percent of his or her personal income will be paid in taxes, as will 50 percent of the corporate profits. Whereas steep taxes are assessed on those who manage to succeed at risky undertakings, the government hands out subsidies to those who take it easy. Under these circumstances, it is difficult for people to listen to calls for more entrepreneurship

by the bureaucrats at the Ministry of Economy, Trade, and Industry.

In order to correct this state of affairs, the system of incentives must be overhauled. Those who take risks, work hard, and succeed should be rewarded. Support for those who rely on subsidies and public-works outlays should be phased out. This may mean more bankruptcies and higher unemployment in the short term. There are many energetic persons in Japan who would strive valiantly to succeed under an enhanced system of incentives.

Achieving Transparency of the Public Sector

The public sector in Japan is inefficient and lacks transparency. Increasing numbers of Japanese have begun to criticize public-works projects. Major construction companies have borne the brunt of the current economic slowdown and are desperate to receive more public-works contracts. The construction industry, composed of more than 560,000 construction companies, which directly employ 6 million people and indirectly provide employment for more than 10 million more, depends on public works. Every year, the construction industry joins hands with its allies in the government to obtain 50 trillion yen ($459 billion, about 11% of the nation's gross domestic product) from the public coffers, which are controlled by the bureaucracy. As is well known, these Diet members receive "votes for cash," and the bureaucrats are assured a place of employment after retirement (amakudari). This "iron triangle" made up of construction companies, the Diet, and bureaucrats continues to thrive. The financially strapped local governments have joined the triangle, calling for more public-works projects.

In the late 1990s, Japan distributed large amounts of funds for public-works projects in the name of "pump-priming measures" to facilitate economic recovery. Japan has spent more than $1 trillion, much of it on bridges, tunnels, airports, concert halls, and pavements, aimed at propping up the economy and satisfying political promises. The goal has been old-fashioned pump priming in the manner of John Maynard Keynes, who was the leading proponent of government spending as a means of restarting economic growth. So in Japan, airport runways have been added when an extension would suffice. Tunnels have been dug instead of constructing simple roads. The cobblestone sidewalks in a graceful old

Government-sponsored projects to construct or improve public facilities and infrastructure such as bridges, roads, dams, and dikes along the rivers have been used as pump-priming measures to stimulate the economy. The construction industry thrives on public projects such as this road-building on the north side of Tokyo. Photo by P.P. Karan.

graveyard have been dug up—and relaid. Many towns are getting a multimillion-dollar concert hall.

No one is certain how many jobs or how much economic growth has been created by public-works spending, but economists generally agree that it has kept the Japanese economy from slipping into a severe recession. Unfortunately, many economists argue, much of the money has been spent profligately, staving off inevitable and necessary changes in the economy and failing to put it back on its feet so that it can move ahead.

Some also have suggested that Japan would have been better served if the money had been used to help start-up companies or to create a better safety net for the unemployed instead of propping up construction companies. With the economic recession, the Japanese people have become more concerned about the future and are controlling their spending, thereby accelerating the economic downturn. As a result, tax revenues have fallen, weakening the social security system that supports the aging society. It is said that the social welfare net in Japan provides only the lowest level of support. As the number of unemployed persons seeking benefits increases, scarce resources will be stretched even further. If even a small portion of public-works expenditures were appropriated for social welfare instead, the Japanese people would feel far more at ease. If social welfare projects were implemented, more jobs would be created and the resulting economic wave would bring greater economic benefits than construction-related public-works projects.

Public works benefit the general contractors,

their subcontractors, and so on; the eventual list of beneficiaries, including the politicians who receive contributions from the construction companies, is a long one. The urge to spend often seems to take precedence over planning. In Hokkaido the authorities decided to build the Doto Jodoshado, a toll road that will eventually cross the island. About 32 miles of the new 160-mile highway have been completed, at a cost of $1.9 billion. But the road has failed to attract drivers, largely because an existing highway running parallel to it is free. Officials have tried to attract drivers by offering prizes, a golf competition, and the chance to drive a snowplow. The campaign succeeded in increasing the average number of cars using the toll road to 862 a day, but the route still has the distinction of being the least used in Japan.

Examples of expensive public projects are found all across the nation. For instance, in Hamamatsu, a city of about 555,000 southwest of Tokyo, almost $1.9 billion of public and private money was spent to build a concert hall and performance center. Act City Hamamatsu, which opened in 1994, features a $3 million organ and a costly high-tech, four-stage performance hall. So grand is Act City that Hamamatsu's across-the-prefecture rival, Shizuoka, with a population of about 471,000, decided that it needed one too. The Granship Shizuoka, designed by the leading Japanese architect, Arata Isozaki, has a meeting hall with a view of Mount Fuji and six booths for simultaneous translators, and its main hall can be used for sporting events, because all of its forty-six hundred seats are removable. It opened in March

1999, about forty miles from its competitor, at a cost of $672 million in public money.

The New Tomei Expressway (a six-lane luxury highway under construction between Tokyo and Nagoya), being built at a cost of $1 million for every 6 yards (5.5 m), is another example of expensive public projects. Sixty percent of the new highway runs across the mountains, rivers, and deep valleys of central Japan through tunnels and bridges, or on concrete pylons (Brooke 2002). Truck traffic along the old Tomei Expressway has declined since 1995 with the erosion of Japan's manufacturing base. The New Tomei will have double the number of lanes along the same route. In view of Japan's Florida-style demographics and European-style rail network, it appears unlikely that many aging Japanese will choose to speed along the new high-toll expressway. Since 1990 vehicle sales have dropped by nearly one-fourth.

The plethora of public projects has already led to huge deficits for the central and local governments. As bonds have been continually issued to finance more public works, the combined debt of the national and local governments has increased (in 2000) to more than 600 trillion yen ($5.56 trillion), nearly 132.9 percent of gross domestic product (compared to 60.2 percent for the U.S.), by far the highest ratio in any industrialized nation. Consequently, the central government has to earmark 40 percent of its annual general budget, and local governments an average of 20 percent of their budgets, for debt repayment. From a financial perspective, public projects have become a nightmare, with the once-wealthy Tokyo and Osaka metropolitan and Kanagawa prefectural governments facing major financial stress.

Public works have also modified the physical geography and natural landscape of Japan. Most of the coastline is covered by *tetorapotto* (concrete blocks used to protect coastlines and make artificial harbors). Rivers are contained within levees; mountainsides have been planted with cedar forests. Taller buildings and deeper subways are being built in urban areas. The construction industry, bureaucrats, and some Diet members are clamoring for larger projects. Among the construction works being promoted is a plan to build two more bridges linking Shikoku and Honshu in addition to the existing three bridges, which were completed in recent years. There are also proposals to extend the shinkansen lines to Tohoku

and Hokkaido, and to Hokuriku and Kyushu. These projects would become the largest public works of the twenty-first century thus far.

The state should spend for the public to boost economic demand. This should not be done by any further feeding of the concrete and construction industry, which has left Iriomote's Nakama River as Japan's only riverbank not cased in concrete; by replicating the Seikan Tunnel from Hokkaido to Honshu, the construction costs of which exceeded Europe's Channel Tunnel; or by building expressways to nowhere or highways to hamlets. Instead, funds should be spent on "soft" infrastructure: the creation of social provisions that will cradle and underpin Japan's pensioners of tomorrow. For example, spending could be used to provide better health care, more housing, more social workers, and more facilities for the aged. In addition, Japan's streets, public transportation, and public buildings could be renovated to improve ease of access for those with mobility problems. Such spending would not only boost the economy in the short term, but it would also launch societal changes.

Japanese people are demanding a change in policy priorities and have begun to hold local plebiscites on public projects such as the reclamation of bays and the construction of dams. Citizens are insisting on their participation in public-works project decisions, hitherto made solely by the Ministry of Construction. Traditionally, local leaders and regional assemblies have denied people the opportunity to express their views on public-works projects. As a result of popular movements, large-scale public-works projects in many areas cannot generally proceed smoothly without the support of local citizens' groups.

THE CHALLENGE OF STRUCTURAL REFORM

The years of poor economic performance in the 1990s have been attributed to inefficient decision making in private industries based on poor administrative policies, especially the rigidity of the inefficient and opaque postwar administration and fiscal system, excessive regulations, and the government's failure to address such lingering problems as bad loans and industrial overcapacity (Benton and Teramoto 2002). Japan's fiscal policies, which were preoccupied with achieving a quick economic rebound through massive spending on public-works projects and were dependent upon new issues of government bonds, are on the brink of collapse.

In order to achieve an economic recovery, Japan will have to confront the challenge of structural reform head-on and open up new economic frontiers by taking steps to encourage individuals and firms to engage in free and creative economic activities. To realize sustainable economic growth, structural reforms must be carried out with long-term perspectives. To renovate industry, business regulations must be boldly reformed. Expectation is running high that information technology (IT) will be a trump card to increase productivity. It is important, however, to enable small and medium-sized companies to utilize IT, as well as major corporations. This will require a new system to train people in the field.

It is also important to build a safety net to provide peace of mind to the residents of Japan. A safety net is a prerequisite to achieving a vital and competitive society in which people can afford to take risks. Japan holds a staggering 1.3 quadrillion yen ($10 trillion) in individual financial assets. Such assets are not being spent to boost consumption because the people harbor a strong sense of anxiety about their postretirement livelihoods. The government must try to dispel this anxiety by presenting a vision of the future of the nation's social security system, including pensions and medical care, that can allay people's concerns.

The best way to stimulate the economy is to deal with the aftereffects of the bubble economy, namely, to dispose of bad loans and implement structural reform such as administrative and fiscal reforms, decentralization, and financial and industrial reconstruction. Blindly boosting fiscal spending has a limited effect in buoying the economy. At stake is whether Japan will be able to implement effective policies by combining timely and flexible fiscal and monetary policies with structural reforms that require a step-by-step, sustained approach (Sakaiya 2001). Many of these structural reforms have been delayed because of resistance from politicians and bureaucrats.

The downside of many of the needed reforms is that they tend to promote inequality. Although Japan's economy stagnated in the 1990s and is shrinking now at about 2 percent annually, the country is still overwhelmingly middle-class. The rich are not getting richer, nor are the poor getting much poorer. But if local areas are left to fend for themselves, some will inevitably lose the competition to develop new industries. Without the safety net of the central government, the price of failure could be high.

REFERENCES

Allen, G.C. 1981. *The Japanese Economy*. London: Weidenfeld and Nicolson.

Belson, Ken. 2002. Japan's official forecast sees little growth next year. *New York Times*, December 20.

Benton, Caroline, and Yoshiya Teramoto. 2002. Revolutionizing Japanese corporate governance. In *Asian Post-Crisis Management*, ed. Usha C.V. Haley and Fraank-Jurgen Richter, 281–298. New York: Palgrave.

Brooke, James. 2002. Japan slows down, but not its road builders. *New York Times*, January 8.

Drysdale, Peter. 1995. The question of access to Japanese market. *Economic Record* 71 (September): 271–283.

Dunning, J.H. 1998. Globalization and the new geography of foreign direct investment. *Oxford Development Studies* 26 (1): 47–70.

Farrell, Roger. 2002. Research issues in Japanese FDI. In *Foreign Direct Investment: Research Issues*, ed. Bijit Bora, 75–90. New York: Routledge.

Flath, David. 2000. *The Japanese Economy*. Oxford: Oxford Univ. Press.

Horiuchi, Akiyoshi. 2000. Japan's bank crisis and the issue of governance. In *Reform and Recovery in East Asia: The Role of the State and Economic Enterprise*, ed. Peter Drysdale, 28–58. London: Routledge.

Ito, Motoshige. 1997. The future of the Japanese distribution system. *Social Science Japan* 11 (November): 7–9.

Ito, T. 1992. *The Japanese Economy*. Cambridge, MA: MIT Press.

Karan, P.P. 2001. *Japan in the Bluegrass*. Lexington: Univ. Press of Kentucky.

Karan, P.P., and C. Jasparro. 2000. Geography of Japanese investments in Southeast Asia. *Reitaku International Journal of Economic Studies* 8 (1): 13–30.

Komiya, R. 1990. *The Japanese Economy: Trade, Industry, and Government*. Tokyo: Univ. of Tokyo Press.

Mikuni, Akio, and R. Taggart Murphy. 2002. *Japan's Policy Trap: Dollars, Deflation, and the Crisis of Japanese Finance*. Washington, DC: Brookings Institution Press.

Sakaiya, Taichi. 2001. Rebuilding the Japanese economy for a "knowledge-value" society. *Japan Quarterly* 48 (2): 3–8.

Wood, C. 1992. *The Bubble Economy*. London: Sidgwick and Jackson.

Chapter 11

第 十一 章

DEVELOPMENT AND RESTRUCTURING
OF INDUSTRY

In comparing Japan's history of industrialization and modernization with that of the West, several important differences stand out. In the first place, the process of modernization took place over a much longer period of time in the West. Western capitalism first appeared about five hundred years ago; then the Industrial Revolution occurred in Britain starting about 1750; and finally industrial corporate capitalism started to appear in the second half of the nineteenth century.

In contrast, Japan changed from a traditional commercial agrarian economy to a technological one in a single generation. The zaibatsu were the central institution in this transformation, and an understanding of the history of the zaibatsu is essential to understanding how Japan developed as a modern technological society (Morikawa 1992).

Industrialization began following the arrival of Commodore Perry in Edo Bay in 1853. Spurred on by this military and industrial threat from the West, Japan began a concerted effort to transform its antiquated economic system. In the West, industrial capitalism evolved from the ground up; but Japan's leaders decided to impose industrialization from the top down by using the power of government and government bureaucracies to import Western technology and Western knowhow.

Some countries, such as Canada, relied heavily on foreign capital to industrialize; but Japan's leaders decided to use Japanese capital and Japanese economic structures as much as possible. They did this because they were not simply seeking to modernize Japanese. Rather they were determined to build a strong economic base, owned and controlled by Japanese private and public interests, to protect the nation's political and economic autonomy. Thus, although Japan's nineteenth-century leaders vigorously imported Western technology, they did not encourage Western corporations to enter Japan's domestic market in force to build Japan's new economic infrastructure.

What exactly were the zaibatsu, and how did they contribute to Japan's economic modernization? A zaibatsu is a group of diversified businesses owned exclusively by a single family or an extended family group. Zaibatsu existed in a variety of sizes, ranging from the enormous Mitsui, Mitsubishi, and Sumitomo industrial and financial combines to medium-sized and small business groups. The zaibatsu form was not unique to Japan, but the huge scale and the number of zaibatsu formed in the course of industrialization were distinctively a Japanese phenomenon. Of the ten major zaibatsu, Mitsui and Sumitomo originated during the Tokugawa shogunate, and the other eight (Mitsubishi, Yasuda, Asano, Furukawa, Fujita, Okura, Nakajima, and Nomura) during the first half of the Meiji era.

Initially the Meiji government had to take the lead in industrialization, managing directly a variety of enterprises ranging from arsenals and shipyards to telegraph services and mines. When the government found entrepreneurs willing to cooperate in its industrialization program, it formed close connections with them and supplied generous assistance, thereby creating a new type of political merchant. In the 1880s, when the government turned over the industrialization of the country to private individuals, the families that undertook this task played a significant part in, and profited from, the government's initial efforts to privatize industries. Many of these families moved from finance and mining to shipping, shipbuilding, and metalworking. Some of them formed trading companies both to export their products and to import the new materials and technol-

Field Report

The Birth of Mitsui, One of Japan's Zaibatsu

In the 1620s, the Mitsui family brewed sake near the shrine at Ise, sacred to the divine ancestors of the Japanese nation. The shrine was visited by many pilgrims, and the Mitsui supplied them sake. In 1673 the family had enough money to open a shop in Edo to sell cotton cloth. They sold goods at fixed prices (not subject to bargaining) and welcomed customers with little to spend since the family preferred many small sales for cash. The shop resembled the modern department store. Today the Mitsui Company operates department stores all over Japan under the name Mitsukoshi.

Mitsui's business in Edo was brisk, and the family opened shops in Kyoto and Osaka in the 1680s. By the 1690s, the family's financial expertise had won for the Mitsui Company appointments as financial agent for the shogun, the emperor, and several daimyo. Their wealth continued to grow, and the Mitsui financed the draining of some of the marshland and land reclamation for agriculture, whose production was added to the family's fortune. In 1881 the minister of finance suggested that government-built industries be sold to private owners such as the great Mitsui family. Mitsubishi Shipping Company merged with the one owned by the Mitsui. Family-owned enterprises such as Mitsui's received government encouragement and cooperation. Indeed, cooperation between government and privately owned companies is one of the most distinctive features of the Japanese economy. In the first half of the twentieth century, Mitsui became one of the largest private economic empires in the world.

After World War II, the U.S occupation dissolved the great family financial empires in Japan such as the Mitsui. Concentrations of economic power were considered undemocratic. Furthermore, the zaibatsu were accused of having led Japan down the path of conquest. In truth some of the zaibatsu had opposed the war and advocated peaceful trade as the best path to national growth. In 1932 members of a Japanese patriotic society had killed the head of Mitsui Corporation, the greatest of these zaibatsu, who had advocated making profits through peaceful progress, rather than through war.

ogy necessary for industrialization. Simultaneously they established banks and insurance companies to support their industrial and trading activities. By the beginning of the twentieth century, these mutually supporting multibusiness groups had become a continuing source of capital for the ongoing transfer of modern industrial technology. Gradually family members withdrew from all but the highest positions in their zaibatsu and were replaced by trained managers who had much better engineering and technical skills, as well as knowledge of foreign languages.

During World War I and then in the 1920s, the zaibatsu provided the pool of capital and managerial skills needed to bring to Japan the more technologically advanced science-based industries—chemicals, electric appliances, electric industrial machinery, and improved metalworking. In the 1930s the military had a major impact on the operations and investments of zaibatsu enterprises. Following World War II the supreme commander for the Allied Powers dissolved the zaibatsu and prohibited holding companies.

Most scholars believe that technological societies could have developed within any political ideology, such as liberal capitalism or Marxist communism. Japan offers a third alternative, what might be called *bureaucratic capitalism*. The development of Japan's industrial society serves as an example to many non-Western nations in Asia and Africa. The steps Japan followed in its economic modernization, particularly the way old traditional wealth was transformed into modern industrial capital and the way government and private capital were able to achieve high levels of economic growth and development without sacrificing Japanese autonomy, provide lessons for others to consider.

Financial institutions such as commercial banks and insurance companies are the most important large shareholders of the Japanese firms. There is also a much higher degree of concentrated ownership of firms as compared to the United States. Financial institutions take a significantly larger equity position in the firms than they do in the United States. Management ownership appears to be rather less important in Japan than in the United States.

From Zaibatsu to Keiretsu

In the 1950s the large corporations that had belonged to the zaibatsu before their breakup revived the old zaibatsu corporate names. However, these postwar corporate groups were not owned exclusively by a single family. These new groups, often called *keiretsu*, are characterized by mutual shareholding among their constituent firms and consultation among the member firms' top managers, but they are much looser groupings than the prewar zaibatsu (Yoshitomi 1990). The keiretsu formed out of zaibatsu include the Mitsui keiretsu, the Mitsubishi keiretsu, and the Sumitomo keiretsu. Sanwa, Fuyo, Toshiba, Matsushita, and Dai-Ichi are among the other large keiretsu. Coordination of keiretsu activities is achieved through periodic meetings of the presidents of the most important companies in each group. General trading companies and keiretsu banks also serve a coordinating function. To some extent, members show a preference for purchasing products from other members of the group, and this preference is stronger in the case of helping out fellow firms with the introduction of new products such as supercomputers.

For many years the Japanese model of keiretsu, the strong family ties between suppliers and automakers, was held up as a model for the rest of the world. The Japanese recession has exposed the weakness of the keiretsu, an institution where parts suppliers are linked with one automaker in a symbiotic relationship. The keiretsu structure had a weak foundation since it was predicated on having numerous small manufacturers devote all their resources to one company; the small manufacturers thus were

Field Report
Toyota Keiretsu

The founding of Toyota dates back to 1918, when Toyoda Sakichi established Toyoda Spinning and Weaving. The automotive aspect of the Toyoda family business began in 1933 as the Automobile Department of the Toyoda Automatic Loom Works, and it became independent of the parent in 1937. As Toyota expanded, it spun off departments into separate companies, which were integrated into the Toyota keiretsu (Toyota Auto Body, Aisin Seiki, Toyoda Gosei, and others). After the war, the association expanded. In 1984 the Toyota keiretsu included about 220 firms, of which 80 percent had plants in Aichi or the surrounding prefectures. Nearly 175 suppliers are organized into a supplier organization named Kyoho-Kai, literally meaning "a club for coprospering with Toyota." Toyota implements a common strategy and set of rules for these suppliers to follow, and their association, Kyoho-Kai, facilitates the process.

Toyota has formed an organization of local suppliers in the United States—the Bluegrass Automotive Manufacturers Association—to help develop better suppliers. Toyota exercises considerable control and influence over its suppliers, such as the Kaito Manufacturing Company, which makes automotive lighting and is a member of the Toyota keiretsu. Toyota uses shareholding leverage to strengthen relationships within its keiretsu.

Toyota maintains close relations with the Mitsui keiretsu and enjoys observer status in Mitsui's premier presidential council (Nimoku-Kai). Toyota also serves on Tokai Bank's Presidential Council (Wakaba-Kai) and holds a stake in Tokai Bank, one of the world's largest banks. A comparison of Toyota's keiretsu structure in Japan with the Toyota network in the United States reveals that Toyota has transplanted essential elements of a keiretsu structure to mid-America and has organized the elements into a group structure patterned after its keiretsu in Japan.

effectively controlled by that company. This system has now turned into a high cost for small suppliers who are saddled with high labor costs.

More recently, American interest in keiretsu has revolved around the impact of these enterprise groupings on manufactured items imported to Japan (Gibson and Roe 1993; Sheard 1994). Even if the ties are not as exclusive as in the prewar zaibatsu, the preference for ingroup business transactions certainly act as an import barrier. Within the past few years, several hundred Japanese auto-parts companies have followed their keiretsu parents to middle America. For example, 73 percent of the companies that belong to Toyota's keiretsu in Japan are now in business in the United States.

JAPANESE MANUFACTURING STRATEGY

A striking characteristic of Japanese factories is the extent of process control; both technically and socially, the labor and production system is controlled down to the very last detail. The underlying characteristics of management and organization are closely interwoven with Japanese culture. This explains why the work content, working conditions, and working relationships in the factories look so different from those in Western cultures. Since the economic and social systems in Japan are fundamentally different from those in the West, the Japanese practice may not work in the West.

Any Japanese factory has to meet a number of requirements. The ways in which the requirements are met are quite different from methods adopted in the West. For example, in order to reduce costs, a factory will farm out a great deal of work to subcontractors or satellite factories. Sometimes more than half of the work is farmed out. For the same purpose of economy, young girls or part-time women workers are hired as temporary production personnel. Cost reduction is also achieved by reducing the number of components and parts used in production.

The requirements of high quality and delivery reliability for incoming goods are achieved through long-established relations with subcontractors and the technical support given to them. The same applies to the detailed inspection and reliability examination of components.

Great diversity of products and rapid introduction of new types are achieved by designing products on a modular basis, by designing for ease of assembly, and by having development groups work in parallel (almost simultaneously on succeeding generations of a product). Sales is the driving force for the current products, and "development" for the new products. There are integrating functions in the organization that control these management practices.

In order to motivate employees, "participation" and indoctrination procedures are used; quality circles play a major part here. In selecting new personnel, the ability to be motivated is an important criterion, among other things, and job applicants have to pass an entry examination. The system of rewards and appraisal compels everyone, from high to low, to cooperate and work for results.

INDUSTRIAL REGIONS

Industries in Japan may be grouped into five types based on their formation, networks, and location of suppliers and customers. First, there are large numbers of localized or regionally based industries (*jiba sangyo*) for which a particular area has become famous (Itakura 1981). These are small firms specializing in the manufacture of a specific product, using local capital and labor. Examples of products made by such firms are lacquerware (made in Kyoto, Kanazawa, Wajima, Wakamatsu, Hirosaki, Takayama, and Takamatsu); bamboo ware (Odawara and Beppu); steel kettles (Morioka); copperware (Takaoka); ceramic goods (Nagoya); wire, fans, and handbags (Toyooka); and gloves (Takeuchi and Ide 1980). These industries are widespread over many communities in Japan. The second group of industries were developed in company towns (*kigyo*

Toyota City, a company town, is the home of the Toyota Motor Corporation. Toyota is located to the east of Nagoya in the Chukyo industrial region. Photo by P.P. Karan.

Muroran in Hokkaido is a major industrial center with steel plants, cement factories, oil refineries, and shipyards clustered along the coast. Muroran initially developed as a shipping center for coal from the Ishikari coalfield; the establishment of a steel mill during the Meiji period led to the development of other related industries. Photo by Cotton Mather.

jokamachi) by major industrial firms such as Nippon Steel (Kamaishi and Muroran), Toyota Motor Manufacturing (Toyota City), Hitachi Engineering (Hitachi), Asahi Chemicals (Nobeoka in Miyazaki), and Matsushita (Kodama). They usually employ hub-and-spoke mass production and have national and international markets for their products (Murata 1980a; Kawase et al. 2000). The third group is made up of large industrial districts located on reclaimed coastal lands along the Pacific. These industries have a relatively weak local network, and their suppliers and customers are also nonlocal (Sargent 1980). The fourth and fifth types of industries specialize in high-technology products and are located in high-tech industrial centers, called technopolises. These types of industries are discussed in chapter 12.

Most of Japan's principal industrial regions have developed around ports (see fig. 11.1), chiefly be-

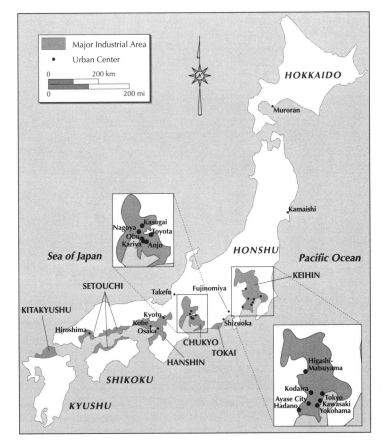

Fig. 11.1. Industrial regions.

cause Japanese industry depends heavily on imported raw materials. Also, a large proportion of the manufactured goods are exported to foreign markets. There are five major manufacturing regions in the country (Murata 1980b). A study by Katsutaka Itakura (1988) reveals that manufacturing industries in these regions are moving out of the metropolitan areas into rural areas or small towns. This trend continues at the present time. Kenkichi Nagao (1996) has analyzed regional changes in the Japanese manufacturing industry between 1970 and 1990. Japanese manufacturers are also increasingly moving production to overseas locations, fleeing high input costs in Japan. This "hollowing out" of manufacturing accelerated in the 1990s (Katz 2001), so that overseas manufacturing as a percentage of total manufacturing by Japanese firms increased from 3 percent in 1985 to 14 percent by 1999. In the 1990s the growth of manufacturing overseas dwarfed the minimal domestic growth in Japan.

The Keihin Region

This region extends along Tokyo Bay and nearby inland areas with major concentrations in Tokyo, Kawasaki, and Yokohama. Manufacturing activity now covers parts of seven prefectures—Tokyo,

Kanagawa, Saitama, Chiba, Ibaraki, Tochigi, and Gumma Prefectures. The Keihin region ranks first in Japan in the value of industrial goods produced. Factories are widely scattered throughout the region, but the principal industrial zone is found on the Tokyo Bay waterfront. Another district follows the Sumida River in eastern Tokyo.

The heart of this industrial region is the coastal belt between Tokyo and Yokohama. Between Kawasaki and Yokohama are large steel mills, oil refineries, petrochemical plants, shipyards, food-processing plants, and thermoelectric plants. The area of heaviest concentration of industry is on the waterfront from Tokyo to Kawasaki and Yokohama, where sites have been developed on reclaimed land. A little farther inland are the automobile manufacturing, electric machinery, secondary food-processing, and precision-machine industries. The machinery industry is concentrated in the area extending from southern Tokyo to Kawasaki and Yokohama (Takeuchi 1987). The machinery industry developed on the low-lying reclaimed land in the south beginning in the 1920s. The precision-machinery industry developed in the north in the 1960s along main roads. Motor vehicle plants of Nissan, Isuzu, Hino, and Honda are located in this outer zone of the Keihin

The Keihin industrial region extends along the lower reaches of the Sumida River and on reclaimed land along the coastal belt between Tokyo and Yokohama. Large heavy industries have developed on the filled-land sites. Farther inland are automobile plants and precision-machine tool industries. Large factories have close linkage with subcontractors that produce parts for the parent factories. Photo by P.P. Karan.

Parts suppliers such as this one in Arakawa Ward of Tokyo are located at various places in the Keihin industrial area. Photo by P.P. Karan.

industrial district. Leading electric machinery makers such as Toshiba, Hitachi, and Sony are also located in the area. The large factories in the north maintain close links with subcontractors in the south that produce parts for the parent factories. Subcontractors function in a complex linkage of groups of factories that produce finished products with groups of parts producers. In recent years overcrowding, congestion, and pollution, as well as the shortage of water supply, have led industries to move to the outskirts of the region.

A number of factors have contributed to the industrial dominance of this region. Tokyo not only is the political and cultural center of Japan; it also possesses leading banking and commercial facilities. Tokyo and Yokohama are major overseas ports; foreign raw materials are easily assembled at these points, and export of manufactured goods is facilitated. This is also a rail hub giving access to domestic markets and domestic raw materials. The population concentration of nearly 39 million people provides not only the largest single market in the nation, but also a skilled labor supply.

The Chukyo Industrial Region

This region is centered on the city of Nagoya and extends east to Toyohashi in Aichi Prefecture, west to southern Mie Prefecture, and north into Gifu Prefecture. The major industries are chemical fibers in the cities of Gifu and Okazaki; automobiles in Toyota; petroleum refining and petrochemicals in Yokkaichi; and steel, transport equipment, and machinery in

Nagoya. Industrial plants are concentrated on the coastal area and along the main railways and highways within a thirty-mile radius of central Nagoya. The steel industry developed in 1910, and the metal, machinery, and chemical industries were established in the 1930s. Oil refining was located at the site of the old Naval Fuel Depot in Yokkaichi in 1956, and since then the site has become a major focus of the petrochemical industry in Japan. An integrated steel plant was located at Tokai to supply steel to the Toyota Motor Corporation plants at Toyota City.

By supplying a wide range of chemical products, the Yokkaichi industrial complex played a major role in supporting postwar growth of the Japanese economy. Now renovation of the old facilities is essential to maintain its level of competitiveness. The renovation is hampered by the large number of restrictions placed on the layout of plants and the use of land. But in April 2003 the government approved a Special Zone designation for the area, which will ease regulatory restrictions. Companies in the industrial complex are now updating their existing plants and building new facilities to start new ventures. Meanwhile, regulatory easing in the electricity sector has encouraged development of the Yokkaichi industrial complex as a hub for fuel cell development. This is just one way the industrial complex is metamorphosing into a center for internationally competitive high-tech industry.

There are three major industrial concentrations in the Chukyo region. The first is along the Ise Bay coast, with heavy chemical industries in the vicinity

Field Report

Japan Johnson

Bilateral trade disputes between America and Japan still garner headlines in newspapers, but many American companies are operating successfully in Japan. Seven out of every ten Japanese shave with Schick. When the Japanese have a yen for a carbonated drink, they will reach for a Coke or some other drink made by Coca-Cola, and the Japanese VCRs that Americans buy are, in all likelihood, held together with glue made by Loctite Corporation, a Connecticut-based company with operations in Japan.

American companies have been successfully operating in Japan for years. One such company is Japan Johnson, located in Oiso, a seaside resort in Kanagawa Prefecture and also in the Keihin industrial region. It is meeting Japanese needs with a parade of popular "Made in Japan" products. A hundred years after its founding in Racine, Wisconsin, in 1868, S.C. Johnson & Son Inc. had established its name as the world's largest maker of waxes and insecticides. In Japan, Johnson has come to be recognized as more than shiny floors and dead bugs—much more.

A Japan Johnson product, Kabi Killer, that zaps mold, the scourge of Japanese housewives for generations, is a hit product in Japan. An immediate best seller, Kabi Killer now racks up millions of dollars in annual sales, making it number one in its category and the company's top-selling product. Although it accounts for more than 10 percent of the company's 35-billion-yen annual sales, Kabi Killer is just one of the many Japan Johnson products that have carved out the largest share in their respective markets. Others include Skin Guard (insect repellent), Katameru Temple (oil solidifier), Crew (glass cleaner), Kamtarch (spray starch), and Java (scale remover for bathtubs). Most of these products are made-in-Japan success stories. Even when Johnson sells a U.S. product, such as Pledge, it is adapted to the needs of the Japanese consumer.

Not only its products, but also the company itself, has become thoroughly Japanized; only two of its six hundred employees—a researcher and an English teacher—are expatriates. But the system itself has not lost its American touch. The U.S. parent company has introduced several innovations, including a five-day workweek, mandatory retirement at sixty-five, and a profit-sharing plan, that set Japan Johnson apart from the pack.

Unlike the many foreign companies that have tried to market their products outside Japan's multilayered distribution system—often with limited success—Japan Johnson has worked within the system, cultivating close relationships with local wholesalers and distributors. Nonetheless, Japan Johnson believes that a good marketing strategy, though of central importance, is meaningless without good products.

Companies in the United States still complain about bureaucratic red tape and cultural stonewalling, but companies like Japan Johnson operating in Japan play a different tune. For companies that have unique products, Japan is a necessary market. A soft dollar and lower political and economic barriers make the Japanese market particularly attractive.

How, then, does one go about cracking the Japanese market? Based on the experiences of several companies, including Kodak, Warner-Lambert, Kentucky Fried Chicken, and Loctite, there seem to be several keys to success. The companies that have done the best are ones that have Japanized their product, their distribution and marketing, and very often their personnel.

Tailor the product to match Japanese tastes. Kentucky Fried Chicken, which went into Japan in 1970 and now has nearly 1,000 restaurants, found that the Japanese and other foreign eaters aren't big on mashed potatoes and gravy. Instead, KFC Japan sells french fries, and a lot of them. The coleslaw is less sweet. Other choices include grilled rice balls and a fried salmon sandwich. The company posted sales of nearly $598 million in 2000.

(continued on the following page)

Field Report: *Japan Johnson* (continued)

Nearly 70 percent of KFC Japan's customers are young women. With the customer base in mind, KFC offers promotions such as tote bags. The company planned to open 100 new KFCs in 2001. At Tricon Inc., the Louisville-based company that owns KFC, Pizza Hut, and Taco Bell brands, international sales account for about 28 percent of revenue. A life-size statue of Colonel Sanders stands outside KFC outlets in Japan.

Coca-Cola, which has an estimated 60 percent of the carbonated beverage market, does not use artificial coloring in its products, because the company found that the Japanese prefer all-natural ingredients. Orange Fanta, for example, is duller, more the color of mandarin oranges, rather than the glow-in-the-dark variety Americans are used to seeing.

Eastman Kodak made shrewd product changes. It developed a film that can be processed in white light, which is a big plus because many graphics-arts businesses do not have darkrooms. In Japan Kodak sells between 70 and 80 percent of all professional film. Its approximately 15 percent share in the amateur market has grown since it introduced, among other things, a film that has more reds and vivid colors.

Learn Japanese business practices. The easiest way is to hook up with a Japanese company, through either a joint venture or tight distribution ties. In 1970 the giant conglomerate Mitsubishi, which is Japan's biggest chicken producer, formed a joint venture with Kentucky Fried Chicken. The Japanese company helped shape the design of the stores—the freestanding ones in America were out of place in Japan—and helped with marketing and business contacts.

Hire Japanese. Most major companies operating in Japan, including IBM, Coke, and Tupperware, have very few Americans.

And finally, be patient. It generally takes five years to turn red ink into black. Kentucky Fried Chicken lost money for five years, but now Japan is its fastest-growing market.

---

of Nagoya Port and petrochemical industries on the western side of the bay at Yokkaichi. The second area of concentration is in western Mikawa, which is dominated by the motor vehicle industry at Toyota City. Many parts factories of the Toyota Group are located in Kariya, adjacent to Toyota City. A large number of factories in the area are linked to Toyota as suppliers of parts for the motor assembly plants (Suganuma 2001).

Toyota, Japan's motor city, with a population of 350,000, has prospered because of its namesake, Toyota Motor Manufacturing, one of Japan's richest corporations. Toyota City has a robust tax roll and low unemployment. But because the Japanese auto market is in a long, slow decline, Toyota is opening plants overseas in China, Poland, and the United States in order to keep growing. Toyota has not opened an assembly plant in Japan since 1992. The job market in Toyota City peaked a decade ago. Every year Toyota Motor builds more cars and buys more parts overseas, and its hundreds of local suppliers must compete with foreign rivals by cutting prices. Many are closing their doors, and local leaders are trying to attract new industries in emerging fields like cell technology and advanced materials that can contribute to Toyota's next generation of vehicles.

As the plants close, thousands of workers employed by small auto-part suppliers must fend for themselves. Nearly 65,500 employed directly by Toyota face different pressures. Despite the company's record profit of 945 billion yen ($8.6 billion) in 2002, Toyota refused to raise the base salary of its workers for the first time in 2003. The action by the company did not provoke protest from the Toyota workers' union. Unions in Japan are organized by company, not by industry, and are less willing to confront management.

An uncanny parallel is beginning to emerge with

Field Report

Toyota: An Example of Successful Japanese Enterprise

In the second half of the twentieth century, the Toyota Motor Corporation was representative of a successful Japanese manufacturing enterprise. Toyota had been established back in the 1930s, but the foundations of its competitiveness grew between 1945 and 1960. During a period of insufficient capital and facilities in the late 1940s, Toyota focused its efforts on improving productivity without large-scale investment in plant and equipment. The improvements that characterized this period reflected "soft" rather than "hard" changes: establishing standard operating procedures, leveling the production rate, introducing product-flow layout, and adding multitask assignments to job descriptions.

The company's fortunes were aided by the outbreak of the Korean War; Toyota's increased production leaned heavily on the supply of trucks to the American armed forces during the conflict. Between 1951 and 1955 Toyota initiated a plan to replace outmoded equipment and increase mechanization to double its production capacity. It introduced the American concept of training within industry (TWI). A training program within the factory itself that focused on

continuous production improvement was an integral part of the TWI. After 1955 it was made clear within Toyota that activities for improvement (*kaizen*) were the responsibility of foremen and work group leaders. Total Quality Control (TQC) was instituted on a companywide basis in the late 1960s. The well-known "just-in-time" (JIT) concept had actually developed before the war by the firm's founder Kiichiro Toyoda, but the *kanban* method itself was introduced in the late 1950s.

With these changes in production under way, Toyota built the Motomachi plant in 1959, Japan's first high-volume assembly factory specially designed for passenger automobiles. The Toyota System, which made the company a very successful enterprise, had its roots in the 1950s focus on improvement. The company's subsequent expansion after the 1960s provided a solid basis for its continuing international competitiveness. Toyota's drive in the 1990s to create the ultimate low-polluting, high-mileage eco-car through the fusion of the fuel cell system and hybrid technology seems poised to make it a benchmark for the automobile industry.

the rusting old car towns of Michigan, which saw factories move to nonunion southern states or lower-wage countries. Although Toyota City has not yet experienced the industrial decline that has began to consume Osaka, where a substantial number of factories are closing and moving to China, the signs of decay in the city's signature industry and its move overseas is a source of concern in western Mikawa.

Although Toyota is better known as an automaker, Chukyo is also the base of the Mitsubishi motor vehicle factories.

The third area of industrial concentration lies to the northwest of Nagoya, with Ichinomiya as its center. This area specializes in the textile industry and utilizes the high level of weaving skill that has long characterized this part of Japan. There are some large textile factories in Ichinomiya, but most of the factories are small and located among merchants' and

The Mitsubishi Motors plant in Nagoya. As part of industrial restructuring in Japan, this plant was closed in 2000. Photo by P.P. Karan.

farmers' houses. The textile industry is no longer a growing sector, and future growth will be limited.

Nagoya, the major industrial node, developed early as an administrative center, its location on the Tokaido—the main highway from Tokyo to Kyoto—facilitating its industrial growth. Before World War II Nagoya became an aircraft center, and since the war a leading automobile center. Its ceramic industry, based on local clays, is the largest in Japan.

The Tokai Industrial Region

This industrial area lies between the Keihin and Chukyo industrial regions, along the Pacific coast in Shizuoka Prefecture. Industries include musical instruments, motorcycles, paper, processed foods, and textiles. Shizuoka, Shimizu, and Hamamatsu are major centers of manufacturing. Manufacturing developed in the Tokai region in the 1880s with cotton spinning and paper mills. Silk reeling started in the 1890s with the increasing exportation of raw silk. The growth of paper mills led to the development of a papermaking machinery industry.

After World War II all industries except the silk reeling experienced major growth. The industries are located along National Road 1 and the Tokaido railway. Many factories from the Keihin region have relocated in Tokai because of lack of space for expansion in Keihin. There are three major areas of industrial concentration in Tokai: (1) Fuji and Numazu cities on the lowlands below Mount Fuji, (2) Shizuoka and Shimizu cities, and (3) Hamamatsu and its neighborhood. Fuji and Numazu have pulp and paper, chemical, synthetic textile, and photographic film industries. Large factories in the area are served by Tagonoura Port. Shizuoka has lumber-processing industries for making lacquerware and furniture. There are several large and small tea-processing factories. Shimizu, a port, has aluminum, oil-refining, and shipbuilding industries. Shizuoka Prefecture is important for fisheries and is a leading producer of mandarin oranges; the canning of oranges, bonito, and tuna is important in Shimizu. Hamamatsu has significant piano and motorcycle manufacturers. Motorcycle enterprises such as Honda, Suzuki, and Yamaha are located in Hamamatsu and adjacent towns.

The Hanshin Industrial Region

The Hanshin industrial region extends along Osaka Bay, with Osaka and Kobe as principal manufacturing centers. In recent years the industrial area has expanded in the west to Himeji and in the northeast to Kyoto and Otsu. It now extends south to Wakayama. Sometimes this larger industrial area (Osaka-Kyoto-Kobe) is called the Keihanshin or the Kinki industrial belt. The main manufacturing industries in this region are metals, iron and steel, electric machinery, textiles, chemicals, and food processing. Manufacturing industries dealing with general machinery, metal fabricating, plastics, printing and publishing, pulp and paper, and food processing extend into Higashi Osaka and Yao east of the Kinki expressway along the Kintetsu–Nara railway (Nagao 2000).

Modern industry in this area started in the 1890s. The Osaka Artillery Arsenal, established in 1879, became the foundation of metal and machinery industries. The Hyogo Shipbuilding Arsenal, started in 1883, became the center of the shipbuilding industry. In 1889 Sumitomo opened a copper wire mill and later added production of steam locomotives and aluminum. Industries developed rapidly during World War I. Textile industries, with spinning, were concentrated in farming villages around Osaka. Since the 1930s emphasis has been placed on heavier industries such as steel, copper, aluminum, electrical equipment, and machinery, established by Japanese corporations such as Mitsubishi and Matsushita. This region has now become a primary metal-producing center, with associated engineering industries. Shipbuilding, machinery, aircraft, and foundries are well-developed industries.

Within the Hanshin region industries are concentrated on the reclaimed land along Osaka Bay from the southern part of Osaka Port to Kashiwada and Sakai, the area east of Osaka city, along the River Yodo north of Osaka city, from Osaka to the Nara area with the focus on Yamato-Koriyama, and in the area from Kyoto to Lake Biwa in Shiga Prefecture. The industrial concentration along Osaka Bay, called the Sakai-Senhoku district, has iron and steel, shipbuilding, oil-refining, and petrochemical industries. The inland area east of Osaka city is characterized by machinery and metal factories with close linkage to larger factories located on Osaka Bay. Along the River Yodo, north of Osaka city, electric machinery and equipment factories of Sanyo, Matsushita, Sharp, and Mitsubishi are located. Machinery, electric precision-instrument, chemical, and food-processing indus-

Tokuyama city is the commercial and industrial center of the Shunan region along the Inland Sea. It is important in the manufacture of materials as well as oil refining and chemical industries. Photo by Cotton Mather.

tries are along the highway from Osaka to Nara. The Kyoto–Lake Biwa area is famous for rayon synthetic fiber, silk textiles, porcelain, and sake.

The Setouchi Industrial Region

This area comprises the southern part of Chugoku, facing the Inland Sea, and the northern part of Shikoku. The principal industrial centers are Hiroshima and Okayama on the Chugoku side of the Inland Sea, and Takamatsu and Matsuyama on the Shikoku side. Sanyo, on the north side of the Inland Sea, is relatively more important in manufacturing than the southern part in Shikoku. The major industries are iron and steel (the Kawasaki Group), chemicals, shipbuilding, transport machinery, oil refining (the Mitsubishi Group), and petrochemicals. Integrated steel plants are located in the Fukuyama district in Hiroshima Prefecture. Mitsui and Idemitsu have petrochemical complexes at Iwakuni and Tokuyama.

Manufacturing in the coastal areas of the Seto Inland Sea developed rapidly after World War II. The transfer of old military land and reclamation of additional land from the sea for industrial sites provided land for new growth industries. The rapid industrial growth led to pollution of the sea in the early 1960s, which has restricted further development.

The Kitakyushu Industrial Region

This industrial area is located in northern Kyushu and the western part of Yamaguchi Prefecture in Honshu. The principal industries are iron and steel, cement, chemicals, fertilizers, glass, ceramics, and metals. The availability of local coal from the Chikuho field and raw materials from China led to the rapid development of industries in this area after 1900. The shift of Japan's industrial structure from heavy industries such as steel and cement has led to the relative decline of industries in this area.

The cities of Moji, Tobata, Yawata, Kokura, Wakamatsu, and Shimonoseki (across the strait on Honshu) are major industrial centers. The early growth of the Yawata Iron and Steel Works, one of the largest industrial establishments in Japan, was strongly subsidized by the Japanese government. Kitakyushu's fortunes were built on steel. At the heart of the economy is the Yawata steelworks. Founded in 1901, the factory became part of Nippon Steel, still the world's biggest steel company. Because of the wealth of coal in the area, other energy-intensive companies, such as chemicals and glass, were also started there. In 1950 Kitakyushu's companies accounted for 5 percent of Japanese output. In its heyday in the 1970s, the Yawata works alone employed 46,000 people. Now it employs 8,000, and some of its land is used for a theme park. Kitakyushu contributes just 0.7 percent of the country's GDP.

An energetic local government is striving for change in this region. Its models for change are places such as Birmingham in Britain and Baltimore in America, old industrial towns that have managed to adapt. Pollution in the area has been reduced significantly. An offshore airport is being built in Kitakyushu; its port is being deepened. Fukuoka, thirty-eight miles away from Kitakyushu, is the larg-

Iron and steel, cement, chemical, and metal industries began to develop in the Kitakyushu region after 1900, based on local coal from the Chikuho field and raw materials from China. A shift in Japan's industrial structure has led to the decline of these industries, and this area is going through massive industrial restructuring. The restructuring of the steel industry in Kitakyushu has depressed the local economy. Several projects are under way to revive the sagging local economy. Photo by P.P. Karan.

est city of the region with a population of more than 1 million. This is where companies have their regional headquarters. One of Japan's biggest shopping centers, Canal City, opened here in April 1996. The port of Kitakyushu lies directly on the Sea of Japan trade route, within six hundred miles of the major Chinese commercial ports of Shanghai, Qingdao, and Dalian. Kitakyushu is making the most of its prime location and turning the port into an international hub for distribution; this will invigorate the overall economy of northern Kyushu.

Other industrial centers in Japan include cities in Hokuriku along the Sea of Japan, with a concentration of manufacturing activity at Fukui, Kanazawa, Toyama, and Niigata; southern Hokkaido, with principal activity at Muroran (steel) and Tomakomai (paper); Hitachi in northeastern Ibaraki Prefecture; and Kamaishi in southeastern Iwate Prefecture, an important steel-producing center since 1858 that is now in decline.

INDUSTRIAL RESTRUCTURING IN JAPAN

Steel, chemical, shipbuilding, automobile, and other industries played a critical role in propelling the economic growth of Japan between 1950 and the 1980s. As domestic and export demand for Japanese heavy products expanded in the 1950s and 1960s, there were major investments in new plants and equipment. Government agencies such as the Ministry of International Trade and Industry (MITI), now the Ministry of Economy, Trade, and Industry (METI), were closely involved in the reconstruction, development, and expansion of heavy industries.

In the 1970s Japan's heavy industries began to experience problems of excess capacity and declining profits as a result of growing protection in export markets, shifting of domestic demand patterns, and competition from other Asian countries. In response to these changing conditions, the industries have pursued a series of restructuring strategies, such as rationalization of capacity, reinvestment in new technologies, and diversification into new areas of business. The steel industry experienced a major restructuring in 1970 through the merger of Yawata Iron and Steel Company and Fuji Iron and Steel Company to form Nippon Steel. There were cutbacks in employment in parent companies and among suppliers, resulting in unemployment in traditional areas of heavy industry. In 1998 the domestic output of steel declined sharply to 91 million tons, the level of more than twenty years before, because of the sluggish economy. In 2000 the steel production of Japan had rebounded to 98 million tons.

Japan is in the beginning of a full-scale economic restructuring, prompted most basically by slowing growth rates, technological change, and intense competition. The result is a move away from the ingrown business practices that have characterized its economy since World War II, to a more open system closer to that of the Western nations.

All across Japan factories are being forced to restructure operations (Banasick 1999), doing things they never would have considered just a few years ago:

Cutting payrolls and capital spending and, on the part of unprofitable businesses, bailing out. After thirty years and more than 10 million cars,

Nissan Motor Company decided to close its main plant at Zama, south of Tokyo, in 1995. It transferred car production from Zama to a newer, more efficient factory halfway across the country. The end of auto production directly affected 2,500 of Nissan's 4,000 Zama workers, who were transferred to other facilities. Nippon Steel Corporation banked the last blast-furnace operations at its Hirohata, Hyogoken, works in June 1993 and withdrew from unprofitable product lines, such as personal computers. It cut the personnel at its iron and steel division by 4,000 people or 15 percent. The company had closed its blast furnaces in Yawata and Kamaishi in 1989. At Toshiba Corporation, structural reform included retraining employees and shifting them to the information, communications, and multimedia divisions, where there was growth potential. The aim of restructuring at Nissan, Nippon, Toshiba, and others was the same: survival in the face of a more-serious-than-anticipated decline in consumer spending and capital investment, and a surge in the value of the yen that makes Japanese products more expensive than those produced in other countries.

Rethinking long-standing relationships with local suppliers and buying more components abroad. NEC switched its purchases of components away from captive suppliers in high-cost Japan to cheaper suppliers of products such as computer motherboards in Taiwan, China, and other low-cost countries. This will produce profound changes among the legions of subcontractors and local businesses that rely on the factories to buy their products.

Streamlining product lines. For example, Ajinomoto reduced its number of products from 4,000 to 2,500. Kikkoman Corporation has gone from 5,000 products to 2,500 (Fruin 1991). Ricoh cut its products from 7,000 to 6,200, and unprofitable lines such as printers were curtailed.

Rethinking the sacred commitment to lifetime employment and other management practices that large Japanese companies thought were the ba-sis of their competitive strength. Big Japanese companies traditionally have guaranteed lifetime employment for workers, but the recession has strained—and sometimes broken—those paternalistic ties. Some companies are encouraging workers to leave voluntarily or take early retirement. Minolta Camera Company reduced its workforce by 1,700 by getting employees to leave voluntarily, and Nippon Telegraph and Telephone persuaded 15,000 of its workers to leave the company.

These changes are the inevitable consequences of a strengthening yen and the painful end of the 1980s economic boom. The slowing Japanese economy in recent years and the resulting sharp decline in corporate profits have prompted some of the changes in business practices. Company profits have fallen, and the surge in the yen has increased the pressure to make changes. The toughest challenge for Japan results from the end of an era of rapid growth and the beginning of a period of slower growth in the 1990s.

Economic globalization and the rapid advancement of information technology have plunged the Japanese steel industry into fierce competition as customers seek the lowest prices. All the five major steel companies (Nippon Steel, NKK, Kawasaki Steel, Sumitomo Metal Industries, and Kobe Steel) suffered operating losses in the 1990s. Profits declined, and investments were cut. In other industrialized countries, mergers or takeovers would have occurred. But in Japan steelmakers have resisted the market. Largely because of the keiretsu system of relationships, large mergers are rare in Japan. With cross-holdings of equity and "safe shares," the system demands that a huge number of parties all agree to any merger before it can go ahead. So each company tries to tackle its problems alone. Japan is an expensive place to make steel, however much restructuring its steelmakers attempt. The wages of Japanese steelworkers are four times as high as those of South Korea. In the long run exports will fall and imports, which now make up only 7.5 percent of the market, will grow. The big customers' need for "just-in-time" delivery has kept the imports from increasing because local manufacturers can provide "just-in-time" delivery more easily than importers can.

NKK, Japan's second-largest steelmaker, and

Kawasaki, the third-largest, announced an alliance plan that was to take effect at the end of 2002. The move was expected to accelerate the wave of restructuring in the steel industry. The planned integration was to create a firm with the world's largest steel output, exceeding that of South Korea's POSCO or Pohang Iron and Steel Company, the current number-one steel producer in the world (26.5 million tons in 1999), or that of Nippon Steel, Japan's largest steelmaker (25.6 million tons in 1999). By joining forces, NKK and Kawasaki expected to wield a stronger influence in the global steel market. The goal is to become a globally competitive steelmaker by cutting back operational costs, including those for research and development, and streamlining operations. With the merger, it is inevitable that companies such as Sumitomo Metal Industries, which has close ties with Nippon Steel, will review its business strategies. Kobe Steel is also expected to reorganize.

Kitakyushu and Kamaishi: Two Examples of Restructuring in the Steel Industry

Kitakyushu is the home of the huge Yawata Steel Works, built by the Japanese government in 1901 and now owned by Nippon Steel, the world's largest steel company until recently. Yawata's location was convenient for using coal from the nearby Chikuho mines and iron ore from China. Production at Yawata reached a peak of 2.45 million tons during the early 1940s. In the 1950s, as Japan entered its high-growth period, Yawata Steel embarked upon large plant expansions. A new integrated steelworks was constructed at Tobata, about 4 miles (6.4 km) from the Yawata works. New plants were also built at Sakai, near Osaka, and Kimitsu, near Tokyo. Fuji Iron and Steel Company constructed plants at Nagoya and Oita. In 1970 Yawata and Fuji merged into Nippon Steel. South Korea's Pohang Iron and Steel Company (POSCO) displaced Nippon Steel as the world's largest steelmaker in 1998.

In 1969 a plan was instituted to rationalize and modernize the old Yawata works. The plan was to concentrate on raw materials handling, iron and steel making, and mass production of coil and sheet products at Tobata and production of high-grade steel at Yawata. The modernization and restructuring of the Yawata works resulted in energy savings and improvements in quality. There was also reduction in the workforce at the plants as well as in the number

of suppliers and subcontractors that provide materials, equipment, specialized technologies, and labor.

In 1987 Nippon Steel announced another restructuring strategy, aimed at the rationalization of the basic steel business, the reduction of the steel-making labor force, and diversification into new manufacturing and service businesses. By 1989 Nippon Steel closed its blast furnaces at Yawata and Kamaishi (in northern Honshu). Three other blast furnaces at Sakai, Muroran, and Hirohata were closed in the 1990s. The company concentrated production at four works at Yawata, Nagoya, Kimitsu, and Oita, in order to reduce employment and give the company a highly productive base for steelmaking.

As a part of its restructuring strategy, Nippon Steel is also pursuing a long-term plan for diversification based on by-products and skills derived from its basic steel business. The company hopes to capitalize on its expertise in automation, software development, instrumentation, and system technologies to develop new businesses and products. Nippon is also moving into urban development and the provision of community services, constructing new apart-

Nippon Paper Mill at Yatsushiro, Kyushu. The mill imports wood from Russia. Photo by P.P. Karan.

ment buildings, developing large leisure and sports facilities, providing dwellings and medical services for the elderly, and offering training courses and conference management services.

Dealing with employment security of the workforce is a major concern. Workers have been shifted between jobs, locations, divisions, and companies. As employees approach retirement age in large companies, they often go on *shukko,* outplacement with suppliers or unrelated companies. To accelerate retirement, the company offers financial incentives for early retirement for workers over age fifty.

At Kitakyushu the cumulative impact of Nippon Steel's restructuring strategies were severe. But the city and the area are gradually recovering. Nippon Steel has located some of its new businesses at Yawata and has developed a leisure park at Kitakyushu to attract visitors to the depressed industrial area. METI (the Ministry of Economy, Trade, and Industry) has provided financial incentives for leisure development. Kitakyushu has been trying to develop new sources of employment such as high-technology industries, small businesses, and services (Shapira 1994).

Kamaishi is a prime example of what the Japanese call a company castle town, one whose inhabitants are as dependent on a single employer as they once were on a feudal lord (Wiltshire 1998). It is a good case study of the effect of plant closing, because the city is an isolated economy, surrounded on three sides by mountains and bordered on the fourth by the Pacific Ocean.

Japan's modern steel industry was born here in 1857, when the country's first blast furnace succeeded in making pig iron. It was produced from ore that was carried by oxen down from the nearby mountains, in bags made from the bark of grape vines. By the early 1960s, the town had a population of 92,000 and had three movie theaters. Nippon Steel employed about 8,000 people in Kamaishi on three shifts.

Starting in the 1960s, the plant became uncompetitive, and there was no more room to expand. The company began building larger, more modern plants elsewhere and transferred workers to those locations. In the 1970s and 1980s, Japan's steel industry found itself awash in excess capacity. In the restructuring process Nippon Steel closed the first of its two Kamaishi blast furnaces in 1984 and the second in 1989. In 1993 the only steel-related activity in Kamaishi was making wire for radial tires.

About 28 percent of the wholesalers and retailers in the city have gone out of business or have reduced the size of their businesses. No movie theaters remain. The closing of the blast furnaces threatened to turn this isolated company town into a ghost town. But although Kamaishi has clearly suffered—for example, its population has shrunk in three decades from 92,000 to 52,000 today—it has not faded away.

A combination of government subsidies to help businesses reorganize, industrial promotion plans, and efforts by Nippon Steel cushioned the blow and created jobs for many of the former steelworkers. The task of finding new jobs for the former mill workers fell to the Nippon Steel management. The key factor has been the policy of providing workers with jobs for life, which, though under pressure, is still honored by Japan's major companies. Nippon Steel, the world's largest steelmaker, kept the factory operating long after it became unprofitable and closed it only gradually, transferring workers to other plants. When it could no longer transfer workers, the company scrambled to create almost any business it could to employ steelworkers in Kamaishi. The result: former steelworkers are now involved in businesses from truck bodies and office furniture to growing miniature Brazilian orchids—as well as making meat substitutes from soy protein. The most urgent and important task was to create new jobs, and Nippon Steel intended to do anything it could toward that end.

Has all this worked? The results were mixed because the former steelworkers had little experience in other businesses. The truck-body business is still struggling for success. The soy food company has found a market in Taiwan among a religious sect that needed meatless food. Nippon Steel has also tried more conventional approaches to keep workers employed. It is trying to offer work that it once performed in the factory, such as diagnostic testing of machinery or computer programming, as services for sale. The company's in-house grocery store has become a supermarket, and company housing is now being rented.

The downtown area of Kamaishi, far from being a ghost town, is still lively and apparently vibrant, with no shuttered stores. But despite the Herculean effort to create jobs, unemployment in Kamaishi has been running about 5 percent since 1985 in a workforce of about 24,000. The new businesses employ 2,300, including 700 former steel plant workers. Although the population of Kamaishi continues to fall, the rate of decline has now eased. And much of the current shrinkage reflects the fact that young people in Japanese small cities tend to move to the big cities.

There are questions of whether even large Japanese companies will be able to maintain the tradition of lifetime employment. But at a time when U.S. factories are closing because of production costs or economic restructuring, the experience of Kamaishi could be instructive. Japan is known abroad for its policies for building industries, but it also adopted policies in the 1970s and 1980s to remove excess capacity from industries in which the nation had lost international competitiveness, such as textiles, shipbuilding, and aluminum. Japan has been successful in picking losers and closing them down.

Murayama: A Case Study of Restructuring in the Automobile Industry

Japan's automobile industry is widely scattered across the nation, although there are major con-

centrations in the Tokyo and Nagoya regions (see fig. 11.2). For nearly forty years the Nissan Motor Company's plant at Murayama, outside Tokyo, was a flagship factory employing more than 5,000 people and producing 435,000 cars a year. With a weak home market and economic distress, Nissan found itself unable to borrow money. It turned to the French government and Renault. Renault bought stakes in Nissan in early 1999 and decided to close the Murayama plant to restore the automaker to long-term profitability. The land on which the plant sits is being sold to a Buddhist religious order, and the factory's equipment has been auctioned off or scrapped. Production of six models was shifted to three surviving plants. Several hundred people lost their jobs. The closing of the Murayama plant has become a symbol of the new order in the Japanese auto industry.

The company has decided to shift all production of its export-only Maxima sedan out of Japan to an existing plant in Tennessee. And it plans to open a $1 billion minivan and sports-utility factory in Can-

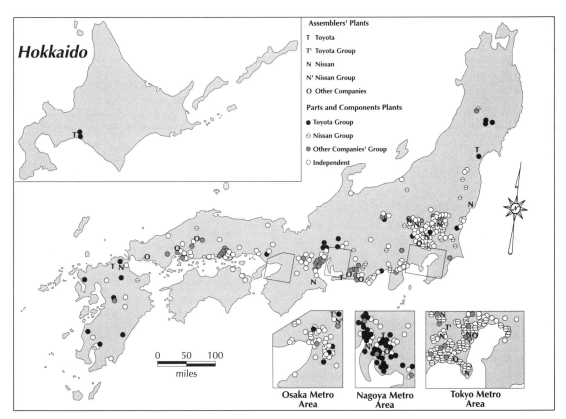

Fig. 11.2. Distribution of motor vehicle industries. Based on a map by Yasuo Miyakawa in *Geographical Review of Japan* 72 (1999): 81.

ton, Mississippi. With the home market declining and demand for Japanese models still strong in North America, it makes sense to make cars where the buyers are. Doing so avoids currency swings and helps sell cars to consumers wary of buying "foreign" brands. In its American push, Nissan is rushing to catch up with Honda and Toyota, both of which have been steadily expanding output in the United States.

Japanese automakers are cutting domestic production. In 2000 only 10.1 million vehicles were made in Japan, down from 13.5 million in 1990. Meanwhile, the number made overseas has grown by almost half. Honda Motor Company has trimmed its domestic plant workers by about 2,000 or 7 percent; since 1990 it has boosted offshore production by 30 percent. Toyota closed two Japanese assembly lines in 2000; but it has kept production of its most expensive cars in Japan. Mazda and Mitsubishi also plan to close one factory each and cut jobs at home.

For Nissan, the closures of Murayama and two smaller plants were going to boost operating capacity to an average of 74 percent in 2001, up from 52 percent in 2000. The company's increased efficiency, plus continued cost-cutting gains, is expected to boost profit. Nissan's actions also underscore a major change: the Japanese unions' growing acceptance of job cuts, since downsizing can lead to sustainable profitability. Nevertheless, Japanese restructuring is less brutal than it would be in America. Nissan executives made an important concession by agreeing, in principle, to offer workers at closed plants other jobs. More than two-thirds of the employees in Murayama transferred, including 700 who went to a plant in Oppama, near Yokohama. However, keeping their jobs meant leaving Murayama, where many of the employees had spent their entire working lives. Four hundred workers who did not want to relocate either accepted early retirement or simply left their jobs. An additional 200 employees, who could not make up their minds, stayed behind in Murayama, stamping replacement parts at a small facility on the factory lot which was scheduled to close in 2004, at which time they had the choice of moving or joining the unemployment line. Some workers who moved to Oppama did not want to sell their homes in Murayama and transfer their kids to new schools. They work Monday through Friday in Oppama and drive the fifty miles to Murayama on weekends.

It is projected that Japan may lose 143,000 of about 800,000 auto and parts-assembly positions, in addition to nearly 100,000 such jobs that have disappeared in the past decade. This will put further pressure on the government to address unemployment. More company towns will feel the pain that Murayama has suffered. A new government agency, Industrial Revitalization Corporation (IRC), was recently set up to aid Japan's ailing industries. The mission of the IRC is to help money-losing Japanese companies get rid of overcapacity and debt, and release them back into the economy with a clean bill of health.

REFERENCES

Banasick, S. 1999. Restructuring of the electrical machinery industry in northern Japan, 1980–1995. *Pennsylvania Geographer* 37 (1): 2–16.

Fruin, M. 1991. *Kikkoman, Clan, Company*. Tokyo: Kodansha.

Gibson, R., and M. Roe. 1993. Understanding the Japanese keiretsu: Overlaps between corporate governance and industrial organization. *Yale Law Review* 102:871–906.

Itakura, Katsutaka. 1981. *Jiba sangyo no Hhattatsu* [The Development of Community-Based Industries]. Tokyo: Taimeido.

———. 1988. Changes in the distribution of manufacturing employment in Japan, 1960–1985. *Science Reports of Tohoku University*, ser. 7 (Geography), 38 (2): 85–103.

Katz, Richard. 2001. Hollowing out accelerates in the late 1990s. *Japanese Economy* 29 (5–6): 20–28.

Kawase, Masaki, Koichi Tanaka, Satoshi Yokoyama, and Zoltan Zahoran. 2000. Industrial linkages in the electrical machinery industry in the Hitachi Industry Area. *Annual Report, Institute of Geoscience*, Univ. of Tsukuba. 26:3–8.

Morikawa, Hidemasa. 1992. *Zaibatsu: The Rise and Fall of Family Enterprise Groups in Japan*. Tokyo: Univ. of Tokyo Press.

Murata, Koji. 1980a. The formation of industrial areas. In *Geography of Japan*, 299–264. Tokyo: Teikoku-Shoin.

———. 1980b. *An Industrial Geography of Japan*. London: Bell and Hyman.

Nagao, Kenkichi. 1996. Regional employment changes in Japanese manufacturing industry, 1970–1990: An extended shift-share analysis. *Geographical Review of Japan* A 69:303–326.

———. 2000. Re-discovery of industrial districts in Japanese metropolitan areas: An examination of Higashi-Osaka City. *Osaka City University Economic Review* 35 (2): 37–46.

Sargent, John. 1980. Industrial location in Japan since 1945. *GeoJournal* 4:205–214.

Shapira, Philip. 1994. Industrial restructuring and economic development strategies in a Japanese steel town: The case of Kita Kyushu. In *Planning for Cities and Regions in Japan*, ed. Philip Shapira, Ian Masser, and David W. Edgington, 155–183. Liverpool: Liverpool Univ. Press.

Sheard, P. 1994. Keiretsu, competition, and market access. Discussion Paper 94–17, Osaka Univ., Faculty of Economics.

Suganuma, Unryu. 2001. The geography of Toyota Motor Manufacturing Company. In *Japan in the Bluegrass*, ed. P.P. Karan, 61–97. Lexington: Univ. Press of Kentucky.

Takeuchi, Atsuhiko, and Sakuo Ide. 1980. Jiba Sangyo: Localized industry. In *Geography of Japan,* 299–319. Tokyo: Teikoku-Shoin.

———. 1987. Two Elements supporting high position of Tokyo Region in the national system of Japanese machinery industry. *Geographical Reports of Tokyo Metropolitan University* 22:128–138.

Wiltshire, Richard. 1998. Diversification and employment in Kamaishi city: A future reconsidered. *Science Reports of Tohoku University*, ser. 7 (Geography), 48 (1–2): 85–104.

Yoshitomi, M. 1990. Keiretsu: An insider guide to Japan's conglomerates. *International Economic Insights* 1 (Sept.–Oct.): 10–17.

Chapter 12

第 十二 章

POSTINDUSTRIAL JAPAN

Since the mid-1970s, when manufacturing employment began to decline, a major transformation has been ushering Japan from the industrial into the postindustrial era. The passage into postindustrial society is marked by structural shifts from the production of goods to the provision of services and by the growing importance of technology and information as factors in production. The most obvious characteristic of economic life in the postindustrial society is that the majority of the labor force is no longer employed in agriculture (primary economic activity) or manufacturing (secondary sector), but in services. In 2002 the service or tertiary industries (retail and wholesale trade, banking, finance, real estate, business services, personal services, and public administration) accounted for nearly 65.9 percent of the national labor force (see fig. 12.1). The growing size of the tertiary sector in Japan is the most important indicator of the progression of the country into a postindustrial society characterized by a prosperous service-and-technology-oriented society based on information and research.

THE DEVELOPMENT OF TECHNOLOGY IN JAPAN

Japan, which began to industrialize much later than most nations of the West, invested considerable time and capital in laying the industrial, economic, and

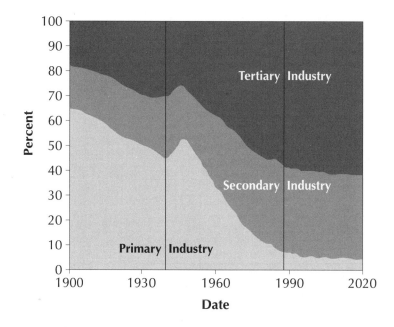

Fig. 12.1. Changes in employment structure since 1900. Based on data from *Japan Times* (Tokyo) archives, 2000.

educational foundations for technologies that were already in use abroad. From the beginning of the Meiji period (1868–1912) the Japanese government promoted the development of industry and technology as part of its plan to create a wealthy and strong nation. Victories in the Sino-Japanese War of 1894–95 and the Russo-Japanese War and economic prosperity during World War I spurred the development of industry and technology. The Institute of Physical and Chemical Research was organized in 1917 under the joint sponsorship of government and industry for the purpose of developing and applying creative technology. Of particular significance was the rapid development of Japan's heavy and chemical industries in the 1930s as part of a general mobilization of industry and technology by the military, and significant advances were made in shipbuilding, optics, and aircraft technologies (Morris-Suzuki 1994).

Although most of Japan's technology has been imported, here are some early examples of Japanese technological innovation: a power loom designed by Toyoda Sakichi; the seasoning Ajinomoto, developed in 1908 by Ikeda Kikunae; the high-performance alloy KS Magnetic Steel, developed in 1917 by Honda Kotaro; a nitrogen-fixation process developed in 1920 by the National Chemical Laboratory for Industry; and the Yagi antenna, the most commonly used television and radio antenna configuration, developed in 1926 by Yagi Hidetsugu (Goto and Odagiri 1997).

Following World War II, industry, under the supervision of the Japanese government, again turned to Western technology, which it adapted to domestic needs and standards. The Science and Technology Agency was established in 1956 to coordinate technological development, and the Ministry of International Trade and Industry (MITI) provided guidance to prevent excessive competition and the consequent payment of unreasonably high licensing fees and royalties for imported technologies (Nishioka and Takeuchi 1986). While assisting in the introduction of foreign technology, the ministry was also able to foster the development of domestic technologies.

Although dependence on foreign technology remains a characteristic of Japanese industrial innovation, the implementation of this technology has not been merely imitative. The Japanese have endeavored not only to improve imported technology but also to adapt it to serve new purposes. For example, although all the fundamental technology for televi-

sion, including video recording, is based on foreign patents, Japanese engineers succeeded in developing video recording for home use. Major Japanese enterprises are intensely competitive and constantly endeavor to be the first to introduce advanced technology from abroad. The smaller manufacturers that serve them as subcontractors then swiftly adopt technologies introduced by large enterprises.

By the mid-1980s Japan had caught up with the United States in the technological level of certain production processes, such as the manufacture of automobiles, television sets, and semiconductors. Japan had also introduced advanced technology in such areas as the prevention of pollution and environmental science. According to a survey made in 1985 by MITI, Japanese technologies for high-tensile steel, videocassette recorders, and plants for the solar generation of electric power were unexcelled by any similar foreign technologies. By 1990 fine ceramics, semiconductor memories, and spectrum analyzers had achieved a high level of technological excellence. Areas in which Japan still lagged behind the West included the technology related to production of airplane engines and microprocessors, as well as database technology, biotechnology, and information technology industries.

The technological revolution in postwar Japan has been effected largely through liberal investments made by private industry for the development of innovative applications of foreign technologies. Whereas in the United States 47 percent of funds for research and development was supplied in 1989 by the government, in Japan only 18 percent was supplied by the government, the remainder coming from private investors. The emphasis placed by Japanese enterprises on developing improved applications of existing technology, rather than expending funds for the development of new technology whose commercial application may be impractical, has resulted in the relatively swift transformation of imported technologies into innovative industrial products, which, if commercially successful, provide a generous return on investment.

After a decade of recession and stagnation, Japan is turning up unexpected ways to harness technology and create surprising new ways to pamper the consumer. A metamorphosis is slowly taking place in Japanese mood and method, particularly in technologies that make life more convenient and alter the way companies do business. Take the new mobile videophone from Kyocera, or the new microwave from Sharp that automatically cooks from recipes found on the Internet, or the new washing machine with an eighteen-minute cycle that scrubs people instead of clothes, or the nifty personal locators that fit into a pocket and use satellite data to generate a map showing one's whereabouts. Global positioning systems may have been invented in America, but many Japanese mothers use them in the form of locators that fax maps to them showing the whereabouts of their children or elderly parents.

Japan's last wave of successes was with cars and audiovisual products and, in the 1970s and 1980s, with Walkmans and sedans and compact-disc players. That wave has subsided, and now Japanese companies are scrambling to race ahead of the rest of the world by reaching into millions of homes and transforming their kitchens, bathrooms, televisions, and every other aspect of life in an aging society. That is, of course, no guarantee that these futuristic devices will catch on with consumers or that technology or the market will not shift in other, unanticipated directions. Japan has always been a king in new gadgetry, even though it has lagged in the Internet and in information technology and is struggling to catch up to the United States.

There is no country like Japan when it comes to fusing and cross-fertilizing technologies to create something new. The United States almost always invents the new paradigms, but Japan often transforms them into popular new products. In the process of recapturing its technological prowess, Japan is coming up with original applications and snazzy designs that may once again captivate the world. If the momentum grows, it might help cultivate the spirit of creation that will help Japan reinvent an economy that is threatening to wind down in the twenty-first century.

THE GROWTH OF THE SEMICONDUCTOR INDUSTRY

A little more than fifty years ago, a phenomenon of then-modest proportion occurred that continues to be felt in ways that were not even dreamed of at the time: Sony Corporation of Japan started selling transistor radios. They were hardly high-tech wonders. They were not even the first transistor radios. But they embodied in their mass-produced simplicity an edict that has since guided Japan's electronics indus-

try to become the fastest-rising contributor to Japan's economic growth. The objectives were simple: make it small, efficient, and inexpensive. The results were sales worth billions.

The key to bringing about such success has been microelectronics, a field that involves semiconductors and integrated circuits. These terms, together with *chips* and *ICs*, are often used interchangeably, but *semiconductor* is the popular term for a device made of materials that can regulate the flow of electricity in predictable ways. Copper, for example, moves electricity at a certain speed, whereas more exotic materials like tungsten, niobium, or gallium-arsenide compounds can move it at different, much faster speeds.

In simplest terms, *integrated circuits* are devices that may put several kinds of semiconductors on one very small piece of material, usually a strip of silicon about as big as a fingernail. There are other buzzwords that have become bywords. *Integration* refers to the combining of tiny circuits that are comparable in function to the big banks of vacuum tubes that preceded them not too many years ago. Imagine all the electrical wiring of a forty-story office building shrunk to the size of a pumpkin seed. That's integration. Now the electronics industry has very large integrations and ultra-large-scale integrations, which are extensions of the same idea: make it small, efficient, and inexpensive.

Just as the transistor replaced vacuum tubes to make possible Sony's lighter, less energy-hungry, less expensive radios in the 1950s, the ICs make possible far more amazing and practical electronic wonders. The results are found virtually everywhere. Microwave ovens remember the proper temperature and cooking times for favorite recipes because of their semiconductor memory. Stereos and TV sets that use the devices can fit into a pocket. Sewing machines use chips instead of mechanical cams to create fancy stitches, and automobile fuel flow and ignition timing are controlled by the microcomputers that made an industry famous.

Japan's semiconductor industry got its start through the acquisition of U.S. technology in the early 1950s when Kobe Kogyo imported transistor technology from RCA and Sony imported similar technology from Western Electric. The technology gap between the United States and Japan was closed in the 1970s. In contrast to the U.S. semiconductor industry, whose main achievements were in industrial machinery, the semiconductor industry in Japan centered on consumer products. In the United States venture-business specialty firms, which started out as small enterprises, form the heart of the semiconductor industry. In Japan the industry is based in large corporate manufacturers such as NEC, Toshiba, Hitachi, and Fujitsu.

Japan's electronics industry increased its production value to nearly $146 billion by 1990. At its peak in the mid-1980s, Japan's electronics manufacturers accounted for 80 percent of the world's semiconductor output. Japanese companies took over the world market for dynamic random-access memory chips (D-RAMs), the main type of computer memory chip, forcing all but a couple of American companies to drop out. Rather than concentrate on high-cost specialty devices like microprocessors, Japanese manufacturers emphasized memories and other control circuits that add to a product's profit advantage, the so-called value added factor, while holding down the cost of manufactures. Japan's early success in the electronics industry was based on government nurturing. Foreign companies were able to operate wholly owned subsidiaries only after 1975. Japan sheltered its fledgling manufacturers by prohibiting semiconductor imports in the 1970s.

In the 1990s South Korean companies began challenging Japan's leadership in D-RAMs. Meanwhile, the Japanese companies were not able to make much of an inroad into the advanced chips, like microprocessors, that are the province of American companies. And, owing in part to Sematech, the consortium based in Austin, Texas, that started in 1987, the American manufacturers of chip-making machinery improved in competitiveness. Until 1996, when its federal funding ended, Sematech spent about $200 million a year, half from the Defense Department and half from its member companies.

In the mid-1990s the Japanese government and semiconductor manufacturers started a series of consortiums and cooperative research programs to catapult the country into the front ranks of the world's computer-chip production. The companies and the government decided to support research to develop advanced technology and to improve the competitiveness of the Japanese industry, which was hurt as South Korean companies encroached on their mar-

kets and the American industry revived. Now, Japan once again sees itself as playing catch-up.

Table 12.1. World semiconductor sales ranking, 2000

Rank	Maker	Market share (%)
1	Intel (USA)	13.4
2	Toshiba (Japan)	5.0
3	NEC (Japan)	5.0
4	Samsung (South Korea)	4.9
5	Texas Instruments (USA)	4.1
6	Motorola (USA)	3.6
7	ST Microelectronics (France, Italy)	3.6
8	Hitachi (Japan)	3.3
9	Hyundai (South Korea)	3.1
10	Infineon (Germany)	3.0

Source: *Asahi Shimbun Japan Almanac* (Tokyo: Asahi Shimbun, 2002).

In the 1980s the sudden increase in Japanese exports of ICs to the United States and Europe led to trade frictions and affected the locational strategies of the Japanese manufacturers. Increasing foreign production became a major strategy of manufacturers. By 1991 Japan had 25 plants in the United States, 9 in the European Community, 35 in Asia, and 3 in Brazil. The United States is the center of Japanese overseas production. NEC, Toshiba, Hitachi, Fujitsu, and Mitsubishi Electric have expanded production in the United States. In Europe, NEC and Fujitsu have plants in Ireland and the United Kingdom; Hitachi, Toshiba, and Mitsubishi have plants in Germany. The Asian plants in Singapore, Thailand, and Malaysia concentrate on the assembly of chips, which are produced in Japan, the United States, and the United Kingdom.

THE LOCATION OF HIGH-TECHNOLOGY INDUSTRIES

High-technology industries are knowledge-intensive industries such as those involving microelectronics, optical fibers, mechatronics (industrial robots and medical electronics), semiconductors, new materials, and aerospace, information, and communication systems. Success in attracting high-technology industries to an area depends to a large extent on access to research and development centers such as universi-

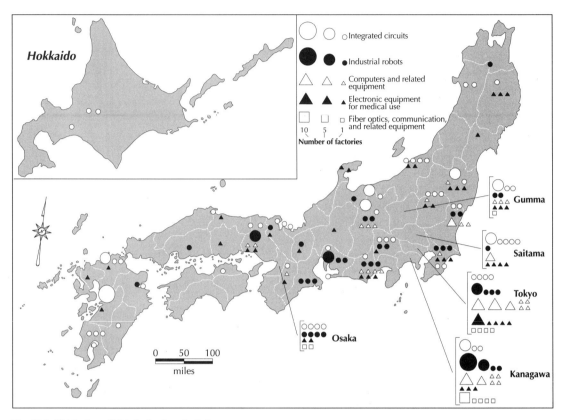

Fig. 12.2. Distribution of high-technology factories.

ties and research institutes. In such locations the industries can constantly collect up-to-date information in order to cope with the rapidly evolving technology. Living conditions are also important and include desirable physical and cultural environments.

Integrated circuits (microchips and silicon chips) form the heart of electronic products from microwave ovens to weapon systems to, of course, computers. Fujitsu, Hitachi, and NEC produce ICs. Several U.S. companies procure parts from Japan. Japan has a major lead in robotics (Matshushita, Toshiba, Kawasaki, and Hitachi are leaders in this field) and a significant share of the world's silicon chip market. Of the world's top semiconductor companies in 2000, three were Japanese (see table 12.1); in 1991 six of the top ten were Japanese.

The Japanese semiconductor industry began in southern Tokyo's Minato and Shinigawa Wards. Since Toshiba was established in the area more than one hundred years ago, many electric machinery manufacturers have concentrated in southern Tokyo. This electronic complex has expanded to Kawasaki and Yokohama and includes, besides Toshiba, plants of Nippon Electric (NEC), Fujitsu, Sony, and Oki Electric (Aoki 2000). In the early 1960s, Japan's electronics and communications industries were concentrated in this region, forming an engineering complex that subsequently spawned the semiconductor industry (Takeuchi 1993).

Semiconductor manufacturers developed in the 1960s in southern Tokyo. Since the 1970s, semiconductor manufacturers have moved their production bases into Kyushu, Tohoku, and other areas (see fig. 12.2). But the research and development functions and the nucleus of the industry have remained in the Tokyo and Osaka regions. The Tokyo region, together with Tsukuba, also has a concentration of IC-related research laboratories and pilot and trial production centers. As decentralization of the plants progressed in the 1980s, Kyushu became the favored location. In the 1980s Kyushu began to be called Silicon Island. Semiconductor plants also began to locate in areas such as Chugoku, Shikoku, Tohoku, and Hokkaido. The industry has spread out in different

NEC's research and development facilities in western Tokyo. Japan's semiconductor industry started in Tokyo in the 1960s. Today, the Tokyo region has most of the nation's research and development facilities; the bulk of the mass production plants are located at various places in other prefectures, from Hokkaido to Kyushu. The R&D plants of NEC, Toshiba, Hitachi, Fujitsu, and Sony are in the Tokyo region. Photo by P.P. Karan.

areas of the country such that the IC productivity is greater in provincial areas than in the metropolitan regions.

Despite the spread-out location of the semiconductor industry, three areas of major concentration can be noted: the Tokyo area, the Osaka area, and Kyushu. In the Japanese semiconductor industry, Tokyo functions as the central core for research and development of products, and the Osaka region as a subcenter forming a strong national network system. Kyushu has production plants of most of the major semiconductor manufacturers.

In the Tokyo region most factories are concentrated in Tokyo, Chiba, Saitama, and Kanagawa Prefectures. Factories in this area manufacture products that require close contact and information exchange between users and makers, and the developers depend upon universities for basic research. Tokyo and Kanagawa Prefectures have more than 37 percent of the private research institutes and 39 percent of the scientific researchers in Japan. At the Hirayama Industrial Complex in Hino, western Tokyo, about fifty high-technology companies and research institutes have assembly plants or laboratories.

Toshiba, Fujitsu, Hitachi, and Nippon Electric Corporation (NEC) are among the major firms in this region. Toshiba was founded in 1939 by merging a firm that made heavy electric apparatus—Shibaura Engineering Works, which went back to 1875 and which had diversified from general to electrical engineering after 1900—and a firm that produced consumer electric appliances. Making a start in computers as early as the 1950s, Toshiba made a bold decision to exit from mainframe computing in 1978 and then, from 1983 on, to concentrate on laptops—a move based on American market research. Industrial electronics, however, accounted for over half of Toshiba's sales in the 1980s.

Fujitsu was founded by Fuji Electric as a subsidiary specializing in communications equipment. Now Fujitsu ranks as a leading Japanese computer maker. NEC was established by Western Electric as its affiliated company specializing in communications equipment. With its strategy of "C&C" (computers and communications), NEC is now a leading company in computers and semiconductor devices. Toshiba, Fujitsu, and NEC have been based in the Keihin region throughout their histories. Toshiba has more than ten factories in Kanagawa. Fujitsu's central factory is located in Kawasaki. NEC has factories in Kawasaki and Yokohama. All three companies have their R&D centers in Kawasaki and production centers for memory devices in Kyushu. Hitachi has concentrated its manufacturing activities around the Tokyo region. Sony and Oki Electric have their research laboratories and R&D plants in the Tokyo area and their production centers in Kyushu.

A second concentration of high-tech industries is in the Osaka and Nagoya Metropolitan Areas, which also contain a large number of research institutes. Mitsubishi Electric, Matsushita, Sharp, Sanyo, and Rohm have their R&D facilities in the Osaka region. The majority of Osaka-based manufacturers have established production plants in Kyushu. Toshiba has established a new development and production center in Nagoya.

The third concentration is in Kyushu, where factories (assembly plants and integrated plants) produce standard goods. It is not important for these factories to have contact with research and development sources. These mass-producing factories require a large, high-quality labor force, a large land area, and clean air and water. These factors have induced them to locate in Kyushu and small cities elsewhere. Technology-intensive high-value-added products can bear high transport costs, a fact that motivates the location of high-tech plants near airports or within easy access to airports by expressways. With the development of highways, trucking has become the dominant form of transportation for companies such as NEC, which are located a bit away from airports. These companies use trucks for 70 percent of their transport from factory to airport.

Both NEC and Toshiba established large-scale integrated plants in Kyushu; their satellite assembly plants and subcontracting plants are located near them. In the 1970s the availability of labor was an important consideration, but because of the progress of automation in the 1980s, production plants no longer require so much local labor. There is greater demand for highly skilled labor for development work.

BIOTECHNOLOGY INDUSTRIES

When biotechnology industries, such as genetic, cellular, and protein engineering, emerged in the 1970s, Japan found itself lagging behind other industrially advanced nations. In order to bring the biotechnologies and products to Japan, Japanese companies entered into licensing agreements with American and European companies. In the meantime, the Japanese government encouraged cooperation between private industries, academia, and national research centers to promote biotech industries. Market movements over the past several years have centered on medical products. Several new physiologically activated materials that implement biotechnology have been developed in Japan (Saxonhouse 1986).

Enzymes with unique capabilities and qualities are also giving rise to bioproducts with important commercial applications, such as biosurfactants and biocosmetics. Significant results are coming out of the development of biosensors and other bioelectronic devices produced by combining Japan's excellent electronic technology with enzymes and microbial cells.

Osaka is a subcenter of semiconductor R&D plants. Mitsubishi, Matsushita, Sanyo, Sharp, and Rohm have their R&D facilities in the Osaka region. Matsushita, Sanyo, and Sharp entered the production of ICs after having developed their bases in the manufacturing of consumer electric-appliance products. Diffusion plants, which supply semiproducts to assembly plants, are also located in the Osaka Metropolitan Area. Photo by P.P. Karan.

Biotech applications in environmental cleanup can be expected to expand with the growing use of genetically altered microbes. Currently hopes are centered on closed-system wastewater treatment and treatment of industrial waste. Because of strong domestic and international demands for this kind of bioremediation, this industry is expected to grow in accordance with government policy. Healthy growth in the edible-goods field, resulting from the development of genetically engineered plants, will continue in the future. In addition to the growth in edible enzymes, amino acids, and some other fields that are applicable to the food and beverage industry, there is also a strong possibility that formulated foods will be developed in which unwanted elements such as allergens and unpleasant smells are removed and desirable qualities and factors added. A robust growth in the biofood market is expected.

The National/Panasonic (Matsushita) semiconductor plant in Yatsushiro, Kyushu. Kyushu has large integrated semiconductor plants. These are usually branch plants of companies located in Tokyo or Osaka. Photo by P.P. Karan.

NEC's large semiconductor assembly plant in Kumamoto. Kumamoto is a leading microchip-producing region in Japan. The Kyushu NEC and Mitsubishi Electric Kumamoto plants are connected to forty-three IC-related companies in the area. Photo by P.P. Karan.

In the field of chemical products, growth is expected in the production of a whole range of enzymes, and there is a good chance that vitamins and nucleic acids will be produced using recombinant DNA technology. Virus-resistant agricultural plants such as rice and tomatoes have been released, and full-blown genetically engineered plants began to appear in 2000. In the livestock field, a rise in the use of transgenic experimental animals and veterinary drugs using recombinant DNA technology is anticipated. In the field of marine products, Japan is expected to produce seaweed using cell fusion.

The largest gene analysis center in Japan, in Mie Prefecture, is owned by Takara Shuzo Company, a liquor producer. In addition to the human genome, the center also studies the genetic makeup of marine mammals, including whales. Influenced by the growth of genome-related businesses, theme-related investment trusts investing in biotechnology and genetic companies have flooded the market in Japan. In June 2000, Daiwa Asset Management Company, an affiliate of Daiwa Securities, launched an investment trust called Idenshi Joho Kakumei (Genetic Information Revolution), or I-Bio for short.

Another area of Japan that is emerging as a center of biotech industries is Kobe. In 1998 the city launched the Kobe Medical Industry Development Project as an initiative to create jobs and revitalize the local economy, devastated by the Great Hanshin-Awaji earthquake of 1995. The project is intended to make Kobe's Port Island a hub for advanced biomedical research institutions, hospitals, and industries. The faculty of Kobe University and other public universities and Port Island companies are cooperating to advance linkages among industry, academia, and government to promote biotech industry. In April 2003 the Institute of Biomedical Research and Innovation (IBRI) began full operation as the core facility of this biomedical industry city. The institute conducts research on medical products and on clinical applications of regenerative medicine. The neighboring Center for Development Biology, the bioresearch arm of the Institute of Physical and Chemical Research (RIKEN), has research teams working on the mechanisms behind cell regeneration. Other advanced facilities near these two research centers are the Kobe International Business Center, a facility for biotechnology companies, and the Transnational Research Informatics Center, a data management center for genome analysis and clinical trials. Spring 2004 saw the opening of the Biomedical Accelerator, which is equipped with a number of special features such as an experimental cell cultivation facility. This resource-rich research and development environment has attracted more than forty biomedical enterprises to Port Island, and Kobe is transforming itself into a biomedical industry city along the lines of Minnesota's Medical Alley and California's Biotech Bay.

In order for biotechnology industries to grow in the twenty-first century, Japan will need to (1) promote basic and original research, (2) remove reliance on foreign countries for access to research infrastructure such as biological data from genome analysis, and (3) develop a mechanism that will rapidly and prudently transfer to private companies the fruits of research and technology developed at public institutions.

Several prefectures and regions across Japan are looking toward the biotechnology industry as a good bet for long-term economic development to replace jobs in the declining manufacturing industries. They are developing strategies to grow their own clusters of biotech companies. As noted earlier, biotechnology is a collaborative enterprise between companies and universities. Several factors will determine the success of the efforts to develop clusters. Most important is a strong scientific base comprised of human resources and medical institutions, with a foundation of public and privately supported research that can be commercialized or applied in the development of biotech products. Beyond this, local governments in Japan must also actively promote a business climate through loans, grants, and a favorable regulatory environment. Some communities are making efforts to promote a good quality of life to lure people and companies from other places. A research park with buildings housing the full continuum of science, including applied research, technology transfer, and corporate research and development, has become the tool of choice for localities in Japan seeking to encourage biotechnology growth.

THE INFORMATION TECHNOLOGY (IT) INDUSTRY

Japan lags behind the United States in the fast-proliferating field of information technology (Kitahara 1983). But Japan seems to have a good chance of taking a lead in this field. In 2000 the number of Internet users in Japan rose 59.7 percent to 27.6 million. Furthermore, 41 percent of the Japanese used mobile phones, far above the 27 percent U.S. rate. In 1999 the total number of mobile phones in Japan (56.9 million) exceeded that of regular fixed phones (55.5 million) for the first time. Also, 7.5 million people in Japan use mobile phone–based Internet services. This market, spearheaded by NTT DoCoMo's I-mode service, is expected to sustain high growth in the coming years.

Despite the economy's weak performance during the 1990s, the IT industry has been robust, as evidenced by the phenomenal growth in the number of IT-related companies. Japan expects to win the next round of development in IT, which will deal with how to hook up all the devices—from mobile phones to home appliances—to the Net. By 2005, for example, Japan will move into an all-devices-online phase after going through Internet-for-personal-computers and Internet-for-household-appliances phases.

In other areas of the IT revolution, Japan's situation does not look bright. For example, Japan ranks twenty-first in the world as an e-commerce environment. This could be serious for the Japanese IT industry, because every country is vying for a share of the booming market. But Internet sales were projected to make a rapid jump in 2003 (see fig. 12.3).

What is the reason for Japan's low position

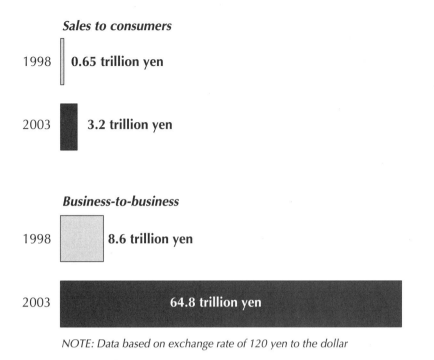

NOTE: Data based on exchange rate of 120 yen to the dollar

Fig. 12.3. Japan's e-commerce sales, 1998, and projection for 2003. Based on data from the *Daily Yomiuri* (Tokyo) archives, 2000.

among the Group of Seven[1] industrial nations in e-commerce? The broad context of the Japanese political and economic system offers some insight. For the sake of international competitiveness the Japanese government actively intervenes in markets to promote the producer's interests. In the past this system was touted as a model for other countries to follow. But in the 1990s it became evident that the system was maintained at the expense of the consumers and could not adapt to the tides of change.

Historically, various ministries, especially the MITI/METI and the Ministry of Posts and Telecommunications, have battled over the IT industry. In June 1998 the Diet passed the Basic Law on the Administrative Reform of the Central Government, aimed at creating a slimmer and more efficient administration. The central government underwent a major reorganization. The Administrative Reform

Council suggested that the Ministry of Economy, Trade, and Industry, which replaced MITI, and the Ministry of Public Management, Home Affairs, and Posts and Telecommunications be put in charge of the IT industry. But the reforms to unify jurisdictional authority over the IT industry have not materialized. Neither METI nor Posts and Telecommunications wants to give up control over the IT industry, which is viewed as the key to Japan's future success. The cost of this bureaucratic rivalry has been enormous. It has often delayed the policy-making process and may be the main culprit in Japan's slowness to adapt to the changing environment.

Among other reasons for Japan's lag in the IT industry are these: (1) telecommunications costs remain higher than the international average, (2) the telecommunications infrastructure is quite weak in capacity and speed, and (3) IT-related businesses still have to cope with many regulations and old-fashioned business practices. Progress in the information technology industry will depend on whether Japan can create a system in which huge amounts of information can be transmitted quickly and inexpensively. The most contentious issue has

---

[1] The United States, Canada, the United Kingdom, France, Germany, Japan, and Italy. The group also now includes Russia and often is called G-8. They meet each year in June. The United States hosted the 2004 meeting in Sea Island, Georgia.

been the structure of the NTT, the telecommunications giant.

In July 1999 the Japanese government split NTT into three companies, two regional carriers (NTT East and NTT West) and a long-distance and international one under a holding company to induce competition among different services. But the split was riddled with pitfalls. NTT DoCoMo, a cell-phone service company that existed before the split, is partially (64%) owned by NTT. Part of the reason the NTT split was not effective was that NTT DoCoMo has not completely separated from NTT. With NTT DoCoMo under the NTT holding company's umbrella, it is hard to say that the government is serious about promoting competition between the two. NTT's monopolistic power has not weakened. The government's Regulatory Reform Committee submitted a set of recommendations in December 2000. Among other things, it suggested scrapping the current NTT holding company structure and transforming it into several independent business entities to encourage fair and effective competition. NTT is strongly opposed to the proposed abolition of its holding company structure, claiming that its international competitiveness would be adversely affected. In fiscal 1999 the NTT group's pretax profit ranked first in Japan at 825 billion yen. This figure is up 13 percent from a year earlier and puts Toyota Motor Corporation's 797 billion yen firmly in second place.

NTT's access fees have remained high, to the detriment of the Japanese IT industry. The telephone monopoly is lowering prices, but not enough to level the playing field for the IT industry. Partly because of high telephone costs of Internet connection, Japanese schools have had a later start and a lower percentage of links than those in the United States (see fig. 12.4).

THE INTERNET ECONOMY

U.S. industries have spent years embracing Internet technologies to cut costs, boost sales, and enhance productivity, but Japan has just recently jumped on the bandwagon. The growth of the Internet is spurring a wave of entrepreneurism not seen since the building boom after World War II. The economy is splitting into the "new" and the "old" as investors, despite the recent economic slowdown, reward companies with Internet strategies. High-tech start-ups are luring employees from older manufacturing industries and businesses, where age and experience, not performance, define careers. And more people realize that Japan needs to catch up to avoid falling further behind in a globally networked economy.

For years, Japan has been under pressure to deregulate its economy, the world's second-largest. Change has come, albeit sometimes at a glacial pace. For the first time, banks are now being sold to foreigners and airlines are discounting tickets. Although historically resistant to foreign investment, Japan

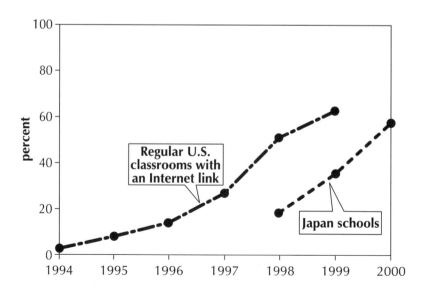

Fig. 12.4. Schools connected to the Internet in Japan and the United States, 1994–2000.
Based on data from the *Daily Yomiuri* (Tokyo) archives, 2000.

welcomed a record $14 billion in 1999. The growth of the Internet and network technologies is hastening the pace of that change. Spending is rising on computer software and hardware to make Japanese companies more efficient. In 2000, 25 percent of Japan's capital outlays went to high-tech products, up from 15 percent in 1998. Companies are getting into the Net. Toshiba and Fujitsu are retooling to focus on information technologies. NTT DoCoMo has emerged as the world leader in Internet wireless connectivity. NEC expected 25 percent of its sales to be over computer networks by 2001. Sony is pushing into the Internet from all angles. It even hopes to set up an online bank. Already, almost 40 percent of Sony's new PlayStation 2 game machine sales in Japan are online. Sony has started selling other products directly to Japanese consumers, cutting out the middlemen. In Japan five layers of people, each adding cost, can sit between the producers and buyers. Being able to cut costs and move the goods in a global market is a must for Japan.

Perhaps more important, with the growth of the Internet economy, Japan is beginning to talk about changes to bedrock societal values. In January 2000 a government-commissioned advisory panel suggested that individuals in group-oriented Japan be empowered and that students spend more time being creative. It also said that Japan needs to brush up on its English, the language of the Internet and of the global economy. Although students study English for years, a heavy emphasis on studying grammar has left Japan, along with North Korea, with the worst English skills in Asia.

For decades, Japan's traditions served the country well. From the ashes of World War II, it rose to world prominence in the 1980s as a manufacturer of high-quality goods. In today's knowledge-based economy, different strengths are needed, strengths like entrepreneurship, innovation, and risk-taking. Individualism and risk-taking are revered in the United States. Enterprising youngsters like Bill Gates and Jerry Yang of Yahoo founded high-tech marvels. In Japan the group and conformity are highly valued. Unfortunately, Japanese society still tends to frown on displays of individual excellence. The nail that sticks up is often hammered down.

Most Japanese companies, too, are ill-positioned to adapt to change. In a global market where an online bookseller like Amazon.com can change an entire industry, companies have to move fast to adapt. To maintain harmony, Japanese companies rely on the time-consuming process of making decisions through consensus. Despite some reforms, Japan's regulations still prevent a lot of free-market forces from operating, and the government has been backtracking on job-costing reforms. The most likely effect: slowing the flow of money into venture capital funds, which fueled the rapid growth of Internet industries in the United States.

Despite obstacles, a small number of Japan's young entrepreneurs are chasing a growing market. Japan's Internet population, 18.5 million in 1999, was expected to reach 60 million by 2003. In May 2000, 1,279 Internet companies were operating in Tokyo's 23 wards. Because nearly a quarter of these firms are based in Minato and Shibuya Wards, Japan's own version of the Silicon Alley has been created. About 60 percent of Internet firms in Japan (those that could not exist without the World Wide Web) are located in Minato (267), Shibuya (204), Shinjuku (112), Chiyoda (125), and Chuo (73) wards. Of these, 37 percent were in Minato and Shibuya Wards, and a notable concentration were in Akasaka, Shibuya, and Ebisu. (See a report on e-commerce in Japan on the Internet at http://www.fujitsu.co.jp/hypertext/fri/reports/88.html, in Japanese).

Japan's Silicon Alley began to develop in the Akasaka-Shibuya areas around 1994. The area has an abundance of entertainment facilities, restaurants, and cafés where young Internet entrepreneurs gather to discuss Web site design businesses, swap tips, and network. These areas are now often referred to as Bit Valley. Grassroots IT business organizations such as the Bit Valley Association have become active, and efforts are being made to reduce high telephone charges, which remain the biggest hurdle faced by the IT businesses wanting to expand. Although specific support measures such as preferential tax treatment for IT start-ups have yet to emerge, the Tokyo Metropolitan Government has started to establish liaisons with young would-be entrepreneurs and their supporters to invigorate private-sector business in Tokyo.

Kyoto, Japan's old traditional city, is nurturing start-ups to build a bright high-tech future. Amid the Buddhist temples, pottery artists, and kimono weavers of this former capital of Japan are some of the country's most nimble companies. Among them, game-maker Nintendo, custom-chip-maker Rohm,

The Shibuya district of Tokyo, with stores and small Internet firms. Shibuya has emerged as a major focus of Internet firms founded by young entrepreneurs. The area is often referred as Silicon Alley or Bit Valley. Generally the Internet firms have offices in the alleys behind stores and banks. Photo by P.P. Karan.

and electric component leader Murata Manufacturing are high-tech manufacturers who grew to global prominence in recent decades. Now Kyoto is trying to lead another wave: giving birth to Internet, multimedia, and software-based industries. In 2000 Kyoto, 320 miles south of Tokyo, was home to an estimated three hundred high-tech start-ups, including Honya-san, which aims to be the Amazon.com of Japan. But to grab a fair share of the global networked economy, Japan needs a lot more entrepreneurs, and Kyoto is trying to encourage their emergence. Among other things, this city of 1.3 million offers to start-ups:

Mentors. In 1997 Kyoto executives formed a committee to review the business plans of aspiring entrepreneurs. A grade of A can be taken to local banks for loans that the city then guarantees.

Links to academia. Kyoto's forty universities and colleges make easy mixing of faculty, entrepreneurs, and bright minds possible.

A place to call home. Many new companies are clustered in the Kyoto Research Park, considered to be among Japan's top new-company incubators. The privately run park supplies low-cost office space, high-speed data lines, and a network of services for start-ups.

Kyoto is trying to shape younger minds, too. At the Center for Entrepreneurship Education, materials are being developed to spur creativity in 12- to 15-year-olds by asking them to come up with ideas.

Student interns are sent to start-ups, and local CEOs hold seminars. Japanese companies don't need obedient employees anymore. They need employees with ideas.

Gifu Prefecture, located in the geographic center of Japan, is emerging as a center of research and development for the IT-related companies after creating Softopia Japan in 1996. In the same year, the International Academy of Media Arts and Sciences was established as an educational institute for cultivating tech-savvy human resources, and in 1998 Technoplaza, a center for fostering a cooperative blend of information technology and artisanship, was opened. In 2001 the prefecture established the Institute for Advanced Media Arts and Science. Both this and the earlier International Academy of Media Arts and Science are known as IAMAS. In 2003 Gifu opened its high-speed broadband fiber optic network, the Gifu Information Super Highway, for use by the private sector. Gifu Prefecture's vigorous support for advanced technology has made it a national leader in IT. Formulation of an environment that attracts the best-qualified personnel to support IT-related industry—both from within Japan and from abroad—is essential for further progress.

There are signs of changes generated by the IT Revolution. Call centers and data centers are rapidly being relocated to remote areas such as Sapporo and Naha. Similarly, physical distance has proved to be no problem for companies such as the American cyberbookstore Amazon.com, which has established operations in Japan. Hoping to gain tax advantages, more and more companies are locating their headquarters in places that used to be considered remote, and opportunities for various economic activities are increasingly available in out-of-the-way places. In short, IT is creating profound changes in the very structure of Japanese society by changing the relationship between central and peripheral regions. The advantages and disadvantages associated with physical location and physical distances, which have always played a part in decisions regarding the siting of businesses and the size of markets, are losing their significance. For Japanese companies pursuing economic activity in cyberspace, the law of economy of scale is losing relevance. Thousands of virtual stores are selling a variety of products, with only a few employees responsible for marketing billions of yen worth of products each year. This ratio of employees to sales was unimaginable in the old economy. A handful of employees serve several million customers in the bill-paying services offered by the Japanese telecommunications companies through the use of mobile telephones. The development of IT is contributing to the breakdown of the traditional distribution system that involved many layers of middlemen.

SCIENCE CITIES AND THE TECHNOPOLIS

In order to foster the growth of technology, Japan built science cities at Tsukuba in the 1960s (Cavasin 1999) and in Kansai in the 1980s. Tsukuba, 40 miles (64.4 km) northeast of Tokyo, is a national research center funded by the central government. Kansai Science City, about 6 miles (9.7 km) north of Nara, is located between Kyoto and Osaka atop the Keihanna hills. Kansai Science City was built through a public-private partnership. The basic initiative there has come from the private sector. Kansai Science City comprises several clusters of universities, research institutes, and housing scattered across the site (see fig. 12.5).

Tsukuba has nearly fifty national research and educational institutes. However, the extreme vertical integration of Japanese government agencies prevents research institutes from sharing facilities and thus leads to an excessive duplication of equipment.

Fig. 12.5. Technopolis centers. Based on a map by Nathalie Cavasin, Waseda University.

Interaction between public research/scientific establishments and private-sector enterprises has been poor, discouraging the development of joint research and spin-off firms and activities.

Unlike Tsukuba, Kansai Science City was developed jointly by representatives of private industry, existing academic institutes, and national and local governments. This project was first promoted by the Osaka Prefectural Government in the late 1970s. The Kansai Science City Promotion Act was passed in 1987 by the national Diet, establishing this as a national project, a category that confers special tax treatment and special privileges for enterprises setting up research facilities in the new science city. Osaka, Nara, and Kyoto Prefectures are responsible for infrastructure development and new housing. The goal of Kansai Science City is to maximize opportunities for public and private research institutes to foster development and growth of new technologies.

In 1983 the Technopolis Law was passed by the national Diet to foster growth of high-technology industries (Tatsuno 1986). By 1990 there were twenty-six technopolis centers (planned cities with concentrations of high-technology industries). Specific activities such as space research, optics, biotechnology, integrated circuits, and medical electronics are undertaken in each technopolis. The technopolis designation included such requirements as the existence of a "mother" city with a population of two hundred thousand or more, an airport or bullet train station, and a potential for high-technology industry. Upon designation, prefectures became eligible for various kinds of financial assistance, including tax exemptions, direct subsidies, and low-interest loans. Incentives were also made available directly to companies that located in the technopolises. These included accelerated depreciation for machinery and buildings, tax breaks, low-interest loans, and relocation assistance. In addition to high-technology production centers, each technopolis was also expected to have a local innovative research and development capacity to help trigger the development of such industries locally. One of the main objectives of the technopolis policy was to shift the Japanese industrial base away from exploitation of imported technologies and toward a world role in the development of leading-edge high-technology industry. By concentrating facilities for research and development, manufacturing, marketing, and services in compact centers of high technology in a network of technopolises, Japan expected to reap advantages of logistical convenience, close communications, close contact, and the synergy that would arise from the existence of a critical mass. It also expected to stimulate economic growth in various regions of the country.

The three technopolises within two hundred miles of Tokyo—Utsunomiya, Hamamatsu, and Toyama—have grown rapidly. Another five—Koriyama, Kofu, Asama, Yamagata, and Sendai-Hokubu—have also expanded. The remaining eighteen have not performed well. Some of them have recorded a decline in manufacturing employment; two have experienced a decline in population. Most of the firms in technopolises are branch plants making parts for shipment to Tokyo, Osaka, or overseas. Major business corporations have established research laboratories close to their headquarters rather than to their factories. For example, NEC's basic research facilities are in Kawasaki, close to its Tokyo headquarters, and its mass-production plants are in Kumamoto, Kyushu. Therefore, there is little technology transfer between incoming factories and local industries.

The program has failed to achieve its original objective of a satellite technopolis city integrating research and development, educational facilities, and production facilities for high-technology industry. Close links between local universities and industry have not developed because of restrictive regulations and the structure of Japanese professional and social relationships, which inhibit spin-offs from university research into new companies. With the exception of the technopolises located within two hundred miles of Tokyo—Utsunomiya, Kofu, Hamamatsu, Toyama, Koriyama, Asama, Yamagata, and Sendai-Hokubu—the program has not been very successful in generating new activity. Since proximity to headquarters has replaced proximity to the factory as the key locational factor for research facilities, technopolises close to Tokyo and Osaka have attracted research laboratories.

In 2002, under the government's Big-Boned Policy, a bold program of collaboration between industry, academia, and government was put forward to enhance Japan's economic competitiveness. As a result of this collaboration, new companies that turn the results of research into viable, commercial products are slowly springing up, and new ideas are being licensed for commercial use. Two notable examples are the development and retailing of gene-therapy medication resulting from collaboration between Osaka University and Daiichi Seiyaku, a pharmaceutical company, and the establishment of GalPharma, a biotechnology venture business developing anticancer drugs in Takamatsu through cooperation between Kagawa Medical University and Fuso Pharmaceutical Industries. Collaboration is viewed as a key for Japan's economic revival. Technology Licensing Organizations (TLOs) are facilitating collaboration by acting as intermediaries between industry and academia. The model for Japan's TLOs is Stanford University's Office of Technology Licensing, founded in 1970.

FUTURE PROSPECTS

Ever since the early 1950s, when the Korean War stimulated the Japanese economy and America promoted Japan as a bulwark against Communism, Japan's economic and business policy has been based on high growth rates. Many features of Japanese corporate behavior, including the priority given to market share over profits and the system of lifetime employment, were sustained in a period of long-term expansion. Primed by access to the vast American market and by cut-rate prices for Western—mostly American—technologies, the Japanese economy expanded at double-digit rates from the 1950s to the mid 1970s. In the latter half of the 1970s, it slowed to about 5 percent, then to an average of 4 percent in the 1980s. The surge in the late 1980s was an aberration fueled by cheap credit and an unprecedented boom in land and stock values. The price of the excess, revealed by a growing number of bankruptcies and a weakened financial sector in the 1990s, will continue to be paid for several years.

When Japan faced other economic crises, such as the oil shocks of the 1970s and the *endaka* or high-yen shock in 1985, there was always a way to respond that allowed it to preserve its traditional practices and its hard-to-penetrate domestic markets. The oil shocks were overcome by high manufacturing productivity and a surge in exports. When endaka arrived, Japan leveraged its new wealth in real estate and stocks into an asset-buying spree at home and abroad. But now there appears to be no way to avoid making changes in the system. With Japan's trade surplus hitting a record low of $140 billion, it is clear that the export escape route is closed by political reality.

Japanese companies are discovering that many of their usual advantages have been eroded. Manufacturing, for example, the leading force in Japan's global expansion, is in trouble because rivals have become more competitive. Another advantage Japan has lost is its free ride in technology. For most of the postwar period, Japan paid little for technologies that were important to its industrial development. Most American companies simply underestimated Japan's potential, and the U.S. government was more concerned with security than with economic issues. Both of these conditions ended with the cold war.

Japan once verged on global technological dominance. Now it is conceding leadership in many key emerging commercial technologies, chiefly to a resurgent United States. Japanese industry is floundering in a creativity crisis and has lost market share—even in strongholds like semiconductors, automobiles, and computers. America's Intel Corporation replaced Japan's NEC as the world's largest semiconductor maker. American automakers are making a comeback, and U.S. computer firms—despite their many problems—are expanding their market-share lead. More tellingly, Japan is missing out as U.S. companies forge new markets and seize control of key technologies and standards that are expected to yield the highest profits in the future. Control of the most profitable computer markets—microprocessors and operating systems—continues to elude Japanese companies. The memory chips they produced so well, in contrast, yield only modest profits and are available from many competing companies. Other traditional Japanese cash cows, like cars, audiovisual equipment, and VCRs, now face saturated markets and low profit margins. Little distinguishes one company's products from another's.

Even in the long-lost markets such as consumer electronics, American firms are winning technological leads in new areas like multimedia, high-definition television, and handheld electronic communicators. By setting the technical standards, American computer, software, and semiconductor manufacturers can control the markets and profit from patent royalties.

The very corporate and government structures that nurtured Japan's industrial growth in the past share part of the blame. The system created to catch up with the West is ill-equipped for moving ahead with original technology. Much of Japan's technological development has involved catching up with, and then perfecting, areas of technology invented elsewhere. Among Japan's recent hit products, for example, Philips of the Netherlands proposed compact discs; Ampex developed VCRs, and liquid crystal displays were begun by RCA.

Japanese companies hesitate to move into uncharted technological waters. Instead, they continue to do what they have done so well in the past—honing new technologies often developed abroad and finding inexpensive applications in consumer products (Hemmert and Oberlander 1998). Japan's own attempts to pioneer new technology have not been dazzling. Projects for magnetically levitated trains, nuclear and superconducting ships, advanced rockets, and high-definition TV have been plagued by unexpected snags. Japanese companies failed to take the technological lead during the boom years in the 1980s because they did not pursue original research. The challenge ahead will center on the need to be innovative at the frontiers of research, new-product design, and process technology—all three.

Increasingly, Japan will have to pay more for intellectual property; it will also have to increase spending on basic research, which, unlike the nation's investment in applied research, remains far below that of the United States and Europe. In the twenty-first century Japan faces a new world, and Japan, a mature economy, must begin to reinvent itself.

The changes are by no means bad for the Japanese. In time, they should result in a greater emphasis on domestic consumption over investment, perhaps making Japan a more comfortable place to live. The changes could further open the Japanese economy to foreign companies, offering its people wider selections at lower prices. And Japanese companies that survive the shakeout would emerge as more efficient competitors both at home and abroad.

REFERENCES

Aoki, Hidekazu. 2000. Factory location in electronic products and regional production linkages: The example of Sony Group. *Human Geography* 57 (5): 23–42.

Cavasin, Nathalie. 1999. Science cities and technopolis in Japan: Innovative networks and regional planning. In *Urban Growth and Development in Asia*, ed. Graham P. Chapman, Ashok K. Dutt, and Robert W. Bradnock, 2:74–91. Brookfield, VT: Ashgate.

Goto, A., and H. Odagiri. 1997. *Innovation in Japan.* Oxford: Clarendon Press.

Hemmert, Martin, and Christian Oberlander. 1998. *Technology and Innovation in Japan: Policy and Management for the Twenty-first Century.* London: Routledge.

Kitahara, Yasusada. 1983. *Information Network System: Telecommunications in the Twenty-first Century.* London: Heinemann Educational Books.

Morris-Suzuki, Tessa. 1994. *The Technological Transformation of Japan: From the Seventeenth to the Twenty-first Century.* Cambridge: Cambridge Univ. Press.

Nishioka, H., and A. Takeuchi. 1986. High technology industry in Japan. In *The Development of High Technology Industry,* ed. M. Broheny and D. Macoaid, 262–295. London: Croom Helm.

Saxonhouse, Gary R. 1986. Industrial policy and factor markets: Biotechnology in Japan and the United States. In *Japanese High Technology Industries,* ed. Hugh T. Patrick. Seattle: Univ. of Washington Press.

Takeuchi, Atsuhiko. 1993. Location dynamics of the Japanese semiconductor industry in the rapid technological innovation. *Geographical Review of Japan* B 66:91–104.

Tatsuno, Sheridan. 1986. *The Technopolis Strategy: Japan, High Technology, and the Control of the 21st Century.* New York: Prentice-Hall.

Chapter 13

第 十 三 章

THE CHALLENGE OF
ENVIRONMENTAL PRESERVATION

Environmental degradation in Japan has accompanied the development of modern industry since the Meiji period. Environmental problems caused by drainage from the refineries at the Ashio Copper Mine in Tochigi Prefecture, operated by the Furukawa Company, go back to 1878. They provoked intense political struggles in the period 1890 to 1905. The pollution in Ashio is of such long standing that it is referred to as the origin of Japan's environmental problems (Nimura 1997). The acid wastewater polluted large areas of agricultural land in the lower reaches of the Watarase River, damaging farm products, killing fish, and doing serious damage to the health of residents along the river. About 29,650 acres (12,000 ha) of land were deforested by sulfurous acid gas from the refineries by 1893. In the 1890s death rates outstripped birthrates in the town of Ashio, which was home to about thirty thousand people. Japan's national policy of militarization needed Ashio's copper exports, which earned the foreign exchange to help buy steel. Copper was one of Japan's leading exports, and Ashio produced some 40 percent and was Japan's most important copper mine. The mine was closed in 1973, when the copper seam was exhausted, but refineries continued operating, using imported ore, until the early 1980s. Although the efforts to restore the environment in the area have been under way for nearly forty years, it is still a long way from full recovery.

The Besshi copper mine, on Shikoku Island, caused pollution problems from the seventeenth century on. After 1885 the expansion of mining and smelting at Besshi intensified pollution and provoked forty years of intense complaint and political tussle. To avoid the political problems of Ashio, the government encouraged mine owners to install antipollution devices. In 1910 the Ministry of Agriculture,

responding to agitation by farmers, ordered Sumitomo, the mine owner, to restrict Besshi's operations during a forty-day period of rice maturation. This practice reduced but did not resolve the antipollution struggles. After 1925 desulfurizing equipment and a 157-foot (48-m) smokestack diffused local pollution and defused political pressure. After 1905 the Hitachi copper mine also caused increased local pollution and public protest. The matter was resolved by building a 509-foot (155-m) stack in 1914–15 (Miura 1975, 286–305). The Kosaka copper mine near Ashita faced similar pollution problems and public protest (Okada 1990).

The discharge from chemical industries polluted coastal areas around Tokyo Bay after 1920. The use of coal as the major source of energy for industry caused widespread but localized air pollution. However, environmental degradation as a devastating side effect of rapid Japanese development has occurred only since the 1950s.

Air and water pollution reached very high levels in Japan by 1970 and then subsided. Both the pollution and its abatement were linked tightly to Japan's politics—international, national, and local. In Japan, crowded cities and polluting industries lived close to each other, and until the mid-1960s the state scarcely regulated the big companies. Powerful nationalism translated into determined efforts to industrialize rapidly regardless of the social and environmental costs. Michio Hashimoto (1989) has described the period from the Meiji restoration in 1868 to about 1965 as "polluter's paradise" in Japan.

Since the 1950s concern over environmental problems has gone through a series of distinct stages (Barrett and Therivel 1991). Until the mid-1960s there was widespread apathy concerning the environment on the part of the government as well as

By the late 1960s awareness of environmental degradation began to strike the national consciousness. The pollution of air (Kawamura 1985) and water became serious in major industrial areas, and many respiratory diseases were named after the industrial cities where they frequently occurred: Kawasaki asthma, or Yokkaichi asthma. Environmental pollution in Japan was at its worst between 1965 and 1975. Inadequate disposal of industrial waste led to widespread contamination of the environment and the emergence of various diseases related to air and water pollution. Rapid urbanization (Tamura 1993), industrialization, a lag in construction of capital facilities such as sewage systems, and a public policy that heavily favored economic growth over public health and a clean environment contributed to the emergence of serious pollution problems. Bays, inland seas, lakes, and other water areas such as Tokyo, Ise, and Osaka Bays and Lakes Biwa, Kasumigaura, and Suwa suffered considerable pollution from organic substances and industrial wastes. Eiichiro Fukui (1969) noted the rise in urban temperatures related to rapid urbanization in Japan, and Tomomasa Taniguchi (1999) has analyzed the changes in water quality of the Sumida River in Tokyo.

Calls for the government and industry to take responsibility for environmental protection led to the passage in 1967 of pollution control laws. These laws were successful in the removal of toxic substances from the water and the reduction of sulfur oxides in the air. Photochemical smog first appeared in Tokyo in July 1970. The Environmental Agency, attached to the prime minister's office and responsible for environmental conservation and pollution control, was established in 1971. However, the oil crisis of 1973, the decline of industries such as shipbuilding and textiles, the slump in the steel industry, and other economic issues had subdued the public pressures for a clean environment by the late 1970s. The right of the victims of pollution-related diseases to compensation was established in relation to diseases such as the Niigata Minamata disease (1971), Yokkaichi asthma (1972), and Kumamoto Minamata disease (1973). In the 1970s Japan adopted the Polluter Pays Principle, according to which the polluting enterprises had to accept financial responsibility for damages they inflicted on the community. A Nature Conservation Law was passed in 1972 to serve as the basis for all legal measures to protect the environment.

Chisso Corporation industrial plant in Minamata, a city of 35,000 people in Kumamoto Prefecture, Kyushu. It lies astride a small river that empties into Minamata Bay, an arm of the Yatsushiro Sea. Methyl mercury was dumped into the sea by Chisso Company as an unwanted by-product of manufacturing acetaldehyde, a substance used to make plastics. Minamata disease is the name given to mercury poisoning that developed in people who ate contaminated seafood taken from Minamata Bay. The disease was recognized in 1956, and a Chisso scientist discovered its cause in 1959, but not until 1973 did a court rule that Chisso was at fault; the company then agreed to pay each victim a lump sum of $60,000 plus annual fees and medical expenses. There were 2,262 patients eventually officially recognized, of whom 879 were alive in 2000. Several thousand others have milder symptoms and were not officially recognized for compensation. Photo by P.P. Karan.

the public. Although the pollution-related Minamata disease caused by mercury from the Chisso Corporation plant was reported in 1956, until the mid-1960s Japan's major industries succeeded in primary capital accumulation by forgetting the diseconomies of environmental pollution and by spending the larger portion of profits on new production equipment. A local citizens' movement brought the awareness of the tragedy to the Japanese public (Iijima 1970).

Field Report

A Japanese Town Staggered by Ecological Disaster

Much as Hiroshima echoes the horrors of atomic war, Minamata, a small town in Kyushu, is a living monument to ecological apocalypse. More than a generation has passed since tons of lethal mercury dumped into Minamata Bay by a giant chemical company traveled up the food chain, killing 700 people and crippling as many as 9,000 others in Minamata; officials have recognized only 2,262 victims of Minamata disease for compensation. Today, the town is still staggering from the consequences. As of March 2000, 879 victims were still alive.

The ghosts are everywhere in this town of 35,000; in hospitals where palsied, brain-damaged victims wait to die; in workshops where partially functional victims strive to exercise basic life skills; in courtrooms where legal battles against the polluter rage on; in the harbor once bulging with fishing boats, now filled in with earth; and in the depressed economy. One-third of the population was lost. Families were broken up. Deep social divisions persist because of the way the disaster has shaped Minamata's fortunes. And then there is the lingering social stigma of a city whose very name is associated with gruesome disease and death.

At Hiroshima, the human destruction was painfully clear as soon as the bomb was dropped. At Minamata, the death and paralysis crept up slowly. The suffering is still going on. Minamata. The very name sears the memory. More recent environmental crises in Bhopal, India (Karan 1986), and in Chernobyl in the former Soviet Union may eventually cause greater human and property loss. But neither evokes the poignant images of Minamata: the twisted bodies of children; the cats hurling themselves into the bay to commit suicide; the anguished faces of survivors; and always the sea, the great source of civilization and livelihood in Japan, transformed into the town's cup of poison.

When the cup spilled, it soiled more than Minamata. As many as 50,000 people who lived within 35 miles (56 km) of the bay and who consumed its fish have suffered symptoms of mercury poisoning. Facing the Shiranui Sea on the island of Kyushu, Minamata was for centuries a simple fishing village. In 1908 the first factory opened here, a chemical company named Chisso Corporation (Huddle and Reich 1991). Chisso built a large factory in the middle of the town and spewed its chemical wastes down a long, open pipe that drained into the bay a half mile downhill. The wastes contained mercury that had been used in the production of acetaldehyde, a component of plastics. As the plastics industry boomed, up to 600 tons of mercury were dumped, mostly after World War II. In 1956 mercury levels in the bay stood at four hundred times the safe level.

The effects surfaced in the 1950s. Fish bellied up. Seabirds dropped into the water and drowned. An outbreak of "cat dancing disease," in which cats staggered, salivated, convulsed, and collapsed, wiped out Minamata's feline population. In April 1956, a six-year-old girl hospitalized for imbalance and delirium became the first officially recognized human victim. Within months, another fifty cases were reported.

Although a Chisso scientist discovered the cause of the disease in 1959, the company continued to dump mercury-laden wastes for another nine years while deaths and injuries mounted. A court verdict in 1973 found Chisso negligent, and compensation paid to victims between 1973 and 1990 has amounted to over $665 million. The company's duplicity, once revealed, ignited among victims a fury rare in a rural Asian society.

Minamata has not recovered from the loss of the four thousand Chisso jobs or the death of the fishing industry after the bay was closed. Tourists who once flocked here for hot springs and natural beauty stopped coming for fear of getting sick. Chisso's sprawling complex of smokestacks, electric generators, and warehouses still dominates the city of wooden frame, tile-

(continued on the following page)

Field Report: *A Japanese Town Staggered by Ecological Disaster* (continued)

roofed houses and tidy vegetable gardens dropped on narrow, winding streets. At Minamata's southern tip, huge cranes piled tons of earth into the bay, dealing the final blow to a centuries-old culture and economy rooted in the sea. The loss of the sea stripped Minamata of its soul. Minamata may have become faded memory to most of the world forty-five years after it set alarm bells everywhere ringing with the dangers of environmental pollution. The Ministry of Environment declared Minamata Bay safe in 1997, after a 48.5-billion-yen ($394 million) effort to dredge or contain in landfill the mercury accumulated at the bottom of the bay.

Yet here, in the eye of the disaster, the lessons of environmental crisis of over four decades ago are woven into life's fabric, undiminished in their pain and prevalence.

The national government sets general standards for environmental protection, but much of the implementation of the policies is done at the prefectural or municipal level. Local governments and citizen groups then negotiate with industrial firms to establish standards for specific facilities. These standards are invariably stricter than the national standards and permit a great deal of local citizen involvement. This involvement strengthens a community's willingness to accept a new facility and supports a healthy industry-community relationship (OECD 1994).

Although some areas in Japan face serious environmental problems, the thrust of public environmental concern shifted in the 1980s. New environmental issues such as groundwater contamination by organic solvents in the effluents from high-tech semiconductor factories, the pollution of rivers and streams from agricultural chemicals used to maintain the golf courses (Sugitani 1998), and acid rain are now attracting major public concern. Extensive land reclamation schemes, often in coastal tidal flats renowned for their scenery (Kim, Je, and Lee 1999), and the development of housing and industrial complexes such as the western Tokyo Nishi-Tama plan have aroused concern among environmentalists. The large number of visitors to national parks and the conflict between economic demands and the need to preserve areas of natural wilderness have led to a keen awareness among the public of the impact of overdevelopment on the environment (Uda, Sumiya, and Shimoyamada 2000).

Acid rain in areas facing the Sea of Japan comes from China, South Korea, and North Korea. Trees killed by acid rain have been observed in those parts of Japan, especially in Shimane and other nearby prefectures. In recent years construction of golf courses has caused environmental concern. The use of huge amounts of underground water for sprinkling the greens has caused land subsidence and drying up of ponds, marshes, lakes, and springs. Chemicals used to enhance the growth of grasses contaminate the water supplies. The Live Tree Trust Movement, a conservation group, has used the tree rights to halt the construction of golf courses in Gifu Prefecture. Under the law, land and tree rights can be sold separately, which means that developers buying land for golf courses must get permission from both the land owners and the tree owners.

TOXIC WASTES

After decades of ignoring the dangers of toxic chemicals and hazardous waste, Japan is pockmarked with thousands of dangerous hot spots—from garbage dumps and clandestine toxic-waste sites to aging incinerators belching dioxin (Wakakura and Iduka 1999). Japan's incinerators churn out almost 40 percent of the world's emissions of dioxin and furan—a related contaminant—according to a report issued in 1999 by the United Nations Environment Program. An incinerator spewing dioxin-laden exhaust onto the grounds of a U.S. Navy base at Atsugi southwest of Tokyo has turned into a sore point for U.S.-Japan relations. Dioxin and many of the other poisons are hard to detect, and their impact on health is tough to pin down. But the problem is not confined to one poison and one place, as Minamata's pollution was.

A series of surveys by the city of Tokyo uncovered more than ninety toxic substances around the Suginami Waste Transfer Station, including dioxin, one of the deadliest known to man. More than four hundred people living near the site have reported frightening symptoms since the plant opened in 1996. Suginami symbolizes the danger. Other toxic trouble spots tend to be messy and smelly: big garbage sites and, in remote hills, incinerators scorching the sides of forest slopes with deadly fumes.

The toxic threat is energizing Japan's environmental movement. Citizens' groups—small, underfunded, but combative—are testing air and water themselves, then demanding that bureaucrats take action. The government does not appear to be listening. The environment and health, it seems, still take a distant back seat to the imperatives of economic growth. Official Japan is starting to talk the environmental talk: bureaucrats and politicians spin visions of a "recycling society," and every company, it seems, "loves the Earth." But the old ways die hard. In Aichi Prefecture the government had planned to clear a pristine forest area to build thousands of houses for the 2005 World Exposition, whose theme is "Living in harmony with nature." Under pressure from a citizens' group and the World Expo ruling body in Paris, the government backed down in March 2000.

Bigger ministries with mandates to promote economic growth regularly trample on the turf of the chronically underfunded Ministry of Environment. The concrete-happy Ministry of Land, Infrastructure, and Transport, which is in charge of Japan's rivers, gets more funding for managing—and damming—these waterways than the Ministry of Environment's entire budget (Kerr 2001). Just as official Japan dithered while mercury poisoning took dozens of lives in Minamata, the government appears to be hoping that the toxic waste problem will just go away. The residents of Suginami Ward have gotten the runaround. A citizens group demanded the closure of the plant five months after it opened. The pleas by the citizens' group Get Rid of Suginami Sickness have been ignored.

The Suginami plant is just a rest stop along the highway of waste running from homes and businesses in Japan's urban area to its final disposal grounds, usually in the countryside. Chronically short of dump sites, Japanese cities ship much of their garbage to surrounding rural communities. That is where the waste wars start to get really nasty. One such place is Hinodecho, once a quiet village nestled in the mountains to the west of Tokyo. In 1984 a big dump site was built at Hinodecho, and garbage trucks that rumbled in every day from the suburbs of Tokyo carried an awful cargo, dioxin-laced ash. Dioxin, a by-product of pesticides and paper production, is also released when plastics are burned. It has been linked to cancer and is suspected of disrupting the hormones that regulate biological processes. The Hinedo Forest, Water, and Life Society, a citizens group, failed to stop the construction of another dump site in 1991.

As in other countries, the use of new plastics and chemicals has soared in Japan. A great quantity of both end up in the 1.2 million tons of garbage and industrial waste that Japan churns out every day, enough to fill six hundred thousand trucks like those that deposit their cargo at the Hinodecho dump. The growing flood of household and industrial waste is straining the system. Japan is quickly running out of places to put its waste, and a not-in-my-backyard sentiment is growing. As a result some of the refuse gets shipped overseas: in January 2000 Japan had to retrieve thousands of tons of medical and other waste illegally shipped to the Philippines by a Japanese company. The rest of the overflow ends up in clandestine dumps at the side of quiet dirt roads in the mountains. The number of illegal toxic waste sites has doubled to nearly thirteen hundred since the mid-1990s, according to Japan's Ministry of Health, Labor, and Welfare.

Dioxin contamination is a global issue, but Japan is one of the world's worst offenders. Short of space, the country favors burning—there are about 1,800 household-waste incinerators in Japan (the United States has about 250) and thousands more licensed and unlicensed hazardous-waste incinerators. Many are pouring dioxin into the air at levels far above what most of the rest of the world considers safe. In 1997 an incinerator outside the town of Nose was shut down. Less than an hour's drive from Osaka, Nose was once known for its rolling green hills and flavorful chestnuts. Now it is infamous as one of the most dioxin-polluted spots in Japan.

As noted above, Japan's promotion of "rampant industrialization without fear of consequences" has resulted in radical transformation of the environment (Taylor 1999, 554; McCormack 1998, 36). Bureaucratic autonomy has led to the exclusion of nongovernment organizations from environmental policymaking (Schreurs 1996). Institutional barriers to public participation in environmental policymaking have hampered the development of the environmental movement in Japan. Big business, the state bureaucracy, and the ruling Liberal Democratic Party dominate the environmental decision-making structure (Imura 1997; Ren 2000), marginalizing public interest groups (Broadbent 1998). Despite these limitations, Japanese grassroots environmental movements are playing a crucial role in pushing environmental reforms in several areas of Japan.

In Japan the challenge is to find a balance between the need for development and the preservation of the nation's precious natural beauty and environment, and to design and carry out a strategy for environmentally integrated development.

GRASSROOTS ENVIRONMENTAL MOVEMENTS IN JAPAN

Since the early 1960s grassroots environmental movements have been a major force in environmental politics in Japan. Rooted in local communities, they have confronted Japan's sociopolitical structure in an effort to preserve local environments and ways of life from pollution (Ui 1989) and technological hazards. Japanese environmental movements represent an amalgamation of new political energy composed of old conservationists, young deep ecologists, former socialists, and thousands of local activists and concerned citizens protesting against the ever-increasing number of cases of environmental destruction. These grassroots environmental movements embrace a new kind of politics, replacing the old politics of the industrial society with a new post-material, value-oriented politics. They stand for a new postmodern environmental consciousness, signaling new relations between society and nature and emphasizing the combination of thought and action.

The literature on environmental movements falls into two main paradigms: (1) studies that focus on environmentalist thought and ideology—"identity theories," which conceptualize movements in abstract terms and judge empirical conflicts as potential sources of new collective identity and as forces for change (Capra and Spretnak 1984; Corgrove 1982; Pepper 1984), and (2) studies that concentrate on the actual development of environmental groups and organizations—"resource mobilization" theories, which define movements empirically as organizations and groups and are concerned with their

successes and failures (Cohen 1985; Eyerman 1984; Eyerman and Jamison 1990; Lowe and Goyder 1983; Milbrath 1984). The intellectual roots and ideological message of the movements are examined in the first group of studies; the characteristics and environmental activism of the movements are analyzed in the second group.

A gap in the literature has emerged as the students of ideology have increasingly left the field of empirical research to roam the heady space of theory and as the empiricists have become bogged down in surveys and quantitative data. As a result the most important aspect of the new grassroots environmental movements—at one and the same time projecting a new set of ideas and mobilizing support for new forms of political activity—has tended to get lost, or at least neglected by social scientists. This chapter links the identity paradigm's interest in ideology with the empirical concerns of the resource mobilizers. The synthesis provides grounds for a more fruitful analysis of complex phenomena and also identifies criteria for determining when and under what circumstances a movement emerges. A grassroots movement emerges when a distinct set of interests is present in the consciousness of activists and is reflected in the movement's organization, and when these interests form the basis not only for collective identity but also for coordination and cooperative action.

In addition, Japanese environmental grassroots groups are notably oriented around struggles that deal with control over localities and the social construction of place. This is dissimilar to the more diffuse environmental groups dominant in Europe and the United States, but it does mirror the emergence of a wide range of grassroots movements oriented around struggles over urban growth (Cox and Mair 1988) and public facility siting (Alviano and Mercer 1996; Lake 1987). Contestations over place and local autonomy are an integral characteristic of Japanese grassroots movements.

Popular images of Japan invoke a cultural tradition of conformity characterized by an intense desire to avoid conflict and to ensure social harmony. Yet the history of Japanese environmental movements belie the stereotype of Japanese passivity and nonconfrontation. Japanese grassroots movements blossomed during the 1970s, as rapid development led to widespread environmental degradation and

Fig. 13.1. Environmental movements.

industrial pollution (see fig. 13.1). This period saw the birth of up to three thousand citizens' movements, with estimates of between 60,000 and 135,000 people directly involved (Cole 1994). These numbers declined during the 1980s but rose again throughout the 1990s. Unlike many environmental groups in the West, Japanese grassroots environmental groups tend to be small and focus on single issues and local goals (Griffith 1990). They are typically made up of adults in their thirties or older, as op-

posed to the younger people and students who dominate environmental groups in western Europe and the United States. Many professionals are involved, and women play a primary role. Japanese grassroots environmental groups use a variety of methods in their efforts to change government policy, including direct action, petitions, and lawsuits. Typically these groups are not organized hierarchically, which makes them more difficult to integrate into existing power structures (Mason 1999). As a result the Japanese environmental movement is far less unified than that of many other nations. Yet the success these groups have had in bringing about changes in Japan's environmental laws and policies has been unique and striking (McKean 1981). As political historian Junnosuke Masumi notes, in Japan "pollution control legislation had its roots in antipollution movements" (1995, 96).

This chapter focuses on several environmental movements spread across Japan from Hokkaido to the southern Ryukyu Islands. All of them are characterized by "lococentrism" (Funabashi 1992) and evince high levels of concern for the local environmental problem. After the problem is resolved, there is a tendency for the movement to dissipate or at least remain local, rather than to form broader networks or create a national environmental movement (Schreurs 1994). During field studies each locality was visited and the leaders of the movements were interviewed. The salient features of each movement are discussed below.

The Citizens' Movement against Industrial Pollution in Support of the Minamata Victims　Japan's most powerful and effective environmental movement emerged from the tragedy at Minamata (see fig. 13.2). In the latter part of the 1960s Minamata area residents began to organize in support of the

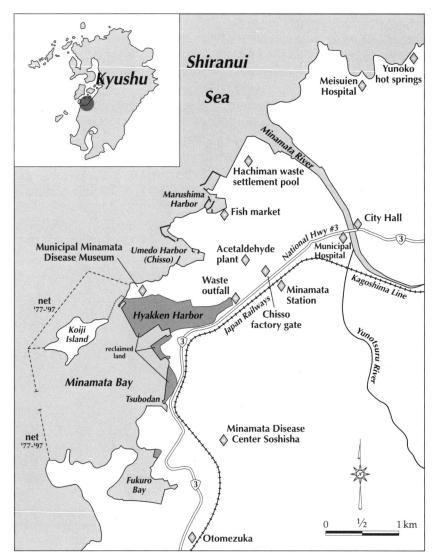

Fig. 13.2. Minamata. Based on a map by Timothy S. George.

ailing victims (George 2001). Another outbreak of Minamata disease occurred in Niigata Prefecture in northern Honshu in 1965. This event was marked by the first lawsuit ever by pollution victims seeking compensation. A groundswell of popular indignation grew over these incidents in the early 1970s. The first victory came in 1973 when the courts decided in favor of the patients' demands for compensation from the polluting company.

The Minamata movement, based on the past suffering of the affected citizens, has created a community that gives the utmost consideration to the environment and ecosystems. The attention of the group is focused on environmental disruption caused by industry. To date more than 2,000 people have been certified as Minamata disease patients. In addition, approximately 2,300 people are fighting for official recognition that they have the disease and hence qualify to collect benefits.

On July 29, 1997, the governor of Kumamoto Prefecture declared the mercury levels in fish and shellfish from Minamata Bay safe for consumption. Following the declaration, the net was removed that had for twenty-three years prevented mercury-polluted fish in the bay from entering the sea—a measure to curb the spread of environmentally induced disease.

Largely through the efforts of the environmental movement, in 1977 a restoration project was launched in Minamata to remove 1.5 million cubic meters of sediment through dredging and landfilling with new sediment. The project, lasting fourteen years, created a reclaimed area of 143.3 acres (58 ha). More importantly, in conjunction with a number of other major pollution cases in the 1960s, the Minamata case led to grassroots protests that eventually resulted in the passage of tough national environmental laws by the Japanese session of parliament known as the "Pollution Diet" in 1970. Many other coastal areas in Kyushu, as well as the rest of Japan, are threatened by industrial and urban pollution.

The Movement by Fishers against the Building of CTS in Shibushi Bay (Kyushu) and Kin Bay (Okinawa) and the Construction of Thermal Power Plants at Date (Hokkaido) and Nanao (Ishikawa Prefecture) Sharp opposition to the impacts of Japan's rapid economic growth and industrial transformation has arisen far from the me-

tropolis by people engaged in fishing, whose livelihood and society are being destroyed by the success of economic growth. The fishing people of the Osumi Peninsula, situated on the southern tip of Kyushu at Shibushi Bay, and those of Kin Bay in Okinawa have organized to oppose the construction of Central Terminal Stations or CTS (a system of strategic petrol storage), and the people of Date in Hokkaido and Nanao in Ishikawa Prefecture oppose the building of thermal power plants in their scenic fishing areas.

Typical of the antidevelopment ethos of these movements is a statement by a fisherman at Shibushi Bay: "Rather than eating beefsteak under smog, we would choose to eat rice-balls under a blue sky."[1] In Kin Bay, a few hundred local villagers formed a grassroots group called the Association to Protect Kin Bay (APKB) in 1973 and marched on the town hall of Yonashiro after Mitsubishi's purchase of the rights to coastal waters was disclosed to the public. The villagers almost succeeded in convincing local assemblymen to sign a pledge opposing the sale, but they were disrupted by the deployment of riot police. Kin Bay is home to coral reefs and a large and diverse aquatic population that is vulnerable to the oil spills frequently accompanying CTS operations. In addition, children living in the vicinity suffer from eye inflammations believed to be linked to air pollution from nearby Henza Island's oil refinery.

The APKB formed as a loose alliance of concerned citizens, fishers, village elders, housewives, and working people, with no established leaders or official representatives. Although unallied with the strongly represented labor and peace movements in Okinawa, the APKB developed a coherent political ideology, claiming that behind the Japanese government and the decision to build the CTS "is Japanese capital and big business, with Mitsubishi at the forefront. This is the giant which has transformed the Japanese islands into a polluted wasteland" (Toya 1974, 18). The APKB was eventually able to persuade Okinawa's governor to refuse permission for the CTS construction, but this was eventually overturned by Japanese courts, and the CTS were built.

---

[1] This quotation is from a September 9, 1995, interview, one of a series of interviews by the author conducted in the Shibushi Bay and Kin Bay areas in September 1995. The interviewees were members of the environmental movements.

The Kin Bay movement, though ultimately unsuccessful in stopping construction of the CTS, has continued to oppose other development projects that have degraded the local environment. Traditional folk songs of the islanders have been modified so that they speak of preserving the environment. These artistic expressions have been fully used to convey the movements' opposition in an effective and colorful manner. One member of the movement noted that islanders "joined the movement to preserve the Kin Bay in order to resist the forces which threatened to rip off the basis of their survival. They believe that the sea is necessary to support their way of life. The issue at stake is, for them, the right to survive. Establishing the right to survive means to gain control of the basis of their own existence. This is why they continue their struggle to save the environment."[2]

In a similar situation, the fishers of Nanao opposed the construction of an oil-burning electric power station along the coast facing the Sea of Japan. They formed a chain of fishing boats to halt the construction. In Date, Hokkaido, local fishers organized a movement to oppose the construction of another such plant that would emit huge amounts of thermal wastewater, destroying the aquatic ecosystem of the coastal area. The Date fishers' movement succeeded in attracting support from the Ainu, an indigenous people with a hunting and fishing tradition. The Ainu were stripped of their land by the rice-growing Japanese settlers and during the last century have been forced to assimilate into Japanese culture and social life.

The Movement Opposing the Nuclear Waste Storage Facility at Rokkasho in Aomori Prefecture

Most of Japan's radioactive waste consists of nuclear power plants' waste products. In 1992 Japan completed construction of a disposal facility for low-level nuclear waste as part of one of the largest nuclear complexes in the world, Japan's Nuclear Fuel Cycle Facility (NFCF) in the village of Rokkasho in northern Honshu (Pickett and Suzuki 1999). This complex includes a reactor-fuel plant that enriches uranium ore from the United States, Canada, Australia, and Africa; facilities for low-level radioactive waste disposal; a temporary high-level radioactive waste storage site; and a plutonium reprocessing cen-

ter. The storage facility consists of forty concrete pits constructed on the bedrock 32.8 feet (10 m) beneath the ground. Five thousand drums of waste material will be placed in each pit and then covered with earth. Local communities are located as close as 0.62 mile (1 km), and nearby villages are at serious risk from radioactive contamination of the water table.

Local citizens' environmental groups in Rokkasho and in Aomori Prefecture have long opposed the storage of nuclear waste in the area. In 1985 villagers unsuccessfully petitioned for a prefectural vote on the NFCF. In 1986, mobilized by public reaction to the Chernobyl disaster, a coalition movement began to form (Shimada 1994). The group was initially composed of local fishing people, but farmers soon joined as well. A protest called the Battle at Sea took place, in which local fishers attempted to block Japan's Marine Security Guard from surveying the coast as part of the planning efforts for the NFCF. The Ten Thousand Plaintiffs Coalition filed lawsuits against the NFCF in 1989 and by 1990 had a million signatures on a petition (De Angelis 1995). Despite these efforts, the facilities at Rokkasho are already storing shipments of radioactive waste, and other parts of the complex are being constructed.

The Rokkasho antinuclear movement is not a NIMBY (Not in My Backyard) movement. Instead, it represents the new consciousness of Japanese grassroots environmental activists concerned with their society's level of consumption. As Kei Shimada, a leading figure in the movement, writes, "People have taken the arrogant attitude that dangerous and dirty things should be sent off to 'isolated places' far removed from the big cities. I would like people to consider the victims of our society's mass consumption of electric power" (1994, 36).

Citizens' environmental groups elsewhere in Japan also have opposed the storage and transport of nuclear waste. An accident in March 1997 involving a fire and explosion at Japan's only nuclear waste reprocessing plant in Tokai, 70 miles (113 km) northeast of Tokyo, has raised additional public concern in Aomori about radioactive waste storage at Rokkasho. Japan's susceptibility to major earthquakes is a further cause for concern about nuclear waste storage. Japan is banking heavily on conventional uranium-based nuclear power and on advanced systems using plutonium to relieve its almost complete dependence on imported oil and coal. As the gov-

---

[2] Kin Bay resident, interview by author, September 7, 1995.

ernment promotes nuclear power, questions about the safety of Japan's nuclear program continue to worry many Japanese citizens.

The Sanrizuka Farmers Movement against the Expansion of Narita Airport Sanrizuka, in the southeastern part of the city of Narita, is the site of the New Tokyo International Airport, which opened in 1978. Its completion and opening was delayed until 1978 because of fierce opposition from local inhabitants. For more than thirty years, the airport authority has tried to clear land around Narita airport for a second runway, and during those years more than three hundred farmers have moved away, but the "Farming Seven" refuse. They stay defiantly in their homes and muddy fields as one of the world's busiest airports struggles along with a single runway.

The airport authority has been held hostage by the farmers because the modern Japanese legal system gives property owners unusually strong rights against land acquisition. These laws were drafted in reaction to the state's dictatorial power before World War II. In addition, the state bungled badly years earlier when it failed to ask for local input before deciding to locate the airport at Sanrizuka. Six people have died in fierce protests, and thousands have been injured. In recent years there have been at least seven small explosions at the airport, all attributed to radicals supporting the farmers.

The radical component of this movement is linked to antiwar protests started during the Vietnam War. As the farmers' protests were beginning, the U.S. military was using Japanese airports to transport American troops to the battlefield, and antimilitary protesters bolstered the farmers' movement opposing the airport. In general, however, the Sanrizuka farmers' movement is rooted in the local community. As such, it has been surprisingly successful in confronting the social-political structure of Japan since the 1970s. The Sanrizuka movement marked a turning point for grassroots local environmental movements in Japan. Its methods and actions have been emulated by numerous subsequent local grassroots movements.

The Movement Opposing Further Development around Lake Shikotsu, Hokkaido Shikotsu-Toya National Park in southern Hokkaido consists of three sections—Lakes Toya and Shikotsu, and Noboribetsu

Spa. The area contains a number of volcanoes, caldera lakes, and hot springs. Lake Shikotsu is a caldera lake tucked among soaring cliffs, with deep blue water that never freezes. The lake is stocked with trout, attracting many anglers in the game-fishing season. Its pristine beauty has rendered it a site for one of the countless disputes in Hokkaido pitting preservationists against developers.

The picture-postcard image of a green and peaceful landscape in Hokkaido is belied by areas of clearcut forests, rivers running in concrete conduits for flood control, and paved-over shorelines that have wiped out fishing beds. Lake Shikotsu, one of the exceptions to this rule, rests in a green canyon surrounded by steep peaks, including at least two active volcanoes where white sulfurous fumes seep from crevices. Somehow Lake Shikotsu has been spared the tawdry tourist traps that encrust the shores of nearby Lake Toyay.

Until the end of World War II, the forests belonged to the emperor of Japan. Although the forests around Lake Shikotsu became part of a national park, the government permitted companies to cut down trees surrounding the lake, a process that accelerated for construction related to the 1972 winter Olympics at nearby Sapporo. The pressure on Lake Shikotsu and other parts of Hokkaido are a reflection of changing living patterns throughout Japan.

Hokkaido has long been renowned as a wild frontier region like Alaska, with an economy based on fishing and lumbering. But as these industries have stagnated in recent years, the island has turned increasingly to tourism. In the early 1990s there were more than 3.5 million tourists on an island with about 5.6 million residents. Environmentalists note that added difficulties have come because of incentives adopted by the Japanese government, which in recent years has sought to encourage more and more leisure pursuits in a country known for its hardworking labor force. The controversial 1987 Resort Law, for example, offers incentives to developers to build golf courses, condominiums, and ski areas in various mountain and seashore communities, to the distress of those at Lake Shikotsu and elsewhere who feel that this is not a harmonious way to enjoy nature. In 1990 Japanese branches of the Friends of the Earth and the World Wide Fund for Nature pointed out that the Resort Law seemed well intentioned but that new

Lake Toya, Hokkaido. Located within Shikotsu-Toya National Park, this lake is one of the northernmost ice-free lakes in Japan. Development along the lakeshore threatens the environmental integrity of the lake. Photo by P.P. Karan.

resort construction was seriously endangering Japan's environment.

Environmentalists are opposed to the building of hotels, souvenir shops, and spas in the mountainous forests around Lake Shikotsu. In recent years, local groups have begun fighting the developers. Some groups have also sprung up to battle the construction of hydroelectric dams and nuclear power plants in Hokkaido. Among the most active groups are those representing the aboriginal people of Hokkaido, the Ainu.

The Movement to Save Kushiro (Hokkaido) and Hakata Bay (Kyushu) Wetlands On the Pacific coast of eastern Hokkaido near the city of Kushiro lies one of Japan's largest remaining wetlands, Kushiro Marsh. Called Kushiro Shitsugen in Japanese, it was 45,196 acres (18,290 ha) in size in 1985. Its present size is less than two-thirds of that. Although 66,375 acres (26,861 ha) of land were designated as a national park in 1987, nothing protects the periphery from developers of homes and leisure facilities, or from the local paper industry's desire to fell more trees. The spongy vegetation of the marsh

provides a safe nesting habitat for the rare Japanese red-crowned crane. Development activities on the periphery of the marsh are also affecting the water table.

National park land in Japan is classified into three categories, two of which permit development in varying degrees. Only 16,037 acres (6,490 ha) of the 66,375 acres (26,861 ha) of Kushiro National Park belong to the strict category that prohibits any development. In 1985 the marsh was about 7,413 acres (3,000 ha) smaller than in 1980. Civic groups and organizations dedicated to environmental preservation, such as the Kushiro branch of the Japanese Society for Preservation of Birds, have tried to keep the swampy area from development. Nearly 40 percent of Japan's wetlands have already been lost owing to industrial development, waste disposal, and reclamation, and the remainder is severely threatened.

Hakata Bay in Kyushu opens up to the narrowest span of water separating Japan from the Asian continent. Its shallow Wajiro tidal flats are an important nesting and feeding site for the birds migrating along the Pacific coast. Since 1959 municipal planners have undertaken a series of reclamation

Kushiro, Hokkaido. The city of Kushiro lies on the edge of the Kushiro Marsh, Japan's largest remaining wetland. Although 66,375 acres (26,861 ha) were designated a national park in 1987, nothing protects the periphery from development. Photo by P.P. Karan.

projects around most of the coastline. The Wajiro tidal flats is the only section still relatively untouched by development. A municipal project in the nearby city of Fukuoka plans to fill part of Hakata Bay to build a container port, a housing complex, and a scientific research center. The city officials contend that new local commercial development will create employment opportunities. The citizens' groups opposed to the project claim that further port facilities will do little for the region's economy.

The Movement Opposing Golf Course Construction on Mount Kotan, Hokkaido   The spectacle of forests or terraced rice paddies dotted with bamboo and straw scarecrows being transformed into precisely trimmed fairways, bunkers, and greens, with towering concrete clubhouses, is leaving many Japanese uneasy about the cultural and environmental

price being paid for the construction of expensive and exclusive golf courses. As a consequence of the wholesale construction of golf courses after the passage of the Resort Law, by 1994 there were more than two thousand completed golf courses in Japan (McCormack 1998). Protests have broken out in numerous locations around Japan where golf course construction is planned. A diverse coalition of citizens' groups oppose the development of golf courses because the agricultural chemicals used to maintain acres of greens pollutes the environment and requires the clearing of forests and dairy areas.

In the area of Mount Kotan, Hokkaido, a group of Ainu women banded together and formed the Group to Save Mount Kotan's Lake and Forest. This movement was created to oppose the conversion of traditional Ainu land into a golf course. Besides the land's symbolic value, it was also a place where edible plants grew and had been picked by Ainu villag-

A golf course at Aso, Kumamoto Prefecture. Fueled by environmentalism and concern about changes in Japan's traditional landscape, a wave of opposition to new course construction has swept Japan. Citizens' groups in many localities claim that agricultural chemicals used to maintain acres of greens will pollute the environment. Photo by P.P. Karan.

ers for countless generations. The group gathered support in nearby villages and elsewhere in Japan, and eventually the construction plan was abandoned (Totsuka 1993). On the national scale, a coalition of groups has formed the Global Anti-Golf Movement, which has blocked construction of more than three hundred Japanese golf courses (McCormack 1998). Following Japan's example, grassroots antigolf movements have recently sprouted up in dozens of places in Southeast Asia and the Pacific.

The Movement to Protect the Ikego Forest, Zushi City In an area of rampant urbanization south of Tokyo, the last significant green open space is the magnificent Ikego Forest in the city of Zushi. Its rolling hills and lush woodlands are home to a rare diversity of wildlife, including many endangered species. The Ikego hills are covered with thick forests of broad-leaved laurel, chestnut, maple, and oak trees, as well as wild cherry trees and wild camellias. Ikego is also home to more than 107 species of birds. Within the Ikego Forest, profoundly important archaeological sites have been discovered, attesting to five thousand years of human occupancy, including religious objects and dwellings dating back to the Jomon period (8,000 BC–300 BC).

Despite the urban sprawl around it, the Ikego Forest is in good condition. This is only because the Japanese military used Ikego, before and during World War II, for underground munitions storage. When the U.S. military took over in 1945, it used Ikego for the same purpose, and the forest cover was unharmed. This situation is changing quickly. A joint project of the United States and Japan will cut the trees and raze the hills to build a massive U.S. military housing facility. The construction plan calls for 854 housing units and other facilities typical of an American suburb.

When the citizens of Zushi first learned of these plans in the 1980s, they organized a movement to save the Ikego Forest. Led by the women of the town, the movement sought preservation of Ikego as a park and wildlife sanctuary. In consecutive elections, citizens expressed their opposition to the project and succeeded in removing a prodevelopment mayor and installing a new city council. Nearly 87 percent of Zushi citizens are against the development plans. A decade of opposition by the citizens of Zushi has been effective in slowing the development.

Santama: A Grassroots Environmental Movement in Western Tokyo Santama Mondai Chosa Kenkyukai, abbreviated as Santamaken, is a fifty-three-member movement aiming at comprehensive environmental conservation in western Tokyo. Literally translated, the name means a group studying problems in the area called Santama in western Tokyo. The group was formed in 1973. One of Santamaken's most appreciated activities so far is its conservation efforts on the Nogawa, the third-largest tributary of the Tama River. The Nogawa used to be a limpid stream, flowing along the cliff line of Musashino Heights in western Tokyo. The river originates in Kokubunji and runs 12.4 miles (20 km) through the cities of Koganei, Mitaka, Chofu, and Komae, before joining the rivers of Iruma and Senkawa in Setagaya-ku.

In the early 1960s, when the area was developed, the river was polluted. Large pieces of trash, such as bicycles and televisions, were found in the river, which smelled bad and foamed. Flies flourished in the area in the summer. One day, a person walking along the river was speechless when he discovered carp in the smelly water. He thought the river had died, but after seeing the fish he realized it was still alive, and he decided to form a group dedicated to cleaning up the river. Although it was polluted, there were some areas where fresh springwater flowed into the river. The carp seemed to be looking for this fresh water.

Believing that it was possible to clean up the river by capitalizing on the flow of spring water and by controlling the inflow of household water, Santamaken started researching the dynamics of the river. For twenty years now, the group has published a quarterly bulletin to report on activities undertaken in its environmental campaigns. It also organizes symposiums and treks along the river so that people can see what is happening. Santamaken is one among several grassroots groups dedicated to conservation in the Kanto region.

The Movement against the Construction of an Airport on Ishigaki Island Ishigaki Island, in the southern part of the Ryukyu chain, is a small island framed on the southeast side by the Shiraho Coral Reef, which contains the largest assemblage of blue coral in the world, home to more than one hundred species (Cross 1990). Elsewhere in the Ryukyus, most of the coral has been damaged by industrialization and development projects, which suffocate the coral through soil erosion, stream siltation, and the deposition of silt offshore. Both the Shiraho reef itself and the livelihood of Ishigaki's fishing people have been endangered by plans to construct a major airport on Ishigaki. This project was proposed in order to spur domestic tourism to the southern Ryukyus, but some speculate that its main purpose was to free an already existing airport for use by U.S. armed forces and Japan's Self-Defense Forces.

The plan was initially formulated in the late 1970s and has been opposed since that time by a coalition of local fishing villagers and environmentalists who ultimately organized into the Okinawa-Yaeyama-Shiraho Save the Ocean, Save our Lives Association (Suzuki 1986). In this instance, local grassroots organizations were able to attract the attention of the wider international environmental community (Suganuma 2002). Scientists from the Cousteau Society and the World Wildlife Fund came and studied the area. Local protests continued unabated, some resulting in political violence. Pressure from the international community eventually led to a study by Japan's Environment Agency, which declared that the site would be moved a few kilometers to the north, where it would cause no damage to the reef. Protests continued, especially in light of findings by the World Wide Fund for Nature Japan, whose study determined that construction at the new location would also threaten the reef. Ultimately the protests were successful. The plan was shelved as construction delays and cost increases jeopardized the entire project.

In 1997 the Japan Environment Agency finally announced a new plan to incorporate the Shiraho reef into a national park in order to protect the aquatic ecosystem of the area.

The Citizens' Movement to Preserve Old Kyoto

An unlikely coalition of Buddhist priests, architects, planners, and housewives has organized out of concern that old Kyoto has been nearly destroyed by a burst of development in the 1980s. Futuristic steel and raw concrete structures illuminated with neon have replaced scores of traditional wooden shops and homes on Kyoto's many narrow streets. The historic character of Japan's most traditional city is being altered by a wave of ultramodern architecture.

The emotional controversy that has arisen over the prospect of a huge glass and steel structure dominating Kyoto's skyline, once a patchwork of tiled roofs and graceful wooden pagodas, goes beyond style to the question of the city's historic legacy. Kyoto is the repository of much of what Japanese admire in their culture. The imperial capital for more than one thousand years, Kyoto is home to grand Shinto shrines as well as exquisitely austere Zen Buddhist temples and gardens.

Until recently, Kyoto had a height limit of around 150 feet (46 m) on most buildings. The concern had always been that taller buildings would wreck the lovely vistas. But under pressure from developers, the city raised the limit in 1990 to about 200 feet (61 m). There is fear that the planned 200-foot height could

Manza Beach viewed from Manzamo, Okinawa. The curved sand beach is pure white, and the coral-rich ocean is literally emerald green. Tourism and military activities on Okinawa threaten the environmental integrity of the area. Photo by P.P. Karan.

The high-density development around and above the Kyoto railway station is dominated by Kyoto Tower, a 430-foot-tall (131-meter-tall) structure meant to look like the candle in Buddhist temples—but with a circular restaurant and observation deck. The tower has sparked controversy over the scale of buildings and the extent to which they harmonize with Kyoto's historic character. A group of local citizens has been organized to save the city's skyline from huge glass and steel structures. Photo by P.P. Karan.

result in a new wave of taller buildings. The Kyoto Tower, built in the 1980s, and the huge steel and glass Kyoto Railway Station complex (with hotel, department store, and shopping mall), built in the 1990s, overwhelm the graceful wood pagodas of the city. The continuing concern of the citizens' groups in the city is over the scale of future buildings and the extent to which their features harmonize with more traditional structures.

Japan has experienced severe environmental problems since at least the early 1950s; the rapid economic growth of the 1960s and 1970s caused heavy pollution of air and water, and unchecked development destroyed portions of the natural environment. By the early 1980s, Japan had succeeded in hammering down critical pollution levels, especially of air pollutants and ozone-depleting and greenhouse gases. However, during the steady economic growth of the 1980s, mass production, mass consumption, and mass waste prevailed further, and the population grew ever more concentrated in urban areas. Greenery diminished in cities, and rural forests and farms lost their sound management. Environmental assessments determined that although Japan had largely improved its air quality and energy efficiency, water pollution and especially nature protection were still in poor shape in the late 1980s. The passage of the Resort Law has been especially damaging to previously untouched sections of coastline and other natural areas.

With their environment deteriorating around them, grassroots movements to save the local envi-

ronment have gained major momentum. Most successful environmental initiatives in Japan have originated from local governments under pressure by local residents and grassroots movements (Miyamoto 1992). These have then eventually been drafted into national environmental policy. Today the growing grassroots movements continue their formidable influence on thought and practice regarding the environment. With their value-oriented politics and will to exert their own desires on the social construction of place, the growing number and strength of Japanese grassroots movements will ensure their continuing pivotal role in forcing private-sector enterprises and local governments to face up to their responsibility to protect the environment.

REFERENCES

Alviano, P., and D. Mercer. 1996. The Dandenong offensive industry zone: A case study in environmental conflict. *Australian Geographer* 27 (1): 101–115.

Barrett, B.F.D., and Riki Therivel. 1991. *Environmental Policy and Impact Assessment in Japan*. London: Routledge.

Broadbent, Jeffrey. 1998. *Environmental Policies in Japan: Networks of Power and Protest*. New York: Cambridge Univ. Press.

Capra, F., and C. Spretnak. 1984. *Green Politics*. London: Hutchinson.

Cohen, J.L. 1985. Strategy or identity: New theoretical paradigms and contemporary social movements. *Social Research* 52 (4): 663–716.

Cole, J. 1994. The right to demand: Citizen activism and environmental politics in Japan. *Journal of Environment and Development* 3 (2): 77–95.

Corgrove, S. 1982. *Catastrophe or Cornucopia*. Chichester, UK: Wiley.

Cox, Kevin, and A. Mair. 1988. Locality and community in the politics of local economic development. *Annals of the Association of American Geographers* 78:307–325.

Cross, M. 1990. International conservationists in last-ditch battle to save Japanese coral. *New Scientist* 19:25.

De Angelis, F. 1995. Rokkasho: Japan's nuclear village. *Earth Island Journal* (Spring): 18.

Eyerman, R. 1984. Social movements and social theory. *Sociology* 18 (1): 71–82.

Eyerman, R., and A. Jamison. 1990. *Social Movements: A Cognitive Approach.* Cambridge: Polity Press.

Fukui, Eiichiro. 1969. The recent rise of temperature in Japan. *Science Reports of Tokyo Kyoiku Daigaku* [Tokyo Univ. of Education] 10 (97–98): 145–164.

Funabashi, H. 1992. Environmental problems in post-war Japanese society. *International Journal of Japanese Sociology* 1:3–18.

George, Timothy S. 2001. *Minamata: Pollution and the Struggle for Democracy in Postwar Japan.* Cambridge: Harvard Univ. Press for Harvard Asia Center.

Griffith, J. 1990. The environmental movement in Japan. *Whole Earth Review,* Winter, 90–96.

Hashimoto, Michio. 1989. History of air pollution control in Japan. In *How to Conquer Air Pollution: A Japanese Experience,* ed. H. Nishimura, 1–94. Amsterdam: Elsevier.

Huddle, Norie, and Michael Reich. 1991. *Island of Dreams: Environmental Crisis in Japan.* Rochester, VT: Schenkman. 102–132.

Iijima, N. 1970. Kogai and the community resident's movement: The case of the Minamata disease. *Japanese Sociological Review* 21 (1): 25–45.

Imura, H. 1997. Japan. In *National Environmental Policies: A Comparative Study of Capacity Building,* ed. M. Janicke and H. Weidner. Berlin: Springer.

Karan, P.P. 1986. Technological hazards in the Third World. *Geographical Review* 76:195–208.

Kawamura, Takeshi. 1985. Recent changes of atmospheric environment in Tokyo and its surrounding area. *Geographical Review of Japan* B 58:83–94.

Kerr, A. 2001. *Dogs and Demons: Tales from the Dark Side of Japan.* New York: Hall and Wang.

Kim, D.-S., J.-G. Je, and S.-W. Lee. 1999. Tidal flats in Japan: Development and conservation. *Ocean Research* 20 (2): 221–235.

Lake, R. 1987. *Resolving Locational Conflict.* New Brunswick, NJ: Center for Urban Policy Research.

Lowe, P., and J. Goyder. 1983. *Environmental Groups in Politics.* London: Allen and Unwin.

Mason, R.J. 1999. Whither Japan's environmental movement? An assessment of problems and prospects at the national level. *Pacific Affairs* 72 (7): 187–207.

Masumi, Junnosuke. 1995. *Contemporary Politics in Japan.* Berkeley: Univ. of California Press.

McCormack, Gavan. 1998. From number one to number nothing: Japan's fin de siècle blues. *Japanese Studies* 18 (1): 31–44.

———. 2001. *The Emptiness of Japanese Affluence.* Armonk, NY: M.E. Sharpe.

McKean, M. 1981. *Environmental Protest and Citizens Politics in Japan.* Berkeley: Univ. of California.

Milbrath, Lester W. 1984. *Environmentalists: Vanguard for a New Society.* Albany: State Univ. of New York Press.

Miura, Toyohiko. 1975. *Taiki osen kara mita kankyo hakai no rekishi* [History of Environmental Destruction from the Perspective of Air Pollution]. Tokyo: Rodo Kagaku Sosho.

Miyamoto, K. 1992. Environmental problems in Asian countries and the responsibility of Japan. *Keiei Kenkyu* 43 (4): 1–9.

Nimura, Kazuo. 1997. *The Ashio Riot of 1907: A Social History of Mining in Japan.* Ed. Andrew Gordon. Trans. Terry Boardman and Gordon. Durham, NC: Duke Univ. Press.

OECD. 1994. *Environmental Performance Reviews: Japan.* Washington, DC: Organization for Economic Cooperation and Development.

Okada, Yuko. 1990. Kosaka kozan engai mondai to hantai undo, 1901–17 [The movement against smoke pollution at the Kosaka Copper Mine, 1901–17]. *Shakai-Keizai Shigaku* 56:59–89.

Pepper, D. 1984. *The Rise of Modern Environmentalism.* London: Croom Helm.

Pickett, Susan, and Tatsujiro Suzuki. 1999. Spent fuel and high level waste policy in Japan: Science, society, and rigid decisions. *Social Science Japan* 16 (August): 24–29.

Ren, Y. 2000. Japanese approaches to environmental management: Structural and institutional features. *International Review for Environmental Strategies* 1 (1): 79–96.

Schreurs, Miranda. 1994. Policy laggard or policy leader: Global environmental politics in Japan. *Journal of Pacific Asia* 2:3–38.

———. 1996. International environmental negotiations, the state, and the environmental NGOs in Japan. Occasional Paper no. 14, Harrison Program on the Future Global Agenda, Washington, DC.

Shimada, Kei. 1994. Nuclear curse in Rokkasho-Mura. *Ampo, Japan-Asia Quarterly Review* 25 (2): 33–36.

Suganuma, Unryu. 2002. Economic growth vs. environmental conservation in Okinawa: The case of the Ishigaki Island Airport construction. *Regional Development Dialogue* 23 (1): 69–79.

Sugitani, T. 1998. Opposition movement against golf course development in Miyoshi Village, Chiba, Japan. *Geographical Review of Japan* B 71:31–44.

Suzuki, M. 1986. Battle for the Shiraho Coral Reef. *Japan Environment Review* (Spring): 10–18.

Tamura, Toshikazu. 1993. Large-scale residential development as a factor in environmental change in Japan. *Science Reports of Tohoku University,* 7th ser. (Geography) 43 (1): 1–12.

Taniguchi, Tomomasa. 1999. Changes in the water quality of the Sumida River in Tokyo from 1900 to 1960 estimated from literary works. *Science Reports of Tohoku University,* 7th ser. (Geography) 49 (2): 227–232.

Taylor, J. 1999. Global environmentalism: Rhetoric and reality, *Political Geography* 18:535–562.

Totsuka, M. 1993. The golf war on Mt. Kotan. *Ampo, Japan-Asia Quarterly Review* 24 (3): 12–14.

Toya, Eiji. 1974. Okinawa citizens' struggle against Mitsubishi and the CTS. *Ampo, Japan-Asia Quarterly* 6 (2).

Uda, T., M. Sumiya, and K. Shimoyamada. 2000. Beach changes triggered by seaward development of towns, expansion of coastal forest, and construction of detached breakwaters on Ariake-Ishihama coast in northern Ibaraki Prefecture. *Chikei* 21 (1): 17–30.

Ui, Jun. 1989. Anti-pollution movements and other grass-roots organizations. In *Environmental Policy in Japan,* ed. Shigeto Tsuru and Helmut Weidner, 109–119. Berlin: Sigma Rainer Bohn Verlag.

Wakakura, M., and Y. Iduka. 1999. Trends in chemical hazards in Japan. *Journal of Loss Prevention in the Process Industries* 12 (1): 79–84.

Chapter 14

第 十四章

FACING THE CHALLENGES

As Japan enters the twenty-first century, the country faces several critical challenges to realize the great potential that the new era holds. Earlier chapters of this book have highlighted realities of contemporary Japan and the environmental, social, demographic, political, and economic challenges facing the nation. Reforms are required in order to meet the needs of the twenty-first century and ensure a vigorous nation in the future ("Future hinges on reality check" 2000). In modern times major changes were imposed on Japan from outside at the end of the Tokugawa shogunate and again at the end of World War II. Now, at the beginning of the twenty-first century, Japan itself must initiate the needed social, economic, and political changes. Japan's profound cultural and institutional legacy makes swift and basic reform very difficult to carry out. In the Japanese cultural environment, before any decisions can be made, great efforts must go into shaping a broad agreement. During the 1990s several detailed economic reform packages proposed by the government died because one or more groups disliked them. The government must do all it can to formulate and implement decisive but flexible measures to invigorate the nation. Political, business, and academic leaders must play a central role in the struggle toward reforms and must not only design strategies for carrying out the tasks facing the country but also implement the measures they arrive at.

THREE MAJOR TRANSITIONS

More than one hundred years ago, on November 18, 1901, the government-operated Yawata Iron and Steel Works opened. The newspaper (*Yomiuri Shimbun*, November 19, 1901) reported that the opening ceremony began at 10.30 a.m., that guests arrived on several extra trains from Moji, and that every household in the cities of Moji and Kokura raised the national flag and hung lights. Thousands of people flocked from neighboring prefectures to see the ceremony. The dawning of the twentieth century coincided exactly with the real beginnings of the modernization process for industry in Japan, as symbolized by the opening of the iron and steel works, which was equipped with the first blast furnace in the country.

In Europe and the United States, the invention of the steam locomotive in the eighteenth century brought about the Industrial Revolution, and the ensuing major industrial growth in the nineteenth century was led by the introduction of electrical power and the internal combustion engine. Industrialization advanced rapidly. But Japan lagged behind the West because of its policy of seclusion from the rest of the world during the Edo period (1603–1868). After the Meiji Restoration in 1868, Japan started to introduce technologies from Europe and the United States, importing and absorbing the achievements of the Industrial Revolution in a short period. The Meiji government made its top priority promoting new industries. Building a system rich in resources, including manpower, it succeeded in catching up with the West. Among other things, the dissolution of the four-class feudal system, the establishment of prefectures in place of feudal domains, the development of the bureaucratic administrative system, and the introduction of Western-style education made it possible for Japan to take in and firmly establish technologies from the Industrial Revolution.

After a period of light industries such as textiles, steel was fully launched with the opening of the Yawata Iron and Steel Works. Japan's shipbuilding technology soon caught up with the global standard, and electricity became a commonly used energy source in factories. As a result, Japan gradually developed into a modern industrial nation.

Half a century ago, Japan demonstrated its ability to rise from the rubble and overcome the terrible blows of defeat in World War II. Despite that trauma—during which production fell to 10 percent of the prewar level, and the real national per capita income dropped to the level of the early twentieth century—the government and the private sector joined hands in the postwar restoration process. The government introduced a system designed to restore the industrial base that was centered on increasing production of coal and steel. A series of bold structural reforms, including the dissolution of zaibatsu conglomerates, the establishment of the Antimonopoly Law, and labor reforms were carried out under the instruction of the occupation forces. Following the special procurement boom sparked by the 1950–53 Korean War, Japan left postwar chaos behind in less than ten years and entered its major economic development period.

These two major transformations in Japan were prompted by the Meiji Restoration and by defeat in World War II—events that cut across politics, economy, and society. Japan was left with no option but to move ahead; changes were imposed from outside. The entire country was united in its effort to catch up with Europe and the United States as soon as possible under the banners of "encouraging new industries" and "postwar restoration."

Now after the passage of a century, Japan is undergoing its third transition. The system that enabled its growth and prosperity is buckling. In order to put the Japanese economy back on the path of growth, the country must build a new system. Despite that need, a clear consensus on how to proceed does not exist. There is no consensus on national goals similar to the overwhelming focus on economic growth following World War II.

In the mid-1990s Japan began to reform its industrial structure. It developed a plan focusing on selected areas of projected growth, including telecommunications and biotechnology. Deregulation measures were introduced, legal systems were upgraded to revive industry, and changes were made in both fiscal and taxation systems. But the efforts were found lacking. The private sector, which took the lead in the earlier transitions, is failing to act in a timely fashion. There is resistance to change from industries that long have enjoyed the protection of regulations and business customs. Current moves for change, therefore, do not have the momentum of those in the past transitions, which were driven by popular support for reform of industrial structures. Some firms have managed to drastically improve their business performance by exploring new markets such as cellular phones and Internet-related industries. Japan is trying to pull out of the stagnation that began with the collapse of the bubble economy. There have been some recent improvements, but there remains a tendency toward uniformity of thinking and dependence on government (*Global Trends 2015* 2000).

SOCIAL REFORMS FOR SUSTAINABLE DEVELOPMENT

Bringing about a self-sustaining recovery of the Japanese economy and accelerating the information technology revolution are important stated national goals of Japan for the twenty-first century. But it is also important to deal with fundamental problems in Japanese society and reform the social system to respond to these concerns. First, the policy debate must be encouraged by reforming the process of policymaking and increasing the transparency of the administration. Japan is facing many serious challenges, such as structural reforms, restructuring of the government, and the creation of an integrated security framework and harmony between humans and technology, which are essential for achieving sustainable growth. However, policy debate in these areas has been very low-key—even in the June 2000 general election. Although the direction and policy of the nation is shaped by the government, the decision-making process must be open to the people and accommodating enough to give consideration to all possible viewpoints and ideas to ensure that optimal choices are made. In the past two general elections (2000 and 2003), there was no constructive policy debate on concrete issues between the ruling coalition and the opposition.

As explained earlier, since the Meiji Restoration of 1868 political parties have mostly depended on bureaucrats for policymaking and have yet to make themselves capable enough to devise appropriate policies themselves. Years of corruption and economic mismanagement on the part of successive governments have also had the effect of shattering the confidence bureaucrats had in the ability of politicians to run an administration. The Japanese leaders in the business community, academia, think tanks, the press, and civic groups do not tend to make policy proposals independently of the government.

In the twenty-first century, social activities will be increasingly interlinked, and social interests may confront each other to a greater extent. It will therefore be necessary, first, for Japan to reform the social system so that many entities from various fields can participate in the policymaking process through discussion and debate.

Second, Japan must increase its social flexibility and mobility. As a result of deregulation and structural reform, private enterprises have changed their strategy from receptive restructuring to proactive restructuring, and workers have started to move from company to company. However, there still is a sense of conservatism, egalitarianism—*yokonarabi*—and negativism. There is a strong tendency in Japan to maintain vested interests. This tendency makes businesses and people depend on government protection and discourages creativity. In recent years, the Japanese government has employed private-sector experts and intellectuals to assist in policymaking. The mobility of these experts and intellectuals across sectors may need improvement.

Since the end of World War II, a sense of egalitarianism and the pursuit of increased market share

by businesses have contributed to a successful catch-up kind of growth. But now, in the challenging information technology age, when being first with ideas is paramount, mobility of highly talented persons and flexibility in enterprises are strong requirements. In order to maintain the dynamism of its economic society and to survive in the globalized market with megacompetition, Japan will need to change the taxation and wage systems so that outstanding people who cultivate their skills and creativity are fully rewarded.

Interaction between, and integration of, different technologies, cultures, and ideas leads to the creation of new values. Japan has been a homogeneous society. In a homogeneous society, people feel comfortable with the status quo, but the inertia that accompanies such comfort may hinder the creation of new values. Japan will need to make much more effort to work in association with people of other countries and with different areas of expertise if it is to make a contribution to the twenty-first-century world in the age of globalization.

Third, in the twenty-first century the driving force of the international order will shift from land, natural resources, population, and military strength to soft power such as information capability, technological creativity, cultural attractiveness, communicative ability, and diplomatic discipline.

Japan has the qualities and talents necessary for

Science Hall at Nagoya University. Institutions of higher education in Japan require substantial strengthening to meet the challenges of the information- and knowledge-based world of the twenty-first century. Many experts say the problems call for much bolder action than the incremental steps taken so far. The Fundamentals of Education Law, enacted more than fifty years ago, has become outdated and needs to be revamped to meet the needs of the twenty-first century. According to a report released in 2001 by the National Institute for Educational Policy Research, nearly half of Japanese schools reported violence, higher dropout rates, and problems like student prostitution. Not long ago Japanese schools were the envy of much of the world for their reputation for producing high-achieving and conspicuously well-balanced youth. Sociologists have found causes for the decline in everything from a seemingly endless economic morass to an awkward shift toward greater individuality, indulgent child rearing, and high expectations by overly demanding parents. Photo by P.P. Karan.

soft power (Takahashi 2000). But it needs to create a national social environment or consensus that will help develop Japan's qualitative capacity and intelligence. Japan is part of a knowledge-based economy—a result of the information technology revolution. Intelligence will determine competitive power in the global economy. However, press reports indicate that the educational attainments of young Japanese have been declining gradually, from primary and middle school education right through to higher education. Actually, TOEFL (Test of English as a Foreign Language) results clearly show that the proficiency level in English of Japanese is ranked at the bottom among Asian countries. According to a survey on international competitiveness made in 1999 by the International Institute for Managing Development in Lausanne, Switzerland, the competitiveness of Japanese higher education was ranked 45th out of 47 surveyed countries. In order to prosper in the twenty-first century, Japan will need to undertake a campaign to raise the standard of human resources.

The twenty-first century will be the age of intellectual competition. Individuals and corporations with knowledge will flourish. Japan will need to develop a society in which the results of competition and the fruits of efforts are recognized, while maintaining the ties of social trust that bind Japan together.

Fourth, Japanese political parties and leaders need to have a clear vision for the future, propose solutions to complex problems with reasonable premises, and reach a national consensus. Japan is fac-ing and will continue to face various challenging issues. An aging society, a low birthrate, changing lifestyles, and delayed information technology development are examples in the domestic sphere; the collective security mechanism, global environmental destruction, human rights, and poverty are examples in the international arena.

THE AGING SOCIETY AND THE FALLING BIRTHRATE

As discussed earlier (chapter 6) Japan's future will be influenced by three demographic issues: trends in life expectancy, marriage and childbearing, and immigration. Since 1950 men's life expectancy at birth has increased by fifteen years in Japan. For women the gains have been even greater. Japan now has the longest life expectancy in the world. At the same time, fertility rates have plummeted. By 1990 the total fertility level in Japan was below the replacement level of 2.1 children per woman. As a result, the proportion of the population age 65 and older has increased dramatically. The proportion of elderly in the population grew from 5 percent in 1920 to 16 percent in 2000 and is projected to increase to 26 percent in 2025, which will be the highest percentage in the world. Between 2000 and 2025, the old-age dependency ratio is expected to double—from one elderly person (age 65 and above) for every five people in the working-age population (ages 20–64) to one elderly person for every two people of working age.

The proportion of Japan's population aged 75 and

An elderly woman enjoying the cherry blossoms at the Botanical Gardens in Sapporo. Japan's birthrate is dropping and the population is aging. Japanese women marry at twenty-six or later on average, later than in any other country except Sweden. The mystery is why they wed at all. The young men, raised by their mothers to excel at school and work and not required to do anything else, expect their wives to pamper them the same way. Young women are putting off marrying as long as they can. Older women who married decades ago sometimes express their resentment at the bitter end; they insist that they be buried in individual graves rather than alongside their husband, a practice called *shigo rikon*—divorce after death. Photo by P.P. Karan.

older is rising even faster than the general elderly population. This group will comprise more than half of the elderly by 2025. And the fastest-growing population segment of all is the group of people aged 85 and older. This increase in the number of "old old" has particularly important implications for the provision of financial support and personal care.

Longer life expectancy means an increasing proportion of "old old" among the elderly. Thus, even if the average age at retirement remains the same, a smaller proportion of the elderly will be in the workforce. In 1960, 60 percent of Japanese men 65 and older were working or seeking employment; this figure dropped to 37 percent in 1995. Elderly women are much less likely to work than elderly men. A significant proportion of elderly Japanese are employed in agriculture, particularly as young people leave the farms to seek employment opportunities in urban areas.

In Japan, the elderly have traditionally relied on their children for personal care and financial support. Characterizing such family support systems is a difficult task. When a family includes children, working-age parents, and elderly grandparents, both financial support and other types of care often flow in more than one direction. One way to observe trends in family support for the elderly is to look at coresidence—how many elderly people live with their adult children. In 1972, 67 percent of all Japanese households that included a person age 65 or older consisted of an elderly person or couple living with their adult children. By 1995 this proportion had dropped to 46 percent.

Improvements in life expectancy mean that a growing proportion of the elderly have spouses still living, but the proportion living alone is also increasing. In Japan the proportion of all-elderly households that consisted of an elderly person living alone rose from 8 percent in 1970 to 17 percent in 1989. Older parents living alone may still have frequent contact with their children and may receive substantial financial support. A study by Naohiro Ogawa and Robert D. Retherford (1997) asked elderly people in Japan, the United States, and Germany about their sources of income (see table 14.1). Elderly Japanese mentioned children as a source of income much more often than elderly in the other two countries. The proportion of elderly Japanese mentioning chil-

Table 14.1. Income sources for the elderly (age 60 and above) in Japan, the United States, and Germany, 1996.

Income Sources	Income Sources (%)			Primary Income Source (%)		
	Japan	U.S.	Germany	Japan	U.S.	Germany
Work	35	26	7	22	16	6
Public pensions	84	83	84	57	56	77
Private pensions	8	33	24	2	13	10
Savings	21	24	21	2	2	2
Assets	11	34	12	3	9	2
Children	15	3	3	4	0	0
Public assistance	1	2	1	0	0	1
Other	4	7	4	2	2	0
No answer	0	2	0	8	2	2

Source: Ogawa and Retherford 1997

dren as an income source has fallen, however—from 30 percent in 1981 to 15 percent in 1996. Only 4 percent of elderly Japanese in 1996 listed children as their primary support.

When an elderly person becomes infirm, personal caregiving may become even more important than financial support. In Japan, family caregivers for the elderly tend to be middle-aged women. Since caring for the elderly may conflict with work outside the home, the rising labor-force participation rates of middle-aged women have important implications for the ability of families to care for elderly relatives. A comparison of the projected number of impaired elderly—those who suffer from senile dementia, who are bedridden, or both—with the projected number of nonworking middle-aged women suggests that the burden on primary caregivers will increase four- or fivefold between 1990 and 2025. In 1990 in Japan, there were 7 impaired elderly persons for each 100 nonworking women aged 40–49. In 2025, there will be an estimated 46 impaired elderly persons for each 100 nonworking women aged 40–49.

One motivation for personal saving is support for old age. There are several indications that this "pension motive" is increasingly important in Japan. Surveys of young adults in Japan, for example, indicate that few are counting on family as a major source of support when they retire. In Japan the ability of the elderly to support themselves financially has improved considerably over time, largely because of the expansion of the public pension system. In 1996, 84 percent of Japanese retirees aged 60 and above were receiving public pension benefits. More than half reported that their pensions were their primary source of income (see table 14.1). Largely because of the rapid growth in pension benefits, elderly Japanese have enjoyed the fastest income gains of any age group. In Japan the pension system is mostly "pay-as-you-go," which means that current benefits are paid out of current contributions. As the population ages under such a system, the pensions of a growing number of retirees must be paid for by a shrinking number of taxpayers of working age.

A recent projection indicates that the contribution rate for Japan's largest public pension scheme will have to rise from 16.5 percent of wages in 1995 to 35 percent in 2025 to pay for all anticipated benefits. Up to now, the Japanese government has used general tax revenues to fill the growing gap between pension benefits and payroll contributions. Major pension reforms were implemented in 1986, partly to slow down the growth of contribution rates and government subsidies.

The Japanese government is seeking to shift some of the burden of caring for the elderly back to families and to the elderly themselves. In 1990 the government launched a ten-year project called the Golden Plan to expand nursing home capacity and to improve social services for the elderly who live at home. The plan calls for improvements in both day-care services and short-term stays in nursing homes to help families who are looking after elderly relatives at home. The government is also considering a new scheme to provide home nursing services, although the financial implications are problematic. Given the expanding elderly population and the shrinking availability of family caregivers, the Japanese government's efforts to shift some of the responsibility for elderly care back to the families are not likely to be successful.

Financial support for the elderly is also likely to become a more serious problem. The elderly may be forced to draw increasingly on their personal savings as public pension schemes are stretched to the limit. They may also work longer. In 1994 the Japanese government raised the minimum pensionable age to 60, to take effect in 1998. It will rise gradually to 65 over the next twenty years. Private employers are being encouraged to keep their workers on after retirement age, either by prolonging their current employment or by finding them another position, usually at reduced pay. Some 70 percent of all companies with thirty or more employees are offering their workers such positions when they reach retirement age. Nevertheless, labor force participation among the elderly has declined slightly in recent years as a result of Japan's current economic recession.

Of course, the aging society does not mean only doom and gloom. A decrease in the population will reduce the burden on the environment and alleviate some of the housing and land-use problems facing urban areas. Having fewer children in school may encourage smaller pupil-to-teacher ratios, and the pressure of school entrance examinations on children may lighten. However, the reality is that the issues requiring immediate attention far outweigh the positive aspects.

THE FUTURE OF THE COUNTRYSIDE

Japan's production shifted from an agricultural base and light manufacturing before World War II to heavy industry and increasingly to services. Although the role of agriculture in the national economy has been declining, the rural sector has a disproportionately large political voice in the nation. Agricultural import barriers (quotas, tariffs, and testing procedures) and subsidies (about $49 billion in 1998) have kept food prices high in Japan but have benefited the rural areas. Rural parts of Japan also benefit from public-works spending.

As import barriers are gradually lowered and public-works projects are cut, rural areas are going to feel the impact. The strength of the farmer's influence may be shrinking in the future. In July 1999 the Basic Law on Food, Agriculture, and Rural Areas took effect to assist development of agriculture and rural areas. It replaced the 1961 Basic Agricultural Law. Like the 1961 law, the 1999 legislation was passed amid rising concerns for the future of agriculture and the rural countryside. The increasing number of aging farmers and the dwindling number of farmers overall pose critical problems for maintaining the vitality of farming and rural areas. Across the nation, the number of people working full time in farming has dropped steadily, to about 2.8 million today, down from 3.9 million in 1980 and from 12 million in 1960.

Who will run the family farms in the future? Generally the eldest son is expected to operate the family farm. Many of these young people who traditionally would have taken over the family farm have been absorbed into secondary- and tertiary-level industries. There are numerous cases of farmers who leave agriculture because none of their children plan to continue the family farm. In many villages the older generation continued to operate farms until about twenty-five years ago. This older generation began to retire from agriculture in the 1990s, and cultivated land was abandoned.

As a result of the easing of agricultural regulations, it is now possible to develop large agricultural corporations. Young people are taking jobs in these corporations. In Toyama Prefecture, for example, of 71 people who inherited family farms between 1992 and 1996, 68 took jobs in agricultural corporations (Odagiri 2000). Young people in Japan are more inclined to work for large agricultural corporations than on the small family farm. In many parts of the country, young people are moving to rural villages, which bodes well for the future of the countryside. In addition, a growing number of people who migrated to urban centers for jobs in the 1960s and 1970s are returning to the village after retirement. The movement of these people is beginning to revitalize the countryside. Positive government agricultural policy that supports this trend will ensure the survival of agriculture and the vitality of rural areas.

THE HIGH-TECHNOLOGY ROAD

Japan has viewed high technology as an area of unprecedented opportunity. Science Cities and tech-

Men of a Japanese farm household in Kumamoto Prefecture look at the vinyl greenhouses used for growing vegetables as well as rice seedlings and ponder the future of farming and the countryside. Forces of globalization have impacted farming in Japan. In addition, an increasing number of aging farmers and the depopulation of rural areas pose serious problems for the vitality of agriculture, rural areas, and the traditional aesthetics of Japanese culture. Photo by Cotton Mather.

nopolis centers were established to achieve Japan's dominance in technology. Japan is attempting to use information technology as the linchpin to drive its economic restoration. With anticipated cuts in telecom costs, the information technology revolution will start changing the face of business in a wide range of industries. It will also influence consumers' lifestyles through the emergence of new products and services. As information technology (IT) took hold worldwide because of the great potential new technology offers, Japan wasted time for almost a decade as it dealt with the aftermath of the bubble economy's collapse. The twenty-first century in Japan begins with the expectation that IT will bring technological changes on the scale that the locomotive, electricity, and the automobile brought in the past. But there can be little hope that the IT initiative will lead to sustainable growth of the national economy. This is so because businesses in general, which hold the key to success or failure for the IT revolution, are not prepared to embark on competition in real earnest to enhance their productivity on the strength of IT. Furthermore, years of tight controls and regulations in the technology sector have created complex challenges for the industry.

The immediate task facing Japan is to adopt measures to ensure that progress is made in research and development by providing more general funding for priority projects for advancement in each scientific discipline. If Japan is to keep up as far as technology is concerned, it must produce a large number of capable people with great creativity and drive.

One successful example of high-technology development in 2002 is in Sapporo. Here, young entrepreneurs, many of them Hokkaido University graduates, have established their own businesses. There are so many enclaves of the high-tech ventures that they have been collectively dubbed Sapporo Valley. Venture companies have managed to thrive in this area without relying on government subsidies—and some of them are competing internationally. There are about three hundred IT-related companies in Sapporo, including about thirty firms concentrated in the area to the north of Sapporo Station and in Sapporo Techno Park, an industrial complex for high-tech firms in the city's suburbs.

The roots of Sapporo Valley go back to a microcomputer study group set up by a Hokkaido University faculty member in electronic information engineering. The history of Sapporo Valley is similar to the history of Silicon Valley, which grew out of the venture firms set up by students from Stanford University. Business circumstances in Sapporo Valley are different from those in Bit Valley in Shibuya, Tokyo, which is the most famous center of IT-related ventures in Japan. Whereas about three hundred companies in Shibuya are competing in new Internet- based services, such as Web site search services and online transactions, Sapporo Valley's niche is technological expertise. Because IT-related projects cannot be completed solely within Hokkaido, companies in Sapporo have established links or subsidiaries with companies all over the world, including Silicon Valley. The success in Sapporo reveals that Japanese entrepreneurs can take a lead in high technology as long as the country keeps educating and nurturing talented people, and as long as it provides increased opportunities for young entrepreneurs.

THE CHANGING LIFESTYLES OF THE YOUNG

More and more young people are turning away from the middle-class Japanese way of life—a job in a big company, a house in the suburbs, a wife and two children. Instead, young Japanese today drift from one low-skilled job to the next and join the ranks of growing permanent part-timers or *furita*. Young Japanese who dislike job restrictions are attracted to part-time work and are unconcerned about the future. They live at home with their parents, pay no rent and have no bills, and do no housework. During the 1990s the number of *furita* rose, and it continues to grow (Kamaii 2000).

According to surveys by the Ministry of Health, Labor, and Welfare, two in every five young Japanese have no desire to work as permanent salaried company employees. Older Japanese view the furita as a symptom of social sickness that Japan has acquired with its affluence. With Japan's shrinking working population, these young part-timers represent a serious waste of Japan's major and only resource—people. Since young people are staying at home and not marrying, the birthrate keeps falling, making the financial condition of Japan's pension system worse.

The economic, political, and social troubles have delayed any Japanese effort to play a greater role in world affairs. The country's population and impor-

Increasingly, Japanese youths are dropping out of college, drifting from one part-time job to another, and living with their parents well into their thirties. Among young Japanese the *freeter* phenomenon (a hip hybrid word composed of the English *free* and the German *arbeiter* or worker) is expanding, stoked by several factors: family affluence, a lack of corporate jobs, attachment to family and home, and a generational revolt. Living with parents, freeters don't pay rent, buy groceries, or do their own laundry, so they have money to spend on themselves. These young Japanese with no children, no dreams, no hope, and no job skills could become a major burden on society, as they contribute to the decline of the birthrate and do not contribute to social insurance. Photo by P.P. Karan.

tance would entitle it to a permanent seat on the United Nations Security Council, which Japan wants. To gain one, however, Japan will have to overcome its scruples about sending troops abroad, so it can participate in peacekeeping operations. Despite public opposition, Japan did send a one-thousand-strong noncombatant military contingent to Iraq in March 2004 to help purify local water supplies, rebuild schools, and provide medical care in the southern part of the country. The government is building momentum for a historic rethinking of the constraints placed on Japan's military by the war-renouncing constitution written by the United States.

In January 2001 Japan implemented a major administrative reform and reorganization of the central government to promote political initiative over that of the bureaucracy and to provide efficient services for the twenty-first century. The change in voter attitudes in recent elections has undermined the power of the old machine politics, but still crucial administrative and electoral reforms are needed to advance Japan in the new century. Japan remains a country with fundamental strengths that include an educated labor force, a competitive market, high

technology, and a great determination to succeed. Japan's economy, politics, and society for decades have displayed an awesome combination of stability and dynamism that can hardly be discounted even now. But the nation that for so many years looked like a combination of political cipher and economic steamroller is changing in ways that for all the present stress and turmoil should eventually benefit its citizens as well as the rest of the world. That augurs well for the future of Japan in the twenty-first century.

REFERENCES

Future hinges on reality check. 2000. Editorial. *Daily Yomiuri* (Tokyo), October 17.

Global Trends 2015: A Dialogue about the Future with Nongovernmental Experts. 2000. Washington, DC: U.S. Central Intelligence Agency.

Kamaii, Yoshihiko. 2000. Freelancers: An increasing social phenomenon. *Social Science Japan* 18 (April): 8–9.

Odagiri, Tokumi. 2000. Who will carry on? Young Japanese and agriculture. *Social Science Japan* 18 (April): 12–14.

Ogawa, Naohiro and Robert D. Retherford. 1997. Shifting costs of caring for the elderly back to families in Japan: Will it work? *Population and Development Review* 23 (1): 59–94.

Takahashi, Yuzo. 2000. A network of tinkerers. *Technology and Culture* 41 (3).

FURTHER READINGS

GEOGRAPHIC STUDIES

Among the early postwar geographers in the United States was Robert Hall, founder of the Japanese Studies Center at the University of Michigan, who published a number of studies on settlement patterns and cities of Japan. But Glenn Trewartha's *Japan: A Geography* (Madison: Univ. of Wisconsin Press, 1965) is the classic standard English-language geography of Japan. Edward Ackerman's *Japan's Natural Resources and Their Relation to Japan's Economic Future* (Chicago: Univ. of Chicago Press, 1953) assesses Japan's natural resources in detail. Clarence Glacken provides a study of the Ryuku Islands after the war in *The Great Loochoo: A Study of Okinawan Village Life* (Berkeley: Univ. of California Press, 1955). Shannon B. McCune's *Ryuku Islands* (Harrisburg, PA: Stackpole Books, 1975) provides a geographic survey of the islands. Paul Wheatley and Thomas See offer an excellent survey of Japanese urbanism in *From Court to Capital: A Tentative Interpretation of the Origins of the Japanese Urban Tradition* (Chicago: Univ. of Chicago Press, 1978). *Nagoya: The Changing Geography of a Japanese Regional Metropolis*, Studies in Geography, no. 17 (Chapel Hill: Department of Geography, Univ. of North Carolina, 1982), by John D. Eyre, is a comprehensive geography of a Japanese city. David H. Kornhauser's two books *Urban Japan: Its Foundations and Growth* (New York: Longman, 1976) and *Japan: Geographical Background to Urban-Industrial Development* (New York: Longman, 1978) provide an excellent overview of Japanese urban development. Andre Sorensen's *Making of Urban Japan: Cities and Planning from Edo to the Twenty-first Century* (London: Routledge, 2002) examines the phenomenon of Japanese city planning.

Among the many geographers who have written on agricultural topics are John D. Eyre, discussing irrigation (in *Geographical Review* 45 [1955]: 197–216); Richard F. Hough, dealing with raw silk (*Annals of the Association of American Geographers* 58 [1968]: 221–249); and George H. Kakiuchi, writing on strawberry farming (*Economic Geography* 36 [1960]: 171–183). Forest R. Pitts's *Rural Prosperity in Japan: Studies on Economic Life in Japan,* Occasional Papers, no. 8 (Ann Arbor: Center for Japanese Studies, Univ. of Michigan, 1964), surveys the agrarian situation in Japan in the early 1960s. Gil Latz's "Agricultural Development in Japan: The Land Improvement District in Concept and Practice," Geography Research Paper no. 225, Univ. of Chicago, 1989; Mary McDonald's "Displacing Rice: Factories in the Fields of Farm Power in Tohoku" (Ph.D. diss., Univ. of California at Berkeley, 1990); and Todd Stradford's "Changes in the Agricultural Landscape of Kochi Prefecture, Japan, 1987 to 1990" (Ph.D. diss., Univ. of Oklahoma, Norman, 1994) are examples of innovative research on twentieth-century agricultural policies of Japan.

Geographers who handle contemporary topics include David Edgington and Roman Cybriwsky, who have made substantive contributions to our understanding of the structure of urban patterns. Cybriwsky's *Tokyo: The Shogun's City at the 21st Century* (Chichester, UK: Wiley, 1998) explores the changing geography of Japan's largest city. *Japan at the Millennium: Joining Past and Future* (Vancouver: Univ. of British Columbia Press, 2003), edited by David Edgington, contains a series of thoughtful essays on economic and political systems, identity and youth, and urban living and beauty. Recent contributions of Japanese geographers have been summarized by P.P. Karan in *Human Geography* (*Jimbun Chiri*) 52 (3) (2000): 79–83; and 54 (4) (2002): 35–

37. *Human Geography* is published by the Human Geographical Society of Japan, Kyoto. *Geographical Review of Japan*, series B, published by the Association of Japanese Geographers, Tokyo, contains original research contributions of Japanese geographers in English. Susumu Kurasawa's *Social Atlas of Tokyo* (Tokyo: Univ. of Tokyo Press, 1986) should be of special interest to geographers and other social scientists. Noritaka Yagasaki's *Japan: Geographical Perspectives on an Island Nation* (Tokyo: Teikoku-Shoin, 2002) is the best textbook on the geography of Japan in English by a noted Japanese geographer.

ECONOMIC AND URBAN STUDIES

Japan's New Economy: Continuity and Change in Twenty-first Century, edited by Magnus Blomstrom, Byron Gangnes, and Summer La Croix (New York: Oxford Univ. Press, 2001), analyzes the demographic, structural, and institutional changes transforming Japan's economy. David Flath's *Japanese Economy* (Oxford: Oxford Univ. Press, 2000) is an excellent overview of Japan's economy. *Japan: The System That Soured*, by Richard Katz (Armonk, NY.: M.E. Sharpe, 1998), examines the features of the country's economic system that led to the current economic problems. In *Arthritic Japan: The Slow Pace of Economic Reforms* (Washington, DC: Brookings Institution Press, 2001), Edward J. Lincoln examines the slowness of economic reforms and explains why the road toward reform will be difficult. In *Japanese Phoenix: The Long Road to Economic Revival* (Armonk, NY.: M.E. Sharpe, 2003), Richard Katz predicts that Japan will recover and that its economic achievements will once again earn the world's admiration. *Japanese Economics and Economists since 1945* (New York: Routledge, 2000), edited by Aiko Ikeo, presents an incisive study of Japanese economics since 1945. *Japan Almanac*, published annually by Asahi Shimbun, Tokyo, is an excellent source of economic and social data for Japan. The development, culture, and global power of Japan are analyzed from the political economy perspective by Peter Wallace Preston in *Understanding Modern Japan: A Political Economy of Development, Culture and Global Power* (Thousand Oaks, CA: Sage, 2000). Gavan McCormack's *Emptiness of Japanese Affluence* (Armonk, NY: M.E. Sharpe, 2001) provides an illuminating analysis of the political economy of exploitation that prevails in contemporary Japan. Japan's financial crisis is the topic of a comprehensive study by Koichi Hamada and Munehisa Kasuya, *Financial Crisis in Japan: Past, Present, and Future* (Northampton, MA: Edward Elgar, 2003). Ulrike Schaede and William Grimes's edited volume *Japan's Managed Globalization: Adapting to the Twenty-first Century* (Armonk, NY.: M.E. Sharpe, 2003) analyzes Japan's policies for managing globalization.

Theodore C. Bestor, the noted anthropologist, has written extensively on Tokyo. His most recent work is *Tokyo's Marketplace Culture and Trade in the Tsukiji Wholesale Market* (Berkeley: Univ. of California Press, 2003). Botund Bognar's *Tokyo* (New York: Wiley, 1997) examines the architecture of the city. William H. Coaldrake explores architecture as a symbol of authority in *Architecture and Authority in Japan* (New York: Routledge, 1996). The role of Tokyo as a global city is discussed in Saskia Sassen, *The Global City: New York, London, Tokyo* (Princeton, NJ: Princeton Univ. Press, 2001). Moriko Kira and Mariko Terada's book *Japan, towards Totalscape: Contemporary Japanese Architecture, Urban Planning, and Landscape* (Rotterdam, Netherlands: NAI Publishers, 2000) provides an interesting discussion of urban and rural landscapes.

Strategic Networks: The Art of Japanese Interfirm Cooperation (New York: International Business Press, 2000), by Frank-Jurgen Richter, discusses the driving forces of strategic networks in Japan and provides an outlook for entrepreneurship in the twenty-first century. Michael E. Porter, Hirotaka Takeuchi, and Mariko Sakakibara, *Can Japan Compete?* (Basingstoke, UK: Macmillan, 2000), is a thought-provoking analysis of Japan's industrial policy and international competitive capacity. Hiromitsu Ishi gives a comprehensive review of Japan's fiscal policy in *Making Fiscal Policy in Japan: Economic Effects and Institutional Settings* (New York: Oxford Univ. Press, 2000).

The Organization for Economic Cooperation and Development's *Economic Surveys: Japan 2002* (Washington, DC: OECD, 2003) is an excellent survey of the Japanese economy, with a full discussion of structural reform and sources of growth. Cultural differences between Japanese and American business negotiation styles are reviewed by James D. Hodgson, Yoshiro Sano, and James L. Graham in *Doing Business with the New Japan* (Lanham, MD: Rowman and Littlefield, 2000). Kazuo Nishiyama provides a good synthesis of and insight into the corporate culture of Japan in *Doing Business with Japan: Successful Strategies for Intercultural Communication* (Honolulu: Univ. of Hawaii Press, 2000).

HISTORY AND POLITICS

Conrad D. Totman's *History of Japan* (Malden, MA: Blackwell, 2000) is a good general survey of the history of Japan. *A Modern History of Japan: From Tokugawa Times to Present* (New York: Oxford Univ. Press, 2003), by Andrew Gordon, provides a wealth of information for the general reader. *The Rise of Modern Japan* (New York: St. Martin's Press, 2000), by William G. Beasley, is a well-researched and useful survey of Japan from the overthrow of the Tokugawa to the unraveling of postwar patterns in the 1990s. Marius B. Jansen provides an authoritative historical survey from the Tokugawa period to the present in *The Making of Modern Japan* (Cambridge, MA: Belknap Press of Harvard Univ., 2000). The two volumes of *Japan: A Documentary History* (Armonk, NY.: M.E. Sharpe, 1996), by David J. Lu, present primary source materials in translation on pivotal changes in Japan's social, economic, and political institutions; culture; and religion, from the dawn of history to the present. *Modern Japan: A Social and Political History* (New York: Routledge, 2002), by Elise K. Tipton, provides a concise and fascinating introduction to the social, cultural, and political history of modern Japan. The daily lives of the people during the Edo period are discussed in Matsunosuke Nishiyama, *Edo Culture: Daily Life and Diversions in Urban Japan, 1600–1868* (Honolulu: Univ. of Hawaii Press, 1997).

For readers interested in the Pacific war against Japan, *Pearl to V-J Day: World War II in the Pacific* (Washington, DC: Air Force History and Museums Program, 2000) contains contributions on military technology, strategic intelligence, submarine warfare, the sea and air wars, and the decision to drop the atomic bomb.

George H. Kerr's study *Okinawa, the History of an Island People* (Boston: Tuttle, 2000) is a good introduction to the island. The debate over the contemporary identity of Okinawa is discussed in Laura Elizabeth Hein, *Islands of Discontent: Okinawan Responses to Japanese and American Power* (Lanham, MD: Rowman and Littlefield, 2003). Terrorism in Japan is discussed by Ian Reader in *Religious Violence in Contemporary Japan: The Case of Aum Shinrikyo* (Honolulu: Univ. of Hawaii Press, 2000). *Introduction to Japanese Politics* (Armonk, NY:

M.E. Sharpe, 2000), by Louis D. Huges, explains the political life of Japan as well as the forces that shape it. *The Pursuit of Power in Modern Japan* (New York: Oxford Univ. Press, 2000), by Chushichi Tsuzuki, examines the complexity of the nation's internal politics. Tomohito Shinoda, *Leading Japan: The Role of the Prime Minister* (Westport, CT: Praeger, 2000), makes a significant contribution to the understanding of the prime minister's role in Japanese politics and government. The breakdown and failure of Japan's policy coherence in the 1990s and their impact on the political economy are analyzed in essays edited by Jennifer Amyx and Peter Drysdale, *Japanese Governance: Beyond Japan Inc.* (New York: RoutledgeCurzon, 2003).

The Challenges of the U.S.-Japan Military Arrangement (Armonk, NY: M.E. Sharpe, 2002), by Anthony DiFilippo; and *The Japan-U.S. Alliance: New Challenges for the 21st Century* (Washington, DC: Japan Center for International Exchange, 2000), by Nishihara Masashi, give in-depth analyses of the U.S.-Japan security alliance and its implications for Japan and the Asia-Pacific region. *Japan's Comfort Women* (New York: Routledge, 2001), by Yuki Tanaka, tells the appalling story of the comfort women who were forced to enter prostitution to serve the Japanese Imperial Army. The everyday life of Koreans who live in Japan is discussed in essays edited by Sonia Ryang in *Koreans in Japan* (New York: Routledge, 2000). Kevin Cooney's *Japan's Foreign Policy Maturation* (New York: Routledge, 2002) examines the restructuring of Japanese foreign policy since the end of the cold war. Unryu Suganuma provides an excellent review of Japan's territorial dispute with China in *Sovereign Rights and Territorial Space in Sino-Japanese Relations: Irredentism and the Diaoyu/Senkaku Islands* (Honolulu: Association of Asian Studies and Univ. of Hawaii Press, 2000). The relationship between Japan and Russia is examined by Gilbert Rozman, *Japan and Russia: The Tortuous Path to Normalization, 1949–1999* (New York: St. Martin's Press, 2000); and by Richard M. Connaughton, *Rising Sun and Tumbling Bear: Russia's War with Japan* (New York: Sterling, 2003).

SOCIAL, CULTURAL, AND ENVIRONMENTAL STUDIES

A clear and readable introduction to Japanese society is Joy Hendry's *Understanding Japanese Society*

(New York: Routledge, 2003). John Sargent's *Perspectives on Japan: Towards the Twenty-first Century* (New York: St. Martin's Press, 2003) discusses social conditions in contemporary Japan. The role of liberal democratic institutions such as community groups and associations in Japan is analyzed in a volume edited by Frank J. Schwartz and Susan J. Pharr, *The State of Civil Society in Japan* (New York: Cambridge Univ. Press, 2003). The political power of the Japanese farmer is discussed by Aurelia George Mulgan, *The Politics of Agriculture in Japan* (London: Routledge, 2000). A collection of previously published pieces by a distinguished sociologist, Robert N. Bellah, *Imaging Japan: The Japanese Tradition and Its Modern Interpretation* (Berkeley: Univ. of California Press, 2003), explores the ways in which Japanese society and culture have developed over the last millennium and a half and discusses the implicit controversy involved in defining Japanese tradition. The expanded and updated fourth edition of H. Paul Varley's *Japanese Culture* (Honolulu: Univ. of Hawaii Press, 2000) is a rich portrait of Japanese culture. Michael Ashkenazi and John R. Clammer's *Consumption and Material Culture in Contemporary Japan* (New York: Kegan Paul, 2000) has essays on convenience stores; representations of infanticide and abortion; cultural heritage and consumption; prostitution; dating, mating and marriage; and love, sex, and materialism in Japan. David E. Kaplan and Alec Dubro, *Yakuza: Japan's Criminal Underworld* (Berkeley: Univ. of California Press, 2003), is an interesting account of organized crime in Japan.

Several authors have produced research on a great variety of topics related to women. Yuko Ogasawara, *Office Ladies and Salaried Men: Power, Gender, and Work in Japanese Companies* (Berkeley: Univ. of California Press, 1998), is a fine introduction to the status of women working in Japanese companies. The Japanese housewife is the subject of Robin M. LeBlanc's comprehensive study *Bicycle Citizens: The Political World of the Japanese Housewife* (Berkeley: Univ. of California Press, 1999). Joanna Liddle and Sachiko Nakajima, in *Rising Suns, Rising Daughters: Gender, Class, and Power in Japan* (New York: Zed Books, 2000), examine the history of feminism and women's social conditions. Barbara Hamill Sato, *The New Japanese Woman: Modernity, Media, and Women in Interwar Japan* (Durham, NC: Duke Univ. Press, 2003), is a deeply insightful account of the status of

women in Japan. The relationships between the old and the young are explored in an excellent study by Leng Leng Thong, *Generations in Touch: Linking the Old and Young in a Tokyo Neighborhood* (Ithaca, NY: Cornell Univ. Press, 2001). Anne Allison, *Nightwork: Sexuality, Pleasure, and Corporate Masculinity in a Tokyo Hostess Club* (Chicago: Univ. of Chicago Press, 1994), is a stimulating study of the hostess club in Japan. Donald Richie's intriguing book *The Image Factory: Fads and Fashions in Japan* (London: Reaktion Books, 2003) investigates fads and fashions of Japan and their inherent meanings and potential for Japanese enterprise and society.

Japanese Cybercultures (New York: Routledge Curzon, 2003), edited by Mark McLelland and Nanette Gottlieb, analyzes the different applications and uses of the Internet in Japan. *Technology and Innovation in Japan* (London: Routledge, 1998), edited by Martin Hemmert and Christian Oberlander, provides an excellent overview of technology policy. A volume edited by Jane M. Bachnik, *Roadblocks on the Information Highway: The IT Revolution in Japanese Education* (Lanham, MD: Lexington Books, 2003), claims that lags in implementing information technology in Japanese education are created by contradictory and challenging responses of the social environment. A revealing new look at culture and technology is offered in Ian Inkster and Fumihiko Satofuka, *Culture and Technology in Modern Japan* (New York: I.B. Tauris, 2000).

Drawing upon nearly two years of multistate fieldwork in Brazil and Japan, Takeyuki Tsuda has written a comprehensive ethnography that examines the ethnic experiences and reactions of both Japanese Brazilian immigrants and their native Japanese hosts in *Strangers in the Ethnic Homeland: Migrant Nationalism and the Making of Japan's Newest Immigrant Minority* (New York: Columbia Univ. Press, 2003). Emigration and immigration patterns are examined in a volume edited by Mike Douglass and Glenda Susan Roberts, *Japan and Global Migration: Foreign Workers and the Advent of a Multicultural Society* (Honolulu: Univ. of Hawaii Press, 2003). Family policy and social and welfare services are discussed in a volume edited by John W. Traphagan and John Knight, *Demographic Change and the Family in Japan's Aging Society* (Albany: State Univ. of New York Press, 2003). A comprehensive discussion of care for the elderly population is provided by Susan Orpett

Long, *Caring for the Elderly in Japan and the U.S.: Practices and Policies* (New York: Routledge, 2000).

Shigeyuki Okajima and Ken'ichi Takada, *Echoes of the Environment: Interviews with 12 Japanese Leaders* (Tokyo: Otowa Shobo Tsurumi Shoten, 2000), offers a revealing look at the perceptions and attitudes of Japanese leaders on ecology, environmental protection, and policy. The relationship between wildlife and humans is analyzed by John Knight, *Waiting for Wolves in Japan: An Anthropological Study of People-Wildlife Relations* (Oxford: Oxford Univ. Press, 2003). Miranda A. Schreurs, a distinguished scholar of environmental politics, has written extensively on Japan's environmental policy. Her most recent book, *Environmental Politics in Japan, Germany, and the United States* (New York: Cambridge Univ. Press, 2003), is an excellent analysis of approaches to environmental protection in the three nations.

INDEX

Note: Page numbers in italic type refer to photographs.